THE NORTH CAROLINA ALMANAC

AND BOOK OF FACTS

1989—1990

THE NORTH CAROLINA ALMANAC

AND BOOK OF FACTS

1989—1990

Edited by
James A. Crutchfield

Project Editor
Julia M. Pitkin

Assistant
Mary Ann Drewry McNeese

RUTLEDGE HILL PRESS
Nashville, Tennessee

Dedicated to the citizens of North Carolina, especially those who helped in compiling this almanac.

Published in Nashville, Tennessee, by Rutledge Hill Press, Inc., 513 Third Avenue South, Nashville, Tennessee 37210

Typography by ProtoType Graphics, Inc., Nashville, Tennessee

Library of Congress Cataloging-in-Publication Data

The North Carolina almanac and book of facts, 1989-1990 / edited by
James A. Crutchfield ; project editor, Julia M. Pitkin, assistant,
Mary Ann Drewry McNeese.
p. cm.
Includes index.
ISBN 0-934395-91-8 ISBN 0-934395-90-X (pbk.)
1. North Carolina—Miscellanea. 2. Almanacs, American—North
Carolina. I. Crutchfield, James Andrew, 1938-
F254.N963 1988
975.6'043—dc19 88-29842
CIP

Manufactured in the United States of America
1 2 3 4 5—93 92 91 90 89

PREFACE

The successful publication of *The North Carolina Almanac and Book of Facts* in 1986 has proven the need for an accurate, up-to-date, inexpensive handbook containing vital information about North Carolina. In that edition we indicated our desire to update the almanac regularly; its wide acceptance has made that vision a reality.

To my knowledge, *The North Carolina Almanac and Book of Facts* represents the first effort to put between two covers a compendium of facts about North Carolina. While there are volumes of statistical data and scores of lists, descriptions, and information about individual subjects of interest to North Carolinians, what makes *The North Carolina Almanac and Book of Facts* unique is that all these figures, tables, charts, essays, and other information have been synthesized into one easy-to-read volume.

The North Carolina Almanac and Book of Facts is sure to become one of the most used volumes in homes, libraries, and offices. Since Rutledge Hill Press plans to update this book regularly, the publisher would be happy to hear from you, the reader, regarding information you believe future editions should include. In fact, numerous suggestions from readers of the first edition have been incorporated into what we hope will become known as "the Encyclopedia of North Carolina."

—James A. Crutchfield

ACKNOWLEDGEMENTS

In compiling *The North Carolina Almanac and Book of Facts,* many books, institutions, state departments, and individuals were consulted. We would like to acknowledge these sources for the information provided that made this almanac possible.

Sources used for each section are as follows:

Agriculture: *North Carolina Agricultural Statistics, 1987,* Agricultural Statistician, North Carolina Department of Agriculture; *Profile, North Carolina Counties Update, Fall 1987,* Office of State Budget and Management and Management Information Services; Carl Cross, Agricultural Statistician, U.S. Department of Agriculture, Statistical Reporting Service; James Olson, State Statistician, North Carolina Department of Agriculture.

Airlines: *Rand McNally 1987 Commercial Atlas and Marketing Guide.*

Airports: Ms. Monte Stevenson, North Carolina Department of Transportation, Aeronautics Division.

Alcohol: North Carolina Department of Commerce, Alcoholic Beverage Control Board.

Arts: Mary Cook, North Carolina Arts Council.

Banking: George Briggs, Public Information, Federal Reserve Bank, Atlanta, Georgia; Ms. Mary W. Chick, Public Services Assistant, Charlotte Branch, Federal Reserve Bank of Richmond.

Chambers of Commerce: *North Carolina Chambers of Commerce, 1988 Directory; Worldwide Chamber of Commerce Directory;* Ms. Bonnie Young, North Carolina Association of Chamber of Commerce Executives.

Climate: Dave Epperson, State Climatologist, North Carolina State University, Department of Marine, Earth and Atmospheric Sciences.

Congressional Medal of Honor: *America's Medal of Honor Recipients.*

Constitution: Thad Eure, Secretary of State.

Corps of Engineers Lakes: Public Affairs Office, Department of the Army, Wilmington District; Sheila B. Roy, Public Affairs Specialist.

County Government Expenditures: Evan L. Anderson, Office of State Budget and Management.

County Name Origins: *The American Counties; The North Carolina Gazetteer.*

County Seats: *Directory of the State and County Officials of North Carolina, 1988,* Thad Eure.

Courts: *Directory of the State and County Officials of North Carolina, 1988,* Thad Eure.

Crime: *Crime in North Carolina, 1986 Uniform Crime Report;* Department of Corrections, Division of Prisons; Department of Human Resources, Division of Facilities Service; Dick Brown, North Carolina State Bureau of Investigation; George Barnes, Department of Corrections; David Guth, Public Information Officer, Department of Corrections; Tom Ritter, Department of Human Resources.

Day Care Facilities: Juanita Cowan, Child Day Care Section, Division of Facility Services, Department of Human Services.

Economics: *County-Level Projections of Economic Activity and Population, North Carolina, 1990-2035,* Bureau of Economic Analysis, U.S. Department of Commerce; *North Carolina Business Climate,* Business/Industry Development Division, North Carolina Department of Commerce; *North Carolina Economic Development Report, 1986,* North Carolina Department of Commerce; *North Carolina Long-Term Economic-Demographic Projections, 1987,* Office of State Budget and Management, Management and Information Services.

Education: *Directory of the State and County Officials of North Carolina, 1988,* Thad Eure; Education Directory, North Carolina State Board of Education; Kay Bullock.

Elections: State Board of Elections; Dot Anderson.

Employment: Joe W. Richardson, Employment Security Commission of North Carolina.

Endangered Species: U.S. Department of the Interior, Fish and Wildlife Service; Dr. George Drewry.

Energy: *North Carolina Energy Outlook,* Mary H. Novak; State of North Carolina Department of Commerce, Energy Division; Paul ("Chris") Mogenson.

Famous North Carolinians: *The Encyclopedia of the South; Notable Names in American History; Young Reader's Picturebook of Tar Heel Authors,* Richard Walser and Mary Reynolds Peacock.

Festivals and Events: North Carolina Division of Travel and Tourism, North Carolina Department of Commerce.

Firsts: *North Carolina Business Climate,* Business/Industry Development Division, North Carolina Department of Commerce.

Flora and Fauna: *The Encyclopedia of Americana International Edition,* Grolier Inc.; The U.S. Department of the Interior, Fish and Wildlife Service.

Foreign Trade Zones: *North Carolina Business Climate,* Business/Industry Development Division, North Carolina Department of Commerce, Ms. Toni Lerew.

Forts: *American FORTS Yesterday and Today,* Bruce Grant.

Game Lands: *1987–88 Hunting and Fishing Maps for North Carolina Game Lands,* North Carolina Wildlife Resources Commission, George Smith.

Government: *Directory of the State and County Officials of North Carolina, 1988,* Thad Eure.

Governors: *Notable Names in American History; North Carolina Governors, 1585–1974,* Beth G. Crabtree, Division of Archives and History.

Higher Education: *Education Directory of North Carolina,* North Carolina State Board of Education.

Highways: North Carolina Department of Transportation; *Profile, North Carolina Counties Update, Fall 1987,* Office of State Budget and Management, Management and Information Services.

Historical Societies: *Directory of Historical Agencies in North America,* 13th Edition, Betty Pease Smith, Editor.

Historic Sites: *Guide to North Carolina Historical Highway Markers,* Division of Archives and History; *North Carolina Business Climate,* Business/Industry Development Division, North Carolina Department of Commerce.

History: *Colonial North Carolina—A History,* Hugh T. Lefler and William S. Powell; *The Encyclopedia of Southern History,* edited by David C. Roller, Robert W. Twyman, and Michael Pinkston; *Historical Statistics of the South, 1790—1970,* Donald B. Dodd and Wynelle S. Dodd.

Housing: *Profile, North Carolina Counties Update, Fall 1987,* Office of State Budget and Management, Management and Information Services.

Indians: *The Indians of the Southeastern United States,* John R. Swanton.

Labor: *1980 Census of Population,* U.S. Department of Commerce; William Scheideler, Office of State Budget and Management.

Land Area: *1980 Area Measurement Report,* U.S. Department of Commerce, Bureau of the Census, Geography Division; U.S. Bureau of Geography, Division of Computer Graphics; William Scheideler, Office of State Budget and Management.

Legislature: *Directory of the State and County Officials of North Carolina, 1988,* Thad Eure.

Libraries: *Statistics & Directory of North Carolina Public Libraries, July 1, 1986—June 30, 1987,* Division of State Library, North Carolina Department of Cultural Resources; Ms. Betty Bass, North Carolina State Library.

License Tag Identification: *The License Plate Book,* Thomson C. Murray.

Manufacturing: Information Services, North Carolina Department of Commerce, Technical Support Division.

Medical Resources: *Family Care Homes Licensed by the North Carolina Department of Human Resources, April 1988,* Division of Facility Services; *North Carolina Health Manpower Data Book (October 1986);* Paul Buescher; Lise Fondren; Hazel Hadley; Earlean Strickland.

Military Posts and Terminal: *1987 North Carolina Transportation Map,* North Carolina Department of Transportation.

Miss North Carolina: Doug Huff and Steve Zaytoun, directors of Miss North Carolina Pageant.

Museums: *The Official Museum Directory (1986).*

National Forests: U.S. Department of Agriculture, Forest Service; Pat Robinson.

National Historic Landmarks: *Catalogue of National Historic Landmarks,* U.S. Department of the Interior.

National Parks: *1987 North Carolina Transportation Map,* North Carolina Department of Transportation.

National Wildlife Refuge: U.S. Department of the Interior, Fish and Wildlife Service; James Glenn, Mackay Island National Wildlife Refuge; John Taylor, Alligator River National Wildlife Refuge.

Natural Resources: *Productive National Resources in North Carolina,* North Carolina Department of Natural Resources and Community Development; Don Follmer, Director of Public Affairs.

Newspapers: *North Carolina Newspaper Directory, 1987,* North Carolina Press Association.

Occupations: *Employment and Wages in North Carolina, Fourth Quarter, 1986,* Labor Market Information Division, Employment Security Commission of North Carolina; Janice Pierce.

Population: *1987 Projection Series,* Office of State Budget and Management; *Population Comparison—Large Cities in the Southeast,* U.S. Department of Commerce, Bureau of the Census;

Profile, North Carolina Counties Update, Fall 1987, Office of State Budget and Management, Management and Information Services; North Carolina Department of Human Resources, Division of Social Services, Planning and Information Services.

Ports and Waterways: *North Carolina Business Climate;* Business/Industry Development Division, North Carolina Department of Commerce; *North Carolina Economic Development Report, 1986,* North Carolina Department of Commerce; *North Carolina Ports, A World of Difference,* North Carolina State Ports Authority; William T. Stover, Department of Commerce, Ports Authority.

Public Assistance: *North Carolina Department of Human Resources; Profile, North Carolina Counties Update, Fall 1987,* Office of State Budget and Management, Management and Information Services; *Supplemental Security Income, State and County,* U.S. Department of Health and Human Services, Social Security Administration; Quentin Uppercue; Pat Fowlkes.

Radio: *Broadcasting/Cablecasting Yearbook, 1987,* Broadcasting Publications, Inc.; *TV and Radio Directory,* The Working Press of the Nation.

Railroads: Kim Nagel, North Carolina Department of Commerce, Utilities Commission.

Regions: Bob Paciocco, Mid-East Commission, Washington, North Carolina.

Religion: *The World Almanac and Book of Facts, 1988.*

Research Triangle Park: *North Carolina Business Climate,* Business/Industry Development Division, North Carolina Department of Commerce.

Revolutionary War: Mary Ann McNeese.

Rivers: *Water Resources Development in North Carolina, 1987,* U.S. Army Corps of Engineers; The North Carolina Gazetteer, William S. Powell.

Roanoke Settlement: James A. Crutchfield.

Social Security: Social Security Administration, Department of Health and Human Services; Rick Jernigan.

Sports: Atlantic Coast Conference Service Bureau; *Reader's Digest Almanac and Yearbook;* Joe Franks, Nashville Sounds; Brian Morrison, Atlantic Coast Conference; Keith Strawn, North Carolina Sports Hall of Fame; Rick Strunk, North Carolina High School Athletic Association.

State Forests: North Carolina Department of Natural Resources and Community Development.

State Parks: *1987 North Carolina Transportation Map,* North Carolina Department of Transportation; *Discover North Carolina Parks and Recreation,* North Carolina Department of Natural Resources and Community Development.

State Symbols: *The Old North State Fact Book,* North Carolina Department of Cultural Resources, Division of Archives and History.

Taxes: *North Carolina State and Local Taxes, 1987,* North Carolina Department of Revenue; Nicole Underwood, Tax Research Division.

Television: *TV and Radio Directory,* The Working Press of the Nation.

Tourist Attractions: *North Carolina,* North Carolina Division of Travel and Tourism, Department of Commerce.

Vehicle Registration: North Carolina Department of Transportation, Motor Vehicles Division.

Voters, Registered: North Carolina State Board of Elections; *Profile, North Carolina Counties Update, Fall 1987,* Office of State Budget and Management, Management and Information Services.

War Between the States: *History of the Civil War,* Patricia L. Faust, editor; James A. Crutchfield.

Zip Codes: *1988 National Five-Digit Zip Code & Post Office Directory,* U.S. Postal Service.

CONTENTS

Index

THE NORTH CAROLINA ALMANAC

AND BOOK OF FACTS

AGRICULTURE

North Carolina led the nation in 1987 as the largest producer of flue-cured tobacco, total tobacco products, sweet potatoes, and turkeys. The state ranked second in the production of cucumbers for pickles.

The most important cash field products for 1987 were tobacco, soybeans, corn, peanuts, and sweet potatoes, in that order.

Sales of broilers led the livestock market, with hogs, turkeys, dairy products, and eggs in second to fifth places respectively.

The average gross income per farm realized in 1986 was $61,073, while the average net income was $18,016.

In 1986, North Carolina ranked twelfth in the nation in crop receipts with a total of $1,970,812,000; eleventh in livestock, dairy, and poultry receipts with a total of $1,957,740,000. The state ranked thirty-first in government payments with receipts totaling $42,581,000 and twelfth in the nation on *total cash receipts* with $3,971,133,000.

In round numbers, in 1987 there were 72,000 farms with a total combined acreage of 10,800,000, for an average of 150 acres per farm, compared to the national average of 461 acres per farm.

Top Ten Counties in Farm Cash Receipts, 1985

Rank	*All Crops*	*Livestock, Dairy and Poultry*
1	Robeson	Union
2	Johnston	Duplin
3	Pitt	Wilkes
4	Sampson	Wayne
5	Nash	Chatham
6	Columbus	Moore
7	Wilson	Sampson
8	Duplin	Randolph
9	Wayne	Iredell
10	Halifax	Nash

Farms

Following is a chart showing the number of farms and average size in acres according to the 1980 census. (The 1985 census information is not available until 1989.) Also listed are the acres of harvested cropland per county and estimated farm income in 1985.

County	Number of Farms 1980	Average Size (in acres) 1980	Acres of Harvested Cropland 1985	Estimated Farm Income (000) 1985
Alamance	972	118	39,200	$ 37,420
Alexander	658	90	14,400	48,410
Alleghany	568	137	17,200	22,354
Anson	390	267	51,500	43,096
Ashe	1,504	86	25,300	29,016
Avery	291	70	4,200	13,124
Beaufort	815	194	144,100	58,058
Bertie	724	248	89,200	62,881
Bladen	919	162	76,100	46,182
Brunswick	476	129	30,100	20,811
Buncombe	1,529	73	22,900	33,428
Burke	409	87	13,800	17,765
Cabarrus	580	142	40,100	13,102
Caldwell	459	95	16,400	14,069
Camden	131	385	53,800	13,609
Carteret	162	418	29,400	9,583
Caswell	870	163	26,600	21,422
Catawba	669	122	37,400	16,394
Chatham	1,028	115	28,200	79,394
Cherokee	322	93	7,900	9,810
Chowan	259	211	41,800	23,815
Clay	224	84	5,100	4,811
Cleveland	933	131	60,100	38,574
Columbus	1,690	112	105,900	75,419
Craven	562	164	59,900	38,996
Cumberland	642	185	70,900	37,775
Currituck	143	377	53,100	15,621
Dare	6	(D)	1,500	948
Davidson	1,214	94	45,800	25,884
Davie	680	115	27,700	22,244
Duplin	1,856	134	132,500	225,741
Durham	304	135	11,600	9,999
Edgecombe	615	356	120,700	72,965
Forsyth	893	67	19,000	14,413
Franklin	878	156	66,100	50,077
Gaston	386	125	21,000	11,716
Gates	282	241	44,100	26,971
Graham	197	53	1,400	2,051
Granville	1,041	166	40,000	37,899
Greene	670	160	72,900	59,125
Guilford	1,354	100	46,900	36,187
Halifax	565	382	123,500	79,475
Harnett	1,163	139	80,600	50,325
Haywood	1,043	78	11,900	$ 24,938
Henderson	608	101	27,700	43,882
Hertford	349	260	52,500	32,996
Hoke	209	347	48,000	17,489
Hyde	189	591	80,800	20,304
Iredell	1,306	125	61,400	62,512
Jackson	275	68	3,700	10,967
Johnston	2,253	118	150,300	107,211
Jones	314	235	50,300	20,477
Lee	457	115	14,600	15,041
Lenoir	839	169	102,500	81,040
Lincoln	560	124	34,300	22,865
Macon	429	69	6,800	14,551
Madison	1,481	72	13,100	13,719
Martin	728	200	81,700	60,736
McDowell	274	89	6,600	7,060
Mecklenburg	429	107	22,700	27,415
Mitchell	454	63	4,900	5,798
Montgomery	288	172	16,400	24,065
Moore	861	113	27,300	86,880
Nash	997	215	94,900	114,359
New Hanover	80	156	5,000	3,285
Northampton	513	330	103,800	68,373
Onslow	578	131	51,000	29,890
Orange	599	151	31,700	25,538
Pamlico	136	324	43,400	13,474
Pasquotank	253	292	73,900	27,829
Pender	514	179	53,800	25,569
Perquimans	343	252	71,900	26,898
Person	753	171	34,300	23,961
Pitt	1,070	219	157,500	115,296
Polk	211	130	8,100	5,402
Randolph	1,527	107	65,600	67,527
Richmond	273	209	27,000	20,306
Robeson	1,943	160	224,300	103,979
Rockingham	1,286	115	35,800	34,132
Rowan	956	134	63,300	34,321
Rutherford	612	110	23,700	10,411
Sampson	1,818	145	177,900	143,966
Scotland	142	630	42,900	14,819
Stanly	689	168	92,300	42,530
Stokes	1,569	77	23,600	24,179

County	Number of Farms 1980	Average Size (in acres) 1980	Acres of Harvested Cropland 1985	Estimated Farm Income (000) 1985	County	Number of Farms 1980	Average Size (in acres) 1980	Acres of Harvested Cropland 1985	Estimated Farm Income (000) 1985
Surry	1,605	90	39,700	$ 57,422	Washington	347	367	87,600	$ 45,347
Swain	89	(D)	1,900	1,597	Watauga	885	63	9,200	23,370
Transylvania	204	87	6,500	8,406					
Tyrrell	141	485	51,000	21,518	Wayne	1,350	147	154,200	156,526
Union	1,263	160	140,300	220,428	Wilkes	1,332	96	26,800	125,176
Vance	502	145	25,500	19,349	Wilson	910	158	96,700	73,701
Wake	1,291	125	60,600	63,810	Yadkin	1,301	89	50,200	42,330
Warren	470	197	30,700	25,473	Yancey	861	64	6,000	9,193
					State Total	72,792	142	5,130,000	$4,140,595

(D) Withheld to avoid disclosing data for individual farms.

County Agricultural Extension Offices

Alamance
201 W. Elm St.
Burlington 27215
919-227-2036

Alexander
255 Liledoun Rd.
Taylorsville 28681
704-632-4451

Alleghany
County Office Bldg.
Sparta 28675
919-372-5597

Anson
McLaurin St.
Wadesboro 28170
704-694-9351

Ashe
County Office Bldg.
Jefferson 28640
704-246-3021

Avery
Courthouse
Newland 28657
704-733-2415

Beaufort
Agriculture Bldg.
111 W. 2nd St.
Washington 27889
919-946-0111

Bertie
Agriculture Bldg.
Windsor 27983
919-794-3194

Bladen
P.O. Box 248
Elizabethtown 28337
919-862-4591

Brunswick
Government Center
Box 109
Bolivia 28422
919-253-4425

Buncombe
331 College St.
P.O. Box 7667
Asheville 28801-3558
704-255-5524

Burke
Human Resource Center
Morganton 28655
704-433-4050

Cabarrus
745 Cabarrus Ave. W.
Concord 28025
704-782-6130

Caldwell
611 Lower Creek Dr.
Lenoir 28645
704-758-8451

Camden
County Office Bldg.
S. Camden Ave.
Camden 27921
919-338-0171

Carteret
Courthouse Square
Beaufort 28516
919-728-8421

Caswell
Agriculture Bldg.
P.O. Box 220
Yanceyville 27379
919-694-4158

Catawba
P.O. Box 389
Newton 28658
704-464-7880

Chatham
P.O. Box 278
Pittsboro 27312
919-542-3974

Cherokee
Office Bldg.
Murphy 28906
704-837-2210

Chowan
County Office Bldg.
P.O. Box 1030
Edenton 27932
919-482-8431

Clay
Community Service Bldg.
Hayesville 28904
704-389-6301

Cleveland
130 S. Post Rd.
Shelby 28150
704-482-4365

Columbus
P.O. Box 569
Whiteville 28472
919-642-5700

Craven
Agriculture Bldg.
P.O. Box 1340
New Bern 28560
919-633-1477

Cumberland
301 South
County Office Bldg.
Fayetteville 28302
919-484-7156

Currituck
Courthouse
Currituck 27929
919-232-2261

Dare
Administration Bldg.
Manteo 27954
919-473-1101

Davidson
301 E. Center St.
Lexington 27292
704-246-2687

Davie
County Office Bldg.
Mocksville 27028
704-634-6297

Duplin
Box 458
Kenansville 28349
919-296-1996

Durham
County Agriculture Bldg.
721 Foster St.
Durham 27701
919-688-2240

Edgecombe
Administration Bldg.
Box 129
Tarboro 27889
919-823-8131

Forsyth
1450 Fairchild Dr.
Winston-Salem 27101
919-767-8213

Franklin
307 E. Nash St.
Louisburg 27549
919-496-3344

Gaston
P.O. Box 276
Dallas 28034
704-922-0301

Gates
County Agriculture Bldg.
Gatesville 27938
919-357-1400

Graham
Smith Howell Bldg.
Robbinsville 28771
704-479-3361

Granville
P.O. Box 926
Oxford 27565
919-693-8806

Greene
County Office Complex
Snow Hill 28580
919-747-5831

Guilford
3309 Burlington Rd.
Greensboro 27402
919-375-5876

Halifax
Agricultural Bldg.
Halifax 27839
919-583-5161

Harnett
P.O. Box 11357
Lillington 27546
919-893-3339

Haywood
Federal Building
203 S. Haywood St.
Waynesville 28786
704-456-3575

Henderson
740 Glover St.
Hendersonville 28739
704-692-0216

Hertford
County Office Bldg. #1
Winton 27986
919-358-7822

Hoke
Box 578
Raeford 28376
919-875-3461

Hyde
Courthouse
Swan Quarter 27885
919-926-3201

Iredell
P.O. Box 311
Statesville 28677
704-873-0507

Jackson
102 Scotts Creek Rd.
Community Service Bldg.
Sylva 28779
704-586-4009

Johnston
301 Highway N.
Box 1457
Smithfield 27577
919-934-5003

Jones
Agriculture Bldg.
Box 218
Trenton 28585
919-448-3011

Lee
225 Steele St.
Lee County Agricultural Bldg.
Sanford 27330
919-775-5624

Lenoir
Pink Hill Hwy.
P.O. Box 757
Kinston 28501
919-527-2191

Lincoln
115 W. Main St.
Lincolnton 28092
704-732-3361

Macon
Courthouse
Franklin 28734
919-524-6426

Madison
Roberts Bldg.
Main & Lower Bridges Sts.
Marshall 28753
919-649-2411

Martin
Agriculture Bldg.
Box 1148
Williamston 27892
919-792-1621

McDowell
County Administration Bldg.
Marion 28752
704-652-7121

Mecklenburg
301 Billingsley Rd.
Charlotte 28202
704-336-2561

Mitchell
Annex Bldg.
Box 67
Bakersville 28705
704-688-2051

Montgomery
P.O. Box 467
Troy 27371
919-576-6011

Moore
Agricultural Bldg.
S. Ray St.
Carthage 28327
919-947-5800

Nash
County Agricultural Center
Nashville 27856
919-459-4111

New Hanover
6206 Olennder Dr.
Wilmington 28401
919-256-9933

Northampton
Agriculture Bldg.
Main St.
Jackson 27845
919-534-2711

Onslow
College & Warlick Sts.
Jacksonville 28540
919-455-4164

Orange
109 Court St.
Hillsborough 27278
919-732-4301

Pamlico
Courthouse
P.O. Box 8
Bayboro 28515
919-745-4121

Pasquotank
P.O. Box 1608
Elizabeth City 27909
919-338-3954

Pender
Office Bldg.
Box 834
Burgaw 28425
919-259-1235

Perquimans
County Office Bldg.
Hertford 27944
919-426-5428

Person
County Office Bldg.
304 S. Morgan St.
Roxboro 27573
919-599-1195

Pitt
1717 W. 5th St.
Greenville 27834
919-830-6367

Polk
Annex Extension Bldg.
Columbus 28722
704-894-8428

Randolph
2222 S. Fayetteville St.
Asheboro 27203
919-629-2131

Richmond
Courthouse
Box 1358
Rockingham 28379
919-895-2762

Robeson
County Government Complex
Box 392
Lumberton 28358
919-738-8111

Rockingham
Rt. 8 Box 701-C
Reidsville 27320
919-342-8230

Rowan
1216 W. Innes St.
Salisbury 28144
704-633-0571

Rutherford
601 N. Main St.
Rutherfordton 28139
704-287-2211

Sampson
E. Rowan St.
Clinton 28328
919-592-7161

Scotland
County Complex
Laurinburg 28352
919-277-2422

Stanly
Courthouse
Albemarle 28001
704-983-7269

Stokes
Community Services Bldg.
Danbury 27016
919-593-8179

Surry
Agricultural Bldg.
Box 324
Dobson 27017
919-386-9274

Swain
Drawer I
Bryson City 28713
704-488-9273

Transylvania
Community Service Bldg.
Brevard 28712
704-884-3109

Tyrrell
Agriculture Bldg.
Box 208, Broad St.
Columbia 27925
919-796-1581

Union
Courthouse
500 N. Main
Monroe 28110
704-289-3801

Vance
306 Young Ave.
Henderson 27536
919-438-8188

Wake
4001-E. Cary Dr.
Raleigh 27602
919-839-7070

Warren
101 S. Main St.
Warrenton 27589
919-257-3640

Washington
P.O. Box 70
Plymouth 27962
919-793-2163

Watauga
Courthouse, Box 18
Boone 28607
704-264-3061

Wayne
206 S. George
Box 68
Goldsboro 27530
919-731-1520

Wilkes
Wilkes County Office Bldg.
Wilkesboro 28697
919-651-7347

Wilson
Agricultural Center
Box 3027
2020 S. Goldsboro St.
Wilson 27893
919-237-0113

Yadkin
County Office Bldg.
Yadkinville 27055
919-679-2061

Yancey
Courthouse, Rm. 7
Burnsville 28714
919-682-6186

AIRLINES

The following airlines serve North Carolina airports.

Airborne Express (air freight only)
Air-Lift Associates, Inc.
Air Wisconsin
American Airlines
American Eagle
Bankair, Inc.
Christman Air System
Continental Airlines
Corporate Air (air freight only)
Delta Air Lines
Delta Connection-Atlantic Southeast
DHL Airlines, Inc. (air freight only)
Direct Air, Inc.
Eastern Air Lines, Inc.
Eastern Metro Express
Federal Express (air freight only)
Flying Tiger Line (air freight only)
Ozark Air Lines, Inc.
New York Air
Pan American World Airways, Inc.
People Express Airlines, Inc.
Piedmont Aviation, Inc.
Piedmont Commuter System
Piedmont Regional Airlines
Saber Aviation, Inc. (air freight only)
Summit Airlines, Inc. (air freight only)

Tennessee Airways, Inc.
Trans World Airlines, Inc.
United Airlines
USAir, Inc.
Wheeler Airlines
Zantop International Airlines, Inc. (air freight only)

AIRPORTS

City	*Airport name*	*Runway length (in feet)*
Ahoskie	Tri-County Airport	3,950
Albemarle	Stanly County Airport	4,700
Andrews-Murphy	Andrews-Murphy Airport	4,560
Asheboro	Asheboro Municipal Airport	3,900
Asheville	Asheville Regional Airport	8,001
Beaufort-Morehead City	Michael J. Smith Field	4,252
Burlington	Burlington Municipal Airport	3,700
Chapel Hill	Horace Williams Airport	3,500
Charlotte	Charlotte-Douglas Intl. Airport	10,000
Clinton	Sampson County Airport	4,300
Currituck	Currituck County Airport	4,000
Edenton	Edenton Municipal Airport	5,300
Elizabeth City	Elizabeth City/CGAB Municipal Airport	7,219
Elizabethtown	Bladen County Airport	5,000
Elkin	Elkin Municipal Airport	4,000
Englehard-Swan Quarter	Hyde County Airport	4,700
Erwin-Lillington	Harnett County Airport	3,700
Fayetteville	Fayetteville Municipal Airport	7,204
Franklin	Macon County Airport	3,800
Gastonia	Gastonia Municipal Airport	3,500
Goldsboro	Goldsboro-Wayne Airport	3,700
Greensboro	Piedmont Triad Intl. Airport	10,000
Greeneville	Pitt-Greeneville Airport	5,000
Hatteras	Hatteras-Billy Mitchell Airport	3,000
Hickory	Hickory Municipal Airport	6,400
Jacksonville	Albert J. Ellis Airport	7,100
Kenansville-Warsaw	P. B. Raefort (Duplin Cty) Airport	4,800
Kill Devil Hills	Kill Devil Hills-First Flight Airport	3,000
Kinston	Eastern Regional JetPort	6,001
Laurinburg-Maxton	Laurinburg-Maxton Airport	6,500
Lexington	Lexington Municipal Airport	3,300
Lincolnton	Lincolnton-Lincoln Cty Airport	4,800
Lumberton	Lumberton Municipal Airport	5,000
Manteo	Dare County Regional Airport	3,850
Monroe	Monroe Municipal Airport	4,800
Morganton-Lenoir	Morganton-Lenoir Airport	4,000
Mount Airy	Mount Airy-Surry County Airport	3,500
Mount Olive	Mount Olive Municipal Airport	3,700
New Bern	Simmons-Nott Airport	4,804
Ocean Isle Beach	Ocean Isle Beach Airport	4,000
Ocracoke Island	Ocracoke Island Airport	3,000
Oxford-Henderson	Henderson-Oxford Airport	5,000
Plymouth	Plymouth Municipal Airport	3,700
Raeford	Raeford/Hoke Airport	3,400
Raleigh-Durham	Raleigh-Durham Airport	10,000

City	Airport name	Runway length (in feet)
Reidsville	Rockingham County Airport	5,200
Roanoke Rapids	Halifax County Airport	4,000
Rockingham-Hamlet	Richmond County Airport	5,000
Rocky Mount-Wilson	Rocky Mount-Wilson Airport	5,999
Roxboro	Person County Airport	5,000
Rutherford-Spindale-Forest City	Rutherford County Airport	4,400
Salisbury	Rowan County Airport	4,200
Sanford	Sanford-Lee County Airport	3,800
Shelby	Shelby Municipal Airport	4,300
Siler City	Siler City Municipal Airport	3,800
Smithfield	Johnston County Airport	4,400
Southern Pines-Pinehurst	Moore County Airport	5,503
Southport-Long Beach	Brunswick County Airport	4,000
Spruce Pine-Newland	Avery County Airport	3,000
Star-Troy	Montgomery County Airport	3,500
Statesville	Statesville Municipal Airport	5,000
Sylva	Jackson County Airport	2,819
Tarboro	Tarboro-Edgecombe Airport	4,000
Wadesboro	Anson County Airport	3,500
Wallace	Wallace Municipal Airport	4,000
Washington	Warren Field Airport	5,000
West Jefferson	Ashe County Airport	4,300
Whiteville	Columbus County Airport	3,700
Wilkesboro	Wilkes County Airport	4,250
Williamston	Martin County Airport	3,700
Wilmington	New Hanover County Airport	7,999
Wilson	Wilson Industrial Air Center	4,500
Winston-Salem	Smith Reynolds Airport	6,655

ALCOHOL

The following chart shows the counties in which liquor sales are legal only in certain cities, and the "wet" cities. Liquor sales are legal in counties that are not listed.

The accompanying map shows the counties that prohibit the sale of liquor county-wide, the counties that allow the sale of liquor in certain cities and those which allow it county-wide.

County	City
Alexander	Taylorsville
Anson	Ansonville
	Morven
	Polkton
	Wadesboro
Ashe	West Jefferson
Avery	Banner Elk
	Elk Park
	Beech Mountain
	Seven Devils
Bladen	East Arcadia
	Elizabethtown
	White Lake
Brunswick	Bald Head Island
	Belville
	Boiling Springs Lake
	Calabash
	Caswell Beach
	Long Beach
	Navassa
	Ocean Isle
	Shallotte

County	City
	Southport
	Sunset Beach
	Yaupon Beach
Burke	Morganton
	Hickory
Cabarrus	Concord
	Mt. Pleasant
Caldwell	Granite Falls
	Lenoir
	Blowing Rock
Cherokee	Andrews
	Murphy
Cleveland	Shelby
	Kings Mountain
Columbus	Bolton
	Brunswick
	Chadbourn
	Fair Bluff
	Lake Waccamaw
	Tabor City
	Whiteville
Davidson	High Point
	Lexington
	Thomasville
Duplin	Faison
	Kenansville
	Wallace
	Warsaw
Gaston	Bessemer City
	Cherryville
	Gastonia
Harnett	Angier
	Coats
	Dunn
	Erwin
	Lillington
Haywood	Canton
	Maggie Valley
	Waynesville
Henderson	Hendersonville
	Laurel Park
Jackson	Sylva
Lee	Broadway
	Sanford
Lincoln	Lincolnton
Macon	Highlands
Madison	Hot Springs
McDowell	Marion
Montgomery	Biscoe
	Candor
	Mount Gilead
	Troy
Moore	Cameron
	Carthage
	Little River Township
	McNeil Township
	Mineral Springs Township
	Sandhill Township
Polk	Tryon
Randolph	Liberty
	Randleman
	High Point
Robeson	Fairmont
	Lumberton
	Maxton
	Pembroke
	Red Springs
	Rowland
	St. Paul
Rutherford	Lake Lure
	Rutherfordton
Sampson	Clinton
	Garland
	Newton Grove
	Roseboro
Stanly	Norwood
Swain	Bryson City
Transylvania	Brevard
	Rosman
Union	Monroe
	Stallings
	Waxhaw
	Weddington
Watauga	Blowing Rock
	Beech Mountain
	Boone
	Seven Devils

Map of Liquor Sales

ARTS

In 1971, North Carolina became the first state in the nation to have a cabinet-level state department, the *Department of Cultural Resources,* to administer programs in the arts, history, and libraries. The state justly takes pride in the fact that it also has the first state-supported symphony, the first outdoor drama, and the first residential state high school and college for the arts. In 1986–87, the state contributed $4.5 million to the North Carolina Arts Council. The state legislature allotted $1,545,102 to the North Carolina Symphony and $2,599,108 to the North Carolina Museum of Art. The state museums received $394,951,000 for 1986–87 from state and federal funding, and the state symphonies received $151,950,000 of state and federal monies.

In 1964, the North Carolina Arts Council was established by executive order, and became a statutory state agency in 1967. The council consists of twenty-four members appointed to three-year terms by the governor. The stated purpose is to enrich the cultural life of the state by nurturing and supporting excellence in the arts and by providing opportunities for every North Carolinian to experience the arts. Art is now a basic component of the State Education Program of the North Carolina Department of Public Instruction. Funding for the council's programs and services is provided by the North Carolina General Assembly and the National Endowment for the Arts, a federal agency in Washington, D.C.

Included is a list of art related events, broken down by locality. For additional information, contact the appropriate source as listed.

For other crafts guilds and events, contact the visual/literary arts director, NC Arts Council, Dept. of Cultural Resources, Raleigh, 27611; 919-733-2821.

For details about other music, dance, and theater companies, contact the music/dance and theater directors, NC Arts Council, Dept. of Cultural Resources, Raleigh, 27611; 919-733-2821.

To inquire about other special holiday events contact the Division of Travel and Tourism, Dept. of Commerce, Raleigh, 27611; 919-733-4171.

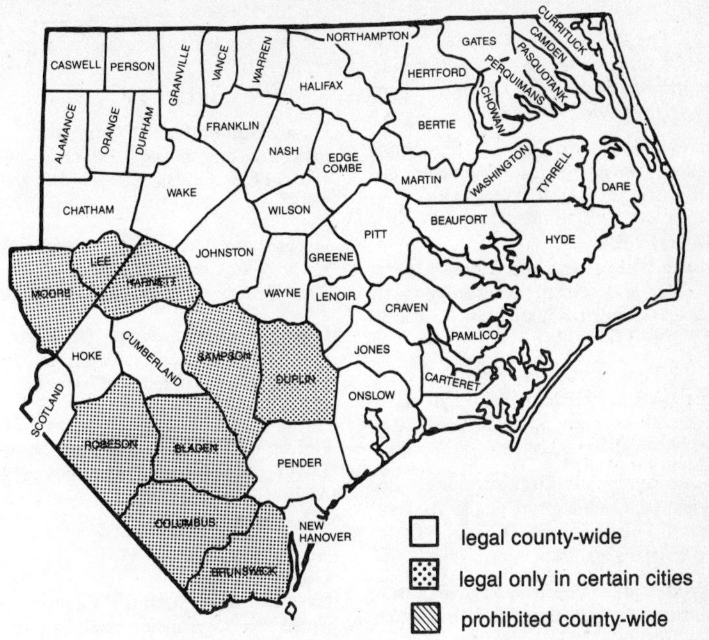

For information about local arts agencies in each county, contact the community development section, NC Arts Council, Dept. of Cultural Resources, Raleigh, 27611; 919-733-7897.

The Council maintains a computerized directory of arts organizations and artists in the state, available for a nominal fee. Contact the Information Manager, 919-733-2111.

ASHEVILLE

Asheville Symphony Orchestra, October—April season. Robert Hart Baker, Music Director and Conductor; Randall Rosenbaum, General Manager; P.O. Box 2852 (28802), 704-254-7046.

Southern Highland Handicraft Guild (Crafts), Folk Art Center featuring members' work, open seven days a week, year-round; P.O. Box 9545 (28815), 704-298-7928.

BATH

Blackbeard: *Knight of the Black Flag* (Outdoor Drama), Late June—August; historical pageant about Blackbeard, the pirate; P.O. Box 209 (27809), 919-923-3971.

BOONE

Horn in the West (Outdoor Drama), Historical pageant about Daniel Boone, other settlers of western North Carolina; P.O. Box 295 (28607), 704-264-2120.

BRASSTOWN

John C. Campbell Folk School (Crafts), classes year-round; (28902), 704-837-2775.

BREVARD

Brevard Music Center, Henry Janiec, Conductor; P.O. Box 592 (28712), 704-883-8188.

CHAPEL HILL

Playmakers Repertory Company (Theater), October—April season; classical, contemporary productions; 203 Graham Memorial, University of North Carolina (27514), 919-962-1122.

Touch, The Mime Trio (Theater), Late fall—early summer touring season; original mime productions; 376 Wesley Court (27514), 919-929-8187.

University of North Carolina Symphony Orchestra, David Serrins, Conductor; 602 Churchill Dr. (27514), 919-966-1330.

CHARLOTTE

Charlotte Opera/North Carolina Opera, September—May season; major productions, special tours; Spirit Square, 110 E. 7th St. (28202), 704-332-7177.

Charlotte Pops Orchestra, June—July; outdoor concerts in Freedom Park, light classical pieces, show tunes; Spirit Square, 110 E. 7th St. (28202), 704-332-6136.

Charlotte Symphony Orchestra Inc., Leo B. Driehuys, Conductor; Douglas A. Patti, Manager; Spirit Square, 110 E. 7th St. (28202), 704-332-6136.

GM Productions (Theater), Regular season; black-oriented productions; P.O. Box 34692 (28234), 704-332-2044.

University of North Carolina Symphony, Robert Glazer, Conductor; Judy Lewandowski, Manager; (28211), 704-597-2474.

CHEROKEE

Unto These Hills (Outdoor Drama), June—August; historical pageant about Cherokee Indians; P.O. Box 398 (28719), 704-497-2111.

DURHAM

Messiah, December; performed in Duke University Chapel, featuring the University Choir, guest singers, and instrumentalists. For information contact: Choral Activities, Duke University, Duke Station (27706), 919-684-3898.

FLAT ROCK

Flat Rock Playhouse, professional repertory company, state theater of North Carolina, featuring drama, contemporary comedy; June—Labor Day; southwest of Asheville (28713), 704-693-0731.

GREENSBORO

Eastern Philharmonic Orchestra, Sheldon Morgenstern, Music Director and Conductor; Mr. Clare E. Humphrey, Executive Director; 200 N. Davie St. (27401), 919-373-4712.

Frank Holder Dance Company, modern dance concerts, tours; September—May season; 314 S. Greene St. (27401), 919-275-8573.

Greensboro Opera, grand opera, nationally known guest artists; October performance; 2000 Dellwood Dr. (27408), 919-288-0741.

Greensboro Symphony Orchestra, Dr. Peter Paul Fuchs, Conductor; Margaret B. Faison, Manager; 200 N. Davie St. (27401), 919-373-4523.

University of North Carolina Symphony, David H. Moskovitz, Conductor; Aycock Auditorium, University of North Carolina School of Music (27412), 919-379-5789.

GREENVILLE

East Carolina Summer Theatre, professional repertory, major musicals a specialty; July; East Carolina University (27834), 919-757-6829.

HALIFAX

First for Freedom, (Outdoor Drama), historical pageant about the Revolution in North Carolina; late June—July; P.O. Box 1776 (27839), 919-583-3011.

HICKORY

Western Piedmont Symphony, Martin Bellar, Conductor; Marian C. Belk, Manager; P. E. Monroe Auditorium, Old City Hall, 30 Third St. NW (28601), 704-324-8603.

HIGH POINT

North Carolina Shakespeare Festival, professional repertory company offering classical, including Shakespeare, and contemporary productions; July—August, also fall touring productions; 305 N. Main St. (27260).

KENANSVILLE

The Liberty Cart, (Outdoor Drama), historical pageant depicting 100 years of eastern North Carolina history; P.O. Box 470 (28349), 919-296-0721.

MANTEO

The Lost Colony, (Outdoor Drama), historical play about Roanoke voyages, first English settlements in America; June—August; special activities in conjunction with America's 400th Anniversary Celebration through 1987; P.O. Box 40 (27954), 919-473-2127.

MARS HILL

Southern Appalachian Repertory Theatre, offering dramas, musicals, comedy, premieres of new works by professional theater; June—August; Mars Hill College (28754), 704-689-1203.

PEMBROKE

Strike at the Wind, (Outdoor Drama), historical pageant about Henry Berry Lowrie and Lumbee Indians; July—August; P.O. Box 1059 (28372), 919-521-2480.

PENLAND

Penland School of Crafts, classes in contemporary crafts. For information, contact the school (28765), 704-765-2359.

RALEIGH

A Christmas Carol, contemporary state production by Theatre in the Park; December; P.O. Box 12151 (27605), 919-755-6058.

Carolina Pops Orchestra, outdoor concerts, show tunes, light classical pieces; June—August; P.O. Box 19102 (27619), 919-828-5766.

Carolina Regional Theater, classical, contemporary productions; October—May; touring season; 1 E. South St. (27601), 919-834-8650.

City of Raleigh Arts Commission, meets regularly the second Tuesday of each month at 7:30 p.m. The public is welcome; P.O. Box 590 (27602), 919-890-3195.

National Opera, classic opera in English; September—May touring season, cities and schools across state; P.O. Box 12800 (27605), 919-890-6081.

North Carolina Symphony Orchestra, Gerhardt Zimmerman, Conductor; Tom McGuire, Executive Director; P.O. Box 28026 (27611), 919-733-2750.

Raleigh Civic Symphony, Robert Petters, Conductor; Stewart Theater, North Carolina State University; Jones Auditorium, Meredith College; North Carolina State University Music Dept., P.O. Box 5937 (27650), 919-737-2981.

SEAGROVE

Jugtown Pottery, demonstrations, large sales shop, established 1917, open year-round Monday—Saturday; Rt. 2 (27341), 919-464-3266.

Seagrove Pottery and Potters Museum, working pottery, demonstrations, sales shop, open year-round, best selection in spring, irregular schedule; (27341), no phone.

SNOW CAMP

The Sword of Peace, (Outdoor Drama), historical pageant about Quakers and other Alamance County settlers in Revolution; July—August; P.O. Box 535 (27349), 919-376-6948.

VALDESE

From This Day Forward, (Outdoor Drama), historical pageant about Waldensian settlements in western North Carolina, July—August; P.O. Box 112 (28690), 919-874-0176.

WAXHAW

Listen and Remember, (Outdoor Drama), Revolutionary War era historical pageant based on the family of Andrew Jackson; P.O. Box 1776 (28173), 704-283-8528.

WILMINGTON

Curtain Call Company, professional repertory company, contemporary comedy a specialty, summer productions, year-round touring; 4642 Riplee Dr. (28401), 919-799-6079.

UNCW Community Orchestra, Joe Hickman, Conductor; Richard Deas, Manager; Sarah Graham Kenan Memorial Auditorium, P.O. Box 3725 (28406), 919-791-4330.

WINSTON-SALEM

North Carolina Dance Theater, ballet and modern dance concerts, tours; September—May season; Seven Vintage Ave. (27107), 919-761-2190.

Piedmont Chamber Orchestra, Dr. George Trautwein, Conductor; Roger R. Jones, Executive Director; Crawford Hall, 200 Waughtown (27107), 919-784-7170.

Piedmont Craftsmen, Inc., Piedmont Crafts Fair, early November; all media by professional members; sales shop open all week year-round; 300 S. Main St. (27101), 919-725-1516.

The Nutcracker, December; ballet performances from North Carolina School of the Arts in Winston-Salem, Charlotte, and Raleigh with Winston-Salem, Charlotte, and North Carolina Symphonies; North Carolina School of the Arts, P.O. Box 12189 (27107), 919-784-7170.

Wake Forest University Symphony, David B. Levy, Conductor; Scales Fine Arts Center, Box 7345, Reynolda Station (27109), 919-761-5372.

Winston-Salem Symphony, Peter Perret, Conductor; Alan W. Cooper, General Manager; regular season, R. J. Reynolds Auditorium; summer pops series, June—July, outdoors at Graylyn estate; 610 Coliseum Dr. (27106), 919-725-1035.

BANKING

According to the Federal Reserve Bank's regional office in Atlanta, Georgia, as of June 30, 1987, there was a total of 67 commercial banks in North Carolina with total assets of $52,240,885,000 and total deposits of $38,330,294,000. There were 139 savings and loan associations with total assets of $1,949,064,400 and $1,642,775,500 deposits.

Commercial Banks

The following chart shows the number of commercial banks headquartered in North Carolina by county, with total assets and deposits as of June 30, 1987, as reported by the Federal Reserve Bank.

County	Banks	Total Assets	Total Deposits	County	Banks	Total Assets	Total Deposits
Alamance	1	1,327,200	1,138,300	Lee	2	1,288,400	1,141,200
Avery	1	2,981,300	2,346,100	Lincoln	1	6,668,200	6,058,000
Bladen	1	1,131,300	973,600	Macon	1	3,822,300	3,413,400
Buncombe	1	5,948,200	5,297,900	Mecklenburg	6	249,970,710	155,754,100
Cabarrus	1	17,833,600	15,830,800	Montgomery	2	1,555,970	1,360,210
Caldwell	1	21,633,600	19,211,400	Nash	2	17,687,500	15,522,880
Catawba	1	11,111,800	9,467,100	New Hanover	1	2,102,500	1,804,900
Cherokee	1	5,072,100	4,368,200	Orange	1	4,000,700	3,337,700
Cleveland	1	15,682,500	12,376,800	Pender	1	657,700	475,700
Columbus	2	17,760,290	15,649,440	Randolph	2	1,721,810	1,545,750
Cumberland	2	190,240	140,090	Robeson	2	17,391,200	15,544,450
Currituck	1	4,685,400	4,106,800	Rockingham	1	9,621,900	8,489,900
Davidson	1	24,700,200	20,177,600	Rowan	2	3,752,780	3,330,520
Durham	3	13,904,300	12,104,620	Scotland	1	1,805,400	1,697,700
Forsyth	3	105,080,810	82,653,690	Stanly	1	5,191,700	4,547,100
Granville	1	8,786,300	7,210,800	Surry	2	1,016,050	891,460
Guilford	7	5,387,160	4,810,200	Union	1	3,069,700	2,760,100
Hyde	1	10,645,300	9,793,300	Wake	2	31,252,350	27,242,220
Iredell	1	3,123,700	2,834,300	Wayne	1	18,939,500	17,065,000
Johnston	2	583,270	523,250	Wilson	2	34,805,500	28,610,610

Top 50 Commercial Banks

Listed below are the top 50 commercial banks in North Carolina ranked by deposits as of June 30, 1987, as reported by the Federal Reserve Bank.

Name	*City*	*Assets*	*Deposits*
NCNB NB OF NC	Charlotte	11,813,333	8,486,614
Wachovia B&TC NA	Winston-Salem	10,452,066	8,219,403
First Union NB NC	Charlotte	12,724,070	6,685,159
Branch BKG&TC	Wilson	3,427,962	2,819,053
First-Citizens B&TC	Raleigh	2,951,018	2,570,014
Southern NB of NC	Lumberton	1,772,986	1,540,030
United Carolina BK	Whiteville	1,744,455	1,536,691
Central Carolina B&TC NA	Durham	1,283,571	1,115,183
Peoples B&TC	Rocky Mount	933,943	813,214
Planters NB&TC	Rocky Mount	834,807	739,074
High Point B&TC	High Point	338,600	309,000
Security B&TC	Salisbury	303,757	270,068
Lexington ST BK	Lexington	247,002	201,776
Bank of Granite	Granite Falls	216,336	192,114
Barclays BK	Charlotte	210,093	188,676
Southern B&TC	Mt. Olive	189,395	170,650
First Charter NB	Concord	178,336	158,308
Fidelity BK	Fuquay-Varina	174,217	154,208
First BK	Troy	147,077	128,762
Republic B&TC	Charlotte	150,530	127,269
First NB of Shelby	Shelby	156,855	123,768
First NB of Randolph Cty	Asheboro	129,283	116,716
Mid-South B&TC	Sanford	116,967	104,085
East Carolina BK	Engelhard	106,453	97,933
Peoples BK	Newton	111,118	94,671
First NB of Reidsville	Reidsville	96,219	84,899
Yadkin Valley B&TC	Elkin	93,748	84,136
Traid BK	Greensboro	84,058	77,061
Union BK of Oxford	Oxford	87,863	72,108
Mechanics & Farmers BK	Durham	79,968	70,917
First Charlotte B&TC	Charlotte	77,603	68,961
Farmers & Merchants BK	Granite Quarry	71,521	62,984
Lincoln BK of NC	Lincolnton	66,682	60,580
First Commercial BK	Asheville	59,482	52,979
Bank of Stanly	Albemarle	51,917	45,471
Citizens BK	Murphy	50,721	43,682
Heritage BK	Lucama	52,588	42,008
Bank of Currituck	Moyock	46,854	41,068
Bank of Four Oaks	Four Oaks	42,894	38,594
Randolph B&TC	Asheboro	42,898	37,859

Name	City	Assets	Deposits
Carolina Mountain BK	Highlands	38,823	34,134
Village BK	Chapel Hill	40,007	33,377
Citizens NB	Winston-Salem	37,430	32,285
Bank of Iredell	Statesville	31,237	28,343
Columbus NB	Whiteville	31,574	28,253
Bank of Union	Monroe	30,697	27,601
Guaranty ST BK	Durham	26,891	24,362
Avery County BK	Newland	29,813	23,461
Central ST BK	High Point	26,627	22,779
American B&TC	High Point	25,559	22,234

Top 50 Savings and Loan Associations

Listed below are the top 50 savings and loan associations in North Carolina ranked by deposits as of June 30, 1987, as reported by the Federal Reserve Bank.

Name	City	Assets	Deposits
First Home FS&LA	Greensboro	1,224,259	829,768
First American SVG BK FSB	Greensboro	944,554	639,366
First FS&LA	Hendersonville	447,965	424,668
Raleigh FSB	Raleigh	462,928	421,308
North Carolina FS&LA	Matthews	590,077	401,245
Old Stone BK NC FSB	High Point	444,020	397,708
Gate City FS&LA	Greensboro	426,631	388,736
Piedmont FS&LA	Winston-Salem	451,869	383,116
First FS&LA	Raleigh	605,106	381,686
Home FS&LA	Charlotte	396,682	364,189
Southeastern S&LC	Charlotte	387,036	336,260
Asheville FS&LA	Asheville	377,504	323,166
Pioneer SVG BK	Rocky Mount	379,991	304,260
Cooperative S&LA	Wilmington	324,306	299,125
First FS&LA	Winston-Salem	316,258	283,846
First FS&LA	Charlotte	297,684	277,536
Heritage FS&LA	Monroe	338,882	276,993
First Financial SVG BK	Kinston	298,060	271,624
Mutual S&LA	Charlotte	286,018	249,906
Preferred SVG BK	High Point	319,226	244,281
East Coast FS&LA	Goldsboro	261,994	229,310
First Southern SVG BK	Asheboro	243,007	206,796
Citizens SVG BK	Newton	220,462	203,403
Security FS&LA	Durham	216,392	200,576
Clyde S&LA	Clyde	225,468	196,213
Workmens FSB	Mt. Airy	211,352	192,731

Name	*City*	*Assets*	*Deposits*
First Fed of The Carolinas	High Point	240,247	192,256
Home S&LA	Durham	230,996	190,507
C K FSB	Concord	200,575	183,724
Financial First FSB	Burlington	202,067	178,183
United FS&LA	Rocky Mount	278,046	175,294
Home FS&LA	Fayetteville	173,789	162,521
Citizens S&LA	Concord	161,372	148,899
Home FS&LA	Salisbury	180,237	145,055
First FS&LA	Southern Pines	151,900	139,938
Carolina SVG BK	Wilmington	159,506	136,979
Essex SVG BK	Elizabeth City	145,520	133,786
Citizens FS&LA	Salisbury	145,433	123,622
Watauga S&LA	Boone	130,454	122,023
Fidelity FS&LA	Hickory	128,294	120,118
Summit S&LA	Sanford	136,939	120,022
First FS&LA	Sanford	121,133	112,282
Brevard FS&LA	Brevard	119,825	111,579
Surety FS&LA	Morganton	126,055	111,293
Macon S&LA	Franklin	117,771	110,706
Community FS&LA	Burlington	124,379	109,619
Gaston FS&LA	Gastonia	122,098	109,259
Peoples FS&LA	Wilmington	122,032	109,183
First FS&LA of PI	Greeneville	122,080	106,448
First SVG BK FSB	Hickory	131,650	104,774

BOUNDARIES

North Carolina is touched by portions of four states. These states and a brief history of each follow.

South Carolina. Both Carolinas—North and South—were named alternately for French King Charles IX and English Kings Charles I and II. In 1690, North and South Carolina became separate entities, and in 1712, they became known as North and South Carolina.

Georgia. Named after the English King George II, the charter for the state was granted in 1732 to James Oglethorpe. The colony was originally intended as a place of refuge for debtors.

Tennessee. Originally part of North Carolina, Tennessee became a territory of the United States in 1790, and later, in 1796, achieved statehood as the 16th state of the Union.

Virginia. One of the original thirteen colonies, it was named after Elizabeth, the Virgin Queen.

CHAMBERS OF COMMERCE

A Chamber of Commerce is a voluntary organization of the business community. It unites business and professional individuals and firms, thus creating a central agency which lends itself to improving business and building a better community.

The major responsibility of the Chamber of Commerce is the community's economic well-being. It works to increase wealth and prosperity by facilitating the growth of existing businesses and fostering new ones. This new wealth can be directed toward establishing and improving educational and cultural facilities in order to create the proper business climate for attracting more business and industry.

The Chamber of Commerce meets this responsibility in three steps:

1. It examines community needs to determine what must be done to make it a better place to live and do business.

2. It channels community resources to the fulfillment of these needs.

3. It organizes and develops the necessary leadership to guarantee that the organization will become an effective force for expansion and improvement.

The following list includes all Chambers of Commerce in North Carolina.

Ahoskie Chamber of Commerce
(Hertford County)
310 S. Catherine Creek Road
Post Office Box 7
Ahoskie 27910; 919-332-2042

Albemarle Chamber of Commerce
(Stanly County)
116 E. N Street
Post Office Box 909
Albemarle 28002-0909; 704-982-8116

Angier Chamber of Commerce
(Harnett County)
111 Depot Street
Post Office Box 47
Angier 27501; 919-639-2500

Apex Chamber of Commerce
(Wake County)
400 W. Williams Street
Apex 27502; 919-362-6456

Asheboro-Randolph Chamber of Commerce (Randolph County)
317 East Dixie Drive
Post Office Box 2007
Asheboro 27204; 919-625-6121

Asheville Chamber of Commerce
(Buncombe County)
151 Haywood Street
Post Office Box 1010
Asheville 28802; 704-258-3858

Belhaven Chamber of Commerce
(Beaufort County)
114 Pamlico Street
Post Office Box 147
Belhaven 27810-0147; 919-943-3770

Belmont Chamber of Commerce
(Gaston County)
26 E. Woodrow Avenue
Post Office Box 368
Belmont 28012; 704-825-5307

Bessemer City Chamber of Commerce
(Gaston County)
117 W. Pennsylvania Avenue
Post Office Box 1342
Bessemer City 28016; 704-629-2979

Black Mountain-Swannanoa Chamber of Commerce (Buncombe County)
Executive Plaza
201 E. State Street
Black Mountain 28711; 704-669-2300

Blowing Rock Chamber of Commerce
(Watauga County)
Main Street
Post Office Box 406
Blowing Rock 28605; 704-295-7851

Boone Chamber of Commerce
(Watauga County)
701 Blowing Rock Road
Boone 28607; 704-264-2225

Brevard Chamber of Commerce
(Transylvania County)
35 W. Main Street
Post Office Box 589
Brevard 28712; 704-883-3700

Burlington Chamber of Commerce
(Alamance County)
610 S. Lexington Avenue
Post Office Box 450
Burlington 27215; 919-228-1338

Burnsville Chamber of Commerce
(Yancey County)
2 Town Square
Room 3
Burnsville 28714; 704-682-7413

Canton Chamber of Commerce
(Haywood County)
Post Office Box 1026
Canton 28716; 704-648-2400

Carolina Beach Chamber of Commerce
(New Hanover County)
(Pleasure Island)
201 Lumberton Avenue
Carolina Beach 28428; 919-458-8434

Cary Chamber of Commerce
(Wake County)
114 W. Chatham Street
Post Office Box 51
Cary 27511; 919-467-1016

Chadbourn Chamber of Commerce
(Columbus County)
208-A Brown Street
Chadbourn 28431; 919-654-3445

Chapel Hill-Carrboro Chamber of Commerce (Orange County)
104 S. Estes Drive
Post Office Box 2897
Chapel Hill 27515; 919-967-7075

Charlotte Chamber of Commerce
(Mecklenburg County)
129 W. Trade Street
Post Office Box 32785
Charlotte 28232; 704-377-6911

Cherokee Chamber of Commerce
(Swain County)
Post Office Box 465
Cherokee 28719; 704-497-9195

Cherryville Chamber of Commerce
(Gaston County)
116 S. Mountain Street
Post Office Box 305
Cherryville 28021; 704-435-3451

Chimney Rock Chamber of Commerce
(Rutherford County)
Post Office Box 32
Chimney Rock 28720; 704-625-4403

Clayton Chamber of Commerce
(Johnston County)
108 S. Barbour Street
Post Office Box 246
Clayton 27520; 919-553-6352

Clinton Chamber of Commerce
(Sampson County)
414 Warsaw Road
Post Office Box 467
Clinton 28328; 919-592-6177

Columbus Chamber of Commerce
(Polk County)
Post Office Box 831
Columbus 28722; 704-894-8237

Concord-Cabarrus County Chamber of Commerce (Cabarrus County)
23 Union Street N.
Post Office Box 1029
Concord 28026; 704-782-4111

Cullowhee Chamber of Commerce
(Jackson County)
Route 67
Box 112-H
Cullowhee 28723; 704-293-9648

Dunn Chamber of Commerce
(Harnett County)
209 W. Divine Street
Post Office Box 548
Dunn 28334; 919-892-4113

Durham Chamber of Commerce
(Durham County)
201 N. Roxboro Street
Post Office Box 3829
Durham 27702; 919-682-2133

Eden Chamber of Commerce
(Rockingham County)
370 W. Meadow Road
Eden 27288; 919-623-6828

Edenton-Chowan Chamber of Commerce
(Chowan County)
116 E. King Street
Post Office Drawer F
Edenton 27932; 919-482-3400

Elizabeth City Chamber of Commerce
(Pasquotank County)
502 E. Ehringhaus Street
Post Office Box 426
Elizabeth City 27909; 919-335-4365

Elizabethtown-White Lake Chamber of Commerce (Bladen County)
108 W. Broad Street
Post Office Box 306
Elizabethtown 28337; 919-862-4368

Enfield Chamber of Commerce
(Halifax County)
Post Office Box 625
Enfield 27823; 919-445-3146

Farmville Chamber of Commerce
(Pitt County)
104 E. Wilson Street
Post Office Box 150
Farmville 27828; 919-753-4670

Fayetteville Chamber of Commerce
(Cumberland County)
519 Ramsey Street
Post Office Box 9
Fayetteville 28302; 919-483-8133

Forest City Chamber of Commerce
(Rutherford County)
102 W. Trade Street
Forest City 28043; 704-245-2144

Franklin Chamber of Commerce
(Macon County)
180 Porter Street
Franklin 28734; 704-524-3161

Fuquay-Varina Chamber of Commerce
(Wake County)
525 N. Main Street
Post Office Box 156
Fuquay-Varina 27526; 919-552-4947

Garner Chamber of Commerce
(Wake County)
401 Circle Drive
Post Office Box 222
Garner 27529; 919-772-6440

Gastonia Chamber of Commerce
(Gaston County)
601 W. Franklin Blvd.
Post Office Box 2168
Gastonia 28053; 704-864-2621

Goldsboro Chamber of Commerce
(Wayne County)
200 E. Spruce Street
Post Office Box 1107
Goldsboro 27530; 919-734-2241

Granite Falls Chamber of Commerce
(Caldwell County)
Post Office Box 10
Granite Falls 28630; No number available

Greensboro Chamber of Commerce
(Guilford County)
330 S. Greene Street
Greensboro 27402; 919-275-8675

Greenville Chamber of Commerce
(Pitt County)
302 S. Greene Street
Greenville 27834; 919-752-4101

Hamlet Chamber of Commerce
(Richmond County)
56 Main Street
Post Office Box 466
Hamlet 28345; 919-582-3233

Havelock Chamber of Commerce
(Craven County)
Post Office Box 21
Havelock 28532; 919-447-1101

Henderson-Vance County Chamber of Commerce
414 S. Garnett Street
Post Office Box 1302
Henderson 27536; 919-438-8414

Hendersonville Chamber of Commerce
(Henderson County)
330 N. King Street
Hendersonville 28739; 704-692-1413

Hertford Chamber of Commerce
(Perquimans County)
Post Office Box 27
Hertford 27944; 919-426-5657

Hickory Chamber of Commerce
(Catawba County)
470 Hwy 64–70, S.W.
Post Office Box 1828
Hickory 28603; 704-328-6111

Highlands Chamber of Commerce
(Macon County)
Post Office Box 404
Highlands 28741; 704-526-2112

High Point Chamber of Commerce
(Guilford County)
704 N. Main Street

Post Office Box 5025
High Point 27262; 919-889-8151

Hillsborough Chamber of Commerce
(Orange County)
228 S. Churton Street
Hillsborough 27278; 919-732-8156

Jackson Chamber of Commerce
(Northampton County)
Highway 305 N.
Post Office Box 97
Jackson 27845; 919-534-5161

Jacksonville Chamber of Commerce
(Onslow County)
1 Marine Boulevard N.
Post Office Box 765
Jacksonville 28540; 919-347-3141

Jamesville Chamber of Commerce
(Martin County)
Water Street
Post Office Box 215
Jamesville 27846; 919-792-5006

Kannapolis Chamber of Commerce
(Cabarrus County)
316 W. Main Street
Post Office Box 249
Kannapolis 28082; 704-932-4164

Kenansville Chamber of Commerce
(Duplin County)
Post Office Box 596
Kenansville 28349; 919-296-0369

Kernersville Chamber of Commerce
(Forsyth County)
100 S. Main Street
Kernersville 27284; 919-993-4521

Kill Devil Hills Chamber of Commerce
(Dare County)
Mustian Street & Ocean Bay Blvd.
Post Office 1757
Kill Devil Hills 27948; 919-441-8144

King Chamber of Commerce
(Stokes County)
710 Kirby Road
King 27201

Kings Mountain Chamber of Commerce
(Cleveland County)
219 N. Battleground Avenue
Post Office Box 794
Kings Mountain 28086; 704-739-5051

Kinston-Lenoir County Chamber of Commerce
301 N. Queen Street
Post Office Box 157
Kinston 28501; 919-527-1131

LaGrange Chamber of Commerce
(Lenoir County)
Post Office Box 444
LaGrange 28551; 919-527-1500

Laurinburg Chamber of Commerce
(Scotland County)
606 Atkinson Street
Post Office Box 1025
Laurinburg 28352; 919-276-7420

Lenoir-Caldwell County Chamber of Commerce
222 Main Street N.W.
Post Office Box 510
Lenoir 28645; 704-754-0782

Lexington Chamber of Commerce
(Davidson County)
235 E. Center Street
Post Office Box C
Lexington 27293; 704-246-5929

Liberty Chamber of Commerce
(Randolph County)
239 S. Fayetteville Street
Post Office Box 986
Liberty 27298; 919-622-4937

Lillington Chamber of Commerce
(Harnett County)
823 Main Street
Post Office Box 967
Lillington 27546-0967; 919-893-3751

Lincolnton-Lincoln County Chamber of Commerce
106 E. Courtsquare
Post Office Box 247
Lincolnton 28092; 704-735-3096 or 3060

Louisburg Chamber of Commerce
(Franklin County)
105 Market Street
Post Office Box 652
Louisburg 27549; 919-496-3056

Lowell Chamber of Commerce
(Gaston County)
101 W. First Street
Lowell 28098; 704-824-3518

Lumberton Chamber of Commerce
(Robeson County)
800 N. Chestnut Street
Post Office Box 1008
Lumberton 28359; 919-739-4750

Madison Chamber of Commerce
(Stokes County)
112 W. Murphy Street
Madison 27025; 919-548-6248

Maggie Valley Chamber of Commerce
(Haywood County)
Rt. 1, Post Office Box 87
Maggie Valley 28751

Marion Chamber of Commerce
(McDowell County)
17 N. Garden Street
City Hall Building
Marion 28752; 704-652-4240

Marshville Chamber of Commerce
(Union County)
Post Office Box 337
Marshville 28103; 704-624-2813

Matthews Chamber of Commerce
(Mecklenburg County)
119 S. Trade Street
Post Office Box 601
Matthews 28106; 704-847-3649

Mint Hill Chamber of Commerce
(Mecklenburg County)
7151 Matthews-Mint Hill
Post Office Box 23077
Mint Hill 28212; 704-545-9726

Mocksville Chamber of Commerce
(Davie County)
107 N. Salisbury Street
Post Office Box 843
Mocksville 27028; 704-634-3304

Monroe-Union County Chamber of Commerce
903 Skyway Drive
Post Office Box 1789
Monroe 28110; 704-289-4567

Mooresville Chamber of Commerce
(Iredell County)
480 N. Main Street
Post Office Box 628
Mooresville 28115; 704-664-3898

Morehead City Chamber of Commerce
(Carteret County)
3401 W. Arendell Street
Post Office Box 1198
Morehead City 28557; 919-726-6831

Morganton Chamber of Commerce
(Burke County)
110 E. Meeting Street
Post Office Box 751
Morganton 28655; 704-437-3021

Mount Airy Chamber of Commerce
(Surry County)
134 S. Renfro Street
Post Office Box 913
Mount Airy 27030; 919-786-6116

Mount Olive Chamber of Commerce
(Wayne County)
123 N. Center Street
Mount Olive 28365; 919-658-3113

Murfreesboro Chamber of Commerce
(Hertford County)
116 E. Main Street
Post Office Box 393
Murfreesboro 27855; 919-398-4886

Murphy Chamber of Commerce
(Cherokee County)
115 U.S. 64 W.
Murphy 28906; 704-837-2242

Newbern-Craven County Chamber of Commerce
101 Middle Street
Post Office Drawer C
New Bern 28560; 919-637-3111

Newland Chamber of Commerce
(Avery County)
Post Office Box 668
Newland 28657; 704-733-4737

North Wilkesboro Chamber of Commerce
(Wilkes County)
Midtown Plaza
Post Office Box 727
North Wilkesboro 28659; 919-838-8662

Oxford Chamber of Commerce
(Granville County)
104 College Street
Post Office Box 820
Oxford 27565; 919-693-6125

Pembroke Chamber of Commerce
(Robeson County)
Post Office Box 1075
Pembroke 28372; No number available

Plymouth Chamber of Commerce (Washington County)
811 Washington Street
Plymouth 27962; 919-793-4804

Raeford-Hoke Chamber of Commerce (Hoke County)
101 N. Main Street
Post Office Box 1260
Raeford 28376; 919-875-5929

Raleigh Chamber of Commerce (Wake County)
800 S. Salisbury Street
Post Office Box 2978
Raleigh 27602; 919-833-3005

Red Springs Chamber of Commerce (Robeson County)
125 W. Third Avenue
Red Springs 28377; 919-843-5441

Reidsville Chamber of Commerce (Rockingham County)
142 N. Scales Street
Post Office Box 1020
Reidsville 27320; 919-349-8481

Richlands Chamber of Commerce (Onslow County)
Post Office Box 752
Richlands 28574; 919-324-4848

Roanoke Valley Chamber of Commerce (Halifax County)
1013 Roanoke Avenue
Post Office Box 519
Roanoke Rapids 27870; 919-537-3513

Robbinsville Chamber of Commerce (Graham County)
Post Office Box 1206
Robbinsville 28771; 704-479-3790

Rockingham Chamber of Commerce (Richmond County)
220 E. Washington Street
Post Office Box 86
Rockingham 28379; 919-895-9058

Rocky Mount Chamber of Commerce (Edgecombe County)
437 Falls Road
Post Office Box 392
Rocky Mount 27802-0392; 919-442-5111

Roxboro Chamber of Commerce (Person County)
211 N. Main Street
Post Office Box 209
Roxboro 27573; 919-599-8333

Rutherfordton-Spindale Chamber of Commerce (Rutherford County)
222 N. Main Street
Rutherfordton 28139; 704-287-3090

St. Pauls Chamber of Commerce (Robeson County)
Post Office Box 243
St. Pauls 28384; 919-865-5122

Salisbury-Rowan County Chamber of Commerce
620 W. Innes Street
Post Office Box 559
Salisbury 28144; 704-633-4221

Sanford Chamber of Commerce (Lee County)
110 Charlotte Avenue
Post Office Box 519
Sanford 27330; 919-775-7341

Scotland Neck Chamber of Commerce (Halifax County)
Post Office Box 237
Scotland Neck 27874; 919-826-3917

Shallotte Chamber of Commerce (Brunswick County)
U.S. Hwy 17 at N.C. 130
Post Office Box 1380
Shallotte 28459; 919-754-6644

Shelby Chamber of Commerce (Cleveland County)
200 S. Lafayette Street
Post Office Box 879
Shelby 28150; 704-487-8521

Siler City Chamber of Commerce (Chatham County)
311 N. 2nd Avenue
Post Office Box 255
Siler City 27344; 919-742-3333

Smithfield-Selma Chamber of Commerce (Johnston County)
114 S. 4th Street
Post Office Box 467
Smithfield 27577; 919-934-9166

Southern Pines Chamber of Commerce (Moore County)
125 S.E. Broad Street
Post Office Box 458
Southern Pines 28387; 919-692-3926

Southport Chamber of Commerce
(Brunswick County)
Route #5, Box 52
Southport 28461; 919-457-6964

Sparta Chamber of Commerce
(Alleghany County)
First Citizens Bank Bldg.
Post Office Box 337
Sparta 28675; 919-372-5473

Spring Lake Chamber of Commerce
(Cumberland County)
Post Office Box 191
Spring Lake 28390; 919-488-3515

Spruce Pine Chamber of Commerce
(Mitchell County)
Rte. 1, Box 796
Spruce Pine 28777; 704-765-9483

Statesville Chamber of Commerce
(Iredell County)
115 E. Front Street
Post Office Box 1064
Statesville 28677; 704-873-2892

Sylva Chamber of Commerce
(Jackson County)
18 N. Central Street
Sylva 28779; 704-586-2155

Tabor City Chamber of Commerce
(Columbus County)
5 W. 5th Street
Tabor City 28463; 919-653-2031

Tarboro Chamber of Commerce
(Edgecombe County)
112 W. Church Street
Post Office Drawer F
Tarboro 27886; 919-823-7241

Taylorsville Chamber of Commerce
(Alexander County)
104 W. Main Avenue
Post Office Box 578
Taylorsville 28681; 704-632-8141

Thomasville Chamber of Commerce
(Davidson County)
6 W. Main Street
Post Office Box 727
Thomasville 27361; 919-475-6134

Troy Chamber of Commerce
(Montgomery County)
Post Office Box 637
Troy 27371; 919-572-2572

Tryon Chamber of Commerce
(Polk County)
401 N. Trade Street
Tryon 28782; 704-859-6236

Wadesboro Chamber of Commerce
(Anson County)
1704 Morven Road
Post Office Box 305
Wadesboro 28170; 704-694-4181

Wake Forest Chamber of Commerce
(Wake County)
100 Front Street
Post Office Box 728
Wake Forest 27587; 919-556-1519

Wallace Chamber of Commerce
(Duplin County)
1536 Old Teachey Road
Post Office Box 552
Wallace 28466; 919-285-4044

Warsaw Chamber of Commerce
(Duplin County)
Post Office Box 585
Warsaw 28398; 919-293-7804

Washington Chamber of Commerce
(Beaufort County)
102 Stewart Pkwy.
Post Office Box 665
Washington 27889; 919-946-9168

Waynesville Chamber of Commerce
(Haywood County)
511 Walnut Street
Post Office Box 125
Waynesville 28786; 704-456-3021

Wendell Chamber of Commerce
(Wake County)
115 N. Pine Street
Post Office Box 562
Wendell 27591; 919-365-6319

West Jefferson Chamber of Commerce
(Ashe County)
#12 Bank Mountain Road
Post Office Box 31
West Jefferson 28694; 919-246-9550

Whiteville Chamber of Commerce
(Columbus County)
601 S. Madison Street
Post Office Box 509
Whiteville 28472; 919-642-3171

Williamston Chamber of Commerce
(Martin County)
105 W. Main Street
Post Office Box 311
Williamston 27892; 919-792-4131

Wilmington Chamber of Commerce
(New Hanover County)
514 Market Street
Post Office Box 330
Wilmington 28402; 919-762-2611

Wilson Chamber of Commerce
(Wilson County)
220 Broad Street
Post Office Box 1146
Wilson 27894; 919-237-0165

Windsor Chamber of Commerce
(Bertie County)
York Street
Post Office Box 572
Windsor 27983; 919-794-4277

Winston-Salem Chamber of Commerce
(Forsyth County)
500 W. 5th Street
Post Office Box 1408
Winston-Salem 27102; 919-725-2361

Yanceyville Chamber of Commerce
(Caswell County)
Post Office Box 29
Yanceyville 27379; 919-694-6106

Zebulon Chamber of Commerce
(Wake County)
Post Office Box 546
Zebulon 27597; 919-269-6320

Source: World-Wide Chamber of Commerce Directory

CLIMATE

North Carolina's Sun Belt Climate offers moderate temperatures. Winter weather rarely interferes with business operations, and rainfall provides ample water supplies. The state experiences four distinct seasons, with picturesque weather during the extended seasons of spring and fall.

The climate varies dramatically among regions of the state. North Carolina rises nearly 7,000 feet in altitude across its 500-mile breadth, from the Atlantic Ocean to Mount Mitchell, the highest peak east of the Mississippi. The year-round average temperature is 20 degrees higher on the coast than in the higher mountains. The southern coast's average annual temperature is comparable to that of inland northern Florida, while Mount Mitchell's average temperature falls below that of Buffalo, N.Y.

Temperatures across the state are usually comfortable. In Raleigh, the centrally located capital, the average summer high is in the mid-80s, and the average winter low remains above 30 degrees. In the Piedmont, temperatures may drop as low as 10 or 12 degrees once in an average winter and occasionally may climb near 100 degrees in the summer.

Precipitation varies widely across the state. The southern mountains are the rainiest region in the Eastern United States, with an annual average of more than 80 inches. Fifty miles to the north, the valley of the French Broad River is the driest point south of Virginia and east of the Mississippi, with annual precipitation of 27 inches. East of the mountains, average rainfall is 40 to 55 inches.

Average winter snowfall varies from about one inch per year on the Outer Banks and southern coast to eight inches in the northern Piedmont and southern mountains. Higher elevations receive as much as 50 inches a year.

Month	Weather Station	TEMPERATURES Daily Maximum	Daily Minimum	Record High	Year	Record Low	Year
Jan.	Asheville	47.5	26.0	78	1975	−16	1985
	Raleigh	50.1	29.1	79	1952	−9	1985
	Wilmington	55.9	35.3	82	1975	5	1985
Feb.	Asheville	50.6	27.6	77	1986	−2	1967
	Raleigh	52.8	30.3	84	1977	5	1971
	Wilmington	58.1	36.6	85	1962	11	1958
Mar.	Asheville	58.4	34.4	83	1985	9	1980
	Raleigh	61.0	37.7	92	1945	11	1980
	Wilmington	64.8	43.3	89	1974	9	1980
Apr.	Asheville	68.6	42.7	89	1972	22	1987
	Raleigh	72.3	46.5	95	1980	23	1985
	Wilmington	74.3	51.8	95	1967	30	1983
May	Asheville	75.6	51.0	91	1969	29	1986
	Raleigh	79.0	55.3	97	1953	31	1977
	Wilmington	80.9	60.4	98	1953	40	1981
June	Asheville	81.4	58.2	96	1969	35	1966
	Raleigh	85.2	62.6	104	1954	38	1977
	Wilmington	86.1	67.1	104	1952	48	1983
July	Asheville	84.0	62.4	96	1983	46	1967
	Raleigh	88.2	67.1	105	1952	48	1975
	Wilmington	89.3	71.3	102	1977	59	1972
Aug.	Asheville	83.5	61.6	100	1983	42	1986
	Raleigh	87.1	66.8	101	1983	46	1965
	Wilmington	88.6	70.8	102	1954	55	1982
Sept.	Asheville	55.8	77.9	92	1975	30	1967
	Raleigh	81.6	60.4	104	1954	37	1983
	Wilmington	83.9	65.7	98	1975	44	1981
Oct.	Asheville	68.7	43.3	86	1986	21	1976
	Raleigh	71.6	47.7	98	1954	19	1962
	Wilmington	75.2	53.7	95	1954	27	1962
Nov.	Asheville	58.6	34.2	81	1974	8	1970
	Raleigh	61.8	38.1	88	1950	11	1970
	Wilmington	66.8	43.9	87	1974	20	1970
Dec.	Asheville	50.3	28.3	78	1971	−7	1983
	Raleigh	52.7	31.2	79	1978	4	1983
	Wilmington	59.1	37.2	81	1984	9	1983

Month	Weather Station	PRECIPITATION Water Equivalent Normal	Maximum Monthly	Year	Minimum Monthly	Year	Snow, Ice Pellets Maximum Monthly	Year
Jan.	Asheville	3.48	7.47	1978	0.45	1981	17.6	1966
	Raleigh	3.55	7.52	1954	0.87	1981	14.4	1955
	Wilmington	3.64	7.08	1964	1.09	1981	2.9	1965
Feb.	Asheville	3.60	7.02	1982	0.44	1978	25.5	1969
	Raleigh	3.43	6.00	1983	1.00	1968	17.2	1979
	Wilmington	3.44	8.74	1983	1.01	1976	12.5	1973

		PRECIPITATION						
		Water Equivalent					*Snow, Ice Pellets*	
Month	*Weather Station*	*Normal*	*Maximum Monthly*	*Year*	*Minimum Monthly*	*Year*	*Maximum Monthly*	*Year*
Mar.	Asheville	5.13	9.86	1975	0.77	1985	13.0	1969
	Raleigh	3.69	7.78	1983	1.03	1985	14.0	1960
	Wilmington	4.04	8.09	1983	0.93	1967	6.6	1980
Apr.	Asheville	3.84	7.26	1979	0.25	1976	11.5	1987
	Raleigh	2.91	6.10	1978	0.23	1976	1.8	1983
	Wilmington	2.98	8.21	1961	0.33	1957		
May	Asheville	4.19	8.83	1973	1.59	1985	T	1979
	Raleigh	3.67	7.67	1974	0.92	1964		
	Wilmington	4.22	9.12	1956	1.13	1983		
June	Asheville	4.20	8.94	1987	1.28	1986		
	Raleigh	3.66	9.38	1973	0.55	1981		
	Wilmington	5.65	12.87	1962	0.89	1984		
July	Asheville	4.43	9.92	1982	0.46	1986		
	Raleigh	4.38	10.05	1945	0.80	1953		
	Wilmington	7.44	15.12	1966	1.65	1961		
Aug.	Asheville	4.79	11.28	1967	0.52	1981		
	Raleigh	4.44	10.49	1955	0.81	1950		
	Wilmington	6.64	14.06	1981	1.66	1968		
Sept.	Asheville	3.96	9.12	1977	0.16	1984		
	Raleigh	3.29	12.94	1945	0.23	1985		
	Wilmington	5.71	18.94	1984	1.07	1981		
Oct.	Asheville	3.29	7.05	1971	0.30	1978	T	1977
	Raleigh	2.73	7.53	1971	0.44	1963		
	Wilmington	2.97	9.81	1964	0.17	1953		
Nov.	Asheville	3.29	7.76	1979	1.19	1981	9.6	1968
	Raleigh	2.87	8.22	1948	0.61	1973	2.6	1975
	Wilmington	3.19	7.87	1972	0.49	1973	T	1976
Dec.	Asheville	3.51	8.48	1973	0.16	1965	16.3	1971
	Raleigh	3.14	6.65	1983	0.25	1965	10.6	1958
	Wilmington	3.43	6.57	1982	0.48	1955	4.0	1970

T = Trace

COASTLINE AND SHORELINE

General coastline figures represent lengths of the seacoast outline. The coastlines of sounds and of bays are included to a point where they narrow to the width of 30 minutes of latitude and the distance across at such point is included. Tidal shorelines include the outer coast, offshore islands, sounds, bays, and rivers to the head of tidewater or to a point where tidal waters narrow to a width of 100 feet.

Coastline	*Shoreline*
301	3,375

CONGRESSIONAL DISTRICTS

North Carolina is divided into eleven Congressional districts, as shown on the accompanying map. The representatives are listed, along with their Washington, D.C. addresses and telephone numbers, and their local addresses and telephone numbers.

DISTRICT 1

Congressman Walter B. Jones—(D)
241 Cannon House Office Building
Washington, D.C. 20515
202-225-3101

108 E. Wilson Street
P.O. Drawer 90
Farmville, NC 27828
919-753-3082

DISTRICT 2

Congressman I. T. Valentine, Jr.—(D)
1510 Longworth Office Building
Washington, D.C. 20515
202-225-4531

Suite 124 Station Square
Rocky Mount, NC 27801
919-446-1147

P.O. Box 3654
Durham, NC 27702
919-541-5201

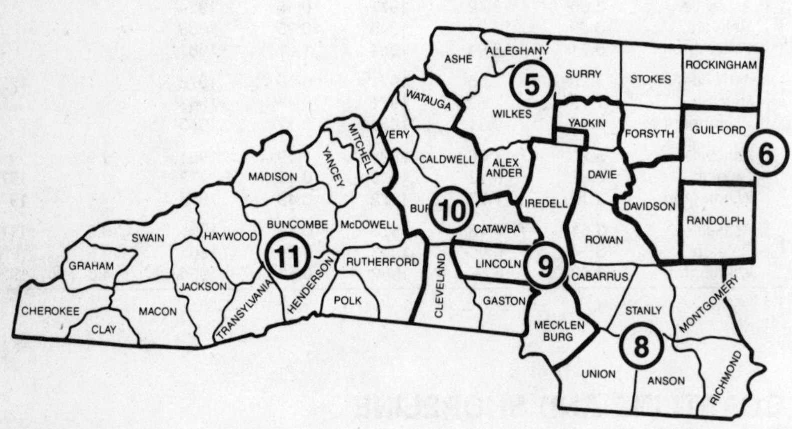

Congressional Districts

DISTRICT 3

Congressman Martin Lancaster—(D)
1408 Longworth House Office Building
Washington, D.C. 20515
202-225-3415

103 Federal Building; 34 N. John St.
Goldsboro, NC 27530
919-736-1844

DISTRICT 4

Congressman David E. Price—(D)
1223 Longworth House Office Building
Washington, D.C. 20515
202-225-1784

1777 Durham-Chapel Hill Blvd., Suite 100
Chapel Hill, NC 27516
919-967-8500

225 Hillsborough St., Suite 330
Raleigh, NC 27603
919-856-4611

241 Sunset Avenue
Federal Building, Suite 101
Asheboro, NC 27203
919-626-3060

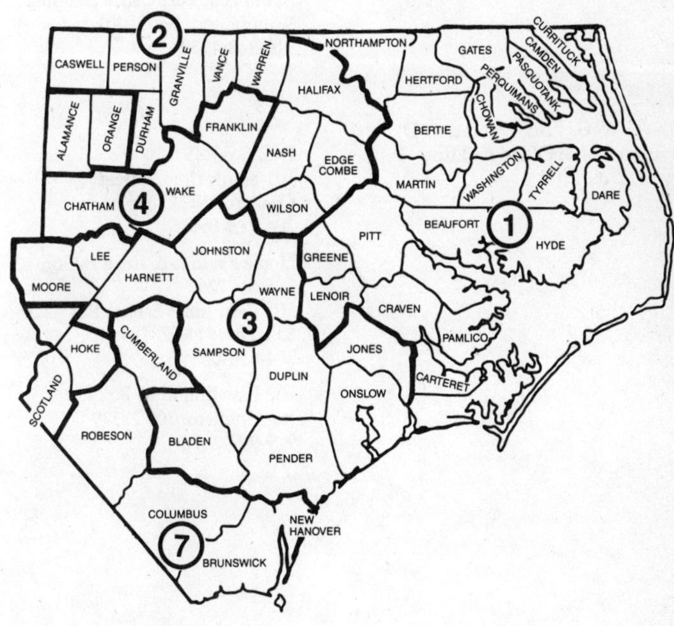

DISTRICT 5

Congressman Stephen L. Neal—(D)
2463 Rayburn House Office Building
Washington, D.C. 20515
202-225-2071

Room 421, Federal Building
Winston-Salem, NC 27101
919-761-3125

DISTRICT 6

Congressman J. Howard Coble—(R)
430 Cannon House Office Building
Washington, D.C. 20515
202-225-3065

P.O. Box 299
Greensboro, NC 27402
919-333-5005

P.O. Box 814
Graham, NC 27253
919-229-0159

510 Ferndale Boulevard
High Point, NC 27260
919-886-5106

DISTRICT 7

Congressman Charles G. Rose, III—(D)
2230 Rayburn House Office Building
Washington, D.C. 20515
202-225-2731

Room 218, Federal Building
Fayetteville, NC 28301
919-323-0260

Room 208, Post Office Building
Wilmington, NC 28401
919-343-4959

DISTRICT 8

Congressman W. G. "Bill" Hefner—(D)
2161 Rayburn House Office Building
Washington, D.C. 20515
202-225-3715

P.O. Box 385
101 South Union Street
Concord, NC 28025
704-933-1615

Home Savings & Loan Building, Suite 225
507 West Innes Street, Box 4220
Salisbury, NC 28144
704-636-0635

202 East Franklin, Box 1503
Rockingham, NC 28379
919-997-2070

DISTRICT 9

Congressman J. Alex McMillan—(R)
401 Cannon House Office Building
Washington, D.C. 20515
202-225-1976

401 West Trade Street, Room 222
Charlotte, NC 28202
704-372-1976

207 West Broad Street
Statesville, NC 28677
704-872-7331

Municipal Building/Courthouse
Mooresville, NC 28115
704-663-1976

U.S. Post Office Building, Room 301
326 East Main
Lincolnton, NC 28092
704-735-1976

DISTRICT 10

Congressman T. Cass Ballenger—(R)
116 Cannon House Office Building
Washington, D.C. 20515
202-225-2576

832 E. Garrison Blvd.
Gastonia, NC 28054
704-864-9922

310 Tenth Avenue Dr., NE
P.O. Box 1830
Hickory, NC 28603
704-327-6100

DISTRICT 11

Congressman James McClure Clark—(D)
217 Cannon House Office Building
Washington, D.C. 20515
202-225-6401

Biltmore Building, Suite 434
1 N. Pack Square
Asheville, NC 28801
704-254-1747

319 W. Main St.
Sylva, NC 28779
704-586-6031

301 W. Main St.
Spindale, NC 28160
704-286-4890

CONGRESSIONAL MEDAL OF HONOR

The Congressional Medal of Honor is the highest United States military decoration and is awarded in the name of Congress to members of the Armed Forces for gallantry and bravery beyond the call of duty in action against the enemy. North Carolina recipients of the Congressional Medal of Honor follow. An asterisk (*) indicates a posthumous award.

War Between the States

Franks, William J. *Rank and organization:* Seaman, U.S. Navy. *Born:* 1830, Chatham County. *G.O. No.:* 32, 16 April 1864.

Stoddard, James. *Rank and organization:* Seaman, U.S. Navy. *Born:* 1838, North Carolina. *G.O. No.:* 32, 16 April 1864.

Trogden, Howell G. *Rank and organization:* Private, Company B, 8th Missouri Infantry. *Place and date:* At Vicksburg, Miss., 22 May 1863. *Born:* 1840, Cedar Falls. *Date of issue:* 3 August 1894.

Indian Campaigns

Brown, Lorenzo D. *Rank and organization:* Private, Company A, 7th U.S. Infantry. *Place and date:* At Big Hole, Mont., 9 August 1877. *Born:* Davidson County. *Date of issue:* 8 May 1878.

Jones, William H. *Rank and organization:* Farrier, Company L, 2d U.S. Cavalry. *Place and date:* At Little Muddy Creek, Mont., 7 May 1877; at Camus Meadows, Idaho, 20 August 1877. *Born:* Davidson County. *Date of issue:* 28 February 1878.

McBryar, William. *Rank and organization:* Sergeant, Company K, 10th U.S. Cavalry. *Place and date:* Arizona, 7 March 1890. *Born:* 14 February 1861, Elizabethtown. *Date of issue:* 15 May 1890.

Spanish-American War

Barrow, David D. *Rank and organization:* Seaman, U.S. Navy. *Born:* 22 October 1877, Reelsboro. *G.O. No.:* 521, 7 July 1899.

Parker, Pomeroy. *Rank and organization:* Private, U.S. Marine Corps. *Born:* 17 March 1874, Gates County. *G.O. No.:* 521, 7 July 1899.

Philippine Insurrection

Johnston, Gordon. *Rank and organization:* First Lieutenant, U.S. Signal Corps. *Place and date:* At Mount Bud Dajo, Jolo, Philippine Islands, 7 March 1906. *Born:* 25 May 1874, Charlotte. *Date of issue:* 7 November 1910. *G.O. No.:* 207.

Ray, Charles W. *Rank and organization:* Sergeant, Company I, 22d U.S. Infantry. *Place and date:* Near San Isidro, Luzon, Philippine Islands, 19 October 1899. *Born:* Pensacola, Yancey County. *Date of issue:* 18 April 1902.

Mexican Campaign

Anderson, Edwin A. *Rank and organization:* Captain, U.S. Navy. *Born:* 16 July 1860, Wilmington. *G.O. No.:* 177, 4 December 1915. *Other Navy award:* Distinguished Service Medal.

Johnston, Rufus Zenas. *Rank and organization:* Lieutenant Commander, U.S. Navy. *Born:* 7 June 1874, Lincolnton. *G.O. No.:* 177, 4 December 1915. *Other Navy award:* Navy Cross.

Staton, Adolphus. *Rank and organization:* Lieutenant, U.S. Navy. *Place and date:* Vera Cruz, Mexico, 22 April 1914. *Born:* 28 August 1879, Tarboro.

World War I

*__Blackwell, Robert L.__ *Rank and organization:* Private, U.S. Army, Company K, 119th Infantry, 30th Division. *Place and date:* Near St. Souplet, France, 11 October 1918. *Born:* Person County. *G.O. No.:* 13, W.D., 1919.

Parker, Samuel I. *Rank and organization:* Second Lieutenant, U.S. Army, Company K, 28th Infantry, 1st Division. *Place and date:* Near Soissons, France, 18–19 July 1918. *Born:* Monroe. *G.O. No.:* 1, W.D., 1937.

World War II

*__Eubanks, Ray E.__ *Rank and organization:* Sergeant, U.S. Army, Company D, 503d Parachute Infantry. *Place and date:* At Noemfoor Island, Dutch New Guinea, 23 July 1944. *Born:* February 1922, Snow Hill. *G.O. No.:* 20, 29 March 1945.

*__Halyburton, William David, Jr.__ *Rank and organization:* Pharmacist's Mate Second Class, U.S. Navy Reserve. *Born:* 2 August 1924, Canton. *Citation:* For conspicuous gallantry and intrepidity at the risk of his own life above and beyond the call of duty while serving with Marine Rifle Company in the 2d Battalion, 5th Marines, 1st Marine Division, during action against enemy Japanese forces on Okinawa Shima in the Ryukyu Chain, 10 May 1945.

Herring, Rufus G. *Rank and organization:* Lieutenant, U.S. Naval Reserve, LCI (G) 449. *Place and date:* Iwo Jima, 17 February 1945. *Born:* 11 June 1921, Roseboro.

Lucas, Jacklyn Harold. *Rank and organization:* Private First Class, U.S. Marine Corps Reserve, 1st Battalion, 26th Marines, 5th Marine Division. *Place and date:* Iwo Jima, Volcano Islands, 20 February 1945. *Born:* 14 February 1928, Plymouth.

Murray, Charles P., Jr. *Rank and organization:* First Lieutenant, U.S. Army, Company C, 30th Infantry, 3d Infantry Division. *Place and date:* Near Kayersberg, France, 16 December 1944. *Born:* Baltimore, Maryland. *Entered service at:* Wilmington, N.C. *G.O. No.:* 63, 1 August 1945.

Thompson, Max. *Rank and organization:* Sergeant, U.S. Army, Company K, 18th Infantry, 1st Infantry Division. *Place and date:* Near Haaren, Germany, 18 October 1944. *Born:* Bethel. *G.O. No.:* 47, 18 June 1945.

*__Warner, Henry F.__ *Rank and organization:* Corporal, U.S. Army, Antitank Company, 2d Battalion, 26th Infantry, 1st Infantry Division. *Place and date:* Near Dom Butgenbach, Belgium, 20–21 December 1944. *Born:* 23 August 1923, Troy. *G.O. No.:* 48, 23 June 1945.

The Korean Conflict

Crump, Jerry K. *Rank and organization:* Corporal, U.S. Army, Company L, 7th Infantry Regiment, 3d Infantry Division. *Place and date:* Near Chorwon, Korea, 6 and 7 September 1951. *Born:* 18 February 1933, Charlotte. *G.O. No.:* 68, 11 July 1952.

*__George, Charles.__ *Rank and organization:* Private First Class, U.S. Army, Company C, 179th Infantry Regiment, 45th Infantry Division. *Place and date:* Near Songnae-dong, Korea, 30 November 1952. *Born:* 23 August 1932, Cherokee. *G.O. No.:* 19, 18 March 1954.

*__Womack, Bryant E.__ *Rank and organization:* Private First Class, U.S. Army, Medical Company, 14th Infantry Regiment, 25th Infantry Division. *Place and date:* Near Sokso-ri, Korea, 12 March 1952. *Born:* Mill Springs. *G.O. No.:* 5, 12 January 1953.

Vietnam

*__Ashley, Eugene, Jr.__ *Rank and organization:* Sergeant First Class, U.S. Army, Company C, 5th Special Forces Group (Airborne), 1st Special Forces. *Place and date:* Near Lang Vei, Republic of Vietnam, 6 and 7 February 1968. *Born:* 12 October 1931, Wilmington.

*__Durham, Harold Bascom, Jr.__ *Rank and organization:* Second Lieutenant, U.S. Army, Battery C, 6th Battalion, 15th Artillery, 1st Infantry Division. *Place and date:* Republic of Vietnam, 17 October 1967. *Born:* 12 October 1942, Rocky Mount.

Joel, Lawrence. *Rank and organization:* Specialist Sixth Class (then Sp5c), U.S. Army, Headquarters and Headquarters Company, 1st Battalion (Airborne), 503d Infantry, 173d Airborne Brigade. *Place and date:* Republic of Vietnam, 8 November 1967. *Born:* 22 February 1928, Winston-Salem.

Miller, Franklin D. *Rank and organization:* Staff Sergeant, U.S. Army, 5th Special Forces Group, 1st Special Forces. *Place and date:* Kontum Province, Republic of Vietnam, 5 January 1970. *Born:* 27 January 1945, Elizabeth City.

Patterson, Robert Martin. *Rank and organization:* Sergeant, U.S. Army, Troop B, 2d Squadron, 17th Cavalry. *Place and date:* Near La Chu, Republic of Vietnam, 6 May 1968. *Born:* 16 April 1948, Durham.

*__Stout, Mitchell W.__ *Rank and organization:* Sergeant, U.S. Army, Battery C, 1st Battalion, 44th Artillery. *Place and date:* Khe Gio Bridge, Republic of Vietnam, 12 March 1970. *Born:* 24 February 1950, Knoxville, Tennessee. *Entered service at:* Raleigh, N.C.

CONSTITUTION

North Carolina is governed in accordance with the constitution of 1868 as amended.

Constitution of North Carolina

(As of July 1, 1985)

PREAMBLE

We, the people of the State of North Carolina, grateful to Almighty God, the Sovereign Ruler of Nations, for the preservation of the American Union and the existence of our civil, political and religious liberties, and acknowledging our dependence upon Him for the continuance of those blessings to us and our posterity, do, for the more certain security thereof and for the better government of this State, ordain and establish this Constitution.

ARTICLE I

Declaration of Rights

That the great, general, and essential principles of liberty and free government may be recognized and established, and that the relations of this State to the Union and government of the United States and those of the people of this State to the rest of the American people may be defined and affirmed, we do declare that:

Section 1. *The equality and rights of persons.* We hold it to be self-evident that all persons are created equal; that they are endowed by their Creator with certain inalienable rights; that among these are life, liberty, the enjoyment of the fruits of their own labor, and the pursuit of happiness.

Section 2. *Sovereignty of the people.* All political power is vested in and derived from the people; all government of right originates from the people, is founded upon their will only, and is instituted solely for the good of the whole.

Section 3. *Internal government of the State.* The people of this State have the inherent, sole, and exclusive right of regulating the internal government and police thereof, and of altering or abolishing their Constitution and form of government whenever it may be necessary to their safety and happiness; but every such right shall be exercised in pursuance of law and consistently with the Constitution of the United States.

Section 4. *Secession prohibited.* This State shall ever remain a member of the American Union; the people thereof are part of the American nation; there is no right on the part of this State to secede; and all attempts, from whatever source or upon whatever pretext, to dissolve this Union or to sever this Nation, shall be resisted with the whole power of the State.

Section 5. *Allegiance to the United States.* Every citizen of this State owes paramount allegiance to the Constitution and government of the United States, and no law or ordinance of the State in contravention or subversion thereof can have any binding force.

Section 6. *Separation of powers.* The legislative, executive, and supreme judicial powers of the State government shall be forever separate and distinct from each other.

Section 7. *Suspending laws.* All power of suspending laws or the execution of laws by any authority, without the consent of the representatives of the people, is injurious to their rights and shall not be exercised.

Section 8. *Representation and taxation.* The people of this State shall not be taxed or made subject to the payment of any impost or duty without the consent of themselves or their representatives in the General Assembly, freely given.

Section 9. *Frequent elections.* For redress of grievances and for amending and strengthening the laws, elections shall be often held.

Section 10. *Free elections.* All elections shall be free.

Section 11. *Property qualifications.* As political rights and privileges are not dependent upon or modified by property, no property qualification shall affect the right to vote or hold office.

Section 12. *Right of assembly and petition.* The people have a right to assemble together to consult for their common good, to instruct their representatives, and to apply to the General Assembly for redress of grievances; but secret political societies are dangerous to the liberties of a free people and shall not be tolerated.

Section 13. *Religious liberty.* All persons have a natural and inalienable right to worship Almighty God according to the dictates of their own consciences, and no human authority shall, in any case whatever, control or interfere with the rights of conscience.

Section 14. *Freedom of speech and press.* Freedom of speech and of the press are two of the great bulwarks of liberty and therefore shall never be restrained, but every person shall be held responsible for their abuse.

Section 15. *Education.* The people have a right to the privilege of education, and it is the duty of the State to guard and maintain that right.

Section 16. *Ex post facto laws.* Retrospective laws, punishing acts committed before the existence of such laws and by them only declared criminal, are oppressive, unjust, and incompatible with liberty, and therefore no ex post facto law shall be enacted. No law taxing retrospectively sales, purchases, or other acts previously done shall be enacted.

Section 17. *Slavery and involuntary servitude.* Slavery is forever prohibited. Involuntary servitude, except as a punishment for crime whereof the parties have been adjudged guilty, is forever prohibited.

Section 18. *Courts shall be open.* All courts shall be open; every person for an injury done him in his lands, goods, person, or reputation shall have remedy by due course of law; and right and justice shall be administered without favor, denial, or delay.

Section 19. *Law of the land; equal protection of the laws.* No person shall be taken, imprisoned, or disseized of his freehold, liberties, or privileges, or outlawed, or exiled, or in any manner deprived of his life, liberty, or property, but by the law of the land. No person shall be denied the equal protection of the laws; nor shall any person be subjected to discrimination by the State because of race, color, religion, or national origin.

Section 20. *General warrants.* General warrants, whereby any officer or other person may be commanded to search suspected places without evidence of the act committed, or to seize any person or persons not named, whose offense is not particularly described and supported by evidence, are dangerous to liberty and shall not be granted.

Section 21. *Inquiry into restraints on liberty.* Every person restrained of his liberty is entitled to a remedy to inquire into the lawfulness thereof, and to remove the restraint if unlawful, and that remedy shall not be denied or delayed. The privilege of the writ of habeas corpus shall not be suspended.

Section 22. *Modes of prosecution.* Except in misdemeanor cases initiated in the District Court Division, no person shall be put to answer any criminal charge but by indictment, presentment, or impeachment. But any person, when represented by counsel, may, under such regulations as the General Assembly shall prescribe, waive indictment in noncapital cases.

Section 23. *Rights of accused.* In all criminal prosecutions, every person charged with crime has the right to be informed of the accusation and to confront the accusers and witnesses with other testimony, and to have counsel for defense, and not be compelled to give self-incriminating evidence, or to pay costs, jail fees, or necessary witness fees of the defense, unless found guilty.

Section 24. *Right of jury trial in criminal cases.* No person shall be convicted of any crime but by the unanimous verdict of a jury in open court. The General Assembly may, however, provide for other means of trial for misdemeanors, with the right of appeal for trial de novo.

Section 25. *Right of jury trial in civil cases.* In all controversies at law respecting property, the ancient mode of trial by jury is one of the best securities of the rights of the people, and shall remain sacred and inviolable.

Section 26. *Jury service.* No person shall be excluded from jury service on account of sex, race, color, religion, or national origin.

Section 27. *Bail, fines, and punishments.* Excessive bail shall not be required, nor excessive fines imposed, nor cruel or unusual punishments inflicted.

Section 28. *Imprisonment for debt.* There shall be no imprisonment for debt in this State, except in cases of fraud.

Section 29. *Treason against the State.* Treason against the State shall consist only of levying war against it or adhering to its enemies by giving them aid and comfort. No person shall be convicted of treason unless on the testimony of two witnesses to the same overt act, or on confession in open court. No conviction of treason or attainder shall work corruption of blood or forfeiture.

Section 30. *Militia and the right to bear arms.* A well regulated militia being necessary to the security of a free State, the right of the people to keep and bear arms shall not be infringed; and, as standing armies in time of peace are dangerous to liberty, they shall not be maintained, and the military shall be kept under strict subordination to, and governed by, the civil power. Nothing herein shall justify the practice of carrying concealed weapons, or prevent the General Assembly from enacting penal statutes against that practice.

Section 31. *Quartering of soldiers.* No soldier shall in time of peace be quartered in any house without the consent of the owner, nor in time of war but in a manner prescribed by law.

Section 32. *Exclusive emoluments.* No person or set of persons is entitled to exclusive or separate emoluments or privileges from the community but in consideration of public services.

Section 33. *Hereditary emoluments and honors.* No hereditary emoluments, privileges, or honors shall be granted or conferred in this State.

Section 34. *Perpetuities and monopolies.* Perpetuities and monopolies are contrary to the genius of a free state and shall not be allowed.

Section 35. *Recurrence to fundamental principals.* A frequent recurrence to fundamental principles is absolutely necessary to preserve the blessings of liberty.

Section 36. *Other rights of the people.* The enumeration of rights in this Article shall not be construed to impair or deny others retained by the people.

ARTICLE II
Legislative

Section 1. *Legislative power.* The legislative power of the State shall be vested in the General Assembly, which shall consist of a Senate and a House of Representatives.

Section 2. *Number of Senators.* The Senate shall be composed of 50 Senators, biennially chosen by ballot.

Section 3. *Senate districts; apportionment of Senators.* The Senators shall be elected from districts. The General Assembly, at the first regular session convening after the return of every decennial census of population taken by order of Congress, shall revise the senate districts and the apportionment of Senators among those districts, subject to the following requirements:

(1) Each Senator shall represent, as nearly as may be, an equal number of inhabitants, the number of inhabitants that each Senator represents being determined for this purpose by dividing the population of the district that he represents by the number of Senators apportioned to that district;

(2) Each senate district shall at all times consist of contiguous territory;

(3) No county shall be divided in the formation of a senate district;

(4) When established, the senate districts and the apportionment of Senators shall remain unaltered until the return of another decennial census of population taken by order of Congress.

Section 4. *Number of Representatives.* The House of Representatives shall be composed of 120 Representatives, biennially chosen by ballot.

Section 5. *Representative districts; apportionment of Representatives.* The Representatives shall be elected from districts. The General Assembly, at the first regular session convening after the return of every decennial census of population taken by order of Congress, shall revise the representative districts and the apportionment of Representatives among those districts, subject to the following requirements:

(1) Each Representative shall represent, as nearly as may be, an equal number of inhabitants, the number of inhabitants that each Representative represents being determined for this purpose by dividing the population of the district that he represents by the number of Representatives apportioned to that district;

(2) Each representative district shall at all times consist of contiguous territory;

(3) No county shall be divided in the formation of a representative district;

(4) When established, the representative districts and the apportionment of Representatives shall remain unaltered until the return of another decennial census of population taken by order of Congress.

Section 6. *Qualifications for Senator.* Each Senator, at the time of his election, shall be not less than 25 years of age, shall be a qualified voter of the State, and shall have resided in the State as a citizen for two years and in the district for which he is chosen for one year immediately preceding his election.

Section 7. *Qualifications for Representative.* Each Representative, at the time of his election, shall be a qualified voter of the State, and shall have resided in the district for which he is chosen for one year immediately preceding his election.

Section 8. *Elections.* The election for members of the General Assembly shall be held for the respective districts in 1972 and every two years thereafter, at the places and on the day prescribed by law.

Section 9. *Terms of office.* The term of office of Senators and Representatives shall commence on the first day of January next after their election.

Section 10. *Vacancies.* Every vacancy occurring in the membership of the General Assembly by reason of death, resignation, or other cause shall be filled in the manner prescribed by law.

Section 11. *Sessions.*

(1) *Regular Sessions.* The General Assembly shall meet in regular session in 1973 and every two years thereafter on the day prescribed by law. Neither house shall proceed upon public business unless a majority of all of its members are actually present.

(2) *Extra sessions on legislative call.* The President of the Senate and the Speaker of the House of Representatives shall convene the General Assembly in extra session by their joint proclamation upon receipt by the President of the Senate of written requests therefor signed by three-fifths of all the members of the Senate and upon receipt by the Speaker of the House of Representatives of written requests therefor signed by three-fifths of all the members of the House of Representatives.

Section 12. *Oath of members.* Each member of the General Assembly, before taking his seat, shall take an oath or affirmation that he will support the Constitution and laws of the United States and the Constitution of the State of North Carolina, and will faithfully discharge his duty as a member of the Senate or House of Representatives.

Section 13. *President of the Senate.* The Lieutenant Governor shall be President of the Senate and shall preside over the Senate, but shall have no vote unless the Senate is equally divided.

Section 14. *Other officers of the Senate.*

(1) *President Pro Tempore—succession to presidency.* The Senate shall elect from its membership a President Pro Tempore, who shall become President of the Senate upon the

failure of the Lieutenant Governor-elect to qualify, or upon succession by the Lieutenant Governor to the office of Governor, or upon the death, resignation, or removal from office of the President of the Senate, and who shall serve until the expiration of his term of office as Senator.

(2) *President Pro Tempore—temporary succession.* During the physical or mental incapacity of the President of the Senate to perform the duties of his office, or during the absence of the President of the Senate, the President Pro Tempore shall preside over the Senate.

(3) *Other Officers.* The Senate shall elect its other officers.

Section 15. *Officers of the House of Representatives.* The House of Representatives shall elect its Speaker and other officers.

Section 16. *Compensation and allowances.* The members and officers of the General Assembly shall receive for their services the compensation and allowances prescribed by law. An increase in the compensation or allowances of members shall become effective at the beginning of the next regular session of the General Assembly following the session at which it was enacted.

Section 17. *Journals.* Each house shall keep a journal of its proceedings, which shall be printed and made public immediately after the adjournment of the General Assembly.

Section 18. *Protests.* Any member of either house may dissent from and protest against any act or resolve which he may think injurious to the public or to any individual, and have the reasons of his dissent entered on the journal.

Section 19. *Record votes.* Upon motion made in either house and seconded by one fifth of the members present, the yeas and nays upon any question shall be taken and entered upon the journal.

Section 20. *Powers of the General Assembly.* Each house shall be judge of the qualifications and elections of its own members, shall sit upon its own adjournment from day to day, and shall prepare bills to be enacted into laws. The two houses may jointly adjourn to any future day or other place. Either house may, of its own motion, adjourn for a period not in excess of three days.

Section 21. *Style of the acts.* The style of the acts shall be: "The General Assembly of North Carolina enacts:".

Section 22. *Action on bills.* All bills and resolutions of a legislative nature shall be read three times in each house before they become laws, and shall be signed by the presiding officers of both houses.

Section 23. *Revenue bills.* No laws shall be enacted to raise money on the credit of the State, or to pledge the faith of the State directly or indirectly for the payment of any debt, or to impose any tax upon the people of the State, or to allow the counties, cities, or towns to do so, unless the bill for the purpose shall have been read three several times in each house of the General Assembly and passed three several readings, which readings shall have been on three different days, and shall have been agreed to by each house respectively, and unless the yeas and nays on the second and third readings of the bill shall have been entered on the journal.

Section 24. *Limitations on local, private, and special legislation.*

(1) *Prohibited subjects.* The General Assembly shall not enact any local, private, or special act or resolution:

(a) Relating to health, sanitation, and the abatement of nuisances;

(b) Changing the names of cities, towns, and townships;

(c) Authorizing the laying out, opening, altering, maintaining, or discontinuing of highways, streets, or alleys;

(d) Relating to ferries or bridges;

(e) Relating to non-navigable streams;

(f) Relating to cemeteries;

(g) Relating to the pay of jurors;

(h) Erecting new townships, or changing township lines, or establishing or changing the lines of school districts;

(i) Remitting fines, penalties, and forfeitures, or refunding moneys legally paid into the public treasury;

(j) Regulating labor, trade, mining, or manufacturing;

(k) Extending the time for the levy or collection of taxes or otherwise relieving any collector of taxes from the due performance of his official duties or his sureties from liability;

(l) Giving effect to informal wills and deeds;

(m) Granting a divorce or securing alimony in any individual case;

(n) Altering the name of any person, or legitimating any person not born in lawful wedlock, or restoring to the rights of citizenship any person convicted of a felony.

(2) *Repeals.* Nor shall the General Assembly enact any such local, private, or special act by partial repeal of a general law; but the General Assembly may at any time repeal local, private, or special laws enacted by it.

(3) *Prohibited acts void.* Any local, private, or special act or resolution enacted in violation of the provisions of this Section shall be void.

(4) *General laws.* The General Assembly may enact general laws regulating the matters set out in this Section.

ARTICLE III
Executive

Section 1. *Executive power.* The executive power of the State shall be vested in the Governor.

Section 2. *Governor and Lieutenant Governor: election, term, and qualifications.*

(1) *Election and term.* The Governor and Lieutenant Governor shall be elected by the qualified voters of the State in 1972 and every four years thereafter, at the same time and places as members of the General Assembly are elected. Their term of office shall be four years and shall commence on the first day of January next after their election and continue until their successors are elected and qualified.

(2) *Qualifications.* No person shall be eligible for election to the office of Governor or Lieutenant Governor unless, at the time of his election, he shall have attained the age of 30 years and shall have been a citizen of the United States for five years and a resident of this State for two years immediately preceding his election. No person elected to the office of Governor or Lieutenant Governor shall be eligible for election to more than two consecutive terms of the same office.

Section 3. *Succession to office of Governor.*

(1) *Succession as Governor.* The Lieutenant Governor-elect shall become Governor upon the failure of the Governor-elect to qualify. The Lieutenant Governor shall become Governor upon the death, resignation, or removal from office of the Governor. The further order of succession to the office of Governor shall be prescribed by law. A successor shall serve for the remainder of the term of the Governor whom he succeeds and until a new Governor is elected and qualified.

(2) *Succession as Acting Governor.* During the absence of the Governor from the State, or during the physical or mental incapacity of the Governor to perform the duties of his office, the Lieutenant Governor shall be Acting Governor. The further order of succession as Acting Governor shall be prescribed by law.

(3) *Physical incapacity.* The Governor may, by a written statement filed with the Attorney General, declare that he is physically incapable of performing the duties of his office, and may thereafter in the same manner declare that he is physically capable of performing the duties of his office.

(4) *Mental incapacity.* The mental incapacity of the Governor to perform the duties of his office shall be determined only by joint resolution adopted by a vote of two-thirds of all the members of each house of the General Assembly. Thereafter, the mental capacity of the Governor to perform the duties of his office shall be determined only by joint resolution adopted by a vote of a majority of all the members of each house of the General Assembly. In all cases, the General Assembly shall give the Governor such notice as it may deem proper and shall allow him an opportunity to be heard before a joint session of the General Assembly before it takes final action. When the General Assembly is not in session, the

Council of State, a majority of its members concurring, may convene it in extra session for the purpose of proceeding under this paragraph.

Section 4. *Oath of office for Governor.* The Governor, before entering upon the duties of his office, shall, before any Justice of the Supreme Court, take an oath or affirmation that he will support the Constitution and laws of the United States and of the State of North Carolina, and that he will faithfully perform the duties pertaining to the office of Governor.

Section 5. *Duties of Governor.*

(1) *Residence.* The Governor shall reside at the seat of government of this State.

(2) *Information to General Assembly.* The Governor shall from time to time give the General Assembly information of the affairs of the State and recommend to their consideration such measures as he shall deem expedient.

(3) *Budget.* The Governor shall prepare and recommend to the General Assembly a comprehensive budget of the anticipated revenue and proposed expenditures of the State for the ensuing fiscal period. The budget as enacted by the General Assembly shall be administered by the Governor.

The total expenditures of the State for the fiscal period covered by the budget shall not exceed the total of receipts during that fiscal period and the surplus remaining in the State Treasury at the beginning of the period. To insure that the State does not incur a deficit for any fiscal period, the Governor shall continually survey the collection of the revenue and shall effect the necessary economies in State expenditures, after first making adequate provision for the prompt payment of the principal of and interest on bonds and notes of the State according to their terms, whenever he determines that receipts during the fiscal period, when added to any surplus remaining in the State Treasury at the beginning of the period, will not be sufficient to meet budgeted expenditures. This section shall not be construed to impair the power of the State to issue its bonds and notes within the limitations imposed in Article V of this Constitution, nor to impair the obligation of bonds and notes of the State now outstanding or issued hereafter.

(4) *Execution of laws.* The Governor shall take care that the laws be faithfully executed.

(5) *Commander in Chief.* The Governor shall be Commander in Chief of the military forces of the State except when they shall be called into the service of the United States.

(6) *Clemency.* The Governor may grant reprieves, commutations, and pardons, after conviction, for all offenses (except in cases of impeachment), upon such conditions as he may think proper, subject to regulations prescribed by law relative to the manner of applying for pardons. The terms reprieves, commutations, and pardons shall not include paroles.

(7) *Extra sessions.* The Governor may, on extraordinary occasions, by and with the advice of the Council of State, convene the General Assembly in extra session by his proclamation, stating therein the purpose or purposes for which they are thus convened.

(8) *Appointments.* The Governor shall nominate and by and with the advice and consent of a majority of the Senators appoint all officers whose appointments are not otherwise provided for.

(9) *Information.* The Governor may at any time require information in writing from the head of any administrative department or agency upon any subject relating to the duties of his office.

(10) *Administrative reorganization.* The General Assembly shall prescribe the functions, powers, and duties of the administrative departments and agencies of the State and may alter them from time to time, but the Governor may make such changes in the allocation of offices and agencies and in the allocation of those functions, powers, and duties as he considers necessary for efficient administration. If those changes affect existing law, they shall be set forth in executive orders, which shall be submitted to the General Assembly not later than the sixtieth calendar day of its session, and shall become effective and shall have the force of law upon adjournment sine die of the session, unless specifically disapproved by resolution of either house of the General Assembly or specifically modified by joint resolution of both houses of the General Assembly.

Section 6. *Duties of the Lieutenant Governor.* The Lieutenant Governor shall be President of the Senate, but shall have no vote unless the Senate is equally divided. He shall perform such additional duties as the General Assembly or the Governor may assign to him. He shall receive the compensation and allowances prescribed by law.

Section 7. *Other elective officers.*

(1) *Officers.* A Secretary of State, an Auditor, a Treasurer, a Superintendent of Public Instruction, an Attorney General, a Commissioner of Agriculture, a Commissioner of Labor, and a Commissioner of Insurance shall be elected by the qualified voters of the State in 1972 and every four years thereafter, at the same time and places as members of the General Assembly are elected. Their term of office shall be four years and shall commence on the first day of January next after their election and continue until their successors are elected and qualified.

(2) *Duties.* Their respective duties shall be prescribed by law.

(3) *Vacancies.* If the office of any of these officers is vacated by death, resignation, or otherwise, it shall be the duty of the Governor to appoint another to serve until his successor is elected and qualified. Every such vacancy shall be filled by election at the first election for members of the General Assembly that occurs more than 30 days after the vacancy has taken place, and the person chosen shall hold the office for the remainder of the unexpired term fixed in this Section. When a vacancy occurs in the office of any of the officers named in this Section and the term expires on the first day of January succeeding the next election for members of the General Assembly, the Governor shall appoint to fill the vacancy for the unexpired term of the office.

(4) *Interim officers.* Upon the occurrence of a vacancy in the office of any one of these officers for any of the causes stated in the preceding paragraph, the Governor may appoint an interim officer to perform the duties of that office until a person is appointed or elected pursuant to this Section to fill the vacancy and is qualified.

(5) *Acting officers.* During the physical or mental incapacity of any one of these officers to perform the duties of his office, as determined pursuant to this Section, the duties of his office shall be performed by an acting officer who shall be appointed by the Governor.

(6) *Determination of incapacity.* The General Assembly shall by law prescribe with respect to those officers, other than the Governor, whose offices are created by this Article, procedures for determining the physical or mental incapacity of any officer to perform the duties of his office, and for determining whether an officer who has been temporarily incapacitated has sufficiently recovered his physical or mental capacity to perform the duties of his office. Removal of those officers from office for any other cause shall be by impeachment.

(7) *Special Qualifications for Attorney General.* Only persons duly authorized to practice law in the courts of this State shall be eligible for appointment or election as Attorney General.

Section 8. *Council of State.* The Council of State shall consist of the officers whose offices are established by this Article.

Section 9. *Compensation and allowances.* The officers whose offices are established by this Article shall at stated periods receive the compensation and allowances prescribed by law, which shall not be diminished during the time for which they have been chosen.

Section 10. *Seal of State.* There shall be a seal of the State, which shall be kept by the Governor and used by him as occasion may require, and shall be called "The Great Seal of the State of North Carolina." All grants or commissions shall be issued in the name and by the authority of the State of North Carolina, sealed with "The Great Seal of the State of North Carolina," and signed by the Governor.

Section 11. *Administrative departments.* Not later than July 1, 1975, all administrative departments, agencies, and offices of the State and their respective functions, powers, and duties shall be allocated by law among and within not more than 25 principal administrative departments so as to group them as far as practicable according to major purposes. Regulatory, quasi-judicial, and temporary agencies may, but need not, be allocated within a principal department.

ARTICLE IV
Judicial

Section 1. *Judicial power.* The judicial power of the State shall, except as provided in Section 3 of this Article, be vested in a Court for the Trial of Impeachments and in a General Court of Justice. The General Assembly shall have no power to deprive the judicial department of any power or jurisdiction that rightfully pertains to it as a coordinate department of the government, nor shall it establish or authorize any courts other than as permitted by this Article.

Section 2. *General Court of Justice.* The General Court of Justice shall constitute a unified judicial system for purposes of jurisdiction, operation, and administration, and shall consist of an Appellate Division, a Superior Court Division, and a District Court Division.

Section 3. *Judicial powers of administrative agencies.* The General Assembly may vest in administrative agencies established pursuant to law such judicial powers as may be reasonably necessary as an incident to the accomplishment of the purposes for which the agencies were created. Appeals from administrative agencies shall be to the General Court of Justice.

Section 4. *Court for the Trial of Impeachments.* The House of Representatives solely shall have the power of impeaching. The Court for the Trial of Impeachments shall be the Senate. When the Governor or Lieutenant Governor is impeached, the Chief Justice shall preside over the Court. A majority of the members shall be necessary to a quorum, and no person shall be convicted without the concurrence of two-thirds of the Senators present. Judgment upon conviction shall not extend beyond removal from and disqualification to hold office in this State, but the party shall be liable to indictment and punishment according to law.

Section 5. *Appellate division.* The Appellate Division of the General Court of Justice shall consist of the Supreme Court and the Court of Appeals.

Section 6. *Supreme Court.*

(1) *Membership.* The Supreme Court shall consist of a Chief Justice and six Associate Justices, but the General Assembly may increase the number of Associate Justices to not more than eight. In the event the Chief Justice is unable, on account of absence or temporary incapacity, to perform any of the duties placed upon him, the senior Associate Justice available may discharge those duties.

(2) *Sessions of the Supreme Court.* The sessions of the Supreme Court shall be held in the City of Raleigh unless otherwise provided by the General Assembly.

Section 7. *Court of Appeals.* The structure, organization, and composition of the Court of Appeals shall be determined by the General Assembly. The Court shall have not less than five members, and may be authorized to sit in divisions, or other than en banc. Sessions of the Court shall be held at such times and places as the General Assembly may prescribe.

Section 8. *Retirement of Justices and Judges.* The General Assembly shall provide by general law for the retirement of Justices and Judges of the General Court of Justice, and may provide for the temporary recall of any retired Justice or Judge to serve on the court from which he was retired. The General Assembly shall also prescribe maximum age limits service as a Justice or Judge.

Section 9. *Superior Courts.*

(1) *Superior Court districts.* The General Assembly shall, from time to time, divide the State into a convenient number of Superior Court judicial districts and shall provide for the election of one or more Superior Court Judges for each district. Each regular Superior Court Judge shall reside in the district for which he is elected. The General Assembly may provide by general law for the selection or appointment of special or emergency Superior Court Judges not selected for a particular judicial district.

(2) *Open at all times; sessions for trial of cases.* The Superior Courts shall be open at all times for the transaction of all business except the trial of issues of fact requiring a jury. Regular trial sessions of the Superior Court shall be held at times fixed pursuant to a calendar of courts promulgated by the Supreme Court. At least two sessions for the trial of jury cases shall be held annually in each county.

(3) *Clerks.* A Clerk of the Superior Court for each county shall be elected for a term of four years by the qualified voters thereof, at the same time and places as members of the

General Assembly are elected. If the office of Clerk of the Superior Court becomes vacant otherwise than by the expiration of the term, or if the people fail to elect, the senior regular resident Judge of the Superior Court serving the county shall appoint to fill the vacancy until an election can be regularly held.

Section 10. *District Courts.* The General Assembly shall, from time to time, divide the State into a convenient number of local court districts and shall prescribe where the District Courts shall sit, but a District Court must sit in at least one place in each county. District judges shall be elected for each district for a term of four years, in a manner prescribed by law. When more than one District Judge is authorized and elected for a district, the Chief Justice of the Supreme Court shall designate one of the judges as Chief District Judge. Every District Judge shall reside in the district for which he is elected. For each county, the senior regular resident Judge of the Superior Court serving the county shall appoint for a term of two years, from nominations submitted by the Clerk of the Superior Court of the county, one or more Magistrates who shall be officers of the District Court. The number of District Judges and Magistrates shall, from time to time, be determined by the General Assembly. Vacancies in the office of District Judge shall be filled for the unexpired term in a manner prescribed by law. Vacancies in the office of Magistrate shall be filled for the unexpired term in the manner provided for original appointment to the office.

Section 11. *Assignment of Judges.* The Chief Justice of the Supreme Court, acting in accordance with rules of the Supreme Court, shall make assignments of Judges of the Superior Court and may transfer District Judges from one district to another for temporary or specialized duty. The principle of rotating Superior Court Judges among the various districts of a division is a salutary one and shall be observed. For this purpose the General Assembly may divide the State into a number of judicial divisions. Subject to the general supervision of the Chief Justice of the Supreme Court, assignment of District Judges within each local court district shall be made by the Chief District Judge.

Section 12. *Jurisdiction of the General Court of Justice.*

(1) *Supreme Court.* The Supreme Court shall have jurisdiction to review upon appeal any decision of the courts below, upon any matter of law or legal inference. The jurisdiction of the Supreme Court over "issues of fact" and "questions of fact" shall be the same exercised by it prior to the adoption of this Article, and the Court may issue any remedial writs necessary to give it general supervision and control over the proceedings of the other courts. The Supreme Court also has jurisdiction to review, when authorized by law, direct appeals from a final order or decision of the North Carolina Utilities Commission.

(2) *Court of Appeals.* The Court of Appeals shall have such appellate jurisdiction as the General Assembly may prescribe.

(3) *Superior Court.* Except as otherwise provided by the General Assembly, the Superior Court shall have original general jurisdiction throughout the State. The Clerks of the Superior Court shall have such jurisdiction and powers as the General Assembly shall prescribe by general law uniformly applicable in every county of the State.

(4) *District Courts; Magistrates.* The General Assembly shall, by general law uniformly applicable in every local court district of the State, prescribe the jurisdiction and powers of the District Courts and Magistrates.

(5) *Waiver.* The General Assembly may by general law provide that the jurisdictional limits may be waived in civil cases.

(6) *Appeals.* The General Assembly shall by general law provide a proper system of appeals. Appeals from Magistrates shall be heard de novo, with the right of trial by jury as defined in this Constitution and the laws of this State.

Section 13. *Forms of action; rules of procedure.*

(1) *Forms of Action.* There shall be in this State but one form of action for the enforcement or protection of private rights or the redress of private wrongs, which shall be denominated a civil action, and in which there shall be a right to have issues of fact tried before a jury. Every action prosecuted by the people of the State as a party against a person charged with a public offense, for the punishment thereof, shall be termed a criminal action.

(2) *Rules of procedure.* The Supreme Court shall have exclusive authority to make

rules of procedure and practice for the Appellate Division. The General Assembly may make rules of procedure and practice for the Superior Court and District Court Divisions, and the General Assembly may delegate this authority to the Supreme Court. No rule of procedure or practice shall abridge substantive rights or abrogate or limit the right of trial by jury. If the General Assembly should delegate to the Supreme Court the rule-making power, the General Assembly may, nevertheless, alter, amend, or repeal any rule of procedure or practice adopted by the Supreme Court for the Superior Court or District Court Divisions.

Section 14. *Waiver of jury trial.* In all issues of fact joined in any court, the parties in any civil case may waive the right to have the issues determined by a jury, in which case the finding of the judge upon the facts shall have the force and effect of a verdict by a jury.

Section 15. *Administration.* The General Assembly shall provide for an administrative office of the courts to carry out the provisions of this Article.

Section 16. *Terms of office and election of Justices of the Supreme Court, Judges of the Court of Appeals, and Judges of the Superior Court.* Justices of the Supreme Court, Judges of the Court of Appeals, and regular Judges of the Superior Court shall be elected by the qualified voters and shall hold office for terms of eight years and until their successors are elected and qualified. Justices of the Supreme Court and Judges of the Court of Appeals shall be elected by the qualified voters of the State. Regular Judges of the Superior Court may be elected by the qualified voters of the State or by the voters of their respective districts, as the General Assembly may prescribe.

Section 17. *Removal of Judges, Magistrates and Clerks.*

(1) *Removal of Judges by the General Assembly.* Any Justice or Judge of the General Court of Justice may be removed from office for mental or physical incapacity by joint resolution of two-thirds of all the members of each house of the General Assembly. Any Justice or Judge against whom the General Assembly may be about to proceed shall receive notice thereof, accompanied by a copy of the causes alleged for his removal, at least 20 days before the day on which either house of the General Assembly shall act thereon. Removal from office by the General Assembly for any other cause shall be by impeachment.

(2) *Additional method of removal of Judges.* The General Assembly shall prescribe a procedure, in addition to impeachment and address set forth in this Section, for the removal of a Justice or Judge of the General Court of Justice for mental or physical incapacity interfering with the performance of his duties which is, or is likely to become, permanent, and for the censure and removal of a Justice or Judge of the General Court of Justice for willful misconduct in office, willful and persistent failure to perform his duties, habitual intemperance, conviction of a crime involving moral turpitude, or conduct prejudicial to the administration of justice that brings the judicial office into disrepute.

(3) *Removal of Magistrates.* The General Assembly shall provide by general law for the removal of Magistrates for misconduct or mental or physical incapacity.

(4) *Removal of Clerks.* Any Clerk of the Superior Court may be removed from office for misconduct or mental or physical incapacity by the senior regular resident Superior Court Judge serving the county. Any Clerk against whom proceedings are instituted shall receive written notice of the charges against him at least ten days before the hearing upon the charges. Any Clerk so removed from office shall be entitled to an appeal as provided by law.

Section 18. *District Attorney and Prosecutorial Districts.*

(1) *District Attorneys.* The General Assembly shall, from time to time, divide the State into a convenient number of prosecutorial districts, for each of which a District Attorney shall be chosen for a term of four years by the qualified voters thereof, at the same time and places as members of the General Assembly are elected. Only persons duly authorized to practice law in the courts of this State shall be eligible for election or appointment as a District Attorney. The District Attorney shall advise the officers of justice in his district, be responsible for the prosecution on behalf of the State of all criminal actions in the Superior Courts of his district, perform such duties related to appeals therefrom as the Attorney

General may require, and perform such other duties as the General Assembly may prescribe.

(2) *Prosecution in District Court Division.* Criminal actions in the District Court Division shall be prosecuted in such manner as the General Assembly may prescribe by general law uniformly applicable in every local court district of the State.

Section 19. *Vacancies.* Unless otherwise provided in this Article, all vacancies occurring in the offices provided for by this Article shall be filled by appointment of the Governor, and the appointees shall hold their places until the next election for members of the General Assembly that is held more than 30 days after the vacancy occurs, when elections shall be held to fill the offices. When the unexpired term of any of the offices named in this Article of the Constitution in which a vacancy has occurred, and in which it is herein provided that the Governor shall fill the vacancy, expires on the first day of January succeeding the next election for members of the General Assembly, the Governor shall appoint to fill that vacancy for the unexpired term of the office. If any person elected or appointed to any of these offices shall fail to qualify, the office shall be appointed to, held, and filled as provided in case of vacancies occurring therein. All incumbents of these offices shall hold until their successors are qualified.

Section 20. *Revenues and expenses of the judicial department.* The General Assembly shall provide for the establishment of a schedule of court fees and costs which shall be uniform throughout the State within each division of the General Court of Justice. The operating expenses of the judicial department, other than compensation to process servers and other locally paid non-judicial officers, shall be paid from State funds.

Section 21. *Fees, salaries, and emoluments.* The General Assembly shall prescribe and regulate the fees, salaries, and emoluments of all officers provided for in this Article, but the salaries of Judges shall not be diminished during their continuance in office. In no case shall the compensation of any Judge or Magistrate be dependent upon his decision or upon the collection of costs.

Section 22. *Qualification of Justices and Judges.* Only persons duly authorized to practice law in the courts of this State shall be eligible for election or appointment as a Justice of the Supreme Court, Judge of the Court of Appeals, Judge of the Superior Court, or Judge of District Court. This section shall not apply to persons elected to or serving in such capacities on or before January 1, 1981.

ARTICLE V
Finance

Section 1. *No capitation tax to be levied.* No poll or capitation tax shall be levied by the General Assembly or by any county, city or town, or other taxing unit.

Section 2. *State and local taxation.*

(1) *Power of taxation.* The power of taxation shall be exercised in a just and equitable manner, for public purposes only, and shall never be surrendered, suspended, or contracted away.

(2) *Classification.* Only the General Assembly shall have the power to classify property for taxation, which power shall be exercised only on a State-wide basis and shall not be delegated. No class of property shall be taxed except by uniform rule, and every classification shall be made by general law uniformly applicable in every county, city and town, and other unit of local government.

(3) *Exemptions.* Property belonging to the State, counties, and municipal corporations shall be exempt from taxation. The General Assembly may exempt cemeteries and property held for educational, scientific, literary, cultural, charitable, or religious purposes, and, to a value not exceeding $300, any personal property. The General Assembly may exempt from taxation not exceeding $1,000 in value of property held and used as the place of residence of the owner. Every exemption shall be on a State-wide basis and shall be made by general law uniformly applicable in every county, city and town, and other unit of local government. No taxing authority other than the General Assembly may grant exemp-

tions, and the General Assembly shall not delegate the powers accorded to it by this subsection.

(4) *Special tax areas.* Subject to the limitations imposed by Section 4, the General Assembly may enact general laws authorizing the governing body of any county, city or town to define territorial areas and to levy taxes within those areas, in addition to those levied throughout the county, city, or town, in order to finance, provide, or maintain services, facilities, and functions in addition to or to a greater extent than those financed, provided, or maintained for the entire county, city, or town.

(5) *Purposes of property tax.* The General Assembly shall not authorize any county, city or town, special district, or other unit of local government to levy taxes or property, except for purposes authorized by general law uniformly applicable throughout the State, unless the tax is approved by a majority of the qualified voters of the unit who vote thereon.

(6) *Income tax.* The rate of tax on incomes shall not in any case exceed ten per cent, and there shall be allowed personal exemptions and deductions so that only net incomes are taxed.

(7) *Contracts.* The General Assembly may enact laws whereby the State, any county, city or town, and any other public corporation may contract with and appropriate money to any person, association, or corporation for the accomplishment of public purposes only.

Section 3. *Limitations upon the increase of State debt.*

(1) *Authorized purposes; two-thirds limitation.* The General Assembly shall have no power to contract debts secured by a pledge of the faith and credit of the State, unless approved by a majority of the qualified voters of the State who vote thereon, except for the following purposes:

(a) to fund or refund a valid existing debt;

(b) to supply an unforeseen deficiency in the revenue;

(c) to borrow in anticipation of the collection of taxes due and payable within the current fiscal year to an amount not exceeding 50 per cent of such taxes;

(d) to suppress riots or insurrections, or to repel invasions;

(e) to meet emergencies immediately threatening the public health or safety, as conclusively determined in writing by the Governor;

(f) for any other lawful purpose, to the extent of two-thirds of the amount by which the State's outstanding indebtedness shall have been reduced during the next preceding biennium.

(2) *Gift or loan of credit regulated.* The General Assembly shall have no power to give or lend the credit of the State in aid of any person, association, or corporation, except a corporation in which the State has a controlling interest, unless the subject is submitted to a direct vote of the people of the State, and is approved by a majority of the qualified voters who vote thereon.

(3) *Definitions.* A debt is incurred within the meaning of this Section when the State borrows money. A pledge of the faith and credit within the meaning of this Section is a pledge of the taxing power. A loan of credit within the meaning of this Section occurs when the State exchanges its obligations with or in any way guarantees the debts of an individual, association or private corporation.

(4) *Certain debts barred.* The General Assembly shall never assume or pay any debt or obligation, express or implied, incurred in aid of insurrection or rebellion against the United States. Neither shall the General Assembly assume or pay any debt or bond incurred or issued by authority of the Convention of 1868, the special session of the General Assembly of 1868, or the General Assemblies of 1868–69 and 1869–70, unless the subject is submitted to the people of the State and is approved by a majority of all the qualified voters at a referendum held for that sole purpose.

(5) *Outstanding debt.* Except as provided in subsection (4), nothing in this Section shall be construed to invalidate or impair the obligation of any bond, note, or other evidence of indebtedness outstanding or authorized for issue as of July 1, 1973.

Section 4. *Limitations upon the increase of local government debt.*

(1) *Regulation of borrowing and debt.* The General Assembly shall enact general laws relating to the borrowing of money secured by a pledge of the faith and credit and the contracting of other debts by counties, cities and towns, special districts, and other units, authorities, and agencies of local government.

(2) *Authorized purposes; two-thirds limitation.* The General Assembly shall have no power to authorize any county, city or town, special district, or other unit of local government to contract debts secured by a pledge of its faith and credit unless approved by a majority of the qualified voters of the unit who vote thereon, except for the following purposes:

(a) to fund or refund a valid existing debt;

(b) to supply an unforseen deficiency in the revenue;

(c) to borrow in anticipation of the collection of taxes due and payable within the current fiscal year to an amount not exceeding 50 per cent of such taxes;

(d) to suppress riots or insurrections;

(e) to meet emergencies immediately threatening the public health or safety, as conclusively determined in writing by the Governor;

(f) for purposes authorized by general laws uniformly applicable throughout the State, to the extent of two-thirds of the amount by which the unit's outstanding indebtedness shall have been reduced during the next preceding fiscal year.

(3) *Gift or loan of credit regulated.* No county, city or town, special district, or other unit of local government shall give or lend its credit in aid of any person, association, or corporation, except for public purposes as authorized by general law, and unless approved by a majority of the qualified voters of the unit who vote thereon.

(4) *Certain debts barred.* No county, city or town, or other unit of local government shall assume or pay any debt or the interest thereon contracted directly or indirectly in aid or support of rebellion or insurrection against the United States.

(5) *Definitions.* A debt is incurred within the meaning of this Section when a county, city or town, special district, or other unit, authority, or agency of local government borrows money. A pledge of faith and credit within the meaning of this Section is a pledge of the taxing power. A loan of credit within the meaning of this Section occurs when a county, city or town, special district, or other unit, authority, or agency of local government exchanges its obligations with or in any way guarantees the debts of an individual, association, or private corporation.

(6) *Outstanding debt.* Except as provided in subsection (4), nothing in this Section shall be construed to invalidate or impair the obligation of any bond, note, or other evidence of indebtedness outstanding or authorized for issue as of July 1, 1973.

Section 5. *Acts levying taxes to state objects.* Every act of the General Assembly levying a tax shall state the special object to which it is to be applied, and it shall be applied to no other purpose.

Section 6. *Inviolability of sinking funds and retirement funds.*

(1) *Sinking funds.* The General Assembly shall not use or authorize to be used any part of the amount of any sinking fund for any purpose other than the retirement of the bonds for which the sinking fund has been created, except that these funds may be invested as authorized by law.

(2) *Retirement funds.* Neither the General Assembly nor any public officer, employee, or agency shall use or authorize to be used any part of the funds of the Teachers' and State Employees' Retirement System or the Local Governmental Employees' Retirement System for any purpose other than retirement system benefits and purposes, administrative expenses, and refunds; except that retirement system funds may be invested as authorized by law, subject to the investment limitation that the funds of the Teachers' and State Employees' Retirement System and the Local Governmental Employees' Retirement System shall not be applied, diverted, loaned to, or used by the State, any State agency, State officer, public officer, or public employee.

Section 7. *Drawing public money.*

(1) *State treasury.* No money shall be drawn from the State Treasury but in consequence of appropriations made by law, and an accurate account of the receipts and expenditures of State funds shall be published annually.

(2) *Local treasury.* No money shall be drawn from the treasury of any county, city or town, or other unit of local government except by authority of law.

Section 8. *Health care facilities.* Notwithstanding any other provisions of this Constitution, the General Assembly may enact general laws to authorize the State, counties, cities or towns, and other State and local governmental entities to issue revenue bonds to finance or refinance for any such governmental entity or any nonprofit private corporation, regardless of any church or religious relationship, the cost of acquiring, constructing, and financing health care facility projects to be operated to serve and benefit the public; provided, no cost incurred earlier than two years prior to the effective date of this section shall be refinanced. Such bonds shall be payable from the revenues, gross or net, of any such projects and any other health care facilities of any such governmental entity or nonprofit private corporation pledged therefor; shall not be secured by a pledge of the full faith and credit, or deemed to create an indebtedness requiring voter approval of any governmental entity; and may be secured by an agreement which may provide for the conveyance of title of, with or without consideration, any such project or facilities to the governmental entity or nonprofit private corporation. The power of eminent domain shall not be used pursuant hereto for nonprofit private corporations.

Section 9. *Capital projects for industry.* Notwithstanding any other provision of this Constitution, the General Assembly may enact general laws to authorize counties to create authorities to issue revenue bonds to finance, but not to refinance, the cost of capital projects consisting of industrial, manufacturing and pollution control facilities for industry and pollution control facilities for public utilities, and to refund such bonds.

In no event shall such revenue bonds be secured by or payable from any public moneys whatsoever, but such revenue bonds shall be secured by and payable only from revenues or property derived from private parties. All such capital projects and all transactions therefor shall be subject to taxation to the extent such projects and transactions would be subject to taxation if no public body were involved therewith; provided, however, that the General Assembly may provide that the interest on such revenue bonds shall be exempt from income taxes within the State.

The power of eminent domain shall not be exercised to provide any property for any such capital project.

Section 10. *Joint ownership of generation and transmission facilities.* In addition to other powers conferred upon them by law, municipalities owning or operating facilities for the generation, transmission or distribution of electric power and energy and joint agencies formed by such municipalities for the purpose of owning or operating facilities for the generation and transmission of electric power and energy (each, respectively, "a unit of municipal government") may jointly or severally own, operate and maintain works, plants and facilities, within or without the State, for the generation and transmission of electric power and energy, or both, with any person, firm, association or corporation, public or private, engaged in the generation, transmission or distribution of electric power and energy for resale (each, respectively, "a co-owner") within this State or any state contiguous to this State, and may enter into and carry out agreements with respect to such jointly owned facilities. For the purpose of financing its share of the cost of any such jointly owned electric generation or transmission facilities, a unit of municipal government may issue its revenue bonds in the manner prescribed by the General Assembly, payable as to both principal and interest solely from and secured by a lien and charge on all or any part of the revenue derived, or to be derived, by such unit of municipal government from the ownership and operation of its electric facilities; provided, however, that no unit of municipal government shall be liable, either jointly or severally, for any acts, omissions or obligations of any co-owner, nor shall any money or property of any unit of municipal government be credited or otherwise applied to the account of any co-owner or be charged with any debt, lien or mortgage as a result of any debt or obligation of any co-owner.

Section 11. *Capital projects for agriculture.* Notwithstanding any other provision of the Constitution the General Assembly may enact general laws to authorize the creation of an agency to issue revenue bonds to finance the cost of capital projects consisting of agricultural facilities, and to refund such bonds.

In no event shall such revenue bonds be secured by or payable from any public moneys whatsoever, but such revenue bonds shall be secured by and payable only from revenues or property derived from private parties. All such capital projects and all transactions therefor shall be subject to taxation if no public body were involved therewith; provided, however, that the General Assembly may provide that the interest on such revenue bonds shall be exempt from income taxes within the State.

The power of eminent domain shall not be exercised to provide any property for any such capital project.

ARTICLE VI
Suffrage and Eligibility to Office

Section 1. *Who may vote.* Every person born in the United States and every person who has been naturalized, 18 years of age, and possessing the qualifications set out in this Article, shall be entitled to vote at any election by the people of the State, except as herein otherwise provided.

Section 2. *Qualifications of voter.*

(1) *Residence period for State elections.* Any person who has resided in the State of North Carolina for one year and in the precinct, ward, or other election district for 30 days next preceding an election, and possesses the other qualifications set out in this Article, shall be entitled to vote at any election held in this State. Removal from one precinct, ward, or other election district to another in this State shall not operate to deprive any person of the right to vote in the precinct, ward, or other election district from which that person has removed until 30 days after the removal.

(2) *Residence period for presidential elections.* The General Assembly may reduce the time of residence for persons voting in presidential elections. A person made eligible by reason of a reduction in time of residence shall possess the other qualifications set out in this Article, shall only be entitled to vote for President and Vice President of the United States or for electors for President and Vice President, and shall not thereby become eligible to hold office in this State.

(3) *Disqualification of felon.* No person adjudged guilty of a felony against this State or the United States, or adjudged guilty of a felony in another state that also would be a felony if it had been committed in this State, shall be permitted to vote unless that person shall be first restored to the rights of citizenship in the manner prescribed by law.

Section 3. *Registration.* Every person offering to vote shall be at the time legally registered as a voter as herein prescribed and in the manner provided by law. The General Assembly shall enact general laws governing the registration of voters.

Section 4. *Qualification for registration.* Every person presenting himself for registration shall be able to read and write any section of the Constitution in the English language.

Section 5. *Elections by people and General Assembly.* All elections by the people shall be by ballot, and all elections by the General Assembly shall be viva voce. A contested election for any office established by Article III of this Constitution shall be determined by joint ballot of both houses of the General Assembly in the manner prescribed by law.

Section 6. *Eligibility to elective office.* Every qualified voter in North Carolina who is 21 years of age, except as in this Constitution disqualified, shall be eligible for election by the people to office.

Section 7. *Oath.* Before entering upon the duties of an office, a person elected or appointed to the office shall take and subscribe the following oath:

"I, ... , do solemnly swear (or affirm) that I will support and maintain the Constitution and laws of the United States, and the Constitution and laws of North Carolina not inconsistent therewith, and that I will faithfully discharge the duties of my office as . . . . , so help me God."

Section 8. *Disqualifications for office.* The following persons shall be disqualified for office: First, any person who shall deny the being of Almighty God.

Second, with respect to any office that is filled by election by the people, any person who is not qualified to vote in an election for that office.

Third, any person who has been adjudged guilty of treason or any other felony against this State or the United States, or any person who had been adjudged guilty of a felony in another state that also would be a felony if it had been committed in this State, or any person who has been adjudged guilty of corruption or malpractice in any office, or any person who has been removed by impeachment from any office, and who has not been restored to the rights of citizenship in the manner prescribed by law.

Section 9. *Dual office holding.*

(1) *Prohibitions.* It is salutary that the responsibilities of self-government be widely shared among the citizens of the State and that the potential abuse of authority inherent in the holding of multiple offices by an individual be avoided. Therefore, no person who holds any office or place of trust or profit under the United States or any department thereof, or under any other state or government, shall be eligible to hold any office in this State that is filled by election by the people. No person shall hold concurrently any two offices in this State that are filled by election of the people. No person shall hold concurrently any two or more appointive offices or places of trust or profit, or any combination of elective and appointive offices or places of trust or profit, except as the General Assembly shall provide by general law.

(2) *Exceptions.* The provisions of this Section shall not prohibit any officer of the military forces of the State or of the United States not on active duty for an extensive period of time, any notary public, or any delegate to a Convention of the People from holding concurrently another office or place of trust or profit under this State or the United States or any department thereof.

Section 10. *Continuation in office.* In the absence of any contrary provision, all officers in this State, whether appointed or elected, shall hold their positions until other appointments are made or, if the offices are elective, until their successors are chosen and qualified.

ARTICLE VII
Local Government

Section 1. *General Assembly to provide for local government.* The General Assembly shall provide for the organization and government and the fixing of boundaries of counties, cities and towns, and other governmental subdivisions, and, except as otherwise prohibited by this Constitution, may give such powers and duties to counties, cities and towns, and other governmental subdivisions as it may deem advisable.

The General Assembly shall not incorporate as a city or town, nor shall it authorize to be incorporated as a city or town, any territory lying within one mile of the corporate limits of any other city or town having a population of 5,000 or more according to the most recent decennial census of population taken by order of Congress, or lying within three miles of the corporate limits of any other city or town having a population of 10,000 or more according to the most recent decennial census of population taken by order of Congress, or lying within four miles of the corporate limits of any other city or town having a population of 25,000 or more according to the most recent decennial census of population taken by order of Congress, or lying within five miles of the corporate limits of any other city or town having a population of 50,000 or more according to the most recent decennial census of population taken by order of Congress. Notwithstanding the foregoing limitations, the General Assembly may incorporate a city or town by an act adopted by vote of three-fifths of all the members of each house.

Section 2. *Sheriffs.* In each county a Sheriff shall be elected by the qualified voters thereof at the same time and places as members of the General Assembly are elected and shall hold his office for a period of four years, subject to removal for cause as provided by law.

Section 3. *Merged or consolidated counties.* Any unit of local government formed by the merger or consolidation of a county or counties and the cities and towns therein shall be deemed both a county and a city for the purposes of this Constitution, and may exercise any authority conferred by law on counties, or on cities and towns, or both, as the General Assembly may provide.

ARTICLE VIII
Corporations

Section 1. *Corporate charters.* No corporation shall be created, nor shall its charter be extended, altered, or amended by special act, except corporations for charitable, educational, penal, or reformatory purposes that are to be and remain under the patronage and control of the State; but the General Assembly shall provide by general laws for the chartering, organization, and powers of all corporations, and for the amending, extending, and forfeiture of all charters, except those above permitted by special act. All such general acts may be altered from time to time or repealed. The General Assembly may at any time by special act repeal the charter of any corporation.

Section 2. *Corporations defined.* The term "corporation" as used in this Section shall be construed to include all associations and joint-stock companies having any of the powers and privileges of corporations not possessed by individuals or partnerships. All corporations shall have the right to sue and shall be subject to be sued in all courts, in like cases as natural persons.

ARTICLE IX
Education

Section 1. *Education encouraged.* Religion, morality, and knowledge being necessary to good government and the happiness of mankind, schools, libraries, and the means of education shall forever be encouraged.

Section 2. *Uniform system of schools.*

(1) *General and uniform system; term.* The General Assembly shall provide by taxation and otherwise for a general and uniform system of free public schools, which shall be maintained at least nine months in every year, and wherein equal opportunities shall be provided for all students.

(2) *Local responsibility.* The General Assembly may assign to units of local government such responsibility for the financial support of the free public schools as it may deem appropriate. The governing boards of units of local government with financial responsibility for public education may use local revenues to add to or supplement any public school or post-secondary school program.

Section 3. *School attendance.* The General Assembly shall provide that every child of appropriate age and of sufficient mental and physical ability shall attend the public schools, unless educated by other means.

Section 4. *State Board of Education.*

(1) *Board.* The State Board of Education shall consist of the Lieutenant Governor, the Treasurer, and eleven members appointed by the Governor, subject to confirmation by the General Assembly in joint session. The General Assembly shall divide the State into eight educational districts. Of the appointive members of the Board, one shall be appointed from each of the eight educational districts and three shall be appointed from the State at large. Appointments shall be for overlapping terms of eight years. Appointments to fill vacancies shall be made by the Governor for the unexpired terms and shall not be subject to confirmation.

(2) *Superintendent of Public Instruction.* The Superintendent of Public Instruction shall be the secretary and chief administrative officer of the State Board of Education.

Section 5. *Powers and duties of Board.* The State Board of Education shall supervise and administer the free public school system and the educational funds provided for its support, except the funds mentioned in Section 7 of this Article, and shall make all needed rules and regulations in relation thereto, subject to laws enacted by the General Assembly.

Section 6. *State school fund.* The proceeds of all lands that have been or hereafter may be granted by the United States to this State, and not otherwise appropriated by this State or the United States; all moneys, stocks, bonds, and other property belonging to the State for purposes of public education; the net proceeds of all sales of the swamp lands belonging to the State; and all other grants, gifts, and devises that have been or hereafter may be made to the State, and not otherwise appropriated by the State or by the terms of the grant, gift, or devise, shall be paid into the State Treasury and, together with so much of the revenue of the State as may be set apart for that purpose, shall be faithfully appropriated and used exclusively for establishing and maintaining a uniform system of free public schools.

Section 7. *County school fund.* All moneys, stocks, bonds, and other property belonging to a county school fund, and the clear proceeds of all penalties and forfeitures and of all fines collected in the several counties for any breach of the penal laws of the State, shall belong to and remain in the several counties, and shall be faithfully appropriated and used exclusively for maintaining free public schools.

Section 8. *Higher education.* The General Assembly shall maintain a public system of higher education, comprising The University of North Carolina and such other institutions of higher education as the General Assembly may deem wise. The General Assembly shall provide for the selection of trustees of The University of North Carolina and of the other institutions of higher education, in whom shall be vested all the privileges, rights, franchises, and endowments heretofore granted to or conferred upon the trustees of these institutions. The General Assembly may enact laws necessary and expedient for the maintenance and management of The University of North Carolina and the other public institutions of higher education.

Section 9. *Benefits of public institutions of higher education.* The General Assembly shall provide that the benefits of The University of North Carolina and other public institutions of higher education, as far as practicable, be extended to the people of the State free of expense.

Section 10. *Escheats.*

(1) *Escheats prior to July 1, 1971.* All property that prior to July 1, 1971, accrued to the State from escheats, unclaimed dividends, or distributive shares of the estates of deceased persons shall be appropriated to the use of The University of North Carolina.

(2) *Escheats after June 30, 1971.* All property that, after June 30, 1971, shall accrue to the State from escheats, unclaimed dividends or distributive shares of the estates of deceased persons shall be used to aid worthy and needy students who are residents of this State and are enrolled in public institutions of higher education in this State. The method, amount, and type of distribution shall be prescribed by law.

ARTICLE X
Homesteads and Exemptions

Section 1. *Personal property exemptions.* The personal property of any resident of this State, to a value fixed by the General Assembly but not less than $500, to be selected by the resident, is exempted from sale under execution or other final process of any court, issued for the collection of any debt.

Section 2. *Homestead exemptions.*

(1) *Exemption from sale; exceptions.* Every homestead and the dwellings and buildings used therewith, to a value fixed by the General Assembly but not less than $1,000, to be selected by the owner thereof, or in lieu thereof, at the option of the owner, any lot in a city or town with the dwellings and buildings used thereon, and to the same value, owned and occupied by a resident of the State, shall be exempt from sale under execution or other final process obtained on any debt. But no property shall be exempt from sale for taxes, or for payment of obligations contracted for its purchase.

(2) *Exemption for benefit of children.* The homestead, after the death of the owner thereof, shall be exempt from the payment of any debt during the minority of the owner's children, or any of them.

(3) *Exemption for benefit of surviving spouse.* If the owner of a homestead dies, leaving a surviving spouse but no minor children, the homestead shall be exempt from the debts of the owner, and the rents and profits thereof shall inure to the benefit of the surviving spouse until he or she remarries, unless the surviving spouse is the owner of a separate homestead.

(4) *Conveyance of homestead.* Nothing contained in this Article shall operate to prevent the owner of a homestead from disposing of it by deed, but no deed made by a married owner of a homestead shall be valid without the signature and acknowledgement of his or her spouse.

Section 3. *Mechanics' and laborers' liens.* The General Assembly shall provide by proper legislation for giving to mechanics and laborers an adequate lien on the subject-matter of their labor. The provisions of Sections 1 and 2 of this Article shall not be so construed as to prevent a laborer's lien for work done and performed for the person claiming the exemption or a mechanic's lien for work done on the premises.

Section 4. *Property of married women secured to them.* The real and personal property of any female in this State acquired before marriage, and all property, real and personal, to which she may, after marriage, become in any manner entitled, shall be and remain the sole and separate estate and property of such female, and shall not be liable for any debts, obligations, or engagements of her husband, and may be devised and bequeathed and conveyed by her, subject to such regulations and limitations as the General Assembly may prescribe. Every married woman may exercise powers of attorney conferred upon her by her husband, including the power to execute and acknowledge deeds to property owned by herself and her husband or by her husband.

Section 5. *Insurance.* A person may insure his or her own life for the sole use and benefit of his or her spouse or children or both, and upon his or her death the proceeds from the insurance shall be paid to or for the benefit of the spouse or children or both, or to a guardian, free from all claims of the representatives or creditors of the insured or his or her estate. Any insurance policy which insures the life of a person for the sole use and benefit of that person's spouse or children or both shall not be subject to the claims of creditors of the insured during his or her lifetime, whether or not the policy reserves to the insured during his or her lifetime any or all rights provided for by the policy and whether or not the policy proceeds are payable to the estate of the insured in the event the beneficiary or beneficiaries predecease the insured.

ARTICLE XI
Punishments, Corrections, and Charities

Section 1. *Punishments.* The following punishments only shall be known to the laws of this State: death, imprisonment, fines, removal from office, and disqualification to hold and enjoy any office of honor, trust, or profit under this State.

Section 2. *Death punishment.* The object of punishments being not only to satisfy justice, but also to reform the offender and thus prevent crime, murder, arson, burglary, and rape, and these only, may be punishable with death, if the General Assembly shall so enact.

Section 3. *Charitable and correctional institutions and agencies.* Such charitable, benevolent, penal, and correctional institutions and agencies as the needs of humanity and the public good may require shall be established and operated by the State under such organization and in such manner as the General Assembly may prescribe.

Section 4. *Welfare policy; board of public welfare.* Beneficient provision for the poor, the unfortunate, and the orphan is one of the first duties of a civilized and a Christian state. Therefore, the General Assembly shall provide for and define the duties of a board of public welfare.

ARTICLE XII
Military Forces

Section 1. *Governor is Commander in Chief.* The Governor shall be Commander in Chief of the military forces of the State and may call out those forces to execute the law, suppress riots and insurrections, and repel invasion.

ARTICLE XIII
Conventions; Constitutional Amendment and Revision

Section 1. *Convention of the People.* No Convention of the People of this State shall ever be called unless by the concurrence of two-thirds of all the members of each house of the General Assembly, and unless the proposition "Convention or No Convention" is first submitted to the qualified voters of the State at the time and in the manner prescribed by the General Assembly. If a majority of the votes cast upon the proposition are in favor of a Convention, it shall assemble on the day prescribed by the General Assembly. The General Assembly shall, in the act of submitting the convention proposition, propose limitations upon the authority of the Convention; and if a majority of the votes cast upon the proposition are in favor of a Convention, those limitations shall become binding upon the Convention. Delegates to the Convention shall be elected by the qualified voters at the time and in the manner prescribed in the act of submission. The Convention shall consist of a number of delegates equal to the membership of the House of Representatives of the General Assembly that submits the convention proposition and the delegates shall be apportioned as is the House of Representatives. A Convention shall adopt no ordinance not necessary to the purpose for which the Convention has been called.

Section 2. *Power to revise or amend Constitution reserved to people.* The people of this State reserve the power to amend this Constitution and to adopt a new or revised Constitution. This power may be exercised by either of the methods set out hereinafter in this Article, but in no other way.

Section 3. *Revision or amendment by Convention of the People.* A Convention of the People of this State may be called pursuant to Section 1 of this Article to propose a new or revised Constitution or to propose amendments to this Constitution. Every new or revised Constitution and every constitutional amendment adopted by a Convention shall be submitted to the qualified voters of the State at the time and in the manner prescribed by the Convention. If a majority of the votes cast thereon are in favor of ratification of the new or revised Constitution or the constitutional amendment or amendments, it or they shall become effective January first next after ratification by the qualified voters unless a different effective date is prescribed by the Convention.

Section 4. *Revision or amendment by legislative initiation.* A proposal of a new or revised Constitution or an amendment or amendments to this Constitution may be initiated by the General Assembly, but only if three-fifths of all the members of each house shall adopt an act submitting the proposal to the qualified voters of the State for their ratification or rejection. The proposal shall be submitted at the time and in the manner prescribed by the General Assembly. If a majority of the votes cast thereon are in favor of the proposed new or revised Constitution or constitutional amendment or amendments, it or they shall become effective January first next after ratification by the voters unless a different effective date is prescribed in the act submitting the proposal or proposals to the qualified voters.

ARTICLE XIV
Miscellaneous

Section 1. *Seat of government.* The permanent seat of government of this State shall be at the City of Raleigh.

Section 2. *State boundaries.* The limits and boundaries of the State shall be and remain as they now are.

Section 3. *General laws defined.* Whenever the General Assembly is directed or authorized by this Constitution to enact general laws, or general laws uniformly applicable throughout the State, or general laws uniformly applicable in every county, city and town, and other unit of local government, or in every local court district, no special or local act shall be enacted concerning the subject matter directed or authorized to be accomplished by general or uniformly applicable laws, and every amendment or repeal of any law relating to such subject matter shall also be general and uniform in its effect throughout the State. General laws may be enacted for classes defined by population or other criteria. General laws uniformly applicable throughout the State shall be made applicable without classification or exception in every unit of local government of like kind, such as every county, or every city and town, but need not be made applicable in every unit of local government in the State. General laws uniformly applicable in every county, city and town, and other unit of local government, or in every local court district, shall be made applicable without classification or exception in every unit of local government, or in every local court district, as the case may be. The General Assembly may at any time repeal any special, local, or private act.

Section 4. *Continuity of laws; protection of office holders.* The laws of North Carolina not in conflict with this Constitution shall continue in force until lawfully altered. Except as otherwise specifically provided, the adoption of this Constitution shall not have the effect of vacating any office or term of office now filled or held by virtue of any election or appointment made under the prior Constitution of North Carolina and the laws of the State enacted pursuant thereto.

Section 5. *Conservation of natural resources.* It shall be the policy of this State to conserve and protect its lands and waters for the benefit of all its citizenry, and to this end it shall be a proper function of the State of North Carolina and its political subdivisions to acquire and preserve park, recreational, and scenic areas, to control and limit the pollution of our air and water, to control excessive noise, and in every other appropriate way to preserve as a part of the common heritage of this State its forests, wetlands, estuaries, beaches, historical sites, openlands, and places of beauty.

To accomplish the aforementioned public purposes, the State and its counties, cities and towns, and other units of local government may acquire by purchase or gift properties or interests in properties which shall, upon their special dedication to and acceptance by resolution adopted by a vote of three-fifths of the members of each house of the General Assembly for those public purposes, constitute part of the "State Nature and Historic Preserve," and which shall not be used for other purposes except as authorized by law enacted by a vote of three-fifths of the members of each house of the General Assembly. The General Assembly shall prescribe by general law the conditions and procedures under which such properties or interests therein shall be dedicated for the aforementioned public purposes.

CORPS OF ENGINEERS LAKES

The U.S. Army Corps of Engineers was formed in 1775 by General George Washington during the Revolutionary War as the engineering and construction arm of the Continental Army. The Corps built fortifications and coastal batteries to strengthen the country's defenses and went on to found the Military Academy at West Point, to help open the West, and to develop the Nation's water resources. Today it is the largest engineering organization in the world.

Although the primary mission of the Corps has always been to provide combat support to our fighting Army, the Nation over the years also needed roads, railroads, lighthouses, bridges, and other works of engineering. Consequently, since the period immediately following the Revolutionary War, the Corps has carried out numerous civil works responsibilities, and since 1824, it has been the principal developer of the Nation's water resources.

Ever responsive to the changing needs and demands of the American people, the Corps has planned and executed national programs for navigation, flood control, water supply, hydroelectric power, recreation, conservation, and preservation of the environment. In its military role, the Corps plans, designs and supervises the construction of modern facilities which are necessary to ensure the combat readiness of our Army and Air force.

Since 1871, when the Corps of Engineers completed their first navigational project on the Roanoke River, 69 projects have been completed by this department to improve rivers and harbors in North Carolina.

The Corps of Engineers have completed 7 units since the late 1940's which are open for public use. Descriptions of these units follow.

B. Everett Jordan Lake. Located on the Haw and New Hope rivers near the geographical center of North Carolina. Area was completed in 1967 and was known as the New Hope Lake. In 1973 Congress changed the name to honor the former Senator Jordan from North Carolina. Area encompasses 46,768 acres, including campsites, picnic areas, beaches, boat launching ramps, a marina, and nature trails. For more information contact the Resource Manager, B. Everett Jordan Lake, P.O. Box 144, Moncure, 27559, 919-542-4501.

Cape Fear River Locks and Dams. Located in the tobacco country of eastern North Carolina on the improved channel between Wilmington and Fayetteville, the facilities are equipped for day-use, boating and picnicking. Shad fishing is popular, but swimming and camping are not permitted.

Pool No. 1. From Wilmington, 2 mi W on US 74–76, 16 mi W on US 74–76, then about 15 mi NW on NC 87, 1 mi NE on state road to lock.
Pool No. 2. From Elizabethtown, about 1 mi SE on NC 87, 1 mi NE on state road to lock.
William O. Huske Pool. From Fayetteville, about 17 mi S on NC 87.

For more information contact the Resource Manager, Cape Fear River Locks and Dams, P.O. Box 1890, Wilmington, 28402.

Falls Lake. Located on the Neuse River 7 miles N of Raleigh off US I-64 E on Six Forks Rd. to SR 2003. 11,000-acre lake with 230 miles of shoreline. Interim facilities for boating, swimming, and picknicking; commercial marina; fishing. For more information contact the Resource Manager, Falls Lake, 11405 Falls of the Neuse, Wake Forest, 27587, 919-846-9332.

John H. Kerr Reservoir. This 50,000-acre lake on the Roanoke River is one of the largest man-made lakes in the southeast, noted for its record striped bass catches and camping facilities. Camp areas are operated by the Corps, the states, and private concessionaires. From Raleigh, N.C., N on US 70 and I-85 (total about 50 miles). For more information contact the Resource Manager, John H. Kerr Reservoir, Rt. 1, Box 76, Boydton, VA 23917, 804-738-6662.

W. Kerr Scott Dam and Reservoir. This 1,470-acre lake located on the Yadkin River is in the heart of scenic country, with Moravian and Cascade Falls in the immediate vicinity and the Blue Ridge Parkway 28 miles away. This area has many historical and cultural attractions. From Winston-Salem, W on US 421 to Wilkesboro, 5 mi W on NC 268. Hunting, camping and fishing are allowed. For more information contact the Resource Manager, W. Kerr Scott Reservoir, P.O. Box 182, Wilkesboro, 28697, 919-921-3390.

COUNTY GOVERNMENT EXPENDITURES

The following charts show expenditures per capita by North Carolina county governments for the fiscal year ending June 30, 1987, using the 1987 projected population. These two charts are, in reality, one; and the total expenditures are on the second. Total state expenditures for fiscal 1983–

1984 was $4,397,000,000; but the information provided below is the latest available on a county-by-county basis.

Major Expenditures Per Capita—Part A

County	General Government	Public Safety	Transportation	Environmental Protection	Economic and Physical Development	Human Services
Alamance	$ 32.94	$ 41.04	$ .58	$ 6.06	$ 16.14	$ 50.13
Alexander	30.08	55.72	.00	12.06	13.56	39.75
Alleghany	64.29	80.81	.00	19.07	31.88	50.25
Anson	36.42	36.39	5.28	6.58	5.92	69.14
Ashe	30.40	36.20	1.46	7.54	9.20	52.13
Avery	43.14	66.38	11.69	12.24	3.66	61.73
Beaufort	28.22	25.29	.00	14.05	3.31	72.52
Bertie	40.31	24.49	.00	13.34	7.63	102.99
Bladen	55.65	33.02	.00	14.06	27.07	74.57
Brunswick	126.87	49.68	.47	18.63	7.86	73.42
Buncombe	40.77	55.76	15.87	8.82	17.19	64.79
Burke	38.16	17.05	.00	18.38	1.36	65.73
Cabarrus	37.14	39.36	.00	5.73	10.23	63.98
Caldwell	25.87	48.22	.00	8.90	3.29	69.07
Camden	58.47	23.43	.00	26.39	8.54	41.26
Carteret	41.11	32.61	2.96	15.59	4.77	53.59
Caswell	33.00	43.50	.00	1.71	35.48	53.90
Catawba	37.07	43.81	.00	6.38	3.15	83.18
Chatham	35.43	54.85	.00	16.55	6.22	31.99
Cherokee	78.66	44.90	.00	13.08	1.98	71.35
Chowan	73.49	36.38	3.23	7.96	7.00	51.35
Clay	47.87	51.30	.00	5.63	4.14	44.89
Cleveland	29.93	35.29	.00	7.59	1.84	83.70
Columbus	52.91	31.70	.00	16.13	6.33	74.79
Craven	27.56	32.32	3.14	10.21	8.59	87.07
Cumberland	29.51	48.59	.35	6.21	17.01	90.76
Currituck	59.70	50.87	.00	18.21	13.23	50.37
Dare	198.17	191.60	14.76	119.65	15.72	78.38
Davidson	24.47	37.74	2.35	7.78	10.52	69.48
Davie	26.31	55.49	.00	10.49	4.44	66.10
Duplin	30.07	31.51	4.39	24.65	5.95	71.93
Durham	41.27	38.70	.00	1.97	11.39	184.68
Edgecombe	28.99	29.06	.00	9.78	26.38	87.13
Forsyth	54.40	43.04	.00	3.15	6.98	80.86
Franklin	31.97	29.83	.00	7.08	8.25	85.65
Gaston	31.80	49.01	.00	12.39	13.30	46.24
Gates	37.97	18.16	.00	14.49	9.17	31.98
Graham	69.37	47.47	.00	27.37	52.34	54.57
Granville	46.55	26.27	.14	9.09	9.17	45.39
Greene	35.07	37.20	.00	17.27	23.90	92.88
Guilford	65.41	52.88	.00	.00	3.39	125.20
Halifax	37.42	31.67	.34	6.37	11.14	148.07
Harnett	22.42	44.31	4.07	10.10	20.65	49.42
Haywood	36.87	39.21	.00	13.63	4.56	61.75
Henderson	32.57	59.91	.00	7.75	13.02	58.66

County	General Government	Public Safety	Transportation	Environmental Protection	Economic and Physical Development	Human Services
Hertford	$ .00	$ .00	$ .00	$ .00	$ .00	$ .00
Hoke	41.20	55.16	.34	10.19	5.27	69.80
Hyde	88.49	96.14	1.44	40.30	5.85	126.16
Iredell	34.20	44.86	.00	7.97	17.63	48.24
Jackson	45.15	47.48	2.19	17.36	11.24	91.95
Johnston	21.95	23.63	.00	5.53	53.71	93.56
Jones	41.95	32.95	.00	13.04	8.53	94.93
Lee	52.69	41.62	.57	11.84	7.40	83.89
Lenoir	19.21	27.62	.00	5.74	12.00	89.03
Lincoln	28.55	33.61	.11	11.28	4.34	45.76
Macon	78.38	61.19	3.40	11.56	9.11	70.63
Madison	43.56	40.15	13.49	13.13	.36	129.53
Martin	37.53	22.98	.95	12.79	6.67	56.11
McDowell	32.86	49.35	.00	12.86	5.21	44.48
Mecklenburg	31.40	53.41	1.21	21.67	5.45	121.32
Mitchell	39.26	49.06	9.49	12.06	14.27	55.98
Montgomery	25.03	40.96	.11	9.82	4.98	69.01
Moore	31.75	29.77	.19	12.00	7.73	63.40
Nash	20.79	36.04	.19	6.26	10.57	77.91
New Hanover	67.41	72.84	34.57	32.44	8.34	92.89
Northampton	71.34	27.84	.27	7.20	23.66	119.15
Onslow	24.23	50.15	9.72	7.71	2.47	67.86
Orange	41.55	42.53	.25	4.10	9.57	69.48
Pamlico	71.08	36.79	.00	12.19	9.04	71.20
Pasquotank	29.45	23.78	.00	5.53	5.65	32.56
Pender	41.91	29.52	.00	15.10	17.05	80.25
Perquimans	47.85	29.55	1.63	3.20	5.31	40.15
Person	43.44	51.51	55.58	6.29	6.23	81.89
Pitt	63.38	26.67	.00	8.25	5.56	87.86
Polk	.00	.00	.00	.00	.00	.00
Randolph	24.91	43.12	.06	7.21	5.68	62.08
Richmond	33.49	43.55	.30	10.04	7.75	48.87
Robeson	28.19	35.66	.00	7.86	5.01	68.44
Rockingham	28.20	42.07	1.16	3.53	3.64	94.79
Rowan	38.06	33.85	.57	12.26	2.38	46.10
Rutherford	27.36	45.07	1.25	10.37	4.27	35.18
Sampson	43.80	42.59	2.92	7.96	16.35	75.96
Scotland	29.56	49.06	.00	12.67	2.71	80.48
Stanly	31.67	34.06	8.18	8.99	38.22	52.47
Stokes	40.16	54.45	.00	9.95	8.38	77.50
Surry	26.15	48.56	.00	11.31	4.26	54.85
Swain	46.10	40.99	.00	9.97	73.70	116.10
Transylvania	75.42	68.40	.08	14.53	7.72	108.80
Tyrrell	.00	.00	.00	.00	.00	.00
Union	31.28	45.80	.00	10.64	8.88	67.73
Vance	23.91	41.93	.14	11.70	11.88	48.34
Wake	52.31	41.26	.61	5.93	13.92	109.08
Warren	39.55	62.92	.00	16.57	21.49	105.48
Washington	40.44	26.65	.00	16.60	10.82	61.57
Watauga	48.44	38.84	.00	16.99	18.42	39.87
Wayne	31.04	27.20	1.45	8.09	4.79	73.72
Wilkes	24.47	34.09	.00	6.34	14.46	61.78

County	General Government	Public Safety	Transportation	Environmental Protection	Economic and Physical Development	Human Services
Wilson	$ 33.65	$ 45.11	$ .27	$ 14.25	$ 3.70	$ 90.71
Yadkin	26.08	33.30	.00	10.58	7.70	75.58
Yancey	43.38	35.53	7.75	24.62	8.35	164.40
State Total	$4,169.28	$4,193.26	$231.52	$1,226.48	$1,114.53	$7,161.66

Major Expenditures Per Capita—Part B

County	Culture and Recreation	Utilities	Debt Service	Intergovernmental Expenditures		Social Services	Total County Expenditures
				Schools	Community Colleges		
Alamance	$ 5.48	$ .00	$ 9.70	$ 82.17	$ 6.77	$ 12.26	$ 263.27
Alexander	6.30	7.73	28.86	70.13	.00	9.78	273.97
Alleghany	.00	.00	4.47	88.22	.00	5.28	344.27
Anson	11.21	84.94	45.63	71.24	11.45	20.96	405.16
Ashe	18.33	.00	5.91	103.67	1.35	16.28	282.47
Avery	6.69	.00	2.99	80.97	3.97	.00	293.46
Beaufort	2.59	.00	5.91	81.37	11.22	15.76	260.24
Bertie	.73	.00	20.53	49.36	.94	25.00	285.32
Bladen	9.87	.00	.00	99.73	9.93	24.34	348.24
Brunswick	16.04	215.73	27.12	99.38	4.18	12.89	652.27
Buncombe	19.26	3.47	21.08	159.96	9.00	12.82	428.79
Burke	3.21	19.47	.00	154.41	9.07	.00	326.84
Cabarrus	12.12	25.72	19.12	90.76	.67	11.67	316.50
Caldwell	6.47	6.74	12.65	95.70	10.57	13.59	301.07
Camden	4.56	.00	8.29	83.15	.00	12.89	266.98
Carteret	11.25	.00	28.09	73.85	8.67	12.09	284.58
Caswell	4.82	16.38	.00	71.22	.39	6.11	266.51
Catawba	9.11	.00	23.30	114.86	9.51	9.14	339.51
Chatham	2.99	25.95	10.37	105.76	.33	12.81	303.25
Cherokee	6.58	.00	2.08	63.64	4.06	.00	286.33
Chowan	6.74	23.23	16.93	106.38	.00	14.15	346.84
Clay	9.02	26.32	3.01	85.67	2.74	16.76	297.35
Cleveland	2.26	.79	17.74	82.87	5.31	15.13	282.45
Columbus	12.93	.00	14.61	99.00	12.69	25.20	346.29
Craven	5.29	45.33	12.50	89.64	9.32	14.17	345.14
Cumberland	17.19	.00	19.30	95.91	9.08	14.52	348.43
Currituck	10.34	.00	14.55	.00	.00	.00	217.27
Dare	38.25	117.37	70.06	137.60	1.54	7.70	990.80
Davidson	11.11	.00	7.73	74.73	7.22	10.33	263.46
Davie	9.28	.00	32.80	91.06	.00	7.16	303.13
Duplin	8.70	26.35	2.73	60.24	16.64	24.66	307.82
Durham	18.31	30.33	18.23	196.25	9.65	14.32	565.10
Edgecombe	4.14	.00	9.67	73.59	8.88	25.30	302.92
Forsyth	23.48	.00	17.30	156.87	5.36	12.08	403.52
Franklin	7.10	.00	6.03	216.14	.00	.00	392.05
Gaston	11.46	.00	13.18	.00	.00	19.58	196.96
Gates	8.57	30.08	15.63	.00	.21	19.35	185.61
Graham	4.84	.00	3.18	69.00	1.40	17.08	346.62
Granville	8.24	.00	10.92	87.82	2.55	15.65	261.79
Greene	4.44	11.77	3.55	95.46	1.58	19.49	342.61

County	Culture and Recreation	Utilities	Debt Service	Intergovernmental Expenditures: Schools	Intergovernmental Expenditures: Community Colleges	Social Services	Total County Expenditures
Guilford	$ .00	$ .00	$ 28.90	$ 180.45	$ 9.43	$ 15.30	$ 480.96
Halifax	4.80	30.37	20.73	71.61	5.65	33.18	401.35
Harnett	5.32	12.06	.00	59.59	.00	18.99	246.93
Haywood	12.99	.00	22.15	.00	.00	.00	191.16
Henderson	14.02	2.60	18.98	81.61	11.74	10.84	311.70
Hertford	.00	.00	.00	.00	.00	.00	0.00
Hoke	7.07	.00	4.17	55.59	.29	20.90	269.98
Hyde	.88	72.97	8.77	133.24	.00	21.91	596.15
Iredell	9.73	.00	4.16	97.39	8.48	11.02	283.68
Jackson	10.03	34.62	19.78	81.66	12.14	15.23	388.83
Johnston	2.40	6.63	16.40	92.43	5.60	20.52	342.36
Jones	7.16	20.26	7.33	64.43	1.37	18.99	310.94
Lee	26.88	10.32	51.09	154.74	19.87	.00	460.91
Lenoir	.50	.00	42.56	199.24	10.45	20.95	427.30
Lincoln	9.56	6.56	17.96	66.99	.43	10.78	235.93
Macon	16.53	.00	55.75	.00	.00	5.32	311.87
Madison	5.05	.00	3.76	48.59	.00	214.60	512.22
Martin	3.93	10.07	20.16	136.49	14.52	21.84	344.04
McDowell	9.94	.00	10.93	82.62	38.63	16.02	302.90
Mecklenburg	24.96	.00	52.50	187.39	13.67	10.15	523.13
Mitchell	2.99	.00	10.34	81.62	4.12	14.66	293.85
Montgomery	4.02	22.23	24.14	70.97	7.05	9.39	287.71
Moore	7.27	23.96	12.10	109.99	18.90	.00	317.06
Nash	1.97	2.54	4.03	126.57	13.17	17.21	317.25
New Hanover	16.67	155.80	64.48	135.54	6.28	20.58	707.84
Northampton	1.60	183.62	3.34	57.29	.00	24.02	519.33
Onslow	9.44	8.05	12.12	65.58	6.02	6.81	270.16
Orange	2.39	.00	9.23	145.64	.00	8.92	333.66
Pamlico	11.78	50.75	21.11	72.49	9.63	27.64	393.70
Pasquotank	.25	17.18	11.29	128.35	8.76	18.90	281.70
Pender	7.48	.00	11.92	106.72	.31	24.16	334.42
Perquimans	4.49	25.88	27.01	183.98	.00	21.99	391.04
Person	5.58	4.62	19.86	109.14	17.24	15.46	416.84
Pitt	1.74	.00	13.41	142.82	17.83	21.70	389.22
Polk	.00	.00	.00	.00	.00	.00	0.00
Randolph	6.12	.00	14.19	76.13	6.29	10.70	256.49
Richmond	5.60	33.85	32.19	70.71	12.14	15.39	313.88
Robeson	4.48	20.93	33.05	60.54	4.51	24.54	293.21
Rockingham	.13	.00	2.62	.00	.00	14.68	190.82
Rowan	17.48	.00	4.53	92.24	6.93	13.63	268.03
Rutherford	5.08	.00	11.24	88.17	16.55	20.42	264.96
Sampson	12.15	.00	4.48	94.49	9.39	20.12	330.21
Scotland	12.60	.00	42.19	124.08	.00	27.17	380.52
Stanly	9.90	17.25	14.44	87.73	17.59	10.11	330.61
Stokes	8.65	.00	19.58	133.18	.00	10.33	362.18
Surry	2.54	.00	10.85	85.56	10.64	12.49	267.21
Swain	11.58	.00	13.12	43.62	.91	.00	356.09
Transylvania	20.64	4.24	17.19	99.32	3.76	7.87	427.97
Tyrrell	.00	.00	.00	.00	.00	.00	0.00
Union	12.96	30.62	47.20	113.89	.15	9.94	379.09

County	Culture and Recreation	Utilities	Debt Service	Intergovernmental Expenditures: Schools	Intergovernmental Expenditures: Community Colleges	Social Services	Total County Expenditures
Vance	$ 3.26	$ .00	$ 6.79	$ 76.62	$ 6.53	$ 22.31	$ 253.41
Wake	13.65	.00	34.78	221.61	10.72	10.74	514.61
Warren	8.36	8.19	11.55	91.90	1.21	29.95	397.17
Washington	.93	28.82	33.40	83.63	.00	25.09	327.95
Watauga	19.61	.00	21.80	77.27	2.56	9.90	293.70
Wayne	.10	.00	1.70	110.16	24.95	20.18	303.38
Wilkes	5.02	.00	19.29	79.11	12.53	12.04	269.13
Wilson	6.44	3.78	5.03	105.36	14.06	30.43	352.79
Yadkin	2.12	.00	5.23	68.49	.00	11.92	241.00
Yancey	10.04	.00	7.02	73.13	3.75	12.06	390.03
State Total	$828.16	$1,566.47	$1,649.67	$9,145.48	$623.00	$1,626.24	$33,535.75

COUNTY NAME ORIGINS

North Carolina contains 100 counties. Each county name, the year of its establishment, and a brief biographical sketch (when available) of the person for whom it was named, follow.

Alamance County. Established 1849; named for the BATTLE OF ALAMANCE CREEK, May 16, 1771, or for the Great Alamance Creek.

Alexander County. Established 1847; named in honor of WILLIAM JULIUS ALEXANDER. Was a member of the state legislature.

Alleghany County. Established 1859; named for the ALLEGEWI Indian tribe. An Indian word *Oolikhanna* which translates "beautiful stream."

Anson County. Established 1749; named in honor of GEORGE LORD ANSON. An English admiral who circumnavigated the world in 1744. Was First Lord of the Admiralty, 1751–56 and 1757–62.

Ashe County. Established 1799; named in honor of SAMUEL ASHE. One of the North Carolina Council of Thirteen before the constitution, was president in 1776; was a representative to the Fourth Provincial Congress at Halifax in 1776; the state constitutional convention, 1776; was state chief justice, 1777–95; served as the ninth governor, 1795–98.

Avery County. Established 1911; named in honor of WAIGHTSTILL AVERY. Was a representative to the Mecklenburg Convention in 1775; state legislature, 1776; state attorney general, 1777–79; colonel in Revolutionary War, 1779; State Senate, 1796. Was challenged to a duel by Andrew Jackson.

Beaufort County. Established 1705; named in honor of HENRY SOMERSET IV, DUKE OF BEAUFORT. Became one of the Lord Proprietors of South Carolina in 1709 by buying a share from the Duke of Albemarle. County originally named Archdale for Governor John Archdale; the name was changed to Beaufort about 1712.

Bertie County. Established 1722; named in honor of JAMES and HENRY BERTIE. They were Lord Proprietors who owned one-eighth of Carolina.

Bladen County. Established 1734; named in honor of MARTIN BLADEN. Served as comptroller of the Mint, 1714; commissioner of trade and plantations, 1717–46.

Brunswick County. Established 1764; named for the former TOWN OF BRUNSWICK which was located on the Cape Fear River, settled about 1725, and is now a State Historic Site.

Buncombe County. Established 1791; named in honor of EDWARD BUNCOMBE. Was a colonel in the state militia, 1771; county court clerk, 1774–77; colonel of state Minute Men, 1775; served in the battle of Brandywine, 1777; was wounded in the battle of Brandywine, 1777 and died while being held prisoner of the British, 1778.

Burke County. Established 1777; named in honor of THOMAS BURKE. Was a physician; lawyer; battle of Brandywine volunteer; member of the Continental Congress, 1776–81; governor, 1781–82. Was held as prisoner of the British for four months, but he escaped January 16, 1782.

Cabarrus County. Established 1792; named in honor of STEPHEN CABARRUS. Was speaker of the House of Representatives and served on the University of North Carolina's first board of trustees.

Caldwell County. Established 1841; named in honor of JOSEPH CALDWELL. A professor of mathematics who served as the first president of the University of North Carolina, 1804–12, 1817–35.

Camden County. Established 1777; named in honor of SIR CHARLES PRATT, EARL OF CAMDEN. English political leader and jurist opposed to American Colony taxation who thought the Stamp Act was unconstitutional.

Carteret County. Established 1722; named in honor of JOHN CARTERET, EARL OF GRANVILLE. Served in House of Lords, 1711; was England's ambassador to Sweden, 1719. Was Secretary of State, 1721–24. He was a proprietor who, in 1729, refused to sell his share of one-eighth of Carolina, one of the most thickly settled and wealthiest parts of the colony. His rights were reverted to the State in 1776.

Caswell County. Established 1777; named in honor of RICHARD CASWELL. Served in the state assembly, 1754–71; as speaker, 1769–71; was a Continental Congress delegate, 1774–76; Halifax convention, 1776. He was governor for 2 terms, 1775–79, 1784–87 and state Senator, 1788.

Catawba County. Established 1842; named for the CATAWBA Indian tribe.

Chatham County. Established 1771; named in honor of WILLIAM PITT, EARL OF CHATHAM. An English statesman who entered Parliament in 1735. Was the Secretary of State and House of Commons Leader, 1756.

Cherokee County. Established 1839; named for the CHEROKEE Indian tribe. The Chickasaw word *chiluk-ki* translates "cave people."

Chowan County. Established 1681; named for the CHOWAN RIVER, that was probably named for the Chowan Indian tribe whose name translates to mean "they of the south."

Clay County. Established 1861; named in honor of HENRY CLAY. A Kentucky legislator; served in U.S. House of Representatives; 1808–09; U.S. Senate, 1810–11; U.S. Secretary of State in President John Quincy Adams' cabinet; and unsuccessful candidate for the presidency, 1824, 1832, and 1834 on the Whig ticket.

Cleveland County. Established 1841; named in honor of BENJAMIN CLEAVELAND. A state militia officer who was a hero at the battle of King's Mountain, 1780. Spelling of county name changed in 1887.

Columbus County. Established 1808; named in honor of CHRISTOPHER COLUMBUS. Italian navigator who sailed from Spain and discovered San Salvador in 1492.

Craven County. Established 1705; named in honor of WILLIAM CRAVEN, EARL OF CRAVEN. One of the eight proprietors of Carolina. He was the second Baron Craven of Hamsted-Marshall, 1697; Lord Palatine of the Province of Carolina. Originally named Archdale County, was changed in 1712.

Cumberland County. Established 1754; named in honor of WILLIAM AUGUSTUS, DUKE OF CUMBERLAND. The second son of King George II and Queen Caroline; commander of the English troops at the battle of Culloden in Scotland in 1745. Privy Councillor, 1742, and officer of the army, 1742–57.

Currituck County. Established 1681; named for the CURRITUCK Indian tribe.

Dare County. Established 1870; named in honor of VIRGINIA DARE. She was the first English child to be born in America. Was the granddaughter of John White, who was made governor of the Virginia Colony, sent out by Sir Walter Raleigh in 1587.

Davidson County. Established 1822; named in honor of WILLIAM LEE DAVIDSON. A brigadier general of the North Carolina militia who fought in the battle of Camden, 1780, and was killed in the battle of Cowan's Pass, 1781.

Davie County. Established 1836; named in honor of WILLIAM RICHARDSON DAVIE. Distinguished soldier of the Revolution, member of the Federal Convention of 1787, governor of North Carolina, minister to France, and one of the University of North Carolina's founders.

Duplin County. Established 1750; named in honor of THOMAS HAY, LORD DUPLIN. English nobleman, member of the Board of Trade and Plantations.

Durham County. Established 1881; named for the town of Durham, that was named for Dr. Bartlett Snipes Durham (1822–58), who donated the land for the railroad station.

Edgecombe County. Established 1741; named in honor of BARON RICHARD EDGECUMBE. Was lord of England's treasury, 1716. Served as treasurer of war and paymaster general of His Majesty's services in Ireland.

Forsyth County. Established 1849; named in honor of BENJAMIN FORSYTHE. A military officer; second lieutenant of the state infantry, 1800; captain of the riflemen, 1808; served in state legislature, 1807–08; led assault at Gananoque Upper Canada, 1812; was killed near Odelltown, New York, 1814.

Franklin County. Established 1779; named in honor of BENJAMIN FRANKLIN. A printer who founded the Pennsylvania "Gazette," 1728; clerk of Pennsylvania General Assembly; postmaster of Philadelphia; provincial assembly; deputy postmaster general of the British North American Colonies; Continental Congress; signed the Declaration of Independence, 1776; Pennsylvania constitutional convention, 1776; commissioner and minister to France, 1776–85; governor of Pennsylvania, 1785–88; federal constitutional convention, 1787.

Gaston County. Established 1846; named in honor of WILLIAM GASTON. Served in State Senate, 1800; House of Represenatives, 1807–09; State Senate, 1812, 1818–19. Served as U.S. Representative, 1813–17; State House of Representatives, 1824, 1827–29, and 1831; Supreme Court judge, 1833–44. He wrote the state song "The Old North State."

Gates County. Established 1779; named in honor of HORATIO GATES. Military officer in Continental Army, 1775, became major general, 1776; defeated Burgoyne at the battle of Saratoga, 1777 and was awarded the congressional medal for the surrender of the British Army, 1777; fought in the battle of Camden, 1780. Served in New York state legislature, 1800–01.

Graham County. Established 1872; named in honor of WILLIAM ALEXANDER GRAHAM. After serving in the state legislature, was U.S. Senator, 1840–43; governor, 1845–49; was Secretary of the Navy, 1850–52; ran unsuccessfully for office of vice president, 1852; State Senate, 1854, 1862, and 1865. Served in Confederate Senate, 1863.

Granville County. Established 1746; named in honor of JOHN CARTERET, EARL OF GRANVILLE. Served in House of Lords, 1711; was England's ambassador to Sweden, 1719. Was Secretary of State, 1721–24. He was a proprietor who, in 1729, refused to sell his share of one-eighth of Carolina, one of the most thickly settled and wealthiest parts of the colony. His rights were reverted to the State in 1776.

Greene County. Established 1799; named in honor of GENERAL NATHANAEL GREENE. Revolutionary War leader whose action at the Battle of Guilford Courthouse was responsible for saving North Carolina from the British; presided at the court of inquiry for Major André.

Guilford County. Established 1771; named in honor of FRANCIS NORTH, THE FIRST EARL OF GUILFORD. He was knighted in 1671; served as attorney general of England, 1675–82; became Baron Guilford in 1683.

Halifax County. Established 1758; named in honor of GEORGE MONTAGU DUNK, EARL OF HALIFAX. Was president of the Board of Trade, 1748–61; lord lieutenant of Ireland, 1761–63; First Lord of the Admiralty, 1762; Secretary of State, 1762; lord privy seal, 1770.

Harnett County. Established 1855; named in honor of CORNELIUS HARNETT. Served in state legislature, 1770–71; Wilmington Committee of Safety, 1774; delegate to Continental Congress, 1777–80; was the author of the Halifax Resolves, 1776. He died of a disease he contracted while being held prisoner of the British.

Haywood County. Established 1808; named in honor of JOHN HAYWOOD. Was treasurer of the state, 1787–1827.

Henderson County. Established 1838; named in honor of LEONARD HENDERSON. Judge of the Appellate Court, 1808–18; Supreme Court, 1818–29; Chief Justice Supreme Court, 1829.

Hertford County. Established 1759; named in honor of FRANCIS SEYMOUR CONWAY, MARQUIS OF HERTFORD. Was Privy Councillor of Ireland, 1749; ambassador to Paris, 1763–65; lord lieutenant of Ireland, 1765–66; lord chamberlain of the Household, 1766–82.

Hoke County. Established 1911; named in honor of ROBERT FREDERICK HOKE. Confederate Army officer who surrendered at Durham Station, North Carolina, 1865. Served as president of the Georgia, Carolina and Northern Railway Company, of Seaboard Air Line.

Hyde County. Established 1705; named in honor of EDWARD HYDE, EARL OF CLARENDON. Was appointed by William of Orange as governor of New York and New Jersey, 1701. Served as deputy governor of North Carolina, 1711–12.

Iredell County. Established 1788; named in honor of JAMES IREDELL. Served as captain of a volunteer company in the War of 1812; state legislature, 1813 and 1816–28; Speaker, 1817–22; Judge of Superior Court, 1819; governor, 1827–28; U.S. Senate, 1828–31; Supreme Court reporter, 1840–52.

Jackson County. Established 1851; named in honor of ANDREW JACKSON. The seventh president of the United States, 1829–37; the first territorial governor of Florida; represented Tennessee in the House of Representatives and Senate; was a judge of the Tennessee Supreme Court, 1798–1804; decorated major general who fought in the Creek War, 1813; defeated British in 1815 at battle of New Orleans.

Johnston County. Established 1746; named in honor of GABRIEL JOHNSTON. A university professor from Scotland who was governor from 1734–52.

Jones County. Established 1778; named in honor of WILLIE JONES. A member of the radical Whig faction and member of the Safety Council, 1776.

Lee County. Established 1907; named in honor of ROBERT EDWARD LEE. A graduate of the U.S. Military Academy, 1829. He resigned as colonel in 1861 from the U.S. Army after being wounded in the Mexican War; was commander-in-chief of the Confederate Army, surrendered at Appomattox Court House; was president of Washington College.

Lenoir County. Established 1791; named in honor of WILLIAM LENOIR. A military man who served as the first president of the board of the University of North Carolina.

Lincoln County. Established 1779; named in honor of BENJAMIN LINCOLN. A military man in the Continental Army who received the sword of Cornwallis, 1781; was Secretary of War,

1781-83. Served as lieutenant governor of Massachusetts, 1788 and was the Collector of the Port in Boston, Massachusetts, 1789-1808.

Macon County. Established 1828; named in honor of NATHANIEL MACON. Served in Revolutionary War; State Senate, 1780-82, 1784, and 1785; U.S. Representative, 1791-1815; Speaker of the House, 1801-07; U.S. Senator, 1815-28; president of the state constitutional convention, 1835.

Madison County. Established 1851; named in honor of JAMES MADISON. A congressman from Virginia who served as Secretary of State in President Jefferson's cabinet, 1801-09; was president of the United States, 1809-17.

Martin County. Established 1774; named in honor of JOSIAH MARTIN. Was the last royal governor, 1771-75.

McDowell County. Established 1842; named in honor of JOSEPH MCDOWELL. He fought against the Cherokees, 1776; led the state militia at the King's Mountain battle, 1780; state legislature, 1785-88; State Senate, 1791-95; U.S. Constitutional Convention, 1788-89; U.S. Representative, 1797-99.

Mecklenburg County. Established 1762; named in honor of CHARLOTTE SOPHIA, PRINCESS OF MECKLENBURG-STRELITZ. She married King George III of England, 1761.

Mitchell County. Established 1861; named in honor of ELISHA MITCHELL. A professor at the University of North Carolina who discovered the highest peak of the mountains in the state. He was killed in a fall and was buried on the mountain, 1857.

Montgomery County. Established 1779; named in honor of RICHARD MONTGOMERY. A Provincial Congress delegate, 1775; served as brigadier general in the Continental Army; was killed leading assault against Quebec, 1775.

Moore County. Established 1784; named in honor of ALFRED MOORE. A Revolutionary War captain; state attorney general, 1782; United States Supreme Court Associate Justice, 1799-1804.

Nash County. Established 1777; named in honor of FRANCIS NASH. Served as justice of the peace, 1763; legislature, 1764; assembly, 1771, 1773-75; provincial council, 1775; served as brigadier general and was killed in battle of Germantown.

New Hanover County. Established 1729; named for HANOVER, GERMANY in honor of King George I of England, who came from Hanover.

Northampton County. Established 1741; named for NORTHAMPTON, ENGLAND.

Onslow County. Established 1734; named in honor of ARTHUR ONSLOW. A member of British Parliament; Chancellor to Queen Caroline, 1729; treasurer of the navy, 1734-42; was speaker of the House of Commons, 1728-61, was the third member of his family to have been speaker.

Orange County. Established 1752; probably named for WILLIAM V OF THE HOUSE OF ORANGE, whose mother, Anne, controlled affairs of state, instead of William III, who died fifty years prior to the formation of the county.

Pamlico County. Established 1872; named for the PAMLICO Indian Tribe.

Pasquotank County. Established 1681; named for the PASQUOTANK Indian Tribe, whose name means "divided tidal river."

Pender County. Established 1875; named in honor of WILLIAM DORSEY PENDER. U.S. Military Academy graduate; Confederate Army captain, 1861; became major general, 1863; was killed at the battle of Gettysburg, July 18, 1863.

Perquimans County. Established 1679; named for the PERQUIMAN Indian Tribe.

Person County. Established 1791; named in honor of THOMAS PERSON. Was a justice of the peace; a sheriff; a member of the state assembly, 1764; provincial council, 1775; a member of the council of safety, 1776; justice of the peace, 1776; state legislature; state Senate, 1787 and 1791.

Pitt County. Established 1760; named in honor of WILLIAM PITT, EARL OF CHATHAM. An English statesman who entered Parliament in 1735. Was the Secretary of State and House of Commons leader, 1756.

Polk County. Established 1855; named in honor of WILLIAM POLK. Served in the Revolutionary War; served in state legislature, 1785-88 and 1790; was Internal Revenue supervisor for the State, 1791-1808.

Randolph County. Established 1779; named in honor of PEYTON RANDOLPH. Was the King's attorney for Virginia, 1748; served in the Virginia House of Burgesses, 1764-74 and was speaker, 1766; chairman of the correspondence committee, 1773; Virginia Convention president, 1774, 1775; member of the Continental Congress, 1774-75.

Richmond County. Established 1779; named in honor of CHARLES LENNOX, DUKE OF RICHMOND. He was the British Minister Extraordinary in Paris, 1765; Secretary of State for the Southern Department, 1766. He was in favor of the American colonies and wanted the troops withdrawn, 1778.

Robeson County. Established 1787; named in honor of THOMAS ROBESON. Member of the Provincial Convention, 1775-76; Army colonel who was leader in the Elizabethtown battle, paid the troops with his own money and was not reimbursed.

Rockingham County. Established 1785; named in honor of CHARLES WATSON WENTWORTH, MARQUIS OF ROCKINGHAM. Was prime minister of Great Britian when the Stamp Act was repealed, 1765-66; he was in favor of the American colonies being independent.

Rowan County. Established 1753; named in honor of MATTHEW ROWAN. Member of the general assembly, 1729; justice of the peace, 1735, 1737; state surveyor general, 1736; commander-in-chief and president of the council (acting governor), 1753-54.

Rutherford County. Established 1779; named in honor of GRIFFITH RUTHERFORD. Member of the legislative council of the Territory South of the River Ohio, 1775; brigadier general, fought against Indians, 1776; State Senate, 1784; was president of the Tennessee legislative council, 1796.

Sampson County. Established 1784; named in honor of JOHN SAMPSON. A colonel in the military; member of the state council during the term of Josiah Martin, the last royal governor.

Scotland County. Established 1899; named for SCOTLAND, GREAT BRITAIN.

Stanly County. Established 1841; named in honor of JOHN STANLY. Served in state legislature, 1798-99; U.S. Representative, 1801-03, 1809-11.

Stokes County. Established 1789; named in honor of JOHN STOKES. A military officer, wounded at Waxhaw Massacre, 1780; district court judge, 1783; State Senate, 1786-87; House of Representatives, 1789; was made U.S. District Court Judge but he died on the way to attend his first session.

Surry County. Established 1771; named in honor of the COUNTY OF SURREY IN ENGLAND, where William Tryon, incumbent governor, was born.

Swain County. Established 1871; named in honor of DAVID LOWRIE SWAIN. Served as governor, 1832-35; president of the University of North Carolina, 1835-68.

Transylvania County. Established 1861; named derived from Latin words *trans* and *sylva* meaning "beyond the woods."

Tyrrell County. Established 1729; named in honor of JOHN TYRRELL. A Lord Proprietor of Carolina.

Union County. Established 1842; name is descriptive. County was formed from parts of two other counties.

Vance County. Established 1881; named in honor of ZEBULON BAIRD VANCE. Was Buncombe County prosecuting attorney, 1852; state legislature, 1854; U.S. Representative, 1858–61; Confederate Army officer, 1861; governor two terms, 1862–65, 1877–79; U.S. Senator, 1879–94.

Wake County. Established 1771; named in honor of MARGARET WAKE. The maiden name of Governor William Tryon's wife.

Warren County. Established 1779; named in honor of JOSEPH WARREN. A physician; was president of the Provincial Congress, 1775; Continental Army officer, was killed at the battle of Bunker Hill, 1775.

Washington County. Established 1799; named in honor of GEORGE WASHINGTON. Revolutionary War leader; presided over federal constitutional convention, 1787; president of the United States, 1789–1797; when war with France was threatened, was made commander-in-chief of the U.S. Army, 1798 until his death December 14, 1799.

Watauga County. Established 1849; named for the WATAUGA RIVER.

Wayne County. Established 1779; named in honor of ANTHONY WAYNE. Was nicknamed "Mad Anthony"; Pennsylvania legislature, 1774–75; military colonel, wounded at battle of Three Rivers, 1776; became brigadier general, 1777; was captured at Stony Point and awarded gold medal and thanks from Congress, 1779; Pennsylvania legislature, 1784; U.S. Representative from Georgia, 1791–92.

Wilkes County. Established 1778; named in honor of JOHN WILKES. A member of English Parliament; supported the colonies side in the American Revolution.

Wilson County. Established 1855; named in honor of LOUIS DICKEN WILSON. Served general assembly 19 years, representing Edgecombe County. Was a military officer; died of a fever at Vera Cruz.

Yadkin County. Established 1850; named for the YADKIN RIVER.

Yancey County. Established 1833; named in honor of BARTLETT YANCEY. Served as U.S. Representative, 1813–17; State Senate, 1817–27.

COUNTY SEATS

County	County Seat	Zip Code	County	County Seat	Zip Code
Alamance	Graham	27253	Buncombe	Asheville	28802
Alexander	Taylorsville	28681	Burke	Morganton	28655
Alleghany	Sparta	28675	Cabarrus	Concord	28025
Anson	Wadesboro	28170	Caldwell	Lenoir	28645
Ashe	Jefferson	28640	Camden	Camden	27921
Avery	Newland	28657	Carteret	Beaufort	28516
Beaufort	Washington	27889	Caswell	Yanceyville	27379
Bertie	Windsor	27983	Catawba	Newton	28658
Bladen	Elizabethtown	28337	Chatham	Pittsboro	27312
Brunswick	Bolivia	28422	Cherokee	Murphy	28906

County	County Seat	Zip Code	County	County Seat	Zip Code
Chowan	Edenton	27932	Mitchell	Bakersville	28705
Clay	Hayesville	28904	Montgomery	Troy	27371
Cleveland	Shelby	28150	Moore	Carthage	28327
Columbus	Whiteville	28472	Nash	Nashville	27856
Craven	New Bern	28560	New Hanover	Wilmington	28402
Cumberland	Fayetteville	28302	Northampton	Jackson	27845
Currituck	Currituck	27929	Onslow	Jacksonville	28540
Dare	Manteo	27954	Orange	Hillsborough	27278
Davidson	Lexington	27292	Pamlico	Bayboro	28515
Davie	Mocksville	27028	Pasquotank	Elizabeth City	27909
Duplin	Kenansville	28349	Pender	Burgaw	28425
Durham	Durham	27702	Perquimans	Hertford	27944
Edgecombe	Tarboro	27886	Person	Roxboro	27573
Forsyth	Winston-Salem	27102	Pitt	Greenville	27834
Franklin	Louisburg	27549	Polk	Columbus	28722
Gaston	Gastonia	28052	Randolph	Asheboro	27203
Gates	Gatesville	27938	Richmond	Rockingham	28379
Graham	Robbinsville	28771	Robeson	Lumberton	28358
Granville	Oxford	27565	Rockingham	Wentworth	27375
Greene	Snow Hill	28580	Rowan	Salisbury	28144
Guilford	Greensboro	27420	Rutherford	Rutherfordton	28139
Halifax	Halifax	27839	Sampson	Clinton	28328
Harnett	Lillington	27546	Scotland	Laurinburg	28352
Haywood	Waynesville	28786	Stanly	Albemarle	28001
Henderson	Hendersonville	27536	Stokes	Danbury	27016
Hertford	Winton	27986	Surry	Dobson	27017
Hoke	Raeford	28376	Swain	Bryson City	28713
Hyde	Swan Quarter	27885	Transylvania	Brevard	28712
Iredell	Statesville	28677	Tyrrell	Columbia	27925
Jackson	Sylva	28779	Union	Monroe	28110
Johnston	Smithfield	27577	Vance	Henderson	27536
Jones	Trenton	28585	Wake	Raleigh	27611
Lee	Sanford	27330	Warren	Warrenton	27589
Lenoir	Kinston	28501	Washington	Plymouth	27962
Lincoln	Lincolnton	28092	Watauga	Boone	28607
Macon	Franklin	28734	Wayne	Goldsboro	27530
Madison	Marshall	28753	Wilkes	Wilkesboro	28697
Martin	Williamston	27892	Wilson	Wilson	27893
McDowell	Marion	28752	Yadkin	Yadkinville	27055
Mecklenburg	Charlotte	28230	Yancey	Burnsville	28714

COURTS

The General Court of Justice in North Carolina is composed of an Appellate Division, a Superior Court Division, and a District Court Division. The Appellate Division consists of the Supreme Court and the Court of Appeals. The Supreme Court has exclusive authority to make rules of procedure and practice for the Appellate Division.

The Constitution of North Carolina provides for an Administrative Office of the Courts to carry out the provisions of Article IV of the Constitution.

Administrative Office of the Courts
Justice Building, 2 East Morgan Street
P.O. Box 2448, Raleigh 27602

Only persons qualified to practice law in the state are eligible for election or appointment as a Justice of the Supreme Court, Judge of the Court of Appeals, Judge of the Superior Court, or Judge of the District Court.

THE SUPREME COURT

The Supreme Court has jurisdiction to review upon appeal any decision of the courts below, upon any matter of law or legal inference.

The Supreme Court consists of a chief justice and 6 associate justices elected by qualified voters of the state for terms of 8 years and until their successors are elected and qualified.

The Supreme Court
Justice Building, 2 East Morgan Street
P.O. Box 1841, Raleigh 27602

Chief Justice
James G. Exum

Associate Justices
John Webb
Louis B. Meyer
Burley B. Mitchell, Jr.
Harry C. Martin
Henry E. Frye
Willis P. Whichard

THE COURT OF APPEALS

The Court of Appeals has appellate jurisdiction over lower courts in cases in which the Supreme Court has no exclusive appellate jurisdiction.

The Court of Appeals consists of a chief judge and 11 associate judges elected by qualified voters of the state to terms of 8 years and until their successors are elected and qualified.

The Court of Appeals
Ruffin Building
P.O. Box 888
Raleigh, 27611

Chief Judge
Robert A. Hedrick

Associate Judges
S. Gerald Arnold
Robert F. Orr
Hugh A. Wells
K. Edward Greene
Charles L. Becton
Clifton E. Johnson
Eugene H. Phillips
Sidney S. Eagles, Jr.
John C. Martin
Sarah E. Parker
Jack Cozart

THE SUPERIOR COURT

The Superior Court has original general jurisdiction throughout the state.

Each regular Superior Court judge will reside in the district for which he is elected. Superior Court judges rotate from district to district within the division in which they reside. The General Assembly may provide by general law for the selection or appointment of special or emergency Superior Court judges not selected for a particular judicial district.

THE DISTRICT COURT

District Court judges are elected for terms of 4 years. Judges reside in the district for which they are elected. When more than one District judge is elected for a district, the Chief Justice of the Supreme Court designates one of the judges as Chief District Judge.

The following list shows the counties in each Judicial District, as well as the Superior and District Court Judges. The Chief District judge is the first District judge listed.

JUDICIAL DISTRICTS

FIRST DIVISION

1st District: Camden, Chowan, Currituck, Dare, Gates, Pasquotank, and Perquimans. *Superior Court:* J. Herbert Small, Thomas Watts. *District Court:* John T. Chaffin, Grafton G. Beaman, J. Richard Parker.

2nd District: Beaufort, Hyde, Martin, Tyrrell, and Washington. *Superior Court:* William C. Griffin. *District Court:* Hallett S. Ward, James W. Hardison, and Samuel G. Grimes.

3rd District: Carteret, Craven, Pamlico and Pitt. *Superior Court:* David E. Reid, Jr., Herbert O. Phillips, III. *District Court:* E. Burt Aycock, Jr., James Randal Hunter, H. Horton Rountree, James E. Martin, James E. Ragan, III, Willie Lee Lumpkin, III.

4th District: Duplin, Jones, Onslow, and Sampson. *Superior Court:* Henry L. Stevens, III, James R. Strickland. *District Court:* Kenneth W. Turner, Wayne Kimble, Jr., William M. Cameron, Jr., Stephen M. Williamson, Leonard W. Thagard.

5th District: New Hanover and Pender. *Superior Court:* Bradford Tillery, Napoleon B. Barefoot. *District Court:* Gilbert H. Burnett, Jacquelin Morris-Goodson, Charles E. Rice, Elton G. Tucker.

6th District: Bertie, Halifax, Hertford, and Northampton. *Superior Court:* Richard B. Allsbrook. *District Court:* Nicholas Long, Harold P. McCoy, Jr., Robert E. Williford.

7th District: Edgecombe, Nash, and Wilson. *Superior Court:* Frank R. Brown, Charles B. Winberry, Jr. *District Court:* George M. Britt, Allen W. Harrell, Quentin T. Sumner, Albert S. Thomas, Jr.

8th District: Greene, Lenoir, and Wayne. *Superior Court:* Paul M. Wright, James D.

Llewellyn. *District Court:* J. Patrick Exum, Kenneth R. Ellis, Rodney R. Goodman, Arnold O. Jones, Joseph E. Setzer, Jr.

SECOND DIVISION

9th District: Franklin, Granville, Person, Vance, and Warren. *Superior Court:* Robert H. Hobgood, Jr., Henry W. Hight, Jr. *District Court:* Claude W. Allen, Jr., Ben U. Allen, J. Larry Senter, Charles W. Wilkinson.

10th District: Wake. *Superior Court:* Henry V. Barnette, Jr., Edwin S. Preston, Jr., Robert L. Farmer, Donald W. Stephens. *District Court:* George F. Bason, Stafford G. Bullock, George R. Greene, William A. Creech, Joyce A. Hamilton, Russell G. Sherrill, III, Fred M. Morelock, Louis W. Payne, Jr., Jerry W. Leonard.

11th District: Harnett, Johnston, and Lee. *Superior Court:* Wiley F. Bowen. *District Court:* Elton C. Pridgen, Edward H. McCormick, William A. Christian, Owen Henry Willis, Jr.

12th District: Cumberland and Hoke. *Superior Court:* Darius B. Herring, Jr., E. Lynn Johnson, Coy E. Brewer, Jr. *District Court:* Sol G. Cherry, Warren L. Pate, John S. Hair, Jr., Lacy S. Hair, Anna Elizabeth Keever, Patricia Ann Goodson.

13th District: Bladen, Brunswick, and Columbus. *Superior Court:* Giles R. Clark. *District Court:* William C. Gore, Jr., Dewey J. Hooks, Jr., David G. Wall, Jerry A. Jolly.

14th District: Durham. *Superior Court:* Thomas H. Lee, Anthony M. Brannon, J. Milton Read, Jr. *District Court:* David O. LaBarre, Carolyn D. Johnson, Orlando F. Hudson, Jr., Richard Chaney.

15-A District: Alamance. *Superior Court:* J. B. Allen, Jr. *District Court:* W. S. Harris, Jr., James Kent Washburn, Spencer B. Ennis.

15-B District: Chatham and Orange. *Superior Court:* F. Gordon Battle. *District Court:* Stanley Peele, Lowry M. Betts, Patricia S. Hunt.

16th District: Robeson and Scotland. *Superior Court:* B. Craig Ellis. *District Court:* John S. Gardner, Herbert L. Richardson, Ms. Adelaide G. Behan, Charles G. McLean.

THIRD DIVISION

17-A District: Caswell and Rockingham. *Superior Court:* Melzer A. Morgan, Jr. *District Court:* Peter M. McHugh, Robert R. Blackwell, Phillip W. Allen.

17-B District: Surry and Stokes. *Superior Court:* James M. Long. *District Court:* Clarence W. Carter, Jerry Cash Martin.

18th District: Guilford. *Superior Court:* W. Douglas Albright, Thomas W. Ross, Ralph R. Walker, Joseph John. *District Court:* Lawrence McSwain, William L. Daisy, Edmund Lowe, Robert E. Bencini, Paul Thomas Williams, J. Bruce Morton, Sherry Fowler Alloway, William A. Vaden.

19-A District: Cabarrus and Rowan. *Superior Court:* Thomas W. Seay, Jr., James C. Davis. *District Court:* Robert M. Davis, Sr., Clarence E. Horton, Jr., Adam C. Grant, Jr., Frank M. Montgomery.

19-B District: Montgomery and Randolph. *Superior Court:* Russell G. Walker, Jr. *District Court:* Richard M. Toomes, William M. Neely.

20th District: Anson, Moore, Richmond, Stanly, and Union. *Superior Court:* F. Fetzer Mills, William H. Helms. *District Court:* Donald R. Huffman, Kenneth W. Honeycutt, Ronald W. Burris, Michael Earle Beale, Tanya T. Wallace.

21st District: Forsyth. *Superior Court:* William Z. Wood, Judson D. DeRamus, Jr., William H. Freeman, Robert A. Collier, Jr., C. Preston Cornelius. *District Court:* Abner Alexander, R. Kason Keiger, James A. Harrill, Jr., William B. Reingold, Roland H. Hayes, Loretta C. Biggs.

22nd District: Alexander, Davidson, Davie, and Iredell. *Superior Court:* Robert A. Collier, Jr., C. Preston Cornelius. *District Court:* Lester P. Martin, Jr., Samuel A. Cathey, Robert W. Johnson, George T. Fuller.

23rd District: Alleghany, Ashe, Wilkes, and Yadkin. *Superior Court:* Julius A. Rousseau, Jr. *District Court:* Samuel L. Osbourne, Michael E. Helms, Edgar B. Gregory.

FOURTH DIVISION

24th District: Avery, Madison, Mitchell, Watauga, and Yancey. *Superior Court:* Charles C. Lamb, Jr. *District Court:* Robert H. Lacey, Roy Alexander Lyerly, Charles Philip Ginn.

25th District: Burke, Caldwell, and Catawba. *Superior Court:* Forrest A. Ferrell, Claude S. Sitton. *District Court:* Timothy S. Kincaid, L. Oliver Noble, Jr., Ronald E. Bogle, Stewart L. Cloer, Jonathan L. Jones.

Judicial Divisions and Districts

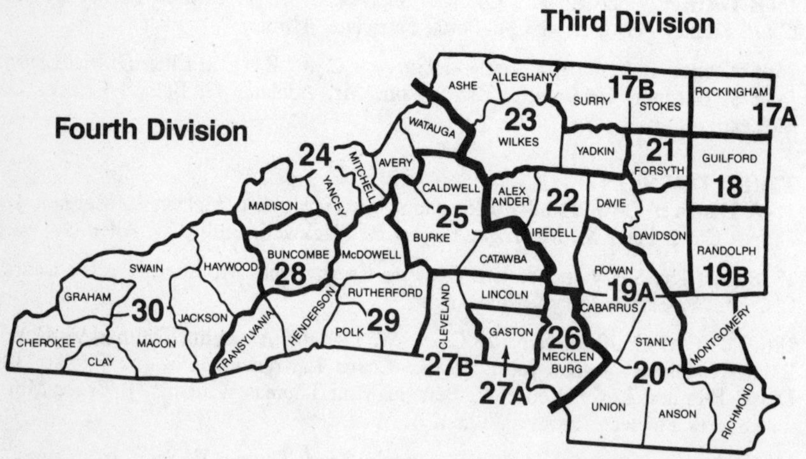

26th District: Mecklenburg. *Superior Court:* Frank W. Snepp. Jr., W. Terry Sherrill, Kenneth A. Griffin, Chase B. Saunders, Robert M. Burroughs, Sr. *District Court:* James E. Lanning, Robert P. Johnston, William H. Scarborough, L. Stanley Brown, Daphene L. Cantrell, T. Patrick Matus, II, Resa L. Harris, William G. Jones, Marilyn Bissell, Richard A. Elkins.

27–A District: Gaston. *Superior Court:* Robert W. Kirby, Robert E. Gaines. *District Court:* Timothy L. Patti, Berlin H. Carpenter, Jr., Harley B. Gaston, Jr., Larry B. Langson, Shirley L. Fulton.

27–B District: Cleveland and Lincoln. *Superior Court:* John Mull Gardner. *District Court:* George W. Hamrick, John M. Gardner, James T. Bowen, III, Catherine C. Stevens.

28th District: Buncombe. *Superior Court:* Robert D. Lewis, C. Walter Allen. *District Court:* Gary S. Cash, Robert L. Harrell, Peter L. Roda, Earl J. Fowler, Jr.

29th District: Henderson, McDowell, Polk, Rutherford, and Transylvania. *Superior Court:* Hollis M. Owens, Jr. *District Court:* Robert T. Gash, Zoro J. Guice, Jr., Loto Jane Greenlee, Thomas N. Hix.

30th District: Cherokee, Clay, Graham, Haywood, Jackson, Macon, and Swain. *Superior Court:* James U. Downs, Janet Marlene Hyatt. *District Court:* Steven J. Bryant, John J. Snow, Jr., Danny E. Davis.

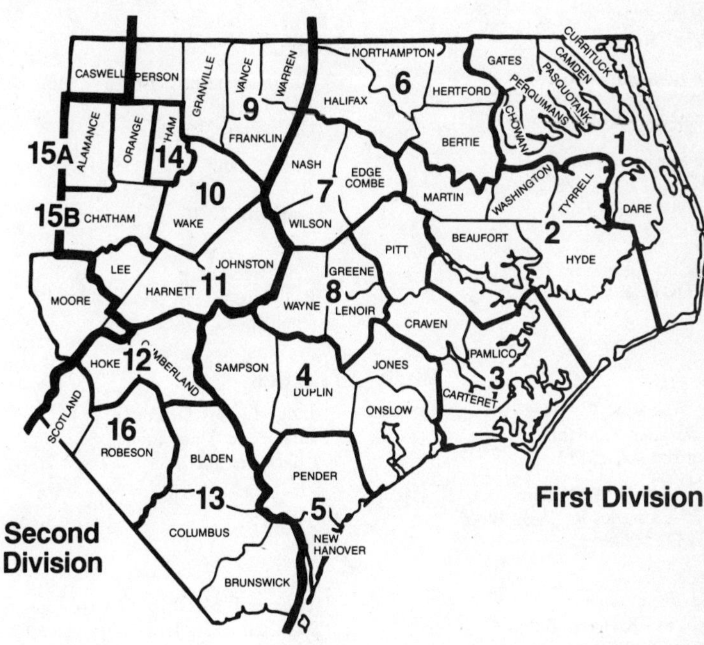

THE FEDERAL JUDICIARY

United States Fourth Circuit Court of Appeals

Judge J. Dickson Phillips
P.O. Box 3617
Durham, 27702

Judge Sam J. Ervin, III
P.O. Drawer 2146
Morganton, 28655

United States District Courts in North Carolina

Eastern District

Judge Franklin T. Dupree, Jr.
P.O. Box 27585
Raleigh, 27611

Judge W. Earl Britt
P.O. Drawer 27504
Raleigh, 27611

Terrence W. Boyle
P.O. Box 429
Elizabeth City, 27909

Judge James C. Fox
P.O. Drawer 2143
Wilmington, 28402

Judge John D. Larkins, Jr.
P.O. Box 126
Trenton, 28585

Attorney:
Margaret P. Currin
P.O. Box 26897, Federal Bldg.
Raleigh, 27611

Clerk:
J. Rich Leonard
P.O. Box 25670
Raleigh, 27611

Middle District

Judge Eugene A. Gordon
Box 3285
Greensboro, 27402

Judge Hiram H. Ward
246 Federal Bldg., 251 Main St.
Winston-Salem, 27101

Judge Richard C. Erwin
P.O. Box 89
Greensboro, 27402

Judge Frank W. Bullock, Jr.
P.O. Box 3807
Durham, 27701

Attorney:
Robert H. Edmonds, Jr.
P.O. Box 1858
Greensboro, 27402

Clerk:
J. P. Creekmore
P.O. Box V-1
Greensboro, 27402

Western District

Judge Woodrow W. Jones
P.O. Box 741, Courthouse
Rutherfordton, 28139

Judge James B. McMillan
Rm. 254, Charles R. Jonas Bldg.
Charlotte, 28202

Judge Robert D. Potter
Charles R. Jonas Bldg.
Charlotte, 28202

Attorney:
Charles R. Brewer
260 Charles R. Jonas Bldg.
Charlotte, 28202

Clerk:
Thomas J. McGraw
204 Charles R. Jonas Bldg.
Charlotte, 28202

CRIME

North Carolina ranked thirty-second in crime rate per 100,000 population in 1985 according to the Federal Bureau of Investigation's publication, *Crime in the United States.*

During 1986, the month having the most crimes reported was August, while February had the fewest number of crimes reported. The most common offense was larceny from motor vehicles. The most common offenders (arrestees) were black males, age 18, as reported in Crime in North Carolina—1986 Uniform Crime Report issued by the NC Department of Justice, State Bureau of Investigation, Division of Criminal Information.

The index crime percent distribution for reported crimes in 1986 is as follows (percentages do not add to 100% due to rounding): larceny, 55.9%; murder, .2%; motor vehicle theft, 4.8%; aggravated assault, 8.1%; burglary, 28.3%; robbery, 2.0%; and rape, .6%.

The approximate number of crime index offenses that were reported to the North Carolina law enforcement officers every 24 hours were as follows: 1 murder; 4 rapes; 15 robberies; 59 aggravated assaults; 206 burglaries; 408 larcenies; and 35 motor vehicle thefts.

To combat crime, North Carolina had a total of 13,623 full-time law enforcement employees in 1986. There were 9,815 male and 1,094 female sworn officers and the remaining 2,714 were civilian employees.

There are 99 county and 50 municipal jails in the state, with an average population of 20,000 per month serving 30- to 120-day sentences.

The state prison population was reported on March 3, 1988, to have reached critical overcrowded status with 17,568 inmates.

The probation population totaled 64,727 in 1986 and the parole population was 5,142.

Charts showing the number of serious crimes, prison, probation, and parole population, as well as full-time police employee data follow.

Number of serious crimes in North Carolina reported to the Police Information Network by type of offense, by county—1986

County	Total Crime Index	Murder	Rape	Robbery	Aggravated Assault	Breaking and Entering	Larceny	Motor Vehicle Theft
Alamance	3,484	5	22	36	246	937	2,078	160
Alexander	346	1	1	0	15	169	143	17
Alleghany	138	0	1	3	36	34	57	7
Anson	633	2	4	2	149	183	262	31
Ashe	268	1	0	0	15	115	125	12
Avery	259	1	1	0	57	77	107	16
Beaufort	1,423	3	11	19	139	468	742	41
Bertie	415	4	1	6	77	121	187	19
Bladen	506	2	3	3	93	216	175	14
Brunswick	772	2	4	6	47	282	399	32

County	Total Crime Index	Murder	Rape	Robbery	Aggravated Assault	Breaking and Entering	Larceny	Motor Vehicle Theft
Buncombe	7,432	13	53	115	363	1,899	4,589	400
Burke	1,901	4	4	12	142	582	1,039	118
Cabarrus	3,246	8	11	40	168	930	1,969	120
Caldwell	2,558	8	13	25	215	799	1,412	86
Camden	106	0	0	1	22	34	43	6
Carteret	1,955	2	6	14	86	502	1,266	79
Caswell	345	2	1	2	33	145	149	13
Catawba	4,713	7	23	58	630	1,235	2,540	220
Chatham	894	5	4	3	76	321	439	46
Cherokee	226	1	0	1	28	77	103	16
Chowan	325	2	0	1	18	116	182	6
Clay	89	0	0	0	5	55	25	4
Cleveland	2,678	6	11	30	166	825	1,522	118
Columbus	1,578	5	17	20	133	578	753	72
Craven	2,410	7	10	20	171	700	1,382	120
Cumberland	18,034	18	166	492	1,535	5,162	9,532	1,129
Currituck	178	1	1	3	7	75	83	8
Dare	1,289	0	4	3	143	440	663	36
Davidson	3,277	7	15	33	151	1,171	1,675	225
Davie	535	0	4	4	27	242	236	22
Duplin	882	2	5	8	96	279	462	30
Durham	11,131	24	54	292	416	3,080	6,762	503
Edgecombe	5,383	10	27	105	449	1,496	3,102	196
Forsyth	14,827	22	127	400	2,374	3,912	7,256	736
Franklin	538	11	9	10	22	266	187	33

CRIME RATES 1982

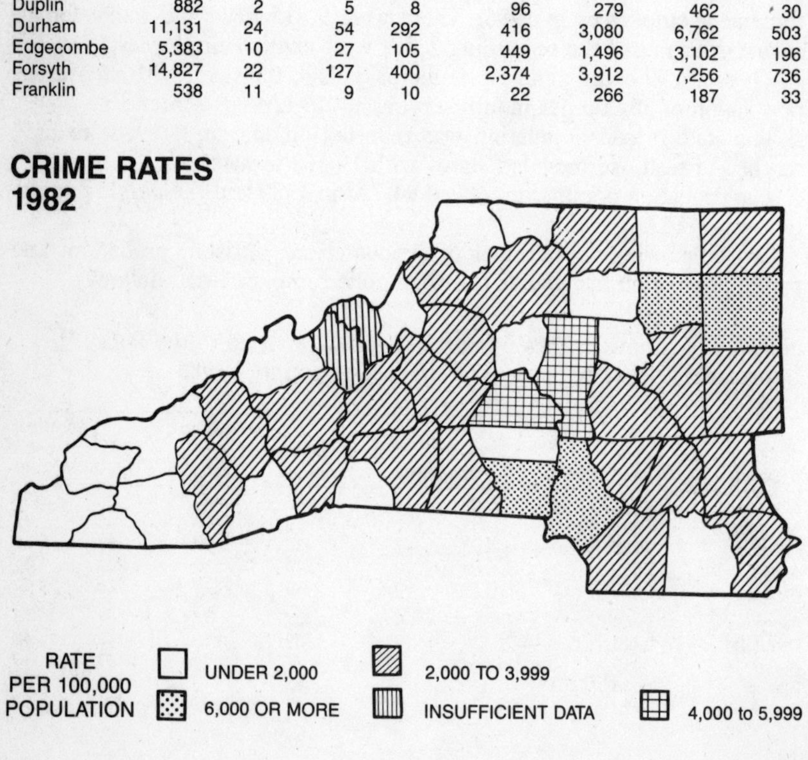

County	Total Crime Index	Murder	Rape	Robbery	Aggravated Assault	Breaking and Entering	Larceny	Motor Vehicle Theft
Gaston	9,316	10	47	215	606	2,756	5,197	485
Gates	149	0	1	0	28	56	58	6
Graham	17	0	0	0	0	10	5	2
Granville	1,586	6	9	21	255	524	720	51
Greene	186	1	1	2	12	109	54	7
Guilford	18,711	35	98	450	1,391	4,453	11,530	754
Halifax	1,461	3	8	13	126	487	768	56
Harnett	2,641	9	21	27	318	766	1,346	154
Haywood	1,127	2	7	7	60	360	624	67
Henderson	1,897	5	13	19	109	543	1,082	126
Hertford	754	3	3	11	92	223	405	15
Hoke	866	3	6	13	100	357	332	55
Hyde	33	0	1	0	0	2	30	0
Iredell	3,567	8	18	53	222	1,102	2,023	141
Jackson	457	2	1	1	10	187	255	1
Johnston	2,785	7	11	31	183	928	1,463	162
Jones	77	0	1	3	17	27	25	4
Lee	2,045	1	15	19	161	628	1,104	117
Lenoir	2,708	5	7	65	266	735	1,560	70
Lincoln	800	1	2	5	46	159	526	61
Macon	257	1	0	0	20	135	92	9
Madison	9	0	0	0	1	5	2	1
Martin	610	2	3	5	37	189	365	9
McDowell	607	2	4	5	23	245	286	42
Mecklenburg	40,403	58	334	1,545	4,072	11,229	21,333	1,832

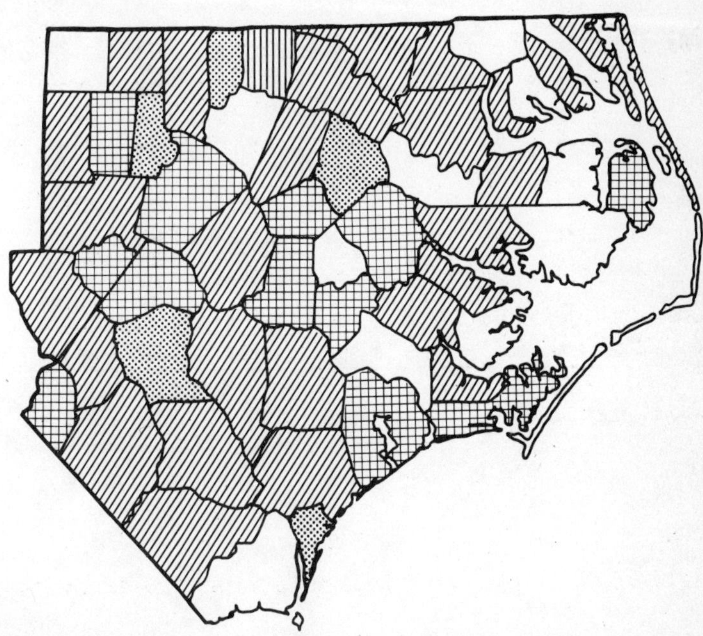

County	Total Crime Index	Murder	Rape	Robbery	Aggravated Assault	Breaking and Entering	Larceny	Motor Vehicle Theft
Mitchell	36	0	0	1	2	7	17	9
Montgomery	756	0	6	6	195	200	315	34
Moore	1,274	5	2	12	51	430	703	71
Nash	1,068	6	1	12	39	424	535	51
New Hanover	8,481	13	52	120	358	2,270	5,256	412
Northampton	282	0	2	1	25	133	107	14
Onslow	5,367	4	20	74	471	1,460	3,114	224
Orange	4,568	3	26	40	158	1,179	2.916	246
Pamlico	137	1	2	0	8	67	52	7
Pasquotank	852	1	1	17	136	271	404	22
Pender	135	0	2	0	5	61	64	3
Perquimans	218	0	0	3	58	60	95	2
Person	779	1	8	6	140	233	334	57
Pitt	4,698	4	49	78	227	1,314	2,853	173
Polk	169	1	4	0	22	51	76	15
Randolph	2,709	12	8	26	233	916	1,383	131
Richmond	1,230	5	2	10	112	336	692	73
Robeson	3,362	22	22	71	229	885	1,924	209
Rockingham	2,192	5	3	14	225	587	1,272	86
Rowan	2,694	2	9	44	115	942	1,486	96
Rutherford	1,247	5	12	9	90	363	694	74
Sampson	861	4	2	4	65	293	425	68
Scotland	1,288	5	1	14	58	389	787	34
Stanly	1,071	2	10	14	68	327	597	53
Stokes	418	1	2	4	27	106	252	26
Surry	1,277	2	1	11	80	434	667	82
Swain	72	0	0	0	3	54	15	0
Transylvania	438	0	3	2	32	119	252	30
Tyrrell	117	0	0	1	30	42	39	5
Union	2,376	4	5	36	269	735	1,225	102
Vance	2,402	0	9	30	177	788	1,324	74
Wake	18,729	25	109	412	1,036	4,162	11,883	1,102
Warren	71	0	0	1	9	34	26	1
Washington	329	1	2	1	51	98	151	25
Watauga	975	1	6	1	31	221	686	29
Wayne	3,361	5	25	66	152	960	2,003	150
Wilkes	1,173	11	2	11	54	331	710	54
Wilson	824	2	3	3	123	248	390	55
Yadkin	355	1	0	3	21	96	209	25
Yancey	0	0	0	0	0	0	0	0
State Totals	266,238	506	1,635	5,435	21,694	75,364	148,764	12,842

The following chart indicates the number of individuals in the prison, probation, and parole populations, as well as the number of law enforcement personnel by county.

County	Clients in the Prison, Probation and Parole Populations			Law Enforcement Personnel		
	Prison Admissions 1986	Probation Population March, 1988	Parole Population March, 1988	Sworn Officers	Civilians	Total
Alamance	528	1,168	95	186	47	233
Alexander	34	299	9	18	7	25
Alleghany	8	81	2	11	5	16
Anson	92	310	26	36	10	46
Ashe	38	180	5	20	9	29
Avery	13	105	1	43	7	50
Beaufort	149	585	39	54	13	67
Bertie	38	221	15	19	5	24
Bladen	77	382	25	37	15	52
Brunswick	98	535	31	82	20	102
Buncombe	277	1,041	87	315	45	360
Burke	117	697	44	104	27	131
Cabarrus	351	888	82	195	17	212
Caldwell	112	581	44	97	30	127
Camden	12	31	4	2	1	3
Carteret	108	376	24	109	23	132
Caswell	82	166	16	18	10	28
Catawba	289	1,057	81	220	35	255
Chatham	28	322	13	45	26	71
Cherokee	32	219	7	20	4	24
Chowan	34	125	8	23	6	29
Clay	8	75	1	6	4	10
Cleveland	217	407	59	103	33	136
Columbus	88	612	34	69	29	98
Craven	184	640	37	110	48	158
Cumberland	513	2,326	164	396	116	512
Currituck	23	84	11	12	3	15
Dare	35	164	6	70	12	82
Davidson	186	1,238	91	163	42	205
Davie	39	211	9	30	8	38
Duplin	136	551	31	61	12	73
Durham	533	2,511	183	400	90	490
Edgecombe	106	593	46	160	51	211
Forsyth	697	2,216	231	529	117	646
Franklin	65	350	16	33	19	52
Gaston	266	1,170	138	337	52	389
Gates	7	42	5	4	0	4
Graham	15	68	1	8	0	8
Granville	102	367	29	90	18	108
Greene	32	147	10	17	1	18
Guilford	669	2,805	288	802	179	981
Halifax	156	703	46	76	47	123
Harnett	200	718	57	89	29	118
Haywood	71	498	37	81	2	83
Henderson	130	439	52	82	20	102

County	Clients in the Prison, Probation and Parole Populations: Prison Admissions 1986	Probation Population March, 1988	Parole Population March, 1988	Law Enforcement Personnel: Sworn Officers	Civilians	Total
Hertford	67	217	11	36	22	58
Hoke	75	332	29	34	7	41
Hyde	19	42	4	7	5	12
Iredell	242	1,232	72	132	13	145
Jackson	20	208	7	43	5	48
Johnston	240	682	61	102	43	145
Jones	14	84	9	6	5	11
Lee	132	545	41	73	20	93
Lenoir	160	707	49	99	17	116
Lincoln	85	246	22	54	4	58
Macon	18	175	3	32	2	34
Madison	11	132	2	22	0	22
Martin	71	230	34	33	3	36
McDowell	61	239	15	18	12	50
Mecklenburg	832	5,180	387	933	294	1,227
Mitchell	11	93	2	23	8	31
Montgomery	97	236	19	41	9	50
Moore	157	530	40	104	32	136
Nash	94	709	50	59	14	73
New Hanover	426	1,301	143	287	79	366
Northampton	51	209	16	18	13	31
Onslow	308	1,158	61	153	50	203
Orange	99	668	37	194	37	231
Pamlico	21	102	4	7	5	12
Pasquotank	93	270	21	43	8	51
Pender	25	255	17	24	5	29
Perquimans	24	68	7	9	1	10
Person	82	305	21	41	8	49
Pitt	384	1,104	90	214	72	286
Polk	21	83	4	19	10	29
Randolph	183	742	42	123	15	138
Richmond	200	537	59	65	29	94
Robeson	441	1,878	160	155	55	210
Rockingham	435	682	85	168	21	189
Rowan	344	1,055	100	132	32	164
Rutherford	137	389	45	67	23	90
Sampson	108	526	34	65	19	84
Scotland	150	479	44	51	8	59
Stanly	77	381	29	82	8	90
Stokes	100	251	18	36	7	43
Surry	261	623	53	84	32	116
Swain	20	105	4	22	12	34
Transylvania	35	131	10	43	12	55
Tyrrell	10	39	2	3	4	7
Union	198	880	8	117	16	133
Vance	115	499	33	62	6	68
Wake	1,140	4,487	279	711	180	891
Warren	29	128	13	16	4	20
Washington	49	126	8	12	11	23
Watauga	43	173	8	70	16	86

County	Prison Admissions 1986	Probation Population March, 1988	Parole Population March, 1988	Sworn Officers	Civilians	Total
	Clients in the Prison, Probation and Parole Populations			*Law Enforcement Personnel*		
Wayne	166	1,154	75	117	43	160
Wilkes	138	801	57	73	13	86
Wilson	137	594	36	118	32	150
Yadkin	54	265	19	30	7	37
Yancey	10	88	3	15	4	19
	Sum of Counties 15,515	Out of State 2,068	Out of State 350	Total Males 9,815 Females 1,094		
State Total	16,547	64,727	5,142	10.909	2,714	13,623

Crime in the United States—1985

The source for the table below is the Federal Bureau of Investigation's publication, Crime in the United States, 1985. The number of index offenses and crime rates per 100,000 population are estimated for 100% population coverage.

State	# Offenses	Rate	Pop.	State	# Offenses	Rate	Pop.
Alabama	158,513	3,942.1	4,021,000	Montana	37,577	4,549.3	826,000
Alaska	30,619	5,877.0	521,000	Nebraska	59,335	3,694.6	1,606,000
Arizona	226,793	7,116.2	3,187,000	Nevada	61,538	6,574.6	936,000
Arkansas	84,571	3,585.0	2,359,000	New Hampshire	32,454	3,251.9	998,000
California	1,718,473	6,518.0	26,365,000	New Jersey	385,239	5,094.4	7,562,000
Colorado	223,555	6,919.1	3,231,000	New Mexico	94,050	6,486.2	1,450,000
Connecticut	149,330	4,704.8	3,174,000	New York	993,811	5,588.5	17,783,000
Delaware	30,859	4,961.3	622,000	North Carolina	257,792	4,121.4	6,255,000
Florida	860,889	7,574.2	11,366,000	North Dakota	18,354	2,679.4	685,000
Georgia	305,381	5,110.1	5,976,000	Ohio	449,882	4,187.3	10,744,000
Hawaii	54,814	5,200.6	1,054,000	Oklahoma	179,080	5,425.0	3,301,000
Idaho	39,276	3,908.1	1,005,000	Oregon	180,830	6,729.8	2,687,000
Illinois	611,324	5,299.7	11,535,000	Pennsylvania	360,028	3,037.4	11,853,000
Indiana	215,234	3,914.1	5,499,000	Rhode Island	45,723	4,723.5	968,000
Iowa	113,713	3,942.9	2,884,000	South Carolina	162,013	4,840.5	3,347,000
Kansas	107,190	4,375.1	2,450,000	South Dakota	18,697	2,640.8	708,000
Kentucky	109,812	2,947.2	3,726,000	Tennessee	198,419	4,166.7	4,762,000
Louisiana	249,303	5,563.6	4,481,000	Texas	1,075,295	6,568.7	16,370,000
Maine	42,739	3,671.7	1,164,000	Utah	87,470	5,317.3	1,645,000
Maryland	235,973	5,372.8	4,392,000	Vermont	20,801	3,888.0	535,000
Massachusetts	276,999	4,757.8	5,822,000	Virginia	215,634	3,779.1	5,706,000
Michigan	578,566	6,366.3	9,088,000	Washington	287,856	6,528.8	4,409,000
Minnesota	173,348	4,134.2	4,193,000	West Virginia	43,615	2,252.8	1,936,000
Mississippi	85,333	3,265.7	2,613,000	Wisconsin	191,798	4,016.7	4,775,000
Missouri	219,568	4,366.0	5,029,000	Wyoming	20,437	4,015.1	509,000
				United States	12,430,026	5,206.5	238,740,000

Note: North Carolina ranks thirty-second (32nd) in crime rate per 100,000 population.

DAY CARE FACILITIES

There are 2,596 licensed day care facilities in North Carolina with a total capacity of 109,026. The total capacity of the 6,502 registered homes is 12,599.

The following charts show the number of licensed day care centers and registered homes including capacities for each per county, as of November, 1987.

Licensed Day Care Facilities

County	Licensed Centers	Total Capacity	County	Licensed Centers	Total Capacity
Alamance	44	1,838	Gaston	94	3,619
Alexander	8	286	Gates	4	64
Alleghany	4	136	Graham	4	74
Anson	9	220	Granville	8	216
Ashe	8	262	Greene	9	157
Avery	5	154	Guilford	129	7,901
Beaufort	14	507	Halifax	15	354
Bertie	6	200	Harnett	25	733
Bladen	11	282	Haywood	21	485
Brunswick	16	503	Henderson	27	983
Buncombe	69	2,619	Hertford	11	306
Burke	36	1,035	Hoke	13	382
Cabarrus	26	1,289	Hyde	2	52
Caldwell	29	937	Iredell	28	913
Camden	2	0	Jackson	12	334
Carteret	18	833	Johnston	39	1,586
Caswell	4	99	Jones	3	57
Catawba	56	2,689	Lee	30	907
Chatham	14	312	Lenoir	22	1,034
Cherokee	10	202	Lincoln	24	837
Chowan	6	110	Macon	9	319
Clay	5	104	Madison	5	141
Cleveland	35	1,164	Martin	17	341
Columbus	23	707	McDowell	10	341
Craven	20	1,195	Mecklenburg	238	12,250
Cumberland	89	5,359	Mitchell	6	241
Currituck	6	88	Montgomery	9	369
Dare	9	382	Moore	24	923
Davidson	42	1,830	Nash	26	943
Davie	12	292	New Hanover	40	2,211
Duplin	19	530	Northampton	9	138
Durham	74	3,329	Onslow	29	1,409
Edgecombe	26	1,001	Orange	45	1,805
Forsyth	103	5,665	Pamlico	2	62
Franklin	13	408	Pasquotank	12	280

County	Licensed Centers	Total Capacity	County	Licensed Centers	Total Capacity
Pender	3	92	Surry	26	957
Perquimans	4	61	Swain	10	227
Person	10	320	Transylvania	9	347
Pitt	42	1,927	Tyrrell	1	0
Polk	4	96	Union	39	1,353
Randolph	31	1,165	Vance	27	870
Richmond	22	794	Wake	147	9,125
Robeson	52	2,276	Warren	8	112
Rockingham	23	843	Washington	5	127
Rowan	43	1,291	Watauga	13	403
Rutherford	15	512	Wayne	45	1,898
Sampson	22	661	Wilkes	22	831
Scotland	24	692	Wilson	16	950
Stanly	26	829	Yadkin	16	420
Stokes	13	377	Yancey	5	136
			State Total	2,596	109,026

Registered Day Care Homes

County	Registered Homes	Total Capacity	County	Registered Homes	Total Capacity
Alamance	151	279	Cumberland	5	2
Alexander	31	78	Currituck	44	40
Alleghany	18	62	Dare	86	229
Anson	47	74	Davidson	20	72
Ashe	4	6	Davie	81	151
Avery	5	8	Duplin	353	722
Beaufort	52	113	Durham	73	97
Bertie	9	6	Edgecombe	144	359
Bladen	43	73	Forsyth	24	63
Brunswick	72	103	Franklin	91	184
Buncombe	78	120	Gaston	7	9
Burke	84	177	Gates	0	0
Cabarrus	51	129	Graham	55	93
Caldwell	2	11	Granville	21	49
Camden	28	40	Greene	330	615
Carteret	10	12	Guilford	35	79
Caswell	151	377	Halifax	112	276
Catawba	80	162	Harnett	18	23
Chatham	8	12	Haywood	45	54
Cherokee	12	22	Henderson	16	52
Chowan	3	3	Hertford	16	52
Clay	4	89	Hoke	16	19
Cleveland	87	113	Hyde	6	15
Columbus	78	110	Iredell	98	208
Craven	203	313	Jackson	7	0

County	Registered Homes	Total Capacity	County	Registered Homes	Total Capacity
Johnston	98	194	Randolph	99	226
Jones	6	10	Richmond	76	51
Lee	64	134	Robeson	42	74
Lenoir	37	104	Rockingham	79	120
Lincoln	24	30	Rowan	83	155
Macon	8	21	Rutherford	15	23
Madison	4	0	Sampson	50	83
Martin	37	136	Scotland	37	63
McDowell	6	6	Stanly	50	101
Mecklenburg	541	969	Stokes	28	25
Mitchell	5	6	Surry	59	81
Montgomery	16	35	Swain	2	8
Moore	70	181	Transylvania	5	2
Nash	55	131	Tyrrell	5	17
New Hanover	152	328	Union	61	138
Northampton	8	8	Vance	58	110
Onslow	169	360	Wake	680	1,405
Orange	224	315	Warren	16	32
Pamlico	14	8	Washington	36	72
Pasquotank	19	19	Watauga	15	35
Pender	35	80	Wayne	100	97
Perquimans	4	1	Wilkes	22	59
Person	21	36	Wilson	48	132
Pitt	91	246	Yadkin	25	73
Polk	4	5	Yancey	3	6
			State Total	6,502	12,599

ECONOMICS

In the past North Carolina's economy has been dominated by agriculture as well as the manufacture of textiles, furniture, and tobacco products. Since the late 1940s, farm employment has drastically declined and there has been a dramatic change in the state's industrial base. Current trends in business now show that the five fastest growing industries in the state are nonelectrical machinery, rubber and plastics, electrical machinery, instruments, and printing and publishing, in that order.

The five slowest growing industries are leather products, textile mill products, tobacco products, apparel and products, and lumber and wood products.

Population is projected to top 7.2 million by the year 2000. During the next 12 years, the nonwhite population is expected to increase twice as fast as the white population—22.6 percent as opposed to 11.6 percent.

The median age is expected to increase from 31.7 to 36.5 years in the year 2000, and the retirement age population, 65 and older, is expected to reach almost a million.

While the civilian labor force growth is expected to slow to a rate of 1.1 percent, it is predicted to reach 3.76 million by the year 2000, but the rate of employment increase will decline during that time.

The state's nonmanufacturing sector will be the primary source of new jobs, in view of past trends. Many of these jobs will be in business, health, and professional service categories with higher wages.

The average hourly manufacturing wage in the state is expected to increase from 1986's $7.55 to $17.12 in 2000, an average increase of 1 percent annually after adjusting for inflation.

It is expected that in 1988 housing starts in North Carolina will peak at around 88,500 units before falling back to a more sustainable rate of 75,000 to 80,000 in the 1990's.

Personal Income

The following chart shows the total estimated personal and per capita income by county for the state in 1984.

County	Total (in millions of dollars)	Per Capita	County	Total (in millions of dollars)	Per Capita
Alamance	$ 1,154,689	$11,300	Duplin	$ 372,548	$ 8,971
Alexander	273,977	10,400	Durham	1,985,902	12,471
Alleghany	86,445	8,755	Edgecombe	574,514	9,863
Anson	229,686	8,784	Forsyth	3,526,919	13,794
Ashe	188,970	8,185	Franklin	274,187	8,604
Avery	118,136	7,917	Gaston	1,846,639	10,925
Beaufort	391,906	9,187	Gates	85,154	9,192
Bertie	179,930	8,405	Graham	52,465	7,355
Bladen	233,406	7,591	Granville	312,107	8,592
Brunswick	358,795	8,212	Greene	150,316	9,165
Buncombe	1,842,619	11,128	Guilford	4,294,863	13,201
Burke	764,113	10,233	Halifax	440,718	7,865
Cabarrus	1,064,900	11,573	Harnett	505,637	8,179
Caldwell	659,328	9,617	Haywood	482,497	10,141
Camden	50,831	8,673	Henderson	794,660	12,238
Carteret	425,468	9,095	Hertford	199,718	8,342
Caswell	165,981	7,510	Hoke	140,554	6,349
Catawba	1,312,633	11,812	Hyde	44,095	7,451
Chatham	409,034	11,605	Iredell	911,749	10,560
Cherokee	144,692	7,241	Jackson	228,961	8,470
Chowan	118,599	9,186	Johnston	706,775	9,388
Clay	50,418	7,202	Jones	74,670	7,627
Cleveland	842,255	9,965	Lee	434,999	11,046
Columbus	411,139	7,941	Lenoir	581,832	9,539
Craven	768,991	10,055	Lincoln	476,137	10,687
Cumberland	2,393,590	9,523	Macon	207,913	9,112
Currituck	110,445	8,576	Madison	130,601	7,604
Dare	142,290	8,692	Martin	249,452	9,188
Davidson	1,260,983	10,723	McDowell	332,875	9,195
Davie	292,286	10,882	Mecklenburg	6,103,107	14,099

County	Total (in millions of dollars)	Per Capita
Mitchell	$ 131,587	$ 9,204
Montgomery	209,716	8,949
Moore	626,668	11,536
Nash	812,159	11,569
New Hanover	1,191,946	10,794
Northampton	157,313	6,892
Onslow	1,128,134	9,512
Orange	983,903	12,158
Pamlico	100,275	9,262
Pasquotank	295,755	10,094
Pender	194,808	8,159
Perquimans	85,890	8,736
Person	268,739	8,931
Pitt	938,066	9,888
Polk	176,271	12,234
Randolph	1,064,209	11,038
Richmond	391,674	8,585
Robeson	771,602	7,312
Rockingham	865,655	10,142
Rowan	1,111,897	10,901
Rutherford	$ 538,985	$ 9,630
Sampson	442,961	8,769
Scotland	292,594	8,662
Stanly	530,067	10,626
Stokes	342,953	9,831
Surry	615,551	10,206
Swain	80,113	7,476
Transylvania	262,706	10,554
Tyrrell	41,374	10,089
Union	907,665	11,889
Vance	348,075	9,157
Wake	4,801,069	14,236
Warren	135,570	8,347
Washington	144,397	9,929
Watauga	285,881	8,467
Wayne	915,009	9,326
Wilkes	609,179	10,067
Wilson	712,636	11,025
Yadkin	307,846	10,505
Yancey	112,864	7,359
State Total	$66,902,861	$10,852

Projected Long-Term Economic Indicators

	1985	1990	1995	2000
Employment (000)				
Total Nonagricultural	2,645.5	2,958.8	3,092.6	3,234.2
Manufacturing	827.4	845.2	825.9	802.6
Nondurables	485.7	500.6	461.8	429.5
Durables	341.7	344.6	364.1	373.1
Nonmanufacturing	1,818.1	2,113.5	2,266.6	2,431.6
Average Hourly Earnings—Mfg. ($)	7.29	8.87	12.12	17.12
Average Nonfarm Wage Rate ($)	17,468	21,336	29,247	41,106
Total Personal Income ($ Bil.)	72.67	98.50	139.86	204.33
Farm	0.85	1.04	1.25	1.66
Nonfarm	71.82	97.46	104.50	149.33
Wages	46.26	63.13	90.49	133.03
Other	25.56	34.33	48.12	69.64
Total Population (000)	6,260.7	6,613.8	6,931.0	7,241.6
Per Capita Income ($)	11,607	14,894	20,178	28,216
Real Disposable Income Per Capita (1972 $)	4,257	4,595	4,883	5,221

	1985	1990	1995	2000
Retail Sales (1972 $)	16.66	18.80	19.75	20.85
Durable Goods	7.85	8.55	9.18	9.93
Nondurable Goods	8.81	10.25	10.57	10.92
Housing Starts (000)	85.68	80.56	73.15	76.32
Single Family	61.23	58.78	55.66	56.27
Multi-family	24.45	21.78	17.49	20.05

Source: Data Resources, Inc., Regional Information Service, and the N.C. Office of State Budget and Management.

Households with income in 1979 and mean income by type of income, by county 1979. Households may be counted in more than one income type.

	Earnings							
	Total		Wage or Salary		Nonfarm Self-Employment		Farm Self-Employment	
County	Households	Mean Income	Households	Mean Income	Households	Mean Income	Households	Mean Income
Alamance	30,343	$18,185	29,246	$17,510	3,224	$10,544	1,196	$4,774
Alexander	7,486	17,074	7,167	16,146	952	9,398	483	6,529
Alleghany	2,798	13,192	2,525	12,229	415	7,735	454	6,220
Anson	6,622	15,427	6,315	14,541	656	11,269	523	5,617
Ashe	6,337	13,141	5,830	12,134	1,015	10,146	1,159	1,927
Avery	3,925	13,278	3,594	12,771	705	7,400	314	3,183
Beaufort	11,389	14,911	10,511	13,963	1,344	11,072	1,373	5,951
Bertie	5,389	13,483	4,831	12,989	558	7,475	1,006	5,702
Bladen	8,191	13,689	7,535	13,001	844	11,075	1,352	3,557
Brunswick	9,693	15,742	8,855	14,929	1,575	11,239	789	3,402
Buncombe	47,743	17,206	45,812	16,641	5,164	10,368	1,675	3,313
Burke	21,545	16,815	21,098	16,059	1,903	11,908	424	1,924
Cabarrus	25,688	18,307	24,952	17,553	2,535	12,338	680	1,471
Caldwell	19,951	16,575	19,369	15,983	1,850	10,322	369	5,472
Camden	1,570	16,773	1,402	16,193	216	9,670	216	7,139
Carteret	12,298	15,815	11,436	14,796	2,172	10,568	388	6,029
Caswell	5,407	15,555	4,942	15,011	555	9,886	1,047	4,238
Catawba	32,884	18,437	32,057	17,736	3,193	11,140	654	3,305
Chatham	10,538	16,857	9,836	16,162	1,320	10,236	1,083	4,758
Cherokee	4,933	13,056	4,598	12,028	713	10,709	243	6,029
Chowan	3,537	14,996	3,257	14,073	380	14,252	440	4,066
Clay	1,728	12,939	1,597	12,017	259	9,573	181	3,805
Cleveland	23,882	17,694	23,047	17,276	2,288	9,619	1,010	2,384
Columbus	14,137	14,226	12,814	13,431	1,536	8,539	2,857	5,565
Craven	19,668	15,765	18,804	15,280	1,817	9,807	959	5,134
Cumberland	65,602	15,535	63,772	15,114	5,138	9,388	1,622	4,370
Currituck	2,979	15,122	2,778	14,750	359	6,905	194	8,212
Dare	4,219	16,264	3,805	13,780	1,140	13,932	90	3,388
Davidson	34,739	17,604	33,435	16,897	3,655	11,570	1,241	3,473
Davie	7,193	18,347	6,892	17,336	848	11,193	574	5,231
Duplin	11,556	13,636	10,339	12,692	1,395	9,970	2,435	5,109
Durham	47,148	18,329	46,070	17,568	4,163	12,569	893	2,806

County	Earnings: Total Households	Total Mean Income	Wage or Salary Households	Wage or Salary Mean Income	Nonfarm Self-Employment Households	Nonfarm Self-Employment Mean Income	Farm Self-Employment Households	Farm Self-Employment Mean Income
Edgecombe	15,445	$ 15,424	14,809	$ 15,026	1,369	$ 7,746	955	$ 5,337
Forsyth	75,682	20,020	73,523	19,372	6,928	12,502	1,612	2,676
Franklin	8,254	14,571	7,585	13,888	1,035	9,404	1,253	4,145
Gaston	48,040	18,279	46,998	17,697	3,871	11,319	714	3,643
Gates	2,345	15,784	2,169	15,322	199	9,836	443	4,113
Graham	1,904	13,429	1,792	13,076	234	7,926	160	1,759
Granville	8,809	15,870	8,268	14,876	833	13,694	1,387	3,889
Greene	4,570	14,850	4,151	13,237	457	8,413	1,043	8,699
Guilford	98,330	20,167	95,366	19,365	9,528	13,538	2,534	2,890
Halifax	13,683	14,148	12,879	13,343	1,364	10,194	966	8,111
Harnett	16,989	14,716	15,916	13,623	1,893	10,141	2,014	6,946
Haywood	13,445	15,858	12,827	15,440	1,452	8,254	1,046	3,040
Henderson	16,619	16,383	15,629	15,558	2,348	10,669	870	4,662
Hertford	5,939	15,368	5,581	14,203	725	11,339	489	7,736
Hoke	4,948	14,871	4,723	14,165	590	9,912	326	2,552
Hyde	1,664	11,827	1,448	10,237	332	9,290	273	6,491
Iredell	24,640	17,470	23,531	16,939	2,560	9,811	1,570	4,302
Jackson	6,811	14,423	6,463	13,165	878	13,620	287	4,145
Johnston	21,030	15,043	19,154	14,197	2,657	10,465	3,474	4,789
Jones	2,657	13,312	2,377	12,431	312	7,258	545	6,524
Lee	10,827	17,872	10,367	16,902	1,297	11,719	724	4,258
Lenoir	17,247	15,587	16,239	14,807	1,549	12,390	1,636	5,618
Lincoln	12,644	17,599	12,173	17,059	1,440	9,085	501	3,559
Macon	5,540	15,074	5,040	14,010	1,149	10,210	284	4,113
Madison	4,656	13,084	4,128	11,706	593	11,796	1,320	4,244
Martin	7,117	14,262	6,620	13,021	817	8,694	1,067	7,685
McDowell	9,858	15,942	9,543	15,372	1,022	9,726	225	2,289
Mecklenburg	129,804	21,142	126,518	20,317	11,800	14,282	1,842	2,888
Mitchell	3,975	14,479	3,717	13,628	514	10,120	347	4,892
Montgomery	6,348	15,262	6,090	14,655	644	10,188	280	3,836
Moore	14,581	16,403	13,783	15,276	1,985	11,743	1,167	4,553
Nash	19,688	17,383	18,717	16,429	1,964	12,542	1,663	6,069
New Hanover	31,180	18,464	29,994	17,613	3,585	12,560	524	4,571
Northampton	5,394	14,739	5,103	13,243	510	16,667	634	5,398
Onslow	27,218	14,204	26,207	13,661	2,356	9,819	1,085	5,020
Orange	23,889	17,897	23,181	16,905	2,854	8,892	914	1,260
Pamlico	2,745	15,101	2,481	14,053	448	10,888	213	8,021
Pasquotank	7,846	15,036	7,406	14,432	871	9,081	464	6,852
Pender	6,034	15,071	5,692	14,305	728	9,629	683	3,661
Perquimans	2,493	13,538	2,260	12,272	239	8,152	536	7,588
Person	8,376	15,983	7,889	15,166	898	9,934	1,058	5,022
Pitt	26,069	16,022	24,713	15,337	2,662	9,629	2,058	6,328
Polk	3,607	15,506	3,318	14,428	666	11,053	196	3,550
Randolph	28,498	17,481	27,338	16,743	3,239	11,001	1,400	3,450
Richmond	12,423	16,418	12,053	16,005	1,031	9,364	391	3,563
Robeson	25,841	14,625	24,453	13,768	2,490	9,760	2,993	5,665
Rockingham	24,573	17,258	23,437	16,393	2,414	11,386	2,017	6,142
Rowan	29,639	17,379	28,688	16,856	2,781	10,311	945	3,010
Rutherford	15,270	15,991	14,588	15,595	1,669	9,138	721	1,994
Sampson	14,198	13,646	12,893	12,914	1,709	8,059	2,822	4,772

County	Earnings: Total Households	Total Mean Income	Wage or Salary Households	Wage or Salary Mean Income	Nonfarm Self-Employment Households	Nonfarm Self-Employment Mean Income	Farm Self-Employment Households	Farm Self-Employment Mean Income
Scotland	8,243	$ 17,716	8,019	$ 17,250	657	$ 10,046	267	$ 4,124
Stanly	14,260	16,933	13,782	16,161	1,546	9,743	838	4,394
Stokes	9,914	16,457	9,085	16,193	1,193	7,335	1,935	3,769
Surry	17,716	15,712	16,541	14,842	2,346	9,607	2,165	4,762
Swain	2,685	11,967	2,518	11,670	336	8,018	90	589
Transylvania	6,477	17,909	6,163	17,611	811	8,837	165	1,757
Tyrrell	1,037	12,041	952	11,710	109	6,849	181	3,274
Union	20,038	19,325	19,072	18,359	2,214	11,486	1,845	6,326
Vance	9,903	14,849	9,428	14,064	1,015	9,932	860	5,084
Wake	95,365	21,061	92,585	20,264	10,016	11,981	3,254	3,776
Warren	4,042	13,494	3,753	12,259	402	14,873	680	3,758
Washington	3,834	17,055	3,645	16,455	278	9,953	413	6,396
Watauga	9,203	13,514	8,640	12,769	1,523	7,658	849	2,811
Wayne	27,577	15,408	26,147	14,637	2,586	10,338	2,328	6,645
Wilkes	17,290	16,802	16,419	15,981	2,200	9,654	1,187	5,793
Wilson	18,471	16,290	17,549	15,722	1,648	9,477	1,581	5,932
Yadkin	8,609	15,997	7,895	15,415	1,181	8,207	1,728	3,658
Yancey	4,208	12,642	3,833	12,142	669	8,850	550	1,333
State Total	1,719,372	$17,376	1,644,365	$16,671	180,106	$10,984	101,511	$4,766

Interest, Dividend, Rental, Social Security, Public Assistance and all other income.

County	Interest, Dividend, or Net Rental Income Households	Interest, Dividend, or Net Rental Income Mean Income	Social Security Households	Social Security Mean Income	Public Assistance Households	Public Assistance Mean Income	All Other Households	All Other Mean Income
Alamance	13,074	$2,056	10,121	$3,848	2,178	$1,962	6,977	$3,208
Alexander	2,529	1,459	2,049	3,388	464	1,780	1,527	2,255
Alleghany	1,115	2,274	1,257	3,204	283	1,797	690	4,577
Anson	1,895	2,459	2,852	3,369	1,005	2,169	1,694	2,431
Ashe	2,531	2,070	2,713	3,121	877	1,740	1,946	2,566
Avery	1,013	3,405	1,453	3,570	399	2,150	1,027	2,992
Beaufort	3,803	2,610	4,560	3,323	1,391	2,074	2,830	3,923
Bertie	1,473	2,932	2,480	3,072	1,056	1,840	1,257	3,271
Bladen	2,048	2,377	3,221	3,103	1,611	1,965	2,008	3,239
Brunswick	3,371	2,125	3,700	3,777	1,157	2,016	3,186	4,279
Buncombe	21,611	2,747	18,251	3,847	3,882	2,006	14,058	3,965
Burke	7,049	2,289	6,467	3,856	1,317	1,751	4,853	2,473
Cabarrus	10,690	2,270	8,819	4,005	1,722	2,100	5,475	3,027
Caldwell	6,332	2,308	5,820	3,661	1,251	2,102	4,279	2,808
Camden	429	3,102	620	3,377	158	1,982	424	4,571
Carteret	4,685	2,862	3,987	3,630	1,039	1,831	4,523	5,506
Caswell	1,577	2,213	1,891	3,198	866	1,739	1,304	3,519
Catawba	13,180	2,578	8,918	3,966	1,639	1,989	7,200	2,647
Chatham	4,354	2,255	3,331	3,437	827	2,003	2,338	3,031
Cherokee	1,697	2,275	2,534	3,683	779	1,705	1,697	3,002

County	Interest, Dividend, or Net Rental Income		Social Security		Public Assistance		All Other	
	Households	Mean Income	Households	Mean Income	Households	Mean Income	Households	Mean Income
Chowan	1,272	$ 2,474	1,417	$ 3,355	518	$ 1,472	997	$ 3,488
Clay	732	2,970	857	3,358	273	2,136	604	4,779
Cleveland	8,607	2,200	7,998	3,709	2,637	1,820	5,768	2,740
Columbus	3,858	2,596	5,335	3,058	2,398	1,814	3,296	3,063
Craven	6,833	2,279	5,241	3,364	2,380	2,090	5,079	5,498
Cumberland	19,930	1,958	11,457	3,497	6,711	2,069	17,890	5,270
Currituck	1,173	2,504	1,146	3,569	216	2,092	1,062	5,050
Dare	1,969	3,921	1,582	3,823	276	3,311	1,611	6,010
Davidson	12,661	2,362	9,534	3,835	2,120	1,957	6,740	2,890
Davie	3,188	2,698	2,204	3,603	451	2,460	1,677	3,499
Duplin	3,058	2,003	4,454	2,995	1,888	1,909	2,785	2,976
Durham	20,934	2,632	13,836	3,916	4,723	2,124	10,711	4,114
Edgecombe	4,355	2,402	5,401	3,374	2,433	1,953	3,673	3,252
Forsyth	35,798	3,254	21,646	3,937	6,307	2,189	16,954	4,193
Franklin	2,527	2,263	3,486	3,009	1,234	1,783	1,917	2,884
Gaston	17,097	2,445	15,178	3,905	3,901	2,105	10,585	3,185
Gates	745	2,240	956	3,198	338	2,159	548	4,196
Graham	651	2,410	799	3,292	240	1,674	726	3,884
Granville	2,831	2,155	3,180	3,245	1,081	1,729	1,948	3,461
Greene	1,338	2,103	1,423	2,950	629	2,090	1,037	3,168
Guilford	44,008	3,287	27,274	3,904	7,061	1,972	20,781	3,799
Halifax	4,064	3,242	6,544	3,343	3,260	2,159	3,706	2,984
Harnett	5,015	2,216	5,523	3,291	2,047	1,931	3,911	3,523
Haywood	5,742	2,294	5,577	3,899	1,294	2,181	4,484	3,200
Henderson	9,609	3,808	8,174	4,165	1,473	1,850	5,632	5,303
Hertford	1,711	2,893	2,218	3,424	1,054	2,254	1,301	3,389
Hoke	1,151	2,589	1,545	3,294	799	2,424	1,354	3,876
Hyde	615	1,863	784	3,126	263	1,758	469	3,251
Iredell	10,041	2,231	8,347	3,807	1,810	1,833	5,123	3,123
Jackson	2,554	2,753	2,399	3,563	780	1,932	2,210	3,421
Johnston	6,175	2,423	7,271	3,143	2,626	1,920	4,592	2,909
Jones	648	2,872	1,113	2,961	586	1,853	550	3,576
Lee	4,178	2,982	3,388	3,501	1,004	1,879	2,813	3,941
Lenoir	5,430	2,937	5,839	3,302	2,683	2,076	4,065	3,330
Lincoln	4,744	2,142	3,870	3,759	733	1,690	2,881	2,691
Macon	2,962	3,318	2,982	3,675	683	1,767	1,929	4,343
Madison	1,479	2,380	1,990	3,098	810	2,211	1,105	3,818
Martin	2,075	2,613	2,704	3,067	1,107	1,832	1,775	3,069
McDowell	2,895	1,681	3,466	3,731	716	2,030	2,358	3,147
Mecklenburg	60,396	2,784	30,875	3,970	9,829	2,035	26,660	4,034
Mitchell	1,379	1,740	1,829	3,677	720	2,208	1,005	3,828
Montgomery	1,996	1,868	2,437	3,337	640	1,873	1,355	2,702
Moore	6,653	5,775	6,140	3,865	1,517	2,195	4,240	6,861
Nash	6,915	3,056	6,316	3,391	2,528	2,003	4,277	3,399
New Hanover	13,518	2,706	9,886	3,708	2,850	1,876	8,747	4,287
Northampton	1,593	2,968	2,621	3,517	1,564	2,569	1,286	2,979
Onslow	7,868	1,569	4,376	3,040	1,902	1,731	6,575	5,542
Orange	12,902	3,099	5,263	3,813	1,259	2,110	5,043	4,826
Pamlico	910	2,207	1,189	3,308	484	1,564	1,017	4,594
Pasquotank	2,648	2,851	3,022	3,669	809	1,994	2,201	4,051

County	Interest, Dividend, or Net Rental Income		Social Security		Public Assistance		All Other	
	Households	Mean Income	Households	Mean Income	Households	Mean Income	Households	Mean Income
Pender	1,871	$2,353	2,354	$3,337	881	$2,131	1,494	$4,048
Perquimans	869	1,840	1,215	3,389	336	1,722	705	3,899
Person	2,869	2,003	2,960	3,386	884	2,102	2,055	2,788
Pitt	9,226	2,451	7,644	3,286	3,318	2,138	5,704	3,507
Polk	1,897	6,055	1,949	4,208	344	2,259	1,249	5,745
Randolph	10,823	2,313	8,385	3,681	1,393	2,093	5,880	2,775
Richmond	4,317	1,815	5,265	3,761	1,436	2,048	3,615	3,893
Robeson	5,789	3,233	8,879	3,162	4,923	2,013	6,117	3,048
Rockingham	9,111	2,084	9,069	3,755	2,158	2,205	7,142	2,713
Rowan	12,553	2,307	10,856	4,233	1,921	2,152	7,586	3,332
Rutherford	5,498	2,237	6,219	3,739	1,485	2,012	3,766	3,188
Sampson	3,923	2,302	5,427	3,017	2,019	1,961	3,260	2,636
Scotland	2,306	2,300	3,002	3,589	1,498	2,396	2,056	3,448
Stanly	6,135	2,068	5,263	3,816	1,135	1,706	3,787	2,862
Stokes	3,599	1,503	2,997	3,254	680	1,984	1,971	2,735
Surry	7,021	2,358	6,716	3,436	1,451	1,636	4,688	2,513
Swain	772	1,862	1,176	3,464	536	2,188	991	3,023
Transylvania	3,265	2,870	2,534	4,022	569	1,788	1,801	5,153
Tyrrell	338	1,735	565	3,635	229	2,162	356	2,867
Union	7,204	2,178	5,607	3,763	1,659	1,890	3,761	3,623
Vance	2,973	3,452	3,761	3,517	1,644	2,072	2,669	2,992
Wake	45,461	2,532	20,402	3,682	5,951	2,037	17,235	4,587
Warren	1,237	2,212	2,096	3,164	924	1,936	1,123	3,737
Washington	1,092	2,031	1,356	3,550	567	2,085	875	3,641
Watauga	4,040	2,518	2,706	3,253	613	1,830	2,371	3,912
Wayne	8,751	2,109	7,768	3,269	3,675	2,005	6,679	4,039
Wilkes	5,620	2,905	5,276	3,258	1,476	2,091	3,696	2,773
Wilson	6,498	2,840	5,887	3,399	2,446	2,071	4,441	3,554
Yadkin	3,402	1,934	2,968	3,278	602	2,039	1,528	3,065
Yancey	1,235	2,568	1,801	3,277	578	1,935	1,052	3,400
State Total	665,582	$2,628	539,219	$3,642	166,877	$2,016	407,999	$3,758

Poverty status of families, by counties—1969 and 1979.

County	*Families With Incomes Below Poverty Level*				*Families With Female Head With Incomes Below Poverty Level*			
	1969		*1979*		*1969*		*1979*	
	Number	*% of All Families*	*Number*	*% of All Families*	*Number*	*% of All Families With Female Head*	*Number*	*% of All Families With Female Head*
Alamance	2,267	8.8	2,086	7.4	607	22.4	914	22.5
Alexander	623	11.8	490	6.9	123	28.1	139	20.1
Alleghany	600	26.0	451	16.2	135	54.0	63	21.3
Anson	1,580	27.2	888	13.4	539	54.9	356	31.0
Ashe	1,509	27.8	1,290	19.6	195	45.6	221	36.3
Avery	934	28.9	561	14.5	169	46.4	93	25.4
Beaufort	2,350	24.9	1,911	17.3	755	57.5	706	43.7
Bertie	1,814	36.9	1,248	22.9	524	66.9	393	39.3
Bladen	1,961	30.5	1,748	21.3	493	54.4	662	48.0
Brunswick	1,420	22.9	1,719	17.1	384	59.3	498	41.9
Buncombe	5,297	13.5	4,586	10.1	1,498	33.7	1,671	27.4
Burke	1,567	10.0	1,512	7.6	366	22.9	555	21.6
Cabarrus	1,795	8.9	1,766	7.2	604	27.6	724	22.6
Caldwell	1,803	11.9	1,558	8.1	520	35.3	473	22.1
Camden	287	21.5	216	13.2	78	53.8	40	25.5
Carteret	1,404	16.6	1,341	11.5	409	43.1	462	32.9
Caswell	877	19.1	913	16.8	201	34.1	302	40.3
Catawba	1,849	7.5	1,843	6.2	505	21.1	730	19.2
Chatham	1,253	16.1	609	6.4	273	36.1	272	25.9
Cherokee	1,098	25.2	1,034	18.7	185	39.0	161	24.8
Chowan	670	25.0	689	19.7	194	49.4	307	50.9
Clay	461	34.7	381	19.4	82	55.0	36	22.4
Cleveland	2,554	13.5	2,404	10.5	809	37.4	956	28.4
Columbus	3,225	27.7	2,984	21.6	788	53.1	904	42.6
Craven	2,836	18.7	2,869	15.5	886	50.9	1,265	48.4
Cumberland	7,931	17.1	9,024	14.8	3,408	53.2	4,620	46.0
Currituck	352	19.2	481	15.5	95	46.6	107	37.2
Dare	254	13.3	338	8.9	73	36.7	86	21.4
Davidson	2,681	10.4	2,686	8.2	670	30.4	858	22.7
Davie	719	14.0	668	9.5	168	34.9	180	25.0
Duplin	2,821	28.9	2,222	20.1	623	48.8	718	41.1
Durham	4,265	12.8	3,684	9.5	1,968	38.2	2,144	27.4

Edgecombe	3,316	26.4	2,322	15.9	1,142	52.6	1,187	37.7
Forsyth	6,180	11.0	5,588	8.4	2,749	36.2	3,098	27.4
Franklin	1,814	27.9	1,303	16.3	430	45.9	510	34.6
Gaston	3,726	9.5	3,734	8.2	1,245	27.4	1,596	23.9
Gates	526	25.5	396	16.8	112	51.6	134	36.6
Graham	438	24.8	368	17.8	87	54.4	64	40.5
Granville	1,725	24.1	1,095	13.4	384	39.7	367	26.9
Greene	1,164	32.6	825	19.2	234	58.3	280	38.8
Guilford	6,936	9.4	6,996	8.3	2,631	31.2	3,687	26.7
Halifax	3,842	29.9	3,558	25.0	1,168	60.0	1,544	49.5
Harnett	2,595	20.5	2,329	14.5	728	49.1	866	37.1
Haywood	1,842	15.8	1,727	12.7	389	37.2	462	29.5
Henderson	2,409	19.8	1,628	9.3	444	37.9	398	25.6
Hertford	1,559	27.5	1,176	19.9	426	50.7	467	42.6
Hoke	907	26.2	878	18.0	305	56.7	395	37.4
Hyde	457	33.5	393	24.7	87	50.0	127	43.5
Iredell	2,190	11.3	1,867	8.0	633	30.5	731	24.6
Jackson	1,315	25.3	940	14.8	243	49.0	226	28.8
Johnston	4,113	24.8	2,950	14.9	1,063	50.6	976	33.8
Jones	706	29.8	465	17.9	171	50.9	156	38.0
Lee	1,307	16.3	1,057	10.5	464	43.0	432	28.0
Lenoir	3,171	23.7	2,496	15.7	1,165	56.2	1,265	42.1
Lincoln	1,046	12.0	882	7.3	250	31.1	304	22.7
Macon	1,116	24.9	896	14.4	176	43.6	158	30.7
Madison	1,390	31.9	1,039	22.1	181	45.1	127	23.1
Martin	1,761	29.0	1,309	19.3	478	52.6	533	45.1
McDowell	1,242	15.0	916	9.3	252	36.3	231	22.7
Mecklenburg	8,522	9.4	8,917	8.3	3,713	32.6	5,266	28.2
Mitchell	1,088	28.1	617	14.2	192	50.8	132	32.4
Montgomery	967	19.6	672	11.2	266	42.0	231	29.1
Moore	2,003	20.3	1,539	10.8	582	42.5	626	32.8
Nash	3,515	23.6	2,869	15.6	892	47.9	1,032	38.4
New Hanover	3,153	14.3	3,283	11.7	1,427	46.7	1,820	38.7
Northampton	2,023	37.9	1,255	22.3	479	58.4	486	47.4
Onslow	3,943	19.1	3,718	14.8	1,147	58.1	1,315	48.5
Orange	1,413	11.1	1,387	8.2	306	24.7	544	21.7
Pamlico	658	27.6	512	17.5	146	50.2	180	46.9
Pasquotank	1,345	20.3	1,044	14.1	411	50.2	520	43.8

County	Families With Incomes Below Poverty Level				Families With Female Head With Incomes Below Poverty Level			
	1969		1979		1969		1979	
	Number	% of All Families	Number	% of All Families	Number	% of All Families With Female Head	Number	% of All Families With Female Head
Pender	1,268	28.8	998	16.6	329	50.3	387	44.4
Perquimans	761	35.0	536	20.7	186	67.1	163	51.1
Person	1,314	20.1	1,073	13.4	332	46.6	401	35.0
Pitt	4,724	27.1	3,767	17.3	1,405	55.6	1,661	41.3
Polk	637	19.1	384	10.2	176	38.9	102	27.2
Randolph	2,039	9.7	1,775	6.7	480	29.3	486	18.5
Richmond	2,150	21.3	1,457	11.9	823	49.8	639	32.4
Robeson	6,102	31.6	5,285	20.9	1,797	57.8	2,312	43.3
Rockingham	2,352	12.0	2,376	10.1	726	30.7	907	27.8
Rowan	2,502	10.3	2,035	7.3	718	30.1	821	22.4
Rutherford	2,063	15.7	1,630	10.7	511	40.3	483	25.9
Sampson	3,330	28.8	2,339	17.5	863	56.2	780	37.2
Scotland	1,515	23.8	1,269	15.4	643	56.9	629	36.5
Stanly	1,201	10.1	1,158	8.4	280	26.0	374	25.2
Stokes	1,055	16.3	995	10.5	197	38.8	185	19.2
Surry	2,262	15.7	1,899	11.0	463	34.3	490	24.2
Swain	529	25.8	667	23.3	84	38.4	140	34.8
Transylvania	690	13.4	652	9.9	184	40.8	127	22.4
Tyrrell	355	37.9	219	20.2	44	54.3	46	22.8
Union	1,828	13.2	1,569	8.2	500	37.8	534	26.1
Vance	1,775	22.2	1,700	17.8	543	46.8	870	45.6
Wake	6,239	11.2	5,464	7.1	2,011	32.0	2,508	23.3
Warren	1,292	34.3	1,046	24.9	322	50.9	392	45.3
Washington	791	23.7	706	18.1	232	52.0	291	46.7
Watauga	1,197	22.2	1,017	14.1	232	44.0	175	22.8
Wayne	4,677	22.8	3,745	14.6	1,707	53.7	1,774	42.2
Wilkes	2,674	20.1	1,929	11.5	487	37.6	421	25.1
Wilson	3,223	22.9	2,464	14.7	989	51.0	1,138	39.9
Yadkin	1,147	16.5	1,005	11.9	156	31.9	207	25.7
Yancey	1,050	30.3	841	19.2	148	49.0	165	33.5
State Total	211,222	16.3%	183,146	11.6%	63,093	40.8%	73,697	31.6%

EDUCATION

The state commits nearly 80 cents of every tax dollar in its general fund to education, over $2 billion a year, because it believes that education is the foundation for cultural and industrial growth.

Available to every child is a free public kindergarten, with one adult for every 13 children. There is a teacher and an aide in each primary class to implement an intensive reading program.

The state has demanding standards for high school graduation: passing the state competency test and 20 or more credits for graduation. A scholars program, one of only three in the nation, gives special "scholars" recognition to students who take advanced courses and complete 22 or more units.

In addition to the basic subjects, high school students may choose from a wide range of courses, including: aerospace technology, astronomy, aviation science, calculus, computer programming, dance composition, forestry, German, music theory, physics, Shakespeare, and statistics.

More than 5,000 teachers provide instruction in nearly 100 vocational fields. Some of these are agribusiness, construction, food services, health services, machine design, manufacturing, marketing and distribution, and microcomputers.

Cooperative vocational education affords more than 30,000 students practical work experience.

Training for handicapped students is provided for in every school system in North Carolina. There is a school for the blind in Raleigh, and schools for the deaf in Greensboro, Morganton, and Wilson.

Special programs are available throughout the state for gifted and talented students, including two very special schools. The North Carolina School of Science and Mathematics, a residential high school for students excelling in science and math, is the only one of its kind in the nation. Offering 11th and 12th graders advanced study free of charge, the school represents a capital investment of $15 million. The school has had an abnormally high rate of National Merit Scholarship finalists, and nearly all its graduates have won scholarships and advanced placement at prestigious universities.

The North Carolina School of the Arts is the only state-supported high school and college for the performing arts in the nation. Instruction in dance and music, visual arts, design, and production are offered. Graduates perform on Broadway and in opera and ballet on the national level.

For information pertaining to colleges and universities, see chapter entitled Higher Education.

The following list gives the address and phone number of each county board of education.

COUNTY BOARDS OF EDUCATION

Alamance
609 Ray St.
Graham 27253
919-226-8465

Alexander
P.O. Box 128
Taylorsville 28681
704-632-7001

Alleghany
Board of Education Office
Sparta 28675
919-372-4345

Anson
S. Greene St.
Wadesboro 28170
704-694-4418

Ashe
P.O. Box 6
Jefferson 28640
704-246-7175

Avery
Board of Education Bldg.
Newland 28657
704-733-6006

Beaufort
Bath 27808
919-932-3951

Bertie
Colerain 27924
919-356-4387

Bladen
Bladenboro 28320
919-863-3506

Brunswick
Southport 28461
919-457-5241

Buncombe
P.O. Box 575
Weaverville 28787
704-258-2222

Burke
Human Resource Ctr.
Morganton 28655
704-433-4300

Cabarrus
660 Hwy. 29 N.
Concord 28025
704-786-6191

Caldwell
P.O. Box 1590
Lenoir 28645
704-754-5381

Camden
P.O. Box 121
Shiloh 27974
919-335-0831

Carteret
104 N. 7th St.
Morehead City 28557
919-726-5730

Caswell
Administration Bldg.
P.O. Box 160
Yanceyville 27379
919-694-6119

Catawba
Rt. 2, Box 216-D
Claremont 28610
704-428-9921

Chatham
P.O. Box 128
Pittsboro 27312
919-542-3626

Cherokee
Office Bldg.
Murphy 28906
704-837-2722

Chowan
Country Club Drive
Edenton 27932
919-482-3579

Clay
School Circle
Hayesville 28904
704-389-8513

Cleveland
130 S. Post Rd.
Shelby 28150
704-487-8581

Columbus
P.O. Box 213
Riegelwood 28456
919-649-7772

Craven
Rt. 1, Box 328
Dover 28526
919-527-1879

Cumberland
P.O. Box 2357
Fayetteville 28302
919-323-4411

Currituck
Knotts Island 27950
919-429-3163

Dare
Board of Education Bldg.
Manteo 27954
919-473-1101

Davidson
Denton 27239
704-869-2196

Davie
Ruffin St.
Cooleemee 27014
704-284-2941

Duplin
Rt. 2, Box 492
Mt. Olive 28365
919-658-6888

Durham
Schools Administration Bldg.
Durham 27701
919-683-2591

Edgecombe
Box 129
Tarboro 27886
919-823-8131

Forsyth
205 Flintshire Rd.
Winston-Salem 27101
919-765-5892

Franklin
Rt. 2
Louisburg 27549
919-853-2225

Gaston
2041 Shannon Dr.
Gastonia 28052
704-866-6110

Gates
Main St.
Gatesville 27938
919-357-1009

Graham
Smith Howell Bldg.
Robbinsville 28771
704-479-3413

Granville
Rt. 2, Box 302-B
Oxford 27565
919-693-5978

Greene
P.O. Box 496
Snow Hill 28580
919-747-3313

Guilford
120 Franklin Blvd.
Greensboro 27402
919-379-1660

Halifax
Rt. 1, Box 210-B
Halifax 27839
919-445-5800

Harnett
Kipling 27530
919-552-4262

Haywood
Rt. 3, Box 180
Waynesville 28786
704-648-6337

Henderson
125 E. Allen St.
Hendersonville 28739
704-692-8251

Hertford
312 NW St.
Ahoskie 27910
919-332-5007

Hoke
Rt. 3, Box 123-D
Raeford 28376
919-875-4963

Hyde
Rt. 1
Swan Quarter 27885
919-926-4411

Iredell
P.O. Box 709
Statesville 28677
704-872-9501

Jackson
Rt. 66, Box 53-B
Cullowhee 28723
704-227-7342

Johnston
Rt. 1, Box 404
Smithfield 27577
919-934-6031

Jones
P.O. Box 252
Maysville 28535
919-743-6941

Lee
County Office Bldg.
Sanford 27330
919-774-6226

Lenoir
201 E. King St.
Kinston 28501
919-523-9575

Lincoln
Rt. 2, Box 114
Lincolnton 28092
704-735-0116

Macon
P.O. Box 826
Highland 28714
704-524-4414

Madison
Courthouse
Marshall 28753
704-649-2424

Martin
Church St.
Williamston 27892
919-792-1575

McDowell
School Office, S. Main St.
Marion 28752
704-652-4535

Mecklenburg
P.O. Box 33894
Charlotte 28202
704-379-7001

Mitchell
Spruce Pine 28777
704-765-9327

Montgomery
Star 27356
919-428-4854

Moore
Robbins 27325
919-948-2432

Nash
Box 339
Bailey 27807
919-459-7021

New Hanover
4522 Spring View Dr.
Wilmington 28401
919-799-4577

Northampton
Henrico 27842
919-534-2561

Onslow
Georgetown Rd.
Jacksonville 28540
919-455-8702

Orange
P.O. Box 602
Hillsborough 27278
919-732-4398

Pamlico
Board of Education Bldg.
Bayboro 28515
919-745-4171

Pasquotank
Rt. 4, Box 321-E
Elizabeth City 27909
919-330-4724

Pender
Education Bldg., Box 1239
Burgaw 28425
919-259-2187

Perquimans
Rt. 1, Box 320
Belvidere 27919
919-297-2006

Person
County Office Bldg.
Roxboro 27573
919-599-2191

Pitt
108 E. Church St.
Farmville 27828
919-753-4117

Polk
Box 697
Columbus 28722
704-894-8249

Randolph
2222 S. Fayetteville St.
Asheboro 27203
919-629-2131

Richmond
522 Hamlet Ave.
Hamlet 28345
919-582-5860

Robeson
P.O. Box 1328
Lumberton 28358
919-738-4845

Rockingham
Rt. 3, Box 403
Eden 27288
919-627-4806

Rowan
1000 N. Long St.
East Spencer 28039
704-636-6750

Rutherford
219 Fairground Rd.
Spindale 28160
704-287-2211

Sampson
Rt. 1
Ivanhoe 28447
919-532-4322

Scotland
600 S. Main St.
Laurinburg 28352
919-276-2631

Stanly
Box 308
Badin 28009
704-982-0121

Stokes
Board of Education Bldg.
Danbury 27016
919-593-8146

Surry
Surry Community College
Dobson 27017
919-386-8121

Swain
P.O. Box U
Bryson City 28713
704-488-3129

Transylvania
Education Ctr.
Brevard 28712
704-884-4662

Tyrrell
Rt. 2
Columbia 27925
919-796-6131

Union
Courthouse, P.O. Box 499
Monroe 28110
704-289-5511

Vance
128 Church St.
Henderson 27536
919-492-2127

Wake
930 Vance St.
Raleigh 27608
919-755-6901

Warren
Rt. 3, Box 334
Warrenton 27589
919-257-3184

Washington
Courthouse
Plymouth 27962
919-793-5171

Watauga
Box 1790
Boone 28607
704-264-7190

Wayne
301 N. Herman, Box GG
Goldsboro 27530
919-736-1104

Wilkes
201 W. Main St.
Wilkesboro 28687
919-667-1121

Wilson
113 N. Tarboro St.
Wilson 27893
919-243-2900

Yadkin
Box 98
Yadkinville 27055
919-835-5736

Yancey
621 W. Main St.
Burnsville 28714
704-682-6101

Public Schools

The following chart shows the number of public schools and the final enrollment (grades K-12) in the state's public school system for the 1986–1987 school year. Final enrollment is a cumulative total of students enrolled throughout the school year and is not adjusted to reflect withdrawals.

County	Total Schools	'87 Final Enrollment	County	Total Schools	'87 Final Enrollment
Alamance	31	17,404	Hertford	8	4,324
Alexander	10	4,905	Hoke	7	5,213
Alleghany	4	1,713	Hyde	4	1,019
Anson	9	5,082	Iredell	33	16,415
Ashe	11	3,926	Jackson	6	3,935
Avery	9	2,820	Johnston	21	14,820
Beaufort	15	8,451	Jones	6	1,684
Bertie	8	4,344	Lee	13	7,739
Bladen	13	6,256	Lenoir	20	11,553
Brunswick	12	8,967	Lincoln	19	9,020
Buncombe	48	27,666	Macon	11	3,593
Burke	24	12,846	Madison	8	2,842
Cabarrus	28	17,242	Martin	13	5,316
Caldwell	23	12,637	McDowell	11	6,819
Camden	3	1,139	Mecklenburg	106	76,748
Carteret	12	8,018	Mitchell	7	2,506
Caswell	12	3,891	Montgomery	10	4,417
Catawba	37	20,664	Moore	18	9,086
Chatham	12	5,871	Nash	27	17,135
Cherokee	10	3,944	New Hanover	30	20,264
Chowan	4	2,551	Northampton	11	4,257
Clay	2	1,258	Onslow	24	17,982
Cleveland	30	16,140	Orange	17	10,956
Columbus	22	11,041	Pamlico	4	2,138
Craven	20	14,634	Pasquotank	8	5,409
Cumberland	69	46,843	Pender	13	4,901
Currituck	6	2,395	Perquimans	4	1,865
Dare	6	2,856	Person	11	5,600
Davidson	39	22,248	Pitt	32	17,227
Davie	9	4,907	Polk	8	2,074
Duplin	16	8,242	Randolph	28	17,372
Durham	42	26,936	Richmond	16	9,083
Edgecombe	16	8,678	Robeson	44	24,759
Forsyth	55	40,284	Rockingham	30	25,537
Franklin	11	6,088	Rowan	28	16,515
Gaston	54	32,495	Rutherford	24	10,383
Gates	6	1,713	Sampson	22	9,598
Graham	3	1,432	Scotland	14	7,737
Granville	12	6,908	Stanly	19	8,797
Greene	5	2,852	Stokes	15	6,731
Guilford	94	55,114	Surry	22	11,299
Halifax	25	11,059	Swain	5	1,777
Harnett	20	12,212	Transylvania	8	4,144
Haywood	14	7,980	Tyrrell	2	786
Henderson	19	10,508	Union	28	15,594

County	Total Schools	'87 Final Enrollment
Vance	13	7,841
Wake	80	60,474
Warren	9	3,095
Washington	5	3,045
Watauga	9	4,735
Wayne	28	18,748
Wilkes	22	10,957
Wilson	23	12,683
Yadkin	9	4,910
Yancey	9	2,740
Total	1,952	1,131,357

ELECTIONS

Presidential Election Results, 1984

County	Walter Mondale (Democrat)	Ronald Reagan (Republican)	David Bergland (Libertarian)
Alamance	11,230	26,063	68
Alexander	3,581	8,502	20
Alleghany	2,013	2,589	13
Anson	5,015	3,719	11
Ashe	4,009	6,611	22
Avery	1,159	4,702	17
Beaufort	5,987	9,284	27
Bertie	3,953	2,879	29
Bladen	5,064	4,701	12
Brunswick	6,774	9,673	35
Buncombe	23,337	37,698	122
Burke	10,353	18,766	51
Cabarrus	8,477	22,528	43
Caldwell	7,311	17,024	50
Camden	1,075	1,282	5
Carteret	5,882	11,637	35
Caswell	4,157	3,992	19
Catawba	11,700	31,476	61
Chatham	7,458	8,595	39
Cherokee	2,776	4,894	8
Chowan	1,736	2,171	9
Clay	1,340	2,259	19
Cleveland	10,288	17,095	82
Columbus	8,728	9,150	20
Craven	7,186	12,893	41
Cumberland	22,614	31,602	89
Currituck	1,668	2,885	8
Dare	1,839	4,738	16
Davidson	11,469	30,471	54
Davie	2,911	8,201	12
Duplin	6,830	7,708	13
Durham	32,244	29,185	134
Edgecombe	10,545	9,635	24
Forsyth	36,814	59,208	174
Franklin	4,766	5,984	10
Gaston	14,142	39,167	70
Gates	2,225	1,694	7
Graham	1,494	2,514	4
Granville	5,217	6,302	58
Greene	2,772	3,195	8
Guilford	46,027	73,096	186
Halifax	9,278	8,832	30
Harnett	7,106	11,198	15
Haywood	7,958	10,146	24
Henderson	7,222	19,369	80
Hertford	4,498	3,176	16
Hoke	3,214	2,449	11
Hyde	1,004	1,195	3
Iredell	9,999	23,641	55
Jackson	4,367	5,582	22
Johnston	7,833	16,210	24
Jones	2,025	2,062	8
Lee	3,925	8,198	25
Lenoir	8,556	13,321	27
Lincoln	5,996	12,621	38
Macon	3,570	6,661	21
Madison	2,988	3,666	10
Martin	3,870	4,266	12
McDowell	4,076	7,639	17
Mecklenburg	63,190	106,754	337
Mitchell	1,286	4,737	10
Montgomery	3,831	5,109	6
Moore	7,063	14,681	30
Nash	8,588	17,295	23
New Hanover	12,591	23,771	75
Northampton	5,094	3,198	24
Onslow	5,713	13,928	34
Orange	20,564	15,585	108
Pamlico	2,152	2,554	8
Pasquotank	3,854	4,646	6

County	Walter Mondale (Democrat)	Ronald Reagan (Republican)	David Bergland (Libertarian)
Pender	4,354	5,079	16
Perquimans	1,441	1,939	4
Person	3,528	5,854	11
Pitt	13,481	18,983	48
Polk	2,169	4,046	34
Randolph	7,511	25,759	23
Richmond	7,494	6,807	26
Robeson	15,257	12,947	56
Rockingham	10,605	17,895	32
Rowan	10,643	25,207	52
Rutherford	6,862	11,369	33
Sampson	9,115	10,665	13
Scotland	4,028	4,077	11
Stanly	6,138	13,116	29
Stokes	4,950	9,515	28
Surry	7,188	13,340	26
Swain	2,000	2,012	9
Transylvania	3,733	6,956	25
Tyrrell	807	774	1
Union	7,048	16,885	27
Vance	5,880	6,836	15
Wake	50,323	81,251	267
Warren	3,946	2,664	3
Washington	3,114	2,731	7
Watauga	5,163	9,370	41
Wayne	10,011	17,961	30
Wilkes	6,852	18,670	40
Wilson	8,343	12,243	40
Yadkin	3,075	8,976	14
Yancey	3,651	4,296	9
State Total	824,287	1,346,481	3,794

Senatorial Election Results, 1984

County	James B. (Jim) Hunt, Jr. (D)	Jesse Helms (R)	Bobby Yates Emory (L)	Kate Daher (SW)
Alamance	15,501	22,657	302	44
Alexander	4,504	7,493	38	4
Alleghany	2,366	2,335	15	1
Anson	5,451	3,161	18	10
Ashe	4,802	6,069	28	5
Avery	1,630	4,239	18	4
Beaufort	7,203	7,907	44	12
Bertie	4,544	2,618	25	41
Bladen	5,738	4,220	32	29
Brunswick	8,264	8,403	94	34
Buncombe	32,611	31,338	366	112
Burke	12,061	16,642	113	26
Cabarrus	11,978	20,812	117	28
Caldwell	9,232	14,915	93	27
Camden	1,203	1,114	5	0
Carteret	7,565	10,745	94	22
Caswell	4,627	3,414	20	6
Catawba	15,363	27,914	196	30
Chatham	8,767	7,108	64	16
Cherokee	3,477	4,746	14	15

County	James B. (Jim) Hunt, Jr. (D)	Jesse Helms (R)	Bobby Yates Emory (L)	Kate Daher (SW)
Chowan	2,289	1,950	36	7
Clay	1,515	2,079	4	2
Cleveland	12,461	15,202	93	18
Columbus	10,495	8,549	69	24
Craven	9,571	11,355	75	33
Cumberland	30,214	25,578	201	80
Currituck	2,158	2,275	6	3
Dare	3,040	3,708	18	4
Davidson	16,434	27,533	147	39
Davie	3,785	7,156	51	8
Duplin	7,718	6,607	25	7
Durham	40,102	22,981	341	55
Edgecombe	11,845	8,738	34	33
Forsyth	50,961	48,575	353	71
Franklin	5,583	5,208	25	16
Gaston	19,097	35,010	237	52
Gates	2,459	1,364	9	5
Graham	1,746	2,273	3	1
Granville	6,318	5,378	15	6
Greene	3,080	2,811	11	5
Guilford	62,021	61,371	454	104
Halifax	10,497	8,412	37	25
Harnett	9,064	10,033	54	17
Haywood	9,759	8,841	93	47
Henderson	10,202	16,281	132	29
Hertford	5,195	2,766	20	35
Hoke	3,655	1,913	18	5
Hyde	1,120	1,028	6	1
Iredell	13,526	20,480	168	25
Jackson	5,706	4,864	224	17
Johnston	10,089	14,130	85	11
Jones	2,147	1,887	7	1
Lee	5,933	7,030	84	12
Lenoir	9,576	11,759	44	16
Lincoln	7,554	11,186	84	20
Macon	4,524	5,664	30	15
Madison	3,401	3,011	11	11
Martin	4,863	3,718	57	16
McDowell	5,507	6,953	42	14
Mecklenburg	86,450	85,013	923	267

County	*James B. (Jim) Hunt, Jr. (D)*	*Jesse Helms (R)*	*Bobby Yates Emory (L)*	*Kate Daher (SW)*
Mitchell	1,743	4,724	31	5
Montgomery	4,341	4,397	26	10
Moore	9,363	12,836	100	17
Nash	10,830	15,800	67	23
New Hanover	17,829	19,515	168	63
Northampton	5,759	3,034	19	31
Onslow	8,260	12,019	95	24
Orange	24,828	11,139	130	33
Pamlico	2,421	2,195	15	5
Pasquotank	4,908	3,975	13	39
Pender	4,918	4,373	19	3
Perquimans	1,729	1,581	2	3
Person	4,668	5,117	101	16
Pitt	16,946	15,699	128	28
Polk	3,031	3,657	132	6
Randolph	11,478	23,831	109	28
Richmond	8,521	5,994	58	20
Robeson	18,936	11,253	134	67
Rockingham	13,418	14,856	101	40
Rowan	13,722	23,162	132	32
Rutherford	8,618	10,472	110	24
Sampson	10,583	9,802	41	14
Scotland	5,059	3,195	22	10
Stanly	7,927	12,367	61	9
Stokes	6,197	8,350	38	8
Surry	9,442	12,205	145	15
Swain	2,464	1,967	16	4
Transylvania	4,926	5,802	68	13
Tyrrell	883	667	0	1
Union	9,489	14,684	93	30
Vance	6,788	6,288	32	14
Wake	75,974	65,062	750	112
Warren	4,138	2,486	19	11
Washington	3,448	2,296	10	5
Watauga	7,093	7,413	108	15
Wayne	12,536	16,251	185	26
Wilkes	9,275	17,247	91	20
Wilson	11,497	10,595	67	30
Yadkin	3,873	8,048	37	13
Yancey	4,082	3,894	7	3
Total	1,070,488	1,156,768	9,302	2,493

Congressional Election Results, 1984

First Congressional District

County	Walter B. Jones (D)	Herbert W. Lee (R)
Beaufort	8,955	5,692
Bertie	4,918	1,234
Camden	1,511	734
Carteret	10,333	7,789
Chowan	2,623	1,052
Craven	12,067	7,051
Currituck	2,514	1,703
Dare	4,048	2,524
Gates	2,850	841
Greene	4,156	1,573
Hertford	5,377	1,456
Hyde	1,543	583
Lenoir	11,922	8,029
Martin	5,914	1,727
Northampton	5,678	1,483
Pamlico	3,109	1,428
Pasquotank	5,483	2,478
Perquimans	2,122	1,097
Pitt	22,523	9,711
Tyrrell	1,088	411
Washington	4,081	1,557
Total	122,815	60,153

Second Congressional District

County	I. T. Valentine, Jr. (D)	Frank H. Hill (R)
Caswell	5,114	2,431
Durham	29,228	22,299
Edgecombe	15,376	4,447
Granville	7,182	3,992
Halifax	14,531	3,898
Nash	19,138	6,907
Person	5,145	2,876
Vance	8,277	3,393
Warren	4,829	1,268
Wilson	12,675	6,257
Johnston (Part)	797	544
Total	122,292	58,312

Third Congressional District

County	Charles O. Whitley (D)	Danny G. Moody (R)
Bladen	5,211	2,598
Duplin	9,675	4,270
Harnett	11,552	6,605
Jones	2,483	1,321
Lee	6,928	4,124
Onslow	12,696	6,989
Pender	5,808	3,033
Sampson	11,996	7,980
Wayne	17,376	9,092
Johnston (Part)	13,945	8,317
Moore (Part)	2,515	1,767
Total	100,185	56,096

Fourth Congressional District

County	Ike Andrews (D)	William W. Cobey, Jr. (R)
Chatham	9,437	6,391
Franklin	5,988	4,510
Orange	22,255	13,242
Randolph	10,022	24,310
Wake	66,760	68,983
Total	114,462	117,436

Fifth Congressional District

County	Stephen L. Neal (D)	Stuart Epperson (R)
Alexander	4,529	7,296
Alleghany	2,629	2,051
Ashe	5,333	5,400
Forsyth	55,382	44,171
Rockingham	14,709	13,365
Stokes	6,702	7,782
Surry	9,910	10,808
Wilkes	10,637	15,726
Total	109,831	106,599

Sixth Congressional District

County	Robin Britt (D)	Howard Coble (R)	Meryl Lynn Farber (SW)
Alamance	17,028	19,577	103
Davidson	18,925	24,789	47
Guilford	64,310	58,559	135
Total	100,263	102,925	285

Seventh Congressional District

County	Charles G. Rose, III (D)	S. Thomas Rhodes (R)
Brunswick	8,918	7,727
Columbus	10,957	7,263
Cumberland	33,094	22,098
New Hanover	17,830	18,373
Robeson	21,358	8,164
Total	92,157	63,625

Eighth Congressional District

County	W. G. Hefner (D)	Harris D. Blake (R)
Anson	6,027	2,302
Cabarrus	15,628	17,017
Davie	4,462	6,406
Hoke	3,669	1,600
Montgomery	4,752	3,847
Richmond	9,737	4,684
Rowan	16,845	19,858
Scotland	4,939	2,127
Stanly	9,537	10,654
Union	12,480	11,323
Moore (Part)	7,745	10,538
Yadkin (Part)	3,910	5,998
Total	99,731	96,354

Ninth Congressional District

County	D. G. Martin (D)	J. Alex McMillan (R)
Iredell	15,082	18,964
Lincoln	8,677	10,101
Mecklenburg	84,780	78,946
Yadkin (Part)	560	1,409
Total	109,099	109,420

Tenth Congressional District

County	Ted A. Poovey (D)	James T. Broyhill (R)
Burke	9,166	19,379
Caldwell	5,827	18,450
Catawba	10,323	32,553
Cleveland	8,432	18,759
Gaston	12,957	40,562
Watauga	4,418	9,829
Avery (Part)	737	3,341
Total	51,860	142,873

Eleventh Congressional District

County	James McClure Clarke (D)	William M. Hendon (R)
Buncombe	33,525	30,626
Cherokee	3,453	4,473
Clay	1,523	2,040
Graham	1,789	2,195
Haywood	10,171	8,558
Henderson	11,192	15,446
Jackson	5,779	4,719
Macon	4,759	5,430
Madison	3,542	2,786
McDowell	6,072	6,221
Mitchell	1,818	4,582
Polk	3,002	3,617
Rutherford	9,174	9,704
Swain	2,483	1,891
Transylvania	5,398	5,380
Yancey	4,183	3,755
Avery (Part)	421	1,175
Total	108,284	112,598

Gubernatorial Election Results, 1984

County	Rufus Edmisten (D)	James G. (Jim) Martin (R)	H. Fritz Prochnow (L)	Gregory McCartan (SW)
Alamance	14,568	23,193	184	48
Alexander	4,604	7,260	3	1
Alleghany	2,479	2,250	6	0
Anson	5,880	2,788	4	12
Ashe	5,393	5,482	13	3
Avery	1,949	3,991	8	10
Beaufort	7,753	7,303	12	6
Bertie	4,532	1,980	25	53
Bladen	5,592	4,012	28	46
Brunswick	8,194	8,528	30	26
Buncombe	30,033	33,673	201	114
Burke	12,704	16,370	24	6
Cabarrus	11,229	21,685	37	24
Caldwell	9,567	14,827	28	15
Camden	1,412	936	3	1
Carteret	8,781	9,630	28	8
Caswell	5,097	2,877	8	6
Catawba	14,928	28,551	48	27
Chatham	8,667	7,190	34	7
Cherokee	3,244	4,707	21	26
Chowan	2,169	1,740	33	27
Clay	1,463	2,109	4	2
Cleveland	12,951	14,914	28	11
Columbus	11,009	7,843	32	25
Craven	10,282	9,850	46	62
Cumberland	29,497	26,409	104	43
Currituck	2,447	1,935	2	3
Dare	3,007	3,699	20	14
Davidson	16,016	28,171	56	19
Davie	3,848	7,190	5	1
Duplin	8,331	6,078	5	2
Durham	34,975	26,957	268	161
Edgecombe	12,669	7,884	10	34
Forsyth	46,345	53,242	143	60
Franklin	6,078	4,704	16	13
Gaston	18,628	35,730	78	48
Gates	2,748	991	0	5
Graham	1,799	2,207	5	1
Granville	6,638	4,916	8	9
Greene	3,844	2,078	4	1

County	Rufus Edmisten (D)	James G. (Jim) Martin (R)	H. Fritz Prochnow (L)	Gregory McCartan (SW)
Guilford	52,073	71,336	195	97
Halifax	10,993	7,825	28	17
Harnett	9,569	9,327	25	18
Haywood	9,714	8,994	35	20
Henderson	8,675	17,953	42	22
Hertford	4,739	2,159	38	67
Hoke	3,734	1,800	1	15
Hyde	1,352	819	0	3
Iredell	11,379	22,936	49	11
Jackson	5,229	5,286	23	25
Johnston	10,730	13,769	24	17
Jones	2,510	1,542	4	0
Lee	6,263	6,588	43	19
Lenoir	11,806	9,950	16	15
Lincoln	6,910	12,010	16	10
Macon	4,688	5,623	12	7
Madison	3,388	2,962	8	25
Martin	5,422	2,920	44	23
McDowell	6,060	6,482	14	13
Mecklenburg	57,279	114,151	446	215
Mitchell	1,692	4,778	8	2
Montgomery	4,447	4,356	5	4
Moore	8,529	13,703	28	17
Nash	11,585	15,037	29	23
New Hanover	14,870	22,006	69	83
Northampton	5,496	3,113	51	108
Onslow	9,535	10,749	41	17
Orange	20,656	15,083	140	76
Pamlico	2,812	1,836	3	3
Pasquotank	4,333	3,924	30	73
Pender	5,227	4,130	2	2
Perquimans	1,957	1,337	2	3
Person	4,492	4,752	65	43
Pitt	17,620	15,021	75	28
Polk	2,836	3,800	108	11
Randolph	10,846	24,341	56	33
Richmond	8,623	5,942	16	11
Robeson	19,630	10,291	81	113
Rockingham	13,090	15,164	62	25
Rowan	13,591	23,429	38	33

County	Rufus Edmisten (D)	James G. (Jim) Martin (R)	H. Fritz Prochnow (L)	Gregory McCartan (SW)
Rutherford	8,841	10,409	21	13
Sampson	10,557	9,846	15	14
Scotland	4,753	3,207	21	21
Stanly	7,437	12,893	26	5
Stokes	6,653	7,949	7	10
Surry	9,661	11,388	47	23
Swain	2,520	1,898	9	5
Transylvania	4,626	6,151	24	10
Tyrrell	1,027	516	1	0
Union	8,856	15,387	33	14
Vance	7,549	5,472	12	18
Wake	63,798	75,856	528	137
Warren	4,442	2,032	0	6
Washington	4,155	1,842	2	0
Watauga	7,617	7,070	49	23
Wayne	13,003	15,288	129	43
Wilkes	10,499	16,257	24	5
Wilson	10,942	10,205	74	65
Yadkin	4,263	7,645	4	0
Yancey	4,280	3,752	1	1
Total	1,011,209	1,208,167	4,611	2,740

ELECTORAL VOTE

The state of North Carolina has thirteen electoral votes.

ELEVATIONS, LATITUDES, AND LONGITUDES

The average elevation in North Carolina is 700 feet. Mount Mitchell is the highest point in the state with an altitude of 6,684 feet. The Atlantic Ocean is the lowest point at one foot. North Carolina lies between 34° and 36°30′ North latitude and from 76°30′ to 84°30′ West longitude. Similar values for selected locales in the state follow.

City	Altitude	Latitude	Longitude
Asheville	2,242	35°36′	82°32′
Charlotte	735	35°13′	80°56′
Durham	406	36°02′	78°58′
Fayetteville	735	35°13′	80°56′
Greensboro	897	36°05′	79°57′
High Point	912	35°58′	79°59′
Raleigh	400	35°47′	78°42′
Winston-Salem	770	36°05′	80°13′

EMPLOYMENT

The manufacturing work force in North Carolina is the largest in the Southeast and the eighth largest in the nation. North Carolina has the lowest rate of unionization in the nation: 5.9 percent as compared to the 22.6 percent national average. Workmen's compensation rates are among the lowest in the nation.

The following charts reflect the distribution of employment in North Carolina, and labor force estimates as of March, 1986.

North Carolina Employment Trends, 1985–1986

Employment Categories	*1986 (,000)*	*1985 (,000)*	*Net Change (,000)*	*Percent Change (%)*
Manufacturing	831.9	828.6	3.3	0.4
Durable Goods	337.8	341.7	-3.9	-1.1
Lumber & Wood Products	37.7	36.9	0.8	2.2
Furniture & Fixtures	84.6	84.7	-0.1	-0.1
Stone, Clay & Glass	20.4	19.6	0.8	4.1
Primary Metals	11.2	10.9	0.3	2.8
Fabricated Metals	26.5	26.8	-0.3	-1.1
Nonelectrical Machinery	56.4	57.8	-1.4	-2.4
Electrical Machinery	60.5	65.3	-4.8	-7.4
Transportation Equipment	23.7	23.1	0.6	2.6
Instruments & Miscellaneous	16.8	16.6	0.2	1.2
Nondurable Goods	494.1	486.9	7.2	1.5
Food Products	46.8	45.6	1.2	2.6
Tobacco Products	26.0	25.8	0.2	0.8
Textiles	211.3	208.3	3.0	1.4
Apparel	88.9	86.7	2.2	2.5
Paper & Allied Products	21.9	22.3	-0.4	-1.8
Printing & Publishing	27.3	26.2	1.1	4.2
Chemicals	37.6	37.7	-0.1	-0.3
Rubber, Plastic Products	30.1	30.0	0.1	0.3
Petroleum & Leather Products	4.2	4.3	-0.1	-2.3
Nonmanufacturing	1,899.8	1,822.6	77.2	4.2
Mining	4.7	4.8	-0.1	-2.1
Construction	157.3	149.2	8.1	5.4
Transportation/Communications/ Utilities	133.1	130.5	2.6	2.0
Trade	607.1	579.5	27.6	4.8
Financial/Insurance/Real Estate	118.4	109.4	9.0	8.2
Services	452.5	428.7	23.8	5.6
Government	426.7	420.5	6.2	1.5
Total Nonagricultural Wage & Salary Employment	2,731.7	2,651.2	80.5	3.0

North Carolina Preliminary Civilian Labor Force Estimates*

Data for December 1987

County	Labor Force	Employment	Unemployment	Rate	Benchmark 1986 Rate
Alamance	63,210	60,960	2,250	3.6	3.5
Alexander	15,710	15,250	460	2.9	2.6
Alleghany	4,380	4,150	230	5.3	5.0
Anson	11,820	11,270	550	4.7	9.6
Ashe	10,780	10,160	620	5.8	6.6
Avery	8,550	8,080	470	5.5	6.3
Beaufort	18,520	17,330	1,190	6.4	7.3
Bertie	9,750	9,290	460	4.7	5.4
Bladen	12,300	11,420	880	7.2	8.5
Brunswick	18,080	16,300	1,780	9.8	10.8
Buncombe	87,400	84,100	3,300	3.8	5.0
Burke	42,720	41,440	1,280	3.0	4.0
Cabarrus	55,630	53,910	1,720	3.1	3.9
Caldwell	37,650	36,400	1,250	3.3	3.4
Camden	2,400	2,300	100	4.2	4.6
Carteret	23,390	21,400	1,990	8.5	6.2
Caswell	9,070	8,620	450	5.0	6.0
Catawba	68,120	65,670	2,450	3.6	3.7
Chatham	19,800	19,160	640	3.2	3.7
Cherokee	9,080	8,380	700	7.7	5.6
Chowan	5,510	5,240	270	4.9	3.4
Clay	3,050	2,910	140	4.6	5.2
Cleveland	41,330	39,780	1,550	3.8	4.7
Columbus	22,300	21,030	1,270	5.7	7.4
Craven	31,420	30,180	1,240	3.9	4.9
Cumberland	97,130	92,260	4,870	5.0	5.6
Currituck	7,430	7,190	240	3.2	3.7
Dare	12,290	11,270	1,020	8.3	8.5
Davidson	68,660	66,790	1,870	2.7	4.0
Davie	15,230	14,780	450	3.0	7.0
Duplin	19,730	18,680	1,050	5.3	6.1
Durham	100,940	97,960	2,980	3.0	3.5
Edgecombe	30,040	28,360	1,680	5.6	6.5
Forsyth	146,000	141,240	4,760	3.3	3.6
Franklin	17,860	16,980	880	4.9	5.7
Gaston	103,010	98,970	4,040	3.9	4.3
Gates	3,780	3,670	110	2.9	3.6
Graham	2,630	2,080	550	20.9	24.8
Granville	19,660	18,710	950	4.8	5.1
Greene	8,550	8,270	280	3.3	5.6
Guilford	190,870	184,370	6,500	3.4	4.0
Halifax	22,900	21,580	1,320	5.8	6.9
Harnett	27,210	25,720	1,490	5.5	7.6
Haywood	21,700	20,430	1,270	5.9	7.3
Henderson	32,010	30,860	1,150	3.6	4.5

County	Labor Force	Employment	Unemployment	Rate	Benchmark 1986 Rate
Hertford	9,540	8,850	690	7.2	7.2
Hoke	10,080	9,500	580	5.8	5.3
Hyde	2,140	1,830	310	14.5	16.6
Iredell	49,690	48,100	1,590	3.2	4.8
Jackson	12,150	11,310	840	6.9	8.0
Johnston	37,040	34,590	2,450	6.6	6.8
Jones	4,020	3,830	190	4.7	5.6
Lee	20,310	19,040	1,270	6.3	8.6
Lenoir	29,350	27,950	1,400	4.8	5.7
Lincoln	27,000	25,740	1,260	4.7	3.9
Macon	10,650	10,090	560	5.3	5.8
Madison	6,240	6,010	230	3.7	6.1
Martin	10,840	10,280	560	5.2	6.5
McDowell	16,140	15,270	870	5.4	6.5
Mecklenburg	271,750	263,710	8,040	3.0	3.4
Mitchell	7,310	6,790	520	7.1	8.4
Montgomery	12,360	11,880	480	3.9	4.1
Moore	28,020	26,930	1,090	3.9	3.5
Nash	37,640	35,830	1,810	4.8	4.8
New Hanover	67,410	63,600	3,810	5.7	7.0
Northampton	8,050	7,650	400	5.0	6.7
Onslow	36,940	35,680	1,260	3.4	3.8
Orange	50,630	49,560	1,070	2.1	2.6
Pamlico	4,670	4,540	130	2.8	6.2
Pasquotank	12,890	12,410	480	3.7	4.0
Pender	11,670	10,890	780	6.7	8.4
Perquimans	3,740	3,540	200	5.3	4.0
Person	14,770	13,510	1,260	8.5	9.5
Pitt	53,320	51,550	1,770	3.3	3.7
Polk	6,000	5,820	180	3.0	3.5
Randolph	59,600	57,920	1,680	2.8	2.7
Richmond	20,420	19,280	1,140	5.6	6.1
Robeson	47,160	43,650	3,510	7.4	7.7
Rockingham	40,180	37,960	2,220	5.5	6.7
Rowan	60,440	57,740	2,700	4.5	4.3
Rutherford	28,060	27,000	1,060	3.8	5.8
Sampson	21,850	20,690	1,160	5.3	8.4
Scotland	15,590	14,750	840	5.4	5.7
Stanly	26,640	25,080	1,560	5.9	4.7
Stokes	18,870	17,960	910	4.8	4.8
Surry	31,050	29,580	1,470	4.7	5.4
Swain	5,490	4,680	810	14.8	19.1
Transylvania	10,290	9,870	420	4.1	6.4
Tyrrell	1,360	1,140	220	16.2	18.8
Union	44,700	43,490	1,210	2.7	6.3
Vance	18,260	16,820	1,440	7.9	7.5
Wake	230,430	223,920	6,510	2.8	3.0

County	Labor Force	Employment	Unemployment	Rate	Benchmark 1986 Rate
Warren	7,090	6,760	330	4.7	5.4
Washington	5,320	4,970	350	6.6	5.3
Watauga	17,630	17,080	550	3.1	3.4
Wayne	43,460	41,640	1,820	4.2	5.2
Wilkes	32,130	31,150	980	3.1	3.8
Wilson	33,600	31,360	2,240	6.7	7.9
Yadkin	16,210	15,520	690	4.3	4.6
Yancey	10,550	10,180	370	3.5	4.2
State Totals	3,298,200	3,161,300	136,900	4.2	4.8

*Not Seasonally Adjusted
U.S. Unemployment Rate: Unadjusted—5.4
Seasonally Adjusted—5.8

ENDANGERED SPECIES

Action	Common Name	Scientific Name
ECH	Indiana bat	*Myotis sodalis*
ECH	Virginia big-eared bat	*Plecotus townsendii virginianus*
ECH	West Indian (Florida) manatee	*Trichechus manatus*
T	Dismal Swamp southeastern shrew	*Sorex longirostris fisheri*
E	Carolina northern flying squirrel	*Glaucomys sabrinus coloratus*
E	Red wolf	*Canis rufus*
E	Eskimo curlew	*Numenius borealis*
E,T	Bald eagle	*Haliaeetus leucocephalus*
ECH	American peregrine falcon	*Falco peregrinus anatum*
T	Arctic peregrin falcon	*Falco peregrinus tundrius*
E(S/A)	Peregrine falcon	*Falco peregrinus*
E,T	Piping plover	*Charadrius melodus*
E,T	Roseate tern	*Sterna dougalli dougalli*
E	Bachman's warbler	*Vermivora bachmanii*
E	Ivory-billed woodpecker	*Campephilus principalis*
E	Red-cockaded woodpecker	*Picoides borealis*
T(S/A)	American alligator	*Alligator mississippiensis*
E	Kemps (Atlantic) Ridley sea turtle	*Lepidochelys kempii*
ECH	Hawksbill sea turtle (=carey)	*Eretmochelys imbricata*
ECH	Leatherback sea turtle	*Dermochelys coriacea*
T	Loggerhead sea turtle	*Caretta caretta*
TCH	Spotfin chub	*Hybopsis monacha*
ECH	Cape Fear shiner	*Notropis mekistocholas*
TCH	Waccamaw silverside	*Menidia extensa*
E	Shortnose sturgeon	*Acipenser brevirostrum*
T	Noonday snail	*Mesodon clarki nantahala*
E	Tar River spiny mussel	*Elliptio (=Canthyria) steinstansana*
E	Bunched arrowhead	*Sagittaria fasciculata*
T	Heller's blazingstar	*Liatris helleri*
E	Canby's dropwort	*Oxypolis canbyi*
T	Blue Ridge goldenrod	*Solidago spithamaea*

Action	Common Name	Scientific Name
TCH	Mountain golden heather	*Hudsonia montana*
E	Rough-leaved loosestrife	*Lysimachia asperilaefolia*
E	Small whorled pogonia	*Isotria medeoloides*
E	Pondberry	*Lindera melissifolia*

T = Threatened
E = Endangered
CH = With critical habitat designated
(S/A) = Due to similarity of appearance to a listed species (affects mostly trade)
E,T = Different status in different parts of the range

ENERGY

The electric generating capacity of North Carolina is currently 22 gigawatts, including a share of the Harris 1 nuclear unit which began operation last year. Coal-fired generating units provided nearly two-thirds (12.8 gigawatts) of the state's capability last year. The second largest generation source, 21 percent of the total capacity, was 4.3 gigawatts of nuclear capacity. The remaining share was composed of combined cycle, combustion turbine, and hydro pumped storage capacity, used during periods of peak demand and during coal or nuclear baseload plant outages as supplemental generating capacity.

In 1986, 55.6 billion kilowatt hours of electricity were generated using coal, 19.6 billion kilowatt hours using nuclear power, and 4.4 billion kilowatt hours using hydroelectric power, which combined to compose 99 percent of total generation. It is projected that coal and nuclear generation will be relied on increasingly to meet the growing demand for electricity.

The greatest portion of the total amount of electricity used in the state, 39 percent, is purchased by residential electric customers. The second largest users are industrial customers with 34 percent, and most of the remainder is purchased by commercial customers.

In 1986, residential customers purchased 30.4 billion kilowatt hours (kwh) of electricity, 32.4 trillion British thermal units (Btu) of natural gas, only minimal amounts of coal, and a marginal amount of wood.

FAMOUS NORTH CAROLINIANS

Alexander, Nathaniel. See section on Governors (1805—1807).

Ammons, A. R. (1926—). Born in Columbus. A major American poet. His *Collected Poems 1951—1971* won the 1973 National Award for Poetry.

Anderson, George B. (1831-1862). Born in Hillsborough; died in Raleigh. Confederate general. Died of wounds inflicted at Antietam.

Archdale, John. See section on Governors (1694—1696).

Armistead, Lewis A. (1817-1863). Born in New Berne; died in Gettysburg, Pennsylvania. Confederate general. Killed in action at Gettysburg.

Ashe, Samuel. See section on Governors (1795—1798).

Athas, Daphne (1924—). Born in Massachusetts; moved to Chapel Hill in 1938. Author of such works as *Weather of the Heart* (1947), *The Fourth World* (1956), and *Entering Ephesus* (1971).

Atkinson, Henry (1782—1842). Soldier who served in War of 1812; led military expeditions to Yellowstone; commanded forces in the Black Hawk War.

Attakullakulla (1700[?]—1778). Born in North Carolina; died in Running Water Town in Tennessee. Sometimes called "Little Carpenter." Was a celebrated Cherokee chief and devoted friend of the British until the Revolution when he sided with the Americans.

Aycock, Charles B. See section on Governors (1901—1905).

Baker, Laurence S. (1830—1907). Born in Gates County; died in Suffolk, Virginia. Confederate general. Became railroad agent after the War.

Barringer, Rufus (1821—1895). Born in Cabarrus County. After the death of Confederate General James Gordon, he became the brigade commander with the rank of brigadier general. Practiced law after the war.

Barry, John D. (1839—1867). Born in Wilmington; died in Wilmington. Rose from the rank of private to brigadier general in the Confederate Army. Was newspaper man after the War, but died of complications of wounds inflicted by a Union sharpshooter in 1864.

Bassett, John Spencer (1867—1928). Born in Tarboro; died in Washington, D.C. Historian, founded and edited the *South Atlantic Quarterly*. Published many works of history and biography, such as *The Life of Andrew Jackson* (1911) and *Expansion and Reform, 1889—1926* (1926).

Baxter, Elisha (1827—1899). Born in Rutherford County; died in Batesville, Arkansas. Union colonel in the War Between the States. Was governor of Arkansas from 1873 to 1874.

Benton, Thomas Hart (1782—1858). Born in Orange County; died in Washington, D.C. Lawyer and U.S. Senator from Missouri. First man to serve 30 years in the Senate.

Berry, Harriet Morehead (1887—1940). Born in Hillsborough; died in Chapel Hill. Director of the State Geological and Economic Survey. Served as chairman of the Chapel Hill Suffrage League and as vice president of the state League.

Betts, Doris (1932—). Born in Statesville. Author of *Tall Houses in Winter* (1958), *The Scarlet Thread* (1965), and *Beasts of Southern Wild* (1973), all winners of the Sir Walter Raleigh Award.

Bickett, Thomas Walter. See section on Governors (1917—1921).

Blackmer, Sidney (1898—1973). Born in Salisbury. A well-known Hollywood character actor. Played in *The High and the Mighty*.

Blount, William (1749—1800). Born in North Carolina. Was the first and only governor of the Territory of the United States South of the River Ohio, the region relinquished by the North Carolina government to the U.S. in 1790. Senator, 1796.

Blount, Willie (1768—1835). Born in Bertie County; died near Nashville, Tennessee. Was half brother of William Blount. Became governor of Tennessee in 1809, serving until 1815.

Blythe, LeGette (1900—). Born in Huntersville. Writer and newspaperman. A graduate of the University of North Carolina at Chapel Hill, he worked as a journalist until 1950. Author of *Marshal Ney: A Duel Life* (1937), *Shout Freedom!*, a play (1948), *Miracle in the Hills* (1953), a Mayflower Cup winner for nonfiction.

Boyd, James (1888—1944). Born in Dauphin County, Pennsylvania; died in Princeton. Author, publisher and writer for the *Pilot*, a Southern Pines newspaper. Works include *Drums* (1925), *Marching On* (1927), and *Old Pines and Other Stories* (1952), a posthumous collection of his short stories.

Bragg, Braxton (1817—1876). Born in Warrenton; died in Galveston, Texas. West Point graduate. Confederate general. Defeated General Rosencrans at Chickamauga. Became adviser to Jefferson Davis and chief engineer of Alabama. Fort Bragg, the largest military reservation in the U.S., is named in his honor.

Bragg, Thomas. See section on Governors (1855—1859).

Branch, John. See section on Governors (1817—1820).

Branch, Lawrence O'Bryan (1828—1862). Born in Halifax County; died in Virginia. Joined the Confederate army as a private and rose to the rank of brigadier general. Was wounded and died during the battle at Sharpsburg.

Brinkley, David (1920—). Born in Wilmington. Noted television newsman. For years was co-anchor of the "Huntley-Brinkley Report."

Brogden, Curtis H. See section on Governors (1874—1877).

Broughton, J. Melville. See section on Governors (1941—1945).

Brown, Charlotte Eugenia Hawkins (1883—1961). Born in Henderson; died in Greensboro. Educator, taught at the American Missionary Association, and became head of the Palmer Memorial Institute for black children. The first black woman to be admitted to Boston's Twentieth Century Club in 1928.

Bullock, Robert (1828-1905). Born in Greenville; died in Ocala, Florida. Confederate general who served in the U.S. Congress after the War.

Burke, Thomas. See section on Governors (1781—1782).

Burleson, Edward (1798—1851). Born in Buncombe County. Pioneer and politician who fought in the Texas revolution; in 1840 commanded forces against Cherokee Indians in East Texas. A senator and vice-president of Texas Reublic who later lost a bid for president of Texas.

Burns, Otway (1775—1850). Born in Onslow County. During War of 1812 commanded the clipper, *Snap Dragon*, and captured millions of dollars worth of British shipping. Later became a shipbuilder, and state legislator (1821—1835).

Burrington, George. See section on Governors (1724—1725).

Burton, Hutchins G. See section on Governors (1824—1827).

Caldwell, Tod R. See section on Governors (1870—1874).

Cannon, Joseph Gurney (1836—1926). Born in Guilford. U.S. Congressman and conservative Speaker of the House (1903—1911).

Cannon, Newton (1781—1841). Born in Guilford County; died in Nashville, Tennessee. Was the first Whig governor of Tennessee.

Carr, Elias. See section on Governors (1893—1897).

Carteret, Peter. See section on Governors (1670—1672).

Cary, Thomas. See section on Governors (1708—1711).

Cash, W. J. (1900—1941). Born in Gaffney, South Carolina; died in Mexico City, Mexico. Author of *The Mind of the South* (1941), which won him wide literary acclaim.

Caswell, Richard. See section on Governors (1776—1780).

Cheatham, Henry P. (1857—1935). Born in North Carolina(?). Was born in slavery but became a U.S. Congressman and Superintendent of the Colored Ordinance of North Carolina.

Cherry, R. Gregg. See section on Governors (1945—1949).

Chestnutt, Charles W. (1858—1932). Born in Cleveland, Ohio, of North Carolina parents. He became North Carolina's most prominent black author; a protegé of Mark Twain, Booker T. Washington, and William Dean Howells. Wrote *The Conjure Woman* (1899) and *The Wife of His Youth* (1899), collections of short stories.

Clark, Henry T. See section on Governors (1861—1862).

Clarke, Mary Bayard (Devereux) (1827—1886). Born in Raleigh. Compiler of the first anthology of North Carolina poetry, *Wood-Notes: or Carolina Carols* (1854).

Clark, Walter (1846—1924). Born in Halifax. North Carolina Supreme Court judge (1899—1924). Decorated veteran in the Confederate army, his career as a judge was noted for his progressivism.

Clingman, Thomas Lanier (1812—1897). Born in Huntsville; died in Morgantown. Was a brigadier general in the Confederate army. Clingman's Dome in the Great Smoky Mountains is named in his honor.

Cockrill, Ann Robertson (1757—1821). Born in Raleigh; died in Nashville, Tennessee. Was a sister of James Robertson. Became the first teacher in Middle Tennessee.

Coffin, Levi (1789—1877). Born in New Garden; died in Cincinnati, Ohio. Agent for Western Freedman's Aid Association, he became known as one of the key figures of the "underground railroad" that moved slaves to freedom in the North.

Cooper, Anna Julia Haywood (1859[?]—1964). Born in Raleigh. Educator and historian. As a principal in the District of Columbia she advocated higher education for blacks and women, which drew criticism and caused her to lose her job. Author of *The Grimke Family* (1951).

Cosell, Howard (1920—   ). Born in Winston-Salem. Noted television sports commentator. Was associated for years with television's "Monday Night Football" program; author of *I Never Played the Game* (1985).

Cox, William Ruffin (1832-1919). Born in Halifax County; died in Richmond, Virginia. One of the last surviving Confederate generals. Served in the U.S. Congress after the War.

Craig, Locke. See section on Governors (1913—1917).

Crockett, David (1786—1836). Born in Tennessee (when it was still part of North Carolina); died in Texas. Served in the War of 1812; was a U.S. Congressman from Tennessee. Died a hero's death at the Alamo.

Dabney, Charles William (1855—1945). Born in Hampden Sidney, Virginia; died Asheville. Educator. Director of North Carolina Agricultural Experiment Station (1880—1887); president of the University of Tennessee (1887—1904) and the University of Cincinnati (1904—1920).

Daly, Augustin (1838—1899). Theatre manager in New York and London, and playwright. Wrote *Under the Gaslight* (1867), *A Flash of Lightening* (1868), and *Woffington, A Tribute to the Actress and the Woman.*

Daniel, Junius (1828—1864). Born in Halifax County; died in Virginia. Graduated from West Point. Served in the Confederate army as a brigadier general. Saw action at Gettysburg, the Wilderness, and Spotsylvania Court House, where he was killed in action.

Daniel, Robert. See section on Governors (1704—1705).

Daniels, Charlie (1937—). Born in Wilmington. Country music singer and songwriter. Lives in Mt. Juliet, Tennessee.

Daniels, Jonathan Worth (1902—). Born in Raleigh. Journalist, administrative assistant to President Franklin Roosevelt (1943—1945), and author of several popular books, including *A Southerner Discovers New England* and *The Devil's Backbone.*

Daniels, Josephus (1862—1948). Born in Washington; died in Raleigh. Publisher of Raleigh's *State Chronicle* (1885—1904) and *News Observer* (1904—1948). Was U.S. secretary of the Navy (1913—1921); was ambassador to Mexico (1933—1941).

Dargan, Olive Tilford (1869—1968). Born in Grayson County, Kentucky; died in Asheville. Author of numerous plays and short stories, she also wrote novels under the pseudonym Fielding Burke.

Davie, William Richardson. See section on Governors (1798—1799).

Davis, Burke (1913—). Born in Durham. Noted writer of many books relating to the War Between the States, among them *Gray Fox, Our Incredible Civil War,* and *Sherman's March.*

Davis, George (1820—1896). Born in New Hanover County. Member of the Congress and Senate. Was attorney general of the Confederate States of America.

DeSoto, Hernando (1500—1542). Born in Spain, died on the Mississippi River. Governor of Cuba (1537—1542). Considered to be the first white man to set foot in present-day North Carolina.

Dickson, William (1770—1816). Born in Duplin County; died in Nashville, Tennessee. Was educated at Grove Academy in North Carolina. Practiced medicine in Nashville, Tennessee. Dickson County, Tennessee is named in his honor.

Dixon, Thomas, Jr. (1864—1946). Born near Shelby; died in Raleigh. Novelist, lawyer, actor, politician, and clergyman. Wrote 22 novels, 9 plays, and 6 motion pictures. Among his books were *The Leopard's Spots* and *The Clansmen*. The latter was made into a classic silent movie entitled *The Birth of a Nation*.

Dobbs, Arthur. See section on Governors (1754—1765).

Dockery, Thomas P. (1833-1898). Born in North Carolina; died in New York City. Confederate general who became a civil engineer in New York after the War.

Dodd, William Edward (1869—1940). Born in Clayton; died at Round Hill, Virginia. An historian and statesman, he warned Americans following World War I of the dangers of Isolationism. Ambassador to Germany (1933-1937), returning disillusioned to Virginia.

Donnell, Robert (1784—1855). Born in Guilford County; died in Athens, Alabama. Was a circuit riding preacher in Tennessee and Kentucky around 1805. Was responsible for popularizing Cumberland Presbyterianism.

Drummond, William. See section on Governors (1664—1667).

Dudley, Edward B. See section on Governors (1836—1841).

Duke, James Buchanan (1856—1925). Born in Durham; died in New York City. Businessman and philanthropist. Entered the tobacco business early and became president of the American Tobacco Company (1890). Established a trust fund that contributed to numerous charitable institutions; Duke University is named in his honor.

Dykeman, Wilma (1920—). Born in Asheville. Noted Tennessee writer. Among her books are *The French Broad* in the "Rivers of America" series, *The Tall Woman*, and *Tennessee: A Bicentennial History*.

Eastchurch, Thomas. See section on Governors (1676—1678).

Eaton, John Henry (1790—1856). Born in Halifax County; died in Washington, D.C. Educated at the University of North Carolina, he was U.S. secretary of war (1829—1831), when he resigned from Andrew Jackson's cabinet because of his second marriage. Appointed governor of Florida in 1834 and minister to Spain in 1836.

Eden, Charles. See section on Governors (1714—1722).

Ehle, John (1925—). Born in Asheville. Author and advocate for the arts. His writings include *Move Over, Mountain* (1957), *Kingstree Island* (1959), *The Land Breakers* (1964), which won the Sir Walter Raleigh Award.

Ehringhaus, J. C. B. See section on Governors (1933—1937).

Ellis, John W. See section on Governors (1859—1861).

Everard, Richard. See section on Governors (1725—1731).

Fargo, Donna (—). Born in Mount Airy. Real name is Yvonne Vaughn. Country music singer; her "Happiest Girl in the Whole USA" was the Country Music Association's Single of the Year for 1972.

Flack, Roberta (1940—). Born in Black Mountain. Popular singer. Among her best-selling hits are "Killing Me Softly" and "The First Time."

Fletcher, Inglis (1879—1969). Born in Alton, Illinois; died in Edenton. Popular writer of North Carolina historical fiction. Among his more popular books are *Lush Wind for Carolina, Roanoke Hundred,* and *Rogue's Harbor.*

Forney, John H. (1829-1902). Born in Lincolnton; died in Jacksonville, Alabama. Confederate general. After the War, he ran a military academy in Jacksonville, Alabama.

Forney, William H. (1823-1894). Born in Lincolnton; died in Jacksonville, Alabama. Confederate general who served in the U.S. Congress after the War.

Fowle, Daniel G. See section on Governors (1889—1891).

Franklin, Jesse. See section on Governors (1820—1821).

Gardner, Ava (1922—). Born in Smithfield. Movie actress. Played in such films as *Buowani Junction* and *The Barefoot Contessa.*

Gardner, O. Max. See section on Governors (1929—1933).

Garrott, Isham W. (1816-1863). Born in Anson County; died in Vicksburg, Mississippi. Confederate colonel who received his promotion to brigadier general several days after he was killed at Vicksburg.

Gaston, William (1778—1844). Born in New Bern. U.S. Congressman, North Carolina Supreme Court Justice, and author of the State's official song, "The Old North State." A county and a city in North Carolina are named for him.

Gatlin, Richard C. (1809-1896). Born in Lenoir County; died in Mount Nebo, Arkansas. As a major in the U.S. infantry, he was captured by Confederate forces and switched sides. Became adjutant general of North Carolina.

Gatling, Richard Jordan (1818—1903). Born Hertford County; died New York City. Inventor who developed a rapid-firing gun called the Gatling gun. Also worked on machines for sowing grain and other agricultural uses.

Gibson, Don (1928—). Born in Shelby. Country music singer and songwriter. His hits include "Oh, Lonesome Me" and "One Day at a Time."

Gilmer, Jeremy F. (1818-1883). Born in Guilford County; died in Savannah, Georgia. Head of Confederate engineers. After the War, became president of the Savannah Gas Light Company.

Glenn, Robert B. See section on Governors (1905—1909).

Glover, William. See section on Governors (1706—1708).

Golden, Harry (1902—1981). Born in New York City. Moved to North Carolina in 1941. Author of the best seller, *Only in America.*

Gordon, James Byron (1822—1864). Born in Wilkes County; died in Richmond, Virginia. U.S. Congressman; later was a brigadier general in the Confederate army. Died of wounds received in the Battle at Brooks Church.

Gordon, James Byron (1822-1864). Born in Wilkesboro; died in Richmond, Virginia. Rose from the ranks of private to brigadier general in the Confederate Army. Died during Sherman's raid on Richmond.

Govan, Daniel C. (1829-1911). Born in Northampton County; died in Memphis, Tennessee. Was deputy sheriff in Sacramento, California before the War. Became Confederate general commanding Arkansas troops.

Graham, Billy (1918—). Born near Charlotte. Evangelist and author. America's best known evangelist, having preached in crusades around the world, he has been a personal counselor to several presidents. Among his books are *Peace with God, Angels, How to Be Born Again, The Secret of Happiness*.

Graham, William A. See section on Governors (1845—1849).

Grayson, Kathryn (1923—). Born in Winston-Salem. Popular singer of the 1950s. Starred in the movie *Showboat* with Howard Keel.

Green, Paul Eliot (1894—1981). Born in Lillington; died in Chapel Hill. Playwright noted for realistic dramas about black and white tenant farmers in the South. His scripts include *In Abraham's Bosom* (1926), for which he won a Pulitzer Prize, and *Native Son* (1941).

Griffith, Andy (1926—). Born in Mount Airy. TV celebrity, comic. Starred in his own TV series, *The Andy Griffith Show,* popular in the 1960s. Presently has his own series, *Matlock*.

Grimes, Bryan (1828—1880). Born in Pitt County; died near Grimesland. A large slave and plantation owner before the War Between the States. Served in the Confederate army as a major general.

Haas, Ben (1926—1977). Born in Charlotte. Along with Frank G. Slaughter and Manly Wade Wellman, he was one of North Carolina's most prolific writers. Among his books were *The Last Valley* and *Daisy Canfield*.

Hamilton, George IV (1937—). Born in Winston-Salem. Country music singer. His "A Rose and Baby Ruth" sold over a million copies in 1956—1957.

Harriot, Thomas (1560—1621). Born Oxford, England; died near London, England. Was a member of Sir Walter Raleigh's first colony on Roanoke Island in 1585—1586. Wrote the first book ever written about North Carolina.

Harris, Bernice Kelly (1891—1973). Born in Mt. Moriah; died in Durham. Writer and author of *Purslane* (1939), the first novel about North Carolina people ever to receive a literary award.

Harvey, John. See section on Governors (1679).

Harvey, Thomas. See section on Governors (1696—1699).

Hasell, James. See section on Governors (1771).

Hawkins, William. See section on Governors (1811—1814).

Haywood, John (1762—1826). Born in Halifax County; died in Nashville, Tennessee. A judge of both the North Carolina and Tennessee Supreme courts. Writer and founder of the Tennessee Historical Society.

Helms, Jessie (1921—). Born in Monroe. U.S. Senator since 1973. Resides in Raleigh.

Helper, Hinton Rowan (1829—1909). Born in Rowan County; died Washington, D.C. Author. Even though he believed in white supremacy and black inferiority, he wrote *The Impending Crisis of the South: How to Meet It* (1857), an antislavery book attacking the institution as a cause of poverty in the South.

Henderson, Richard (1735—1785). Born in Hanover County, Virginia; died in Millsborough. He was a lawyer and land speculator who worked with Daniel Boone to promote settlement in Kentucky. He organized the plan that resulted in the settlement of Nashville, Tennessee (French Lick) in 1779—1780.

Hewes, Joseph (1730—1779). Born in New Jersey; moved to North Carolina sometime between 1756 and 1763. A signer of the Declaration of Independence for North Carolina.

Heyward, DuBose (1885—1940). Born in Charleston, South Carolina; died in Tryon. Author. His first novel, *Porgy* (1925), was turned into an Ira and George Gershwin musical, *Porgy and Bess*. All his writings deal with unique cultural situations.

Hodges, Luther H. See section on Governors (1954—1961).

Hoey, Clyde R. See section on Governors (1937—1941).

Hoke, Robert F. (1837—1912). Born in Lincolnton; died in Raleigh. Confederate general. Received the thanks of the Confederate Congress for his siege of U.S. fortifications at Plymouth, N.C. After the War, served as director of the North Carolina Railroad Company.

Holden, William W. See section on Governors (1865; 1868—1870).

Holmes, Gabriel. See section on Governors (1821—1824).

Holmes, Theophilus H. (1804—1880). Born in Sampson County. A West Point graduate, he was a Confederate lieutenant general. Led a brigade at the first battle of Manassas and a division during the Seven Days campaign. Later commanded the District of Arkansas.

Holshouser, James E. See section on Governors (1973—1977).

Holt, Thomas. See section on Governors (1891—1893).

Hooper, William (1742—1791). Born in Boston, Massachusetts; moved to North Carolina as a young man. Was a member of Governor Tryon's military against the Regulators. Was one of North Carolina's three signers of the Declaration of Independence.

Horton, George Moses (1797[?]—1883[?]). Born in Northampton County. Author of *The Hope of Liberty,* the best book in its time written by a Southern black.

Houston, David Franklin (1866—1940). Born in Monroe. An educator and public official. Taught political science at the University of Texas; appointed secretary of agriculture by President Woodrow Wilson in 1913, and later secretary of the treasury (1920).

Hunter, Kermit (1910—). Born in West Virginia. Writer of outdoor drama, including *Unto These Hills,* performed at Cherokee, and *Horn in the West,* performed at Boone.

Hyde, Edward. See section on Governors (1711—1712).

Iredell, James. See section on Governors (1827—1828).

Jackson, Stonewall (1932—). Born in Tabor City. A country music singer. "Waterloo" is his biggest hit.

Jarvis, Thomas. See section on Governors (1691—1694).

Jarvis, Thomas Jordan. See section on Governors (1879—1885).

Jenkins, John. See section on Governors (1672—1677).

Johnson, Andrew (1808—1875). Born in Raleigh; died at Carter's Station, Tennessee. Military governor of Tennessee and seventeenth president of the United States.

Johnson, F. Roy (1911—). Born in Gladen County. Author and historian, often called a "one-man folklore society." His works number over twenty, including *Stories of the Old Cherokees* (1975).

Johnson, Gerald W. (1890—1980). Born in Riverton. Author of dozens of books and many magazine articles and reviews. Most of his books were political or social commentaries of a generally liberal view.

Johnston, Gabriel. See section on Governors (1734—1752).

Johnston, George D. (1832-1910). Born in Hillsborough; died in Tuscaloosa, Alabama. Confederate general. After the War, he served as commandant of cadets at the University of Alabama.

Johnston, Joseph E. (1807—1891). Born in Virginia. Led the army of Tennessee throughout the 1865 Carolina campaigns. Surrendered on April 26, 1865.

Johnston, Robert D. (1837-1919). Born in Lincoln County; died in Winchester, Virginia. Confederate general. After the War, he practiced law in Charlotte and was a banker in Birmingham, Alabama, and Winchester, Virginia.

Johnston, Samuel. See section on Governors (1787—1789).

Key, Alexander (1904—). Born in La Plata, Maryland. Author of numerous books for children, including *Return from Witch Mountain,* which was made into a successful movie in 1978.

King, William Rufus de Vane (1786—1853). Born in Sampson County; died in Cahaba, Alabama. Public official and politician. A Congressman from North Carolina (1811—1816) and later a Senator from Alabama. He died soon after taking office as vice-president to President Franklin Pierce in 1852.

Kirkland, William W. (1833-1915). Born in Hillsborough; died in Washington, D.C. A Confederate general who was wounded in action three times. Died at the Soldiers' Home in Washington.

Kitchin, William W. See section on Governors (1909—1913).

Koch, Frederick H. (1877—1944). Born in Kentucky. A renowned teacher of writers at the University of North Carolina.

Kuralt, Charles (1934—). Born in Wilmington. Television newsman. He is the key figure in CBS's "On the Road with Charles Kuralt" news program.

Lane, Ralph. See section on Governors (1585—1586).

Lawson, John (late-1600s—1711). Born in England; died in North Carolina. An early traveler in the North Carolina Country. He was the author of *A New Voyage to Carolina*, published in 1709. Was killed by Tuscarora Indians.

Lefler, Hugh T. (1901—). Born in Davie County. Prizewinning historical writer. His books include *North Carolina* and *North Carolina: The History of a Southern State*.

Leventhorpe, Collett (1815—1899). Born in England. Served in the British army; later immigrated to North Carolina. Joined the Confederate army and was wounded at Gettysburg. Was brigadier general of North Carolina's troops.

Lewis, William G. (1835-1901). Born in Rocky Mount; died in Goldsborough. Confederate general, who served as State Engineer after the War.

Loring, William W. (1818-1886). Born in Wilmington; died in New York City. Confederate general. After the War, he fled to Egypt where he served in the forces of the Khedive. Wrote the book, *A Confederate Soldier in Egypt.*

Ludwell, Philip. See section on Governors (1689—1691).

Macon, Nathaniel (1758—1837). A public official who championed states' rights in the U.S. House of Representatives and Senate.

MacRae, William (1834-1882). Born in Wilmington; died in Augusta, Georgia. Rose from the rank of private to general in the Confederate Army. Surrendered with Lee at Appomattox.

Madison, Dorothea ("Dolley") (1768—1849). Born in Guilford County; died in Washington, D.C. Wife of President James Madison. She also served as White House hostess for President Thomas Jefferson (a widower).

Manly, Charles. See section on Governors (1849—1850).

Martin, Alexander. See section on Governors (1782—1785).

Martin, James G. (1819-1878). Born in Elizabeth City; died in Asheville. Was in charge of the defense of North Carolina during the War Between the States. Was responsible for the best equipped and best organized troops in the South at the outbreak of the War.

Martin, James G. See section on Governors (1985).

Martin, Josiah. See section on Governors (1771—1775).

Mason, Mary Ann (1802—1881). Born in New Bern. Was the first native North Carolinian to write a book for children, *A Wreath from the Woods of Carolina*.

McLean, Angus W. See section on Governors (1925—1929).

McNair, Evander (1820-1902). Born in Richmond County; died in Hattiesburg, Mississippi. Confederate general whose brigade was called the "star brigade of Chickamauga." Later, he commanded Arkansas troops.

McNeill, John Charles (1874—1907). Born near Wagram; died in Scotland County. Poet. Among his writings are *Lyrics from Cotton Land* and *Possums and Persimmons*.

Meredith, Solomon (1810-1875). Born in Guilford County; died in Indiana. Was a United States general during the War Between the States, who earlier had served in the Indiana legislature. After the War, he was a government surveyor in Montana.

Miller, Thomas. See section on Governors (1677).

Miller, William. See section on Governors (1814—1817).

Monk, Thelonious (1920—1982). Born in Rocky Mount. Musician. As a pianist, composer, and arranger, he was an important figure in modern jazz music.

Moore, Daniel K. See section on Governors (1965—1969).

Morehead, John M. See section on Governors (1841—1845).

Morrison, Cameron. See section on Governors (1921—1925).

Murrow, Edward R. (1908—1965). Born in Greensboro. Radio and television newsman. He became popular for his radio coverage of affairs in London during the Battle of Britain.

Nash, Abner. See section on Governors (1780—1781).

Nash, Francis (1720—1777). Born in Prince Edward County, Virginia; died in Pennsylvania. Served in the North Carolina colonial legislature, and was a general in the Continental Army. Nashville, Tennessee, is named in his honor.

Owen, John. See section on Governors (1828—1830).

Page, Walter Hines (1855—1918). Born in Cary; died in Pinehurst. Author, journalist and diplomat. A crusader for reform in the South, both in industry and education. Served as ambassador to Great Britain during World War I.

Patton, Frances Gray (1906—   ). Born in Raleigh. Writer of articles for *New Yorker, Collier's,* and *Harper's* magazines. Author of *Good Morning, Miss Dove,* which was made into a movie.

Pearson, James Larkin (1879—   ). Born near Boomer in Wilkes County. Poet Laureate of North Carolina. Author of such works as *Fifty Acres* (1937) and "My Fingers and My Toes" (1971).

Pender, William Dorsey (1834—1863). Born in Edgecombe County; died in Staunton, Virginia. West Point graduate and a major general in the Confederate army. Wounded in action at Gettysburg and later died.

Penn, John (1740[?]—1788). Born in Virginia; died in Granville County. Moved to North Carolina at an early age. Was one of North Carolina's three signers of the Declaration of Independence.

Pettigrew, James J. (1828-1863). Born in Tyrrell County; died in Maryland. Confederate general who was mortally wounded during the Battle of Falling Waters.

Pierce, Ovid Williams (1910—   ). Writer and educator. His novels include *The Plantation* (1953) and *On a Lonesome Porch* (1960), both of which won the Sir Walter Raleigh Award.

Polk, James K. (1795—1849). Born in Mecklenburg County; died in Nashville, Tennessee. Served as governor of Tennessee and eleventh president of the United States.

Polk, Leonidas (1806—1864). Born in Raleigh; died in Pine Mountain, Georgia. Episcopal bishop and military officer. He was the founder of the University of the South and also commanded corps at Shiloh (1862) and Murfreesboro (1862—1863). Killed in action at the battle of Pine Mountain.

Polk, Leonidas Lafayette (1837—1892). Born Anson County. An agricultural activist and key figure in organizing the Populist Party in 1891. Also active in the North Carolina Grange Association.

Polk, Lucius E. (1833-1892). Born in Salisbury; died in Columbia, Tennessee. Rose in the ranks from private to general in the Confederate Army. After the War, he served in the Tennessee Senate.

Pollock, Thomas. See section on Governors (1712—1714).

Porter, William Sidney ("O. Henry") (1862—1910). Born near Greensboro. One of America's most popular short story writers, among the best being *The Ransom of Red Chief* and *The Gift of the Magi*.

Powell, William S. (1919—). Born near Smithfield. Educator and writer. Author of *North Carolina Lives, The North Carolina Gazetteer,* and *North Carolina: A Bicentennial History* (with Hugh T. Lefler).

Rains, Gabriel J. (1803-1881). Born in Craven County; died in Aiken, South Carolina. Confederate general. Toward the end of the War, he commanded the Confederate Torpedo Bureau.

Rains, George W. (1817-1898). Born in Craven County; died in Newburgh, New York. Confederate general. After the War, he became dean of the Medical College of Georgia.

Ramseur, Stephen D. (1837-1864). Born in Lincolnton; died in Virginia. A brilliant battlefield general of the Confederacy, excelled by few. Was mortally wounded during the Battle of Cedar Creek.

Ransom, Matt W. (1826-1904). Born in Warren County; died in Garysburg. Rose through the ranks of the Confederate Army from private to general. After the War, he served in the U.S. Senate and was Minister to Mexico.

Ransom, Robert (1828—1892). Born in Warren County. A West Point graduate, he was a major general in the Confederate army.

Reed, William. See section on Governors (1722—1724).

Reeves, Del (1934—). Born in Sparta. Had his own radio show in North Carolina at age twelve. Later moved to Nashville, Tennessee, and later became a member of the Grand Ole Opry.

Reid, Christian (1846—1920). Born in Salisbury; died in Salisbury. Pen name for Frances Fisher, a popular post-War Between the States writer. Wrote 46 books in all, including *The Land of the Sky, Benny Kate,* and *The Wargrave Trust*.

Reid, David S. See section on Governors (1851—1854).

Revels, Hiram Rhoades (1822—1901). Born in Fayetteville; died in Aberdeen, Mississippi. Educator and politician, the first black person to serve in the U.S. Senate (from Mississippi). Later named president of Alcorn University (1876—1882).

Rhine, Joseph B. (1895—1980). Founder and director of the Duke University Parapsychology Laboratory.

Rice, Nathaniel. See section on Governors (1752—1753).

Richardson, Robert V. (1820-1870). Born in Granville County; died in Clarkton, Missouri. He grew up in Tennessee, became a general in the Confederate Army, and was murdered in Missouri.

Roberts, Nancy (1924—). Born in South Milwaukee, Wisconsin. Educated at the University of North Carolina. Writer of a series of "supernatural" books, including *Ghosts of the Carolinas* and *An Illustrated Guide to Ghosts and Mysterious Occurrences in the Old North State.*

Roberts, William P. (1841-1910). Born in Gates County; died in Norfolk, Virginia. Was the youngest Confederate general officer. After the War, he served in the State legislature.

Robinson, James Lowry. See section on Governors (1883).

Rounds, Glen (1906—). Born in South Dakota. Prolific writer of books about the people and nature of the American West. After moving to North Carolina in 1945, he turned his attention to North Carolina subjects, with such books as *Swamp Life, Wild Orphans,* and *Rain in the Woods and Other Small Matters.*

Rowan, Matthew. See section on Governors (1753—1754).

Ruark, Robert (1915—1965). Born in Wilmington; died in London, England. Journalist and author. Among his books are *The Old Man and the Boy* and *Something of Value.*

Russell, Daniel L. See section on Governors (1897—1901).

Russell, Phillips (1884—1974). Born in Rockingham. He was a prizewinning historical writer of such titles as *Benjamin Franklin, the First Civilized American* and *John Paul Jones, Man of Action.*

Rutherford, Griffith (1731[?]—1800). Born in Ireland. Assisted in forming the state constitution. Brigadier general during the American Revolution. Rutherford County, Tennessee, is named in his honor.

Sales, Soupy (1926—). Born in Wake Forest. Comedian and television personality.

Sandburg, Carl (1878—1967). Born in Galesburg, Illinois; died near Hendersonville. Lived in North Carolina for 21 years. Most remembered for his biography of Abraham Lincoln.

Sanford, Terry. See section on Governors (1961—1965).

Scales, Alfred M. See section on Governors (1885—1889).

Scott, Robert W. See section on Governors (1969—1973).

Scott, W. Kerr. See section on Governors (1949—1953).

Scruggs, Eugene (1924—). Born in Flint Hill. Bluegrass musician and one-time partner of the "Earl Scruggs and Lester Flatt" act.

Slaughter, Frank Gill (1908—). Born in Washington, D.C. Was raised and educated in North Carolina. A major American novelist, his most widely read books are *In a Dark Garden, The Road to Bithynia,* and *Doctors' Wives,* which was made into a popular movie.

Smith, Benjamin. See section on Governors (1810—1811).

Smith, Betty (Keogh) (1904—1972). Born in Brooklyn, New York; died in Shelton, Connecticut. Moved to Chapel Hill in 1936, where she wrote *A Tree Grows in Brooklyn,* reputed to be one of the ten best selling books of all time.

Smith, Hoke (1855—1931). Born in Catawba County. U.S. Senator and governor of Georgia, and U.S. secretary of the interior (1893—1896).

Sothel, Seth. See section on Governors (1682—1689).

Spaight, Richard Dobbs, Sr. See section on Governors (1792—1795).

Spaight, Richard Dobbs, Jr. See section on Governors (1835—1836).

Steele, John (1764—1815). Born in Salisbury; died in Salisbury. Served in the 1st and 2nd U.S. Congresses from 1789 to 1793. Was comptroller of the treasury from 1796 until 1802.

Steele, Wilbur Daniel (1866—1970). A short story writer who has won several O. Henry awards. Works include *Land's End* (1918) and *Isles of the Blest* (1924).

Stephens, Samuel. See section on Governors (1662—1664).

Stokes, Montford. See section on Governors (1830—1832).

Stone, David. See section on Governors (1808—1810).

Strange, Robert (1796—1854). Born in Manchester, Virginia. Political figure and author. Served as member of state House of Commons, superior court judge, and U.S. Senator. Also wrote *Eonegusky,* or *The Cherokee Chief.*

Sumner, Jethro (1730—1785). Born in Suffolk, Virginia; died in Warren County. Brigadier general in the Continental Army who distinguished himself in the Battle of Eutaw Springs in 1781.

Swain, David L. See section on Governors (1832—1835).

Toon, Thomas F. (1840-1902). Born in Columbus County; died in Raleigh. Was a Confederate general who was active in the Shenandoah Valley campaigns. After the War, he was the Superintendent of Public Instruction for North Carolina.

Tryon, William. See section on Governors (1765—1771).

Tucker, Glenn (1892—). Born in Indiana. Award winning biographer and historian. Author of *High Tide at Gettysburg* and *The War of 1812,* among others. Moved to North Carolina in 1948.

Tucker, William F. (1827-1881). Born in Iredell County; died in Okolona, Mississippi. Confederate general who commanded Mississippi troops at Bull Run, Chattanooga, and Chickamauga. Was murdered in Mississippi.

Turner, James. See section on Governors (1802—1805).

Umstead, William B. See section on Governors (1953—1954).

Vance, Robert B. (1828—1899). Born in Buncombe County. A brigadier general in the Confederate army. Afterwards served in the U.S. Congress (1873—1885).

Vance, Zebulon B. See section on Governors (1862—1865).

Waddell, James I. (1824-1886). Born in Pittsboro; died in Annapolis, Maryland. Was the commander of the Confederate Navy's ship, *CSS Shenandoah*.

Walker, Henderson. See section on Governors (1699—1704).

Walser, Richard (1908—). Born in Lexington. Educator and writer. Author of *Young Readers' Picturebook of Tar Heel Authors*.

Washington, James Augustus (—). Born in Kinston. One of the first doctors to administer medicine by hypodermic needle (1839).

Watson, Doc (1923—). Born in Deep Gap. Country music singer, guitarist, and banjoist. Best known for his renditions of traditional material.

Wellman, Manly Wade (1903—). Born in Portuguese West Africa. Writer of over 70 books on such varied subjects as history, science fiction, and country music. Many of his juvenile books have a North Carolina setting.

Whistler, Anna McNeill (—). Born in Wilmington. The mother of James Whistler, "Whistler's Mother" of American art fame.

White, Hugh Lawson (1773—1840). Born in Iredell County; died in Knoxville, Tennessee. Was the son of Governor James White, the founder of Knoxville, Tennessee, and a judge in Tennessee. He ran against Martin Van Buren in 1836 for the U.S. presidency.

White, James (1749—1821). Born in Rowan County; died in Knoxville, Tennessee. Served in the North Carolina militia from 1779 to 1781. Settled the site of Knoxville, Tennessee, in 1786. Donated the site in Knoxville for the University of Tennessee.

White, John. See section on Governors (1587).

Wicker, Tom (1926—). Born in Hamlet. Journalist and novelist. His latest book, *Unto This Hour*, was a nationwide best-seller.

Wilcox, Cadmus M. (1824-1890). Born in Wayne County; died in Washington, D.C. Confederate general. After the War, he held the post of Chief of the Railroad Division of the U.S. Government Land Office.

Wiley, Calvin Henderson (1819—1887). Born near Greensboro; died in Winston-Salem. North Carolina's first Superintendent of Common Schools. Author of two North Carolina-oriented novels, *Alamance* and *Roanoke*.

Williams, Benjamin. See section on Governors (1799—1802).

Williamson, Hugh (1735—1819). Born in West Nottingham, Pennsylvania; died in New York City. Physician and surgeon-general of North Carolina troops during the Revolutionary War. Was a signer of the U.S. Constitution.

Winslow, John A. (1811-1873). Born in Wilmington; died in Boston, Massachusetts. Served in the U.S. Navy during the War Between the States. After the War, he became Commander of the Pacific Fleet.

Winslow, Warren. See section on Governors (1854—1855).

Worth, Jonathan. See section on Governors (1865—1868).

FERRIES

Reservations are recommended to avoid possible delay in boarding the Cedar Island-Ocracoke Ferry and the Swan Quarter-Ocracoke Ferry. These may be made by telephone, or in person at the departure terminal. For departures from Ocracoke, call 919-928-3841; from Cedar Island, 919-225-3551; and for reservations for departures from Swan Quarter, call 919-926-1111.

Reservations may be made up to 30 days in advance of departure date and are not transferable. These reservations must be claimed at least 30 minutes prior to departure time.

The name of the driver and the vehicle license number are required when making reservations.

The gross load limits at all crossings: any axle, 13,000 lbs.; two axles (single vehicle), 24,000 lbs.; three or more axles, 36,000 lbs.

Cedar Island–Ocracoke Toll Ferry

Capacity: approx. 30 cars
Crossing time: approx. 2¼ hours

Summer Schedule
April 15—November 30

Leave Cedar Island	*Leave Ocracoke*
7:00 AM	7:00 AM
9:30 AM	9:30 AM
12:00 Noon	12:00 Noon
3:00 PM	3:00 PM
6:00 PM	6:00 PM
8:30 PM	8:30 PM

Winter Schedule
December 1—April 14

Leave Cedar Island	*Leave Ocracoke*
7:00 AM	10:00 AM
1:00 PM	4:00 PM

Cherry Branch–Minnesott Beach Free-Ferry Schedule

Capacity: approx. 20 cars
Crossing time: approx. 20 minutes

Year-Round Schedule

Leave Cherry Branch	*Leave Minnesott Beach*
5:45 AM	6:15 AM
6:45 AM	7:15 AM
7:45 AM	8:15 AM
8:45 AM	9:15 AM
9:45 AM	10:15 AM
10:45 AM	11:15 AM
11:45 AM	12:15 PM
1:30 PM	2:00 PM
2:30 PM	3:00 PM
3:45 PM	4:15 PM
4:45 PM	5:15 PM
5:45 PM	6:15 PM
6:45 PM	7:15 PM
7:45 PM	8:15 PM
8:45 PM	9:15 PM
9:45 PM	10:30 PM
11:30 PM	12:15 AM
12:45 AM	1:15 AM

Currituck Sound–Free-Ferry

Capacity: approx. 18 cars
Crossing time: approx. 50 minutes

Year-Round Schedule

Leave Mainland Side	*Leave Knotts Island*
6:15 AM	7:15 AM
9:00 AM	10:00 AM
11:00 AM	12:00 Noon
1:00 PM	2:00 PM
3:45 PM	4:45 PM
5:45 PM	6:45 PM

Hatteras Inlet–Free-Ferry

Capacity: approx. 22 cars
Crossing time: approx. 40 minutes

Summer Schedule
April 15—October 31

Leave Hatteras	*Leave Ocracoke*
5:00 AM	6:00 AM
6:10 AM	7:10 AM
6:50 AM	*7:50 AM
7:30 AM	8:30 AM
* 8:10 AM	9:10 AM
8:50 AM	9:50 AM
9:30 AM	10:30 AM
10:10 AM	*11:10 AM
*10:50 AM	11:50 AM
11:30 AM	12:30 PM
12:10 PM	1:10 PM
12:50 PM	*1:50 PM
* 1:30 PM	2:30 PM
2:10 PM	3:10 PM
2:50 PM	3:50 PM
3:30 PM	4:30 PM
* 4:10 PM	*5:10 PM
4:50 PM	5:50 PM
5:30 PM	6:30 PM
6:10 PM	7:10 PM
7:00 PM	8:00 PM
8:00 PM	9:00 PM
9:00 PM	10:00 PM
10:00 PM	11:00 PM
11:00 PM	

*Priority loading of commercial vehicles in effect June 1—Labor Day (by permit only)

Winter Schedule
November 1—April 14

Leave Hatteras every hour on the hour from 5:00 AM to 5:00 PM and at 7:00 PM, 9:00 PM and 11:00 PM. Leave Ocracoke every hour on the hour from 6:00 AM to 6:00 PM, 8:00 PM and 10:00 PM.

Ocracoke-Swan Quarter Toll-Ferry

Capacity: approx. 30 cars
Crossing time: approx. 2½ hours

Year-Round Schedule

Leave Ocracoke	*Leave Swan Quarter*
6:30 AM	9:30 AM
12:30 PM	4:00 PM

Pamlico River–Free-Ferry

Capacity: approx. 18 cars
Crossing time: approx. 25 minutes

Year-Round Schedule

Leave South Shore (near Aurora, NC)	*Leave North Shore (Near Bayview, NC)*
12:30 AM	5:30 AM
6:15 AM	7:00 AM
8:30 AM	9:15 AM
10:00 AM	11:00 AM
12:00 Noon	1:00 PM
2:00 PM	3:00 PM
4:45 PM	5:30 PM
6:15 PM	7:00 PM
8:00 PM	9:00 PM
10:00 PM	11:00 PM

Southport–Fort Fisher Toll-Ferry Schedule

Capacity: approx. 20 cars
Crossing time: approx. 1 hour

Year-Round Schedule

Leave Southport	*Leave Fort Fisher*
8:00 AM	8:50 AM
9:40 AM	10:30 AM
11:20 AM	12:10 PM
1:00 PM	1:50 PM
2:40 PM	3:30 PM
4:20 PM	5:10 PM
6:00 PM	6:50 PM

Schedules are subject to change without notice.

FESTIVALS AND EVENTS

The following is a partial list of festivals and events with the general dates on which they usually take place. For a more detailed list of events giving actual dates write: North Carolina Travel & Tourism Division, Dept. of Commerce, Raleigh, 27611, 919-733-4171. Call toll-free in the United States and Toronto, Canada; 1-800-VISIT NC. If you desire more detailed information on a specific festival or event and no contact person is listed, consult the chamber of commerce in that area (see Chambers of Commerce chapter).

JANUARY

North Carolina Artists' Exhibition—Asheville—Buncombe County.

Field Trials—Pinehurst—Moore County.

Old Christmas Celebration—Rodanthe—Dare County.

Arts and Crafts Show and Sale—Morehead City—Carteret County, late January, 1 day. (Morehead City Festival Committee, 112 Taylor Street, 28557.)

Watauga and Avery County Winter Festival—Banner, Blowing Rock, Boone, Elk, and Linville (simultaneously), late January—early February, annual, 11 days. (Boone Area Chamber of Commerce, 827 Blowing Rock Rd., Boone, 28607.)

FEBRUARY

Camellia Show—Whiteville—Columbus County.

Camellia Show—Wilmington—New Hanover County.

Festival of Contemporary Arts—Wilson—Wilson County, mid-February—mid-March, annual musical concert series, other arts also. (Festival of Contemporary Arts, Atlantic Christian College, 27893).

The Carolina 500—Rockingham—Richmond County, late February, new stock cars compete in this 500-mile race at the N.C. Motor Speedway. Admission. (919-582-2861.)

St. Thomas Celebration of the Arts—Wilmington—New Hanover, late February—early March, fine arts festival, jazz, performances, celebration. (Thalian Hall, Box 317, 28402, 919-763-9328.)

MARCH

Camellia Show—Elizabeth City—Pasquotank County.

Grand National Stock Car Race—Hillsborough—Orange County.

National Amateur Field Trials—Hoffman—Richmond County.

Block House Steeplechase—Tryon—Polk County.

Old Time Fiddlers' Convention—Union Grove—Iredell County.

Commemoration of Battle at Guilford Courthouse—Greensboro—Guilford County, mid-March, annual, 3 day gala festival, troops in military costumes of the era drill and fire an eighteenth century cannon, Guilford Courthouse National Military Park. (W. W. Danielson, Superintendent, P.O. Box 9334, 27408.)

Old Quawk's Day—Morehead City—Carteret County, mid-March, 2 day celebration inspired by the legend of a shipwrecked mariner, City Park. (Carteret County Chamber of Commerce, P.O. Drawer B, 28557.)

Fine Arts Festival—Winston-Salem—Forsyth County, mid-March, 8 day festival of fine arts on display and in performance, Winston-Salem State University. (Harry E. Pickard, Winston-Salem State University, Columbia Heights, 27107.)

Fine Arts Festival—Elizabeth City—Pasquotank County, mid—late March, 7 day festival of fine arts on display and in performance on the campus of Elizabeth City State University. (Chamber of Commerce, 100 E. Main St., 27909.)

Folk Music Festival—Louisburg—Franklin County, late March, annual, 1 day presentation of traditional American music and dancing, with competitions and awards in bluegrass and folk, at Louisburg College. (Allen DeHart, Louisburg College, 27549.)

Moravian Easter Sunrise Service—Winston-Salem—Forsyth County, traditional Moravian Easter service held in Old Salem. (919-722-6171.)

City Spirit—18th Century Music Festival—Buies Creek—Harnett County, late March, one day musical presentation at Campbell College. (Anne Moore, Project Director, Campbell College, 27506.)

Arts Festival—Winston-Salem—Forsyth County, late March, 2 day arts and crafts show and sale sponsored by the North Carolina Women's Club. (Greater Winston-Salem Chamber of Commerce, P.O. Box 1408, 27102.)

Greater Greensboro Open—Greensboro—Guilford County, late March—early April, premier PGA tournament, testing ground for top pros on their way to the Masters, held at Forest Oaks Country Club. (919-379-1570.)

APRIL

Stoneybrooke Steeplechase—Southern Pines—Moore County.

Hubert Hays Mountain Youth Jamboree—Asheville—Buncombe County, annual 4 day jamboree of folk music, dancing, singing by young performers (grades one to twelve) who have come from nine states to compete in clog, smooth square and western square dancing, and dances of other countries; held in Asheville City Auditorium. (Hubert Hayes, Mountain Youth Jamboree, 30 Maney Ave., 28804.)

Apple Chill Festival—Chapel Hill—Orange County, arts, crafts, informal performances, street festival. (Chapel Hill Park and Recreation Department, 27514, 919-968-2784.)

Old Time Fiddler's Convention—Union Grove—Iredell County, early April, 2–3 day country music competition by performers from the U.S., Mexico, and Canada. (Annual Old Time Fiddlers' Convention, P.O. Box 38, 28689.)

Festival of Music—Charlotte—Mecklenburg County, early April, annual 8 day program of high school band performance. (Chairman, Festival of Music in Freedom Park with High School Bands, 308 E. Fifth Street, 28202.)

Spring Celebration—Davidson—Mecklenburg County, annual 1 day event of piano and organ recitals, choral concerts, an exhibition of the works from the Davidson National Print and Drawing Competition, plays and a humorous debate; held at Davidson College. (Director of Communications, Davidson College, 28036.)

Artsplosure: The Raleigh Arts Festival—Raleigh—Wake County, mid—late April, two-week arts festival, exhibits, performances, special events. (Raleigh Arts Commission, P.O. Box 590, 27602, 919-755-6154.)

Shad Festival—Grifton—Pitt County, mid-April, 3 day event, competition in horseshoe pitching, canoe racing, golf and a horse show, crowning of Shad Queen, a parade, arts and crafts display, square dancing and fish fry. (Mrs. Janet Haseley, Box 147, 28530.)

Pioneer Sunday—Asheville—Buncombe County, mid-April, 1 day reenactment of ping costumes, log cabin and sheds, and outdoor cooking, held at Zebulon Vance Birthplace State Historic Site. (North Carolina Travel Development Section, Division of Economic Development, Dept. of Natural and Economic Resources, Raleigh, 27611.)

North Carolina Azalea Festival—Wilmington—New Hanover County, mid-April, annual 4 day event with garden tours, concerts, a parade, art shows, arts and crafts, a beauty pageant, live music, an air show and boat races. (T. H. Salade, Star Newspapers, P.O. Box 840, 28401.)

Fontana Spring Fling—Fontana Dam—Graham County, late April, annual 4 day festival offers callers and teachers for both western style square dancing and round dancing, "swaps" of calls and dances, workshops, parties and special events. (Fontana Village Resort, 28733.)

Watauga County Spring Festival—Boone, late April, 1 day event featuring displays and demonstrations of arts and crafts, mountain music, and dancing held at Appalachian State University. (Boone Area Chamber of Commerce, 827 Blowing Rock Rd., 28607.)

Arts and Crafts Festival of Southeastern North Carolina—Lake Waccamaw—Columbus County, late April, 2 day event featuring arts, crafts and performing arts, presentations of literature and history held on Boy's Home campus. (Ann A. Hood, Route 2, Box 211, Elizabethtown, 28337.)

Springfest—Charlotte—Mecklenburg County, late April, neighborhood festival centered on restored Fourth Ward downtown. Arts, crafts, and live entertainment. (1 NCNB Plaza, T07-9, 28255, 704-374-5535.)

Earl of Granville Festival—Oxford—Granville County, late April, townwide festival features antique car show, arts and crafts, athletic events, street dances, a parade, and a large fireworks show. (919-693-6125.)

Carolina Dogwood Festival—Statesville—Iredell County, late April, a celebration with athletic events, music, food, a parade and beauty pageant. (704-873-6501.)

Strawberry Festival—Chadbourn—Columbus County, late April—early May, 9 day event featuring a parade, queen's ball, strawberry cooking contest, and an art exhibit, plus tennis and golf tournaments. (Greater Chadbourn Chamber of Commerce, 208-A Brown Street, 28431.)

Triangle Festival of Crafts—Durham—Durham County, late April—early May, 3 day event featuring crafts, music and dance performances, and the screening of films, held at Durham Civic Center. (Durham Arts Council, 810 W. Proctor St., 27707.)

Crafts Festival—Raleigh—Wake County, late April—early May, 4 days of demonstrations and displays by craftsmen from 8 states. (Blue Ridge Hearthside Crafts Association, Inc., P.O. Box 128, Sugar Grove, 28679.)

MAY

World 600—Charlotte—Mecklenburg County, late model auto race.

Bluegrass and Old Time Music Festival—Camp Springs—Rockingham County, annual 3 day event to promote and preserve this traditional music, held at Bluegrass Park. (Carlton Haney, Box 7A, Ruffin, 27326.)

Aulander Day—Aulander—Bertie County, 1 day festival, old fashioned homecoming with athletic events, concerts, and a picnic. (North Carolina Travel Development Section, Division of Economic Development, Dept. of Natural and Economic Resources, Raleigh, 27611.)

Invitational Mountain Dance—Cullowhee—Jackson County, 1 day event featuring various types of mountain dancing, including smooth and precision clogging, also public square dancing held at Western Carolina University. (Office of Public Information, Western Carolina University, 28723.)

Springfest—Raleigh—Wake County, early May, German festival of spring featuring German cultural events and food held at the Civic Center. (919-755-6011.)

"May Fair"—Wilmington—New Hanover County, early May, celebration with arts and crafts, children's games, a country store, and attic treasures held at the Governor Dudley Mansion. (919-762-2511.)

Ashe County Arts Festival—West Jefferson, early May, fine arts, performing arts, and folk arts represented in a series of concerts, displays, exhibits and performances. (Boone Area Chamber of Commerce, 827 Blowing Rock Rd., Boone, 28607.)

Spring Wildflower Pilgrimage—Asheville—Buncombe County, early May, guided field trips along the Blue Ridge Pkwy. to see wildflowers and birdlife. (704-258-6623.)

Sunday in the Park Festival of Arts and Crafts—Wilson—Wilson County, early May, 1 day outdoor show and sale of arts and crafts in city park. (Chamber of Commerce, P.O. Box 979, 27893.)

Civitan Spring Festival—Garner—Wake County, mid-May, fun event with rides, games, and concessions held at Forest Hills Shopping Center. (Garner Civitan Club, P.O. Box 205, 27529.)

Hang-Gliding Spectacular—Nags Head—Dare County, late May. Hang-gliding pilots from across the nation come to compete in this event at Jockey's Ridge State Park. (No admission, 919-441-6247.)

Arts and Crafts Festival—Wilmington—New Hanover County, late May, 2 day event featuring exhibits, arts and crafts displays, food and band concerts all with a colonial theme, held at Greenfield Park. (Lower Cape Fear Council for the Arts, P.O. Box 212, 28401.)

JUNE

Horn in the West—Boone—Watauga County, outdoor drama.

Hobby Crafts Show—Hendersonville—Henderson County.

Eastern Carolina Singing Convention—Wilson—Wilson County.

North Carolina Summer Festival—Winston-Salem—Forsyth County, June—August, annual, 5 week event featuring variety of performing arts; films, popular musical performances, Dance Theatre productions, the Festival Orchestra, and the Piedmont Chamber Players; held at the North Carolina School of the Arts. (North Carolina School of the Arts, P.O. Box 4657, 27107.)

Clogging and Country and Bluegrass Music Festival—Murphy—Cherokee County, early June, 5 day event, old time and country music, and mountain-style dancing. (Cherokee County Chamber of Commerce, 28906.)

Dare Days—Manteo—Dare County, early June, 2 day festival featuring exhibitions, craft displays, and entertainment. (Outer Banks Chamber of Commerce, Kitty Hawk, 27949.)

Early American Moravian Music Festival—Winston-Salem—Forsyth County, mid-June, biennial, 1 week festival, programs combine chamber music, organ recitals, concerts for chorus and orchestra, and seminars. (Early American Moravian Music Festival, Salem College, 27108.)

North Carolina Rhododendron Festival—Bakersville—Mitchell County, mid-June, beauty pageants, food, athletic events, and arts and crafts exhibits held at Bowman Middle School. (704-688-2113.)

Highland Heritage Arts and Crafts Show—Asheville—Buncombe County, mid-June, about 65 exhibitors in 35 mediums show and sell wood carvings, woven goods, pottery, glasswork, and mountain furniture at the Asheville shopping mall. (704-253-6893.)

National Hollerin' Contest—Spivey's Corner—Harnett County, mid-June, contests in ham hollerin', junior hollerin', conch shell and foxhorn blowin', whistlin', and ladies callin', as well as a clogging demonstration and other entertainment. (National Hollerin' Contest, P.O. Box 332, 28334, 919-892-4133.)

Unto These Hills—Cherokee—Swain County, Outdoor Drama, mid-June—late August, Cherokee Indian history from 1540 through their removal from their homeland, daily except Sunday at the Mountainside Theatre. (704-497-2111.)

The Lost Colony—Manteo—Dare County, Outdoor Drama, mid-June—late August, first English settlement in the New World portrayed daily except Sunday at the Fort Raleigh National Historic Site. (919-473-2127.)

Eastern Music Festival—Greensboro—Guilford County, mid-June—July, 6 week event, residential music center, classes, orchestral music, chamber pieces, recital works. (200 N. Davie St., 27401, 919-373-4712.)

American Dance Festival—Durham—Durham County, mid-June—July, International festival of modern dance with performances by world's most prominent companies, classes, professional seminars, public tours, and special events. (P.O. Box 6097, Duke University, College Station, 27708, 919-684-6402. New York office, 212-586-1925.)

Watauga County Arts Festival—Boone, late June, 1 day event features displays and performances in the fine arts, performing arts, and native folk arts. (Boone Area Chamber of Commerce, 827 Blowing Rock Rd., 28607.)

Macon County Arts and Crafts—Franklin, 3rd weekend in June, 4 day event includes demonstration, display, sale, special exhibits and entertainment held at Macon County Fairgrounds. (Eva Thaller, Route 1, 28734.)

Pirate Invasion—Beaufort—Carteret County, late June, pirates invade the town and carry off maidens in an unrehearsed free-for-all on Beaufort's Waterfront. (919-726-6831.)

Singing on the Mountain (Folk and Folk Song Festival)—Linville—Avery County, last Sunday in June, annual 1 day religious event with gospel singing and preaching. In the past, well-known entertainers have participated in this musical tradition held at MacRae Meadow, Grandfather Mountain. (Folk and Folk Song Festival, Grandfather Mountain, 28646.)

Fair—Black Mountain—Buncombe County, late June, annual event featuring food, entertainment, and mountain crafts. (Black Mountain-Swannanoa Chamber of Commerce, 411 W. State St., 28711.)

Old Time Railroaders Day at Tweetsie Railroad—Blowing Rock—Watauga County, late June, 1 day celebration in honor of former employees of Tweetsie (East Tennessee and Western North Carolina) Railroad. (Boone Area Chamber of Commerce, 827 Blowing Rock Rd., Boone, 28607.)

JULY

Fiddlers Convention—Elkin—Surry County.

Highland Games on Grandfather Mountain—Linville—Avery County.

Brevard Music Festival—Brevard—Transylvania County, July—mid-August, 6 weeks of musical activities including performances by the various groups of the Transylvania Music Camp: the Youth Orchestra, Wind Ensemble, Symphony Orchestra, Concert Band, and Chorus; the Brevard Music Center Orchestra, and opera productions are staged by the Brevard Opera Workshop. (Brevard Music Festival, Box 592, 28712, 704-884-2011.)

Festival of the Arts—Brevard—Transylvania County, annual 1 week of diversified events including country fair, crafts shows, flower shows, mineral shows, and pet shows. Also gospel singing, square dancing in the street, and hikes and tours of the forests. (Chamber of Commerce, 28 E. Main St., P.O. Box 589, 28712.)

Elon College Music Festival—Elon College—Alamance County, July—August, annual, orchestral and chamber music concerts, recitals at the Elon College campus. (Elon College Music Festival, Box 2159, 27244.)

Coon Dog Day—Saluda—Polk County, early July, 1 day event featuring coon dogs trials and show, also arts and crafts show, parade, flea market, and the crowning of the Coon Dog Queen. (Mayor E. B. Hall, Box 248, 28773.)

Crepe Myrtle Festival—Angier—Harnett County, early July, around the 4th, annual 1 day event in honor of the flowering shrub. A parade, and festival including horse show, and fireworks display held at Angier High School. (Angier Chamber of Commerce, Box 47, 27501.)

Mountaineer Book Fair—Franklin—Macon County, early July, 3 day literary event with additional festivities for all ages, held at Macon County Fairgrounds. (Adelaide Key, Chairman, P.O. Box 108, 28734.)

Smoky Mountain Art and Craft Show—Murphy—Cherokee County, around the 4th of July, annual 4 day event attended by artists and craftspeople from through out the area to the Old Rock Gym. (Murphy Rotary Club, Box 493, 28906.)

Avery County Crafts Fair and Arts Festival—Banner Elk, early July, 1 day event features exhibitions and concerts in the fine arts, the performing arts, native and folk crafts. (Boone Area Chamber of Commerce, 827 Blowing Rock Rd., 28607.)

Shindig on the Green (Mountain Folk Fair)—Asheville—Buncombe County, early July—early September, annual, every Saturday for 2 months, clog and square dancing, audience participation encouraged, at City-County Plaza. (Chamber of Commerce, P.O. Box 1011, 28802.)

Southern Highlands Craftsmen's Fair—Asheville—Buncombe County, mid-July, 5 day event where craftsmen display and demonstrate: woodcarving, enameling, weaving, spinning, knotting, fringing, instrument making, stained glass, leather work, pottery, jewelry, printing and smithing. Also traditional music and dancing are presented. Held at Civic Center. (Southern Highland Handicraft Guild, P.O. Box 9145, 28805.)

Angier Festival—Angier—Harnett County, mid-July, 3 day event featuring folk music and crafts shows held at the Dixie Campgrounds. (National Folk Festival Association, Inc., 1346 Connecticut Ave., NW, Washington, D.C. 20036.)

Grandfather Mountain Highland Games and Gathering of Scottish Clans—Linville—Avery County, mid-July, more than 100 Scottish clans are represented at Grandfather Mountain for ceremonies, pageantry, dances, and traditional sports. (704-898-4720.)

Greater Raleigh Antique Show—Raleigh—Wake County, early—mid-July, 3 day event where thousands of antiques are on display and for sale at the Raleigh Civic Center. (919-755-6011.)

Festival of Folk Arts and Crafts—Hendersonville—Henderson County, late July, 4 day "walking fair" where various crafts are displayed at several churches within walking distance, in addition to mountain music concerts by local performers and singing and dancing. (Harold McLaughlin, Blue Ridge Technical Institute, 28739.)

Macon County Gemboree—Franklin, late July, annual 4 day event with swap shops and retail sales of gems and minerals from all over the world, also special exhibits, held at the Macon County Fairgrounds. (Franklin Area Chamber of Commerce, P.O. Box 504, 28734.)

Smoky Mountain Folk Festival—Waynesville—Haywood County, late July, crafts, square dancing, music, and an old-time muzzle-loading shoot to celebrate mountain ways. (704-456-6834.)

Guild Fair of the Southern Highlands—Asheville—Buncombe County, late July, folk music and dancing, crafts sales and exhibits all featured at the Civic Center. (704-298-7928.)

AUGUST

Gems and Minerals Festival—Spruce Pine—Mitchell County.

Bluegrass and Old-Time Fiddlers' Convention—Jefferson—Ashe County, early August, bluegrass music, fiddling competition, and food at Ash Park. (919-246-9945.)

Mountain Dance and Folk Festival—Asheville—Buncombe County, early August, annual 3 day event. Oldest festival of traditional mountain music and dance including bluegrass, smooth and clog dancing, string bands, band and team dance competition, held at City Auditorium. (Asheville Chamber of Commerce, P.O. Box 1101, 28802, 704-258-5200.)

Village Arts and Crafts Fair—Asheville—Buncombe County, early August, annual 2 day event, native crafts exhibited and sold at All Souls Church, held concurrently with Mountain Dance and Folk Festival. (Asheville Chamber of Commerce, P.O. Box 1101, 28802.)

Boone Crafts Festival—Boone—Watauga County, early August, 5 day event when more than 75 mountain craftsmen sell their crafts and give demonstrations, also entertainment at the Holiday Inn Conference Center. (Blue Ridge Hearthside Crafts Association, P.O. Box 128, Sugar Grove, 28679.)

Sidewalk Art Show and Sale—Brevard—Transylvania County, early August, annual 1 day event, various art works displayed and sold on the lawn of the courthouse. (Mrs. Harold Matthews, Transylvania Art Guild, 113 Park Ave., 28712.)

Macon County Folk Festival—Franklin, early—mid-August, annual 3 day mountain musical event by local fiddlers and bands, also dance competitions at Franklin High School. (Franklin Area Chamber of Commerce, P.O. Box 504, 28734.)

Mountain Arts and Crafts—Fontana Dam—Graham County, late August, annual 2 day exhibit of artwork and craft pieces held at Fontana Village Resort. (Fontana Village Resort, 28733.)

North Carolina Apple Festival—Hendersonville—Henderson County, late August—early September, annual 16 day event that includes arts and crafts, athletic events, apple-bobbing and -baking contests, beauty pageants, parades, and street dances. (Greater Hendersonville Chamber of Commerce, 330 N. King St., P.O. Box 1302, 28739.)

SEPTEMBER

Pony Penning—Cedar Island—Carteret County.

Square Dance Fun Fest—Fontana Dam—Graham County.

West North Carolina Fair—Hendersonville—Henderson County.

Carolina Streetscene—Winston-Salem—Forsyth County, early September, downtown outdoor festival featuring arts and crafts. (The Arts Council, Inc., 305 W. Fourth St., 27101, 919-722-2585.)

Bluegrass and Old Time Mountain Festival—Black Mountain—Buncombe County, Labor Day weekend, annual event featuring arts and crafts for sale, mountain music and dancing held at Monte Vista Farm. (Asheville Area Chamber of Commerce, P.O. Box 1011, 28802.)

Downtown Street Art Celebration—Durham—Durham County, early September, annual festival presenting displays of arts and crafts; performances of music, dancing, and shows; and the screening of films. (Durham Arts Council, 810 W. Proctor St., 27707.)

Stanly County Arts Festival—Albemarle, 5 day event including visits by the Artrain—a traveling art show, street dancing, performances by clog and square dance teams, films, marching band and drill team performances, and bluegrass music. (Stanly County Arts Council, P.O. Box 909, 28001.)

North Carolina Soybean Festival—Clayton—Johnston County, annual 3 day event including arts and crafts show, beauty pageant, bingo games, a fish fry, karate demonstrations, tours of the Research Station, and youth games. (Clayton Chamber of Commerce, P.O. Box 246, 27520.)

Center Fair—Center—Davie County, 2nd Saturday in September, annual 2 day event including exhibits of field crops, horticulture, canning, household furnishings, crafts and hobbies, plants and flowers, pantry and dairy, and clothing; also competitions in fine arts and crafts for both children and adults; held at Center Community. (Center Community Development Association, c/o Larry Harpe, Route 1, Mocksville, 27028.)

Gourd Festival—Cary—Wake County, 2nd weekend in September, annual 2 day exhibition of gourds and gourd crafts, also craft demonstrations held at Jordan Hall Community Center. (Cary Gourd Club, P.O. Box 666, Fuquay-Varina, 27526.)

Arts and Crafts Show—Maggie Valley—Haywood County, mid-September, 3 day event featuring arts and crafts displays, plus mountain dancing and music at Stallard Plaza. (North Carolina Travel Development Section, Division of Economic Development, Department of Natural and Economic Resources, Raleigh, 27611.)

Festival in the Park—Charlotte—Mecklenburg County, mid-September, 6 day event features arts and crafts, children's activities, drama, music, and various contests held in Freedom Park, free admission. (704-372-8900.)

Playmore Beach Fiddlers' Convention—Morgantown—Burke County, mid-September, annual 3 day event of bluegrass music and dancing at Playmore Beach. (Elbert Phillips, Route 5, Box 717, 28655).

Coharie Indian Pow-Wow—Clinton—Sampson County, mid-September, features Indian cultural activities, arts and crafts, dancing and singing, drumming, and games held at the Coharie Indian Center. (919-564-6901.)

Street Arts Celebration—Durham—Durham County, mid-September, downtown outdoor festival with visual and performing arts, crafts. (Durham Arts Council, 120 Morris St., 27701, 919-682-5519.)

Masters of Hang-Gliding Championship—Linville—Avery County, mid-September, the world's top 28 pilots are invited to compete in this international tournament at Grandfather Mountain. (704-898-4720.)

Old Time Fiddlers' and Bluegrass Convention—Mount Airy—Surry County, mid-September, fiddle contest, and traditional music and dancing. (Old Time Fiddlers and Bluegrass Convention, P.O. Box 161, Route 9, 27030.)

Pioneer Living Day—Asheville—Buncombe County, mid—late September, 1 day re-creation of a typical pioneer day, complete with costumes, outdoor cooking and tours of log cabins at Zebulon Vance Birthplace State Historic Site. (North Carolina Travel Development Section, Division of Economic Development, Department of Natural and Economic Resources, Raleigh, 27611.)

Traditional Wooden Boat Show—Beaufort—Carteret County, late September, many different types and designs of handmade wooden boats are on display both in and out of the water. (919-728-7317.)

Farmer's Festival—Fairmont—Robeson County, late September, 9 day event includes a beauty pageant, parade, arts and crafts displays, flower and farm equipment shows, street square dancing, and a golf tournament. (Fairmont Chamber of Commerce, P.O. Box 27, 28340.)

Mule Day Celebration—Benson—Johnston County, late September, annual event which includes mule pulling, a parade, beauty contests, a street dance, and the Governor's Mule Race. (Travel and Promotion Division, State of North Carolina, P.O. Box 27687, Raleigh, 27611.)

Albemarle Craftsman's Fair—Elizabeth City—Pasquotank County, last Wednesday-Sunday of September, annual event when many varied crafts are exhibited, demonstrated, and sold at the Knobbs Creek Community Center. (Elizabeth City Area Chamber of Commerce, P.O. Box 426, 27909.)

North Carolina Poultry Jubilee—Rose Hill—Duplin County, late September, chicken is served from what is claimed to be the "world's largest frying pan," also a beauty pageant, parade and carnival. (W. H. Saunders, Rose Hill, 28458.)

Denim Fun Days—Erwin—Harnett County, late September—early October, 3 day event when Erwin, which calls itself the "World Denim Capital," celebrates the fabric with this festival. (Division of Travel and Tourism, Department of Commerce, Raleigh, 27611, 919-733-4171.)

OCTOBER

500 Stock Car Race—Charlotte—Mecklenburg County.

500 Stock Car Race—Rockingham—Richmond County.

City Stage Celebration—Greensboro—Guilford County, early October, outdoor festival featuring arts and crafts held downtown. (United Arts Council, 200 N. Davie St., 27401, 919-889-2787.)

Bascom Lamar Lunsford Mountain Music and Dance Festival—Mars Hill—Madison County, first weekend in October, annual 3 day event dedicated to the "Minstrel of the Appalachians" who devoted his life to preserving and promoting the traditions of his native mountains, which are the theme of this festival held on

Mars Hill College campus. (Donald N. Anderson, Director, Southern Appalachian Center, Mars Hill College, 28754.)

Cherokee Fall Festival—Cherokee—Swain County, early October, Indian food, an archery and blowgun competition, a grandstand show, a band competition, and arts and crafts exhibits held at the Cherokee Ceremonial Grounds. (704-497-9195.)

Eastern North Carolina Bluegrass Festival—Angier—Harnett County, early October, annual 3 day event featuring traditional music. (Chamber of Commerce, 27501.)

Fall Festival—Chapel Hill—Orange County, early October, 1 day, old town fair, with bands and dancing, games, and refreshments. (Shirley Harper, Recreation Department, 27514.)

Tobacco Festival—Clarkton—Bladen County, early October, annual event with beauty pageant, parade, dances, a golf tournament, and a Field Day in the Park in honor of the tobacco crop. (Norwood Meggs, Clarkton, 28433.)

Harvest Festival Days—Wendell—Wake County, early October, annual event includes a parade and arts and crafts displays. (Chamber of Commerce, P.O. Box 562, 27591.)

Autumn Leaves Festival—Mount Airy—Surry County, annual 3 day event featuring apple cider and butter, churning, kraut making, quilting, refreshments, and souvenirs; plus bandstands offering country, clogging, gospel, and rock music; craft items, hobbies, and paintings are on display. (Chamber of Commerce, P.O. Box 913, 27030.)

Fontana Fall Jubilee Festival—Fontana Dam—Graham County, early—mid-October, annual 8 day event featuring western style square dancing, round dancing, "swaps" of calls and dances, workshops, parties, and special events. (Fontana Village Resort, 28733.)

Fall Festival—Morgantown—Burke County, mid-October, annual display and sale of handcrafts at the Old Burke County Courthouse Square. (Chamber of Commerce, P.O. Box 751, 28655.)

Southeastern Art Auction and Sale—Greensboro—Guilford County, annual fund-raising event for the C. L. Phillips Memorial Arts Scholarship, which provides assistance to art students at five nearby colleges; open to any southeastern artist; all works must be for sale. (Greensboro Artists' League, Inc., 404-B Fisher Park Circle, 27401.)

North Carolina State Fair—Raleigh—Wake County, annual, livestock shows, agricultural and industrial displays, a carnival midway, and livestock shows are featured at the State Fairgrounds. (919-733-2145.)

Sacred Music Convocation—Davidson—Mecklenburg County, annual 2 day event to appraise and study religious music. Addresses, master classes on various aspects of music, and recitals by organ and choir. (Director of Music, Davidson College Music Department, Davidson College, 28036.)

NOVEMBER

Carolinas' Carrousel—Charlotte—Mecklenburg County.

Rock Fish Rodeo—Elizabeth City—Pasquotank County.

Piedmont Crafts Fair—Winston-Salem—Forsyth County, 1st weekend in November, annual 2 day event includes exhibits, demonstrations and sale of crafts at the Winston-Salem Memorial Coliseum. (Piedmont Craftsmen, Inc., 936 W. Fourth St., 27101.)

Cary Band Day—Cary—Wake County, 2nd Saturday in November, annual 1 day event. Nationally recognized judges officiate at parade and field competition for outstanding bands from the eastern seaboard states.

Southern Flue-Cured Tobacco Festival—Greenville—Pitt County, mid-November, annual event features athletic events, beauty pageant, a clogging contest, a quilting seminar, a tractor-driving contest, a pipe-smoking contest, and an agricultural art contest. (919-756-9687.)

Davie Craft Corner—Mocksville—Davie County, Friday and Saturday before Thanksgiving, annual 2 day show and sale of country crafts produced by the Davie Craft Association, held at the National Guard Armory. (Davie Craft Association, P.O. Box 812, 27028.)

Lake Norman Fiddlers Convention and Buck Dance Contest—Terrell—Catawba County, held on Thanksgiving night, competitions for bluegrass and old time bands, solo guitar, banjo, fiddle, and mandolin; also hog calling, tall tale stories, and buck dancing held at Lake Norman Music Hall. (Mrs. Pauline Lawing, Lake Norman Music Hall Manager, P.O. Box 326, 28682.)

DECEMBER

Anniversary of Wright Brothers' Flight—Kitty Hawk—Dare County.

Christmas in Old Salem—Winston-Salem—Forsyth County, 2nd week in December, annual event. In restored buildings of the original Moravian town of the eighteenth to early nineteeth century, visitors can observe typical work of that era: baking, coffee roasting, gunsmithing, needlework, pottery, tinsmithing, and woodwork; bands, choruses, and other instrumentalists and vocalists perform period pieces; a night watchman announces the hour with a conch shell and chants, children play games typical of the eighteenth century and townspeople in costumes ride by on their horses. (Director of Information, Old Salem December, Inc., Drawer F, Salem Station, 27108.)

Old Wilmington by Candlelight—Wilmington—New Hanover County, mid-December, tours of historic houses and churches are conducted by candlelight and music and refreshments are supplied. (919-762-0492.)

FIRSTS

North Carolina is proud to boast a few of the nations firsts.

1585—The first English colony settled on Roanoke Island on June 26.

1587—Virginia Dare, the first child of English parents born in America, August 18, on Roanoke Island.

1700—Bath became the first community in America to open a public library.

1775—The First Declaration of Independence occurred on May 20 when Mecklenburg County declared its citizens "a free and independent people."

1795—The University of North Carolina at Chapel Hill became the nation's first state university on January 15.

1799—America's first gold nugget was found in Cabarrus County.

1838—America's first silver lode was discovered near Lexington.

1896—The first X-ray photograph was made on January 12 by Dr. Harry Lewis Smith of Davidson College.

1903—Orville and Wilbur Wright piloted the first airplane 120 feet at Kitty Hawk, December 17.

1914—Babe Ruth hit his first unofficial home run as a professional player, 405 feet out of the park. A historic marker has been erected on the site in Fayetteville, in Cumberland County, even though the ball park is gone.

—The first national forest, Pisgah, was established. The main part of this forest had belonged to George Vanderbilt's estate and was donated to the federal government by his widow.

1928—The Asheville Mountain Dance, the nation's first folk festival, was established.

1937—America's first outdoor drama, *The Lost Colony,* opened July 4. It is the story of the strange disappearance of the first English settlement.

—The first national seashore park was authorized by Congress. World War II caused a delay in the establishment of the park.

1949—The nation's first local arts council was founded in Winston-Salem.

1958—Cape Hatteras National Seashore was finally dedicated, becoming the first park of its kind (see 1937).

1963—North Carolina School of the Arts became the nation's first state-supported institution for the performing arts.

FLORA AND FAUNA

North Carolina has a wide variety of natural vegetation, made possible by the wide range of natural conditions. Growing in the high mountains are found subarctic species such as spruce and balsam fir. Along the southern coastal area, palmetto and other subtropical trees flourish. Forests cover more than half of the state.

In the highlands of the Great Smoky Mountains National Park, the dominate species are balsam fir *(Abies balsamea)*, hickory *(Carya)*, oak *(Quercus)*, spruce *(Picea)*, yellow buckeye *(Aesculos octandra)*, and hemlock *(Isuga canadensis)*. Ash *(Fraxinus)*, hickory, oak, and pine *(Pinus)* are the commercial woods indigenous to the Piedmont area. The most prevalent species on the coastal plain are cypress *(Taxodium)*, black gum *(Nyssa sylvatica)*, oak, and pine. Hardy azalea *(Rhododendron),* mountain laurel *(Kalmia latifolia),* and rhododendron *(Rhododendron)* are native shrubs common to the area, as well as sumac *(Rhus)* and yaupon (a holly, *Ilex vomitoria*). Native to the state is one of the most intriguing plants in the world, the insectivorous Venus's-flytrap *(Dionaea muscipula)*.

The state abounds with a variety of wildlife, due in part to the abundant forests and fields, mild climate, and diverse topography. There are more than 200 species of birds and 50 species of mammals. Black bear *(Ursus americanus),* fox *(Velpes velpes),* opossum *(Didelphis virginiana),* raccoon *(Procyon lotor),* and whitetail deer *(Odocoileus virginianus)* are most common. Some of the upland birds are ruffed grouse *(Bonasa umbellus),* quail *(Coturnix),* and wild turkey *(Meleagris gallopavo),* and in the bays and coastal marshes there is an abundance of migratory waterfowl. Trout *(Salmo)* and bass *(Micropterus)* are two of the freshwater game fish. Amberjack *(Seriola),* bluefish *(Pomatomus saltatrix),* dolphin *(Coryphaena),* flounder *(Pleuronectidae)* pompano *(Trachinotus carolinus),* and sea trout *(Cynoscion)* inhabit the sounds, river mouths, and bordering ocean.

FOREIGN TRADE ZONES

There are four foreign trade zones in North Carolina. They are in Charlotte (FTZ #57), convenient to major business and trucking facilities; in Durham County (FTZ #93), near Research Triangle Park and Raleigh-Durham Airport; and at the state ports in Wilmington (FTZ #66) and Morehead City (FTZ #67), with direct access to international shipping.

The United States Customs Service treats foreign goods in a foreign trade zone as if they were not in the United States. Import quotas and duties do not apply until (or unless) the goods leave the zone for use in the United States. If goods are exported, regardless of whether they have been used to manufacture a new product, it is as if they were never in the United States. Manufacturers can realize substantial savings by assembling imported components in the trade zone and paying import duties on the finished product.

FORTS

Fort Amory. Built in 1862 by Federal troops near New Bern, a colonial capital. It was a portion of a mile-long defense works between the Trent and Neuse rivers, in Craven County. Still visible are the deep moat and parts of its pentagonal embankment.

Fort Anderson. Large Confederate fort named in honor of Richard H. Anderson, Confederate army general. The fortification, more than a mile long, was constructed of sand. It was evacuated February 18, 1865, after a strong Union attack, resulting in the fall of Wilmington. The fort is located at Belville, in Brunswick County.

Fort Barnwell. Constructed by and named for Colonel John Barnwell, a South Carolinian. Hundreds of colonists were killed in the Tuscarora massacre in 1711, and

Barnwell, also called Tuscarora Jack, was appointed by Governor Edward Hyde to lead a campaign against the Tuscarora Indians in April, 1712. Remains of this fort are in Craven County.

Fort Bartow. Mounting nine guns, it was a Confederate earth fort which was bombarded on February 7, 1862 by the Federal fleet. The earthworks are found in Manteo, Dare County.

Fort Blanchard. As the smallest on Roanoke Island, this Confederate earth fort mounted four guns, and was surrendered on February 8, 1862. Earthworks are located on Roanoke Island, Dare County.

Fort Bragg. Named for Confederate General Braxton Bragg, a North Carolina native, it is one of the largest U.S. military reservations in the nation with an area of 130,000 square miles. Known as "Home of the Airborne," Fort Bragg was constructed in 1918 on the site used as headquarters of General Francis Marion, the "Swamp Fox," during the Revolutionary War. It is located in Cumberland County.

Fort Branch. Built to protect railroads and the upper Roanoke River Valley, this Confederate fort was located at Rainbow Banks. The earthworks remain near Williamston in Martin County.

Fort Butler. Built in 1838, it was one of the forts used by General Winfield Scott, in command of U.S. forces, to gather the Cherokee Indians before moving them west. This fort is located in Murphy, in Cherokee County.

Fort Caswell. Named for Governor Richard Caswell, this fort was built by the U.S. to guard the mouth of the Cape Fear River near Southport in Brunswick County. It was seized by North Carolina troops in 1861 and later abandoned by the Confederates in 1865.

Fort Clark. Confederate fort located near Hatteras-Ocracoke Ferry Landing, Dare County, Fort Clark was overcome on August 29, 1861 by Union troops after two days of heavy naval bombardment.

Davidson's Fort. Built in 1776 as a shelter for pioneer settlers at the present town of Old Fort in McDowell County.

Fort Defiance. Built in Happy Valley near Patterson in Caldwell County, this fort later gave its name to the farmhouse built in 1788 by General William Lenoir, Revolutionary officer and leader at the Battle of Kings Mountain.

Fort Dobbs. Named for Governor Arthur Dobbs, this log fort was built in 1755–56 near the present Statesville in Iredell County. The hero of the French and Indian War, Colonel Hugh Waddell, here defeated the Cherokee.

Fort Embree. See *Fort Hembree*.

Fort Fisher. Named in honor Colonel Charles F. Fisher of Salisbury, who was killed in the First Battle of Manassas. It is located north of the entrance of the Cape Fear River in New Hanover County. Built by the Confederacy, this huge earthwork fortification was begun in 1861 and not completed until 1864. It reached half a mile across the peninsula from Cape Fear River and then for a mile down the beach to the south. As the last important southern port for blockade running, its fall, January 15, 1865, closed Wilmington and helped to isolate the Confederacy.

Fort Forrest. Confederate fort which protected the west side of Croatan Sound, mounting seven guns. The fort was destroyed on February 8, 1862. The earthworks are located at Manns Harbor in Dare County.

Frontier Fort. This early outpost was used by General Rutherford in the expedition against the Cherokee Indians in September, 1776. It was located near Old Fort in McDowell County and for it the town was named.

Fort Granville. Named in honor of Lord Granville, one of the Lords Proprietors to the original colony, it was located at the northern tip of Core Banks, on Portsmouth Island. Though nothing remains today, the Union forces sustained a hospital and prison there until after the War Between the States.

"Fort Hamby." Captured by citizens' force on May, 1865, a band of army deserters and robbers had used "Fort Hamby" in Wilkes County as a fortified stronghold.

Fort Hampton. Built in Carteret County, very near Beaufort Inlet, it was washed away in a storm in 1815. It was replaced by Fort Macon.

Fort Hancock. Used to protect Cape Lookout Bay, this fort was built in 1778 by Le Chevalier de Chambray and Captain de Cottineau at Shell Point, Harker's Island. It was dismantled in 1780.

Fort Hatteras. Located at Hatteras-Ocracoke Ferry Landing, Dare County, this Confederate fort was captured on August 29, 1861, after two days of heavy naval bombardment by Union troops.

Fort Hembree. On a hill southwest of Hayesville, in Clay County, this fort was used as a collecting stockade in 1838 by General Winfield Scott's United States forces during the removal of the Cherokee Indians.

Fort Hill. This Confederate artillery unit on the Pamlico River near Chocowinity, Beaufort County made it possible for General Daniel Harvey Hill's forces to besiege Washington in the spring of 1863.

Fort Huger. This was the main Confederate fort on Roanoke Island in Dare County. Mounting twelve guns, this fort was surrendered February 8, 1862.

Huggins' Island Fort. Guarding the entrance to Bogue Inlet, this Confederate 6-gun fort was burned, August 19, 1862, by Union troops. The remains are marked by a North Carolina historical marker in Swansboro, Onslow County.

Fort Johnston. Named in honor of Governor Gabriel Johnston, this was the second fort built in North Carolina. As protection against Spanish pirates, Fort Johnston was completed in 1764 on a bluff over the Cape Fear River near Wilmington, in Brunswick County. It was burned by the Whigs in 1775 after Governor Josiah Martin fled from taking refuge there. The U.S. Government built a new fort there which was completed in 1809. Confederates held possession from 1861 until 1865 when Union forces captured it. Only the officers' quarters remain.

Fort Lane. Located southeast of New Bern in Craven County, this fort was built by North Carolina, 1775–76, and called Fort Caswell. It was renamed Fort Lane by the Confederacy. Taken by U.S. troops in 1862, it then became Fort Point.

Fort Macon. Named for Nathaniel Macon, speaker of the House of Representatives and U.S. Senator from Warren County, this brick fort was built by the U.S. Corps of Engineers, 1826–34. It was seized by the Confederates, April 14, 1861 and was the scene of a battle April 25, 1862. It has become a state park and is located in Morehead City, Carteret County.

Fort Nooherooka. This was a palisaded stronghold of the Tuscarora Indians and was the site of the decisive battle of the Tuscarora War in March, 1713, after a two-year struggle. Under Colonel James Moore's command, 950 Indians were killed or captured. This fort was located in the Contentnea Creek west of Snow Hill, in Greene County.

Fort Point. The fort now known as Fort Point was taken by Federal troops in 1862. Prior to that time, it had been held by the Confederacy and was called Fort Lane. Originally this fort was built by North Carolina, 1775–76, to protect New Bern, in Craven County, and was then named Fort Caswell.

Fort Raleigh. When the colonists of Sir Walter Raleigh's second expedition arrived to re-establish the colony which later would become North Carolina, they rebuilt the fort which had been called the *New Fort of Virginia*. It was here that Virginia Dare was born.

Fort Totten. Named for the Chief Engineer of the Federal Army, General Joseph G. Totten. This was one of the forts built around New Bern, Craven County, by Union forces after they seized the town in March, 1862. There was a fort built at each end of the town and one in the center, as well as trenches across the town to the Trent and Neuse rivers.

Fort Williams. Named in honor of General Thomas Williams, this was the principal Union fort at Plymouth, in Washington County. It was the last fort to fall, April 20, 1864.

GAME LANDS

Within the state of North Carolina there are 65 game land areas managed by the North Carolina Wildlife Resources Commission. The total acreage currently under cooperative management is 1,820,070. Of this total, 50 percent is federally owned (U.S. Forest Service and USA Corps of Engineers), 30 percent is corporately owned (timber company, etc.), 15 percent is state owned, and 5 percent is privately owned.

There are 75 landowners involved in the game land program. Annual payments to cooperating landowners amount to $200,000. The amount of payment to each landowner is based on the landowner's pro-rata contribution (acreage) to the program.

Access to the game lands is attained by the purchase of a game lands license, with annual sales amounting to $140,000. Mandatory check-in of big game kills with the nearest cooperator agent applies.

Following is a list of the game land areas with a brief description of each. For more information consult the North Carolina Wildlife Resources Commission, 512 North Salisbury Street, Raleigh, NC 27611.

Alcoa has a combined total of 7,531 acres and is located in Davie, Davidson, Montgomery, Rowan, and Stanly counties. Primary game species available are fox, quail, rabbit, raccoon, deer, waterfowl, and warm water fishes. No camping is permitted.

Angola Bay has 21,134 acres in Duplin and Pender counties. Primary game species available are deer and bear. Unrestricted camping permitted.

Anson has 2,886 acres in Anson County. Primary game species available are fox, quail, rabbit, squirrel, raccoon, and deer. No camping permitted.

Bachelor Bay consists of 9,446 acres in Beaufort, Bertie, and Washington counties. Available game are fox, quail, rabbit, squirrel, raccoon, and deer. No camping permitted.

Bertie, located in Bertie County, has 15,936 acres. Available game are fox, dove, quail, rabbit, squirrel, raccoon, deer, and waterfowl. No camping permitted.

Big Pocosin has 13,242 acres located in Beaufort and Craven counties. Quail, rabbit, squirrel, raccoon, and deer are the primary available species of game. No camping permitted.

H. M. Bizzell, Sr. has 690 acres in Lenoir County. Dove, quail, rabbit, squirrel, raccoon, and deer are the available game species. Unrestricted camping permitted.

Bladen has 31,740 acres located in Bladen County. Available game are fox, dove, quail, rabbit, squirrel, raccoon, deer, bear, and warm water fishes. Camping is allowed in designated areas only.

Bluff Mountain, located in Ashe County, has 1,140 acres. Squirrel, grouse, and turkey are the primary game species available. No camping permitted.

Browntown Farms has 510 acres in Buncombe County. Dove is the available species of game. No camping permitted.

Brushy Mountains, located in Alexander and Caldwell counties, has 3,088 acres. Available game species are fox, squirrel, and raccoon. Unrestricted camping permitted.

Butner and Falls of the Neuse have a combined acreage of 46,034 located in Durham, Granville, and Wake counties. Fox, dove, quail, rabbit, squirrel, raccoon, deer, and waterfowl are the primary game species available at both, as well as turkey and warm water fishes at Falls of the Neuse. Camping is allowed in designated areas only in Butner Game Land, no camping permitted in Falls of the Neuse area.

Carson Woods, located in Ashe County, has 1,007 acres. Primary game available are squirrel, grouse, deer, and warm water fishes. No camping permitted.

Caswell has 16,503 acres located in Caswell County. Fox, dove, quail, rabbit, squirrel, raccoon, deer, turkey, and warm water fishes are the primary game available. Camping is permitted in designated areas only.

Caswell Farm, located in Lenoir County, has 215 acres. Dove is the primary game species available. No camping is permitted.

Chatham and Shearon Harris combined have a total of 12,906 acres. The primary game species available are fox, quail, rabbit, squirrel, raccoon, deer, and turkey. No camping permitted.

Cherokee, located in Ashe County, has 327 acres. Squirrel and grouse are the primary game species available. No camping permitted.

Cherry Farm has 2,000 acres and is located in Wayne County. The primary game species available is dove. No camping permitted.

Chowan Swamp, located in Gates County, has 6,959 acres. Fox, squirrel, raccoon, and deer are available, as well as waterfowl and warm water fishes. Unrestricted camping permitted.

Croatan consists of 156,634 acres and it spans Carteret, Craven, and Jones counties. Fox, dove, quail, rabbit, squirrel, raccoon, deer, and bear are available, as well as turkey and waterfowl. Unrestricted camping permitted.

Dare, located in Dare County, has 57,645 acres. The available game species are fox, dove, quail, rabbit, squirrel, raccoon, deer, waterfowl, and warm water fishes. Unrestricted camping permitted.

Dysartsville spans portions of Burke, McDowell, and Rutherford counties with a total of 12,983 acres. Fox, quail, rabbit, squirrel, raccoon, deer, and turkey are the primary game species available. Unrestricted camping permitted.

Elk Knob is located in Ashe and Watauga counties and has 3,578 acres. The primary game species are rabbit, squirrel, and grouse. Camping is controlled in this area by the land owners.

Falls of the Neuse. See *Butner and Falls of the Neuse*.

Franklin has 5,550 acres located in Franklin County. Fox, rabbit, squirrel, raccoon, and deer are the primary game species available. No camping permitted.

Gardner-Webb has 2,474 acres in Cleveland County. The primary game species available are fox, quail, rabbit, raccoon, and warm water fishes. Unrestricted camping permitted.

Goose Creek, located in Beaufort and Pamlico counties, has 7,599 acres. Fox, quail, rabbit, squirrel, raccoon, deer, bear, waterfowl, and warm water fishes are the primary game species available. Camping is allowed in designated areas only.

Granville has 2,276 acres in Granville County. The primary game species available are fox, quail, rabbit, squirrel, raccoon, deer, and turkey. No camping permitted.

Green River spans Henderson, Polk, and Rutherford with 27,108 acres. Fox, quail, rabbit, squirrel, raccoon, deer, turkey, warm water fishes, and mountain trout are the primary species available. Camping in designated areas only.

Green Swamp has 13,295 acres in Brunswick County. The primary game species available are fox, rabbit, squirrel, raccoon, and deer. No camping permitted.

Guilford County has 756 acres of designated game land. Dove is the primary species available. No camping permitted.

Gull Rock has 18,856 acres located in Hyde County. The primary game species are fox, dove, quail, rabbit, squirrel, raccoon, deer, waterfowl, and warm water fishes. Camping allowed in designated areas only.

Halifax, located in Halifax County, has 8,459 acres. Fox, rabbit, squirrel, raccoon, and deer are the primary game species available. No camping permitted.

Harnett has 1,544 acres in Harnett County. The primary game species available are fox, rabbit, squirrel, and raccoon. No camping permitted.

Hickorynut Mountain, located in Buncombe, McDowell, and Rutherford counties, has 8,953 acres. Fox, rabbit, squirrel, raccoon, and deer are the available game species. No camping permitted.

Hofmann Forest, consisting of 29,654 acres, is located in Jones and Onslow counties. The available species of game are fox and deer. No camping permitted.

Holly Shelter has 48,795 acres in Pender County. Fox, dove, quail, squirrel, deer, and warm water fishes are the primary game species available. Camping is permitted in designated areas only.

Huntsville, located in Robeson County, has 802 acres. The primary game species available are dove, quail, rabbit, squirrel, and deer. Camping is controlled by land owners.

Keith Farms has 2,327 acres in Lee County. Fox, dove, quail, rabbit, and squirrel are the primary game species available. No camping permitted.

Lee, located in Lee County, has 5,402 acres. The available game species are fox, quail, rabbit, squirrel, raccoon, deer, turkey, waterfowl, and warm water fishes. No camping permitted.

Linwood has 126 acres in Davidson County. Dove, quail, rabbit, raccoon, and warm water fishes are the primary game available. Unrestricted camping permitted.

Moore, located in Moore County, has 5,225 acres. The available game species are fox, quail, rabbit, squirrel, raccoon, and deer. No camping permitted.

Nantahala spans Cherokee, Clay, Graham, Jackson, Macon, Swain, and Transylvania counties with a total acreage of 1,043,258. Fox, squirrel, grouse, raccoon, deer, bear, boar, turkey, warm water fishes, and mountain trout are the available game species. Unrestricted camping permitted.

New Hope has 42,357 acres in Chatham, Durham, Orange, and Wake counties. The available game species are fox, dove, quail, rabbit, squirrel, raccoon, deer, turkey, waterfowl, and warm water fishes. No camping permitted.

New Lake is in Hyde and Tyrrell counties and has 11,912 acres. Fox, dove, quail, rabbit, squirrel, raccoon, deer, waterfowl, and warm water fishes. Unrestricted camping permitted.

Northampton has 632 acres in Northampton County. Game species available are fox, rabbit, squirrel, raccoon, and deer. No camping permitted.

North River, located in Currituck County, has 8,730 acres. Fox, squirrel, raccoon, deer, waterfowl, and warm water fishes are the available game species.

Northwest River Marsh has 1,251 acres in Currituck County. The available game are squirrel, raccoon, deer, waterfowl, and warm water fishes. Unrestricted camping permitted.

Orange, with an acreage of 779, is located in Orange County. Fox, quail, rabbit, squirrel, raccoon, deer, and turkey are the available game species. No camping permitted.

Person has 9,128 acres in Person County. Fox, dove, quail, rabbit, squirrel, raccoon, deer, turkey, waterfowl, and warm water fishes are the available game species. No camping permitted.

Pisgah contains 524,343 acres spanning parts of Avery, Buncombe, Burke, Caldwell, Haywood, Henderson, Madison, McDowell, Mitchell, Transylvania, Watauga, and Yancey counties. The available game species are fox, rabbit, squirrel, grouse, raccoon, deer, bear, turkey, warm water fishes, and mountain trout. Unrestricted camping is permitted.

Pungo River in Hyde County has 530 acres. Fox, quail, rabbit, raccoon, deer, waterfowl, and warm water fishes are the available game species. No camping permitted.

Richmond contains 2,000 acres in Richmond County. The available game species are fox, quail, rabbit, squirrel, raccoon, and deer. No camping permitted.

River View Acres in Cabarrus County has 789 acres. Dove, quail, rabbit, squirrel, and raccoon are the available game species. No camping permitted.

Sandhills spans parts of Moore, Richmond, and Scotland counties and contains 62,579 acres. The available game species are fox, dove, quail, rabbit, squirrel, raccoon, deer, and warm water fishes. Camping allowed in designated areas only.

Sauratown Plantation has 5,323 acres in Stokes County. Dove, quail, rabbit, squirrel, raccoon, deer, and warm water fishes are the available game species. Camping is controlled by land owners.

Shearon Harris. See *Chatham and Shearon Harris.*

South Mountains contain 4,745 acres in Burke County. The available game species are squirrel, raccoon, deer, and mountain trout. Unrestricted camping permitted.

Sutton Lake in New Hanover County has 1,585 acres. Dove, quail, rabbit, waterfowl, and warm water fishes are the available game. No camping permitted.

Thurmond Chatham has 7,709 acres in Wilkes County. The available game species are fox, squirrel, grouse, raccoon, deer, turkey, and mountain trout. Camping is allowed in designated areas only.

Toxaway in Transylvania County has 14,720 acres. Fox, squirrel, raccoon, deer, bear, warm water fishes, and mountain trout are the available game species. Camping is allowed in designated areas only.

Uwharrie contains 46,932 acres in portions of Davidson, Montgomery, and Randolph counties. The available game species are fox, dove, quail, squirrel, raccoon, deer, and warm water fishes. Unrestricted camping permitted.

Warren in Warren County has 5,675 acres. Fox, rabbit, squirrel, raccoon, and deer are the primary game species available. No camping permitted.

White Oak River has 100 acres in Warren County. Waterfowl and warm water fishes are available there. No camping permitted.

Vance consists of 4,128 acres in Vance County. The available game species are quail, rabbit, squirrel, raccoon, deer, waterfowl, and warm water fishes.

Yadkin in Caldwell County has 2,848 acres. Fox, rabbit, squirrel, raccoon, and deer are the available game species. Camping is controlled by the land owners.

GEOGRAPHIC CENTER

The geographic center of the state of North Carolina lies 10 miles northwest of Sanford in Chatham County.

GOLD

The first known discovery of gold in North Carolina took place in 1799. A thirteen-year-old boy, Conrad Reed, was shooting fish with a bow and arrows when he broke an arrow on a strange yellow rock. Though the rock was small, it was rather heavy. Thinking that it was pretty, he took the rock home to his mother to use as a doorstop.

Three years later, the lad and his father, a hired German soldier in the Revolutionary War who had settled on a farm in Cabarrus County, took the rock to a jeweler. The jeweler melted down the seventeen pound rock and cast it into a six-inch-long bar. The father, John Reed, agreed to sell it to the jeweler for $3.50 before knowing it was gold. Mr. Reed was angry at the jeweler for tricking him.

Conrad and his father returned home in Cabarrus County and with the help of slaves and others, they found more nuggets, ranging from one grain to twenty-eight pounds.

It is said to have been the first gold ever found in the United States. The word spread rapidly of a gold strike in North Carolina and soon Cabarrus County was teeming with gold seekers.

Reportedly, John Reed sued the jeweler for swindling him and won a settlement of three thousand dollars.

North Carolina was known as the Golden State for about 60 years, beginning in 1803. About 300 mines in Anson, Cabarrus, Davidson, Mecklenburg, Montgomery, Randolph, and Rowan counties netted more than 50 million dollars' worth of gold.

Unfortunately, dishonest promoters and high mining costs meant that the discovery of gold did little more than cast a warm glow on a chapter of North Carolina history.

GOVERNMENT

The government of North Carolina is made up of three major divisions; executive, legislative, and judicial.

The *Executive Cabinet* consists of ten members of the Council of State, headed by the governor as chief executive, and nine executive departments which are each directed by "Secretaries." The exception is the Department of Community Colleges; its head is not a member of the Executive Cabinet.

The governor is elected to a four year term by popular vote, and may serve two consecutive terms. He does not have veto power.

The Council of State members are constitutional officers elected every four years by the North Carolina populace. The governor appoints the administrative heads, called "Secretaries," of the other executive departments to serve at his pleasure.

The *Legislative Branch* of the North Carolina government, which meets in odd-year biennial sessions, consists of a 50-member Senate and a 120-member House of Representatives. Elections for these members are held every two years from districts containing approximately the same population. A list of these members is found in the section entitled *Legislature*.

The *Judicial Branch* is headed by the State Supreme Court. The Chief Justice and six Associate Justices, who are elected by the people at large to serve eight-year terms, make up this body. A list of these justices and the other officers of the courts are found in the section entitled *Courts*.

Most of the 461 incorporated cities and towns within North Carolina have a Mayor/City Council/Manager form of government. Two unique state institutions which assist the local governments are the *North Carolina Institute of Government* (an educational institution designed to help in the professional training of local government administrators) and the *Local Government Commission* (a state government entity which oversees the fiscal capacity to issue bonds).

Following is a list of the names of the members of the Council of State and their addresses, and the Executive Departments and their addresses.

COUNCIL OF STATE

Governor
James G. Martin
The State Capitol
Raleigh, 27611
919-733-4240

Lieutenant Governor
Robert B. Jordan, III
Legislative Office Building
Raleigh, 27611
919-733-7350

Secretary of State
Thad Eure
300 North Salisbury St.
Raleigh, 27611
919-733-3433

State Auditor
Edward Renfrow
Dept. of the State Auditor
300 North Salisbury St.
Raleigh, 27611
919-733-3217

State Treasurer
Harlan E. Boyles
Dept. of the State Treasurer
Albemarle Bldg.
325 North Salisbury St.
Raleigh, 27611
919-733-3951

Department of Public Education
Dr. A. Craig Phillips, Superintendent of Public Instruction
Education Bldg., 114 West Edenton St.
Raleigh, 27611
919-733-3813

Department of Justice
Lacy H. Thornburg, Attorney General
Justice Bldg., 2 East Morgan St.
Raleigh, 27611
919-733-3377

Department of Agriculture
James A. Graham, Commissioner
Agriculture Building
1 West Edenton St.
Raleigh, 27601
919-733-7125

Department of Labor
John C. Brooks, Commissioner
Labor Building
4 West Edenton St.
Raleigh, 27601
919-733-7166

Department of Insurance
James E. Long, Commissioner
Dobbs Bldg.
430 North Salisbury St.
Raleigh, 27611
919-733-7343

EXECUTIVE DEPARTMENTS

Department of Administration
503 Administration Bldg.
116 West Jones St.
Raleigh, 27611
919-733-7232

Department of Commerce
430 North Salisbury St.
Raleigh, 27611
919-733-4962

Department of Community Colleges
116 West Edenton St.
Raleigh, 27603-1712
919-733-7051

Department of Correction
840 West Morgan St.
Raleigh, 27603
919-733-4926

Department of Crime Control and Public Safety
P.O. Box 27687
Raleigh, 27611
919-733-2126

Department of Cultural Resources
Archives–Library Bldg.
109 East Jones St.
Raleigh, 27611
919-733-4867

Department of Human Resources
325 North Salisbury St.
Raleigh, 27611
919-733-4534

Department of Natural Resources and Community Development
P.O. Box 27687
Raleigh, 27611
919-733-4984

Department of Revenue
P.O. Box 25000
Raleigh, 27640
919-733-3991

Department of Transportation
P.O. Box 25201
Raleigh, 27611
919-733-2520

GOVERNORS

OF THE ORIGINAL VIRGINIA COLONY

Lane, Ralph, 1585–1586. Born *c.* 1530, Northamptonshire, England. Was appointed governor by Sir Walter Raleigh, a courier of Queen Elizabeth I who had been granted a patent for the settling of the new territory. Lane had just completed a tour of duty in Ireland with the British Army when he was made lieutenant governor. He and the group of early settlers arrived at Roanoke Island in August, 1585 and remained until a shortage of food, hostile Indians, and a poorly located settlement forced them to give up and return home, June, 1586. Died in Ireland, 1603.

White, John, 1587. When the first group of settlers failed to establish a colony, Sir Walter Raleigh arranged for a second group of settlers to go to the New World, and appointed White to be their governor. This time the settlers were to own land, raise crops, and start a community and twelve men were appointed to assist Governor White. While there, a granddaughter, Virginia Dare, was born. Because of the serious problems they experienced, White was sent to England for provisions. The settlers were to move further inland and leave some sign as to where they had gone. Because of England's war with Spain, White was unable to return until three years later. The only sign of the settlers that was found was the word "Croatoan" carved on a tree. The lost colony was never found.

COMMANDER OF THE SOUTHERN PLANTATION

Stephens, Samuel, 1662–1664. What was later to become North Carolina was at this time a frontier of Virginia and by 1662 the population exceeded 500 and caused Governor Berkeley of Virginia to be concerned. He appointed Stephens to be commander of the Southern Plantation and granted him authority to appoint a sheriff.

UNDER THE LORDS PROPRIETORS

Drummond, William, 1664–1667. A native of Scotland who came to Virginia in 1638, Drummond was appointed governor by Virginia's Governor Berkeley, with six men to serve as a council to aid him. Together they appointed civil and military officers. The first General Assembly met 1665, consisting of freeholders, or their representatives, the governor and council, to make laws which were sent to the Lords Proprietors for approval. Drummond was considered a good man and suited to be governor.

Stephens, Samuel, 1667–1669. Born in Virginia, *c.* 1629; was the first American-born governor. After having served as commander of the "Southern plantation," the Lords Proprietors appointed him governor in 1667. A General Assembly (12 representatives chosen by the colonists, the governor and the council he appointed) met to pass laws, appoint courts and decide on their jurisdiction. Three of the acts they passed were: every person bringing suit in court was to pay 30 pounds of tobacco to help pay the expenses of the governor and council; no suit could be made against an individual for debt until he had been a resident 5 years (to encourage emigration); civil marriage ceremonies were legalized because there were so few ministers. Stephens seemed to satisfy both the people and the Proprietors. He died in 1669.

Carteret, Peter, 1670–1672. Nephew of Lords Proprietor Sir George Carteret, and represented his interests in Carolina. Was speaker of Assembly; secretary of general court; appointed lieutenant colonel of Albemarle forces by Governor Stephens. Was made acting governor by Council when Stephens died in 1669. In 1670 was appointed governor by Lords Proprietors. Because of problems created by rent the colonists couldn't afford and oaths of allegiance that they resented having to make, Carteret returned to England, May 1672.

Jenkins, John, 1672–1677; 1679–1681. A graduate of Clare College, Cambridge, 1642; a holder of a patent of 700 acres; was appointed deputy of Albemarle; became council senior member. Became deputy governor and president of council when Governor Carteret left for England. Jenkins sided with prominent landowners and New England traders who were against restrictions on colonial commerce. While attempting to adjourn the Assembly, he was defeated by the speaker, Thomas Eastchurch, who led the opposition. Eastchurch sailed to England to register complaint against Jenkins for failure to enforce navigation laws and collect custom duties. The Assembly governed the colony for a while, then John Harvey was appointed governor. Within the year he died and Jenkins was again appointed. He died in 1681.

Eastchurch, Thomas, 1676–1678. Was appointed governor, 1676, but never actually served. He went to England to lodge his complaints against Jenkins and the Lords Proprietors appointed him governor but he did not return to Carolina for a long while. He was returning by way of Virginia when armed forces sent by Albemarle colonists came to prevent his return. He died before he could gather forces to help subdue the rebellion.

Miller, Thomas, 1677. A druggist who was against Governor Jenkins and went to England to protest. He was appointed secretary and collector of customs when Eastchurch was appointed deputy governor. Miller was sent on as acting governor when Eastchurch failed to return. When he took advantage of his position, a group of colonists led by John Culpepper revolted ("Culpepper's Rebellion") and Culpepper became appointed governor.

Harvey, John, 1679. He was a precharter settler and an antiproprietary faction leader. Customs duties were collected and lost revenues during the rebellion were compensated for by a tax that was levied and collected under his and his successor's terms. He died after six months in office.

Jenkins, John, 1679–1681 (Second Term).

Sothel, Seth, 1682–1689. Because of the dissension between the proprietor and antiproprietor factions, the Lords Proprietors chose Sothel to be governor because they thought he wouldn't represent either side. He was appointed governor in 1678 but he was captured on his way to Carolina by the Turks and held in Algiers for 5 years. He managed to escape from the pirates and find his way to Carolina to serve as governor from 1682 to 1689. He proved to be one of the most corrupt governors in any of the English colonies. He did things contrary to the government, illegally appointed officials, accepted bribes, disregarded instructions from other proprietors, put his opponents in jail without trial, and took over estates he was responsible for settling. He was tried and expelled by the General Assembly. He died in 1694.

Ludwell, Philip, 1689–1691. A native of the County of Somerset, England who emigrated to Virginia about 1660. Later became a captain of militia, member of the council and a loyal supporter of Governor Berkeley. He was later suspended from the council because he was a leader in the resistance to taxes. He was later appointed governor of the northern part of Carolina. He approved an act which allowed the colonists to hold their land the same as the colonists in Virginia. The Lords Proprietors didn't like this and removed Ludwell from office.

Jarvis, Thomas, 1691–1694. He served as deputy governor during Governor Ludwell's term. His administration was orderly and well managed. There were approximately 70 families living in the colony during this time. He died in 1694.

Archdale, John, 1694–1696. Born in England, *c.* 1642, Archdale was a governor who was also a Quaker, Proprietor and the author of a book. Emigrated to the colony in 1683. He had a good administration with the passage of a bill regulating prices, rents, and transfers and the maintenance of friendly relations with the Indians and Spanish. He returned to England in 1698 and died there, July 4, 1717.

Harvey, Thomas, 1696–1699. He served as deputy governor during Governor Archdale's administration. He was recognized as a leader, a man of good character, interested in the people's welfare. He died July 3, 1699.

Walker, Henderson, 1699–1704. Born in England, *c.* 1660. He was a lawyer and a leader of the Church of England who emigrated to the colony in 1680. He served as attorney general; judge of the admiralty court; superior court justice; president of the council before succeeding Harvey as deputy governor. Under his leadership, legislation was passed organizing parishes, establishing churches, and the levying and collecting of taxes to support them. The Quakers resented this action, and it was later vetoed by the Proprietors. Walker died April 14, 1704.

Daniel, Robert, 1704–1705. A competent and brave Indian fighter who was appointed deputy governor following the death of Walker. The religious question became a political one when the Assembly passed a law which forced out of office all the Quakers who did not take oaths of office and yet they were required to pay taxes which went for the support of the church. The dissension over this issue caused Daniel to be removed from office.

Cary, Thomas, 1705–1706; 1708–1711. A merchant of Charles Town, Cary was sent in 1705 to be deputy governor when Daniel was removed from office. He was even more determined that the Quakers take an oath to hold office. The Quakers were again upset and sent a representative, John Porter, to London to request help from the proprietors. The proprietors sent orders that the Quakers' affirmation be accepted, Cary was to be removed from office, a free assembly was to be elected, the council was to elect a president to serve as governor and to appoint new proprietary deputies. When Porter returned Cary was in South Carolina, and William Glover, as president of the council, was acting governor.

Glover, William, 1706–1708. During Cary's absence, Glover, as president of the council, was acting governor. This arrangement seemed acceptable to everyone, including John Porter and the Quakers, until Glover started to demand the required oath. When Cary returned, he sought to return to the office of governor and Porter and the Quakers strangely took his side. After the two factions prepared for civil war, it was decided that the Assembly determine who should hold office.

Cary, Thomas, 1708–1711 (Second Term). The Assembly decided in Cary's favor and Glover, still claiming to be governor, went to Virginia. Cary appointed many Quakers to office, declared all of Glover's acts to be void, and remained in office until 1711.

Hyde, Edward, 1711–1712. The proprietors appointed Hyde, who was thought to be a cousin of Queen Anne, to be a deputy governor of the northern part of Carolina. He was to have received his commission from the governor of Charles Town, but he died before Hyde's arrival. The fact that he was related to the queen seemed to make such an impression that everyone put aside their quarrels and invited him to take the position as president of the council until the proprietors advised further. Former Governor Cary did not like the way he handled things, however, and gathered supporters to help him rebel against Hyde, but the governor of Virginia sent assistance to Hyde and Cary was arrested and sent to England to be tried for treason. Because of lack of evidence, he was never tried, but the rebellion was ended because of his defeat. He died of yellow fever in 1712, during an epidemic which took many lives.

Pollock, Thomas, 1712–1714; 1722. Serving during the Tuscarora War, Pollock was successful in ending the conflict with the aid of the South Carolina forces. It took a long time to repay the huge debt of the war, but Pollock's administration was effective because vast tracts of land were now available for white settlers, factions were eliminated, and the separation from South Carolina was formalized. Growth and progress were the result of the strengthening of governmental authority. Pollock gave up his office when Charles Eden arrived. When Eden died in 1722, Pollock returned to office, but he died a few months later in August, 1722.

Eden, Charles, 1714–1722. Born in England, 1673. Eden's administration was one of peace and quiet. Progress was made with the passage of nearly 60 laws, some toward increasing trade and others to stop piracy and smuggling. The pirate Blackbeard had been operating off the coast of North Carolina but on November 22, 1718, Blackbeard and half of his men were killed and the rest of his crew were arrested, convicted, and hanged. During November and December of that year 78 pirates were hanged. When piracy ended and hore eliminated, the settlers were able to concentrate on their hunting, farming, trading and the expansion of their borders. Died March 26, 1722 in Edenton.

Pollock, Thomas, 1722 (Second Term).

Reed, William, 1722–1724. Served as deputy of Lords Proprietors, 1713; deputy under Governor Eden, 1715; Currituck Precinct parish vestryman; commissioner to settle Carolina-Virginia boundary line, 1718; colonel in Tuscarora War; member of council 16 years. Reed, as president of the council, was appointed acting governor following Pollock's death. Reed died September, 1728.

Burrington, George, 1724–1725; 1731–1734. As governor, Burrington worked toward developing the Cape Fear area, in spite of being advised against it. The Lords Proprietors removed him from office because South Carolina had been in revolt against them, and with the growth of the Cape Fear area, they feared North Carolina would revolt also. Because he had won the confidence of the General Assembly, his successor's term was made difficult. When the proprietors sold their shares to the Crown, Burrington went to England in an effort to be appointed governor but was not returned to his former office until 1731, when he became the first royal governor of North Carolina. He was unpopular during his second term because of unpopular and undemocratic practices pertaining to elections to the Assembly, paying of rents and holding of court, but he possessed qualities of leadership. His death was especially tragic. He was robbed and murdered and his body thrown in the canal at St. James Park, London.

Everard, Richard, 1725–1731. Everard was the last governor appointed by the proprietors. He had many difficulties during his term because Burrington remained in the colony and was more influential with the Assembly than he was. Also he had bad advice from his former advisers but the colony expanded greatly during his term. He died in England in 1733.

GOVERNORS OF NORTH CAROLINA UNDER THE KING

Burrington, George, 1731–1734 (Second Term).

Johnston, Gabriel, 1734–1752. Born in Scotland in 1699, Johnston was a physician, political writer, and a professor. His term was characterized by an increase in wealth, population, and development of resources. He was greatly concerned about education in the state. There was a dispute over representation in the Assembly and location of the colonial capital. He died July 17, 1752, two years before the Privy Council made a decision.

Rice, Nathaniel, 1752–1753. Rice was a commissioner of peace, New Hanover Precinct and a member and secretary of the council. Was involved in a conflict with Governor Burrington over the sale of lands in the colony. When Burrington left office, Rice served as deputy governor from April 15 to October 27, 1734, when Governor Johnston assumed office. He became acting governor again in 1752. Rice died in January, 1753.

Rowan, Matthew, 1753–1754. A Scotsman who became interested in colonial affairs soon after his emigration to Carolina. Was a church warden in Bath, 1729; Assembly representative, 1730; justice of the peace, New Hanover, 1735; surveyor general of the province, helped run boundary line between North and South Carolina. When Governor Rice died, Rowan became president of the council and commander in chief of the colony for a year until Arthur Dobbs was commissioned governor, 1754. Then he served as councillor to the governor until his death six years later, 1760.

Dobbs, Arthur, 1754–1765. Born in Scotland, April 2, 1689, to Irish parents; was educated in England; served 2 years of military duty; was elected high sheriff; became a member of Irish Parliament, was a supporter of economic and social reform. Was appointed governor of the Carolina colony, 1754. The problems of his administration were matters with the Board of Trade; conflicts between old settlers of the North and the new settlers of the South; war with France. He was opposed to the Navigation Acts and encouraged foreign trade. He sought the establishment of churches and schools. Was granted a leave of absence from his post and was preparing to sail home to Ireland when he died March, 1765.

Tryon, William, 1765–1771. Born in the County of Surrey, England, in 1729; arrived in Brunswick, October, 1764. Problems caused by the Stamp Act, the Sons of Liberty and the Regulators made his administration difficult. He tried to improve the postal service and better establish the Church of England. He was interested in public education and tried to help start a college in Charlotte in 1771 but the King and Privy Council refused to allow it. Tryon Palace was completed in New Bern in 1770 to be used as the governor's residence and the capitol. He died in 1788.

Hasell, James, 1771. Served as judge of the Court of Oyer and Terminer for Beaufort, Carteret, Craven, Hyde and Johnston counties; became chief justice, 1766. Hasell was appointed governor by the council when Governor Tryon left office, and he served approximately one month until Josiah Martin was appointed to the office.

Martin, Josiah, 1771–1775. Born April 3, 1737, in the West Indies. Was appointed as the last royal governor. Was less concerned about the people's rights than loyalty to the Crown. The Stamp Act caused conflict, also certain taxes that supported the courts were discontinued, causing the colony to be without courts. An inquiry into the invasion on the colonists' rights by the Crown was requested the Assembly. A provincial congress met at New Bern, August, 1774 and again in April, 1775 to take positive action. The Assembly also met and dissolved, ending royal rule in the state, April, 1775. Martin escaped on a British warship. He died April 13, 1786 in England.

GOVERNORS OF THE STATE OF NORTH CAROLINA

Caswell, Richard, 1776–1780; 1784–1787. Born August 3, 1729 in Cecil County, Maryland. Moved to North Carolina in 1746. Served as Orange County court clerk; Colonial Assembly member 17 years; active in civil and military affairs during the Revolution. After his first term as governor, was state comptroller 3 years, then elected governor again. He favored a strong central government, though he was a political moderate. Was a Constitutional Convention delegate, 1787. Served in State Senate and was presiding when he was stricken with paralysis. He died November 10, 1789.

Nash, Abner, 1780–1781. Born in Prince Edward County, 1740. Moved to North Carolina at age 23; elected to General Assembly, 1764; active patriot; council of safety member; New Bern's delegate to four provincial congresses. Representation based on property holdings instead of population, conflicts between conservatives and radicals, and the Revolutionary War made his term as governor difficult. Served in Continental Congress from 1781 until death in 1786.

Burke, Thomas, 1781–1782. Born in Galway, Ireland, *c.* 1747, emigrated to Virginia; moved to North Carolina about 1770. Besides being a poet, he was a doctor, lawyer, and a bill collector for merchants. A committee member to prepare a temporary civil government, 1776; helped draft a constitution for the state. Served in Continental Congress; was strong advocate of citizens' and states' rights. Elected governor by General Assembly, 1781; was captured September 12, 1781, and held as prisoner of war until he managed to escape and return to North Carolina. He was criticized severely for violating parole and returning to office. He retired to his home near Hillsborough, bitter and disillusioned. He died in 1783.

Martin, Alexander, 1782–1785; 1789–1792. Born in New Jersey, 1740. Was lawyer; justice of the peace; Royal Attorney; judge; Colonial Assembly member, 1774. Served in Revolutionary War; State Senate, chairman Board of War, 1780, speaker, 1780–1782 and as speaker of the Senate was made acting governor while Governor Burke was held prisoner of war; then elected governor by General Assembly, 1782–1784. Was elected as state's first governor under new federal constitution to three terms, 1789–1792. As governor, he appealed for military readiness, for tolerance of former enemies, and was a strong advocate of education. Was Constitutional Convention delegate; U.S. Congressman, Federalist Party member. He died in 1807.

Caswell, Richard, 1784–1787 (Second Term).

Johnston, Samuel, 1787–1789. Born December 15, 1733 in Scotland; came to North Carolina at age 3. A General Assembly member and superior court clerk. Favored law and order, regulations of lawyers' and officers' fees and measures which would relieve discontent. He opposed the tyranny of the Crown and was a leader of the revolt and the reorganization which followed. As governor he believed in citizens' rights as well as law and order. Was later a director of the United States bank and U.S. Senator. Died 1816.

Martin, Alexander, 1789–1792 (Second Term).

Spaight, Richard Dobbs, Sr., 1792–1795. Born in New Bern, March 25, 1758. Served state legislature, 1781–83; Continental Congress delegate, 1782–85; state representative, 1785–87, speaker of House, 1785. Served House again in 1792, was elected governor by General Assembly, the first native of the state to hold that office. During his term, Raleigh was made state capitol site and Chapel Hill was chosen to be the location of the state university. U.S. Representative, 1798–1801; State Senate, 1801–1802. Was wounded in a duel, September 5, 1802 and died the following day.

Ashe, Samuel, 1795–1798. Born near Beaufort in 1725. Despite having served as an assistant attorney for the Crown, he took sides with the revolutionists. Was president of council of safety; member of committee to draw up the constitution; under new constitution was elected speaker of Senate. Became governor in 1795 after serving 18 years as presiding judge of state superior court. Was also president of the Board of Trustees, University of North Carolina, 1795–1798. Died February 3, 1813.

Davie, William Richardson, 1798–1799. Born in Cumberland County, England on June 22, 1756. Emigrated to South Carolina at age 5. Gained reputation as skillful fighter and resourceful commander during Revolutionary War. A Federalist supporter who was largely responsible for the adoption of the state constitution. He had such a great part in the founding of the University of North Carolina he was titled "father" of the institution. As governor he prosecuted the persons involved in the Tennessee land grant scandal, attempted to settle boundary dispute with South Carolina, and supervised the drawing of the western border of the state. During the War of 1812, he supported the Federalist position. Died November 18, 1820.

Williams, Benjamin, 1799–1802; 1807–1808. Born January 1, 1751 in Johnston County. Was a member of the state convention which ratified the Federal Constitution, 1788. Served U.S. Representatives as a Republican, 1793–1795. As governor, he advocated public education and inland navigation systems to make the state independent of neighboring states' markets. Died July 20, 1814.

Turner, James, 1802-1805. Born December 20, 1766 in Southampon County, Virginia. Moved in 1770 to Warren County, North Carolina. Served with State Volunteers, 1780; House of Commons representative, 1798-1800; State Senate, 1801-1802. Following the death of John Baptista Ashe, governor-elect, Turner was chosen governor by the General Assembly. He sought a public school system which would be financed by state revenue. He also sought transportation improvements but lack of funds prevented very much progress. Died January 15, 1824.

Alexander, Nathaniel, 1805-1807. Born March 5, 1756 in Mecklenburg County. A physician who graduated from Princeton University, 1776. Served 4 years during Revolutionary War as a surgeon; State Senate, 1801-1802; U.S. Representative, 1803-1805. During his term, the number of district courts was increased and district lines were changed. Was a strong advocate for public education and internal improvements and in 1807 he attempted to settle a border dispute with Georgia. Died March 8, 1808 in Salisbury.

Williams, Benjamin, 1807-1808 (Second Term).

Stone, David, 1808-1810. Born February 17, 1770 in Bertie County. Princeton graduate of 1788; became lawyer, 1790; House of Commons, 1790-1795; judge of superior court, 1795-1798; U.S. House of Representatives, 1799-1801; U.S. Senate, 1801-1807. As governor, he urged the expansion of agriculture, the growth of new industries, improvements in transportation and public education. Died October 7, 1818.

Smith, Benjamin, 1810-1811. Born in Brunswick County, January 10, 1756, into wealth and position. He served as aide-de-camp to General Washington during Long Island retreat, 1776; at Moultrie, 1779; defense of South Carolina, 1780. He received 20,000 acres of land in Tennessee for his war efforts, which he donated to the University of North Carolina in 1789 to support its endowment. Served several terms in the State Senate; was speaker, 1795-1799. Served as a member of the first University of North Carolina Board of Trustees. During his term as governor he was in favor of domestic industry; public supported education; encouraged the establishment of a penitentiary system; sought reform of the penal code. Died January 27, 1826.

Hawkins, William, 1811-1814. Born in Pleasant Hill, October 10, 1777. Served as Assistant Indian Agent, 1797; became lawyer, 1801; representative to House of Commons, 1804-1805, 1809-1811; speaker of the House, 1810-1811; three consecutive terms as governor. Served during War of 1812, raised 7,000 volunteers at President Madison's request. When a British fleet arrived at New Bern, he personally inspected the coastal defenses, urging unity from within to meet the threat. Major concerns during his tenure were agriculture, public education, industry, roads and transportation. Died May 17, 1819.

Miller, William, 1814–1817. Born in Warren County, *c.* 1770. Served as state attorney general, 1810; House of Commons, 1810–1814, speaker of the House, 1812–1814. Lack of adequate transportation and public education were problems Governor Miller recognized and made an effort to solve during his term. Served as president of the North Carolina Board of Trustees, 1814–1817. He was the first occupant of the governor's mansion. Was state senator, 1821–1822. President John Quincy Adams appointed him United States Charge d'Affaires to Guatemala, March, 1825, and he died the same year while on that mission.

Branch, John, 1817–1820. Born November 4, 1782 in Halifax County. Graduated with A.B. from the University of North Carolina, 1801; served in State Senate, 1811, 1813–1817, speaker, 1815–1817; and three terms as governor. He strived for internal improvements and sought a less severe penal code, reducing capital offenses and eliminating imprisonment for debt. The State Supreme Court was formed in 1818 because of his call for increasing and improving of the superior court. Served in U.S. Senate, 1823–1829; was appointed to President Andrew Jackson's cabinet as secretary of the Navy, the first North Carolinian to be appointed to a federal cabinet position. He served as governor of the Florida Territory, 1844–1845, having been appointed by President Tyler. He was the last governor before Florida attained statehood. He died January 4, 1863 in Halifax County.

Franklin, Jesse, 1820–1821. Born March 24, 1760, in Orange County, Virginia. About 1778, he and his family moved to Surry County, North Carolina. Served in Revolutionary Army; promoted to major after outstanding service at King's Mountain and at Guilford Courthouse. Served in House of Commons; U.S. Representative, 1795–1797; U.S. Senate, 1799–1805, President Pro Tempore of Senate, 1804; State Senate, 1805–1806; U.S. Senate, 1806–1813. As governor, he sought improvements in the court system, revision of the penal codes, and abolishment of the practice of ear cropping of perjurers. Was in favor of public education and sought state militia reorganization. Died September, 1823 in Surry County.

Holmes, Gabriel, 1821–1824. Born in 1769 near Clinton, in Sampson County. Served House of Commons, 1793–1795; State Senate, 1797, 1801–1802, 1812–1813; University of North Carolina Board of Trustees; Council of State, 1810, 1814–1816. Sought funding for education, also internal improvements but the monies were spread out into so many areas that large gains in any one area were hampered. Died September 26, 1829 in Sampson County.

Burton, Hutchins Gordon, 1824-1827. Born *c.* 1774 in Virginia. Following his father's death, he was raised by his uncle in Granville County, North Carolina. Became lawyer, 1806; House of Commons, 1809; state attorney general, 1810-1816; U.S. Representative, 1819-1824. As governor he stressed the need for public education on the primary level in preference to higher learning. He served 3 terms. Died April 21, 1836; buried in Lincoln County.

Iredell, James, Jr., 1827-1828. Born in Chowan County November 2, 1788. In War of 1812, he commanded a volunteer company in defense of Norfolk, Virginia. Served in House of Commons, 1813, 1816-1820; speaker of the House, 1816-1818; superior court judge. Took office as governor December 1827. He sought internal improvements, namely the building of railroads, development of a coastal port and drainage of the swamps. Served in U.S. Senate, 1828-1831. Died April 13, 1853 in Edenton.

Owen, John, 1828-1830. Born in Bladen County August 1787. Served House of Commons, 1812-1814; State Senate, 1819-1820; council of state, 1824-1827; State Senate, 1827-1828. As governor, he proposed taxing the wealthy land owners to help fund education; also sought internal improvements. Died October 9, 1841, in Chatham County.

Stokes, Montford, 1830-1832. Born March 12, 1762 in Virginia. Was Merchant Marine; served in Continental Navy; was captain of a merchant ship following War of 1812; eventually settled in North Carolina. Served in U.S. Senate, 1816-1823; was president of a convention in Raleigh which attempted to secure more equal representation in the legislature. Was state senator, 1829; House of Commons, 1830. Became governor, December 1830; urged internal improvements and stressed the importance of sound currency. Was appointed to Federal Indian Commission, 1832, by President Andrew Jackson, to supervise the settlement of southeastern Indians in the West. Died in Arkansas, November 4, 1842.

Swain, David Lowry, 1832-1835. Born in Buncombe County, January 4, 1801. Member of the House of Commons, 1824-1830; state superior court judge, 1830-1832. Was the youngest governor; first Whig to serve. He favored the building of railroads; internal improvements; state control and financing of major projects. During his term he was made president of the University of North Carolina, and the University prospered and enrollment increased from 90 to 500. Became state agent responsible for collecting historical material in 1854; was the founder of the State Historical Society; created the first historical museum prior to the founding of the North Carolina Historical Commission. Died August 27, 1868 in Chapel Hill.

Spaight, Richard Dobbs, Jr., 1835-1836 (Democrat). Born in 1796 in New Bern, son of Governor Spaight who served from 1792-1795. Served

House of Commons, 1819; State Senate, 1820–1822; U.S. Representative, 1823. Was the last governor to be elected by the General Assembly. He believed that few improvements were completed because there was a conflict between individual projects, and opposed the religious test for persons in office. Died November 2, 1850.

Dudley, Edward Bishop, 1836–1841 (Whig). Born in New Hanover County on December 15, 1789. Served in House of Commons, 1811–1813; State Senate, 1814; U.S. Representative, 1829–1831. Was the first governor selected by popular vote. During his term, a homestead exemption act was favored because of an agricultural decline. He also sought development of a transportation system, road construction, and the opening of the inlet at Nags Head. Died October 30, 1855.

Morehead, John Motley, 1841–1845 (Whig). Born in Virginia, July 4, 1796; brought to North Carolina at age 2. Served House of Commons, 1821–1822; 1826–1828; became a life member of the Board of Trustees, University of North Carolina in 1828. During his tenure in office, he sought agricultural, educational, and industrial development as well as the improvement of canals, railroad lines and turnpike construction. Died August 27, 1866.

Graham, William Alexander, 1845–1849 (Whig). Born September 5, 1804 in Lincoln County. Served in state legislature, 1833–1840; speaker of the House, 1838–1840; U.S. Senate, 1840–1843. As governor, he was displeased that the stress was on national concerns instead of state affairs. He sought educational developments, and institutions for the deaf, dumb, blind and insane. A school for the deaf and dumb was opened in 1845. Appointed secretary of the Navy by President Fillmore, 1850–1852. Was defeated in his bid for the office of Vice President on the Whig ticket with General Winfield Scott. Died August 11, 1875.

Manly, Charles, 1849–1850 (Whig). Born May 13, 1795 in Chatham County. Clerk of claims settling commission under Treaty of Ghent, 1823; Board of Trustees, University of North Carolina, 1828–1868; House of Commons clerk, 1831–1841, 1844–1847; presidential elector, 1840. As governor, he favored internal improvements, particularly canals and railways, also popular education. During his term, an asylum bill was passed, providing for more humane treatment of the insane. Died May 1, 1871.

Reid, David Settle, 1851–1854 (Democrat). Born in Rockingham County, April 19, 1813. Served in State Senate, 1835–1841; U.S. Representative, 1843–1847. He ran twice for the office of governor on the issue of free suffrage but was defeated the first time. He was strongly opposed to the fact that only landholders were allowed to vote in State Senate elections. He was pro-slavery and against federal interference. Served in U.S. Senate, 1854–1859. Died June 19, 1891.

Winslow, Warren, 1854–1855 (Democrat). Born in Fayetteville, January 1, 1810. Served as speaker of State Senate, 1854–1855. When Governor Reid resigned, Winslow became governor until the next election, less than a month later. Served as U.S. Representative, 1855–1861. Died August 16, 1862.

Bragg, Thomas, 1855–1859 (Democrat). Born in Warren County, November 9, 1810. Served in House of Commons, 1842–1843. During his administration his interests included state railway expansion, internal improvements, and a geological survey of the state. In many ways, this was a time of increasing prosperity. Served in U.S. Senate, 1858–1861; attorney general of the Confederacy. Died January 19, 1872 in Raleigh.

Ellis, John Willis, 1859–1861 (Democrat). Born November 23, 1820 in Rowan County. Served in House of Commons, 1844–1849; superior court judge, 1848–1858. Was candidate of the slaveholding gentry; advocated being prepared for war. The ordinance of secession was passed on May 20, 1861 and the offer of assistance was made to the Confederacy. Forced to retire from office for health reasons, he died July 7, 1861.

Clark, Henry Toole, 1861–1862 (Democrat). Born in Edgecombe County, February 7, 1808. Served in State Senate, 1850–1861; speaker of the Senate, 1858–1861. When Ellis was forced to retire, Clark, as speaker of the Senate, finished out his term. He did much to prepare the state for war but the convention had put an end to volunteering and there was not an adequate defense when it was needed most. Served in State Senate, 1866–1867. Died April 14, 1874.

Vance, Zebulon, 1862–1865; 1877–1879 (Conservative). Born in Buncombe County, May 13, 1830. Served in House of Commons, 1854–1855; co-editor of the Asheville *Spectator,* 1855; U.S. Representative, 1858–1861. He served briefly, but honorably, in the war before being elected overwhelmingly as governor. As governor, he made a serious effort to keep railroads, schools and courts operating despite being labeled as a Northern sympathizer by the Confederacy. His greatest disagreement with the Confederacy was his refusal to allow state officials to be drafted. The hiring of women teachers, normal schools for both races, and expansion of the railroads were goals during his second term. Served in U.S. Senate, 1879–1893. Died April 14, 1894.

Holden, William Woods, 1865; 1868–1870. Born in Orange County, November 24, 1818. After having worked for 2 newspapers, the Hillsborough *Recorder* and the Raleigh *Star,* he was offered and accepted the position of editor of the North Carolina *Standard* in exchange for his becoming a Democrat. It became the most influential newspaper in the state. Served in House of Commons, 1846–1847. After losing the Democratic nomination for governor in 1858, he changed political affiliations more than once. He was appointed provisional governor on May 29, 1865 by President Johnson. He was directed by the President to convene a state convention to repeal secession, abolish slavery and set new elections to replace the provisional government. He was defeated in his bid for governor but was elected in 1868. Although he didn't gain anything, his administration was one of corruption and mismanagement. On March 23, 1871, he was convicted on 6 of 8 counts of impeachment for high crimes and misdemeanors and forbidden to hold state office again. Died March 1, 1892.

Worth, Jonathan, 1865–1868 (Conservative). Born November 18, 1802. As an opponent of nulllification, was elected to House of Commons, 1830–1832; State Senate, 1840–1841. In 1862 was appointed by legislature to be public treasurer and was successful in reducing the state debt by redeeming a large percentage of bonds. As governor, he agreed with President Johnson's reconstruction policies. Died September 6, 1869.

Holden, William Woods, 1868–1870 (Second Term).

Caldwell, Tod Robinson, 1870–1874 (Republican). Born in Burke County, February 19, 1818. Served in House of Commons, 1842–1845, 1848–1849, 1858–1859; State Senate, 1850–1851. Was elected as the first lieutenant governor, serving with Governor Holden and became governor when Holden was impeached. As governor, he sought to reopen the schools closed by war, with emphasis on lower instead of higher levels; revive the state's finances and attempt to settle the state debt. Died while still in office, July 11, 1874.

Brogden, Curtis Hooks, 1874–1877 (Republican). Born in Wayne County, November 6, 1816. After serving in the House of Commons, 1838–1851; State Senate, 1852–1857, 1868–1872; was elected lieutenant governor, 1872 and became governor when Tod Caldwell died. He affirmed every citizen's right to an education, was helpful in getting the University of North Carolina reopened, called for a state Negro college to be founded, sought revisions in the penal code, the building of a state penitentiary and expansion of the railroad system. Was U.S. Representative, 1877–1879. Died January 5, 1901.

Vance, Zebulon, 1877–1879 (Second Term).

Jarvis, Thomas Jordan, 1879–1885 (Democrat). Born in Currituck County, January 18, 1836. Received LL.D. from the University of North Carolina, 1833; opened a school in Pasquotank County. Served in Civil War, was permanently disabled at the battle of Drewry's Bluff in Virginia; State Representative, 1868–1872; speaker of the House, 1870–1872. When Vance resigned, Jarvis, as lieutenant governor took over the office. He favored increased spending for agriculture, education and care of the insane; also settlement of the state debt. Was appointed as ambassador to Brazil by

President Cleveland, 1885–1889. Served in U.S. Senate, 1894–1895. Died June 17, 1915.

Robinson, James Lowry, 1883 (Democrat). Born in Macon County, September 17, 1838. Served in Civil War, 1861–1863, wounded at Battle of Seven Pines. Served as State Representative, 1868–1875, 1885; House speaker, 1872–1875; State Senate, 1876–1877, 1879–1880; President Pro Tempore, 1876–1877; president, 1879–1880. When Governor Jarvis left the state temporarily to attend an exposition, Robinson, as lieutenant governor was sworn into office and he served 4 weeks (Sept. 1–Sept. 28, 1883). As governor, he granted pardons to a dying Cherokee in state prison, and a murderer whom he believed had acted in self-defense. Died in 1887.

Scales, Alfred Moore, 1885–1889 (Democrat). Born in Rockingham County, November 26, 1827. Served in General Assembly, 1852, 1856–1857; House of Representatives, 1857–1859. Served in Civil War and was twice severely wounded; U.S. Congress, 1875–1884. As governor, his interests included extending the school term to 6 months; better teachers; using federal surplus to help fund education; increased railroad expansion and using convicts to help build state roads. Died February 9, 1892.

Fowle, David Gould, 1889–1891 (Democrat). Born in Beaufort County, March 13, 1831. Served in the Civil War alternately with serving in House of Commons, 1862, 1864–1865. As governor he sought the creation of a railroad commission to protect the state against any misuse of the railways power while still allowing for their further expansion. He advocated financing longer school terms by increasing county land taxes. Died while still in office, April 7, 1891.

Holt, Thomas Michael, 1891–1893 (Democrat). Born July 15, 1831, in Alamance County. Was a businessman; served in State Senate, 1876–1877; House of Representatives, 1883, 1885, 1887; House speaker, 1885; lieutenant governor, 1889; president of the Senate, 1889–1891. Became governor when Fowle died. He favored education, including the deaf; helped in the establishment of the State Department of Agriculture; and helped resolve the state debt. Died April 11, 1896.

Carr, Elias, 1893–1897 (Democrat). Born in Edgecombe County, February 25, 1839. During the Civil War, he served in a cavalry regiment. Became involved with the agrarian movement in the 1880s; was president of the Farmers Alliance of North Carolina, 1890. As governor, his emphasis was on education, particularly rural schools and universities; road improvements; and he personally inspected the prisons and convict farms, as well as other state institutions. Died July 22, 1900.

Russell, Daniel Lindsay, 1897–1901 (Republican). Born in Brunswick County, August 7, 1845. Enlisted in a county regiment and was elected captain when the Civil War began, but following an altercation with another officer was court-martialed in 1863. Served in House of Commons, 1864-1865; superior court judge, ruled that blacks could not be barred from public places, 1873; House of Representatives, 1876-1877; U.S. Representative, 1879-1881. As governor, he favored increased education aid, higher taxes for corporations, and legislation to prevent monopolies. Died May 14, 1908.

Aycock, Charles Brantley, 1901-1905 (Democrat). Born in Wayne County, November 1, 1859. A lawyer; co-founder of Goldsboro *Daily Argus* in 1885; was known as the educational governor; sought equal educational opportunities for both races; school terms were lengthened by one month; three colleges were founded; 3,459 schoolhouses were built; teachers' salaries were increased; and illiteracy declined among both races. He was noted for his interest in education, and died while delivering a speech to the Alabama Education Association, April 4, 1912.

Glenn, Robert Broadnax, 1905-1909 (Democrat). Born in Rockingham County, August 11, 1854. Elected to State House of Representatives, 1880; appointed by President Cleveland as U.S. Attorney for the Western District, 1892; State Senate, 1898. A mandatory four month school term; compulsory school attendance; statewide prohibition; lowering of railroad passenger rates and a utilization of water power resources were some of the highlights of his administration as governor. Known as a defender of prohibition, he was later legal advisor to Western Union and Southern Railways. Served on the International Boundary Commission for President Wilson, 1920. Died May 16, 1920.

Kitchin, William Walton, 1909-1913 (Democrat). Born in Halifax County, October 9, 1866. Wake Forest College graduate, 1884; Scotland Neck *Democrat* editor, 1885; taught school periodically; U.S. Representative, 1897-1909. As governor he sought regulation of power companies and public service corporations; factory sanitation; enforcement of child labor laws which prevented employers from hiring children under thirteen; stricter railroad regulations; public political disclosure; and the establishment of a highway commission. Died November 9, 1924.

Craig, Locke, 1913-1917 (Democrat). Born in Bertie County, August 16, 1860. Served in State House of Representatives, 1899, 1901; practiced law in Asheville, 1903-1912. The highway commission sought by the previous administration was instituted in this administration. Other accomplishments include the purchase of Mt. Mitchell, expanding the state park system; school district consolidation; longer school terms; compulsory attendance; legislation for fixed railway rates; and conservation measures were enacted. Died June 9, 1924.

Bickett, Thomas Walter, 1917-1921 (Democrat). Born in Union County,

February 28, 1869. A Wake Forest graduate; taught school 2 years before entering law school; state representative, 1907–1908, sponsored bill making the state legally responsible for the care of the insane; state attorney general, 1909–1917; represented the state before the U.S. Supreme Court in five cases, winning them all, including one pertaining to a border dispute with Tennessee. The establishment of juvenile courts; strengthening of child labor laws; expanded public health services; prison reforms; compulsory school attendance age raised to 14; and a longer school term (6 months) were advancements made during his administration. School curriculums included manual training, home economics, and agricultural courses; home ownership was encouraged; running water and electricity became available in rural areas and tax reforms were all part of this time of modernization. Died December 22, 1921.

Morrison, Cameron, 1921–1925 (Democrat). Born in Richmond County, October 5, 1869. Was Rockingham mayor; State Senator, 1901. During his term, the state's primary road system was developed, with funds for paving coming from taxes on gasoline and automobiles. Also funds were allocated to higher learning; a loan fund was begun for county schools; and banking laws were strengthened. He called for state troops to restore order during the mill strikes, 1921, and the railway strikes, 1922. Served in U.S. Senate, 1930–1932; U.S. Representative, 1943–1945. Died August 20, 1953.

McLean, Angus Wilton, 1925–1929 (Democrat). Born April 20, 1870 in Robeson (now Hoke) County. Was an active member of the Democratic Party; state chairman of Woodrow Wilson's campaign, 1912, 1916; National Democratic Executive Committee, 1916–1924; State Bar Association president, 1917; Assistant Secretary of the Treasury, 1920–1921. As governor, he sought to have sound fiscal management and state government efficiency, and the Department of Revenue was established. The Department of Conservation and Development and the office of Pardon Commissioner were created, and he sought the passage of a bill to establish the Great Smoky Mountains National Park as well as a Salary and Wage Commission. Reestablishing the state's credit was his greatest accomplishment. Died June 21, 1935.

Gardner, Oliver Max, 1929–1933 (Democrat). Born March 22, 1882 and raised in Cleveland County by his sisters, following the death of his parents. Elected to State Senate, 1911, 1915; President Pro Tempore, 1915; lieutenant governor, 1917–1921; State Board of Agriculture, 1921–1939. As governor, he had the problems of industrial strife and the depression to contend with, but he reduced the state budget, centralized governmental functions; and the State Tax Commission was created. Also he abolished chain gangs, introduced a secret ballot law and a workmen's compensation bill; and consolidated the University of North Carolina, North Carolina State College, and North Carolina College for Women into a unified system, an accomplishment of which he was justly proud. Served as chairman of the advisory board of the Office of War Mobilization and Reconversion, 1944; Undersecretary of the Treasury, 1946. He was appointed by President Truman as ambassador to Great Britain but he died before reaching England, February 6, 1947.

Ehringhaus, John Christoph Blucher, 1933–1937 (Democrat). Born in Pasquotank County, February 5, 1882. Served as state representative, 1905, 1907–1908. As governor, he reduced the state deficit, sought to balance the state budget, and there was a surplus of over 5 million dollars when he left office. The state assumed control of public schools; the school term was lengthened to 8 months; and a school book rental system was set up. The prisons were improved and penal reform was sponsored. He later served as special assistant to the U.S. District Attorney. Died July 31, 1949.

Hoey, Clyde Roark, 1937–1941 (Democrat). Born December 11, 1877. He quit school and went to work with the Shelby *Aurora* as a printer's devil at age 12. Began his own newspaper, the Cleveland *Star,* at age 16, when he purchased the bankrupt Shelby *Review.* Studied law; admitted to the bar, 1899. Elected to State House of Representatives before he was legal voting age, 1899–1900, 1901; State Senate, 1903; U.S. Representative, 1919–1921. During his administration as governor, he favored educational measures; increased expenditures for schools thirty percent; granted pay raises for teachers; started Negro college graduate programs; and free textbooks were provided in the elementary schools at his recommendation. Other improvements include the establishment of the State Bureau of Investigation, the Alcoholic Beverage Board of Control, state highway system expansion; tourist and industry promotional programs; and a modern prison parole system. Served in the U.S. Senate from 1945 until his death, May 12, 1954.

Broughton, Joseph Melville, 1941–1945 (Democrat). Born November 17, 1888, in Wake County. After receiving a law degree, he served as principal of Bunn High School, 1910–1912; Winston-Salem *Journal* staff reporter; Raleigh school board member; state senator, 1927–1931. As governor, he supported domestic reform; a better health program; aid to public libraries; black and white teachers' salary equalization; school term lengthened to 9 months; twelfth grade added to schools; agricultural aid increases and greater funding for mental institutions. He served in the U.S. Senate the last 3 months of his life. Died March 6, 1949.

Cherry, Robert Gregg, 1945–1949 (Democrat). Born in York County, October 17, 1891. Raised by his maternal grandparents following the death of his mother. Served in World War I, saw action in France; Mayor of Gastonia, 1919–1923; State Representative, 1931–1941, speaker of the House, 1937–1939. During his term as governor, school expenditures were increased road construction was expanded; but health problems were his main concern and the Good Health Association, which promoted the building of hospitals and clinics, was formed during his administration, and supervised the changing of Camp Butner into a center for the mentally ill. Died June 25, 1957.

Scott, William Kerr, 1949–1953 (Democrat). Born in Alamance County, April 17, 1896. Served in World War I; became farmer; State Farm Agent, 1920–1930; Master of State Grange, 1930–1933; State Commissioner of Agriculture, 1937–1948. As governor, he introduced a "Go Forward" program, using state revenue surplus to fund construction of hospitals and schools; assistance to handicapped, dependent and aged; improvements in care of mentally ill. Appointed first black to Board of Education and supervised modern deep water port construction at Wilmington and Morehead City. Served in U.S. Senate from 1954 until his death, April 16, 1958.

Umstead, William Bradley, 1953–1954 (Democrat). Born in Durham County, May 13, 1895. Was a Kinston school teacher; served in World War I; U.S. Representative, 1933–1939; U.S. Senate, 1947–1948. He suffered a heart attack 2 days after assuming office but determined to serve, he sought to reorganize the Board of Paroles; industrial growth; and presided over the Department of Conservation and Development. He urged moderation on the school desegregation issue, although he criticized the 1954 Supreme Court decision as an invasion of states' rights. Died while in office, November 7, 1954.

Hodges, Luther Hartwell, 1954–1961 (Democrat). Born in Pittsylvania County, Virginia, March 9, 1898. Moved to North Carolina at age three. Served in World War I; was a successful businessman, active in Rotary affairs, 1923–1945, International Convention chairman, 1948. Was elected lieutenant governor, 1952; president of State Senate, 1953; assumed office of governor upon death of William Umstead. As governor, he advocated law and order in the school desegregation issue and made every effort to keep the schools open. He worked to encourage industries to locate in the state. The Research Triangle, a laboratory center between Duke University, University of North Carolina, and North Carolina State College, was incorporated in 1956. Was appointed by President Kennedy as Secretary of Commerce, 1961–1965. Died October 6, 1974.

Sanford, Terry, 1961–1965 (Democrat). Born August 20, 1917, in Scotland County. After working for the Federal Bureau of Investigation for two years, he served and was decorated in World War II. Served as state senator, 1953. As governor, he strongly supported education; seeking community colleges, a school for the gifted, a school of arts; also more teachers, increased teacher salaries, library expansions, and improved curriculum. The greatest industrial growth occurred during his term. Was appointed president of Duke University, 1969.

Moore, Dan Killian, 1965–1969 (Democrat). Born in Buncombe County, April 2, 1906. Was elected state representative, 1941; served in World War II, 1943–1945; superior court judge, 1950–1958; State Board of Water Resources member, 1959–1964. Highway safety, education, agricultural problems, recreation, conservation, and improved health care were some of his concerns as governor. State services were expanded and he traveled to promote industrial growth. During his administration a $300 million road bond issue was passed.

Scott, Robert Walker, 1969–1973 (Democrat). Born in Alamance County, June 13, 1929. Was the son of William Kerr Scott, governor of the state, 1949–1953. Was a dairy farmer, active in National and State Grange, also agricultural organizations. Member of the U.S. Army Counter Intelligence Corps, 1953–1955; lieutenant governor, 1965–1969; president of State Senate, 1965–1967. As governor, he raised large sums of money for education with the passage of tobacco and soft drink tax legislation which he recommended. Gasoline taxes made vast highway expansion possible. Free transportation for handicapped people; kindergartens; high school vocational programs; community college and technical school system expansion were accomplishments of his administration.

Holshouser, James Eubert, Jr., 1973–1977 (Republican). Born October 8, 1934 in Watauga County. Served in State House of Representatives, 1963, 1965–1966, 1969 and 1971; House Minority Leader and Chairman of Republican State Executive Committee, 1966–1972; state campaign manager for Richard Nixon, 1968. Became the first Republican governor since 1896. As governor he wanted the state's financial matters conducted with sound business principles. To promote economy and improve services an Efficient Study Commission was begun. He sought to increase foreign trade; develop a modern transportation system, including a mass transit system; and pledged open communications and more involvement with the press and minority groups. He also called for educational and state parks improvements.

Hunt, James Baxter, 1977–1985 (Democrat). Born in Guilford County, May 16, 1937. Went to Nepal as economic advisor, sponsored by the Ford Foundation, 1964–1966; State Young Democratic Clubs president, 1968; elected lieutenant governor, 1972. As governor, he hoped to remove every trace of discrimination, and have a new beginning. He sought a utilities regulation structure that better suited consumer needs; called for reading to be taught with greater emphasis in the public schools. A black and a woman were appointed to high level posts.

Martin, James G., 1985– (Republican). Born in Chatham County, Georgia, December 11, 1935. Was raised in South Carolina. Served as professor of chemistry at Davidson College, after receiving his doctorate in chemistry from Princeton University in 1960. Was Mecklenburg County Commissioner; commission chairman; president of North Carolina Association of County Commissioners; elected U.S. Representative, 1972, served six terms; Ways and Means Committee member; House Republican Research Committee chairman; became first elected official to receive the Charles Lathrop Parsons Award, given by the American Chemical Society for outstanding public service by an American chemist. He is the second Republican governor to be elected in this century.

HIGHER EDUCATION

Higher education in the state had its beginning in 1795 when the University of North Carolina at Chapel Hill, the oldest state university in the nation, first began with a faculty of 2 and a class of 41. With 16 campuses across the state, the University of North Carolina system educates more than 120,000 students. The average tuition is about $700 per year for state residents, due to strong financial support by the state.

There are 38 private colleges and universities, with a total enrollment of approximately 53,000 additional students. Nearly $20 million is appropriated to these schools annually by the North Carolina Legislature to help equal the funding between public and private colleges and universities.

Among the nation's top research universities are UNC-Chapel Hill, North Carolina State University in Raleigh and Duke University in Durham. Within the state there are five law schools and four major medical schools. Business administration degrees are offered at nine UNC campuses. More than 1,600 engineers graduate each year from the state's engineering schools. There are four medical schools in North Carolina which graduate more than 400 new doctors each year.

One out of seven adults in the state, about 600,000 people, are enrolled in the 58 community colleges, technical colleges and technical institutes. Nearly the entire population, 99 percent, live within 30 minutes of a community college or technical institue. Anyone 18 or older, regardless of whether they completed high school, is eligible for admission, and the cost is minimal.

Each of the community colleges is administered locally by a board under the guidance of the state Board of Community Colleges. The address and phone number of this department is: Department of Community Colleges, Raleigh, 27611, 919-733-7051.

The North Carolina Industrial Training Program is entirely funded by the state. More than $12 million was appropriated by the state legislature for the 1983–1985 biennium. For any new or expanding plant that creates as many as 12 new jobs, the industrial training service is available as long as a company creates enough new jobs to justify the state's investment. About 150,000 people have been trained in this system since 1957.

Higher education is also accessible to the handicapped; all campuses of the University of North Carolina system offer special assistance. Educating the handicapped has become a special mission at St. Andrews Presbyterian College in Laurinburg, where severely disabled students live in a rehabilitation center on campus.

PUBLIC INSTITUTIONS

● **Universities**

1 Appalachian State University
Boone 28608
2 East Carolina University
East Fifth Street, Greenville 27834
3 Elizabeth City State University
P.O. Box 172, Elizabeth City 27909
4 Fayetteville State University
Fayetteville 28301
5 North Carolina Agricultural and Technical State University
1600 East Market Street, Greensboro 27411
6 North Carolina Central University
Durham 27707
7 North Carolina School of the Arts
200 Waughtown Street, Winston-Salem 27117
8 North Carolina State University at Raleigh
Box 7103, Raleigh 27695
9 Pembroke State University
Pembroke 28372
10 University of North Carolina at Asheville
Asheville 28814
11 University of North Carolina at Chapel Hill
Chapel Hill 27514
12 University of North Carolina at Charlotte
Charlotte 28223
13 University of North Carolina at Greensboro
Greensboro 27412
14 University of North Carolina at Wilmington
601 South College Road, Wilmington 28403
15 Western Carolina University
Cullowhee 28723
16 Winston-Salem State University
Winston-Salem 27102

○ **Community Colleges and Technical Institutes**

17 Anson Technical College
Ansonville 28007
18 Asheville-Buncombe Technical College
Asheville 28801
19 Beaufort County Community College
Washington 27889
20 Bladen Technical College
Dublin 28332
21 Blue Ridge Technical College
Flat Rock 28731
22 Brunswick Technical College
P.O. Box 30, Supply 28462
23 Caldwell Community College and Technical Institute
Lenoir 28645
24 Cape Fear Technical Institute
Wilmington 28401
25 Carteret Technical College
Morehead City 28557
26 Catawba Valley Technical College
Highway 64–70, Hickory 28601
27 Central Carolina Technical College
1105 Kelly Drive, Sanford 27330
28 Central Piedmont Community College
1141 Elizabeth Avenue, Charlotte 28235
29 Cleveland Technical College
137 South Post Road, Shelby 28150
30 Coastal Carolina Community College
Jacksonville 28540
31 College of the Albemarle
Riverside Avenue, Elizabeth City 27909
32 Craven Community College
New Bern 28560
33 Davidson County Community College
Davidson 28036

34 Durham Technical Institute
1637 Lawson Street, Durham 27703
35 Edgecombe Technical College
P.O. Box 550, Tarboro 27886
36 Fayetteville Technical Institute
P.O. Box 35236, Fayetteville 28303
37 Forsyth Technical Institute
2100 Silas Creek Parkway, Winston-Salem 27103
38 Gaston College
Dallas 28034
39 Guilford Technical Community College
P.O. Box 309, Jamestown 27282
40 Halifax Community College
Weldon 27890
41 Haywood Technical College
Clyde 28721
42 Isothermal Community College
P.O. Box 804, Spindale 28160
43 James Sprunt Technical College
P.O. Box 398, Kenansville 28349
44 Johnston Technical College
Smithfield 27577
45 Lenoir Community College
P.O. Box 188, Kinston 28501
46 Martin Community College
Kehukee Park Road, Williamston 27892
47 Mayland Technical College
P.O. Box 547, Spruce Pine 28777
48 McDowell Technical College
Marion 28752
49 Mitchell Community College
Statesville 28677
50 Montgomery Technical College
P.O. Drawer 487, Troy 27371
51 Nash Technical Institute
Rocky Mount 27801
52 Pamlico Technical College
Grantsboro 28529
53 Piedmont Technical College
P.O. Box 1197, Roxboro 27573
54 Pitt Community College
P.O. Drawer 7007, Greenville 27834
55 Randolph Technical College
P.O. Box 1009, Asheboro 27203
56 Richmond Technical College
Rockingham 28379
57 Roanoke-Chowan Technical College
Ahoskie 27910
58 Robeson Technical College
Lumberton 28358
59 Rockingham Community College
Wentworth 27375
60 Rowan Technical College
I-85 at Klumac Road, Salisbury 28144
61 Sampson Technical College
Clinton 28328
62 Sandhills Community College
Carthage 28327
63 Southeastern Community College
Whiteville 28472
64 Southwestern Technical College
P.O. Box 67, Sylva 28779
65 Stanly Technical College
Albemarle 28001
66 Surry Community College
Dobson 27017
67 Technical College of Alamance
Haw River 27258
68 Tri-County Community College
Murphy 28906
69 Vance-Granville Community College
Henderson 27536
70 Wake Technical College
9101 Fayetteville Road, Raleigh 27603
71 Wayne Community College
P.O. Box 8002, Goldsboro 27530
72 Western Piedmont Community College
Morganton 28655
73 Wilkes Community College
Wilkesboro 28697
74 Wilson County Technical Institute
902 Herring Avenue, Wilson 27893

PRIVATE INSTITUTIONS

▲ Senior Colleges and Universities

75 Atlantic Christian College
Wilson 27893
76 Barber-Scotia College
Concord 28025
77 Belmont Abbey College
Belmont 28012
78 Bennett College
Greensboro 27420
79 Campbell University
P.O. Box 546, Buies Creek 27506

80 Catawba College
2300 W. Innes St., Salisbury
28144

81 Davidson College
Davidson 28036

82 Duke University
Durham 27706

83 Elon College
Elon College 27244

84 Gardner-Webb College
Boiling Springs 28017

85 Greensboro College
815 W. Market Street,
Greensboro 27401-1875

86 Guilford College
5800 West Friendly Avenue,
Guilford College 27410

87 High Point College
933 Montlieu Ave., High Point
27262

88 Johnson C. Smith University
100 Beatties Ford Road,
Charlotte 28216

89 Lenoir-Rhyne College
Hickory 28603

90 Livingstone College
Salisbury 28144

91 Mars Hill College
Mars Hill 27854

92 Meredith College
3800 Hillsborough Street,
Raleigh 27607

93 Methodist College
Raleigh Road, Fayetteville 28301

94 North Carolina Wesleyan College
Wesleyan College Station,
Rocky Mount 27801

95 Pfeiffer College
Misenheimer 28109

96 Queens College
1900 Selwyn Avenue, Charlotte
28274

97 Sacred Heart College
Belmont 28012

98 St. Andrews Presbyterian College
Laurinburg 28352

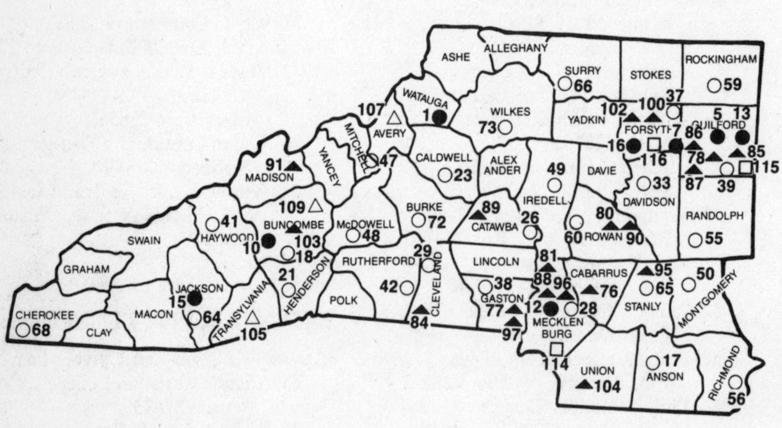

Higher Education

99 St. Augustine's College
Raleigh 27611
100 Salem College
P.O. Box 10548
Winston-Salem 27108
101 Shaw University
Raleigh 27611
102 Wake Forest University
Reynolds Station, Winston-Salem 27109
103 Warren Wilson College
701 Warren Wilson Road,
Swannanoa 28778
104 Wingate College
Wingate 28174

△ Junior Colleges

105 Brevard College
Brevard 28712
106 Chowan College
Murfreesboro 27855
107 Lees-McRae College
Banner Elk 28604
108 Louisburg College
501 North Main Street,
Louisburg 27549
109 Montreat-Anderson College
Montreat 28757
110 Mount Olive College
Mount Olive 28365
111 Peace College
Raleigh 27804
112 St. Mary's College
900 Hillsborough Street, Raleigh 27611

■ Theological Seminary

113 Southeastern Baptist Theological Seminary
Wake Forest 27587

□ Bible Colleges

114 East Coast Bible College
115 John Wesley College
924 Eastchester Drive,
High Point 27260
116 Piedmont Bible College
716 Franklin Street,
Winston-Salem 27101
117 Roanoke Bible College
Elizabeth City 27909

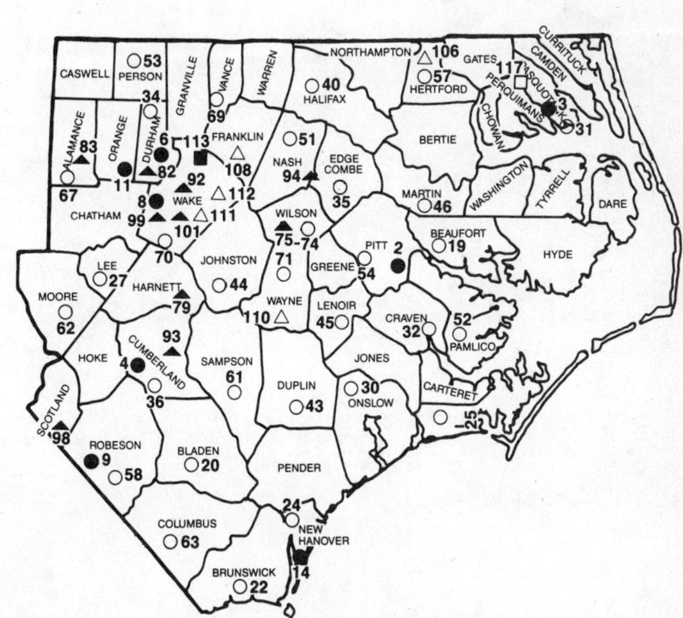

Years of school completed for persons 25 years old and over by race, by county, 1980.

County	Total Persons 25 Years & Over	White			Black			Other Races		
		Elementary (0–8 Years)	High School (1–4 Years)	College (1 or More Years)	Elementary (0–8 Years)	High School (1–4 Years)	College (1 or More Years)	Elementary (0–8 Years)	High School (1–4 Years)	College (1 or More Years)
State Total	3,403,219	595,785	312,832	794,752	225,438	314,269	112,455	14,397	21,314	11,977
Alamance	61,025	10,713	25,865	13,926	3,342	5,506	1,422	83	82	86
Alexander	14,597	4,540	6,888	2,206	289	511	70	35	17	41
Alleghany	6,128	2,315	2,783	884	87	35	14	3	4	3
Anson	14,686	2,126	4,761	1,965	2,178	3,071	533	36	10	6
Ashe	13,975	5,328	6,452	2,040	31	56	23	9	13	23
Avery	8,340	2,668	3,828	1,795	8	27	0	6	8	0
Beaufort	23,942	4,017	9,296	4,063	2,751	3,060	729	2	15	9
Bertie	11,847	1,638	2,810	1,246	2,758	2,825	529	13	21	7
Bladen	17,518	3,343	5,750	2,284	2,401	2,831	697	71	119	22
Brunswick	21,014	4,176	8,940	3,650	1,410	2,133	609	16	65	15
Buncombe	101,638	18,429	46,101	28,709	2,445	4,098	1,354	71	191	240
Burke	43,464	12,694	19,473	8,433	911	1,324	436	27	57	109
Cabarrus	52,379	12,138	23,097	10,856	2,169	3,151	758	21	136	53
Caldwell	39,579	12,000	18,909	6,587	635	1,072	248	27	57	44
Camden	3,391	606	1,372	466	SUPP	SUPP	SUPP	SUPP	SUPP	SUPP
Carteret	24,898	4,388	11,877	6,553	596	1,112	242	13	83	34
Caswell	12,002	2,122	3,788	1,283	2,109	2,288	400	6	6	0
Catawba	62,457	13,386	29,309	14,805	1,479	2,741	567	49	101	20
Chatham	20,824	3,354	8,006	4,391	1,733	2,639	626	20	23	32
Cherokee	11,803	4,235	5,462	1,725	93	113	21	86	59	9
Chowan	7,595	1,116	2,451	1,247	1,335	1,176	217	19	7	27
Clay	4,296	1,393	1,990	866	SUPP	SUPP	SUPP	SUPP	SUPP	SUPP
Cleveland	48,742	10,869	19,978	9,480	3,009	4,289	953	17	72	75
Columbus	29,446	6,293	10,126	4,724	3,218	3,485	982	235	318	65
Craven	36,436	3,868	14,378	8,655	3,524	4,268	1,247	71	263	162
Cumberland	116,793	9,653	41,662	28,388	6,549	16,826	8,595	899	3,022	1,199
Currituck	6,622	1,145	3,499	926	457	438	68	16	55	18
Dare	8,676	1,177	4,310	2,712	185	218	59	2	8	5
Davidson	67,579	16,231	32,839	12,532	2,155	2,840	685	89	139	69
Davie	15,005	3,324	7,475	2,820	467	656	226	17	0	20

Duplin	23,809	4,501	8,801	3,284	2,760	3,579	815	3	32	34
Durham	88,524	8,668	24,744	25,811	7,601	12,065	8,859	55	130	591
Edgecombe	31,308	4,152	9,497	3,774	5,581	6,595	1,662	21	9	17
Forsyth	146,644	19,206	55,420	40,567	8,149	14,514	7,919	176	345	348
Franklin	17,814	2,892	6,030	2,502	2,953	2,793	608	2	34	0
Gaston	95,597	25,580	40,550	19,015	3,552	4,814	1,721	101	129	135
Gates	5,329	603	1,541	688	1,082	1,140	269	0	6	0
Graham	4,324	1,531	2,025	588	0	0	0	98	81	1
Granville	20,301	3,310	6,139	2,720	3,332	3,741	901	36	56	66
Greene	8,906	1,387	3,048	1,164	SUPP	SUPP	SUPP	SUPP	SUPP	SUPP
Guilford	186,981	25,526	65,596	56,095	8,688	18,322	11,314	333	577	530
Halifax	31,802	4,628	9,190	4,299	6,673	5,210	1,076	296	364	66
Harnett	32,685	6,730	13,489	5,737	2,614	3,139	636	151	146	43
Haywood	29,543	7,788	14,877	6,298	95	294	88	45	32	26
Henderson	38,061	7,164	18,370	11,251	455	592	48	69	62	50
Hertford	13,123	1,420	3,028	2,031	3,151	2,507	894	12	73	7
Hoke	10,291	1,107	2,674	1,450	1,538	2,084	368	440	522	108
Hyde	3,416	472	1,275	616	548	450	50	0	5	0
Iredell	49,592	10,363	22,077	10,151	2,152	4,028	675	30	77	39
Jackson	13,859	3,748	5,165	3,610	73	85	40	336	574	228
Johnston	42,390	10,662	17,489	7,053	2,843	3,527	656	36	84	40
Jones	5,531	1,097	1,687	617	SUPP	SUPP	SUPP	SUPP	SUPP	SUPP
Lee	21,513	3,264	8,747	5,297	1,607	1,972	558	19	28	21
Lenoir	34,846	5,137	11,440	6,535	4,480	5,481	1,662	7	42	62
Lincoln	25,095	6,476	11,996	4,747	611	989	229	28	13	6
Macon	13,416	4,020	6,246	2,983	63	60	0	0	22	22
Madison	10,075	3,771	4,493	1,736	32	2	24	3	11	3
Martin	15,029	2,306	4,674	2,180	2,799	2,326	725	0	9	10
McDowell	21,080	6,298	10,028	3,847	331	438	75	34	24	5
Mecklenburg	237,289	17,971	78,478	85,144	13,276	26,851	12,921	407	840	1,401
Mitchell	9,229	3,422	4,204	1,513	12	12	0	22	24	20
Montgomery	13,238	3,090	5,381	2,008	1,060	1,368	282	22	22	5
Moore	31,078	4,661	11,687	8,937	2,134	2,761	694	84	87	33
Nash	39,389	6,018	14,565	7,836	5,399	4,507	861	30	116	57
New Hanover	61,075	6,093	24,759	17,898	3,627	6,232	2,087	43	193	143
Northampton	13,180	1,383	3,350	1,254	3,919	2,601	654	8	0	11
Onslow	43,946	5,313	20,281	9,708	1,565	4,255	1,355	170	884	415
Orange	39,871	3,616	9,233	19,675	2,154	2,983	1,638	55	124	393

County	Total Persons 25 Years & Over	White			Black			Other Races		
		Elementary (0–8 Years)	High School (1–4 Years)	College (1 or More Years)	Elementary (0–8 Years)	High School (1–4 Years)	College (1 or More Years)	Elementary (0–8 Years)	High School (1–4 Years)	College (1 or More Years)
Pamlico	6,291	848	2,637	1,028	625	862	208	29	47	7
Pasquotank	15,894	2,317	5,418	3,011	2,063	1,753	1,208	27	25	72
Pender	13,178	1,799	4,897	1,852	1,631	2,457	492	8	13	29
Perquimans	5,778	995	2,131	760	914	808	170	0	0	0
Person	17,248	3,621	6,375	2,466	1,997	2,087	588	31	65	18
Pitt	47,013	5,351	13,386	13,134	6,614	6,464	1,819	31	68	146
Polk	8,727	1,865	3,499	2,679	290	266	88	13	6	21
Randolph	55,552	14,778	28,194	9,180	1,088	1,600	418	77	187	30
Richmond	26,610	5,903	10,147	4,202	2,556	2,904	678	90	109	21
Robeson	53,240	5,991	12,207	6,388	4,774	6,080	1,401	7,170	7,153	2,076
Rockingham	50,139	12,634	19,942	8,579	3,089	4,659	1,086	59	57	34
Rowan	61,434	13,678	27,036	12,281	2,558	3,912	1,647	64	134	124
Rutherford	32,835	8,964	14,676	5,915	1,336	1,573	316	13	14	28
Sampson	29,138	5,019	10,793	4,182	3,564	4,100	947	140	327	66
Scotland	17,365	2,784	5,183	3,016	2,169	2,496	808	463	375	71
Stanly	29,660	7,525	13,814	5,427	904	1,603	305	21	41	20
Stokes	19,521	5,723	10,225	2,327	468	651	111	6	8	2
Surry	36,345	12,510	16,670	5,539	629	722	168	31	61	15
Swain	6,127	1,815	2,188	906	SUPP	SUPP	SUPP	SUPP	SUPP	SUPP
Transylvania	14,098	3,148	6,569	3,780	121	360	73	6	27	14
Tyrrell	2,346	478	787	289	SUPP	SUPP	SUPP	SUPP	SUPP	SUPP
Union	39,294	6,667	18,944	8,156	2,080	2,708	552	29	124	34
Vance	21,273	3,527	6,620	3,098	3,465	3,621	851	30	40	21
Wake	172,846	12,847	53,954	70,732	9,393	15,356	8,604	185	496	1,279
Warren	9,588	1,021	2,144	920	2,300	2,296	516	170	192	29
Washington	8,209	1,153	2,826	1,224	1,313	1,355	322	2	12	2
Watauga	15,966	4,046	6,136	5,567	76	68	22	7	19	25
Wayne	53,415	7,115	18,578	11,234	5,316	8,324	2,306	167	258	117
Wilkes	34,978	12,142	15,584	5,568	483	827	279	18	52	25
Wilson	36,035	5,680	12,297	6,724	4,974	5,192	1,092	34	20	22
Yadkin	17,872	5,802	8,893	2,304	208	531	72	20	19	23
Yancey	9,328	3,380	4,333	1,448	41	60	29	7	14	16

SUPP—Indicates data are suppressed.

Higher Education Enrollment

The number of in-state undergraduate students enrolled during the fall term in North Carolina public and private institutions of higher learning is shown here by home county of the student.

County	Community College Enrollment 1985–86	Undergraduate Higher Education Fall Enrollment Public 1985–86	Undergraduate Higher Education Fall Enrollment Private 1985–86
Alamance	5,253	1,420	884
Alexander	1,297	177	84
Alleghany	655	82	17
Anson	1,355	249	157
Ashe	1,170	263	65
Avery	997	156	65
Beaufort	1,903	516	115
Bertie	952	255	92
Bladen	1,378	420	83
Brunswick	3,663	382	85
Buncombe	6,124	2,907	588
Burke	5,301	610	207
Cabarrus	3,446	1,105	334
Caldwell	4,336	467	219
Camden	240	118	10
Carteret	3,033	456	118
Caswell	948	172	42
Catawba	5,681	1,146	676
Chatham	1,472	448	119
Cherokee	1,151	201	56
Chowan	435	184	31
Clay	406	58	12
Cleveland	3,854	849	421
Columbus	3,429	575	94
Craven	3,626	785	141
Cumberland	12,660	3,911	1,579
Currituck	389	86	37
Dare	737	191	45
Davidson	4,949	1,130	406
Davie	1,347	326	137
Duplin	2,249	439	162
Durham	4,930	3,111	656
Edgecombe	2,843	712	271
Forsyth	10,072	4,672	1,627
Franklin	816	309	168
Gaston	5,508	1,406	831
Gates	318	141	41
Graham	348	85	16
Granville	1,410	387	144
Greene	1,169	144	77
Guilford	13,460	7,009	1,846
Halifax	2,189	561	189
Harnett	3,379	521	392
Haywood	2,228	591	83
Henderson	3,054	788	213
Hertford	1,108	295	177
Hoke	1,171	232	60
Hyde	126	51	17
Iredell	4,434	902	270
Jackson	1,174	690	33
Johnston	3,859	729	278
Jones	524	102	28
Lee	2,781	504	265
Lenoir	3,113	770	230
Lincoln	1,505	430	154
Macon	758	291	31
Madison	545	107	159
Martin	1,328	401	72
McDowell	1,880	301	107
Mecklenburg	22,951	8,215	2,264
Mitchell	831	97	58
Montgomery	990	171	86
Moore	3,614	579	172
Nash	3,610	808	496
New Hanover	5,038	2,741	304
Northampton	982	282	81
Onslow	7,973	998	188
Orange	2,331	1,664	295
Pamlico	776	118	26
Pasquotank	1,294	610	73
Pender	1,965	323	47
Perquimans	310	114	15
Person	1,417	309	107
Pitt	4,356	2,109	214
Polk	869	137	47
Randolph	3,833	852	264
Richmond	2,435	404	142
Robeson	3,896	1,758	231
Rockingham	3,559	788	206
Rowan	3,908	1,006	582
Rutherford	4,258	452	192
Sampson	2,747	543	183
Scotland	933	411	175
Stanly	2,462	395	291
Stokes	977	297	120
Surry	3,487	497	166
Swain	604	148	18
Transylvania	1,005	329	194
Tyrrell	172	39	17
Union	2,810	725	484
Vance	1,450	379	113
Wake	11,003	9.946	2,053
Warren	568	186	42
Washington	727	238	56
Watauga	1,517	884	61
Wayne	4,934	1,185	393

County	Community College Enrollment 1985–86	Undergraduate Higher Education Fall Enrollment Public 1985–86	Undergraduate Higher Education Fall Enrollment Private 1985–86	County	Community College Enrollment 1985–86	Undergraduate Higher Education Fall Enrollment Public 1985–86	Undergraduate Higher Education Fall Enrollment Private 1985–86
Wilkes	3,870	510	166	Yancey	1,051	108	95
Wilson	3,333	744	575	Sum of Counties	286,967	88,663	26,878
Yadkin	1,655	238	70				

HIGHWAY PATROL COMMUNICATION CENTERS

Troop A
Williamston
919-792-4101

Troop B
Elizabethtown
919-862-3133

Troop C
Raleigh
919-733-3861

Troop D
Greensboro
919-334-5500

Troop E
Salisbury
704-637-0207

Troop F
Newton
704-464-8200

Troop G
Asheville
704-298-4253

Troop H
Monroe
704-283-8559 (day)
704-637-0207 (night)

These stations maintain 24-hour operation. For the number of Highway Patrol stations in other areas, consult the local white pages of the telephone directory.

To call the Highway Patrol, after 5:30 p.m. only, in areas other than the telephone service areas of the above troop headquarters, call 1-800-662-7956, toll-free.

HIGHWAYS

North Carolina boasts possibly the largest state-maintained system in the nation with a network of 76,547.16 miles, as of January 1, 1988. The state serves as a highway hub for the Eastern seaboard and the South.

There are five interstate highways: I-85, I-40, I-77, I-26, and I-95, making North Carolina home to more "long-line" interstate motor carriers than any other state in the nation. All highways and bridges are toll-free.

State Highway System

Figures shown for primary and secondary roads as of December 31, 1986, include both paved and unpaved mileage. The state primary highway system is composed of all Interstate, U.S., and N.C. numbered highways. The state secondary road system is composed of all other state-maintained roads. A small amount of un-numbered roads such as school driveways, state university campuses, rural fire departments, etc., are not included. Source: NC Department of Transportation, Division of Highways, *North Carolina Highway and Road Mileage*

County	*Primary 1986*	*Secondary 1986*	*Paved 1986*	*Unpaved 1986*
Alamance	155.83	768.51	777.06	147.28
Alexander	45.53	509.49	416.87	138.15
Alleghany	83.76	369.67	249.24	204.19
Anson	126.62	699.71	709.82	116.51
Ashe	119.64	680.40	389.34	410.70
Avery	87.12	247.01	187.70	146.43
Beaufort	189.59	689.06	609.12	269.53
Bertie	157.64	480.78	464.33	174.09
Bladen	279.94	589.76	689.86	179.84
Brunswick	196.11	560.57	588.84	167.84
Buncombe	241.25	993.18	904.80	329.63
Burke	150.91	682.93	614.89	218.95
Cabarrus	133.79	822.24	845.24	110.79
Caldwell	125.02	566.20	438.89	252.33
Camden	46.74	152.36	140.68	58.42
Carteret	124.63	264.90	338.98	50.55
Caswell	121.88	494.47	465.61	150.74
Catawba	135.13	845.42	821.48	159.07
Chatham	157.31	870.55	764.06	263.80
Cherokee	86.54	483.24	314.55	255.23
Chowan	53.63	194.38	212.40	35.61
Clay	36.91	214.40	164.13	87.18
Cleveland	184.71	1,029.01	983.36	230.36
Columbus	254.80	981.03	970.19	265.64
Craven	140.72	582.39	540.63	182.48
Cumberland	221.55	1,049.12	1,089.78	180.89
Currituck	70.76	185.54	208.16	48.14
Dare	147.44	105.23	226.43	26.24
Davidson	202.87	1,247.27	1,203.04	247.10
Davie	107.05	391.33	383.51	114.87
Duplin	222.15	930.65	949.13	203.67
Durham	120.50	618.79	551.85	187.44
Edgecombe	188.96	504.61	632.74	60.83
Forsyth	194.98	1,015.91	1,033.83	177.06
Franklin	152.82	621.71	635.89	138.64
Gaston	177.71	780.00	831.99	125.72
Gates	84.12	278.50	259.73	102.89
Graham	56.94	191.26	173.01	75.19
Granville	134.93	708.08	573.36	269.65
Greene	91.91	368.71	387.36	73.26
Guilford	293.55	1,329.71	1,293.11	330.15
Halifax	246.18	650.10	729.95	166.33
Harnett	183.68	842.30	826.10	199.88
Haywood	155.68	442.11	388.56	209.23
Henderson	103.35	716.12	500.00	319.47
Hertford	110.57	336.01	355.44	91.14
Hoke	60.84	373.66	400.02	34.48
Hyde	89.80	187.04	213.06	63.78

County	*Primary 1986*	*Secondary 1986*	*Paved 1986*	*Unpaved 1986*
Iredell	221.69	1,180.72	1,114.89	287.52
Jackson	122.74	459.79	307.35	275.18
Johnston	285.77	1,227.34	1,223.80	289.31
Jones	87.15	236.69	274.52	49.32
Lee	78.11	407.57	437.47	48.21
Lenoir	125.61	615.24	576.23	164.62
Lincoln	104.10	597.72	564.99	136.83
Macon	96.70	577.88	390.92	283.66
Madison	125.30	517.87	348.25	294.92
Martin	137.04	408.46	420.31	125.19
McDowell	133.82	450.33	423.45	160.70
Mecklenburg	260.13	868.81	1,045.75	83.19
Mitchell	79.49	242.32	196.01	125.80
Montgomery	140.04	515.11	549.25	105.90
Moore	173.52	909.80	908.36	174.96
Nash	253.13	792.04	932.90	112.27
New Hanover	90.57	326.59	403.47	13.69
Northampton	156.76	427.42	467.33	116.85
Onslow	160.77	555.79	619.69	96.87
Orange	111.55	659.62	574.39	196.78
Pamlico	59.20	207.04	194.70	71.54
Pasquotank	47.94	232.30	216.89	63.35
Pender	208.93	487.87	591.55	105.25
Perquimans	31.64	272.58	217.15	87.07
Person	95.45	577.55	405.68	267.32
Pitt	239.29	810.53	813.04	236.78
Polk	59.99	361.85	269.35	152.49
Randolph	212.00	1,406.67	1,191.02	427.65
Richmond	113.76	621.48	647.40	87.84
Robeson	339.31	1,417.41	1,520.36	236.36
Rockingham	240.60	937.93	846.14	332.39
Rowan	142.20	1,032.10	972.57	201.73
Rutherford	133.57	920.24	730.48	323.33
Sampson	244.89	1,211.71	1,255.04	201.56
Scotland	89.38	466.79	497.33	58.84
Stanly	124.30	731.07	706.55	148.82
Stokes	140.61	803.45	621.87	322.19
Surry	158.01	957.63	720.15	395.49
Swain	62.89	192.92	176.07	79.74
Transylvania	104.49	298.06	263.41	139.14
Tyrrell	46.34	144.04	144.18	46.20
Union	175.73	1,171.16	1,111.14	235.75
Vance	81.36	372.34	379.75	73.95
Wake	283.70	1,527.06	1,512.83	297.93
Warren	86.20	528.83	427.21	187.82
Washington	68.46	222.08	215.51	75.03
Watauga	91.44	467.65	277.84	281.25

County	Primary 1986	Secondary 1986	Paved 1986	Unpaved 1986
Wayne	175.06	863.94	921.48	117.52
Wilkes	148.94	1,128.84	751.24	526.54
Wilson	144.56	579.33	632.29	91.60
Yadkin	91.01	584.77	470.89	204.89
Yancey	89.49	293.56	236.32	146.73
Total	14,128.82	62,453.31	59,164.88	17,417.25

Accidents, Persons Injured, and Persons Killed

These figures represent the number of reportable accidents in 1986. A reportable accident is one which involves a motor vehicle on a trafficway resulting in injury, death, or property damage of $500 or more. The number of persons injured or killed is determined from the investigating officers' reports which are filed within 24 hours of the accident. The state figure represents the sum of county totals. Source: NC Department of Transportation, Division of Motor Vehicles, *North Carolina Traffic Accident Facts*

County	Accidents 1986	Persons Injured 1986	Persons Killed 1986
Alamance	2,411	1,863	15
Alexander	475	304	7
Alleghany	200	124	1
Anson	512	460	7
Ashe	427	219	3
Avery	406	259	5
Beaufort	938	661	17
Bertie	447	373	12
Bladen	513	400	11
Brunswick	991	878	24
Buncombe	4,286	2,880	30
Burke	1,797	1,261	20
Cabarrus	2,277	1,731	22
Caldwell	1,723	1,169	14
Camden	102	107	0
Carteret	1,371	870	11
Caswell	372	304	12
Catawba	3,437	2,134	25
Chatham	924	639	20
Cherokee	319	269	5
Chowan	191	110	3
Clay	121	113	2
Cleveland	1,920	1,387	23
Columbus	1,277	1,068	31
Craven	1,495	1,180	16
Cumberland	6,065	4,446	42
Currituck	372	339	10
Dare	507	297	8
Davidson	2,772	2,140	26
Davie	447	409	4
Duplin	787	553	11
Durham	5,223	3,239	28
Edgecombe	1,120	743	15
Forsyth	7,321	4,926	42
Franklin	659	497	9
Gaston	4,631	3,417	35
Gates	221	137	10
Graham	111	89	2
Granville	759	520	15
Greene	308	211	3
Guilford	10,360	7,507	70
Halifax	1,116	848	15
Harnett	1,519	1,291	32
Haywood	987	564	11
Henderson	1,714	1,108	14
Hertford	525	343	16
Hoke	358	303	7
Hyde	79	52	1
Iredell	2,088	1,353	17
Jackson	474	272	12
Johnston	1,826	1,475	44
Jones	249	189	8
Lee	1,070	700	15
Lenoir	1,587	1,221	19
Lincoln	1,019	715	15
Macon	307	240	6
Madison	312	134	2
Martin	555	435	6
McDowell	924	552	12
Mecklenburg	18,044	11,906	85

County	Accidents 1986	Persons Injured 1986	Persons Killed 1986	County	Accidents 1986	Persons Injured 1986	Persons Killed 1986
Mitchell	252	141	4	Rutherford	1,273	970	21
Montgomery	430	332	3	Sampson	1,006	915	30
Moore	1,072	772	17	Scotland	647	502	18
Nash	1,910	1,340	30	Stanly	935	719	5
New Hanover	3,615	2,750	16	Stokes	534	447	17
Northampton	359	304	11	Surry	1,578	963	14
Onslow	2,940	2,009	38	Swain	173	121	2
Orange	2,020	1,140	23	Transylvania	506	275	2
Pamlico	154	152	4	Tyrrell	63	38	1
Pasquotank	708	418	5	Union	1,834	1,261	23
Pender	534	421	9	Vance	943	559	20
Perquimans	155	145	2	Wake	13,167	8,100	70
Person	647	450	5	Warren	217	195	9
Pitt	2,220	1,563	18	Washington	259	172	7
Polk	247	194	2	Watauga	923	422	7
Randolph	2,169	1,456	32	Wayne	2,114	1,653	16
Richmond	997	829	14	Wilkes	1,319	883	21
Robeson	2,381	1,898	45	Wilson	1,747	1,304	20
Rockingham	1,753	1,208	28	Yadkin	615	414	7
Rowan	2,235	1,657	23	Yancey	217	165	3
				NC Totals	162,216	113,191	1,645

HISTORICAL SOCIETIES

ALBEMARLE
Stanly County Historical Society, Inc.
813 W. Main St., 28001
704-982-1825

ASHEBORO
Randolph County Historical Society
201 Worth St., 27203
919-629-3329

ASHEVILLE
Historic Resources Commission of Asheville and Buncombe County
P.O. Box 7148, 28807
704-255-5434

Preservation Society of Asheville and Buncombe County
P.O. Box 2806, 28802
704-254-2343

Western North Carolina Historical Association, Inc.
283 Victoria Rd., 28801
704-253-9231

Western Office, Division of Archives and History
13 Veterans Dr., 28805
704-298-5024

BEAUFORT
Beaufort Historical Association
P.O. Box 1709, 28516
919-728-5225/728-7647

Carteret Historical Research Association
P.O. Box 1722, 28516
919-354-3215

BOONE
Southern Appalachian Historical Association, Inc.
P.O. Box 295, 28607
704-264-2120

CAMDEN
Camden County Historical Society
919-336-2747

CARY
Cary Historical Society
P.O. Box 134, 27511

CHAPEL HILL
Chapel Hill Historical Society
P.O. Box 503, 27514

CHARLOTTE
Mecklenburg Historical Association
P.O. Box 35032, 28235

CHEROKEE
Cherokee Historical Association
P.O. Box 398, U.S. Hwy. 441 N, 28719

CLIMAX
Old Time Historical Association
P.O. Box 70, 27233
919-685-4407

CLINTON
Sampson County Historical Society
P.O. Box 422, 28328

DURHAM
Forest History Society
701 Vickers Ave., 27701
919-682-9319

Historic Preservation Society of Durham
3008 Ithaca St., 27707
919-489-7810

EDENTON
Edenton Historical Commission
P.O. Box 474, 27932
919-482-3663

ELIZABETH CITY
Pasquotank Historical and Genealogical Society
P.O. Box 523, 27909
919-335-2041

ENGLEHARD
Hyde County Historical Society
P.O. Box 159, Main St., 27824
919-925-4591

FAYETTEVILLE
Cumberland County Historical Society
312 DeVane St., 28305
919-484-5217

FRANKLIN
Macon County Historical Society
Macon County Public Library
P.O. Box 822, 28734

GATESVILLE
Gates County Historical Society
c/o President, 27937
919-357-1733

GERMANTON
Stokes County Historical Society
P.O. Box 250, 27019
919-591-7969

GREENVILLE
Pitt County Historical Society
P.O. Box 5063, 27834
919-752-3129

HERTFORD
Perquimans County Historical Society
P.O. Box 652, 27944

HIGH POINT
High Point Historical Society, Inc.
1805 E. Lexington Ave., 27262
919-885-6859

HILLSBOROUGH
Hillsborough Historical Society
P.O. Box 871, 27278
919-732-8648

JACKSONVILLE
Onslow County Historical Society
P.O. Box 5203, 28540
919-347-5287

JAMESTOWN
Historic Jamestown Society, Inc.
P.O. Box 512, 27282
919-454-3819

MANTEO
Roanoke Island Historical Association, Inc.
P.O. Box 40, 27954
919-473-2127

MARSHALL
Madison County Historical Society
P.O. Box 236, 28753
704-689-1153

MORGANTON
Burke County Historical Society
P.O. Box 151, 28655

NEW BERN
New Bern Historical Society Foundation, Inc.
P.O. Box 119, 28560
919-638-8558

NEWTON GROVE
Catawba County Historical Association, Inc.
P.O. Box 73, 28658
704-465-0383

RALEIGH
Federation of North Carolina Historical Societies
109 E. Jones St., 27611
919-733-7305

Historical Society of North Carolina
109 E. Jones St., 27611
919-733-9375

Mordecai Square Historical Society, Inc.
1 Mimosa St., 27604
919-834-4844

ROSE HILL
Duplin County Historical Society—Leora H. McEachern Library of Local History
P.O. Box 130, 28458
919-289-2654/289-2430

ROXBORO
Person County Historical Society, Inc.
P.O. Box 887, 27573

SHALLOTE
Brunswick County Historical Society
P.O. Box 874, 28459

SHELBY
Cleveland County Historical Association and Museum
P.O. Box 1335, Court Square, 28150
704-482-8186

SMITHFIELD
Johnston County Genealogical Society
305 Market St., 27577
919-934-8146

SOUTHPORT
Southport Historical Society
501 N. Atlantic Ave., 28461
919-457-6940

SPARTA
Alleghany Historical-Genealogical Society, Inc./Floyd Crouse House
P.O. Box 817, 28675
919-372-8864

SWANSBORO
Swansboro Historical Association, Inc.
P.O. Box 21, 28584
919-726-1421/326-5361

TARBORO
Edgecombe County Historical Society
P.O. Box 1258, 27886
919-823-4159

Historic Preservation Fund of Edgecombe County, Inc.
P.O. Box 1595, 26886
919-823-3080

TRENTON
Jones County Historical Society
P.O. Box 219, 28585
919-448-3911

WADESBORO
Anson County Historical Society
P.O. Box 732, 28170
704-694-6694

WALLACE
Duplin County Historical Society
416 E. Main St., 28466
919-285-2432

WENTWORTH
Rockingham County History Society
P.O. Box 84, 27375

WILMINGTON
Lower Cape Fear Historical Society, Inc.
P.O. Box 813, 28402
919-762-0492

WINSTON-SALEM
Old Salem, Inc.
Drawer F, Salem Station, 27108
919-723-3688

YADKINVILLE
Yadkin County Historical Society
E. Main St.
919-679-2795

YANCEYVILLE
Caswell County Historical Association, Inc.
P.O. Box 278, 27379

HISTORIC SITES

ASHEVILLE
Thomas Wolfe Memorial. See section on National Historic Landmarks.

BATH
Historic Bath. North Carolina's oldest town and first meeting place of the Colonial Assembly of the Province. Restored houses in the area. Visitor center. 919-923-3971.

BURLINGTON
Alamance Battleground. Pre-revolutionary battleground, site of 1771 battle between Royal forces and Regulators. Late 18th century farmstead, monuments, markers and visitor center-museum. 919-227-4785.

CARTHAGE
House in the Horseshoe. Plantation home of Philip Alston, Whig leader, and was the scene of Whig-Tory skirmishes in 1780–81. 919-947-2051.

CRESWELL

Somerset Place. Plantation built in the 1830s by Josiah Collins II; located on the shore of Lake Phelps. Was a gathering place for fashionable society. Picnic facilities in adjacent Pettigrew State Park. 919-797-4560.

DURHAM

Bennett Place. Restored farm dwelling where second and largest of four Confederate surrenders ending the War Between the States took place. Visitor center-museum. 919-383-4345.

Duke Homestead. See section on National Historic Landmarks.

EDENTON

Iredell House. Built in 1759, home of James Iredell who was Attorney General of North Carolina, and later named to the U.S. Supreme Court by George Washington. 919-482-2637.

FREMONT

Charles B. Aycock Birthplace. Mid-19th century birthplace of North Carolina's "Educational Governor." Visitor center-museum and 1870 school. 919-242-5581.

HALIFAX

Historic Halifax. Site of first official action by a colony for independence and site of the adoption of North Carolina's first state constitution. Tours through restored 18th and 19th century buildings. Visitor center-museum and archaeological exhibits. 919-583-7191.

KURE BEACH

Fort Fisher. See section on National Historic Landmarks.

KINSTON

The Richard Caswell Memorial and *CSS Neuse*. Grave of North Carolina's first constitutionally elected governor, and site of remains of the ram *Neuse,* one of two iron-clad gunboats completed in North Carolina. 919-522-2091.

MANTEO

***Elizabeth II*.** Designed in the 16th century-style and named for the ship which brought the first English colonists to America. Costumed interpreters and visitor center with exhibits on the Roanoke Voyages. 919-473-1144.

MT. GILEAD

Town Creek Indian Mound. See section on National Historic Landmarks.

NEWTON GROVE

Bentonville Battleground. Markers, trenches. Harper House Field Hospital restoration and visitor center-museum on site of largest War Between the States battle fought in North Carolina. 919-594-0789.

PINEVILLE

James K. Polk Memorial. Restored log house where the 11th president of the U.S. was born November 2, 1795. Visitor center-museum. 704-889-7145.

SEDALIA

Charlotte Hawkins Brown Memorial. Contributions of North Carolina Afro-American citizens are remembered at the site of Palmer Memorial Institute. Visitor center. 919-733-7862.

SOUTHPORT

Brunswick Town. Ruins of colonial seaport and St. Philip's Church and earthworks of Fort Anderson. Visitor center-museum. 919-371-6613.

SPENCER

Spencer Shops. Once Southern Railways central repair shops; now the North Carolina Transportation Museum which displays the development of transportation in the state. 704-636-2889.

STANFIELD

Reed Gold Mine. See section on National Historic Landmarks.

STATESVILLE

Fort Dobbs. Built in 1756, the fort was named for Royal Governor Arthur Dobbs. Visitor center, recreational facilities and exhibits. 704-873-5866.

WEAVERVILLE

Zebulon B. Vance Birthplace. Reconstruction of log house where North Carolina's War Between the States governor was born. Visitor center-museum. 704-645-6706.

HISTORY

Exploration and colonial era. Following the voyage of Christopher Columbus, Spain, France, and England conducted explorations of North Carolina. In 1524 Giovanni da Verrazano, who sailed in the interest of France, recorded the first descriptive account of the Carolina coastline. He observed the Cape Fear River, the Outer Banks, and the presence of friendly Indians. He assumed mistakenly that the Pamlico and Albemarle sounds were part of the Pacific Ocean. Verrazano's accounts were subsequently published by Richard Hakluyt in 1584 and influenced the efforts of Sir Walter Raleigh and others in planting colonies. In 1525 Lucas Vázquez de Ayllón, of Hispaniola, conducted an exploration of the coastline between the Cape Fear and Santee rivers in the interest of Spain. In 1526 he brought a colony of some 500, including women and Negroes, to the lower Cape Fear River. The colony was plagued by loss of supplies and decimated by diseases and in desperation sought to relocate in South Carolina. Within a short time, reduced to 150 survivors, it returned to Santo Domingo.

Subsequent Spanish explorations of the North Carolina mountains were undertaken in 1539–1540 by Hernando De Soto in a futile search for gold. But Spanish explorations of the coastline and the mountains were inconclusive, and this nation withdrew to its frontier bastions in Florida and the Southwest. Following the unsuccessful explorations of Jan Ribault and René de Laudonnière along the South Atlantic coast in the 1560s, France focused attention upon its colonies in Canada and the Mississippi Valley. The development of North Carolina would be left to English colonizers.

In 1584 Sir Walter Raleigh received a patent from Elizabeth I that authorized the establishment of colonies and gave the settlers the same privileges as natives of England. Raleigh sent Philip Amadas and Arthur Barlow on an exploratory voyage in 1584; landing at Roanoke Island in July, the party was hospitably treated by Indians. Six weeks later the explorers returned to England and submitted the most favorable accounts to Raleigh and Queen Elizabeth. In 1585 Raleigh dispatched an expedition of seven ships and possibly as many as 600 men to the West Indies, whence it sailed to Roanoke Island. This extraordinarily talented group spent too much time looking for gold and a passage to the South Seas. Factional discord and the prospect of starvation prompted Richard Grenville, the commander, to dispatch vessels to England for supplies. Ralph Lane was left to command the fort at Roanoke Island and a force of 107 men. In 1586, faced with the prospect of starvation and the threat of an Indian attack, he chose to return to England with the fleet of Sir Francis Drake. Thus ended the first English colony in America.

On July 25, 1587, the John White colony, Raleigh's second attempt to establish an English outpost in America, arrived at Cape Hatteras and proceeded to Roanoke Island. Plagued by hostile Indians and lack of supplies, Governor White returned to England for assistance. Delayed by England's engagement with the Spanish armada in 1588, White did not return to Roanoke Island until August, 1590. He searched in vain for the settlers; and to this day no conclusive evidence has been revealed to account for the fate of the Lost Colony (Croatan Island).

Following the settlement of Jamestown, Va., in 1607, explorers, trappers, and traders ventured into the Albemarle Sound region. When Virginia became a royal colony in 1624, all ungranted land reverted to the crown. Accordingly Charles I granted to his attorney general, Sir Robert Heath, the land incorporated as the province of Carolana between 31° and 36° north latitude, from sea to sea. Heath failed to colonize his 1629 grant and in 1638 transferred it to Lord Maltravers, the duke of Norfolk. The proprietary grant of March 24, 1663, to eight lords proprietors vacated the earlier Heath patent. Charles II thereby rewarded his friends and supporters of the Restoration era. They were men of established reputation and ability, although only one of the original proprietors, Sir William Berkeley, ever came to America. In 1665 the charter was amended to extend northward to 36°30′ north latitude to accommodate settlements already made in the Albemarle Sound; it was also extended southward to 29°.

Extraordinary powers were granted to the proprietors by the charter of 1663. The colony was expected to serve as a buffer against Spanish encroachments on the southern frontier and to provide a reliable source of supply for the naval stores industry. It was among the most favored and perhaps most heavily subsidized of the English colonies. Emigrants were granted the same rights as the king's subjects at home, were entitled to representation in the lawmaking process, and were granted liberty of conscience. Nevertheless, the indecision of the proprietors, their lack of firsthand knowledge of the colony, and their failure to select competent governors thwarted the colony's growth. They spent far more time and money promoting the development of South Carolina. For more than 30 years the proprietors sought to implement a feudalistic scheme of government, the fundamental constitutions of 1669, based upon an artificially contrived landed aristocracy, before the plan was abandoned altogether. Economic experiments that involved crops unsuited to the colony were launched and abandoned after considerable waste of time and money.

Throughout the proprietary era (1663–1729), politics in North Carolina involved incessant factional squabbles between the popular party (consisting of leaders of the legislative branch) and the party of officialdom (usually led by governors and their hirelings). In a bitter struggle that involved conflicting views over violations of trade and navigation, Albemarle partisans resorted to armed rebellion against the proprietary faction in what was known as Culpeper's Rebellion of 1677. Although the uprising led to a change of officialdom, colonists soon found that the administration of Governor Seth Sothel (1683–1689) was the most notoriously corrupt of any in their history. Sothel was tried by the general assembly in 1689, found guilty on 13 charges, and banished forever from politics by an irate citizenry.

From 1689 to 1763, England and France were engaged in a series of intercolonial wars characterized by Lawrence H. Gipson as the "great war for empire." Ultimately North Carolina colonists were involved directly in all of these wars, whether they originated in Europe or America. In a broader sense England's involvement with wars and diplomacy meant that the administration of the colony was neglected. Immediately after the Glorious Revolution, a succession of fairly capable but undistinguished deputy governors was appointed by the proprietors for the county of Albemarle. In this period the settled area gradually extended southward into the Pamlico Sound region, where French Huguenots principally located. In 1706 the legislature incorporated Bath as the first town in North Carolina.

In 1710 New Bern was founded by colonists from Germany, Switzerland, and England under the leadership of Christopher de Graffenried. The settlement of New Bern was launched under the most trying circumstances; almost half the original party died in the Atlantic crossing, and the survivors were plundered by a French privateer upon reaching the Virginia coast. The overland trek to New Bern was arduous, and the settlers arrived too late to plant and harvest crops. Under de Graffenried's dedicated efforts, however, the settlement survived and flourished. New Bern became the largest town in North Carolina during the colonial period.

The Cary Rebellion of 1711 divided the colonists and thwarted growth of the proprietary. It involved a crisis between the Society of Friends (Quakers) and the government of the colony over the enforcement of vestry legislation. The issue of separation of church and state was at stake. Ultimately these differences led to armed clashes in which Governor Edward Hyde routed the Quaker forces. This rebellion left the colonists prone to Indian attacks during the Tuscarora War (1711–1713). The fact that the Tuscarora Indians had been eliminated as middlemen in the conduct of fur trade with the Cherokee on the frontier also provoked hostility. Furthermore the Tuscarora resented the encroachment of settlers in the New Bern area upon their hunting grounds. During the war the suppression and banishment of the Tuscarora were accomplished largely by forces of friendly Indians from South Carolina led by John Barnwell and James Moore. A further hindrance to the Carolina proprietary involved the last stand of piracy in the Western Hemisphere. Driven from South America and the Caribbean, pirates sought refuge along the sounds and rivers of North Carolina. They used the inland waterways of North Carolina as bases from which to prey upon shipping around Charleston and Norfolk. The heyday of piracy was short-lived. By 1718 practically all of these pirates had been captured and executed.

Conceivably proprietary government might have survived these crises and brought a period of expansion and prosperity to North Carolina. However, the proprietors apparently concluded that the venture was unsuccessful, and in 1729 all the lords except John Carteret, the earl of Granville, sold their shares to James II. At this time North Carolina was the most isolated and sparsely settled English colony in America. In marked contrast, the growth of population and expansion of settled areas were phenomenal from 1729 to 1775. Most of the immigrants after 1729 were of non-English extraction. Highland Scots, given an opportunity to settle in America after they were crushed at the battle of Culloden in 1746, were landed on the lower Cape Fear River and settled upstream in this river valley. Heavily subsidized by the English government, they were instrumental in the development of the naval stores industry.

Scotch-Irish and German immigrants traveled over the Great Wagon Road from Pennsylvania through the Shenandoah Valley of Virginia to North Carolina. High land prices, exhaustion and erosion of farmlands, overcrowding of the population, and the Indian menace and mountain barriers on the Pennsylvania frontier all influenced the southward migration of these settlers. Practically all the Scotch-Irish had come to America as indentured labor and after serving their period of indenture were able to acquire title to free land. The best-known German colonists, the United Brethren or Moravians, settled principally in Forsyth County. Devoutly religious, operating under a system of community ownership and management of property, the Moravians established an impressive record for other colonists to follow.

From 1729 to 1775 the population of North Carolina as a royal colony increased from about 35,000 to 345,000. Of this number there were about 80,000 Negroes in 1775. During this period the Cape Fear Valley was developed, and colonists occupied the fertile farmlands of the Piedmont along the Yadkin and Catawba rivers. This growth was accomplished in spite of the ineptitude of royal governors and the "salutary neglect" of the colony. In 1775 only Virginia, Pennsylvania, and Massachusetts exceeded North Carolina in total population.

The spread of population into the Piedmont did not result in adequate reapportionment of representation in the general assembly. Eastern counties were divided and subdivided to counterbalance the influence of the west. Frontiersmen could therefore rightfully complain of taxation without representation. The frustration of yeomen farmers of the west was also aggravated by corrupt land agents and surveyors, tax collectors, sheriffs, and political opportunists who were allowed to hold multiple offices. The protest movement by Regulators of the backcountry in many ways resembled uprisings in other colonies and states, including such well-known events as Bacon's Rebellion in Virginia and Shays's Rebellion in Massachusetts. The vigilante activities of the Regulators of Piedmont North Carolina, which centered in Orange and Alamance counties, were not provoked by more stringent colonial and commercial policies of Parliament after 1763. Nor were the Regulators moved to acts of violence by inadequate representation. Their protests were instead aimed against specific abuses of local and county government, which were particularly severe in the Granville District, lands claimed by the Carteret heirs. The Regulator movement was utterly crushed by Governor William Tryon and forces under his command at the battle of Alamance in 1771. Many of the Regulators moved westward; an impressive number joined Whig forces during the Revolution. There is little evidence, contrary to some myths, that Regulators joined the Tory cause after 1775.

Revolution and the new nation. When British colonial and commercial policies became more exacting after the end of the French and Indian War, colonists in North Carolina responded by appealing to their constitutional rights within the empire. They demonstrated little interest in the Albany Plan of union in 1754, but in defying the Stamp Act of 1765 they willingly endorsed the Stamp Act Congress and used force to coerce royal officials. The general assembly acted in concert with other colonies in an economic boycott of Great Britain that forced repeal of the Townshend Acts of 1767. The impetus for colonial unity was further promoted by a committee of correspondence in 1773 and by support of beleaguered Boston and the Massachusetts Bay Colony in 1774. North Carolina patriots, defiantly challenging Governor Josiah Martin, called for a provincial congress that would be independent of royal control. This congress met in New Bern in 1774, endorsed the proposal for the First Continental Congress, and elected William Hooper, Richard Caswell, and Joseph Hewes to serve as delegates to Philadelphia. With the outbreak of hostilities at Lexington and Concord in April, 1775, Governor Martin found his position in New Bern to be untenable. Ultimately he took refuge on a British warship stationed off the coast. Thereafter, committees of safety and provincial congresses took over governmental powers.

On April 12, 1776, delegates to the fourth provincial congress at Halifax, N.C., drafted what were known as the Halifax Resolves. The resolves empowered North Carolina's delegates in the Continental Congress to "concur" with representatives of other colonies "in declaring Independency" and in "forming foreign alliances." This may well have been the most significant action for American independence by any revolutionary body at the time. The Continental Congress acted decisively when it adopted the resolution for independence submitted by Richard Henry Lee of Virginia. The Declaration of Independence that followed Lee's resolution was signed by North Carolina's delegates Hooper, Hewes, and John Penn.

A substantial number of North Carolinians were Loyalists during the revolutionary era. Highland Scots in particular had many reasons to support the crown. They had taken an oath of allegiance to the house of Hanover before coming to America and were also heavily subsidized producers of naval stores in the Cape Fear Valley. They were promised free land, money, and remission of arrearages in rent, as well as exemption from future rentals, to support the Tory cause. Furthermore, they suspected the motives of Whig political leaders in the Albemarle Sound region. Throughout the Piedmont many colonists were at best neutral in outlook. Whig tactics of violence and intimidation were therefore effective in swaying many of the uncommitted colonists to support the Whig cause even before the outbreak of hostilities. And in many ways Whigs were guilty of excesses fully comparable with alleged British abuses. During the Revolution, Highland Scots recruited military units and in 1776 undertook to rendezvous with British forces along the North Carolina coast. This operation failed utterly when the Scots were crushed at the battle of Moore's Creek Bridge on February 27, 1776. The initial British plan to join Tory forces and drive a wedge into the southern colonies was therefore thwarted, and following the battle of Ft. Moultrie in South Carolina the plan was abandoned. After 1776 Tories within North Carolina posed no major military threat; their efforts were confined largely to harassment of army operations.

After the battle of Moore's Creek Bridge, North Carolina did not become a principal theater of operations until 1780–1781. Its regular army forces, troops of the Continental Line numbering some 6,000, served with distinction under George Washington's command in campaigns across New York, New Jersey, Pennsylvania, and Virginia. An estimated 10,000 North Carolinians served as militiamen who were castigated by their commanders for fleetness of foot in running from the enemy. Both Continentals and militiamen served under General Benjamin Lincoln's command in Georgia and South Carolina in 1779 and 1780, and an inordinately large number was taken prisoner in the ill-advised defense of Charleston. The staggering losses at Charleston and the subsequent battle of Camden left the southern states vulnerable to the British forces led by General Charles Cornwallis. At this juncture the heroic assault by militiamen from the mountain counties upon a British force at the battle of Kings Mountain, October 7, 1780, stalled the advance of Cornwallis' army. Under the command of Nathanael Greene, American forces skillfully retreated across North Carolina and maneuvered British troops into position for the battle of Guilford Courthouse on March 15, 1781. Although Greene was driven from the field of battle, the British losses were so great that this engagement is regarded as a turning point of the Revolution. Thereafter Cornwallis was engaged in a desperate maneuver to evacuate his army from the South. And, finally thwarted in this effort, he surrendered at Yorktown on October 19, 1781.

While the war was under way, the fifth provincial congress at Halifax, which convened on November 12, 1776, launched a new constitution for the independent state of North Carolina. The work of this congress symbolized the transition from colony to commonwealth. Although radical and conservative Whigs were well represented in the congress, neither faction dominated its proceedings. The final draft of the constitution represented a compromise, with moderates holding the balance of power. The constitution of 1776 was based on colonial experience, shaped by English charters and precedents, and drawn in part from the constitutions of other states. The legislative branch dominated the executive and judicial branches and reflected the colonists' dislike and suspicion of governors and judges generally. The framers of the constitution placed considerable emphasis upon a bill of rights. Yet in many ways the document reflected a conservative trend in politics. Property-holding and tax-paying requirements for voting and officeholding were prescribed. Although the separation of church and state was affirmed in principle, the delegates by a curious twist of logic set up religious tests for officeholding, barring ministers from election to the legislature and excluding candidates for any public office who denied the "truth" of the Protestant religion. The constitution cited the obligation of the state to support public schools and higher learning. Ironically, the state failed to take decisive action to support public schools until 1839. The glaring inequities in representation the delegates allowed in 1776, which favored eastern counties and towns, aroused much political disaffection until corrected in the convention of 1835. Furthermore, the constitution contained no provision for amendments and was not submitted to a popular referendum before it was put into effect. The defects of the original state constitution caused incessant controversy between 1776 and 1835.

The rapid recovery of the economy of North Carolina in the aftermath of the Revolution appears to contradict the views of earlier historians that the Confederation era was marked by depression and chaos. The state was occupied with the problems of transition from a wartime to a peacetime economy in attempting to cope with disgruntled veterans and in handling the separatist tendencies of frontiersmen. Disaffection on the frontier was finally resolved when North Carolina ceded its western land claims in 1789. The legislature contented itself with chartering private academies but neglected to support public schools. In 1789 it commenced to erect the apex of an educational pyramid by chartering the state university. When it opened in 1795, the University of North Carolina became the first state institution of higher learning to enroll students. After much haggling, Wake County was finally chosen as the seat of government in 1792, and the first permanent capitol building was completed at Raleigh in 1794.

North Carolina was not prominently represented in the movement that led to the Constitutional Convention of 1787 in Philadelphia. The five delegates who represented the state were drawn from the ranks of the planter aristocracy. They appeared to be principally concerned about restrictions upon the president and sought vainly to provide for his election by Congress. The Tarheel delegates significantly influenced provisions relating to the power of Congress to override a presidential veto, the method of impeachment of the president, the senatorial term of six years, and the decennial census. Although frequently absent, the delegates voted with the slaveholding states and with the small states for the great compromises of the Philadelphia convention. After the Constitution was submitted to the states, the Hillsboro convention of 1788 refused by a vote of 184 to 84 to ratify the document. After the Federalists promised a Bill of Rights, conducted a campaign to educate voters on the advantages of a stronger central government, and pointed out that the new government would become operative regardless of the North Carolina vote, a second convention at Fayetteville in 1789 voted to ratify by 195 to 77.

Rural and agrarian interests of North Carolina opposed the economic and diplomatic policies of the Federalist party after 1789. The state electoral vote was cast for Thomas Jefferson for president in the election of 1796, and from that time until 1824 the electorate was dominated by the Virginia dynasty in presidential politics. Yet in many ways the Jeffersonian Republicans of North Carolina did not share the enlightened views of the founder of the party or his successors. A dissident group of states' rights advocates led by Nathaniel Macon of Warren County, known as Quids, assumed an intransigent role on national issues.

Antebellum era. Archibald D. Murphey, state senator from Orange County (1812–1819), symbolized the spirit of progress and reform that followed the War of 1812. The Murphey program, ably presented in a series of reports to the general assembly, called for the development of a network of canals linking the river systems, the opening of inlets to the sounds, and extension of navigable waterways into the Piedmont. Roads were also projected to lead from canals and rivers into the Piedmont and western counties. However, railroad construction soon eclipsed and rendered futile this ambitious program to link together the east and west.

Murphey also undertook to fulfill the constitutional mandate of 1776 for a public school system. He proposed state support for elementary schools for all white children. His plan included ten regional public academies for students of extraordinary ability. Those specially qualified but unable to pay tuition would also receive free education in the state university. Murphey's advocacy of a state school for the deaf and mute, as well as his views on reforming the curriculum of the state university to include more practical and fewer ornamental subjects, indicates a progressive outlook toward learning. An integral part of the state senator's reform program involved revision of the 1776 constitution to allow more equitable representation in government and to remove many defects from the original document.

Although North Carolina was moved by the spirit of patriotism and nationalism after 1815, the legislature hesitated to enact Murphey's proposals. Generally the state did not support the new nationalist measures of Congress or look with favor upon the U.S. Supreme Court decisions of John Marshall. In this period North Carolina acquired a reputation for backwardness and inertia and was castigated as the "Rip Van Winkle state." Emigration of population, the high rate of illiteracy, and the low per capita income and standard of living contributed to this image. Tarheels salved their consciences for tardy participation in the War of 1812 by providing for the families of three wartime heroes, and the legislature in a fit of patriotism commissioned a statue of George Washington by Canova. In 1822 the legislature provided modest support to agricultural societies, and between 1824 and 1827 Denison Olmsted and Elisha Mitchell, of the University of North Carolina, prepared and published the first state geological survey in the United States.

Enthusiasm for state spending programs was dampened by the Panic of 1819. Nevertheless, North Carolina employed an engineer to survey rivers and sounds and authorized subscription of stock in navigation and canal companies. State funds were also appropriated to construct turnpikes, located principally in the west. Generally the state wasted money on widely scattered local projects, of which only a few were successful. The precedent for state spending on internal improvements was nonetheless established and was later augmented by railroad construction. Indecisive action also characterized the early school program. Long after Murphey left public life, the legislature in 1825 created a literary fund to establish common schools and a literary board to administer it. The fund was derived from dividends, taxes, land sales, and appropriations. However, the receipts were inadequate, some monies were stolen by the state treasurer, and the legislature borrowed heavily from the fund for other than educational purposes. For more than ten years the state languished under a totally inadequate plan for public schools. The legislature, dominated by eastern slaveholding counties, dedicated to parsimony and maintenance of the status quo, and determined to thwart Murphey's program of constitutional and social reform, hampered the impulses for change. Unfortunately, Murphey became insolvent and was imprisoned for debts. It would take North Carolina more than a century to implement and appreciate many of his visionary proposals.

Jeffersonian Republicans dominated state politics after 1815, but sectional animosities and demands for change split the party and led eventually to its demise. Western counties were clamoring for more equitable representation and internal improvements. They resented party caucuses and the general ticket system whereby eastern counties dictated the nomination and election of candidates. The clamor of western counties for constitutional reforms heralded the emergence of a new political era. In 1822 disgruntled legislators called for a convention, and in 1823 an extralegal convention of 47 delegates from 24 western counties met in Raleigh. The general assembly rejected its proposals for a state constitutional convention.

During the presidential election of 1824, Charles Fisher of Salisbury mobilized support of western counties for John C. Calhoun on what was called a "people's ticket." Calhoun supported nationalist measures for internal improvements, including a national road that would run across Piedmont North Carolina, but he found his appeal in northern states eclipsed by the meteoric rise of Andrew Jackson. When Calhoun withdrew from the race, Fisher and his followers endorsed Jackson. Consequently those who aligned with the "people's ticket" believed they were supporting a movement to eliminate the Republican machine, congressional caucuses, and the Virginia dynasty in national politics and to institute a broad spectrum of constitutional and social reform in North Carolina. The Jackson ticket won by a commanding majority in the state in 1824.

After 1824 the party of Jackson experienced a metamorphosis in state politics. The base of its support shifted from western to eastern North Carolina, from yeomen farmers of the backcountry to planter aristocrats of the coastal plain. Jackson's views on slavery, state sovereignty, and federal spending programs generally pleased slaveholders. Small farmers became increasingly weary of Jackson during his second term. Therefore advocates of internal improvements, banking interests disturbed by the veto of the recharter bill of 1832, and critics of the president's handling of the nullification crisis in South Carolina turned to the anti-Jackson or Whig party. The North Carolina Whigs were more inclined to support nationalist measures and were less ardent about states' rights issues. They also championed constitutional reform, reapportionment of representation, public school legislation, state aid to eleemosynary institutions, and tax reforms. The state program of the Whig party was one that under ordinary circumstances would most likely be identified with the tenets of Jacksonian Democracy. Yet the party that inherited Federalist political traditions was destined to carry out a program of progress for North Carolina. Whigs championed the interests of undeveloped and underrepresented counties from the western and sound regions. From 1835 to 1850 this party dominated the political life of the state, thereby terminating eastern control.

The constitutional convention of 1835, one of the early accomplishments of the Whig party, represented a turning point in the history of the state. Whigs first secured in 1835 a popular referendum on the call for a constitutional convention. The majority support for this call resulted from strong western support, with opposition generally in eastern counties. Governor David L. Swain, a Whig, was the floor leader, ably assisted by Whigs William Gaston and John Motley Morehead and by Charles Fisher from the Democratic ranks. The changes incorporated in the state constitution were subject to popular approval. Borough representation and free Negro suffrage were abolished, thereby satisfying demands of slaveholders, who were apprehensive about abolitionist activities. Poll taxes were equalized; Catholics, but not Jews or atheists, were permitted to hold public office. Provisions were added to allow constitutional amendments by either a convention or legislative action.

Under the new constitution, legislative sessions became biennial instead of annual. Election of the governor was removed from the legislature and placed with the electorate—adult white male taxpayers. Equal county representation in the house of commons was abolished, and the 120 members were apportioned according to federal population, with each county guaranteed one representative. The 50 state senators were to be chosen from districts the size of which was determined by amounts paid in state taxes. In this way the convention allowed western control of the house of commons and eastern control of the senate. Whigs scored a major victory when these changes were ratified by a popular majority in 1835. The activities surrounding the convention, the emergence of two fairly evenly balanced political parties, and the emphasis upon party journalism and campaign activities tended to highlight state problems and issues. Perhaps for the first time the problems confronting North Carolina as a state could be treated in a realistic way.

Whigs promoted railroad construction in their efforts to provide a statewide transportation system. Railroads were believed to be superior and cheaper than canals or turnpikes, and with construction from the coast to the mountains the landlocked counties would finally have access to port facilities. Consequently towns vied for railroads; the legislature chartered many private companies in the 1830s, and the sister state Virginia aroused concern by threatening to encroach upon shipping in the Roanoke River valley. The Wilmington & Weldon Railroad (chartered as Wilmington & Raleigh in 1834) became the first significant line to orient traffic from the Roanoke River to Wilmington, N.C. It was chartered as a private company, and its construction was completed in 1840 by state aid of about $1 million. This 161-mile line was the longest railroad in the world in 1840. Ultimately it became a profitable operation and was described as the "lifeline of the Confederacy" during the Civil War. The Raleigh & Gaston Railroad, an 86-mile line connecting Raleigh and the Roanoke River, was completed in 1840 after receiving substantial state aid. This line was not profitable at first, and the state lost almost $1 million from its investment. The losses from state aid to railroad companies did not dampen enthusiasm for more construction, and in 1849 the most ambitious project of all, the North Carolina Railroad, was chartered to connect Goldsboro and Charlotte. The state subscribed two-thirds of the stock in this venture, which opened for development what is presently known as the Piedmont Crescent. This 223-mile project was completed in 1856 and was the pride of the state. The immediate reduction of freight rates and the expansion of agriculture and industry into the Piedmont would affect the economic prosperity of the 1850s. It is noteworthy that when the Democrats returned to power in 1850 they expanded the railroad construction program launched under the Whig party.

Whigs next focused attention upon the development of a public school system. Aware of the shortcomings of the literary fund, they capitalized upon the distribution of the federal surplus in 1837 and directed that it be used to support schools. In 1839 the legislature enacted a public school law to permit counties to vote for or against the principle of state support. Those approving schools would receive, for each district, $40 annually from the literary fund, to be supplemented by $20 and a school building provided by the district. Ultimately all counties voted for schools, and by 1850 there were 2,657 public schools with an enrollment of 100,591 students. This notable expansion of educational opportunities was achieved within a decade.

In 1844 the legislature appropriated $5,000 to create a state school for the deaf and the blind. Counties provided $75 a year in supplements for each student enrolled. This institution was launched in Raleigh in 1845 and in 1851 was expanded to include a department for the blind. Whigs also acted to create a state hospital for the insane in 1848, and this institution, located in Raleigh, was opened in 1856. These pioneering efforts to provide eleemosynary institutions fell short of the goals of many reformers, who envisioned state-supported orphanages and a penitentiary. Although Whigs provided for reassessment of property and levied new taxes on inheritances, incomes, licenses, and luxuries, the state income was inadequate to provide for increased services. Consequently in 1848 the party resorted to borrowing by authorizing the sale of state bonds.

Although the record of the Whig party from 1835 to 1850 was one of extraordinary achievement, events during the 1840s led to its decline and eventual disappearance. Some critics maintained that the Whigs failed to carry out an adequate railroad-building program. Others questioned the lack of administration and efficiency in the public school system and pointed to the unequal distribution of state support under a formula based on the federal population. The resurgent Democratic party capitalized upon the issue of free white manhood suffrage, which the Whigs opposed, and under William W. Holden's editorship the *North Carolina Standard* depicted the party of Jackson as the party of the common man. This strategy represented a dramatic change from the status quo mentality of the 1830s. The election of James K. Polk to the presidency in 1844, in view of his North Carolina background and upbringing, augured favorably for Democratic party prospects. But Whig opposition to the Mexican War and expansion of slavery into the territories became perhaps the most telling issues. Increasingly the Democratic party in North Carolina was identified as most favorable to southern and slaveholding interests. And, as the issues involving slavery and territorial expansion became more heated, the nationalist measures identified with the Whig party were less and less appealing to Tarheels.

The election of David S. Reid, a Democrat, as governor in 1850 terminated an era of Whig party domination. The Democrats also won control of the legislature. They pressed immediately for enactment of a free suffrage amendment, but did not secure ratification of their proposal until 1857. On state issues Democrats expanded the railroad construction program significantly and also contributed state aid to plank roads and navigation companies. A plank road craze swept North Carolina in the 1850s. These roads were expected to provide access to railroads and assist farmers in marketing produce; the cost was about $1,500 per mile. Promoters did not reckon with decay of timbers and the mounting cost of maintenance. By 1860 the movement was of little consequence.

In 1852 Democrats created the office of state superintendent of common schools and elected Calvin H. Wiley, a Whig, to fill the position. Under Wiley's brilliant leadership, textbooks were improved, teachers were certified by examination, salaries were augmented, facilities were expanded and vastly improved, and a spirit of professionalism was brought to the public school system. Emphasis upon quality became the singular contribution of Wiley.

Phenomenal economic prosperity during the 1850s brought additional tax revenues for education and for charitable and correctional services. From 1850 to 1860 land values more than doubled; tobacco production increased from 12 to 33 million pounds; the cotton crop increased from 73,845 bales in 1850 to 145, 514 bales in 1860; and wheat production rose from 2 million bushels in 1850 to 4.7 million bushels in 1860. The bright leaf variety of tobacco was introduced by Abisha and Elisha Slade of Caswell County and with a new curing process became the basis for the bright leaf tobacco industry. New varieties of short-staple cotton facilitated expansion of the cotton economy into Piedmont North Carolina. Much of the agricultural and industrial expansion was made possible by railroad construction. It is noteworthy that between 1850 and 1860 the value of manufactured articles rose from $9.7 million to $16.7 million. There were indications of an industrial transformation before the Civil War. The unparalleled prosperity of the 1850s also convinced many slaveholders of the economic advantages of the peculiar institution and strengthened their defensive attitude. Developments in the decade contradicted much of what Hinton Rowan Helper described in *The Impending Crisis*.

The great revival movement in religion strengthened the membership and influence of churches in the antebellum period. In its broadest sense the movement included missionary and philanthropic work, Sunday school activities, Bible tract publications and church journals, advocacy of temperance, peace proposals, and defense of the rights of women and children. A major function of churches in the early years of the nineteenth century involved the establishment of academies and colleges for men and women. Through involvement in many social issues and reform movements, the churches came to occupy a more important role in the lives of the people. Only a few denominations, most notably the Society of Friends and the Wesleyan Methodists, supported abolition of slavery. The others either took a neutral role or defended the institution. By 1844 the leading Protestant denominations were establishing southern branches.

Disunion and the Civil War. Although the Democratic party after 1850 expanded the state reform programs initiated by Whigs, its position on the question of slavery placed it in a defensive posture in national politics. The great debates over the Compromise of 1850 and the Kansas-Nebraska Act of 1854 made Tarheels aware of their minority interests. And civil crises in Kansas, the emergence of the Republican party in 1854, the spirited debates between Stephen A. Douglas and Abraham Lincoln in 1858, and the wave of hysteria that followed John Brown's Harpers Ferry Raid in 1859 manifestly contributed to the determination of Democrats to uphold sectional interests.

The division of the Democratic party into northern and southern branches in 1860 assured the election of Lincoln to the presidency. Lincoln had no Republican organization or significant following in North Carolina. Predictably, John C. Breckinridge, the southern Democratic candidate, received the majority vote and North Carolina's electoral vote. However, John Bell, the Constitutional Union party candidate who appealed to the nationalist sentiments of old-line Whigs in particular, received 44,990 votes to 48,539 cast for Breckinridge. It is significant that a candidate who espoused nationalism—the Constitution, the Union, and the laws of Congress—almost defeated the prosouthern slaveholding candidate. North Carolinians obviously were not in the vanguard of the secession movement in 1860.

The combined vote for Bell and Douglas, leader of the northern Democrats, exceeded that cast for Breckinridge and indicated that majority sentiment in North Carolina opposed secession. Therefore the Democratic legislature at first refused to call a convention to consider secession. When voters were given an opportunity in February, 1861, to endorse a convention, they rejected the proposal by a vote of 47,323 to 46,672. Conceivably Unionists would have controlled such a gathering, but voters nonetheless feared it might lead to secession. The refusal of Republican leaders to agree to any terms of compromise, as well as Lincoln's determination to reinforce federal garrisons in the South, strengthened the appeal of secessionists in North Carolina. When Confederate troops fired on Ft. Sumter on April 12, 1861, and the president responded by calling upon the states to supply 75,000 soldiers to suppress the insurrection, there remained scant hope that North Carolina could stay in the Union.

Governor John W. Ellis thereupon ordered that U.S. Fts. Caswell and Johnston, the arsenal at Fayetteville, and the branch mint at Charlotte be seized. The legislature in special session called for election of delegates to a convention that met in Raleigh on May 20. This convention rejected the argument that the state could secede from the Union by right of revolution. Instead it resolved that under the right of secession the Union was dissolved. On May 20 the ordinance of secession was adopted unanimously and Tarheels joined the Confederacy.

Although North Carolina had strong Unionist ties, it was never considered a large slaveholding state with an influential planter aristocracy, and was hardly regarded as wealthy or affluent, it nevertheless supplied a greater number of men to the Confederacy (125,000) than any other southern state. It also sustained a greater number of casualties by far than any other Confederate state. Those killed in battle or who died from diseases numbered 40,275. Yet the position North Carolina occupied in the Confederate government aroused constant political wrangling. Confederates, those who supported without reservation the policies of Jefferson Davis and the Confederate government in Richmond, were a decided minority. The majority of North Carolinians belonged to a political faction, known as the Conservative party, with strong reservations about the policies of the Confederate government.

Led by Zebulon B. Vance, who was elected governor in 1862, the Conservatives criticized the use of North Carolina troops on the Virginia front while much of eastern North Carolina was vulnerable to invasion. Vance demanded that his state have more high-ranking generals in the Confederate ranks, and he particularly resented the presence of Confederate recruiters. He insisted that the supply and provisioning of troops be a state function, and he displayed outstanding administrative talents in directing the war effort. He also maintained that his state should have higher-ranking members of the Confederate Cabinet, its diplomatic service, and strategic committee assignments in the Confederate Congress.

Vance took exception to the policies of the Richmond government over suspension of the writ of habeas corpus, and his defense of this venerable constitutional guarantee indicated a concern for civil rights in wartime. When the Conscription Act of 1862 exempted from military service all those who owned 20 or more slaves, Vance complained that the conflict had become "a rich man's war, and a poor man's fight." He strongly objected to the insistence of the Confederate government that goods carried through the Union blockade, principally at Wilmington, be consigned to Confederate account. In 1863 and 1864 Vance determined that peace overtures with the Union were futile, and he sharply criticized William W. Holden, who emerged as a gubernatorial candidate and leader of the peace movement in 1864.

During the Civil War much of eastern North Carolina, along the rivers, sounds, and Outer Banks, was overrun and occupied by Union forces. Ft. Hatteras was captured in 1861; Roanoke Island, New Bern, Washington, Ft. Macon, and Plymouth fell in 1862 (Burnside's North Carolina Expedition). In 1863 Union forces conducted raids upon the Wilmington & Weldon Railroad, upon Goldsboro, and in the Tar River valley near Tarboro. Governor Vance complained that North Carolina troops, engaged principally on the Virginia front, should be used to drive the invader from the state. After repeated Union naval attacks in 1862 and 1864, Ft. Fisher, which commanded approaches to the port of Wilmington and thus protected blockade-runners, fell to naval and amphibious attacks on January 15, 1865. From that point Union forces advanced to Wilmington and over the Wilmington & Weldon Railroad to join William T. Sherman's army advancing from South Carolina (Carolinas Campaign). The "lifeline of the Confederacy" was severed, and the loss of Robert E. Lee's base of supplies and reinforcements made his position in Virginia untenable.

In March, 1865, Sherman's army captured Fayetteville. Advancing toward Goldsboro it defeated Confederate forces at Southwest Creek, at Avarasboro, and in a major battle at Bentonville (March 19–21, 1865). By April 13 Sherman's army passed in review around Capitol Square in Raleigh, and on April 18 General Joseph Johnston surrendered what was left of his Confederate army to Sherman. The final terms of surrender were negotiated at Bennett House, near Durham, on April 26. During the final weeks of the war, North Carolina was invaded by General George Stoneman's army, which marched from Tennessee. This campaign involved destruction of small factories, supply bases, and harassment of the civilian population (Stoneman's Raids). Its principal objective was to capture the Confederate prison at Salisbury, second only to Andersonville in size and by 1865 a veritable deathtrap for most of its occupants. Stoneman seized the prison on April 12. The concept of total war was brought home to North Carolinians by Sherman and Stoneman. Following Lee's surrender at Appomattox and Johnston's surrender at Bennett House, North Carolina was placed under a Union army of occupation commanded by General John M. Schofield on April 29.

Reconstruction and Redemption. Andrew Johnson of Tennessee, a native of Raleigh, undertook to carry on Lincoln's plan for the restoration of the southern states upon succeeding to the presidency on April 15, 1865. He offered amnesty to most Tarheels and in exceptional cases generously extended pardons. William Holden was appointed provisional governor and in this capacity filled offices, processed applications for pardons, and arranged to call a constitutional convention. This convention repealed the ordinance of secession, abolished slavery, and repudiated the state war debt. The heated issue of debt repudiation led to Holden's defeat by Jonathan Worth in the gubernatorial election of 1865. The refusal of North Carolina to grant suffrage to freedmen or to provide public schools for their advancement, the enactment by Conservatives of black codes restricting the rights of freedmen, as well as Holden's defeat and reports of widespread racial violence in the South, convinced Radical Republicans in Congress that harsher measures of Reconstruction were necessary. President Johnson's intransigence and his failure to win support in the congressional elections of 1866 enabled Radical Republicans to override his vetoes and proceed with their own plans for Reconstruction in 1867.

Under congressional Reconstruction, North Carolina was placed in the second military district. The Republican party state organization coincided with the inauguration of Reconstruction measures. In 1868 Republicans controlled the constitutional convention that drafted a completely new fundamental law for the state. Principally written by Albion W. Tourgée of Ohio, this document was one of the most progressive of the state constitutions. It enfranchised freedmen, provided for popular control of county government through elected commissioners, supported the principles of a public school system, and removed previous religious and property-holding restrictions on voting and officeholding. In April, 1868, the new constitution was ratified. Republicans won control of the legislature and the congressional delegation, and

Holden was elected governor over his Conservative party opponent. The principal accomplishment of Reconstruction in North Carolina involved constitutional reform.

Throughout the Reconstruction era, agents of the Freedmen's Bureau established schools, negotiated labor contracts, provided for clinics, dispensaries, and medical care to freedmen, and distributed food and clothing. The bureau agents failed notably in the distribution of abandoned and confiscated lands to freedmen, and further disappointment came with the failure of the Freedmen's Bank in 1874. Bureau agents were accused of using the agency to promote the Republican party, a charge that has not been substantiated. Instead the Union League was launched for the avowed purpose of encouraging freedmen to register and vote as Republicans. After 1867 the Ku Klux Klan undertook through violence and intimidation to discourage the political activities of freedmen and white Republican leaders. This organization bequeathed a legacy of hatred and violence to the state.

Although there were several tangible accomplishments by the Reconstruction regime, it was comparatively short-lived and marred by corruption. The most notable failure involved the fraudulent issuance of railroad construction bonds, in which many Conservatives concurred. Subsequent exposure of these railroad schemes by the Bragg and Shipp commissions tarnished the record of Republicans. When Governor Holden sought to suppress Klan violence in the Piedmont and in his zeal denied the writ of habeas corpus, he was overruled by a federal judge and rejected by national leaders of the Republican party. After Conservatives regained control of the legislature in 1870, they impeached Holden and removed him from office. He thus became the only state governor up to that time removed by impeachment.

Conservatives sought to undo much of the Reconstruction program through constitutional amendments, particularly in the convention of 1875. The convention provided a means for Conservative control of county government by replacing popularly elected county commissioners. Instead county commissioners were to be appointed by justices of the peace, who in turn were appointed by the legislature. In this way local self-government and home rule were denied. In the election of 1876, Conservatives, in anticipation of Samuel J. Tilden's victory, assented to use the Democratic party label. In this celebrated election Zebulon Vance, the Democratic gubernatorial candidate, defeated his Republican opponent Thomas Settle. Joint debates between the candidates were a memorable feature of the campaign.

The Bourbon Democrats, or Redeemers, dominated state politics after the abandonment of Reconstruction. They emphasized economy in government, retrenchment, and scrupulous honesty. No major scandal involving corruption would plague Tarheel Democrats in this period. Bourbons gave special favors to railroads through charters of incorporation and tax exemptions. They either sold or leased valuable state properties to railroads. Generally their tax policies favored business interests, holders of stocks, bonds, and securities, and salaried persons, while bearing down heavily upon farmers and owners of real property. In 1879 Democrats drastically scaled down and repudiated a substantial portion of the state debt, thereby reducing it from about $43,750,000 to some $6,500,000. Shortly thereafter, following the sale of state-owned railroad property, they declared a tax holiday of one year. While these economies were pursued, the party in office neglected public schools, internal improvements, and eleemosynary institutions. If challenged by disaffected interests, Democrats invariably fell back on the campaign slogan of "Radical Reconstruction and Negro misrule," thereby capitalizing on the legacies of Reconstruction, which created an illogical political unity of the white voters. One-party domination was augmented by control of the electoral machinery. Yet independent movements represented a constant threat, Republicans regularly cast more than 40 percent of the total vote, and in 1887 a coalition of independents and Republicans actually secured control of the state house of representatives on the issue of repeal of the odious county government system. The coalition failed to enact this reform, and in 1889 Democrats undertook to discourage further independence through enactment of a repressive election law. A substantial decline in the vote attested to the effectiveness of this legislation.

The most effective criticism of Bourbon policies came from farmers, who in 1887 were encouraged by Leonidas L. Polk, editor of the *Progressive Farmer,* to organize a state association. The 1887 farmers' lobby was instrumental in securing the charter of the agricultural and mechanical college in Raleigh and, in cooperation with the Knights of Labor, created in 1887 the state bureau of labor statistics. In 1887 the Farmers' Alliance was organized in Robeson County, and by 1890 it was active in politics throughout the state. Farmers were emboldened to make demands upon legislative and congressional candidates, and the 1891 legislature was accurately called the "farmers' legislature." In creating a railroad commission and in chartering a normal and industrial college for women and an agricultural and mechanical college for Negroes, both in Greensboro, the farmers achieved a noteworthy reform program.

Although most North Carolina Alliance men preferred to work within the Democratic party, the nomination of Grover Cleveland in 1892 alienated farmers generally and hastened the emergence of a Populist Party ticket at the state level. The Populist state candidates fared badly in 1892, but the combination of Populist and Republican votes exceeded the number cast for Democrats and was an augury of defeat for Bourbon hopefuls in 1894. Instead of making a sincere effort to accommodate Alliance and Populist demands, Bourbon Democrats ignored the advice of their liberal members and assumed a posture of intransigence. They also undertook to repeal the charter of the Farmers' Alliance and to crush its political role. These circumstances made inevitable the coalition of Populists and Republicans in 1894, known to Tarheels as the fusion government. Although the alliance of Populists and Republicans was illogical from the standpoint of national ideology, there were mutual state interests on which the parties could agree. Republicans were preoccupied with reform of the county government system and election machinery. Populists sought restoration of their charter, usury legislation, stronger railroad regulations, and tax reform. Both parties initially made concessions in shaping their state programs and electoral slates.

The record of the fusion government was impressive in securing repeal of the county government system and in restoring local self-government and home rule. Many of the Populist economic reforms were carried out. Negroes were encouraged to take a more active role in politics, although the extent of their vote and officeholding was exaggerated by Democrats. Populists and Republicans were, however, plagued by disagreements over patronage and electoral slates, and by 1897 an open schism over senatorial candidates had developed. Yet, instead of appealing to disaffected Populists, Democrats capitalized upon an emotionally charged "white supremacy" campaign in 1898 to wrest control of the legislature from fusionists. In a campaign marked by violence and intimidation, Democrats regained control of the state. They proceeded in 1899 to draft a suffrage amendment with its infamous Grandfather Clause. In 1900, again pursuing the white supremacy theme, Democrats elected Charles B. Aycock to replace the fusionist governor Daniel L. Russell.

The twentieth century. In the 1900 election voters ratified the suffrage amendment that disfranchised illiterate blacks and enfranchised illiterate whites. The hopes of Republicans and Populists were further dashed by the new election law of 1899. Subsequently Populists either returned to the ranks of Democrats or joined the Republicans. And whatever appeal Republicans might have to the electorate was further undermined by bitter factional squabbling after 1900. There is substantial evidence to indicate that patronage brokers in the Republican ranks were content to allow the party to remain small during the early years of the twentieth century.

The Wilmington race riot erupted in November shortly after the 1898 election. Although it had no effect on the outcome of this white supremacy campaign, it intensified the movement to remove blacks from politics and to replace black laborers with whites. Furnifold M. Simmons, the Democrat state chairman, devised party strategy in 1898 and 1900. He promised denominational interests that state support for the University of North Carolina and other public institutions would not be augmented. Furthermore he promised railroad interests that the party would not demand rate reductions. These commitments indicated a conservative leaning among Democrat leaders.

When former Populists complained of the number of white illiterates and doubted that all who came of voting age after 1908 would be educated (in order to qualify under the suffrage amendment), Aycock turned this criticism to advantage by highlighting the educational issue. The educational crusade became the most noted aspect of his gubernatorial program—increased school support, construction of schoolhouses, and most important a campaign to persuade counties and school districts to levy taxes for the support of common schools.

In the absence of effective Republican or Populist opposition, Democrats divided into liberal and conservative factions. U.S. Senator Furnifold Simmons of New Bern, the acknowledged party leader, headed the conservative faction, known usually as the Simmons machine or dynasty, during the time he served as senator (1901–1931). Simmons by no means dictated party candidates or state legislative policies. Governors Aycock, Robert B. Glenn, and William W. Kitchin were not considered machine candidates. The legislative records, particularly the 1907 and 1913 sessions, were far more liberal and Progressive than Simmons' forces generally favored. With the emergence of the Kitchin family, of Scotland Neck, to prominence in state and national politics, mounting pressures were put upon Democrats to remove Simmons, whom many accused of apostasy to his own party. Josephus Daniels, editor of the *News and Observer;* Chief Justice Walter Clark of the North Carolina supreme court; and Edward J. Justice, most prominent of the Progressive legislators, demanded a reorientation of the party along more liberal lines. In 1912 Aycock, Clark, and Kitchin challenged Simmons in the senatorial primary. Aycock died during the campaign, and Simmons easily defeated his two lesser opponents. Ironically, he soon became a cosponsor of one of the major pieces of legislation in Woodrow Wilson's first administration, the Underwood–Simmons Tariff Act of 1913.

Disfranchisement of Negroes, the overall decline of the electorate, and the reluctance of Democrats to enact a statewide primary law until 1915 qualified in many ways the proud boast that North Carolina was in the mainstream of the Progressive movement and a leader among southern states. The inability of labor to organize, the pervasively low wage scale, the reluctance of the legislature to enact child labor laws or compulsory attendance regulations, and the blighting effects of mill town paternalism retarded Progressive forces during the early years of the twentieth century. Although Simmons was identified with tariff reforms of the Wilson era and Claude Kitchin was instrumental in shaping Progressive tax reforms at the national level, North Carolina Democrats were unable to translate the idealism of Woodrow Wilson into an impressive state reform program. This was perhaps most evident in the failure of the Progressive Democratic convention of 1914 to impress its demands upon the party leaders. The failure of voters to ratify ten proposed constitutional amendments in 1914 revealed basic conservative philosophies of Tarheel Democrats.

During World War I the focus upon defense efforts and expansive training and supply operations in North Carolina shifted emphasis from domestic state programs. A total of 86,457 North Carolinians served in the armed forces, of whom 629 were killed in action. A far greater number, 1,542, died from disease, particularly from the influenza epidemic of 1918.

The accomplishments of state government in the 1920s eclipsed earlier records. From 1913 to 1930 North Carolina taxes increased 554 percent; state expenditures from 1915 to 1925 rose by 847 percent; and from 1920 to 1930 the state bonded debt increased from $13,300,000 to $178,265,000. In this decade business-oriented governors focused on new budgeting and accounting methods, higher tax assessments, highway and school bond issues, and significant increases of support for public schools, higher education, and charitable institutions. Much of the debt burden for schools and roads was assumed by counties and municipalities. In this decade North Carolina deservedly earned its reputation as the "good roads" state of the South.

The administration of Governor O. Max Gardner (1929–1933) coincided with the Great Depression, and his significant accomplishments in time of crisis attest to an extraordinary political ability. In 1931 the legislature provided for overall state control of the highway system; it also assumed responsibility for the constitutional six-month public school term and directed that taxes other than ad valorem levies be used to support public schools. The legislature also provided for consolidation of the three major branches of the University of North Carolina. The 1931 session enacted controls over local and county debts in an effort to curtail the advancing tax burden. Due largely to the impetus of Gardner and his successor J. C. B. Ehringhaus, the legislature in 1933 provided that revenues from a 3 percent sales tax be placed in a general fund largely to support schools and charitable institutions. Although North Carolina was in the depths of a depression, the public school term was extended from six to eight months in 1933.

Enormous economic and social losses that followed the panic of 1929 required drastic federal programs to carry out relief, recovery, and reform. Public works projects, conservation activities, and direct relief grants were launched by the administration of Franklin D. Roosevelt to provide employment and a stimulus to the economy. From 1933 to 1938 North Carolina received $428,053,000 in various federal relief projects. At the height of the New Deal era, more than 10 percent of the state population was employed in various federal relief activities. The per capita expenditure of $123.82 was, however, the lowest in the nation. Farmers received benefit payments for crop control and soil conservation projects; with curtailment of production and revival of prosperity, the income of farmers more than doubled from 1932 to 1935. Benefit payments to farmers amounted to $99,351,000 from 1933 to 1940.

The New Deal program, particularly after the passage of the Wagner Act of 1935, sought to protect the rights of workers to organize and bargain collectively (labor unions). This legislation and subsequent court decisions upholding the powers of the National Labor Relations Board became a powerful stimulus to the growth of organized labor in North Carolina. Further gains for labor were secured in the wages and hours legislation of 1938, which provided to workers in the major industries a minimum 25-cent hourly wage and a 44-hour work week. Under the Social Security Act of 1935, retirement benefits were provided to workers, and payments were made to dependent children and to the needy, blind, and aged. By 1939 the New Deal program had contributed manifestly to the recovery of North Carolina. Tarheels indicated their overwhelming support for the Roosevelt program in the election of 1936 and the election of 1940.

With the outbreak of World War II in Europe in 1939, the concerns of North Carolinians became inextricably linked with foreign policies. The peacetime draft of 1940 and strategies to assist Great Britain affected the lives of many Tarheels before the Japanese attack upon Pearl Harbor in 1941 brought the nation into a two-front war in the Far East and Europe. North Carolina became one of the major training areas for army and marine recruits. Altogether 362,000 Tarheels, including more than 7,000 women, served in the armed forces. Of this number more than 7,000 died in service. On the home front industry and agriculture were converted to wartime production. The state became a major supplier to the armed forces, a construction site for naval vessels at Wilmington, and a quartermaster center of major significance.

During the height of the war, Governor J. Melville Broughton worked with the legislature to secure a nine-month school term (1943) and record-breaking appropriations for education. In 1944 the governor launched a medical care program, whose importance was highlighted by the state's having had the highest rate of rejections of draftees for medical reasons of any American state. The increased revenues available to the state allowed the implementation of a five-year hospital plan (1947–1952) to secure modern hospitals and public health centers for practically every county. Federal matching funds were provided for these projects under the Hill–Burton Act.

The Shelby dynasty in state politics, launched under the aegis of O. Max Gardner in 1928, for 20 years provided the state with a succession of business-oriented governors, half of whom came from the Shelby area. This leadership was known to historians and political scientists as the progressive plutocracy. In 1948 this political machine was challenged successfully by the former state commissioner of agriculture, W. Kerr Scott of Haw River. Scott achieved one of the most notable records in the twentieth century. Under his leadership landmark victories were secured in bond proposals for schools and roads. The state set a world record for road construction between 1948 and 1952. Scott's program included completion of four-year medical and dental schools at the University of North Carolina and a determined campaign to construct hospitals and health centers in all counties of the state. As a farmer he pushed aggressively for rural electrification, improved telephone services, and the concept that all state financial deposits should yield interest payments. Under Scott's administration blacks were first admitted to the University of North Carolina following a federal court order of 1951.

In 1949 Scott appointed the well-known liberal Frank P. Graham, president of the University of North Carolina, to the U.S. Senate. When Graham was challenged and defeated by Willis Smith of Raleigh in the primary campaign of 1950, the race issue was used extensively in North Carolina politics for the first time since 1900. Smith's race-baiting marked a significant political departure in the history of the state. This tactic was also used by Alton Lennon against Scott's bid for a Senate seat in 1954 and by I. Beverley Lake against gubernatorial candidate Terry Sanford in 1960. In both instances the agitation of the race issue failed. Since 1960 the issue was exploited in 1968 and 1972 variously by Richard Nixon and by the followers of George Wallace.

Recent political trends, particularly since the victory of James Earl Carter over Wallace in North Carolina's 1976 presidential primary and Carter's subsequent election, appear to indicate that the race issue has lost much of its emotional impact.

When Luther H. Hodges became governor on November 9, 1954, following the death of William B. Umstead, he brought to the office a background of business experience at national and international levels. Perhaps his greatest achievement was the campaign to attract industry to North Carolina. A major focal point of interest was the creation of the 5,000-acre "research triangle" between Raleigh, Durham, and Chapel Hill. The center presently contains a significant number of research laboratories, both public and private, in the industrial, chemical, and medical fields. In spite of significant progress in construction of industries and laboratories, the relocation of business in North Carolina did not improve significantly the state's average per capita wage for industrial workers. There were even indications that new textile and apparel industries depressed wage levels. Yet the legislature in 1959 became the first in the South to enact a minimum hourly wage law of 75 cents for workers in companies that employed more than five people.

In recent years North Carolina's reputation as a progressive state has been greatly enhanced by the leadership of Governors Terry Sanford (1961–1965) and Robert W. Scott (1969–1973). Stressing quality education for all people, Sanford introduced bold and innovative programs involving a school for the performing arts, a governor's school for high school students of extraordinary ability, and an advancement school for underachievers. The movement to create community colleges and technical schools brought opportunities for higher education into every corner of North Carolina. And a major area of educational activity has involved public television. Significantly larger appropriations for school construction and teachers' salaries were provided during the Sanford and Scott administrations. To finance this ambitious program Sanford defended the extension of sales taxes to food and other consumer items. The governor was not as successful as W. Kerr Scott in securing popular approval for school and road bonds. Indeed, the voters in 1961 rejected all ten items that involved a bond issue referendum. Sanford was more successful in securing constitutional amendments to provide court reform, legislative reapportionment, and tax revision. During his administration a number of cities across the state integrated their schools and, following the much publicized sit-ins at Greensboro, lunch counters commenced to serve customers on an integrated basis. To conservative-minded critics who assailed federal programs and raised the issue of states' rights, the governor responded that the state should assume greater responsibilities and function in a more dynamic and creative way.

Joseph F. Steelman
East Carolina University

Editor's Note

James E. Holshouser, Jr., was elected governor of North Carolina in 1972, the first Republican to attain the office since 1896. Republicans also gained a U.S. Senate seat the same year with the election of Jesse A. Helms. However, in 1976, Democrats regained control of the governorship when James B. Hunt, Jr., was elected. James G. Martin, a Republican, currently serves as North Carolina's governor.

Chronology

The following chronology only scratches the surface of North Carolina's history. For brevity's sake, some important events in the state's past have been omitted. Also, see the sections "Revolutionary War," "War Between the States," "Forts," and "Famous North Carolinians" for more information about these related topics.

1524—The Italian navigator, Giovanni de Verrazzano, in the service of France, explored North Carolina coastal waters.

1540—Hernando de Soto and his Spaniards reached western North Carolina.

1566—Another Spanish expedition, led by Juan Pardo, visited among the Catawba and other Indians.

1578—Sir Humphrey Gilbert was granted patent of discovery.

1583—Sir Humphrey Gilbert drowned in the *Squirrel.*

1584—Walter Raleigh was granted patent of discovery.

—Formal ceremony of possession of what is now North Carolina was held on an island near Roanoke Island, in Queen Elizabeth's name.

1585—Walter Raleigh was knighted, and permitted to call his colony Virginia.

—Sir Richard Grenville sailed for Virginia with seven vessels and 100 colonists.

—New Fort in Virginia completed. Ralph Lane appointed governor of colony of 107 men.

1586—Resentful Indians attacked Lane while on expedition up the Albemarle River. Lane later made a surprise attack on the Indians when he learned that Indians planned to attack the colony.

—Sir Francis Drake brought a ship and crew with stores for Lane. After anchoring, the ship, along with three others, was lost in a hurricane. The colonists decided to return to England with Drake.

—Supply ship arrived to find settlement deserted.

—Sir Richard Grenville arrived with seven ships and stores to find settlement deserted. Grenville left 15 colonists to guard the colony. Two of the colonists were killed by Indians, the rest disappeared.

1587—Grant of arms for "Cittie of Ralegh," in Chesapeake Bay. John White appointed governor.

—Three ships carrying 115 colonists, on the way to Chesapeake Bay, arrived to pick up the 15 colonists left as guards. The pilot instead left the 115 colonists at Roanoke Island.

—John White's daughter, Elenor Dare, gave birth to Virginia Dare.

—White persuaded to leave for England to arrange for supplies.

1588—Sir Richard Grenville, prepared to sail for Virginia with relief stores, was instead sent to join Sir Francis Drake in Armada emergency.

—White sailed for Virginia, but was attacked and looted, and had to return to England.

1590—John White sails to Roanoke Island to find the colony deserted. The word "Croatoan" carved on a tree suggested that the colony had moved to Croatoan Island, but weather prevented White from going to the island. Due to the weather, White was forced to return to England.

1602—Samuel Mace was sent by Raleigh to collect plants from the area south of Carolina Outer Banks.

1603—Sir Walter Raleigh arrested for treason.

1604—Terms of Peace Treaty with Spain agreed in London.

1608—Jamestown colonists sent a search party to look for lost colonists rumored to still be living. No survivors were found.

1609—Jamestown colonists sent a man with two Indian guides to search for lost colonists. Later a second search party was sent inland. No survivors were found.

1629—Charles I of England granted "Carolana" to Sir Robert Heath.

1663—Charles II granted a charter to the territory south of Virginia to eight lords proprietors.

—Population for the North Carolina area already exceeded 500.

1670—John Lederer visits several North Carolina Indian tribes along the Atlantic coast.

1672—William Edmundson, an English Quaker, was the first missionary to visit Albemarle County.

1675—North Carolina's first Indian war erupted between Virginia whites and the Chowan tribe.

1694—The population of the colony was approximately 4,000.

1706—Bath was incorporated as the first town in North Carolina.

1710—New Bern was established by Swiss and German colonists.

1711—Marked the onset of the Tuscarora Indian War.

1713—Upon their defeat at the hands of the whites, members of the Tuscarora tribe migrated to New York to live among the Iroquois.

1718—Off the North Carolina coast, on November 22, Blackbeard and nine of his men were killed and the rest of his crew were arrested, convicted and hanged. During November and December 78 pirates were hanged.

1729—North Carolina became a royal province under George II.

1730—Several North Carolina Cherokee chiefs visited London.

1750—Sixteen-year-old Daniel Boone and his parents moved to the region that was soon to become Rowan County.

1770—Capitol and governor's mansion completed in New Bern.

1774—North Carolina elected delegates to the First Continental Congress.

1775—The Mecklenburg Declaration of Independence was presented.

—Richard Henderson bought a large tract of land in Western North Carolina (later Middle Tennessee) from the Cherokees.

1776—North Carolina was the first colony to instruct its delegates to the Continental Congress to vote for independence. The Halifax resolves were adopted.

—Battle of Moores Creek Bridge was fought.

—The first state constitution was adopted.

—Legislature made provisions for public schools.

1781—Battle of Guilford Court House was fought.

1785—Cherokees ceded more land in the west (Tennessee) to the central government.

1789—North Carolina became the 12th United State by ratifying the Constitution.

1790—Western North Carolina was ceded to the United States Government. It became the Territory of the United States South of the River Ohio. (In 1796, it became the State of Tennessee.)

1792—Raleigh became the state's permanent capital.

1794—First capitol in Raleigh was completed.

—The state adopted a new seal.

1795—James K. Polk was born near Charlotte, North Carolina.

1798—Former state capitol and governor's residence in New Bern was ravaged by fire.

1801—Gold was discovered in Cabarrus County.

1802—Cherokees formed a National Council.

1811—Battle of Tippecanoe won by Americans.

1812—United States declared war on Great Britain. Secretary of War asked for 7,000 North Carolina troops.

—North Carolina's Cherokee and Lumbee Indians served with Americans in the War of 1812.

1813—140 "Fine looking soldiers" left Salisbury for Fort Moultrie.

—Massacre at Fort Mims, Alabama.

1814—Governor Hawkins called for 10 companies of state militia to participate in the Alabama Indian campaigns.

—Washington, D.C. burned at the hand of the British.

1816—Governor William Miller became the first occupant of the "New Governor's Palace" in Raleigh.

1835—State Constitution was amended to favor more democratic forces.

1836—Davy Crockett, born in Tennessee (at the time part of North Carolina) died at the Alamo.

—Sam Houston from Tennessee defeated Santa Anna at San Jacinto.

1845—Texas was admitted to the Union. (James K. Polk, born in North Carolina, was instrumental in the Texas question.)

1847—By January 19, nine North Carolina companies were formed for service in the Mexican War.

1848—Treaty of Guadaloupe-Hidalgo ends the Mexican War.

1861—President Abraham Lincoln called for 75,000 North Carolina troops to quell the "Southern Insurrection." Governor John Ellis refused.

—North Carolina seceded the Union.

1862—Union forces occupied eastern North Carolina.

1863—Over 4,000 North Carolina troops were killed at Gettysburg.

1864—Confederate forces recaptured Plymouth, North Carolina in April, only to lose it again in October.

—The ironside, *Albemarle,* was torpedoed and destroyed.

—Thomas Dixon, Jr., author of *The Leopard's Spots* and other books, was born in Shelby.

—North Carolina-born General James B. Gordon died of wounds received at the Battle of Brooks Church.

1865—The Battle of Bentonville, March 19–21, was the last great battle for North Carolina. Confederates lost 2,825 men. The battle effectively ended the War Between the States.

—General Johnston surrendered to General Sherman a few miles west of Durham.

1868—June 25, North Carolina was readmitted to the Union.

1870—North Carolina's population exceeded 1,000,000 for the first time.

—Governor William Holden became the first governor in United States history to be impeached.

1876—Reconstruction in North Carolina officially ended.

1881—The Reynolds Company, tobacco producers, employed 125 men and cut 300,000 pounds of tobacco.

1890—American Tobacco Company was founded at Durham by James Buchanan Duke.

1892—The University of North Carolina at Greensboro, the first state supported institution for the higher education of women in North Carolina, was established.

1898—Approximately 2,100 officers and 28,000 enlisted men from North Carolina served in the United States Army.

—Worth Bagley, of Raleigh, became the first North Carolina naval officer killed in the Spanish-American War.

1899—North Carolina's 1st Regiment, mustered out of Spanish-American War, landed at Savannah, Georgia.

1903—First airline flight in the United States was conducted at Kitty Hawk by Orville and Wilbur Wright.

—Richard Gatling, inventor of the Gatling Gun, died.

1909—North Carolina Central University at Durham was chartered. Official opening was 1910.

1910—Population for the state went over 2,000,000.

1914—*Charlotte Daily Observer* carried headlines, "War Clouds Cover All Europe and Huge Forces Are Moving."

1916—The tank was first used as an offensive weapon.

—North Carolinian Kiffin Rockwell became the first American to shoot down an enemy plane.

1917—480,491 men registered for the draft.

1920—North Carolina women voted for the first time.

1927—University of North Carolina at Asheville opened its doors.

1928—Five million dollars from the Laura Spelman Rockefeller Memorial was donated toward the creation of the Great Smoky Mountains National Park.

1930—Indian population within the Cherokee Qualla boundary was 3,000 people.

—North Carolina's population passed 3,000,000.

1936—North Carolina dedicated its first highway historical marker.

—Intracoastal Waterway was completed.

1940—Franklin D. Roosevelt dedicated the Great Smoky Mountains National Park.

—450,000 North Carolinians registered the first day of the draft.

1942—Camp LeJeune and Cherry Point marine bases were opened.

1945—Raleigh maintained over 4,000 Victory Gardens.

1947—University of North Carolina at Wilmington was opened.

1950—Population of Raleigh was 65,679; Winston-Salem, 87,811; Charlotte, 134,042.

1952—Restoration begun on Tryon Palace (former state capitol) at New Bern.

1955—*Something of Value*, by Robert Ruark, was published.

1958—Research Triangle was established by three universities.

1961—St. Andrew's Presbyterian College opened doors.

1963—Tercentenary of the Carolina charter was celebrated.

1967—Wake Forest College gained university status.

1970—5,000,000 mark passed in population.

1971—A new state constitution became effective.

1972—James E. Holshouser, Jr., took office as the state's first Republican governor in the 20th century.

1974—"Connemara," Carl Sandburg's home at Flat Rock, was opened to the public.

—B. Everett Jordan, United States senator from 1958 to 1973, died.

1976—Part of the New River, which may have begun to flow 100 million years ago, was incorporated into the National Wild and Scenic River System.

1986—Governor Martin led Governor's Conference with proposal on drug abuse.

HOLIDAYS

When a public holiday falls on Sunday, the following Monday shall be observed as a public holiday. The dates of declared legal public holidays are as follows:

New Year's Day	January 1
Martin Luther King, Jr.'s, Birthday	third Monday in January
Robert E. Lee's Birthday	January 19
Washington's Birthday	third Monday in February
Greek Independence Day	March 25
Anniversary of signing of Halifax Resolves	April 12
Confederate Memorial Day	May 10
Anniversary of Mecklenburg Declaration of Independence	May 20
*Memorial Day	last Monday in May
*Easter	Monday following
Independence Day	July 4
Labor Day	first Monday in September
Columbus Day	second Monday in October
Yom Kippur	
Veterans Day	November 11
Election Day	Tuesday after first Monday in general election years
Thanksgiving Day	fourth Thursday in November
Christmas Day	December 25

*A holiday for all state and national banks only.

HOUSING

County	Year-Round Units(a)		Occupied Units(a)									
	Total		Total		Owner Occupied		Incomplete Plumbing		Overcrowding(b)		Incomplete Plumbing and Overcrowding	
	1980	1970	1980	1970	1980	1970	1980	1970	1980	1970	1980	1970
Alamance	38,144	30,878	35,962	29,851	26,376	21,439	1,325	3,519	1,249	2,624	175	890
Alexander	9,133	6,231	8,528	5,796	7,079	4,774	349	937	343	574	51	211
Alleghany	4,241	3,006	3,596	2,677	2,896	2,155	216	627	115	185	22	87
Anson	9,023	7,428	8,386	6,787	6,244	4,665	933	2,099	804	1,017	226	641
Ashe	8,950	6,829	8,028	6,039	6,646	4,966	800	1,865	278	554	84	327
Avery	6,168	4,242	4,826	3,667	3,904	2,918	315	875	226	469	40	219
Beaufort	15,792	12,533	14,253	11,030	10,467	7,484	1,179	2,965	735	1,195	182	649
Bertie	7,739	6,503	6,897	5,664	4,926	3,528	1,111	2,406	642	963	239	732
Bladen	11,206	8,095	10,113	7,363	8,225	5,373	1,020	2,547	657	1,092	167	691
Brunswick	18,000	11,407	12,411	6,958	10,074	5,648	551	1,497	611	992	87	415
Buncombe	64,712	50,525	60,274	47,248	42,461	33,920	1,502	4,560	1,767	3,598	171	814
Burke	27,000	18,639	25,338	17,645	19,282	13,139	768	2,371	1,011	1,753	73	550
Cabarrus	32,421	24,409	30,610	23,488	22,185	15,843	625	1,973	1,290	2,225	87	450
Caldwell	24,967	17,964	23,331	16,833	17,836	12,593	885	2,521	1,162	1,966	123	631
Camden	2,147	1,739	1,931	1,596	1,508	1,181	218	523	106	173	38	117
Carteret	20,668	11,226	15,128	9,997	11,394	7,798	264	978	429	782	29	177
Caswell	7,506	5,564	6,516	5,119	4,950	3,346	767	1,957	477	880	136	592
Catawba	39,282	29,696	37,308	27,974	27,669	20,428	663	2,329	1,360	2,507	88	531
Chatham	12,861	9,601	12,063	8,943	9,423	6,730	1,079	2,401	490	914	133	544
Cherokee	8,214	5,795	6,847	5,195	5,497	3,895	439	1,300	292	546	52	245
Chowan	4,799	3,409	4,350	3,171	3,019	2,008	301	917	221	369	45	232
Clay	2,955	1,892	2,490	1,688	2,139	1,421	145	419	90	168	20	71
Cleveland	30,294	22,592	28,458	21,422	20,421	14,355	963	2,940	1,427	2,363	140	802
Columbus	18,706	14,742	17,266	13,487	12,855	9,358	1,446	3,587	1,041	1,735	268	945
Craven	25,448	18,871	23,499	17,543	14,631	9,854	1,031	2,619	929	1,622	145	598
Cumberland	81,277	56,831	74,934	52,000	43,690	28,903	1,245	4,242	3,619	5,806	181	1,104
Currituck	4,716	2,599	3,897	2,164	3,155	1,667	235	529	162	206	30	115
Dare	6,112	3,274	5,359	2,465	4,134	1,931	112	303	166	160	9	25
Davidson	43,689	30,690	40,010	29,478	29,794	21,451	915	3,417	1,585	2,825	72	723
Davie	9,459	6,187	8,540	5,870	7,113	4,696	309	976	282	471	21	170
Duplin	15,461	12,512	13,993	11,199	10,594	7,690	1,187	3,086	788	1,345	184	729
Durham	58,331	43,019	55,614	40,921	29,918	21,736	726	2,012	2,144	3,437	87	377

	Year-Round Units(a)		Occupied Units(a)									
	Total		Total		Owner Occupied		Incomplete Plumbing		Overcrowding(b)		Incomplete Plumbing and Overcrowding	
County	1980	1970	1980	1970	1980	1970	1980	1970	1980	1970	1980	1970
Edgecombe	20,262	16,003	18,397	14,709	11,338	7,807	1,531	3,722	1,691	2,513	409	1,383
Forsyth	95,771	70,602	90,146	67,502	58,606	43,718	861	2,408	2,660	4,980	70	380
Franklin	11,131	8,211	9,983	7,622	6,981	4,759	1,458	2,793	688	1,059	270	760
Gaston	59,168	46,117	56,362	44,757	38,762	29,542	923	3,973	2,893	5,171	118	962
Gates	3,163	2,617	2,889	2,396	2,278	1,736	583	1,019	243	361	140	296
Graham	3,473	2,123	2,481	1,956	1,993	1,498	120	507	120	241	15	118
Granville	11,483	8,960	10,445	8,294	7,146	4,664	1,494	2,989	825	1,223	363	880
Greene	5,516	4,465	5,059	3,915	3,299	1,959	747	1,310	445	695	178	522
Guilford	120,258	91,029	114,084	87,827	71,377	55,456	1,602	4,967	3,837	7,133	168	1,000
Halifax	20,071	16,243	18,286	15,036	11,825	8,855	2,831	5,080	1,681	2,626	777	1,897
Harnett	22,041	15,762	20,148	14,692	13,492	9,068	1,105	2,801	1,073	1,592	218	759
Haywood	19,449	14,384	16,997	13,228	12,886	9,940	578	1,649	646	1,128	71	338
Henderson	24,225	16,240	22,389	14,195	17,428	10,693	450	1,265	620	1,125	35	231
Hertford	8,150	6,988	7,499	6,553	5,079	3,830	969	2,323	611	1,024	220	730
Hoke	6,470	4,302	6,024	3,960	4,594	2,669	478	1,257	677	866	131	519
Hyde	2,580	1,932	2,029	1,604	1,572	1,185	253	627	128	235	37	151
Iredell	30,951	23,703	29,128	22,411	22,042	16,467	697	2,279	1,236	2,057	97	465
Jackson	11,073	6,684	8,502	6,056	6,242	4,519	418	1,341	317	676	49	342
Johnston	27,727	20,849	25,157	19,190	17,001	11,424	1,249	4,169	1,108	1,906	166	899
Jones	3,643	3,009	3,203	2,679	2,394	1,846	339	920	232	432	56	252
Lee	13,974	9,737	12,914	9,118	9,381	6,271	528	1,447	528	943	66	384
Lenoir	22,468	17,194	20,674	15,941	12,744	8,783	1,393	3,055	1,179	1,839	244	850
Lincoln	15,810	10,656	14,674	9,960	11,461	7,620	589	1,458	675	977	92	343
Macon	9,830	6,178	7,701	5,197	6,448	4,161	355	997	22	422	28	153
Madison	6,986	5,548	5,844	4,960	4,342	3,557	957	1,983	255	567	87	365
Martin	9,297	7,584	8,615	7,019	5,665	3,972	867	2,256	657	991	205	626
McDowell	13,637	10,145	12,224	9,412	9,615	7,053	534	1,689	561	1,020	58	343
Mecklenburg	155,646	114,757	146,967	109,532	88,631	65,881	1,273	2,472	5,394	8,385	170	522
Mitchell	5,820	4,890	5,263	4,248	4,353	3,428	360	859	187	389	35	148
Montgomery	8,834	6,365	7,760	5,708	6,003	4,262	638	1,367	484	690	80	328
Moore	20,829	13,156	18,582	11,838	14,187	8,815	1,012	2,447	724	1,273	133	575
Nash	25,652	18,461	23,470	17,331	14,718	9,606	2,225	4,408	1,473	2,390	537	1,518
New Hanover	41,103	29,051	37,691	26,623	24,358	16,733	364	1,312	1,073	1,918	51	214
Northampton	8,245	6,863	7,097	6,214	5,287	3,975	1,099	2,644	661	1,144	244	881
Onslow	34,259	24,346	30,307	22,761	16,451	11,117	491	1,728	1,252	2,553	80	445

Orange	28,646	16,997	27,044	16,544	14,943	9,254	782	1,542	752	1,137	96	365
Pamlico	4,105	3,162	3,678	2,886	3,064	2,400	420	912	173	321	55	179
Pasquotank	10,408	8,624	9,723	7,952	6,358	5,094	455	1,212	386	727	80	282
Pender	8,468	6,587	7,511	5,237	6,244	4,129	622	1,661	457	720	88	416
Perquimans	3,811	2,824	3,283	2,500	2,467	1,749	313	763	163	239	47	153
Person	10,624	8,203	9,858	7,536	6,929	4,821	921	2,098	615	1,040	166	601
Pitt	32,832	22,679	30,198	20,914	17,543	10,645	1,706	4,416	1,719	2,568	386	1,381
Polk	5,565	4,504	5,023	3,955	3,978	3,022	253	731	178	320	20	126
Randolph	35,175	24,939	32,917	24,108	25,867	18,513	1,192	3,460	1,066	1,976	111	611
Richmond	17,013	13,066	15,809	12,051	11,689	8,420	911	2,320	893	1,469	181	617
Robeson	33,261	24,059	31,372	22,162	21,271	12,758	2,545	6,444	3,133	4,294	612	2,342
Rockingham	32,083	23,887	29,616	22,486	21,894	15,843	1,350	4,043	1,598	2,559	243	1,024
Rowan	38,832	29,789	35,949	28,714	26,572	20,369	620	1,971	1,211	2,314	56	384
Rutherford	21,172	15,909	19,221	14,993	14,267	10,876	704	2,291	827	1,311	97	436
Sampson	17,978	14,132	16,646	13,032	11,853	8,416	1,304	3,656	1,037	1,601	251	942
Scotland	11,095	7,842	10,343	7,387	7,016	4,320	600	1,953	823	1,249	112	619
Stanly	18,918	14,921	17,378	13,632	13,558	10,294	436	1,288	625	1,004	48	231
Stokes	12,525	7,961	11,252	7,221	9,178	5,474	837	2,054	526	747	101	421
Surrey	23,148	17,293	21,301	16,332	16,559	12,271	1,024	2,901	822	1,477	137	603
Swain	4,599	2,778	3,565	2,394	2,668	1,693	182	566	199	259	19	122
Transylvania	9,299	6,529	8,200	5,906	6,598	4,412	220	723	262	531	28	165
Tyrrell	1,580	1,322	1,381	1,128	1,070	873	160	426	98	169	27	108
Union	23,923	16,619	22,921	15,904	17,362	11,366	944	2,639	1,193	1,698	200	698
Vance	13,642	10,062	12,239	9,406	7,781	5,219	1,172	2,547	982	1,388	294	803
Wake	113,282	71,147	106,525	67,533	65,263	39,742	2,126	4,736	3,300	5,234	357	1,369
Warren	6,490	4,829	5,257	4,339	3,670	2,680	1,042	1,777	470	712	232	517
Washington	5,263	4,194	4,729	3,810	3,504	2,733	372	1,023	336	520	73	299
Watauga	13,390	7,427	10,746	6,525	7,193	4,778	453	1,046	273	512	40	154
Wayne	34,984	25,332	32,300	23,829	19,117	11,902	1,190	3,906	1,466	2,728	170	958
Wilkes	21,908	15,863	20,522	14,960	16,503	11,824	1,123	3,223	794	1,651	124	719
Wilson	23,394	17,774	21,549	16,709	12,344	8,399	1,242	3,328	1,397	2,239	304	1,059
Yadkin	11,034	8,293	10,211	7,881	8,430	6,250	451	1,360	292	505	31	195
Yancey	6,144	4,414	5,277	3,876	4,188	2,989	476	1,193	234	439	62	242
State Total	2,223,007	1,618,103	2,043,291	1,509,564	1,397,425	987,290	83,143	217,027	91,854	153,718	13,951	55,124

(a)These are complete count data from both censuses. Any corrections to published census information are not shown.
(b)For purposes of this table, "Overcrowding" is defined as 1.01 or more persons per room.

INDIAN RESERVATION

North Carolina contains a single Indian reservation. That there is a reservation at all within the state's boundaries is a tribute to the courage of a Cherokee man named Tsali, who gave up his life that his kinsmen might be allowed to stay in their beloved homeland.

In 1830, Andrew Jackson, then United States President, signed into law the Indian Removal Act which called for the eventual expulsion of all Indians east of the Mississippi River and their relocation in the West. Several of the Southeastern tribes soon began to be moved, culminating in the forced marches of the Cherokees in 1838—39, the "Trail of Tears."

During the Army's observance that the Cherokees move peacefully, a few of the more adamant Indians took refuge in the mountains. In the confusion, Tsali killed a U.S. soldier and was immediately sought by government authorities for murder. As time passed, it became painfully apparent to the Army that the wanted Cherokee would never be apprehended. Through negotiations with the Cherokees, the government made the offer that if Tsali surrendered, the renegade Indians would be allowed to remain in their native mountains. The deal was made, Tsali was executed, and the Cherokees who had refused to follow the "Trail of Tears" continued to live in the North Carolina mountains.

Today, the descendants of this brave people maintain their homes on the Qualla Indian Reservation located in Cherokee, Graham, Jackson, Macon, and Swain Counties, North Carolina.

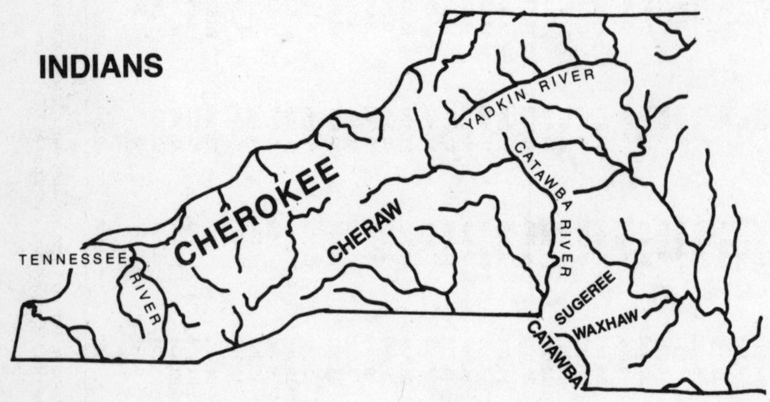

INDIANS

Aboriginal North America, north of Mexico, can be divided into ten "culture areas," namely the Arctic, Subarctic, Northeast Woodlands and Great Lakes, Southeast Woodlands, Great Plains, Southwest, Great Basin, Plateau, California, and Northwest Coast. The culture area in which North Carolina was located was the *Southeast Woodland*. While the environment and terrain of this vast wilderness differed significantly—from the high, cool Appalachian Mountains in the west to the low lying, tidewater plains along the Atlantic Ocean in the east—the several tribes of Indians who made their homes here during the historic period all shared traits and customs more akin to each other than divergent.

The hallmarks of the Southeast Woodland culture were organized village life, well-advanced agricultural techniques, and skilled artisanship. All of the tribes indigenous to North Carolina expressed these traits to one degree or another.

Although, from a cultural standpoint, all North Carolina Indians were affiliated, their languages varied greatly. At least three language families were represented in the state: the *Iroquoian*, the *Siouan*, and the *Algonquian*.

The largest tribe in the entire Southeast, the *Cherokee*, lived in North Carolina as well as parts of Georgia, South Carolina, and Tennessee.

Another large tribe was the *Siouan*-speaking *Cheraw*, among whom de Soto is thought to have visited. A later Spaniard, Juan Pardo, built a fort

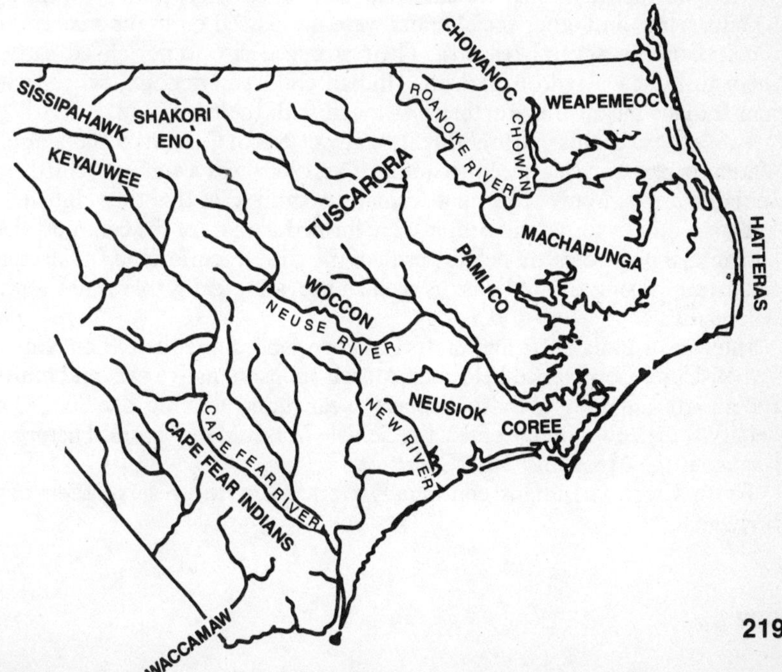

in the Cheraw country in 1566. The *Catawba* was the largest of the eastern Siouian tribes, but by 1946, their population had been reduced to less than 200. The other numerous tribe was the *Tuscarora*. After a disastrous war with the whites in 1711–1713, the majority of this tribe moved to New York State to settle among the Iroquois.

North Carolina contains numerous small tribes, most of them speaking a Siouan tongue and none of them ever numbering over a few hundred individuals. Many of these—like the *Cape Fear*—are extinct today. The Algonquian tribes of the *Hatteras* and the *Pamlico* are likewise extinct.

The accompanying map shows the approximate locations of the homes for the 19 distinct Indian tribes that inhabited North Carolina in about 1600.

Today, there are over 60,000 Indians living in North Carolina. Eleven organized groups (tribes) remain of the dozens of tribes who once inhabited the state. The only federally-recognized tribe in the state, the Cherokee, live in the Great Smoky Mountains, their ancestral homeland.

Tribes of eastern North Carolina and the Piedmont include the *Coharie* of Sampson and Harnett counties, the *Haliwa-Saponi* of Halifax County, the *Cherokee-Powhatan* of Person County, the *Eno-Occaneechi* of Alamance and Orange counties, the *Meherrin* of Hertford County, the *Lumbee* of Robeson and surrounding counties, the *Tuscarora,* also from Robeson County, and the *Waccamaw-Siouan* of Bladen and Columbus counties.

The urban Indian organizations are: Metrolina Native American Association in Charlotte; Guilford Native American Association in Greensboro; and the Cumberland County Association of Indian People in Fayetteville.

Many of the traditional Indian arts, such as basketry, pottery, quilting, woodcarving, and other social crafts were not passed on to the majority of the Indians for several reasons. Their strong desire to get ahead caused them to imitate Anglo-Americans. Indian children attending school with non-Indians meant they further lost touch with their heritage.

In response to this cultural threat, many of North Carolina's Indian population began to re-learn old customs. The 1960s was a time of rebirth for Indian culture. Many tribes not formally organized at this time did so.

Dance groups for young people were formed in most of the communities, and annual powwows are held by each of the tribes, reinforcing Indian consciousness among the Indians, as well as providing enjoyable times for all who gather.

Interest in Indian arts and crafts has experienced a rebirth. The Annual Indian Unity Conference held each March sponsors native arts and crafts. Indian arts and crafts are also displayed year-round at Pembroke State University Indian Resource Center, the Schiele Museum of Natural History in Gastonia, the Museum of the Cherokee.

North Carolina Indians continually work today to preserve their own heritage.

LABOR

The following chart is compiled from data from the 1980 census. It shows how many North Carolinians live close to their work or commute; average travel time; number that drive alone, carpool, use public means, or walk to work.

In addition to the information shown on the chart, it is interesting to note that 46,005 persons worked in their homes.

County	Number Working in County of Residence	Number Working Outside County of Residence	Mean Travel Time (in minutes)	Number That Drive Alone	Number That Carpool	Public Transportation	Walked Only
Alamance	35,971	8,701	18.6	34,424	11,343	672	1,100
Alexander	7,092	4,939	20.0	8,179	11,745	36	275
Alleghany	2,980	733	19.7	2,120	1,418	17	154
Anson	6,951	2,243	21.5	6,401	3,409	96	289
Ashe	6,615	1,508	26.0	4,412	3,756	27	200
Avery	3,450	1,600	23.3	2,895	2,045	62	283
Beaufort	12,428	1,825	20.5	9,610	4,923	69	675
Bertie	5,079	1,812	23.0	4,555	2,370	83	301
Bladen	7,591	2,729	22.5	6,665	3,858	12	298
Brunswick	8,231	3,695	23.6	7,812	4,000	179	460
Buncombe	60,860	4,367	18.5	49,928	14,997	1,288	2,276
Burke	25,611	7,081	17.5	24,164	8,539	143	935
Cabarrus	26,509	11,610	19.9	27,817	11,536	497	1,506
Caldwell	23,572	6,036	18.5	21,669	9,094	53	764
Camden	601	1,374	30.3	1,219	707	17	52
Carteret	11,070	4,080	20.0	10,430	4,574	48	644
Caswell	2,422	5,003	25.2	4,701	2,863	32	341
Catawba	46,536	4,305	16.5	38,410	12,011	171	1,670
Chatham	9,322	5,976	19.7	10,582	5,400	29	572
Cherokee	5,507	824	19.9	4,214	1,977	47	305
Chowan	3,558	797	20.6	2,966	173	28	349
Clay	1,227	912	22.3	1,457	722	8	46
Cleveland	28,505	7,257	18.7	25,186	9,705	224	1,280
Columbus	14,435	2,884	22.0	11,725	5,780	43	724
Craven	25,876	3,378	17.9	18,407	8,504	601	2,907
Cumberland	97,783	5,868	17.3	68,369	23,742	1,503	16,214
Currituck	1,425	2,107	34.3	2,278	1,126	35	187
Dare	4,891	182	14.1	3,699	1,083	10	546
Davidson	32,626	17,103	17.7	39,582	12,690	123	1,399
Davie	5,295	4,601	21.7	7,202	3,201	20	204
Duplin	11,145	4,177	22.1	9,877	5,001	105	775
Durham	57,859	10,061	18.0	49,334	16,246	2,554	3,113
Edgecombe	14,362	7,064	18.0	15,504	6,331	449	914
Forsyth	92,525	9,472	18.0	81,107	23,810	3,386	3,093
Franklin	5,888	5,649	24.2	7,479	4,305	28	495
Gaston	54,416	16,319	17.9	54,752	18,794	500	3,109
Gates	1,334	1,673	34.5	1,759	1,262	31	115
Graham	1,988	308	19.8	1,347	814	7	134
Granville	9,196	3,177	19.9	8,711	3,870	60	475
Greene	2,715	3,177	20.2	4,015	1,974	46	286

County	Number Working in County of Residence	Number Working Outside County of Residence	Mean Travel Time (in (minutes)	Number That Drive Alone	Number That Carpool	Public Transportation	Walked Only
Guilford	125,057	12,313	17.6	111,124	30,600	2,992	4,664
Halifax	15,024	3,257	18.6	12,697	5,138	102	1,091
Harnett	12,580	10,132	21.3	15,099	7,108	14	1,142
Haywood	12,987	3,162	18.9	11,617	4,000	393	619
Henderson	17,166	4,402	18.2	16,117	5,274	55	897
Hertford	6,050	1,706	21.9	5,140	2,688	148	655
Hoke	4,243	3,043	19.8	4,823	2,668	14	195
Hyde	1,697	281	18.7	1,170	582	7	222
Iredell	27,227	8,072	18.7	26,548	9,895	189	1,335
Jackson	7,189	2,035	17.5	5,826	2,869	46	744
Johnston	19,724	9,495	21.9	19,911	8,706	55	1,114
Jones	1,509	1,600	26.6	2,078	1,216	30	116
Lee	12,552	2,465	17.6	11,507	4,280	62	374
Lenoir	20,822	2,515	18.0	16,686	6,423	170	1,087
Lincoln	11,336	7,609	20.3	13,679	5,496	37	314
Macon	5,870	1,172	17.4	5,063	1,840	72	204
Madison	6,117	1,985	26.3	3,258	2,058	33	346
Martin	10,587	1,984	18.4	6,859	2,702	55	512
McDowell	12,711	2,162	19.7	9,110	5,161	254	515
Mecklenburg	202,735	10,156	21.1	144,427	39,245	9,948	5,255
Mitchell	4,063	1,541	25.7	3,382	2,107	64	190
Montgomery	7,580	1,643	17.4	6,534	3,014	89	416
Moore	16,142	3,582	18.5	14,796	5,577	53	572
Nash	20,506	5,830	19.1	20,949	6,523	212	743
New Hanover	36,414	3,614	18.6	32,180	9,044	946	1,319
Northampton	3,978	2,864	20.1	4,746	2,237	58	334
Onslow	51,821	2,435	15.4	24,810	14,532	474	17,202
Orange	23,311	11,468	18.5	21,469	8,326	1,970	3,144
Pamlico	1,974	1,446	28.2	1,964	1,289	56	156
Pasquotank	7,904	2,248	19.7	7,083	2,953	336	670
Pender	3,080	4,593	26.4	5,057	2,876	63	228
Perquimans	1,631	1,746	24.2	2,086	930	9	180
Person	9,818	1,964	20.2	7,941	3,486	50	415
Pitt	31,355	5,016	17.1	26,385	8,661	386	2,307
Polk	2,754	2,021	21.1	3,387	1,315	40	201
Randolph	26,520	14,636	18.3	33,356	11,108	81	929
Richmond	14,045	2,216	17.1	12,869	4,488	139	448
Robeson	27,708	5,872	21.3	23,409	12,046	156	1,438
Rockingham	27,335	6,935	18.8	24,834	10,222	220	918
Rowan	30,830	11,933	17.9	30,371	12,047	792	1,843
Rutherford	18,879	3,138	18.5	15,759	6,037	54	565
Sampson	13,462	5,145	20.7	12,884	5,403	39	704
Scotland	10,354	1,578	16.2	9,042	3,187	58	548
Stanly	17,087	3,415	20.1	15,929	6,123	280	708
Stokes	4,794	8,743	25.8	8,214	5,092	110	235
Surry	21,589	3,589	18.9	16,864	7,669	117	900
Swain	2,972	518	18.2	2,142	1,202	48	141
Transylvania	7,881	848	18.7	5,638	2,776	63	531
Tyrrell	843	354	23.2	690	416	5	117
Union	19,315	11,004	22.8	21,879	8,781	177	911

County	Number Working in County of Residence	Number Working Outside County of Residence	Mean Travel Time (in minutes)	Number That Drive Alone	Number That Carpool	Public Transportation	Walked Only
Vance	11,225	1,520	16.5	9,702	3,377	53	475
Wake	125,725	14,107	19.6	103,238	35,020	4,044	5,330
Warren	2,935	2,421	23.7	3,274	2,008	49	234
Washington	3,888	1,190	18.3	3,554	1,362	58	210
Watauga	10,530	1,527	18.3	7,646	3,129	42	1,417
Wayne	33,124	4,425	16.9	28,947	8,889	159	1,895
Wilkes	20,590	4,005	20.7	17,470	7,863	127	596
Wilson	22,158	3,215	16.8	18,341	6,276	343	996
Yadkin	4,981	6,297	24.0	7,300	4,427	19	383
Yancey	3,495	1,710	26.0	3,094	1,969	46	203
Total	2,046,350	448,505	20.5	1,756,417	658,734	40,100	120,718

LAND AREA

North Carolina contains 52,669.11 square miles and ranks 28th in size in the nation. The following chart lists the counties along with the total land and water areas in square miles.

County	Area in Square Miles: 1980			County	Area in Square Miles: 1980		
	Total Area	Land	Water		Total Area	Land	Water
Alamance	435.03	433.14	1.89	Cumberland	658.46	657.26	1.20
Alexander	263.34	258.64	4.70	Currituck	439.19	255.59	183.60
Alleghany	234.52	234.52	.00	Dare	1,250.94	390.79	860.15
Anson	537.24	533.14	4.10	Davidson	566.58	548.28	18.30
Ashe	426.16	426.16	.00	Davie	266.87	266.59	.28
Avery	247.07	247.07	.00	Duplin	819.42	819.22	.20
Beaufort	957.78	826.10	131.68	Durham	298.54	297.74	.80
Bertie	736.53	700.93	35.60	Edgecombe	505.69	505.69	.00
Bladen	887.82	878.92	8.90	Forsyth	413.92	412.48	1.44
Brunswick	892.99	860.49	32.50	Franklin	494.93	494.38	.55
Buncombe	660.13	659.33	.80	Gaston	363.89	357.29	6.60
Burke	515.15	504.45	10.70	Gates	345.45	338.25	7.20
Cabarrus	364.55	364.08	.47	Graham	301.59	288.69	12.90
Caldwell	474.47	471.17	3.30	Granville	537.10	533.50	3.60
Camden	318.39	240.49	77.90	Greene	266.53	266.37	.16
Carteret	1,052.54	525.57	526.97	Guilford	657.34	650.77	6.57
Caswell	428.41	427.51	.90	Halifax	731.29	723.69	7.60
Catawba	413.16	395.66	17.50	Harnett	601.51	601.11	.40
Chatham	708.76	707.91	.85	Haywood	554.95	554.85	.10
Cherokee	466.73	451.83	14.90	Henderson	374.90	374.39	.51
Chowan	241.85	181.55	60.30	Hertford	362.09	356.09	6.00
Clay	220.51	213.91	6.60	Hoke	392.56	391.16	1.40
Cleveland	468.39	468.19	.20	Hyde	1,361.15	624.22	736.93
Columbus	952.94	938.44	14.50	Iredell	593.82	574.12	19.70
Craven	761.27	701.47	59.80	Jackson	495.12	490.52	4.60

County	Area in Square Miles: 1980 Total Area	Land	Water	County	Area in Square Miles: 1980 Total Area	Land	Water
Johnston	797.09	795.41	1.68	Randolph	789.46	788.83	.63
Jones	470.61	470.01	.60	Richmond	479.59	477.19	2.40
Lee	259.53	259.28	.25	Robeson	950.59	949.19	1.40
Lenoir	402.42	402.32	.10	Rockingham	572.48	568.64	3.84
Lincoln	306.66	298.26	8.40	Rowan	523.32	519.02	4.30
Macon	519.48	516.58	2.90	Rutherford	569.42	567.62	1.80
Madison	451.31	451.31	.00	Sampson	947.35	946.85	.50
Martin	468.26	460.76	7.50	Scotland	320.83	319.33	1.50
McDowell	442.89	437.39	5.50	Stanly	404.98	395.78	9.20
Mecklenburg	549.47	527.77	21.70	Stokes	455.93	452.04	3.89
Mitchell	222.00	222.00	.00	Surry	539.47	539.34	.13
Montgomery	501.55	489.55	12.00	Swain	540.18	525.98	14.20
Moore	705.55	701.25	4.30	Transylvania	380.13	378.28	1.85
Nash	542.44	539.60	2.84	Tyrrell	598.66	406.82	191.84
New Hanover	220.27	184.54	35.73	Union	639.28	639.28	.00
Northampton	549.62	538.32	11.30	Vance	268.79	248.79	20.00
Onslow	820.21	762.61	57.60	Wake	857.01	854.36	2.65
Orange	401.01	400.27	.74	Warren	444.00	427.10	16.90
Pamlico	575.29	340.73	234.56	Washington	413.26	331.63	81.63
Pasquotank	289.38	228.00	61.38	Watauga	314.05	314.05	.00
Pender	878.72	874.82	3.90	Wayne	555.72	553.70	2.02
Perquimans	326.32	246.40	79.92	Wilkes	758.41	752.21	6.20
Person	404.23	398.02	6.21	Wilson	375.52	374.27	1.25
Pitt	656.52	656.52	.00	Yadkin	337.74	335.74	2.00
Polk	238.95	238.30	.65	Yancey	313.60	313.60	.00
				Total	52,669.11	48,843.37	3,825.74

LEGISLATURE

MEMBERS OF SENATE BY DISTRICTS

1st District
Beaufort (part), Bertie (part), Camden, Chowan, Currituck, Dare, Gates (part), Hyde, Pasquotank, Perquimans, Tyrrell, and Washington.
Basnight, Marc (D)
P.O. Box 1025
Manteo, 27954

2nd District
Bertie (part), Edgecombe (part), Gates (part), Halifax (part), Hertford, Martin (part), Northampton, and Warren (part).
Harrington, J. J. (D)
P.O. Drawer 519
Lewiston-Woodville, 27849

3rd District
Carteret, Craven, and Pamlico.
Barker, William H. (D)
P.O. Box 52
Oriental, 28571

4th District
Onslow.
Guy, A. D. (D)
306 Woodland Dr.
Jacksonville, 28540

5th District
Duplin, Jones, Lenoir, and Pender (part).
Hardison, Harold W. (D)
P.O. Box 128
Deep Run, 28525

6th District
Edgecombe (part), Martin (part), Pitt (part), and Wilson (part).
Martin, R. L. (D)
P.O. Box 387
Bethel, 27812

7th District
New Hanover, and Pender (part).
Block, Frank (D)
1108 Seapath Towers
Wrightsville Beach, 28480

8th District
Greene and Wayne.
Barnes, Henson P. (D)
707 Park Ave.
Goldsboro, 27530

9th District
Beaufort (part), Martin (part), and Pitt (part).

Taft, Thomas F. (D)
611 Queen Anne's Rd.
Greeneville, 27834

10th District
Edgecombe (part), Halifax (part), Nash, Warren (part), and Wilson (part).
Ezzell, James E., Jr. (D)
201 Forest Hill Ave.
Rocky Mount, 27801

11th District
Franklin, Vance, and Wake (part).
Speed, James D. (D)
Rt. 6, Box 542
Louisburg, 27549

12th District
Cumberland (part).
Rand, Anthony E. (D)
1600 Morganton Rd.
Fayetteville, 28305

Tally, Lura S. (D)
3100 Tallywood Dr.
Fayetteville, 28303

13th District
Durham, Granville, Orange (part), and Person.
Hunt, Ralph A. (D)
1005 Crete St.
Durham, 27707

Royall, Kenneth C., Jr. (D)
64 Beverly Dr.
Durham, 27707

14th District
Harnett, Lee, and Wake (part).
Johnson, Joseph E. (D)
P.O. Box 750
Raleigh, 27602

Sherron, J. K. (D)
3329 Julian Dr.
Raleigh, 27604

Staton, William W. (D)
205 Courtland Dr.
Sanford, 27330

15th District
Johnston and Sampson.
Warren, Robert D. (D)
Rt. 3, Box 25
Benson, 28504

16th District
Chatham, Moore, Orange (part), and Randolph.
Hunt, Wanda H. (D)
P.O. Box 1335
Pinehurst, 28374

Walker, Russell G. (D)
1004 Westmont Dr.
Asheboro, 27203

17th District
Anson, Montgomery, Richmond, Scotland, Stanly, and Union.
Conder, J. Richard (D)
1401 Carolina Dr.
Rockingham, 28379

Plyler, Aaron W. (D)
2170 Concord Ave.
Monroe, 28110

18th District
Bladen, Brunswick, Columbus, and Cumberland (part).
Soles, R. C., Jr. (D)
P.O. Box 6
Tabor City, 28463

19th District
Forsyth (part) and Guilford (part).
Shaw, Robert G. (R)
P.O. Box 8101
Greensboro, 27419

20th District
Forsyth (part).
Kaplan, Ted (D)
1001 Dalton Rd.
Lewisville, 27023

Ward, Marvin M. (D)
641 Yorkshire Rd.
Winston-Salem, 27106

21st District
Alamance and Caswell.
Daniel, George B. (D)
P.O. Box 179
Yanceyville, 27379

22nd District
Cabarrus and Mecklenburg (part).
Johnson, James C., Jr. (R)
360 Patience Dr.
Concord, 28025

23rd District
Davidson, Davie, and Rowan.
Smith, Paul S. (R)
114 N. Milford Dr.
Salisbury, 28144

Somers, Robert V. (R)
240 Confederate Ave.
Salisbury, 28144

24th District
Alleghany, Ashe, Rockingham, Stokes, Surry, and Watauga.
Goldston, W. D., Jr. (D)
P.O. Box 307
Eden, 27288

Sands, A. P., III (D)
908 Oakcrest Dr.
Reidsville, 27320

25th District
Cleveland, Gaston, Lincoln, and Rutherford.
Harris, J. Ollie (D)
P.O. Box 627,
Kings Mountain, 28086

Marvin, Helen Rhyne (D)
119 Ridge Ln.
Gastonia, 28054

Rauch, Marshall A. (D)
1121 Scotch Dr.
Gastonia, 28052

26th District
Alexander, Catawba, Iredell, and Yadkin.
Allran, Austin M. (R)
515 6th St. NW
Hickory, 28601

Howard, F. Bryan (D)
1420 Mt. Vernon Ave.
Statesville, 28677

27th District
Avery, Burke, Caldwell, Mitchell, and Wilkes.
Kincaid, Donald R. (R)
110 Lakeview Dr.
Lenoir, 28645

28th District
Buncombe, McDowell, Madison, and Yancey.
Swain, Robert S. (D)
Rt. 5, Box 1112
Asheville, 28803

29th District
Cherokee, Clay, Graham, Haywood, Henderson, Jackson, Macon, Polk, Swain, and Transylvania.
Hipps, Charles W. (D)
115 Walnut St.
Waynesville, 28786

Thomas, R. P. (D)
714 Heatherwood Dr.
Hendersonville, 28739

30th District
Hoke and Robeson.
Parnell, David R. (D)
P.O. Box 100
Parkton, 28371

31st District
Guilford (part).
Martin, William N. (D)
P.O. Box 21363
Greensboro, 27420

32nd District
Guilford (part).
Seymour, Mary P. (D)
1105 Pender Lane
Greensboro, 27420

33rd District
Mecklenburg (part).
Richardson, James F.
1739 Northbrook Dr.
Charlotte, 28216

34th District
Mecklenburg (part).
McDuffie, James D. (R)
9041-2 J. M. Keynes Dr.
Charlotte, 28213

35th District
Mecklenburg (part).
Cobb, Laurence A. (R)
3022 Sharon Rd.
Charlotte, 28211

SENATE DISTRICTS

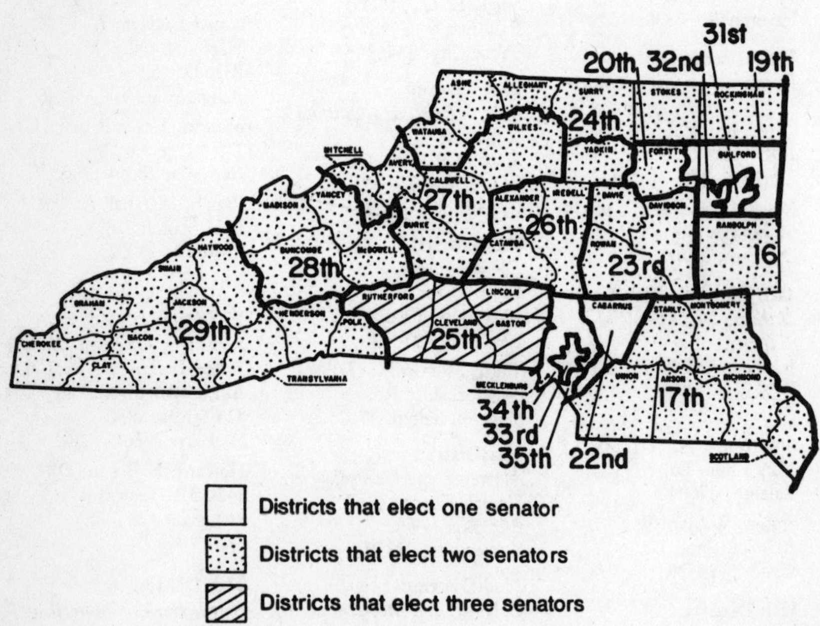

MEMBERS OF SENATE ALPHABETICALLY LISTED

Allran, Austin M. (R)
26th District

Barker, William H. (D)
3rd District

Barnes, Henson P. (D)
8th District

Basnight, Marc (D)
1st District

Block, Frank (D)
7th District

Cobb, Laurence A. (R)
35th District

Conder, J. Richard (D)
17th District

Daniel, George B.(D)
21st District

Ezzell, James E., Jr. (D)
10th District

Goldston, W. D., Jr. (D)
24th District

Guy, A. D. (D)
4th District

Hardison, Harold W. (D)
5th District

Harrington, J. J. (D)
2nd District

Harris, J. Ollie (D)
25th District

Hipps, Charles W. (D)
29th District

Howard, F. Bryan (D)
26th District

Hunt, Ralph A. (D)
13th District

Hunt, Wanda H. (D)
16th District

Johnson, James C., Jr. (R)
22nd District

Johnson, Joseph E. (D)
14th District

Kaplan, Ted (D)
20th District

Kincaid, Donald R. (R)
27th District

Martin, R. L. (D)
6th District

Martin, William N. (D)
31st District

Marvin, Helen Rhyne (D)
25th District

McDuffie, James D. (R)
34th District

Parnell, David R. (D)
30th District

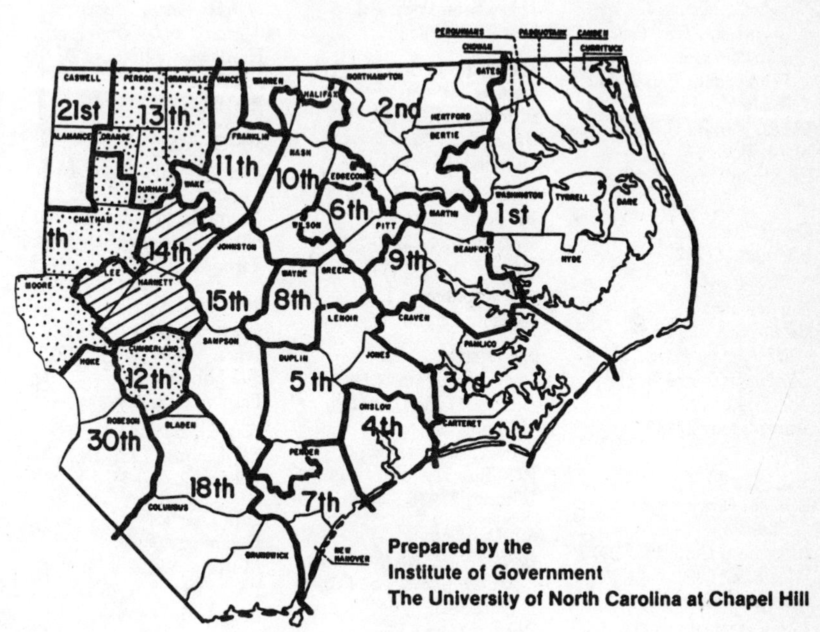

Plyler, Aaron W. (D)
17th District

Rand, Anthony E. (D)
12th District

Rauch, Marshall A. (D)
25th District

Richardson, James F. (D)
33rd District

Royall, Kenneth C., Jr. (D)
13th District

Sands, A. P., III (D)
24th District

Seymour, Mary P. (D)
32nd District

Shaw, Robert G. (R)
19th District

Sherron, J. K. (D)
14th District

Simpson, Daniel R. (R)
27th District

Smith, Paul S. (R)
23rd District

Soles, R. C., Jr. (D)
18th District

Somers, Robert V. (R)
23rd District

Speed, James D. (D)
11th District

Staton, William W. (D)
14th District

Swain, Robert S. (D)
28th District

Taft, Thomas F. (D)
9th District

Tally, Lura S. (D)
12th District

Thomas, R. P. (D)
29th District

Walker, Russell G. (D)
16th District

Ward, Marvin M. (D)
20th District

Warren, Robert D. (D)
15th District

Winner, Dennis J. (D)
28th District

MEMBERS OF THE HOUSE OF REPRESENTATIVES BY DISTRICT

1st District
Camden, Chowan, Currituck, Dare, Gates (part), Pasquotank, Perquimans, Tyrrell, and Washington.
James, Vernon G. (D)
Rt. 4, Box 265
Elizabeth City, 27909

Thompson, R. M. (D)
Queen Anne Dr.
Edenton, 27932

2nd District
Beaufort, Hyde, and Washington (part).
Chapin, Howard B. (D)
212 Smaw Rd.
Washington, 27889

3rd District
Craven, Lenoir, and Pamlico.
Anderson, Gerald L. (D)
P.O. Box 568
Bridgeton, 28519

Lilley, Daniel T. (D)
P.O. Box 824
Kinston, 28501

Perdue, Beverly M. (D)
211 Wilson Point Rd.
New Bern, 28560

4th District
Carteret and Onslow.
Ethridge, W. Bruce (D)
Rt. 2, P.O. Box 27
Swansboro, 28584

Grady, Robert (R)
107 Jean Circle
Jacksonville, 28540

Tyndall, J. Paul (D)
414 Woodhaven Dr.
Jacksonville, 28540

5th District
Bertie (part), Gates (part), Hertford (part), and Northampton.
Brown, Brewster W. (D)
P.O. Box 527
Winton, 27986

6th District
Bertie (part), Hertford (part), Martin (part), and Pitt (part).
Rogers, Gene (D)
908 Woodlawn Dr.
Williamston, 27892

7th District
Halifax (part), Martin (part), and Warren (part).
Hardaway, Thomas (D)
207 McDaniel St.
Enfield, 27832

8th District
Edgecombe (part) and Nash (part).
Mavretic, Josephus L. (D)
601 St. Andrews St.
Tarboro, 27886

9th District
Greene and Pitt (part).
Jones, Walter B., Jr. (D)
302 Hillcrest Dr.
Farmville, 27828

Warren, Edward M. (D)
227 Country Club Dr.
Greenville, 27834

10th District
Duplin and Jones.
Murphy, Wendell H. (D)
Rt. 1, P.O. Box 76-E
Rose Hill, 28458

11th District
Wayne.

Kerr, John H., III (D)
302 Hillcrest Dr.
Goldsboro, 27530

Tart, John (D)
Rt. 1, Box 125-A
Goldsboro, 27530

12th District
Bladen, Pender (part), and Sampson.

Bowen, Ed (D)
Rt. 1, Box 289
Harrells, 28444

Nye, Edd (D)
P.O. Box 8
Elizabethtown, 28337

13th District
New Hanover (part).

Hall, A. M. (D)
223 Ashford Ave.
Wilmington, 28405

Payne, Harry E., Jr. (D)
P.O. Box 1147
Wilmington, 28402

14th District
Brunswick, New Hanover (part), and Pender (part).

Redwine, E. David (D)
P.O. Box 1238
Shallotte, 28459

15th District
Columbus.

Wright, Richard (D)
6 Orange St.
Tabor City, 28463

16th District
Hoke, Robeson, and Scotland (part).

DeVane, Daniel H. (D)
P.O. Drawer N
Raeford, 28376

Hasty, John Calvin (D)
P.O. Box 338
Maxton, 28364

Locks, Sidney A. (D)
P.O. Box 290
Lumberton, 28358

17th District
Cumberland (part).

Edwards, C. R. (D)
1502 Boros Dr.
Fayetteville, 28303

Jeralds, Luther R. (D)
319 Jasper St.
Fayetteville, 28301

18th District
Cumberland (part).

Beard, R. D. (D)
2918 Skye Dr.
Fayetteville, 28303

Raynor, Joseph B., Jr. (D)
2108 Morganton Rd.
Fayetteville, 28305

Warner, Alex (D)
3713 Hillcrest St.
Hope Mills, 28343

19th District
Harnett and Lee.

Etheridge, Bobby R. (D)
Box 295
Lillington, 27546

Wicker, Dennis A. (D)
1201 Burnes Dr.
Sanford, 27330

20th District
Franklin and Johnston.

Brannan, George W. (D)
309 Maplewood Dr.
Smithfield, 27577

Woodard, Barney Paul (D)
P.O. Box 5
Princeton, 27569

21st District
Wake (part).

Blue, Daniel T., Jr. (D)
2541 Albemarle Ave.
Raleigh, 27610

22nd District
Caswell, Granville, Halifax (part), Person, Vance, and Warren.

Church, John T. (D)
420 Woodland Rd.
Henderson, 27536

Crawford, James W., Jr. (D)
509 College St.
Oxford, 27565

Watkins, William T. (D)
P.O. Box 247
Oxford, 27565

23rd District
Durham (part).

Michaux, H. M., Jr. (D)
1722 Alfred St.
Durham, 27713

24th District
Chatham (part) and Orange.

Barnes, Anne C. (D)
313 Severin St.
Chapel Hill, 27514

Hackney, Joe (D)
104 Carolina Forest
Chapel Hill, 27514

25th District
Alamance, Rockingham, and Stokes (part).

Bowman, J. Fred (D)
814 N. Graham-Hopedale Rd.
Burlington, 27215

Holt, Bertha M. (D)
P.O. Box 1111
Burlington, 27215

Hunt, R. Samuel, III (D)
1218 W. Davis St.
Burlington, 27215

McAlister, Robert L. (D)
Rt. 1
Ruffin, 27326

26th District
Guilford (part) and Randolph (part).

Gist, Herman C. (D)
442 Gorrell St.
Greensboro, 27406

27th District
Guilford (part).

Keesee-Forrester, Margaret P. (R)
204 N. Mendenhall St.
Greensboro, 27405

Lineberry, Albert S. (D)
300 Meadowbrook Terrace
Greensboro, 27408

Sizemore, F. J., III (R)
P.O. Box 21927
Greensboro, 27401

28th District
Guilford (part).
Chalk, Richard E. (R)
427 Wright St.
High Point, 27260

Jarrell, Mary (D)
1010 Wickliff Ave.
High Point, 27260

29th District
Forsyth (part) and Guilford (part).
Decker, Michael (R)
6011 Bexhill Dr.
Walkertown, 27051

30th District
Chatham (part) and Randolph (part).
Boyd, William T. (R)
1315 N. Shore Dr.
Asheboro, 27203

31st District
Moore.
Craven, James M. (R)
P.O. Box 44
Pinebluff, 28373

32nd District
Richmond and Scotland (part).
Dawkins, Donald M. (D)
Rt. 3, P.O. Box 358
Rockingham, 28379

33rd District
Anson and Montgomery.
Hightower, Foyle R., Jr. (D)
715 East Wade St.
Wadesboro, 28170

34th District
Cabarrus, Stanly, and Union.
Alexander, William G. (D)
1589 Daybreak Ridge Rd.
Kannapolis, 28081

Barbee, Bobby H., Sr. (R)
P.O. Box 656
Locust, 28097

Privette, Coy C. (R)
306 Cottage Dr.
Kannapolis, 28081

Tallent, Timothy N. (R)
210 Corban Ave., SE
Concord, 28025

35th District
Rowan.
Gardner, Charlotte A. (R)
1500 W. Colonial Dr.
Salisbury, 28144

Ligon, Bradford V. (R)
Rt. 12, P.O. Box 460
Salisbury, 28144

HOUSE OF REPRESENTATIVES DISTRICTS

Prepared by the
Institute of Government
The University of North Carolina at Chapel Hill

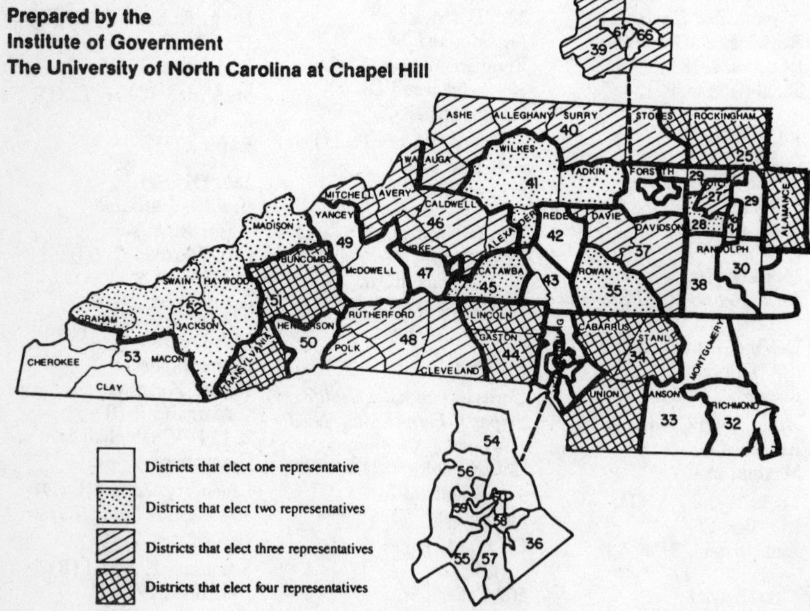

36th District
Mecklenburg (part).
Warren, Raymond (R)
10003 Grand Junction Rd.
Charlotte, 28212

37th District
Davidson, Davie, and Iredell (part).
Cochrane, Betsy L. (R)
P.O. Box 517
Bermuda Run
Advance, 27006

Cromer, Charles L. (R)
Rt. 4, P.O. Box 362
Thomasville, 27360

Hege, Joe H., Jr. (R)
1526 Greensboro St.
Lexington, 27292

38th District
Randolph.
Brubaker, Harold J. (R)
Rt. 9, P.O. Box 268
Asheboro, 27203

39th District
Forysth.
Duncan, Ann Q. (R)
1237 Mashie Dr.
Pfafftown, 27040

Esposito, Theresa H. (R)
207 Stanaford Rd.
Winston-Salem, 27104

Rhodes, Frank E. (R)
4701 Whitehaven Rd.
Winston-Salem, 27106

40th District
Alleghany, Ashe, Stokes (part), Surry, and Watauga (part).
Diamont, David H. (D)
P.O. Box 784
Pilot Mountain, 27041

Hunt, Judy F. (D)
1283 Chestnut Circle
Blowing Rock, 28605

Wilmoth, Wade F. (D)
209 Crest Dr.
Boone, 28607

41st District
Alexander (part), Wilkes, and Yadkin.
Brown, John Walter (R)
Rt. 2, P.O. Box 87
Elkin, 28621

Holmes, George M. (R)
P.O. Box 217
Hamptonville, 27020

42nd District
Iredell (part).

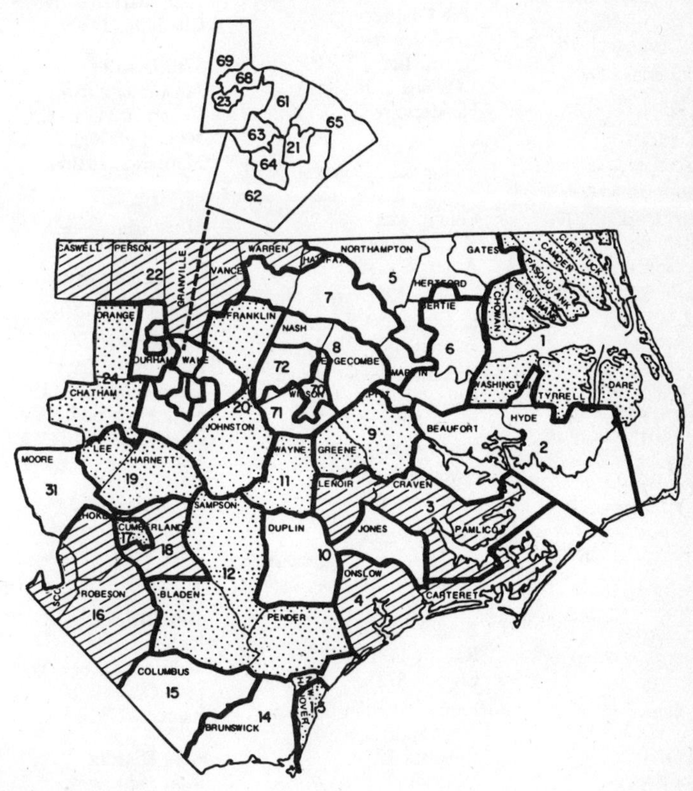

Walker, Lois S. (R)
611 Woods Dr.
Statesville, 28677

43rd District
Alexander (part), Catawba (part), and Iredell (part).
Brawley, C. Robert (R)
Rt. 5, P.O. Box 96
Mooresville, 28115

44th District
Gaston and Lincoln.
Bumgardner, David W., Jr. (D)
P.O. Box 904
Belmont, 28012

Abernathy, J. Vernon (R)
P.O. Box 38
Gastonia, 28054

Rhyne, J. L., Jr. (R)
Rt. 6, P.O. Box 538-R
Lincolnton, 28092

Windley, Walter H. (R)
2138 Winterlake Dr.
Gastonia, 28054

45th District
Burke (part) and Catawba (part).
Huffman, Doris R. (R)
Rt. 4, P.O. Box 81
Newton, 28650

Isenhower, W. Stine (R)
505 2nd Ave. NE
Conover, 28613

46th District
Alexander (part), Avery, Burke (part), Caldwell, Mitchell, and Watauga (part).
Buchanan, Charles (R)
Rt. 1
Green Mountain, 28740

Hughes, James F. (R)
P.O. Box 277
Linville, 28646

Starnes, Edgar V. (R)
P.O. Box 425
Granite Falls, 28630

47th District
Burke (part).
Fletcher, Ray C. (D)
P.O. Box 68
Valdese, 28690

48th District
Cleveland, Polk, and Rutherford.
Hunt, John J. (D)
P.O. Box 277
Lattimore, 28089

Lutz, Edith Ledford (D)
Rt. 3
Lawndale, 28090

Owens, Charles D. (D)
P.O. Box 610
Forest City, 28043

49th District
McDowell and Yancey.
Hunter, Robert C. (D)
P.O. Drawer 1330
Marion, 28752

50th District
Henderson (part).
Justus, Larry T. (R)
P.O. Box 2396
Hendersonville, 28739

51st District
Buncombe, Henderson (part), and Transylvania.
Colton, Marie W. (D)
392 Charlotte St.
Asheville, 28801

Crawford, Narvel J., Jr. (D)
15 Edgemont Rd.
Asheville, 28801

Greenwood, Gordon H. (D)
P.O. Box 487
Black Mountain, 28711

Nesbitt, Martin L. (D)
6 Maple Ridge Ln.
Asheville, 28806

52nd District
Graham (part), Haywood, Jackson, Madison, and Swain.
Beall, Charles M. (D)
Rt. 3, P.O. Box 322
Clyde, 28721

Ramsey, Liston B. (D Speaker)
P.O. Box 337
Marshall, 28753

53rd District
Cherokee, Clay, Graham (part), and Macon.
Enloe, Jeff H., Jr. (D)
Rt. 1, P.O. Box 38
Franklin, 28734

54th District
Mecklenburg (part).
McLaughlin, John B. (D)
P.O. Box 158
Newell, 28126

55th District
Mecklenburg (part).
Mothershead, C. Ivan (R)
P.O. Box 30036
Charlotte, 28230

56th District
Mecklenburg (part).
Foster, Jo Graham (D)
1520 Maryland Ave.
Charlotte, 28209

57th District
Mecklenburg (part).
Grimmer, Harry C. (R)
4000 Highridge Rd.
Matthews, 28105

58th District
Mecklenburg (part).
Easterling, Ruth M. (D)
811 Bromley Rd., #1
Charlotte, 28207

59th District
Mecklenburg (part).
Cunningham, W. Pete (D)
3121 Vallewood Place
Charlotte, 28216

60th District
Mecklenburg (part).
Barnhill, Howard C. (D)
2400 Newland Rd.
Charlotte, 28216

61st District
Wake (part).
Holroyd, Casper (D)
1401 Granada Dr.
Raleigh, 27612

62nd District
Wake (part).

Freeman, William M. (D)
502 Burton St.
Fuquay Varina, 27526

63rd District
Wake (part).
Stamey, Peggy (D)
6201 Arnold Rd.
Raleigh, 27607

64th District
Wake (part).
Wiser, Betty H. (D)
404 Dixie Trail
Raleigh, 27607

65th District
Wake (part).
Fussell, Aaron E. (D)
1201 Briar Patch Ln.
Raleigh, 27609

66th District
Forsyth (part).
Kennedy, Annie B. (D)
3727 Spaulding Dr.
Winston-Salem, 27101

67th District
Forsyth (part).
Burke, Logan (D)
3420 Cumberland Rd.
Winston-Salem, 27105

68th District
Durham (part).
Thompson, Sharon A. (D)
1809 Glendale Ave.
Durham, 27701

69th District
Durham (part).
Miller, George W., Jr. (D)
3862 Somerset Dr.
Durham, 27707

70th District
Edgecombe (part), Nash (part), and Wilson (part).
Fitch, Milton F., Jr. (D)
516 South Lodge St.
Wilson, 27893

71st District
Nash (part) and Wilson (part).
Etheridge, Larry E. (R)
1406 Downing St.
Wilson, 27893

72nd District
Edgecombe (part) and Nash (part).
Cooper, Roy A., III (D)
5016 Netherwood Rd.
Rocky Mount, 27803

MEMBERS OF HOUSE OF REPRESENTATIVES ALPHABETICALLY LISTED

Abernathy, J. Vernon (R)
44th District

Alexander, William G. (D)
34th District

Anderson, Gerald L. (D)
3rd District

Barbee, Allen C. (D)
72nd District

Barnes, Anne C. (D)
24th District

Barnhill, Howard C. (D)
60th District

Beall, Charles M. (D)
52nd District

Beard, R. D. (D)
18th District

Blue, Daniel T., Jr. (D)
21st District

Bowen, Ed (D)
12th District

Bowman, J. Fred (D)
25th District

Boyd, William T. (R)
30th District

Brannan, George W. (D)
20th District

Brawley, C. Robert (R)
43rd District

Brown, Brewster W. (D)
5th District

Brown, John Walter (R)
41st District

Brubaker, Harold J. (R)
38th District

Buchanan, Charles (R)
46th District

Bumgardner, David W., Jr. (D)
44th District

Burke, Logan (D)
67th District

Chalk, Richard E. (R)
28th District

Chapin, Howard B. (D)
2nd District

Church, John T. (D)
22nd District

Cochrane, Betsey L. (R)
37th District

Colton, Marie W. (D)
51st District

Cooper, Roy A., III (D)
72nd District

Craven, James M. (R)
31st District

Crawford, James W., Jr. (D)
22nd District

Crawford, Narvel J., Jr. (D)
51st District

Cromer, Charles L. (R)
37th District

Cunningham, W. Pete (D)
59th District

Dawkins, Donald M. (D)
32nd District

Decker, Michael (R)
29th District

DeVane, Daniel H. (D)
16th District

Diamont, David H. (D)
40th District

Duncan, Ann Q. (R)
39th District

Easterling, Ruth M. (D)
58th District

Edwards, C. R. (D)
17th District

Enloe, Jeff H., Jr. (D)
53rd District

Esposito, Theresa H. (R)
39th District

Etheridge, Bobby R. (D)
19th District

Etheridge, Larry E. (R)
71st District

Ethridge, W. Bruce (D)
4th District

Fitch, Milton F., Jr. (D)
70th District

Fletcher, Ray C. (D)
47th District

Foster, Jo Graham (D)
56th District

Freeman, William M. (D)
62nd District

Fussell, Aaron E. (D)
65th District

Gardner, Charlotte A. (R)
35th District

Gist, Herman C. (D)
26th District

Grady, Robert (R)
4th District

Greenwood, Gordon H. (D)
51st District

Grimmer, Harry C. (R)
57th District

Hackney, Joe (D)
24th District

Hall, A. M. (D)
13th District

Hardaway, Thomas (D)
7th District

Hasty, John Calvin (D)
16th District

Hege, Joe H., Jr. (R)
37th District

Hightower, Foyle R., Jr. (D)
33rd District

Holmes, George M. (R)
41st District

Holroyd, Casper (D)
61st District

Holt, Bertha M. (D)
25th District

Huffman, Doris R. (R)
45th District

Hughes, James F. (R)
46th District

Hunt, John J. (D)
48th District

Hunt, Judy F. (D)
40th District

Hunt, R. Samuel, III (D)
25th District

Hunter, Robert C. (D)
49th District

Isenhower, W. Stine (R)
45th District

James, Vernon G. (D)
1st District

Jarrell, Mary (D)
28th District

Jeralds, Luther R. (D)
17th District

Jones, Walter B., Jr. (D)
9th District

Justus, Larry T. (R)
50th District

Keesee-Forrester, Margaret P. (R)
27th District

Kennedy, Annie B. (D)
66th District

Kerr, John H., III (D)
11th District

Ligon, Bradford V. (R)
35th District

Lilley, Daniel T. (D)
3rd District

Lineberry, Albert S. (D)
27th District

Locks, Sidney A. (D)
16th District

Lutz, Edith Ledford (D)
48th District

Mavretic, Josephus L. (D)
8th District

McAlister, Robert L. (D)
25th District

McLaughlin, John B. (D)
54th District

Michaux, H. M., Jr. (D)
23rd District

Miller, George W., Jr. (D)
69th District

Mothershead, C. Ivan (R)
55th District

Murphy, Wendell H. (D)
10th District

Nesbitt, Martin L. (D)
51st District

Nye, Edd (D)
12th District

Owens, Charles D. (D)
48th District

Payne, Harry E., Jr. (D)
13th District

Perdue, Beverly M. (D)
3rd District

Privette, Coy C. (R)
34th District

Ramsey, Liston B.
(D Speaker)
52nd District

Raynor, Joseph B., Jr. (D)
18th District

Redwine, E. David (D)
14th District

Rhodes, Frank E. (R)
39th District

Rhyne, J. L., Jr. (R)
44th District

Rogers, Gene (D)
6th District

Sizemore, F. J., III (R)
27th District

Stamey, Peggy (D)
63rd District

Starnes, Edgar W. (R)
46th District

Tallent, Timothy N. (R)
34th District

Tart, John (D)
11th District

Thompson, R. M. (D)
1st District

Thompson, Sharon A. (D)
68th District

Tyndall, J. Paul (D)
4th District

Walker, Lois S. (R)
42nd District

Warner, Alex (D)
18th District

Warren, Edward M. (D)
9th District

Warren, Raymond (R)
36th District

Watkins, William T. (D)
22nd District

Wicker, Dennis A. (D)
19th District

Wilmoth, Wade F. (D)
40th District

Windley, Walter H. (R)
44th District

Wiser, Betty H. (D)
64th District

Woodard, Barney Paul (D)
20th District

Wright, Richard (D)
15th District

LIBRARIES

There are 349 public libraries in the state of North Carolina. Of the total libraries, there are 15 regional, 51 county (including municipal serving county), 34 independent municipal, 1 Indian Reservation, and 248 branch units. Eighty-nine counties are served by 69 bookmobiles.

For 1986–87, the NC Department of Cultural Resources, Division of State Library reports a total book stock of 10,245,762, 1.64 volumes per capita. Total book circulation is 25,158,848.

Source of Library Income, 1986–87

	Amount	*%*	*Per Capita*
City or town	$ 8,026,586	13	$1.28
County	36,347,438	59	5.81
State Aid	10,789,462	18	1.73
Federal Aid (LSCA)	1,335,700	2	.21
Other	4,911,091	8	.79
	$61,410,277	100	$9.82

Regional Public Library Collections

Region	*Adult Books*	*Juvenile Books*	*Periodicals*	*Recordings*	*16mm Films*	*Filmstrips*
Albemarle	128,425	53,900	81	2,079	29	422
Appalachian	80,749	29,637	—	1,903	—	—
AMY ①	80,316	24,387	60	4,147	—	652
BHM ②	68,053	23,526	57	3,017	—	204
Central NC	98,720	48,220	205	3,838	4	—

Region	Adult Books	Juvenile Books	Periodicals	Recordings	16mm Films	Filmstrips
CPC ③	180,875*	—	533	4,969	6	121
East Albemarle	85,140	31,577	166	2,800	1	350
Fontana	84,094	41,384	218	5,516	20	426
Gaston-Lincoln	306,619	126,648	271	11,885	738	3,823
Hyconeachee	58,628	29,608	257	1,637	43	312
Nantahala	68,417	27,371	148	2,030	2	485
Neuse	109,823	53,706	269	6,806	—	350
Northwestern	158,368	60,304	107	3,524	88	345
Pettigrew	78,911	28,546	125	1,439	—	334
Sandhill	149,217	53,776	208	3,481	65	392
Total Regional	1,736,355	632,590	2,705	59,071	996	8,216

*Total books—breakdown of adult and juvenile not available.
① Avery-Mitchell-Yancey Regional
② Beaufort-Hyde-Martin Regional
③ Craven-Pamlico-Carteret Regional

Public Library Collections

County	Adult Books	Juvenile Books	Periodicals	Recordings	16mm Films	Filmstrips
Alexander	23,102	13,171	99	1,092	2	168
Bladen	24,852	13,230	105	1,740	78	198
Brunswick	35,312	15,402	65	2,762	6	224
Buncombe	178,811	60,893	397	7,854	77	678
Burke	80,176	26,029	247	2,518	74	311
Cabarrus	87,332	39,516	328	3,336	135	226
Caldwell	48,969	17,221	161	889	58	317
Catawba	67,707	25,797	216	2,242	369	281
Cleveland	49,604	19,167	130	1,924	—	256
Columbus	46,417	26,421	175	2,259	4	947
Cumberland	194,455	62,974	423	7,838	692	557
Davidson	91,297	43,383	204	4,944	67	855
Davie	31,496	11,649	127	743	—	186
Duplin	24,172	20,603	61	764	53	115
Durham	191,224	100,748	655	8,834	556	1,640
Edgecombe	46,344	34,462	116	2,212	—	401
Forsyth	260,649	86,621	825	13,617	835	572
Franklin	35,786	18,451	141	1,789	—	202
Granville	50,626	26,251	152	1,426	15	111
Guilford	439,535	214,576	785	11,765	1,214	—
Halifax	34,624	11,682	79	2,280	1	58
Harnett	46,250	27,439	204	3,152	5	939
Haywood	64,282	30,998	205	5,276	4	544
Henderson	75,443	36,400	281	5,466	65	1,255
Iredell	114,506	39,662	222	5,013	197	853
Johnston	59,700	23,772	104	928	11	245
Lee	55,388	25,722	142	1,404	—	559
Madison	22,980	9,139	35	585	—	153
McDowell	52,815	16,776	158	3,109	24	364
Mecklenburg	625,478	295,586	1,176	36,328	2,481	351
Nash	45,381	29,207	184	824	—	132
New Hanover	141,962	43,278	333	2,815	29	95
Onslow	47,084	24,707	150	382	89	152
Pender	43,143	17,340	96	1,263	—	385
Pitt	87,806	42,716	283	4,177	9	893

County	Adult Books	Juvenile Books	Periodicals	Recordings	16mm Films	Filmstrips
Polk	24,087	6,372	60	1,027	—	40
Randolph	116,592	36,976	351	7,407	242	1,172
Robeson	73,853	28,620	136	1,973	19	891
Rockingham	122,697	49,264	237	4,200	139	388
Rowan	89,556	33,799	388	3,014	—	192
Rutherford	61,749	29,687	57	4,443	—	114
Sampson	43,992	20,210	139	292	1	64
Scotland	45,061	19,477	100	500	1	100
Stanly	71,356	29,964	158	684	16	311
Transylvania	26,538	10,521	118	3,081	1	127
Union	104,951	63,620	320	3,694	202	1,230
Vance	27,706	20,693	95	750	—	108
Wake	658,058*	—	555	111	527	113
Warren	34,615*	—	25	25	—	—
Wayne	48,697	27,213	152	668	15	—
Wilson	73,538	34,239	187	1,825	44	315
Total County	4,455,081 ①	1,961,644	12,142	187,244	8,357	20,388

Grand Total Books 7,109,398

*Total books—breakdown of adult and juvenile not available.

① Total does not include counties where adult/juvenile breakdown was not available.

Public Library Collections

Municipality	Adult Books	Juvenile Books	Periodicals	Recordings	16mm Films	Filmstrips
Ayden	6,004	4,918	18	0	20	91
Bailey	1,485	597	8	—	—	—
Benson	8,274	4,889	6	0	—	—
Bethel	4,344	—	—	—	—	—
Chapel Hill	48,539	15,997	192	1,528	7	32
Clayton	7,993	3,440	29	38	—	5
Dunn	10,673	5,137	22	570	—	12
Enfield	6,778	3,050	10	10	—	—
Farmville	15,530	6,440	96	325	—	110
Forest City	5,219	916	45	—	—	—
Fountain	3,571	1,038	0	100	—	—
Four Oaks	3,752	761	12	0	—	—
Grifton	5,138*	—	—	166	—	—
Hickory	87,664*	—	232	3,392	107	47
High Point	254,454*	—	455	6,461	794	830
Kenly	1,795	223	0	0	—	—
King's Mountain	29,181*	—	42	—	—	—
Mooresville	28,121	10,357	48	48	—	1
Nashville	2,893	1,602	32	0	2	—
Norlina	6,712	1,852	0	0	—	—
Pinehurst	13,160	3,586	56	212	—	68
Roanoke Rapids	16,109	7,263	101	1,229	66	70
Rutherfordton	—	—	70	—	—	—
Scotland Neck	5,864	4,044	25	88	1	42
Selma (Atkinson)	927	352	4	0	—	—
Selma	4,621	2,667	23	72	—	1
Southern Pines	24,950	7,691	99	1,372	—	77
Spencer	6,942	5,205	22	76	—	—

Municipality	Adult Books	Juvenile Books	Periodicals	Recordings	16mm Films	Filmstrips
Spindale	—	—	20	—	—	—
Spring Hope	1,871	1,291	6	—	—	—
Wallace	12,656	5,224	54	32	29	77
Warrenton	1,305	1,177	—	—	1	—
Washington	38,161*	—	75	610	2	12
Whitakers	2,485	591	7	0	—	16
Total Municipal	252,513	100,308	1,809	16,329	1,029	1,491
State Grand Totals	6,263,074 ①	2,694,542	16,656	262,644	10,382	30,095

Grand Total of Books 10,245,762

*Total books—adult/juvenile breakdown not available.

① Total does not include amounts when adult/juvenile breakdown was not available.

Regional Libraries' Circulation of Books

Regional Libraries	Number Adult Non-Fiction	Number Adult Fiction	Total Juvenile	Total Book Circulation	Volumes Circulated Per Capita	Reference Questions Answered
Albemarle	27,578	76,159	72,888	176,625	2.3	35,427
Appalachian	72,604	174,765	154,208	401,577	3.4	15,523
AMY	42,701	191,475	71,376	305,552	6.8	40,616
BHM	23,367	106,344	59,299	189,010	2.5	3,910
Central NC	75,497	93,283	129,741	298,521	2.2	116,829
CPC	84,897	237,115	95,262	417,274	3.0	117,204
East Albemarle	61,721	103,423	82,232	247,376	3.8	31,902
Fontana	70,802	180,858	106,673	358,333	5.9	34,836
Gaston-Lincoln	186,054	399,920	297,731	883,705	4.1	292,784
Hyconeechee	37,669	104,444	101,122	243,235	1.8	41,506
Nantahala	35,019	114,332	65,339	214,690	6.2	48,863
Neuse	86,917	222,196	152,178	461,291	5.3	159,540
Northwestern	75,959	193,803	147,636	417,398	3.1	61,932
Pettigrew	29,093	94,595	50,037	173,725	4.1	35,936
Sandhill	64,977	201,480	120,204	386,661	2.2	145,544

County Libraries' Circulation of Books

County Libraries	Number Adult Non-Fiction	Number Adult Fiction	Total Juvenile	Total Book Circulation	Volumes Circulated Per Capita	Reference Questions Answered
Alexander	13,612	23,750	30,834	68,196	2.6	18,478
Bladen	19,873	61,284	46,508	127,665	4.2	28,632
Brunswick	24,653	80,315	31,672	136,640	3.0	45,774
Buncombe	193,797	333,235	228,500	755,532	4.5	62,493
Burke	42,863	96,113	106,248	245,224	3.2	34,416

County Libraries	Number Adult Non-Fiction	Number Adult Fiction	Total Juvenile	Total Book Circulation	Volumes Circulated Per Capita	Reference Questions Answered
Cabarrus	71,513	97,511	160,509	329,533	3.6	61,762
Caldwell	36,049	97,056	66,782	199,887	2.8	27,864
Catawba	43,554	112,195	94,309	250,058	2.2	114,944
Cleveland	41,320	95,807	64,339	201,466	2.3	39,146
Columbus	23,874	58,263	84,437	166,574	3.2	24,358
Cumberland	250,705	325,736	294,296	870,737	3.4	329,967
Davidson	87,806	129,811	175,017	392,634	3.3	144,174
Davie	16,243	26,176	27,583	70,002	2.5	3,673
Duplin	14,368	27,161	27,438	68,967	1.7	68,551
Durham	187,277	205,491	331,469	724,237	4.5	250,443
Edgecombe	58,397	96,934	120,362	275,693	4.7	48,135
Forsyth	224,393	352,432	836,321	1,413,146	5.5	450,363
Franklin	22,882	40,616	42,791	106,289	3.2	20,750
Granville	16,827	31,744	34,052	83,199*	2.3	16,776
Guilford	221,513	586,975	345,172	1,153,660	3.5	137,235
Halifax	7,182	44,101	12,680	63,963	1.1	3,624
Harnett	15,598	50,690	103,071	169,359	2.7	12,396
Haywood	62,747	168,052	84,745	315,544	6.6	29,060
Henderson	8,891	24,106	110,219	377,029*	5.7	37,417
Iredell	86,057	121,138	107,972	315,167	3.6	38,509
Johnston	27,408	54,409	45,856	127,673	1.7	16,410
Lee	27,651	47,672	39,806	115,129	2.8	22,022
Madison	8,723	35,331	18,937	62,991	3.7	2,938
McDowell	37,725	85,818	47,329	170,872	4.7	27,496
Mecklenburg	575,255	878,101	768,938	2,222,294	5.0	906,738
Nash	47,150	90,895	169,707	307,752	4.3	37,176
New Hanover	120,317	221,116	184,462	525,895	4.7	101,089
Onslow	—	—	127,278	309,976	2.5	42,812
Pender	18,757	43,235	27,924	89,916	3.7	3,525
Pitt	68,460	93,855	192,416	354,731	3.7	48,860
Polk	15,907	53,720	15,886	85,513	5.9	13,100
Randolph	57,694	100,603	100,046	258,343	2.7	60,482
Robeson	34,335	84,068	61,154	179,557	1.7	44,700
Rockingham	49,118	170,169	124,298	343,585	4.0	133,014
Rowan	—	—	134,469	357,238	3.5	29,075
Rutherford	16,763	40,761	29,994	87,518	1.5	14,778
Sampson	25,963	56,515	49,771	132,249	2.6	25,847
Scotland	21,032	40,044	51,517	112,593	3.4	19,965
Stanly	36,877	56,239	50,918	144,034	2.9	23,016
Transylvania	25,341	63,745	33,559	122,645	4.8	18,664
Union	82,172	86,092	144,309	312,573	4.0	2,215,793
Vance	11,575	16,479	21,493	49,547	1.3	13,297
Wake	577,797	853,259	927,443	2,358,499	6.7	384,208
Warren	—	—	—	11,440	0.7	—
Wayne	58,584	140,843	102,225	301,922	3.1	30,966
Wilson	48,614	93,164	76,730	218,508	3.4	41,249
Total County	3,785,482	6,692,825	7,113,791	18,243,394	3.9	6,326,160

*Contains circulations not included in preceding categories.

Municipal Libraries' Circulation of Books

Municipal Libraries	Number Adult Non-Fiction	Number Adult Fiction	Total Juvenile	Total Book Circulation	Volumes Circulated Per Capita	Reference Questions Answered
Ayden	2,057	7,022	12,453	21,532	4.5	2,847
Bailey	135	1,300	720	2,155	3.1	—
Benson	3,567	8,125	5,829	17,521	5.7	1,000
Bethel	14	1,356	1,137	2,507	1.3	—
Chapel Hill	106,925	142,146	164,179	413,250	12.1	66,339
Clayton	6,021	10,641	16,493	33,155	6.5	1,200
Dunn	6,286	17,633	15,913	39,832	4.4	5,485
Enfield	1,821	3,291	4,078	9,190	3.1	970
Farmville	3,992	10,309	8,082	22,383	4.6	4,378
Forest City	6,549	17,365	16,969	40,883	5.0	4,834
Fountain	120	1,186	417	1,723	4.0	—
Four Oaks	166	1,587	721	2,474	1.8	110
Grifton	186	2,596	2,363	5,145	2.6	629
Hickory	42,133	60,023	68,924	171,080	7.0	27,013
High Point	—	—	100,256	368,615	5.6	65,807
Kenly	114	2,023	1,187	3,324	2.2	—
Kings Mountain	—	—	12,251	31,402	3.6	2,330
Mooresville	7,488	31,968	30,939	70,395	7.9	11,603
Nashville	868	2,565	3,603	7,036	2.0	—
Norlina	73	907	278	1,258	1.4	—
Pinehurst	13,091	33,046	4,893	51,030	20.8	4,790
Roanoke Rapids	17,505	35,953	27,753	81,211	5.3	19,613
Rutherfordton	6,669	40,125	21,709	68,503	19.2	17,315
Scotland Neck	1,795	10,245	4,553	16,593	6.1	615
Selma (Atkinson)	99	796	1,091	1,986	0.4	—
Selma	2,233	14,183	10,638	27,054	5.4	1,050
Southern Pines	13,340	44,384	15,174	72,898	7.8	41,560
Spencer	444	6,527	1,878	8,849	3.1	2,985
Spindale	4,109	20,683	25,945	50,737	11.8	10,413
Spring Hope	998	1,347	856	3,201	2.5	607
Wallace	3,934	8,885	6,892	19,711	6.7	4,920
Warrenton	485	820	1,177	2,482	2.5	—
Washington	17,375	29,548	23,228	70,151	7.4	14,423
Whitakers	107	495	613	1,215	2.4	250
Total	270,699	569,080	613,192	1,740,481	6.7	313,086
Grand Total	5,031,036	9,756,097	9,432,909	25,158,848	4.0	7,821,598

LICENSE TAG IDENTIFICATION

License tags for passenger vehicles in North Carolina are identified by three alpha characters (AAA through ZZZ) and three numeric characters. One plate is issued for each vehicle. County of origin is not designated on the license plate.

To trace the owner of a North Carolina registered vehicle, send the license plate number plus $1.00 (fee per inquiry) and a request for an abstract of the registration to the North Carolina Division of Motor Vehicles, Motor Vehicle Building, 1100 New Bern Ave., Raleigh 27697.

MANUFACTURING

North Carolina ranks first in the nation in the manufacture of tobacco products; textile mill products; and furniture and fixtures; ninth in total manufacturing.

In the Southeast, North Carolina ranks first in total manufacturing; tobacco products; textile mill products; lumber and wood products; furniture and fixtures; rubber and miscellaneous plastics; fabricated metal products; machinery, except electrical; electric and electronic equipment; instruments and related products.

The state ranks second in the Southeast in the manufacture of apparel; chemicals and allied products; leather and leather products; third in paper and allied products; stone, clay and glass products.

Following is a list of North Carolina's largest manufacturing establishments based on first quarter 1986 employment, shown in order of rank.

1. Burlington Ind., Inc.
   3330 West Friendly Ave.
   Greensboro 27410
   919-379-2000
   Guilford County
   Product: Textiles and Furniture

2. International Business Machines Corp.
   P.O. Box 12195
   Research Triangle Park 27709
   919-543-5221
   Durham County
   Product: Telecommunications Equipment

   1001 West Harris Blvd.
   Charlotte 28257
   704-598-1000
   Mecklenburg County
   Product: Electronic Circuit Cards

3. R. J. Reynolds Tobacco Co.
   1100 Reynolds Blvd.
   Winston-Salem 27102
   919-773-2000
   Forsyth County
   Product: Cigarettes

4. Cannon Mills Co.
   subs. Pacific Holding Corp.
   P.O. Box 107
   Kannapolis 28081
   704-933-1221
   Cabarrus County
   Product: Textiles

5. American Telephone & Telegraph Co.
   3300 Lexington Rd., SE
   Winston-Salem 27102
   919-784-1110
   Forsyth County
   Product: Telephone Equipment

   Western Electric Co., Inc. (Div. of AT&T)
   204 Graham Hopedale Rd.
   Burlington 27215
   919-228-4000
   Alamance County
   Product: Military Electronics Equipment

6. Cone Mills Corp.
   1201 Maple St.
   Greensboro 27405
   919-379-6246
   Guilford County
   Product: Textiles

7. Collins & Aikman Corp.
   Ca Vel Div.
   1803 North Main St.
   Roxboro 27573
   919-599-1111
   Person County
   Product: Textiles

8. J. P. Stevens & Co., Inc.
   Fifth & Jackson Streets
   Roanoke Rapids 27870
   919-537-4171
   Halifax County
   Product: Textiles

9. Northern Telecom, Inc.
   P.O. Box 13010
   Research Triangle Park 27709
   919-549-5000
   Durham County
   Product: Integrated Network Systems

10. Broyhill Furniture Ind.
    Broyhill Park
    Lenoir 28633
    704-758-3111
    Caldwell County
    Product: Furniture

11. E. I. du Pont de Nemours & Co.
P.O. Box 800
Kinston 28501
919-522-6111
Lenoir County
Product: Polyester Fibers

12. Fieldcrest Mills, Inc.
326 East Stadium Dr.
Eden 27288
919-627-3000
Rockingham County
Product: Textiles

13. General Electric Co.
Spartanburg Hwy.
Hendersonville 28739
704-693-2000
Henderson County
Product: Outdoor Lighting Fixtures

14. Drexel Heritage Furnishings, Inc.
subs. Masco Corp.
Drexel 28619
704-433-3000
Burke County
Product: Furniture

15. Westinghouse Electric Corp.
P.O. Box 9533
Raleigh 27611
919-834-5271
Wake County
Product: Electric Timing Devices

16. Blue Bell, Inc.
301 North Elm St.
Greensboro 27401
919-373-3400
Guilford County
Product: Apparel

17. Fiber Ind., Inc.
subs. Celanese Corp.
P.O. Box 32414
Charlotte 28232
704-554-2000
Mecklenburg County
Product: Polyester Fibers & Yarn

18. Thomasville Furniture Ind.
subs. Armstrong World Ind., Inc.
401 E. Main St.
Thomasville 27360
919-475-1361
Davidson County
Product: Furniture

19. Kayser-Roth Corp.
P.O. Box 820
Burlington 27220
919-229-2232
Alamance County
Product: Hosiery

20. Holly Farms Poultry Ind., Inc.
subs. Federal Co.
P.O. Box 88
Wilkesboro 28697
919-838-2171
Wilkes County
Product: Poultry

21. Perdue Processing
P.O. Box 467
Lewiston 27849
919-348-2581
Bertie County
Product: Poultry Processing

22. Consolidated Foods
Bali Co.
P.O. Box 5070
Statesville 28677
704-872-2785
Iredell County
Product: Foundation Garments

23. Ti-Caro, Inc.
P.O. Box 699
Gastonia 28053
704-867-7271
Gaston County
Product: Textiles

24. ITT Corp.
ITT Continental Baking
P.O. Box 33007
Raleigh 27606
919-832-6686
Wake County
Product: Bakery Goods

25. Weyerhaeuser Co.
P.O. Box 1391
New Bern 28560
919-633-7100
Craven County
Product: Bleached Kraft Pulp

26. Champion Paper
P.O. Box C-10
Canton 28716
704-646-2000
Haywood County
Product: Paper Mill

27. PPG Ind., Inc.
Route 4
Shelby 28150
704-434-2261
Cleveland County
Product: Fiberglass Yarn

28. AMP, Inc.
P.O. Box 55
Winston-Salem 27102
919-725-9222
Forsyth County
Product: Electronic Connectors

29. Burroughs Wellcome Co.
subs. Wellcome Foundation Ltd.
3030 Cornwallis Rd.
Research Triangle Park 27709
919-248-3000
Durham County
Product: Pharmaceuticals

30. Kelly-Springfield Tire Co.
Highway 401 North
Fayetteville 28301
919-488-9295
Cumberland County
Product: Automobile Tires

31. Ithaca Ind., Inc.
P.O. Box 620
Wilkesboro 28697
919-667-5231
Wilkes County
Product: Apparel & Hosiery

32. Doran Textiles
Drawer A
Shelby 28150
704-487-2000
Cleveland County
Product: Textiles

33. Reeves Brothers, Inc.
P.O. Box 188
Cornelius 28031
704-892-8081
Mecklenburg County
Product: Plastic Products

34. Black & Decker Mfg. Co.
P.O. Box 64429
Fayetteville 28306
919-425-1181
Cumberland County
Product: Electrical Hand Tools

35. Abbott Laboratories
P.O. Box 2226
Rocky Mount 27801
919-977-5111
Edgecombe County
Product: I. V. Solutions

36. Macfield Texturing, Inc.
P.O. Box 737
Madison 27025
919-427-4051
Rockingham County
Product: Textiles

37. Travenol Laboratories, Inc.
P.O. Box 1390
Marion 28752
704-756-4151
McDowell County
Product: I. V. Solutions

38. Loew's Theatres Inc.
Lorillard Corp.
P.O. Box 21688
Greensboro 27401
919-373-6600
Guilford County
Product: Cigarettes

39. The Singer Co.
Furniture Division
P.O. Box 1588
Lenoir 28645
704-728-6741
Caldwell County
Product: Furniture

40. Wix Corp.
subs. Dana Spicer
1301 East Ozark Ave.
Gastonia 28052
704-864-6711
Gaston County
Product: Oil Filters

41. Eaton Corp.
Air Controls Plant
P.O. Box 241
Roxboro 27573
919-599-1141
Person County
Product: Tire Valves

42. American Tobacco Co.
201 West Pettigrew St.
Durham 27701
919-682-2101
Durham County
Product: Cigarettes

43. National Spinning Co.
West Third St.
Washington 27889
919-946-8111
Beaufort County
Product: Textiles

44. Union Carbide Corp.
Union Carbide Battery Products Div.
P.O. Box 849
Asheboro 27203
919-672-0363
Randolph County
Product: Batteries

45. Stuart Furniture Ind., Inc.
P.O. Box 220
Asheboro 27203
919-625-6174
Randolph County
Product: Furniture

46. Georgia-Pacific Corp.
P.O. Box 246
Murfreesboro 27855
919-398-4121
Hertford County
Product: Lumber Products

47. Federal Paper Board Co., Inc.
Carolina Operations
Riegelwood 28456
919-655-2211
Columbus County
Product: Paperboard

48. Firestone Tire & Rubber Co.
P.O. Box 1139
Wilson 27893
919-291-4275
Wilson County
Product: Tires

49. Bernhardt Ind., Inc.
1839 Morganton Blvd., SW
Lenoir 28645
704-758-9811
Caldwell County
Product: Furniture

50. Glen Raven Mills, Inc.
Glen Raven 27215
919-227-6211
Alamance County
Product: Textiles

51. Square D Co.
P.O. Box 27446
Raleigh 27611
919-266-3671
Wake County
Product: Electric Controls

52. Lance, Inc.
8600 South Blvd.
Charlotte 28210
704-554-1421
Mecklenburg County
Product: Snack Foods

53. Stedman Corp.
P.O. Box 1288
Asheboro 27203
919-625-2141
Randolph County
Product: Textiles & Apparel

54. Chatham Mfg. Co.
East Main St.
Elkin 28621
919-835-2211
Surry County
Product: Textiles

55. Carolina Mills, Inc.
618 Carolina Ave.
Maiden 28650
704-428-9911
Catawba County
Product: Textiles

56. Tultex Corp.
Tultex Yarn Group
P.O. Box 1865
Gastonia 28052
704-864-7701
Gaston County
Product: Textiles

57. Shuford Mills, Inc.
Highland & 15th St., NE
Hickory 28601
704-328-2131
Catawba County
Product: Textiles

58. Bassett Furniture Ind., Inc.
Bassett Upholstery
P.O. Box 47
Newton 28658
704-464-3354
Catawba County
Product: Furniture

59. West Point-Pepperell, Inc.
Alamac Knitting Div.
P.O. Box 1347
Lumberton 28358
919-739-2811
Robeson County
Product: Textiles

60. Dixie Furniture Co.
South Salisbury St.
Lexington 27292
704-246-5971
Davidson County
Product: Furniture

61. Adams-Millis Corp.
225 North Elm St.
High Point 27260
919-889-7071
Guilford County
Product: Textiles

62. Parkdale Mills, Inc.
1630 West Garrison Blvd.
Gastonia 28052
704-864-8761
Gaston County
Product: Textiles

63. Gilbarco, Inc.
subs. Exxon Corp.
P.O. Box 22087
Greensboro 27420
919-292-3011
Guilford County
Product: Service Station Equipment

64. The Lane Co., Inc.
Hickory Chair Co.
P.O. Box 2147
Hickory 28601
704-328-1801
Catawba County
Product: Furniture

65. BASF Corp.
BASF Fibers Div.
Sand Hill Road
Enka 28728
704-667-7110
Buncombe County
Product: Manmade Fibers

66. Guilford Mills, Inc.
4925 West Market St.
Greensboro 27402
919-292-7550
Guilford County
Product: Textiles

67. Ladd Furniture, Inc.
One Plaza Center, Box HP3
High Point 27261
919-889-0333
Guilford County
Product: Furniture

68. General Tire Inc.
General Tire & Rubber
P.O. Box 7001
Charlotte 28217
704-588-1600
Mecklenburg County
Product: Tires

69. Freightliner Corp.
1400 Tulip Dr.
Gastonia 28052
704-866-8511
Gaston County
Product: Truck Parts

70. Ecusta Corp.
P.O. Box 200
Pisgah Forest 28768
704-877-2211
Transylvania County
Product: Paper

71. American & Efird Mills, Inc.
subs. Ruddick Corp.
P.O. Box 507
Mount Holly 28120
704-827-4311
Gaston County
Product: Textiles

72. Pharr Yarns
subs. Stowe Mills, Inc.
Main Street
McAdenville 28101
704-824-3551
Gaston County
Product: Textiles

73. Henredon Furniture Ind., Inc.
Henredon Road
Morganton 28655
704-437-5261

Burke County
Product: Furniture

74. Liggett & Myers Tobacco Co.
P.O. Box 1572
Durham 27702
919-683-9000
Durham County
Product: Tobacco Products

75. Dayco Southern
P.O. Box 360
Waynesville 28786
704-456-5311
Haywood County
Product: Fan Belts & Radiator Hoses

76. Corning Glass Works
3900 Electronics Drive
Raleigh 27604
919-878-6200
Wake County
Product: Capacitors

77. Siecor Corp.
489 Siecor Park
Hickory 28603
704-327-5000
Catawba County
Product: Computer Optical Cables

78. National Service Ind. Inc.
Block Ind.
P.O. Box 420
Wilmington 28401
919-763-8221
New Hanover County
Product: Apparel

79. Americal Corp.
P.O. Box 1419
Henderson 27536
919-492-2166
Vance County
Product: Textiles

80. Cooper Group, Inc.
3535 Glenwood Ave.
Raleigh 27622
919-781-7200
Wake County
Product: Hand Tools

81. American Thread Co.
P.O. Box 269
Marble 28905
704-837-5171
Cherokee County
Product: Yarns & Thread

82. Harriet & Henderson Yarns, Inc.
Alexander Ave.
Henderson 27536
919-438-3101
Vance County
Product: Textiles

83. Southern Devices, Inc.
subs. Leviton Mfg. Co.
P.O. Box 68
Morganton 28655
704-584-1611
Burke County
Product: Electrical Wiring Devices

84. Rocky Mount Under-Garment Co. Inc.
1536 Boone St.
Rocky Mount 27801
919-446-6161
Edgecombe County
Product: Under-garments

85. Miller Brewing Co.
P.O. Box 3327
Eden 27288
919-627-2100
Rockingham County
Product: Beer

86. Spencer's, Inc.
P.O. Box 988
Mount Airy 27030
919-789-9111
Surry County
Product: Apparel

87. Philip Morris USA
P.O. Box 1098
Concord 28025
704-788-5000
Cabarrus County
Product: Cigarettes

88. Data General Corp.
P.O. Box 786
Apex 27502
919-362-4800
Wake County
Product: Computer Assembly

89. Century Furniture Co.
408 12th St. Dr., NW
Hickory 28601
704-328-1851
Catawba County
Product: Furniture

90. Stanadyne, Inc.
Clark Neck Rd.
Washington 27889
919-975-2553
Beaufort County
Product: Diesel Fuel Injection Components

91. Maro Hosiery Corp.
Influential, Inc.
P.O. Box 309
High Point 27261
919-885-6006
Guilford County
Product: Hosiery

92. AMF Hatteras Yachts
P.O. Box 2690
High Point 27261
919-889-6621
Guilford County
Product: Yachts

93. American Bakeries Co.
P.O. Box 668648
Charlotte 28266
704-394-1181
Mecklenburg County
Product: Bakery Goods

94. Hickory Springs Mfg. Co.
P.O. Box 128
Hickory 28603
704-328-2201
Catawba County
Product: Springs & Foam Products

95. McGregor Corp.
Gilead Mfg. Co.
402 North Main St.
Mount Gilead 27306
919-439-6141
Montgomery County
Product: Undergarments

96. House of Raeford Farms Inc.
520 East Central Ave.
Raeford 28376
919-875-5161
Hoke County
Product: Turkeys & Chickens

97. Wiscassett Mills Co. subs. Pacific Holding Co.
P.O. Box 40
Albemarle 28002
704-982-1181
Stanly County
Product: Textiles

98. Alba-Waldensian, Inc.
210 St. Germain St., SW
Valdese 28690
704-874-2191
Burke County
Product: Textiles & Apparel

99. Renfro Corp.
P.O. Box 908
Mount Airy 27030
919-789-5531
Surry County
Product: Hosiery for Children

100. Coca-Cola Bottling Co. Consolidated
P.O. Box 31487
Charlotte 28231
704-551-4400
Mecklenburg County
Product: Soft Drinks

MEDICAL RESOURCES

There were 9,205 known active physicians with nonfederal, nonresident practices in 1986. This total is broken down as follows: 1,211, family practice; 294, general practice; 1,210, internal medicine; 586, obstetrics/gynecology; 687, pediatrics; 5,202, other specialties; 15, no specialty.

There were 443 nurse practitioners and 593 physician assistants. Registered nurses (RN's) numbered 36,867 while there were 13,259 licensed practical nurses (LPN's).

In other health professions, there were 440 chiropractors, 1,835 dental hygienists, 2,589 dentists, 586 optometrists, 4,019 pharmacists, 1,037 physical therapists, 393 physical therapist assistants, 118 podiatrists, 667 psychological associates, and 926 practicing psychologists.

On the following chart the number of physicians are those nonfederal and nonresident who had active practices within the county. Data was compiled from the *North Carolina Health Manpower Data Book, Effective October 1986*, prepared by The Health Services Research Center of the University of North Carolina at Chapel Hill.

County	*Physicians*	*Midlevel Practitioners*	*Nurses*	*Chiropractors*	*Dentists*	*Optometrists*	*Practicing Psychologists*
Alamance	134	6	616	9	50	15	11
Alexander	9	0	61	2	5	2	1
Alleghany	5	2	34	0	2	1	0
Anson	22	3	138	1	3	2	0
Ashe	15	4	76	1	3	3	0
Avery	21	1	149	1	6	0	2
Beaufort	43	5	273	1	17	3	1
Bertie	9	3	41	0	2	1	0
Bladen	18	3	93	0	6	2	1
Brunswick	34	3	146	3	11	2	1
Buncombe	351	67	2,181	21	94	13	34
Burke	108	17	785	6	27	4	23

County	Physicians	Midlevel Practitioners	Nurses	Chiropractors	Dentists	Optometrists	Practicing Psychologists
Cabarrus	91	6	570	10	30	7	4
Caldwell	54	7	320	5	20	5	0
Camden	1	0	4	0	0	0	0
Carteret	49	9	324	3	14	2	1
Caswell	4	2	19	0	3	0	1
Catawba	146	12	918	11	50	14	7
Chatham	21	5	130	1	10	2	1
Cherokee	20	2	135	2	6	3	1
Chowan	17	0	139	1	5	1	0
Clay	3	0	27	0	2	1	0
Cleveland	87	6	646	5	31	10	2
Columbus	43	13	281	4	9	3	0
Craven	112	10	652	4	33	7	7
Cumberland	220	32	1,445	9	72	14	21
Currituck	3	0	5	0	2	0	0
Dare	19	9	62	0	11	2	1
Davidson	72	5	495	8	24	10	3
Davie	15	4	126	1	8	2	0
Duplin	23	7	158	1	11	4	2
Durham	1,017	121	4,022	13	97	14	90
Edgecombe	36	8	252	2	21	3	0
Forsyth	818	95	3,457	27	160	32	68
Franklin	15	3	84	0	7	2	0
Gaston	131	10	873	13	63	18	7
Gates	3	0	8	0	0	0	0
Graham	4	2	9	0	1	0	0
Granville	50	12	539	0	14	5	30
Greene	7	2	41	0	4	0	2
Guilford	552	93	3,257	30	183	31	80
Halifax	47	4	348	2	13	5	5
Harnett	37	3	295	2	14	6	2
Haywood	56	2	333	7	24	7	3
Henderson	100	10	464	9	32	8	5
Hertford	29	5	229	0	10	3	1
Hoke	5	3	67	0	5	0	1
Hyde	2	2	4	0	1	0	0
Iredell	93	7	699	9	31	12	2
Jackson	44	3	173	1	13	2	9
Johnston	46	3	283	5	16	6	4
Jones	6	0	12	1	0	0	0
Lee	51	4	253	4	14	5	2
Lenoir	77	8	599	2	23	5	6
Lincoln	27	4	167	4	10	4	1
Macon	26	3	131	4	7	4	0
Madison	5	5	40	0	3	1	1
Martin	11	7	93	1	6	3	0
McDowell	22	1	130	4	9	2	2
Mecklenburg	839	33	4,781	40	263	47	84
Mitchell	21	0	108	0	6	1	0
Montgomery	17	2	111	1	7	2	0
Moore	100	8	645	3	26	5	2
Nash	100	8	634	2	19	14	5
New Hanover	227	26	1,214	16	63	11	15

County	Physicians	Midlevel Practitioners	Nurses	Chiropractors	Dentists	Optometrists	Practicing Psychologists
Northampton	4	3	40	0	3	0	0
Onslow	69	4	548	4	32	7	6
Orange	708	54	1,539	6	157	5	123
Pamlico	4	0	13	0	1	0	1
Pasquotank	51	3	339	4	13	6	3
Pender	8	3	80	0	4	1	0
Perquimans	3	0	6	0	2	0	0
Person	16	2	108	2	10	1	0
Pitt	306	39	1,432	5	40	11	29
Polk	23	2	105	1	7	3	1
Randolph	53	4	381	5	31	9	1
Richmond	26	3	258	3	12	5	2
Robeson	90	13	479	5	22	10	4
Rockingham	58	11	382	6	30	10	0
Rowan	94	12	817	11	36	12	19
Rutherford	47	0	292	4	15	7	5
Sampson	47	8	233	2	11	4	1
Scotland	28	4	250	1	7	3	2
Stanly	37	6	218	5	15	6	1
Stokes	10	3	98	1	11	1	0
Surry	54	15	340	4	24	7	1
Swain	9	1	111	0	4	1	1
Transylvania	26	3	140	2	10	2	1
Tyrrell	0	1	8	0	0	0	0
Union	56	1	298	3	15	7	2
Vance	31	7	168	4	12	4	3
Wake	630	61	3,653	34	229	40	127
Warren	10	1	46	0	4	0	0
Washington	7	0	45	1	2	1	0
Watauga	52	1	292	5	18	4	24
Wayne	105	11	831	2	36	8	12
Wilkes	34	13	300	3	14	6	3
Wilson	91	2	643	2	21	6	2
Yadkin	17	2	95	2	6	3	0
Yancey	11	3	32	1	3	3	0
State Totals	9,205	1,036	50,126	440	2,589	586	926

Hospitals, Beds by Type, and Licensed Family Care Homes

County	Number of Hospitals	Beds			Family Care Homes	
		General	Psychiatric	Long-Term Care	Facilities	Residents
Alamance	2	231	71	83	23	122
Alexander	1	65	0	0	2	11
Alleghany	1	46	0	0	0	0
Anson	1	52	0	45	0	0
Ashe	1	76	0	0	0	0
Avery	2	93	24	0	0	0
Beaufort	2	207	0	0	2	11
Bertie	1	49	0	0	4	23
Bladen	1	62	0	0	11	54
Brunswick	2	100	0	0	0	0

County	Number of Hospitals	Beds: General	Beds: Psychiatric	Beds: Long-Term Care	Family Care Homes: Facilities	Family Care Homes: Residents
Buncombe	6	779	350	0	47	269
Burke	4	426	865	0	13	72
Cabarrus	1	458	0	0	6	31
Caldwell	2	165	0	0	4	19
Camden	0	0	0	0	0	0
Carteret	2	133	0	60	3	15
Caswell	0	0	0	0	18	96
Catawba	3	467	112	0	3	15
Chatham	1	68	0	0	2	8
Cherokee	2	111	0	120	3	8
Chowan	1	71	0	56	0	0
Clay	0	0	0	0	0	0
Cleveland	3	462	0	0	20	112
Columbus	1	166	0	0	2	11
Craven	1	278	24	0	0	0
Cumberland	3	539	193	0	8	38
Currituck	0	0	0	0	2	10
Dare	0	0	0	0	0	0
Davidson	2	243	15	0	4	21
Davie	1	81	0	0	2	11
Duplin	1	69	12	20	5	26
Durham	4	1,364	127	0	39	183
Edgecombe	1	127	0	0	2	12
Forsyth	6	1,538	219	0	21	104
Franklin	1	54	15	0	9	42
Gaston	1	399	80	0	3	17
Gates	0	0	0	0	1	2
Graham	0	0	0	0	0	0
Granville	3	111	795	0	7	31
Greene	0	0	0	0	1	6
Guilford	7	1,374	170	0	28	140
Halifax	2	190	20	0	2	11
Harnett	2	190	0	0	4	22
Haywood	1	200	0	0	8	41
Henderson	2	336	0	40	4	21
Hertford	1	141	0	0	14	76
Hoke	1	81	0	0	0	0
Hyde	0	0	0	0	0	0
Iredell	3	487	0	0	4	20
Jackson	1	86	0	0	0	0
Johnston	1	160	20	0	12	63
Jones	0	0	0	0	0	0
Lee	1	142	0	0	3	15
Lenoir	1	322	0	0	5	28
Lincoln	1	110	0	0	1	3
Macon	2	86	22	0	0	0
Madison	0	0	0	0	5	30
Martin	2	61	0	0	5	26
McDowell	1	65	0	0	9	52
Mecklenburg	10	2,055	355	0	18	93
Mitchell	1	112	0	0	6	34
Montgomery	1	90	0	0	5	30

MEDICAL RESOURCES

County	Number of Hospitals	Beds: General	Beds: Psychiatric	Beds: Long-Term Care	Family Care Homes: Facilities	Family Care Homes: Residents
Moore	2	327	59	86	3	17
Nash	2	322	20	0	5	22
New Hanover	3	626	67	0	10	54
Northampton	0	0	0	0	3	15
Onslow	2	150	76	0	7	31
Orange	1	572	63	0	10	50
Pamlico	0	0	0	0	0	0
Pasquotank	1	206	0	0	1	5
Pender	1	57	0	23	5	28
Perquimans	0	0	0	0	4	20
Person	1	65	0	23	2	12
Pitt	2	469	112	0	17	85
Polk	1	74	0	0	4	18
Randolph	1	145	0	0	10	56
Richmond	2	215	10	0	5	26
Robeson	2	264	59	132	10	54
Rockingham	2	230	0	55	26	136
Rowan	1	327	15	0	9	46
Rutherford	1	165	0	0	26	143
Sampson	1	156	0	0	4	19
Scotland	1	125	0	40	8	48
Stanly	1	130	0	0	1	4
Stokes	1	64	0	40	1	5
Surry	2	233	0	64	0	0
Swain	1	48	0	0	0	0
Transylvania	1	64	40	0	2	11
Tyrrell	0	0	0	0	1	5
Union	1	160	0	70	16	86
Vance	1	100	0	0	6	30
Wake	11	1,255	869	0	37	190
Warren	0	0	0	0	4	20
Washington	1	49	0	0	2	6
Watauga	2	175	0	72	2	11
Wayne	2	320	750	0	5	28
Wilkes	1	133	0	0	0	0
Wilson	1	365	23	0	5	27
Yadkin	1	72	0	0	1	5
Yancey	0	0	0	0	1	6
State Total	159	23,041	5,652	1,029	653	3,404

MILEAGE CHART

	ASHEVILLE	BOONE	BURLINGTON	CHAPEL HILL	CHARLOTTE	DURHAM	ELIZABETH CITY	FAYETTEVILLE	GASTONIA	GOLDSBORO	GREENSBORO	GREENVILLE	HENDERSONVILLE	HICKORY	HIGH POINT	KANNAPOLIS	MORGANTON	MURPHY	NEW BERN	RALEIGH	ROCKY MOUNT	STATESVILLE	WILMINGTON	WINSTON-SALEM
ASHEVILLE		95	200	224	115	231	415	256	95	302	178	336	22	74	165	142	54	105	354	241	296	103	318	144
BOONE	95		140	165	100	166	356	204	92	241	112	283	116	49	109	106	46	200	306	189	242	74	302	85
BURLINGTON	200	140		26	114	34	223	82	132	111	21	142	215	129	38	88	155	314	172	60	101	101	174	49
CHAPEL HILL	224	165	26		127	12	196	67	147	82	48	116	234	150	61	110	173	330	143	28	79	122	151	74
CHARLOTTE	115	100	114	127		140	306	141	20	190	91	228	108	51	78	26	68	220	246	143	199	43	203	81
DURHAM	231	166	34	12	140		180	72	159	74	54	108	241	157	70	121	182	340	135	23	67	129	146	81
ELIZABETH CITY	415	356	223	196	306	180		194	326	144	236	108	406	329	253	292	355	523	124	165	112	301	211	265
FAYETTEVILLE	256	204	82	67	141	72	194		162	59	91	106	249	178	100	127	204	356	110	59	95	154	92	118
GASTONIA	95	92	132	147	20	159	326	162		210	112	248	88	44	97	46	49	200	272	163	219	63	223	101
GOLDSBORO	302	241	111	82	190	74	144	59	210		131	49	298	216	139	175	242	406	58	50	44	188	89	156
GREENSBORO	178	112	21	48	91	54	236	91	112	131		163	193	97	17	66	117	283	192	78	123	69	184	27
GREENVILLE	336	283	142	116	228	108	108	106	248	49	163		326	250	174	213	276	446	44	85	41	220	117	193
HENDERSONVILLE	22	116	215	234	108	241	406	249	88	298	193	326		96	176	135	70	119	359	251	307	124	311	172
HICKORY	74	49	129	150	51	157	329	178	44	216	97	250	96		91	56	20	180	277	164	220	28	254	70
HIGH POINT	165	109	38	61	78	70	253	100	97	139	17	174	176	91		52	117	281	199	93	140	63	192	19
KANNAPOLIS	142	106	88	110	26	121	292	127	46	175	66	213	135	56	52		82	248	236	123	179	33	201	55
MORGANTON	54	46	155	173	68	182	355	204	49	242	117	276	70	20	117	82		159	303	190	246	48	280	90
MURPHY	105	200	314	330	220	340	523	356	200	406	283	446	119	180	281	248	159		467	355	411	208	423	256
NEW BERN	354	306	172	143	246	135	124	110	272	58	192	44	359	277	199	236	303	467		112	85	246	87	220
RALEIGH	241	189	60	28	143	23	165	59	163	50	78	85	251	164	93	123	190	355	112		53	136	123	104
ROCKY MOUNT	296	242	101	79	199	67	112	95	219	44	123	41	307	220	140	179	246	411	85	53		192	133	151
STATESVILLE	103	74	101	122	43	129	301	154	63	188	69	220	124	28	63	33	48	208	246	136	192		229	42
WILMINGTON	318	302	174	151	203	146	211	92	223	89	184	117	311	254	192	201	280	423	87	123	133	229		210
WINSTON-SALEM	144	85	49	74	81	81	265	118	101	156	27	193	172	70	19	55	90	256	220	104	151	42	210	

MILITARY POSTS AND TERMINAL

Six military installations are contained in North Carolina.

Camp LeJeune Marine Base. Begun in 1942 and known as the New River Marine Base. Later the name was changed to honor Major General John A. LeJeune (1867–1942), who served in World War I as a Marine Commandant. It is located in Onslow County near Jacksonville. The base encompasses 173 square miles. The base is on both sides of the New River, and 26,000 acres of the base is under water.

Cherry Point Marine Air Station. Begun in 1942, it has been called the largest Marine air station in the world, covering approximately 12,000 acres in Craven County near the town of Havelock. The name was derived from a small community which was situated here prior to the establishment of the station.

Fort Bragg Military Reservation. Established first as a U.S. Field Artillery training center in 1918 as Camp Bragg, in honor of Confederate General Braxton Bragg (1817–1876). In 1922 the name became Fort Bragg when the unit became a U.S. Field Artillery training center. This 200 square mile area covers parts of Cumberland, Hoke, Harnett, and Moore counties. It now serves as headquarters for the airborne.

Pope Air Force Base. Established during World War I. Located in Cumberland County, on the Fort Bragg Military Reservation. Named in honor of Lieutenant Harley Halbert Pope, who died near Fayetteville on the Cape Fear River in an aircraft accident in 1919.

Seymour Johnson Air Base. Established in 1941, and named for a Navy test pilot, Lieutenant Seymour Johnson of Goldsboro. Located in Goldsboro, Wayne County, it served as an Army Air Forces Technical Training School before becoming an Air Force Base.

Sunny Point Army Terminal. An ammunition loading depot in the southeastern portion of Brunswick County, near Southport.

MISS NORTH CAROLINA

Each year a "Miss North Carolina" is selected in competition in Raleigh, usually near the end of June. The winner represents the state in the annual "Miss America" contest. Since the contest's inception in 1937, the following "Miss North Carolinas" have been selected.

1937 Ruth McLean Covington, *Charlotte*
1939 Marguerite Taylor, *Charlotte*
1940 Jeanie D'Arbre, *Forest City*
1941 Joey Augusta Paxton, *Charlotte*
1942 Hilda Ward Taylor, *Goldsboro*
1944 Betsy Marie Dalton, *Winston-Salem*
1945 Dorothy Johnson, *Winston-Salem*
1946 Trudy Riley, *Wilson*
1947 Alice Vivian White, *Fayetteville*
1948 Patsy Ann Osborne, *Lawndale*
1949 Nancy Lee Velverton, *Rocky Mount*
1950 Carolyn Edwards, *Leaksville*
1951 Lu Long Ogburn, *Smithfield*
1952 Barbara Anne Harris, *Salisbury*
1953 Barbara Crockett, *Winston-Salem*
1954 Betty Jo Ring, *Lexington*
1955 Clara Faye Arnold, *Raleigh*
1956 Joan Spinks Melton, *Albemarle*
1957 Elaine Herndon, *Durham*
1958 Betty Lane Evans, *Greenville*
1959 Judith Lynn Kilpfel, *Asheboro*
1960 Ann Farrington Herring, *Winston-Salem*
1961 Maria Beale Fletcher—Miss America 1962, *Asheville*
1962 Janice Elizabeth Barron, *Morganton*

1963 Jeanne Flinn Swanner, *Graham*
1964 Esther Sharon Finch, *Thomasville*
1965 Penelop Clark, *Sanford*
1966 Nannette Jackson Minor, *Charlotte*
1967 Sarah Elizabeth Stedman, *Asheboro*
1968 Elisa Annette Johnson, *New Bern*
1969 Patricia Elaine Johnson, *Raleigh*
1970 Cornelia Collette Lerner, *Asheville*
1971 Patsy Gail Wood, *Garner*
1972 Constance Ann Dorn, *Kinston*
1973 Heather Lee Walker, *Hendersonville*
1974 Susan Lynn Griffin, *High Point*
1975 Susan Lawrence, *Thomasville*
1976 Susie Proffitt, *Forest City*
1977 Kathy Fleming, *Appalachian*
1978 Deborah Shook, *Spivey's Corner*
1979 Monta Anne Maki, *Hickory*
1980 Janet Ward Black, *Charlotte-Mecklenburg*
1981 Lynn Williford, *Wilmington*
1982 Elizabeth Williams, *Greater Greensboro*
1983 Deneen Graham, *Elkin Valley*
1984 Francesca Adler, *Fayetteville*
1985 Joni Bennett Parker, *Fayetteville*
1986 Karen S. Bloomquist, *Durham*
1987 Lori Wrenn Boggs, *Kannapolis*
1988 Lee Beaman, *Henderson*
1989 Kelly Dawn Fletcher

MUSEUMS

ALBEMARLE

Morrow Mountain State Park, Morrow Mountain Rd., 28001, 704-982-4402. *Park Museum:* area artifacts; Indian civilization, plant, and animal exhibits. *Hours & Admission Prices:* June—Labor Day daily 10-5; Labor Day—May Sat.-Sun. 10-5; Mon.-Fri. by appointment; no charge.

Stanly Historical Kitchen Museum, 813 W. Main St., 28001, 704-982-1825. *History Museum:* period kitchen items; dolls; history of Stanly County. *Hours & Admission Prices:* by appointment only; no charge.

ASHEBORO

North Carolina Zoological Park, Rte. 4, Box 83, 27203, 919-879-5606. *Zoological Park:* library, outdoor theater, fast foods, picnic area. *Hours & Admission Prices:* April—Sept. Mon.-Fri. 9-5; Sat.-Sun. holidays 10-6; Oct.—March daily 9-5; adults $3; senior citizens & children $1.

ASHEVILLE

Asheville Art Museum, Asheville Civic Center, 28801, 704-253-3227. *Collections:* crafts; sculpture; contemporary Southeastern American Regional paintings. *Hours & Admission Prices:* Tues.-Fri. 10-5; Sat.-Sun. 1-5; closed holidays; no charge.

Biltmore Homespun Shops, Grovewood Rd., 28804, 704-253-7651. *Textile Museum:* handwoven homespun industries complex c. 1917. *Hours & Admission Prices:* April 8—Oct. Mon.-Sat. 9-4:30; Sun. 1-5; no charge.

Biltmore House & Gardens, One Biltmore Plaza, 28803, 704-274-1776. *Collections:* historic house; arboretum; gardens; library; restaurant. *Hours & Admission Prices:* daily 9–5; adults $15; children 12–17 $15; children under 12 free; closed New Years, Thanksgiving, Christmas.

Colburn Memorial Mineral Museum, Civil Center Complex, 28801, 704-254-7162. *Collections & Activities:* American Indian artifacts, minerals, fossils, gems; identification service; lectures; tours. *Hours & Admission Prices:* Tues.-Fri. 10–5; Sat.-Sun. 1–5; closed holidays; no charge.

Craggy Gardens Visitor Center, Blue Ridge Parkway, 700 Northwestern Bank Bldg., 28805, 704-298-0277. *Collections:* permanent exhibits; natural history of high elevations of Southern Appalachia, particularly heath balds. *Hours & Admission Prices:* May—Oct. daily; holidays 10–5; no charge.

Estes-Winn Antique Automobile Museum, Grovewood Rd., 28804, 704-253-7651. *Transportation Museum:* on the grounds of the Biltmore Homespun Shops. *Hours & Admission Prices:* April 8—Oct. Mon.-Sat. 9–4:30; Sun. 1–5; no charge.

Folk Art Center, Milepost 382, Blue Ridge Pkwy., 28815, 704-298-3202. *Craft Museum:* library; information center; demonstrations; publications; crafts for sale. *Hours & Admission Prices:* daily 9–5; closed major holidays; no charge.

The Health Adventure, 501 Biltmore Ave., 28801, 704-254-6373. *Collections:* general anatomy exhibits; life patterns; substance abuse; health education library. *Hours & Admission Prices:* Mon.-Fri. 8:30–5, or by appointment; adults & children $1; tour 50¢; closed holidays.

Smith-McDowell Museum of Western North Carolina History, 283 Victoria Rd., 28801, 704-253-9231. *History Museum:* decorative arts and artifacts. *Hours & Admission Prices:* May—Oct. Tues.-Fri. 10–4, or by appointment; adults $2; children under 12 $1.

Thomas Wolfe Memorial, 48 Spruce St., 28807, 704-253-8304. *Historic House:* antique furnishings; memorabilia of Thomas Wolfe. *Hours & Admission Prices:* Mon.-Sat. 9–5; Sun. 1–5; adults $1; children 50¢; closed Thanksgiving, Dec. 22–26.

University Botanical Gardens at Asheville, Inc., 151 W. Weaver Blvd., 28804, 704-252-5190. *Botanical Gardens & Historic House:* native flora on site of Civil War battle; primitive furnishings in log cabin. *Hours & Admission Prices:* dawn to 7:30 daily; no charge.

Western North Carolina Nature Center, 75 Gashes Creek Rd., 28805, 704-298-5600. *Nature Center:* living plants and animals; tours; lectures; workshops; permanent exhibitions. *Hours & Admission Prices:* Tues.-Sat. 10–5; Sun. 1–5; adults $1.50; senior citizens & children $1.

ATLANTIC BEACH

Fort Macon State Park, E. Fort Macon Blvd., 28512, 919-726-3775. *Museum & Historic Building:* Civil War artifacts; tours; lectures. *Hours & Admission Prices:* June—Labor Day 9–5:30 daily; Labor Day—May Sat.-Sun. 9–5:30; no charge.

BAILEY

The Country Doctor Museum, Vance St., 27807, 919-235-4165. *Collections:* medical and pharmacy instruments of 18th, 19th, and 20th centuries. *Hours & Admission Prices:* Sun.-Wed. 2–5, or by appointment; no charge.

BATH

Historic Bath State Historic Site, NC Hwy. 92, 27808, 919-923-3971. *Historic Houses:* guided tours; lectures; permanent exhibitions. *Hours & Admission Prices:* Mon.-Sat. 9–5; Sun. 1–5; adults $1; children 50¢; closed Thanksgiving, Dec. 24–25.

BEAUFORT

Beaufort Historical Association, Box 1709, 28516, 919-728-5225. *Historical Buildings:* guided tours; exhibits; lectures; weaving demonstrations; quilting and whittling classes. *Hours & Admission Prices:* Mon.-Sat. 9:30–4:30; summer Sun. 2–4; adults $2.50; children $1; closed major holidays.

North Carolina Maritime Museum, 315 Front St., 28516, 919-728-7317. *Activities:* lectures; exhibits; boatbuilding skills program. *Hours & Admission Prices:* Mon.-Fri. 9–5; Sat. 10–5; Sun. 2–5; no charge; closed Christmas, New Years.

BELHAVEN

Belhaven Memorial Museum, Inc., P.O. Box 220, 27810. *Collections:* 19th–20th century items of coastal Carolina. *Hours & Admission Prices:* daily 1–5, or by appointment; no charge.

BURLINGTON

Alamance Battleground State Historic Site, NC Hwy. 62, 27215, 919-227-4785. *Historic House:* guided tours; exhibitions; lectures. *Hours & Admission Prices:* Mon.-Sat. 9–5; Sun. 1–5; closed Thanksgiving, Christmas; no charge.

BUXTON

Hatteras Island Visitor Center, Buxton, 27920, 919-473-2111. *Park Museum & Historic Houses:* guided tours; exhibitions; lectures. *Hours & Admission Prices:* daily 9–5; closed Christmas Day; no charge.

CHAPEL HILL

The Ackland Art Museum, Columbia and Franklin Sts., University of North Carolina, 27514, 919-966-5736. *Collections:* American and European painting; local folk art; Far Eastern art; sculpture; ancient coins. *Hours & Admission Prices:* Tues.-Sat. 10–5; Sun. 2–6; closed major holidays; no charge.

Coker Arboretum, N.W. corner of Raleigh Rd. & Cameron Ave., UNC Campus, 27514, 919-967-2246. *Collections:* S.E. Asian species; cacti; dwarf conifers. *Hours & Admission Prices:* daily dawn-dusk; no charge.

Morehead Planetarium, E. Franklin St., 27514, 919-962-1237. *Collections:* astronomy; science; art collection; library. *Hours & Admission Prices:* Sun.-Thurs. 12:30–5 & 7:30–9:30; Fri. 12:30–5 & 6:30–9:30; Sat. 10–5 & 7:30–9:30; adults $2.75; students & senior citizens $2; children $1.35; closed Dec. 24–25.

North Carolina Botanical Garden, Totten Center 457A, University of North Carolina, 27514, 919-967-2246. *Facilities:* greenhouse; 320 acres; research plots; lectures; guided tours. *Hours & Admission Prices:* Mon.-Fri. 8–5; Sat. 10–4; Sun. 2–5; closed Thanksgiving, Christmas, New Years; no charge.

CHARLOTTE

Charlotte Nature Museum, 1658 Sterling Rd., 28209, 704-372-6261. *Facilities:* nature center; planetarium; nature trails; lectures; tours; workshops. *Hours & Admission Prices:* Mon.-Sat. 9–6; Sun. 1–6; closed major holidays; 75¢ per person.

Discovery Place, 301 N. Tryon St., 28202, 704-372-6262. *Natural Science & Technology Museum:* lectures; tours; educational programs; arts and science festivals. *Hours & Admission Prices:* Mon.-Fri. 9–5; Sat. 9–6; Sun. 1–6; closed Thanksgiving, Christmas; adults $3; students & senior citizens $2; preschoolers free.

Hezekiah Alexander Homesite, 3500 Shamrock Dr., 28215, 704-568-1774. *Collections:* period furnishings. *Hours & Admission Prices:* Tues.-Sat. 10–5; Sun. 2–5; no charge.

Mint Museum, 2730 Randolph Rd., 28207, 704-337-2000. *Art & History Museum:* in building used as first branch of U.S. Mint, 1835; lectures; tours. *Hours & Admission Prices:* Tues. 10–10; Wed.-Sat. 10–5; Sun. 1–6; closed holidays; no charge.

Wing Haven Garden and Bird Sanctuary, 248 Ridgewood Ave., 29209, 704-332-5770. *Arboretum:* gardens; bird sanctuary; conservation center; outdoor cathedral. *Hours & Admission Prices:* Mon.-Wed. 3–5, or by appointment; no charge.

CHEROKEE

Museum of the Cherokee Indian, U.S. 441, 28719, 704-497-3481. *Activities:* exhibits; library; lectures. *Hours & Admission Prices:* mid-June—Aug. Mon.-Sat. 9–8; Sun. 9–5:30; Sept.—mid-June daily 9–5:30; closed Thanksgiving, Christmas, New Years; adults $3; children $1.50.

Oconaluftee Visitor Center, 150 Hwy. 441 N., 28719, 704-497-9146. *Facilities:* exhibitions; living history pioneer farm. *Hours & Admission Prices:* mid-June—Labor Day daily 8–7; Labor Day—mid-June 8–4:30; closed Christmas; no charge.

CRESWELL

Somerset Place State Historic Site, Pettigrew State Park, 27928, 919-797-4560. *Historic Houses:* dairy; ice and smoke houses; agriculture. *Hours & Admission Prices:* Mon.-Sat. 9–5; Sun. 1–5; closed Thanksgiving, Christmas; no charge.

CULLOWHEE

Mountain Heritage Center, Western Carolina University, 28723, 704-227-7129. *History Museum:* local and Indian history; tours; lectures; educational programs. *Hours & Admission Prices:* Mon.-Fri. 8–5; closed mid-Dec.—Jan. 2; no charge.

CURRIE

Moores Creek National Battlefield, NC Hwy. 210, 28435, 919-283-5591. *Military Museum:* weapons; diorama on site of Revolutionary War battle. *Hours & Admission Prices:* daily 8–5; summer Sat.-Sun. 8–6; closed Christmas, New Years; no charge.

DALLAS

Gaston County Museum of Art and History, 131 W. Main St., 28034, 707-866-3437. *Historic Buildings:* tours; lectures; carriage and sleigh exhibits; textile exhibits. *Hours & Admission Prices:* Tues.-Fri. 10–5; Sat. 1–5; Sun. 2–5; closed holidays; no charge.

DAVIDSON

Davidson College Art Gallery, Davidson College, 28036, 704-892-2000. *Features:* lectures; 15th–20th century graphics. *Hours & Admission Prices:* Jan.—May and Sept.—Dec. Mon.-Fri. 10–5; closed holidays; no charge.

DOBSON

Pick Shin Farm Living Museum and Nature Center, Dobson, 27017, 919-386-8211. *Features:* historic buildings and equipment; lectures; drama; art festivals. *Hours & Admission Prices:* Mon.-Fri. 9:15–2:45, or by appointment; no charge.

DURHAM

Bennett Place State Historic Site, 4409 Bennett Memorial Rd., 27705, 919-383-4345. *Features:* Civil War history; historical building; tours; exhibits. *Hours & Admission Prices:* Mon.-Sat. 9–5; Sun. 1–5; closed Thanksgiving, Christmas; no charge.

Duke Homestead State Historic Site, 2828 Duke Homestead Rd., 27705, 919-477-5498. *Features:* historical buildings and related items of Washington Duke, founder of American Tobacco Co.; tours; lectures; craft workshops. *Hours & Admission Prices:* Mon.-Sat. 9–5; Sun. 1–5; closed Thanksgiving, Christmas; no charge.

Duke University Museum of Art, Box 6845, College Station, 27708, 919-684-5135. *Features:* tours; permanent and temporary exhibitions. *Hours & Admission Prices:* Tues.-Fri. 9–5; Sat. 10–1; Sun. 2–5; closed major holidays; no charge.

Museum of Art, North Carolina Central University, Durham, 27707, 919-683-6211. *Features:* lectures; educational programs; sculpture; paintings; original prints, especially American minority artists. *Hours & Admission Prices:* Tues.-Fri. 9–5; Sun. 2–5, or by appointment; no charge.

North Carolina Museum of Life and Science, 433 Murray Ave., 27704, 919-477-0431/32. *Features:* science education center; exhibits; nature trails; 80-acre nature park. *Hours & Admission Prices:* May—Labor Day Mon.-Sat. 10–6; Sun. 1–6; Labor Day—May Mon.-Sat. 10–5; Sun. 1–5; adults $2.50; senior citizens & children $1.50.

Stagville Preservation Center, Old Oxford Hwy., 27704, 919-477-9835. *Features:* historic buildings; period furnishings. *Hours & Admission Prices:* Mon.-Fri. tours 9–5; closed major holidays; no charge.

Trent Collection in the History of Medicine, Duke University Medical Center Library, 27710, 919-684-3325. *Medical Museum:* on premises research library; lectures. *Hours & Admission Prices:* Mon.-Fri. 8:30–5; no charge.

EDENTON

Historic Edenton, Broad St., 27932, 919-482-3663. *History Museum:* historic buildings; tours; exhibitions. *Hours & Admission Prices:* Mon.-Sat. 10–4:30; Sun. 2–5; no charge for museum; all buildings admission, adults $3, students $1.50; each building tour, adults $1.50, students 75¢.

James Iredell House State Historic Site, 105 E. Church St., 27932, 919-482-2637. *Historic House:* period furnishings; tours; lectures; educational programs. *Hours & Admission Prices:* Mon.-Sat. 10–4:30; Sun. 2–5; closed Thanksgiving, Christmas; 5-house tour, adults $3, students $1.

ELIZABETH CITY

Museum of the Albemarle, Rt. 6, Hwy. 17 S., 27909, 919-335-1453. *History Collections:* Indian artifacts; farm and lumbering items. *Hours & Admission Prices:* Tues.-Sat. 9–5; Sun. 2–5; closed legal holidays; no charge.

FAYETTEVILLE

Arts Council of Fayetteville/Cumberland County, 822 Arsenal Ave., 28302, 919-323-1776. *Features:* exhibits; competitions; tours; concerts; dance recitals; arts festivals. *Hours & Admission Prices:* Mon.-Fri. 9–5; Sat.-Sun. 1–5, or by appointment; closed major holidays; no charge.

Fayetteville Museum of Art, 839 Stamper Rd., 28303, 919-485-5121. *Features:* current local artists works; lectures; educational programs; competition. *Hours & Admission Prices:* Tues.-Fri. 10–5; Sat.-Sun. 1–5; closed major holidays; no charge.

FLAT ROCK

Carl Sandburg Home National Historic Site, P.O. Box 395, 28731, 704-693-4178. *Features:* historic home c. 1838; personal effects; library; tours. *Hours & Admission Prices:* daily 9–5; no charge.

FORT BRAGG

JFK Special Warfare Museum, Ardennes and Marion Sts., Bldg. D-2502, 28307, 919-396-4272/1533. *Military Museum:* exhibits including "Hall of Heros"; items dealing with special forces. *Hours & Admission Prices:* Tues.-Sun. 11:30–4; closed Thanksgiving, Christmas, New Years; no charge.

82nd Airborne Division War Memorial Museum, Gela and Ardennes Sts., 28307, 919-396-5307. *Features:* history of warfare and airborne units; tours; films; lectures. *Hours & Admission Prices:* Tues.-Sat. 10–4:30; Sun. 11:30–4; closed Christmas, New Years; no charge.

FREMONT

Charles B. Aycock Birthplace State Historic Site, U.S. Hwy. 117, 1 mile S. of Fremont, 27830, 919-242-5581. *Features:* historic buildings; tours; lectures; exhibitions. *Hours & Admission Prices:* Mon.-Sat. 9–5; Sun. 1–5; closed Thanksgiving, Christmas; no charge.

GASTONIA

Schiele Museum of Natural History and Planetarium, Inc., 1500 E. Garrison Blvd., 28053, 704-864-3962. *Features:* lectures; films; guided tours; educational programs; native American studies; living history demonstrations; Sequoyah dance team; study workshops. *Hours & Admission Prices:* Tues.-Fri. 9–5; Sat.-Sun., holidays 2–5; closed Christmas week; no charge.

GOLDSBORO

Community Arts Council, Inc., 901 E. Ash St., 27530, 919-736-3335. *Features:* two dimensional works by regional contemporary artists; art classes; workshops; tours; lectures. *Hours & Admission Prices:* Mon.-Fri. 9–5; Sun. 2–5; closed Easter and day after, Memorial Day, July 4, Labor Day, Thanksgiving and day after, Christmas, New Years; no charge.

GREENSBORO

Green Hill Center for North Carolina Art, 200 N. Davie St., 27401, 919-373-4515. *Features:* local contemporary art; lectures; tours; concerts. *Hours & Admission Prices:* Tues.-Fri. 10–5; Sat.-Sun. 2–5; closed legal holidays; no charge.

Greensboro Artists League, 200 N. Davie St., 27401, 919-373-4514. *Features:* gallery; lectures; competition. *Hours & Admission Prices:* Tues.-Fri. 10–5; Sat.-Sun. 2–5; closed major holidays; no charge.

Greensboro Historical Museum, Inc., 130 Summit Ave., 27401, 919-373-2043. *Features:* general exhibits housed in 1892 First Presbyterian Church which was once used as a hospital following Civil War battle of Bentonville, NC; also historic houses. *Hours & Admission Prices:* Tues.-Sat. 10–5; Sun. 2–5; historic houses; Sat. 10–5; Sun. 2–5; closed New Years, Easter, Thanksgiving, Christmas; no charge.

Guilford Courthouse National Military Park, 2332 New Garden Rd., 27410, 919-288-1776. *Military Museum:* Revolutionary War weapons; library for use on premises. *Hours & Admission Prices:* E.S.T. daily 8:30–5; E.D.T. daily 9:30–6; closed Christmas, New Years; no charge.

Irene Cullis Gallery, Greensboro College, 815 W. Market St., 27401, 919-272-7102. *Features:* small collection of modern original prints. *Hours & Admission Prices:* during school year, Mon.-Fri. 10:30–4; Sun. 2–5; closed Easter holidays, Thanksgiving, Christmas.

Mattye Reed African Heritage Center, N.C.A. & T. State University, 27411, 919-379-7874. *Features:* arts and crafts from many African nations. *Hours & Admission Prices:* Mon.-Fri. 9–5, or by appointment; no charge.

The Natural Science Center of Greensboro, Inc., 4301 Lawndale Dr., 27408, 919-288-3769. *Features:* science center and zoo; marine aquarium; solar observatory; botanical courtyard; health theatre. *Hours & Admission Prices:* Mon.-Sat. 9–5; Sun. 2–5; no charge. Zoo: adults $1, children under 12 50¢. Planetarium shows: Mon.-Fri. 11 & 12; Thurs. 4; Sat. 2 & 3; Sun. 2, 3, & 4; students and teachers $1, adults $1.50; closed Easter, Thanksgiving, Christmas, New Years.

Weatherspoon Art Gallery, Walker Ave. and McIver St., University of NC at Greensboro, 27412, 919-379-5770. *Features:* sculpture; graphic arts; modern and contemporary paintings; oriental art. *Hours & Admission Prices:* Tues.-Fri. 10–5; Sat.-Sun. 2–6; closed school holidays and vacations; no charge.

GREENVILLE

Gray Art Gallery, East Carolina University, 5th St., 27834, 919-757-6665. *Features:* educational program; lectures; exhibitions of contemporary works. *Hours & Admission Prices:* Mon.-Fri. 10-5; Sun. 1-4; no charge.

Greenville Museum of Art, 802 Evans St., 27834, 919-758-1946. *Features:* sculpture; water colors; graphic arts; oils. *Hours & Admission Prices:* Tues.-Fri. 10-6; Sat. 11-3; Sun. 1-5; closed major holidays; no charge.

HALIFAX

Historic Halifax State Historic Site, Box 406, 27839, 919-583-7191. *Features:* historic buildings; lectures; guided tours; visitor center. *Hours & Admission Prices:* Mon.-Sat. 9-5; Sun. 1-5; closed Thanksgiving, Christmas; no charge.

HICKORY

Catawba Science Center, 406 3rd Ave., N.W., 28601, 704-322-8169. *Natural History and Science Museum:* located in historic building. *Hours & Admission Prices:* Tues.-Sat. 9-5; Sun. 2-5; closed major holidays; no charge.

Hickory Landmarks Society, Inc. 542 2nd St., N.E., 28601, 704-322-4731. *Historic Homes:* period furnishings; tours; seminars. *Hours & Admission Prices:* April—Oct. Sun. 2-5, or by appointment; adults $1; students 50¢.

The Hickory Museum of Art, 234 Third Ave., N.W., 28601, 704-327-8576. *Features:* sculpture; decorative art; relics; American and European art. *Hours & Admission Prices:* Sept.—July Mon.-Fri. 10-5; Sun. 3-5; closed Easter, July 4, Thanksgiving, Christmas; no charge.

HIGH POINT

High Point Environmental Education Center, Rt. 1, Box 401, Penny Rd., 27260, 919-454-4214. *Features:* nature conservation center; zoological park; botanical garden; hobby workshops. *Hours & Admission Prices:* Mon.-Fri. 8-5; closed Easter, July 4, Thanksgiving, Christmas; no charge.

High Point Historical Society, Inc., 1805 E. Lexington Ave., 27262, 919-885-6859. *History Museum:* photographs and other exhibits pertaining to local history; historic buildings. *Hours & Admission Prices:* Tues.-Fri. 10-5; Sat.-Sun. 2-5; closed major holidays; no charge.

Springfield Museum of Old Domestic Arts, 514 Hayworth Circle, 27262, 919-889-4911. *Features:* historic buildings; Indian artifacts; domestic items. *Hours & Admission Prices:* by appointment; no charge.

HILLSBOROUGH

Orange County Historical Museum, 201 N. Churton St., 27278, 919-732-2201. *Features:* items relating to Orange County history housed in Confederate memorial; tours; lectures; exhibits. *Hours & Admission Prices:* Tues.-Sun. 1:30-4:30; group tours arranged with three days notice; student groups of 10 accompanied by teacher; no charge for Orange County students.

KANNAPOLIS

The Cannon Visitor Center, 200 West Ave., 28081, 704-938-3200. *Museum:* affiliated with Cannon Mills Co.; exhibits on textile art. *Hours & Admission Prices:* Mon.-Fri. 8:30-4:30; closed Monday following Easter, July 4, Labor Day, Thanksgiving, Christmas; no charge.

KILL DEVIL HILLS

Wright Brothers National Memorial, Kill Devil Hills, 27948, 919-473-2111. *Aviation Museum:* replicas of 1902 glider and 1903 flyer located on site of Wright Brothers' experiments. *Hours & Admission Prices:* daily and holidays, 8:30-4:30; summer daily and holidays 8-6:30; closed Christmas; no charge.

KINSTON

Caswell-Neuse State Historic Site, US Hwy 70, W. of Kinston, 28501, 919-522-2091. *Features:* articles depicting life of first elected governor; hull of Confederate gunboat; tours; lectures. *Hours & Admission Prices:* Mon.-Sat. 9–5; Sun. 1–5; closed Thanksgiving, Christmas; no charge.

Community Council For the Arts, 111 E. Caswell St., 28501, 919-527-2517. *Exhibitions:* chiefly by North Carolina artists. *Hours & Admission Prices:* Mon.-Thurs. 8:30–5:30; Fri. 8:30–12:30; closed state holidays; no charge.

KURE BEACH

Fort Fisher State Historic Site, US Hwy. 421, 3 miles S. of Kure Beach, 28449, 919-458-5538. *Visitor Center:* trails; Civil War military earthworks; tours; lectures. *Hours & Admission Prices:* Mon.-Sat. 9–5; Sun. 1–5; closed Thanksgiving, Christmas; no charge.

North Carolina Marine Resources Center/Fort Fisher, off US 421 near Ferry Terminal, S. of Kure Beach, 28449, 919-458-8257. *Marine Museum:* library; nature center; aquarium. *Hours & Admission Prices:* Mon.-Fri. 9–5; Sat.-Sun. 1–5; closed Thanksgiving and day following, Christmas, New Years; no charge.

LAKE JUNALUSKA

World Methodist Museum, 39 Lakeshore Dr., 28745, 704-456-9433. *Features:* Methodist church history; items from 18th century England. *Hours & Admission Prices:* Mon.-Fri. 9–5; summer Mon.-Fri. 9–5; Sat. 9–12 & 1–5; closed holidays; no charge.

LAKE WACCAMAW

Lake Waccamaw Depot Museum, Flemington Dr., 28450, 919-646-3918. *Museum:* marine science and history; housed in turn of the century railroad station; tours; lectures. *Hours & Admission Prices:* May—Aug. Mon., Wed.-Sat. 9–12 & 1–5; Tues., Sun. 1–5; Sept.—April Thurs.-Fri. 2–5; Sat. 9–12 & 2–5; Sun. 2–5; no charge.

LAURINBURG

Indian Museum of the Carolinas, Inc., 607 Turnpike Rd., 28352, 919-276-5880. *Features:* Indian archaeology and ethnology; library for use on the premises; botanical garden; lectures; tours. *Hours & Admission Prices:* closed holidays; call for hours; no charge.

LEXINGTON

Davidson County Historical Museum, Old Courthouse on the Square, 27292, 704-249-7011/ ext. 309. *Features:* local history items; lectures; tours. *Hours & Admission Prices:* Tues.-Fri. 10–4; Sun. 2–4; closed holidays; no charge.

LINVILLE FALLS

Avery County Museum, P.O. Box 86, 28647, 704-765-9872. *Features:* genealogies; historical artifacts; local minerals. *Hours & Admission Prices:* March—Nov. Sun. 3–5; no charge.

LOUISBURG

Louisburg College Art Gallery, N. Main St., 27549, 919-496-2521. *Features:* contemporary, primitive, and American impressionist art. *Hours & Admission Prices:* Jan.—April and Aug.—Dec. Mon.-Thurs. 8:30–5:30; Fri. 8:30–1; closed holidays; no charge.

MANTEO

Elizabeth II State Historic Site, Ice Plant Island on the waterfront, 27954, 919-473-5522. *Features:* replica of 16th century sailing ship; visitor center; exhibits; tours. *Hours & Admission Prices:* Memorial Day—Labor Day Mon.-Sat. 9–7; Sun. 10–6; Labor Day—Memorial Day Mon.-Sat. 9–5; Sun. 1–5; admission $2.

Fort Raleigh National Historic Site, Manteo, 27954, 919-473-2111. *Museum:* located on the place where attempts were made at first colony, 1585–1587. *Hours & Admission Prices:* mid-June—Labor Day daily 8:30–8:15; Labor Day—mid-June daily 9–5; closed Christmas; no charge.

MARION

Carson House Restoration, Inc., Hwy. 70, W. of Marion, 28752, 704-724-4640. *History Museum:* pioneer artifacts housed in historic house. *Hours & Admission Prices:* May—Oct. Mon.-Fri. 10–5; Sat.-Sun. 2–5; adults $1; students 50¢; children under 12 25¢.

MONTREAT

The Historical Foundation of the Presbyterian and Reformed Churches, Inc., P.O. Box 847, 28757, 704-669-7061. *Religious Museum:* items relating to the history of the Presbyterian Church. *Hours & Admission Prices:* Mon.-Fri. 8–5; Sat. 8–1; closed Easter Monday, Labor Day, Thanksgiving, Christmas, New Years; no charge.

MOUNT GILEAD

Town Creek Indian Mound State Historic Site, 9 miles S. of Mount Gilead, on SR 1160, 27306, 919-439-6802. *Visitor Center:* Indian artifacts; archaeology; anthropology. *Hours & Admission Prices:* Mon.-Sat. 9–5; Sun. 1–5; closed Thanksgiving, Christmas; no charge.

MURFREESBORO

Rea Store Museum, P.O. Box 3, 27855, 919-398-4886. *Historic Building:* artifacts and exhibits on the Richard J. Gatling family. *Hours & Admission Prices:* Mon.-Sat. 1–4; adults $3; students $1; children under 6 no charge.

MURPHY

Cherokee County Historical Museum, Inc., Peachtree St., 28906, 704-837-6792. *Features:* local history; library for use on premises; lectures; tours. *Hours & Admission Prices:* Mon.-Fri. 9–5; closed Easter Monday, Memorial Day, July 4, Labor Day, Thanksgiving, Christmas, New Years; no charge.

NEW BERN

Attmore-Oliver House, 511 Broad St., 28560, 919-638-8558. *Museum:* housed in historic house; antique American furnishings. *Hours & Admission Prices:* call for appointment.

New Bern Firemen's Museum, 410 Hancock, 28560, 919-637-3105. *Features:* Civil War and firefighting equipment display. *Hours & Admission Prices:* Tues.-Sat. 9:30–12 & 1–5; Sun. 1–5; closed one week in July, Thanksgiving, Christmas, New Years; adults $1; children 50¢.

Tryon Palace Restoration Complex, 610 Pollock St., 28560, 919-638-5109. *Historic Houses:* including period furnishings and decorative arts. *Hours & Admission Prices:* Mon.-Sat. 9:30–4; Sun. 1:30–4; closed Thanksgiving, Christmas, New Years; combination ticket to see all buildings, adults $7, children $3.

NEWTON

Catawba County Historical Museum, 1716 S. College Dr., Hwy. 321, 28658, 704-465-0383. *Historic Buildings:* featuring general history of the upper Piedmont. *Hours & Admission Prices:* Tues.-Fri. 9–5; Sat.-Sun. 1–5, or by appointment; closed major holidays; no charge.

NEWTON GROVE

Bentonville Battleground State Historic Site, 3 miles N. of US 701 to SR 1008, 3 miles E. on SR 1008, 28366, 919-594-0789. *Visitor Center:* located on Civil War battleground. *Hours & Admission Prices:* Mon.-Sat. 9–5; Sun. 1–5; closed Thanksgiving, Christmas; no charge.

NORTH WILKESBORO

Wilkes Art Gallery, 800 Elizabeth St., 28659, 919-667-2841. *Features:* sculpture; graphics; contemporary paintings, primarily of North Carolina artists. *Hours & Admission Prices:* Mon.-Fri. 10–5; Sun. 3–5; closed major holidays; no charge.

OCRACOKE

Ocracoke Island Visitor Center, Ocracoke, 27960, 919-473-2111. *Park Museum:* wall panel exhibits; lectures; tours. *Hours & Admission Prices:* mid-April—mid-Oct. daily 9–5; mid-March—mid-April, mid-Oct.—Nov. Sat.-Sun. 9–5; closed Dec.—March; no charge.

OLD FORT

Mountain Gateway Museum, Water & Catawba Sts., 28762, 704-668-9259. *Features:* Indian and mountain life artifacts. *Hours & Admission Prices:* Mon.-Sat. 9–5; Sun. 2–5; closed state holidays; no charge.

PEMBROKE

Native American Resource Center, Pembroke State University, College Rd., 28372, 919-521-4214/ext. 282. *Features:* items pertaining to Native American and Lumbee Indians. *Hours & Admission Prices:* Mon.-Fri. 8–5; closed major holidays; no charge.

PINEHURST

World Golf Hall of Fame, Gerald R. Ford Blvd., 28374, 919-295-6651. *Features:* artifacts from all golfing nations. *Hours & Admission Prices:* March—Dec. daily 9–5; closed Christmas; adults $3; children 10–18 $2; children under 10 no charge.

PINEVILLE

James K. Polk Memorial State Historic Site, US Hwy. 521, 1 mile S. of Pineville, 28134, 704-889-7145. *Historic House:* lectures; guided tours. *Hours & Admission Prices:* Mon.-Sat. 9–5; Sun. 1–5; closed Thanksgiving, Christmas; no charge.

RALEIGH

Mordecai Historic Park, 1 Mimosa St., 27604; 919-834-4844. *Historic Buildings:* lectures; tours; exhibitions. *Hours & Admission Prices:* Oct.—May Tues.-Thurs. 11–2; Sat.-Sun. 2–4; June—Sept. Wed.-Thurs. 11–2; Sat. 1–4; Sun. 2–5.

North Carolina Division of Archives and History, 109 E. Jones St., 27611, 919-733-7305. *History Museum:* lectures; tours; exhibitions. *Hours & Admission Prices:* Tues.-Sat. 9–5; Sun. 1–6; closed holidays; no charge.

North Carolina Museum of Art, 2110 Blue Ridge Blvd., 27607, 919-833-1935. *Features:* lectures; tours; exhibits; workshops; art reference library. *Hours & Admission Prices:* Tues.-Sat. 10–5; Sun. 1–5; closed state holidays; no charge.

North Carolina Museum of History, 109 E. Jones St., 27611, 919-733-3894. *Features:* general history; lectures; tours. *Hours & Admission Prices:* Tues.-Sat. 9–5; Sun. 1–6; closed Thanksgiving, Christmas, New Years; no charge.

North Carolina State Museum, 102 N. Salisbury St., 27611, 919-733-7450. *Museum of Natural History:* lectures; tours; exhibitions. *Hours & Admission Prices:* Mon.-Sat. 9–5; Sun. 1–5; closed state holidays; no charge.

North Carolina State University Student Center Art Gallery, P.O. Box 7306, Cates Ave., 27695, 919-737-3503. *Features:* American contemporary art. *Hours & Admission Prices:* daily 10–10; closed school holidays; no charge.

RANDLEMAN

St. Paul Museum, 411 High Point St., 27317, 919-498-2221. *General Museum:* exhibitions; guided tours. *Hours & Admission Prices:* by appointment only; no charge.

REIDSVILLE

Chinqua-Penn Plantation House, Rt. 8, Box 682, 27320, 919-349-4576. *Art Museum:* guided tours; flower, shrub, and herb gardens. *Hours & Admission Prices:* March—mid-Dec. Wed.-Sat. 10–4; Sun. 1:30–4:30; closed July 4, Thanksgiving; adults $3; senior citizens $2; children under 12 and school groups $1.

RICHLANDS

Onslow County Museum, 100 Hargett St., 28574, 919-324-5008. *Features:* general history exhibits housed in 1900 post office. *Hours & Admission Prices:* Wed.-Sun. 1–4; no charge.

ROCKY MOUNT

Rocky Mount Arts & Crafts Center, 1173 Nashville Rd., 27803, 919-972-1163. *Features:* various medias of arts by North Carolina artists. *Hours & Admission Prices:* Mon.-Fri. 8:30–5; Sun. 3–5; closed Memorial Day, Labor Day, Christmas, New Years; no charge.

Rocky Mount Children's Museum, Inc., 1610 Gay St., 27801, 919-972-1167. *Features:* natural and physical science exhibits; planetarium. *Hours & Admission Prices:* Easter—May Mon.-Fri. 10–5; Sun. 2–5; June—Labor Day Mon.-Fri. 10–5; Sat.-Sun. 2–5; Labor Day—Easter Mon.-Fri. 10–5; Planetarium Easter—Labor Day 3 p.m., other times by appointment; call Planetarium for charges; museum no charge.

Stonewall House, 1325 Falls Road Ext., 27801, 919-443-6708. *Historic House:* local historical memorabilia. *Hours & Admission Prices:* every first Sunday 2–5 and by appointment; adults $2.50; groups & senior citizens $2.

SALISBURY

Dan Nicholas Park Nature Center, Rt. 10, Box 832, 28144, 704-636-2089. *Zoo and Nature Center Museum. Hours & Admission Prices:* May—Sept. Mon.-Fri. 9–5; Sat. 10–7; Sun. 12–7; Oct.—April Mon.-Tues., Thurs.-Fri. 10–4; Sat. 10–5; Sun. 12–5; no charge.

Rowan Museum, Inc., 114 S. Jackson St., 28144, 704-633-5946. *Historic House:* regional relics. *Hours & Admission Prices:* Thurs.-Sun. 2–5; July—Aug. and Dec.—Feb. Sat.-Sun. 2–5, or by appointment; no charge.

Salisbury Supplementary Educational Center, 1636 Parkview Circle, 28144, 704-636-3462. *Local History, Art, and Natural Science Museum. Hours & Admission Prices:* Mon.-Fri. 8–4 during school year; no charge.

Waterworks Gallery, No. 1 Water St., 28144, 704-636-1882. *Visual Arts Center:* featuring works by Southeastern artists. *Hours & Admission Prices:* Mon.-Fri. 10–5; Sun. 2–5; closed major holidays; no charge.

SANFORD

House in the Horseshow State Historic Site, US Hwy. 42, W. 12 miles, S. 5 miles on SR 1644, 27330, 919-947-2051. *Historic House:* belonged to Benjamin Williams, governor in 1798; was site of Revolutionary War skirmish. *Hours & Admission Prices:* Mon.-Sat. 9–5; Sun. 1–5; closed Thanksgiving, Christmas; no charge.

Railroad House Museum, Hawkins and Carthage, 27330, 919-775-7341. *Features:* local and railroad history; pottery exhibits. *Hours & Admission Prices:* Mon.-Fri. 9–5; no charge.

SEVEN SPRINGS

Cliffs of the Neuse State Park, Rt. 2, P.O. Box 50, 28578, 919-778-6234. *Park Museum:* lectures; tours; exhibitions. *Hours & Admission Prices:* mid-March—mid-Dec. daily 9–6; mid-Dec.—mid-March Sat.-Sun. 9–6; no charge.

SHELBY

Cleveland County Historical Museum, Courtsquare, 28150, 704-482-8186. *Features:* lectures; tours; art festivals; hobby workshops. *Hours & Admission Prices:* Mon.-Fri. 9–4; Sun. 2–5; closed major holidays; no charge.

SOUTH NAGS HEAD

Bodie Island Visitor Center, Bodie Island Lighthouse, 27959, 919-441-5711. *Park Museum:* historic buildings; natural history. *Hours & Admission Prices:* call for hours; no charge.

SOUTHERN PINES

Weymouth Woods-Sandhills Nature Preserve Museum, 400 N. Fort Bragg Rd., 28387, 919-692-2167. *Features:* nature center; wildlife refuge; bird sanctuary; lectures; tours. *Hours & Admission Prices:* Mon.-Sat. 9–6; Sun. 12–5; no charge.

SOUTHPORT

Brunswick Town State Historic Site, NC Hwy. 133 N., 28461, 919-371-6613. *Features:* local history; lectures; tours. *Hours & Admission Prices:* Mon.-Sat. 9–5; Sun. 1–5; closed Thanksgiving, Christmas; no charge.

SPENCER

Spencer Shops State Historic Site, 411 S. Salisbury Ave., 28159, 704-636-2889. *Transportation Museum:* library; 55-acre park. *Hours & Admission Prices:* Mon.-Sat. 9–5; Sun. 1–5; closed major holidays; no charge.

SPRUCE PINE

Museum of North Carolina Minerals, Milepost 331, Blue Ridge Pkwy. at Hwy. 226, 28777, 704-765-2761. *Features:* exhibitions; lapidary demonstrations. *Hours & Admission Prices:* daily 10–5; closed major holidays; no charge.

STANFIELD

Reed Gold Mine State Historic Site, Reed Mine Rd., Rt. 2, 28163, 704-786-8337.

STATESVILLE

The Arts and Science Museum, Box 585, Museum Rd., 28677, 704-873-4734. *Features:* exhibitions; dance recitals; concerts; arts festivals; lectures; tours. *Hours & Admission Prices:* Tues.-Sun. 2–5; mornings by appointment; closed major holidays; no charge.

TARBORO

The Pender Museum, St. Andrew St., 27886, 919-823-8121. *Features:* historic building; lectures; tours; arts festivals. *Hours & Admission Prices:* Mon.-Fri. 10–4; Sat.-Sun. 2–4 during summer or by appointment (call 823-4159); no charge.

VALDESE

Museum of Waldensian History, Waldensian Presbyterian Church, 28690, 704-874-2531. *Religious Museum:* library; lectures; tours. *Hours & Admission Prices:* Mon.-Sat. by appointment; Sun. 3–5; summer during outdoor drama Thurs.-Sun. 5–8:30; closed national and religious holidays; no charge.

WADESBORO

Anson County Historical Society, Inc., 210 E. Wade St., 28170, 704-694-2090. *General Museum:* lectures; tours; arts festivals. *Hours & Admission Prices:* Sun. 3-5; adults $1; children 25¢.

WAKE FOREST

Wake Forest College Birthplace, Main St., 27587. *Historic Building:* 1820 building that became first Wake Forest College in 1834. *Hours & Admission Prices:* by appointment for tours.

WEAVERVILLE

Zebulon B. Vance Birthplace State Historic Site, 911 Reems Creek Rd., 28787, 704-645-6706. *Park Museum:* lectures; tours. *Hours & Admission Prices:* Mon.-Sat. 9–5; Sun. 1–5; closed Thanksgiving, Christmas; no charge.

WILMINGTON

The Burgwin-Wright House and Gardens, 224 Market St., 28401, 919-762-0570. *Historical Society Museum:* guided tours. *Hours & Admission Prices:* Tues.-Sat. 10–5; closed major holidays, Christmas, New Years; adults $2; students 50¢.

Lower Cape Fear Historical Society, Inc., 126 S. 3rd St., 28401, 919-762-0492. *Decorative Arts Museum. Hours & Admission Prices:* Tues.-Sat. 10–5; adults $2; students 50¢.

New Hanover County Museum, 814 Market St., 28401, 919-763-0852. *History Museum:* local and lower Cape Fear history; natural history. *Hours & Admission Prices:* Tues.-Sat. 9–5; Sun. 2–5; closed major holidays; no charge.

St. John's Museum of Art, Inc., 114 Orange St., 28401, 919-763-0281. *Features:* regional paintings and sculptures. *Hours & Admission Prices:* Tues.-Sat. 10–5; no charge.

USS North Carolina Battleship Memorial, Cape Fear River on Eagles Island, 28401, 919-762-1829. *Historic Ship Museum:* exhibitions; drama; tours. *Hours & Admission Prices:* winter daily 8–sunset; summer daily 8–8; adults $3; children $1.50.

WILSON

Case Art Gallery, Atlantic Christian College, Whitehead and Gold St., 27893, 919-237-3161. *Features:* all types of art media. *Hours & Admission Prices:* Sept.—May Mon.-Fri. 10–4:30; Sat. 1–3; closed spring recess, Thanksgiving, Christmas; no charge.

WINDSOR

Historic Hope Foundation, Inc., Hwy. 308 W., 27983, 919-794-3140. *Historic Buildings:* lectures; guided tours. *Hours & Admission Prices:* March—mid-Dec. Tues.-Sat. 10–4; Sun. 2–5; closed Thanksgiving, New Years; adults $2; children 75¢.

WINSTON-SALEM

Historic Bethabara Park, 2147 Bethabara Rd., 27106, 919-924-8191. *History Museum:* lectures; tours; special events. *Hours & Admission Prices:* April—Nov. Mon.-Fri. 9:30–4:30; Sat.-Sun. 1:30–4:30, by appointment only; no charge.

Museum of Early Southern Decorative Arts, 924 S. Main St., 27101, 919-722-6148. *Features:* lectures; guided tours; exhibitions. *Hours & Admission Prices:* Mon.-Sat. 10:30–5; Sun. 1:30–4:30; closed Christmas; adults $3.50; students $1.75.

Museum of Man, Wake Forest University, Dept. of Anthropology, Wake Forest University, 27109, 919-761-5282. *Anthropology Museum:* educational programs; lectures; films. *Hours & Admission Prices:* Mon.-Sat. 10–5; Sun. 2–5; groups by appointment; no charge.

Nature Science Center, Museum Dr., 27105, 919-767-6730. *Physical and Natural History Museum:* lectures; nature trails. *Hours & Admission Prices:* Mon.-Sat. 10–5; Sun. 1–5; closed major holidays; no charge.

Old-Salem, Inc., Drawer F, Salem Station, 27108, 919-723-3688. *Historic Restoration Village:* lectures; tours; exhibitions. *Hours & Admission Prices:* Mon.-Sat. 9:30–4:30; Sun. 1:30–4:30; closed Christmas; adults $8; children $4.

Piedmont Craftsmen, Inc., 300 S. Main St., 27101, 919-725-1516. *Arts and Crafts Museum:* lectures; fair; monthly exhibits. *Hours & Admission Prices:* Mon.-Sat. 10–5; Sun. 1–5; closed major holidays; no charge.

Reynolda House, Inc., Reynolda Rd., 27106, 919-725-5325. *Art Museum:* American paintings; lectures; tours. *Hours & Admission Prices:* Tues.-Sat. 9:30–4:30; Sun. 1:30–4:30; closed major holidays; adults $4; senior citizens $3; students $2.

The Southeastern Center for Contemporary Art, 750 Marguerite Drive, 27106, 919-725-1904. *Features:* 50 annual exhibitions. *Hours & Admission Prices:* Tues.-Sat. 10–5; Sun. 2–5; closed major holidays; no charge.

NATIONAL FORESTS

Four National Forests are situated in North Carolina. They are administered by the U.S. Forest Service of the U.S. Department of Agriculture. The gross amount of land contained in these forests as of September 30, 1987, is 2,953,502 acres. This total includes state and privately owned acreage. Forty-one percent of this amount, 1,219,306 acres, is federally owned. The address for the administrative offices is: National Forests in North Carolina, 100 Otis St. (P.O. Box 2750), Asheville, 28802, 704-257-4200.

The location of these forests vary from mountains to rolling piedmont hills to sandy pine forests in the coastal plains. There are more than 800 campsites, 490 picnic sites, over 1,300 miles of hiking trails, 7 swimming beaches, and 4 wilderness areas. Also there is stream and lake fishing, as well as hunting in areas managed by North Carolina Wildlife Resources Commission and the Forest Service cooperatively. Forest Service roads and main highways, including portions of the Blue Ridge Parkway make the forests readily accessible.

Croatan National Forest. Established in 1933. Located in parts of Jones, Craven, and Carteret counties on the coastal plain. Covers 308,234 acres, 157,503 of which are federally owned. The name Croatan was derived from the Algonquin Indian name for the "Council Town" that was located in the area.

Nantahala National Forest. Established in 1911. Covering 1,349,000 acres, 518,158 of which are federal lands, it is located in portions of seven counties: Cherokee, Clay, Graham, Jackson, Macon, Swain, and Transylvania, in the southwest portion of the state. Nantahala is a Cherokee Indian name meaning "noon day sun," so named because the sun penetrates to the bottom of the Nantahala Gorge only at noon. The Joyce Kilmer Memorial Forest (Graham County), dedicated to the poet who wrote *Trees and Other Poems,* is located within this National Forest.

Pisgah National Forest. Established in 1911. Contains 1,076,511 acres, of which 496,666 are federally owned. It is located in the western portion of the state, and covers portions of twelve counties: Avery, Buncombe, Burke, Caldwell, Haywood, Henderson, Madison, McDowell, Mitchell, Transylvania, Watauga, and Yancey.

Pisgah derives its name from the mountain from which the promised land was viewed by Moses.

Uwharrie National Forest. Became a National Forest in 1961. Located in the central part of the state along the Pee Dee River, the largest portion is located in Montgomery County, but also in Davidson, Randolph, and Stanly counties. The gross total acreage is 219,757, with 46,979 the federal total. Uwharrie, which means "new home," received its name from German settlers.

NATIONAL HISTORIC LANDMARKS

National Historic Landmarks are buildings, structures, sites, and objects of *national* significance that commemorate and illustrate the history and culture of the United States. Listed are the 26 National Historic Landmarks in North Carolina.

ASHEVILLE

Biltmore Estate. Biltmore Plaza. Built in 1890. Profitable forest management was first practiced here in 1892. Owner George W. Vanderbilt set up the Biltmore Forest School in 1898, the first of its kind in the United States. Biltmore House is a lavish reminder of the opulent tastes of America's most wealthy industrial magnates of the late 19th century.

Wolfe (Thomas) House. 48 Spruce Street. Built in early 20th century. Wolfe, a major American novelist, used his boyhood experiences in this rambling frame house in his novels, the first of which was *Look Homeward, Angel.* Wolfe's mother bought this house in 1906, and he lived here until 1916.

BATH

Palmer-Marsh House. Main Street, south of N.C. 92. Built c. 1774. Well-preserved example of a substantial colonial town house designed as both a place of business and a residence.

CHAPEL HILL

Old East. Built in 1795. The first building constructed on the campus of the first state university in the United States, the University of North Carolina, which was chartered in 1789.

Playmakers Theatre. Cameron Avenue. Built in 1850. One of the oldest structures on the campus of the University of North Carolina, originally named Smith Hall for Governor Benjamin Smith. It became the Playmakers Theatre in 1925.

CONCORD

Reed Gold Mine. 11 miles southeast of Concord on U.S. 601 and N.C. 200. Built in 1799. Nuggets found here set off the first gold rush in the United States. This mine furnished much of the gold minted in Philadelphia before 1829.

DURHAM

Blackwell (W. T.) and Company Tobacco Factory. 201 W. Pettigrew Street. Built in 1874. This factory was the home of Bull Durham smoking tobacco, the first truly national tobacco brand. In processing and promoting Bull Durham, W. T. Blackwell and Company introduced production, packaging, and marketing techniques that made Bull Durham a part of American industrial history and folklore.

Duke Homestead and Tobacco Factory. On N.C. 1025 east of Guess Road, one-half mile north of Durham. Built in 1851. In 1890 Washington Duke organized the American Tobacco Company, preeminent in its time. Duke's frame house and first small tobacco factory of log construction remain.

North Carolina Mutual Life Insurance Company. 114-116 W. Parish Street. Built in 1921. Home office of the North Carolina Mutual Life Insurance Company, a Black-managed enterprise founded in 1898 which achieved success despite the age of "Jim Crow."

EDENTON

Chowan County Courthouse. E. King Street. Built in 1767. Edenton was the first permanent colonial settlement in North Carolina. The present courthouse replaced one completed in 1719.

Cupola House. 408 S. Broad Street. Built c. 1725; remodeled 1750s. Rare example of a Southern colonial house having a Jacobean 2nd-story overhang. The roof is crowned by an octagonal wood cupola.

Hayes Plantation. E. Water Street Extension, Edenton vicinity. Built c. 1801. A large white house with columned porch that displays unusually early tones of Greek Revival, blended with Federal, design.

FAYETTEVILLE

Market House. Market Square. Built in 1838. Patterned after 18th-century English town halls. Meat and produce were sold under the open first floor arcade while the second floor served as the town hall.

FLAT ROCK

Connemara, The Carl Sandburg Farm. One-quarter-mile west of Flat Rock. Built in 1838. Sandburg, the poet, novelist, and writer of a Pulitzer Prize-winning biography of Lincoln, lived here from 1945 until his death in 1967. (Now the Carl Sandburg Home National Historic Site.)

HILLSBOROUGH

Nash-Hooper House. 118 W. Tryon Street. Built in the 18th century by Francis Nash, Revolutionary War hero and general. Home, from 1782 until his death in 1790, of William Hooper, a signer of the Declaration of Independence for North Carolina and a delegate to the Continental Congress (1774–77).

MILTON

Union Tavern. Main Street. Built c. 1800. Workshop studio of Thomas Day, early 19th-century free Black cabinetmaker who achieved recognition for the superior quality of his craftsmanship.

MOCKSVILLE

Coolemee. Mocksville vicinity. Built in 1850–55. A monumental example of the villas that became popular in America as a result of architectural pattern books of the 1850s. An unusually sophisticated villa for its rural Piedmont location.

Helper (Hinton Rowan) House. Vicinity of Mocksville. Helper, author of *The Impending Crisis* (1857), a controversial anti-slavery book, lived here for the first 20 years of his life, and returned in later years. The original log structure is now clapboarded and has modern frame additions.

MOUNT GILEAD

Town Creek Indian Mound. 5 miles southeast of Mount Gilead. Built in late prehistoric period. Ceremonial center for a group of people with a Mississippian-influenced culture who had moved northward into the area.

RALEIGH

Daniels (Josephus) House. 1520 Caswell Street. Secretary of the Navy (1913–21) under President Wilson, Daniels significantly reformed policies by introducing schooling for illiterate sailors, instituting vocational training, opening the Naval Academy to enlisted men, and reforming the naval prison system.

State Capitol. Capitol Square. Built in 1833–40. Example of Greek Revival architecture in its most sophisticated and erudite form. Important representative of the work of three major 19th-century architects. Imposing rotunda, 2-story legislative chambers, rich detail, and subdued colors distinguish the building.

TARBORO

Coolmore. Route 3, Tarboro vicinity. Built in 1859–61. This plantation complex is one of the largest, finest, and best-documented examples of a mid-19th-century Italian villa in the South.

WILMINGTON

Fort Fisher. 18 miles south of Wilmington on U.S. 421. Built in 1862–65. An earthen Confederate stronghold which created an impassable barrier for the blockading Union fleet. Its fall, in January, 1865, helped isolate the Confederacy.

WINSTON-SALEM

Old Salem Historic District. Salem College campus and area near Salem Square. Well-preserved example of an 18th-century planned community, established by Moravians. The city that grew up here became the commercial center of the surrounding Piedmont region.

Salem Tavern. 800 S. Main Street. Built in 1784. The first brick building in Salem, reflecting the architectural heritage of the town's Moravian settlers.

Single Brothers' House. S. Main and Academy Streets. Built in 1768–69. Restored example of German half-timbered construction. Used as a trade school for master craftsmen, journeymen, and apprentices.

NATIONAL PARKS

Ten units of the National Park Service are located in North Carolina.

Appalachian National Scenic Trail. Called the longest marked footpath in the world, this trail extends approximately 2,050 miles from Maine to Georgia, 200 of which are within North Carolina. About 70 of these miles cross the crest of the Great Smoky Mountains. Completed in 1937.

Blue Ridge National Parkway. Extends from Shenandoah National Park in Virginia to the Great Smoky Mountains National Park in North Carolina and Tennessee. Entering North Carolina in the northeast portion of Alleghany County, it continues for 252.1 miles to the southwest. Begun in 1936. Will extend 469 miles when completed.

Cape Hatteras National Seashore. Located in the southeast portions of Dare and Hyde counties, on the Outer Banks. Covers large portions of Hatteras and Ocracoke Islands, as well as the southern part of Bodie Island, 30,319 acres. Campgrounds are provided. Established in 1953.

Cape Lookout National Seashore. Located on Core Banks, Portsmouth Island, and Shackleford Banks, on the Outer Banks of east Carteret County. Established in 1967.

Carl Sandburg Home National Historic Site. Connemara, farm and home of the Pulitzer Prize-winning writer, poet, and novelist. Located one fourth mile west of Flat Rock in Henderson County.

Fort Raleigh National Historic Site. After considerable studies by archaeologists, the remains of this earthen fort were reconstructed in 1950. Located on the northeast shore of Roanoke Island, eastern Dare County.

Great Smoky Mountains National Park. Established in 1926 by Congress. Contains approximately 461,000 acres in portions of Haywood and Swain counties of North Carolina, and Blount, Cocke, and Sevier counties of Tennessee. Museums, nature trails, restorations, and campgrounds are here.

Guilford Courthouse National Military Park. Important battle of the Revolution between armies of American General Nathanael Greene and British General Lord Charles Cornwallis, March 15, 1781. Former county seat, it is located in central Guilford County.

Moores Creek National Battlefield. On February 27, 1776, the first battle of the Revolution in North Carolina took place here. Located in Pender County.

Wright Brothers National Memorial. The Kill Devil Hills Monument National Memorial, Visitor Center, and reconstructed Wright hangar and workshop, on 314 acres.

NATIONAL WILDLIFE REFUGES

In 1903 Theodore Roosevelt established tiny Pelican Island refuge in Florida, beginning the collection of lands and waters of the National Wildlife Refuge System. Today, with more than 425 refuges encompassing over 88 million acres of land and water, the opportunity is afforded for experiencing wildlife habitats of unequaled variety to which you can compare the quality of your own environment.

Ten such refuges are located in North Carolina. A brief description of each follows, including the manager's name, mailing address, and phone number. These refuges are located within Region 4 of the U.S. Department of the Interior, Fish and Wildlife Service, James W. Pulliam, Jr., Director, Richard B. Russell Federal Bldg., 75 Spring St., Room 1240, Atlanta, GA 30303, 404-331-3538.

Alligator River, opened in 1984, located in Dare, Hyde, and Tyrrell counties, has 137,000 acres of inaccessible wetlands that serve as habitat for the American alligator and the red wolf, both of which are endangered species. John Taylor, Manager, P.O. Box 1969, Manteo, 27954, 919-473-1131.

Cedar Island, established in 1964, located in Carteret County, has approximately 12,526 acres including 10,000 acres of irregularly flooded salt marsh and 2,041 acres of woodlands. An important resting and feeding area for migrant and wintering waterfowl, over 270 species of birds can be observed on refuge each year. Larry Ditto, Manager, Rt. 1, Box N-2, Swan Quarter, 27885, 919-926-4021.

Currituck, opened in 1984, is a coastal barrier island in Currituck County with 2,000 acres that provides a natural habitat for wintering migratory waterfowl as well as the mammals and other species common to the area. Because there is no development and no roads, this refuge is relatively inaccessible but the public is allowed to visit. John Taylor, Manager, P.O. Box 1969, Manteo, 27954, 919-473-1131.

Great Dismal Swamp, established in 1973, has 106,000 acres of heavily forested land and water in southern Virginia and Gates, Camden, and Pasquotank counties of North Carolina. Black bear, white-tailed deer, bobcat, and otter inhabit the swamp, as well as the Dismal Swamp short-tailed shrew and the Dismal Swamp log fern, which are seldom seen elsewhere, plus 207 species of birds. James Oland, Manager, P.O. Box 349, Suffolk, VA 23434, 804-441-6253.

Mackay Island, established in 1960, located in Currituck County and southeastern Virginia, has 7,055 acres. It is a wintering ground for migratory waterfowl, particularly greater snow geese. At least 174 species of birds have been sighted on the refuge. William H. Hegge, Manager, P.O. Box 31, Knotts Island, 27950, 919-429-3100.

Mattamuskeet, established in 1934, located in Hyde County, consists of 50,000 acres of water, marsh, timber, and croplands. The largest natural lake in North Carolina, Lake Mattamuskeet, contains about 40,000 acres of the total area. Primarily noted for its waterfowl, the refuge is also habitat for endangered and threatened species such as the bald eagle and the red-cockaded woodpecker. Deer, bobcats, otter, an occasional black bear, 214 species of birds and other wildlife species are indigenous to the area. Larry R. Ditto, Manager, Rt. 1, P.O. Box N-2, Swan Quarter, 27885, 919-926-4021.

Pea Island, opened in 1938, located in Dare County, has 32,000 acres on a coastal barrier island. The refuge provides a winter habitat to thousands of migrating water fowls, raptors, marsh and shorebirds, as well as nesting turtles. John Taylor, Manager, P.O. Box 1969, Manteo, 27954, 919-473-1131.

Pee Dee, established in 1965, contains 8,443 acres on the banks of the Pee Dee River in Anson and Richmond counties. The refuge is used by 166 migratory species of birds, especially geese and ducks, 28 species of mammals, 28 species of amphibians, and 48 species of reptiles. M. Bruce Blihovde, Manager, P.O. Box 780, Wadesboro, 28170, 704-694-4424.

Pungo, established in 1963, has 12,230 acres located in Hyde and Washington counties. The refuge is a wintering ground for thousands of Canada geese, snow geese, whistling swans, mallards, etc., while bird watching for species other than waterfowl is best during the spring and fall migrations. A total of 207 species of birds have been observed since the refuge was established. Larry R. Ditto, Manager, Rt. 1, Box N-2, Swan Quarter, 27885, 919-926-4021.

Swan Quarter, established in 1932 and located in Hyde County, is a tree wilderness, an estuarine marsh habitat for wildlife bordering Pamlico Sound. Though the primary objective of Swan Quarter is to provide a wintering sanctuary for migratory waterfowl, it is an optimum habitat for songbirds, shorebirds, wading birds, raptors, rails, and numerous other varieties including several birds of prey species. Critical habitat is provided for at least four endangered animal species; bald eagles, peregrine falcons, red-cockaded woodpeckers, and American alligator. Larry R. Ditto, Manager, Rt. 1, Box N-2, Swan Quarter, 27885, 919-926-4021.

NATURAL RESOURCES

The North Carolina Department of Natural Resources and Community Development, with its many divisions, implements such efforts as producing more than 50 million tree seedlings each year to aid in reforestation; guarding against sedimentation and erosion; keeping a close check on mining operations; monitoring toxic and chemical wastes; managing and regulating recreational and commercial fishing in the state, to name a few. Some of the resources they work to protect are the following.

Soils and Minerals. There are 73,800 farms that cover nearly six million acres of cropland, making agriculture North Carolina's number one industry. Producing one billion bricks per year for $100 million dollar industry, the state leads the nation in brickmaking. More lithium, the lightest known metal used for everything from air conditioners to aerospace technology, is produced in the state than anywhere else in the world. Scrap mica, used in paint, rubber, and insecticides, and feldspar and pyrophyllite, used in ceramics, tile, china, and glass are found in abundance in the state. Olivine, the heat-resistant mineral used in high temperature manufacturing, is also a product of the state's resources. In fact, minerals contribute more than $429 million to the state's economy and create 5,500 jobs, while the state's 520 mines cover only 0.1 percent of the state's surface land.

Forests. Furniture, lumber, and paper product industries are supported by the vast amount of commercial forests, 18.5 million acres, found in North Carolina. Private ownership constitutes 80 percent of this vast acreage, which covers about 60 percent of the state's land, causing the Tar Heel state to rank fourth in the nation in the number of commercial forest acres. The state ranks first in the nation in the production of hardwood plywood and face veneer, and ninth in hardwood and softwood lumber production. Annual value of these forest products exceeds eight billion dollars, creating employment for 136,000 employees, 17 percent of the state's workforce receiving in excess of $1.5 billion annual payroll.

Wildlife. Hunting and fishing are extremely popular in North Carolina, as evidenced by the fact that 800,000 hunting and fishing licenses are sold annually; nearly $580 million is spent to purchase hunting and fishing equipment; and 1,221,000 people hunt and fish annually in the state. Wildlife enriches the economy as well as enriching the environment.

Public Lands. Due at least in part to the fact that 3,000 miles of public trails, 320 miles of coastline, and 3.6 million acres are set aside for recreation, almost $4 billion is generated by travel and tourism, creating jobs for 154,000 people.

Water. About 11 trillion gallons of water are used annually in North Carolina. Since water is necessary for most manufacturing processes and for agriculture, it is fortunate that there is a relatively generous supply. The state ranks fourth in the 48 contiguous states in the amount of inland waters (rivers, lakes, streams, reservoirs and coastal bays) within its borders, which supply about 40 percent of the household water supply while 60 percent comes from groundwater (wells).

As with all states, much is being done to safeguard the future of these resources as they are necessary for our survival.

Source of information: North Carolina Department of Natural Resources & Community Development, P.O. Box 27687, Raleigh 27611-7687.

NEWSPAPERS

DAILY AND SUNDAY NEWSPAPERS

ABERDEEN
(Moore County)
The Citizen News-Record
P.O.B. 336, 28315
919-944-2356
Circulation: 5,149
Pub. Days: M-F (p.m.)

ASHEBORO
(Randolph County)
The Courier-Tribune
P.O.B. 340, 27204
919-625-2101
Circulation:
(M-F) 16,925
(Sun) 18,395
Pub. Days: M-F (p.m.)
Sun (a.m.)

ASHEVILLE
(Buncombe County)
Asheville Citizen
P.O.B. 2090, 28802
704-252-5611
Circulation: 49,809
Pub. Days: M-F (a.m.)

Asheville Times
P.O.B. 2090, 28802
704-252-5611
Circulation: 13,356
Pub. Days: M-F (p.m.)

Asheville Citizen-Times
P.O.B. 2090, 28802
704-252-5611
Circulation:
(Sat) 62,682
(Sun) 73,130
Pub. Days: Sat-Sun (a.m.)

BURLINGTON
(Alamance County)
The Daily Times-News
P.O.B. 481, 27216
919-227-0131
Circulation:
(M-F) 29,645
(Sat) 29,347
(Sun) 31,425
Pub. Days: M-F (p.m.)
Sat-Sun (a.m.)

CHAPEL HILL
(Orange County)
The Chapel Hill Newspaper
P.O.B. 870, 27514
919-967-7045
Circulation:
(M-F) 5,793
(Sun) 6,827
Pub. Days: M-F (a.m.)
Sun (a.m.)

CHARLOTTE
(Mecklenburg County)
The Charlotte Observer
P.O.B. 32188, 28232
704-379-6300
Circulation:
(M-Sat) 214,700
(Sun) 269,435
Pub. Days: M-Sat (a.m.)
Sun (a.m.)

CLINTON
(Sampson County)
The Sampson Independent

P.O.B. 110, 28328
919-592-8137
Circulation:
(M-F) 8,649
(Sun) 9,106
Pub. Days: M-F (p.m.)
Sun (a.m.)

CONCORD
(Cabarrus County)
The Concord Tribune
P.O.B. 608, 28026
704-782-3155
Circulation:
(M-F) 12,441
(Sun) 13,311
Pub. Days: M-F (p.m.)
Sun (a.m.)

DUNN (Harnett County)
The Daily Record
P.O.B. 1448, 28334
919-892-3117
Circulation: 8,523
Pub. Days: M-F (p.m.)

DURHAM
(Durham County)
Durham Morning Herald
P.O.B. 2092, 27702
919-682-8181
Circulation:
(M-Sat) 43,183
(Sun) 60,732
Pub. Days: M-Sat (a.m.)
Sun (a.m.)

The Durham Sun
P.O.B. 2092, 27702
919-682-8181
Circulation: 20,470
Pub. Days: M-Sat (p.m.)

EDEN
(Rockingham County)
Eden Daily News
P.O.B. 308, 27288
919-623-2155
Circulation: 6,989
Pub. Days: M-F (p.m.)

ELIZABETH CITY
(Pasquotank County)
The Daily Advance
P.O.B. 588, 27909
919-335-0841
Circulation:
(M-F) 11,146
(Sun) 11,869
Pub. Days: M-F (p.m.)
Sun (a.m.)

FAYETTEVILLE
(Cumberland County)
The Fayetteville Times
P.O.B. 849, 28302
919-323-4848
Circulation: 25,678
Pub. Days: M-F (a.m.)

The Fayetteville Observer
P.O.B. 849, 28302
919-323-4848
Circulation: 46,242
Pub. Days: M-F (p.m.)

The Fayetteville Saturday Observer-Times
P.O.B. 849, 28302
919-323-4848
Circulation: 73,483
Pub. Day: Sat (a.m.)

The Fayetteville Sunday Observer-Times
P.O.B. 849, 28302
919-323-4848
Circulation: 73,746
Pub. Day: Sun (a.m.)

FOREST CITY
(Rutherford County)
The Daily Courier
P.O.B. 1149, 28043
704-245-6431
Circulation: 10,482
Pub. Days: M-F (p.m.)

GASTONIA
(Gaston County)
The Gastonia Gazette
P.O.B. 1538, 28053
704-864-3291
Circulation:
(M-Sat) 39,638
(Sun) 43,597
Pub. Days: M-F (p.m.)
Sat-Sun (a.m.)

GOLDSBORO
(Wayne County)
Goldsboro News-Argus
P.O.B. 10629, 27532
919-778-2211
Circulation:
(M-F) 21,862
(Sun) 24,754
Pub. Days: M-F (p.m.)
Sun (a.m.)

GREENSBORO
(Guilford County)
Greensboro News & Record
P.O.B. 20848, 27420
919-373-7000
Circulation:
(M-F) 112,424
(Sat) 119,953
(Sun) 126,037
Pub. Days: M-F (a.m.)
Sat-Sun (a.m.)

GREENVILLE
(Pitt County)
The Daily Reflector
P.O.B. 1967, 27835
919-752-6166
Circulation:
(M-F) 17,200
(Sun) 19,186
Pub. Days: M-F (p.m.)
Sun (a.m.)

HENDERSON
(Vance County)
Henderson Daily Dispatch
P.O.B. 908, 27536
919-492-4001
Circulation: 9,644
Pub. Days: M-Sat (p.m.)

HENDERSONVILLE
(Henderson County)
Times-News
P.O.B. 490, 28793
704-692-0505
Circulation: 17,707
Pub. Days: M-Sun (a.m.)

HICKORY
(Catawba County)

Hickory Daily Record
P.O.B. 968, 28603
704-322-4510
Circulation: 27,487
Pub. Days: M-Sat (p.m.)

HIGH POINT
(Guilford County)
High Point Enterprise
P.O.B. 1009, 27261
919-841-5700
Circulation:
(M-Sat) 31,343
(Sun) 32,019
Pub. Days: M-F (p.m.)
Sat-Sun (a.m.)

JACKSONVILLE
(Onslow County)
The Daily News
P.O.B. 196, 28540-1096
919-353-1171
Circulation:
(M-Sat) 21,875
(Sun) 21,427
Pub. Days: M-F (p.m.)
Sat-Sun (a.m.)

KANNAPOLIS
(Cabarrus County)
The Daily Independent
P.O.B. 147, 28082-0147
704-932-3131
Circulation:
(M-F) 13,118
(Sun) 14,248
Pub. Days: M-F (p.m.)
Sun (a.m.)

KINSTON
(Lenoir County)
Kinston Daily Free Press
P.O.B. 129, 28501
919-527-3191
Circulation:
(M-F) 13,830
(Sun) 14,400
Pub. Days: M-F (p.m.)
Sun (a.m.)

LENOIR
(Caldwell County)
Lenoir News-Topic
P.O.B. 1110, 28645
704-758-7381
Circulation: 13,138
Pub. Days: M-F (p.m.)
Sat (a.m.)

LEXINGTON
(Davidson County)
The Dispatch
P.O.B. 908, 27292
704-249-3981
Circulation: 14,654
Pub. Days: M-Sat (p.m.)

LUMBERTON
(Robeson County)
The Robesonian
P.O.B. 1028, 28739
919-739-4322
Circulation:
(M-F) 15,453
(Sun) 17,123
Pub. Days: M-F (p.m.)
Sun (a.m.)

MARION
(McDowell County)
The McDowell News
P.O.B. 610, 28752
704-652-3313
Circulation: 7,193
Pub. Days: M-F (p.m.)

MONROE (Union County)
The Enquirer-Journal
P.O.B. 5040, 28110-0532
704-289-1541
Circulation:
(M-F) 12,847
(Sun) 13,743
Pub. Days: M-F (p.m.)
Sun (a.m.)

MORGANTON
(Burke County)
The News Herald
P.O.B. 280, 28655
704-437-2161
Circulation:
(M-F) 11,943
(Sun) 11,157
Pub. Days: M-F (p.m.)
Sun (a.m.)

MOUNT AIRY
(Surry County)
The Mount Airy News
P.O.B. 808, 27030
919-786-4141
Circulation: 8,875
Pub. Days: M-F (p.m.)

NEW BERN
(Craven County)
The Sun Journal
P.O.B. 1149, 28560
919-638-8101
Circulation: 15,718
Pub. Days: M-Sat (p.m.)

NEWTON
(Catawba County)
The Observer-News-Enterprise
P.O.B. 48, 28658
704-464-0221
Circulation: 4,062
Pub. Days: M-F (p.m.)

RALEIGH (Wake County)
The News and Observer
P.O.B. 191, 27601
919-829-4500
Circulation:
(M-Sat) 137,746
(Sun) 178,326
Pub. Days: M-Sat (a.m.)
Sun (a.m.)

The Raleigh Times
P.O.B. 191, 27601
919-829-4500
Circulation: 34,234
Pub. Days: M-Sat (p.m.)

REIDSVILLE
(Rockingham County)
The Reidsville Review
P.O.B. 2157, 27323-2157
919-349-4331
Circulation: 7,700
Pub. Days: M-F (p.m.)

ROANOKE RAPIDS
(Halifax County)
Daily and Sunday Herald
P.O.B. 520, 27870
919-537-2505

Circulation:
(M-F) 11,622
(Sun) 12,621
Pub. Days: M-F (p.m.)
Sun (a.m.)

ROCKINGHAM
(Richmond County)
Richmond Co. Daily Journal
P.O.B. 1888, 28379
919-997-3111
Circulation: 8,427
Pub. Days: M-F (p.m.)

ROCKY MOUNT
(Nash County)
The Evening and **Sunday Telegram**
P.O.B. 1080, 27802-1080
919-446-5161
Circulation:
(M-Sat) 13,229
(Sun) 14,287
Pub. Days: M-Sat (p.m.)
Sun (a.m.)

SALISBURY
(Rowan County)
The Salisbury Post
P.O.B. 4639, 28144
704-633-8950
Circulation:
(M-Sat) 25,339
(Sun) 25,428
Pub. Days: M-Sat (p.m.)
Sun (a.m.)

SANFORD (Lee County)
Sanford Herald
P.O.B. 100, 27330
919-776-0534
Circulation: 12,994
Pub. Days: M-Sat (p.m.)

SHELBY
(Cleveland County)
The Shelby Star
P.O.B. 48, 28150
704-484-7000
Circulation: 17,591
Pub. Days: M-Sat (p.m.)

STATESVILLE
(Iredell County)
Statesville Record & Landmark
P.O.B. 1071, 28677
704-873-1451
Circulation: 17,541
Pub. Days: M-F (p.m.)
Sun (a.m.)

TARBORO
(Edgecombe County)
The Daily Southerner
P.O.B. 1199, 27886
919-823-3106
Circulation: 6,210
Pub. Days: M-F (p.m.)

THOMASVILLE
(Davidson County)
The Times
P.O.B. 549, 27360
919-475-2151
Circulation: 8,320
Pub. Days: M-Sat (a.m.)

TRYON
(Polk County)
Tryon Daily Bulletin
P.O.B. 790, 28782
704-859-9151
Circulation: 3,439
Pub. Days: M-F (a.m.)

WASHINGTON
(Beaufort County)
Washington Daily News
P.O.B. 1788, 27889
919-946-2144
Circulation: 10,043
Pub. Days: M-Sat (p.m.)

WILMINGTON
(New Hanover County)
Wilmington Morning Star and **Sunday Star News**
P.O.B. 840, 28402
919-343-2000
Circulation:
(M-Sat) 45,484
(Sun) 53,029
Pub. Days: M-Sat (a.m.)
Sun (a.m.)

WILSON
(Wilson County)
The Wilson Daily Times
P.O.B. 2447, 27894-2447
919-243-5151
Circulation: 17,286
Pub. Days: M-Sat (p.m.)

WINSTON-SALEM
(Forsyth County)
Winston-Salem Journal
P.O.B. 3159, 27102
919-727-7211
Circulation:
(M-Sat) 91,536
(Sun) 100,959
Pub. Days: M-Sat (a.m.)
Sun (a.m.)

NON-DAILY (COMMUNITY) NEWSPAPERS

ABERDEEN
(Moore County)
The Citizen News-Record
P.O.B. 336, 28315
919-944-2356
Circulation: 8,200
Pub. Days: M-W-F (a.m.)

AHOSKIE
(Hertford County)
The News-Herald
P.O.B. 1325, 27910
919-332-2123
Circulation: 5,602
Pub. Days: M-W-F (p.m.)

ALBEMARLE
(Stanly County)
The Stanly News & Press
P.O.B. 520, 28801
704-982-2121
Circulation: 13,369
Pub. Days: T-F

ANDREWS
(Cherokee County)
The Andrews Journal
P.O.B. 250, 28901
704-321-4271
Circulation: 2,425
Pub. Day: Th (a.m.)

ANGIER
(Harnett County)
The Angier Independent
P.O.B. 878, 27501
919-639-4913
Circulation: 1,400
Pub. Day: W (a.m.)

APEX
(Wake County)
Western Wake Herald
P.O.B. E, 27502
919-362-8356
Circulation: 2,962
Pub. Day: W (a.m.)

ARCHDALE
(Randolph County)
Archdale-Trinity News
P.O.B. 4437, 27263
919-434-2716
Circulation: 1,988
Pub. Day: Th (a.m.)

ASHEBORO
(Randolph County)
The Randolph Guide
P.O.B. 1044, 27204-1044
919-625-5576
Circulation: 4,705
Pub. Day: W (p.m.)

BENSON
(Johnston County)
The Benson Review
P.O.B. 9, 27504
919-894-2112
Circulation: 3,268
Pub. Day: W (a.m.)

BLACK MOUNTAIN
(Buncombe County)
Black Mountain News
P.O. Box 8, 28711
704-669-8727
Circulation: 2,481
Pub. Day: Th (a.m.)

BLOWING ROCK
(Watauga County)
The Blowing Rocket
P.O.B. 1026, 28605
704-295-7522
Circulation: 2,037
Pub. Day: F (a.m.)

The Mountain Times
P.O.B. 1010, 28605
704-295-7696
Circulation: 5,600
Pub. Day: Th

BOONE
(Watauga County)
Watauga Democrat
P.O.B. 353, 28607
704-264-3612
Circulation: 10,405
Pub. Days: M-W-F (p.m.)

BREVARD
(Transylvania County)
The Transylvania Times
P.O.B. 32, 28712
704-883-8156
Circulation: 6,287
Pub. Days: M & Th (p.m.)

BRYSON CITY
(Swain County)
The Smoky Mountain Times
P.O.B. 730, 28713
704-488-2189
Circulation: 2,636
Pub. Day: Th (a.m.)

BURNSVILLE
(Yancey County)
The Yancey Journal
P.O.B. 280, 28714
704-682-2120
Circulation: 5,356
Pub. Day: Th (a.m.)

CANTON
(Haywood County)
The Enterprise
P.O.B. 268, 28716
704-648-2381
Circulation: 3,013
Pub. Day: W (p.m.)

CAROLINA BEACH
(New Hanover County)
The Island Gazette
P.O.B. 183, 28428
919-458-8156
Circulation: 3,950
Pub. Day: W (p.m.)

CARY
(Wake County)
The Cary News
P.O.B. 1146, 27511-1146
919-467-2231
Circulation: 6,861
Pub. Days: Sun & W (a.m.)

CASHIERS
(Jackson County)
Cashiers Crossroads Chronicle
P.O.B. 1040, 28717
704-743-5101
Circulation: 1,479
Pub. Day: W (p.m.)

CHADBOURN
(Columbus County)
Columbus County News
P.O.B. 567, 28431
919-654-3762
Circulation: 2,393
Pub. Day: W (p.m.)

CHARLOTTE
(Mecklenburg County)
The Mecklenburg Times
P.O.B. 36306, 28236
704-377-6221
Circulation: 735
Pub. Day: Tu & F

CLARKTON
(Bladen County)
The Southeastern Times
P.O.B. 757, 28337
919-862-2857
Circulation: 2,959
Pub. Days: M & W (p.m.)

CLAYTON
(Johnston County)
The Clayton News
P.O.B. 157, 27520
919-553-7234

Circulation: 2,700
Pub. Day: Tu (a.m.)

CLEMMONS
(Forsyth County)
The Clemmons Courier
P.O.B. 765, 27012
919-766-5505
Circulation: 3,800
Pub. Day: Th (p.m.)

COLUMBUS
(Polk County)
Thermal Belt News Journal
P.O.B. 566, 28722
704-894-3220
Circulation: 2,750
Pub. Days: W & F (a.m.)

CREEDMOOR
(Granville County)
The Butner-Creedmoor News
P.O.B. 726, 27522
919-528-2393
Circulation: 3,714
Pub. Day: Th (a.m.)

DANBURY
(Stokes County)
The Danbury Reporter
P.O.B. 216, 27016
919-593-8191
Circulation: 5,078
Pub. Day: Th (p.m.)

ELIZABETHTOWN
(Bladen County)
The Bladen Journal
P.O.B. 67, 28337
919-862-4163
Circulation: 4,600
Pub. Days: M & Th (p.m.)

ELKIN (Surry County)
(also Jonesville, Yadkin County)
The Tribune
P.O.B. 1009, 28621
919-835-1513
Circulation: 5,636
Pub. Days: M-W-F (p.m.)

FAIRMONT
(Robeson County)
The Times-Messenger
P.O.B. 684, 28340
919-628-7125
Circulation: 1,726
Pub. Day: Th (a.m.)

FOUR OAKS
(Johnston County)
The Four Oaks News
P.O.B. 518, 27524
919-963-2126
Circulation: 1,177
Pub. Day: Tu (a.m.)

FRANKLIN
(Macon County)
The Franklin Press
P.O.B. 350, 28734
704-524-2010
Circulation: 6,593
Pub. Days: M-W-F (p.m.)

FREMONT
(Wayne County)
Wayne-Wilson News Leader
P.O.B. 158, 27830
919-242-6301
Circulation: 947
Pub. Day: Th (a.m.)

FUQUAY-VARINA
(Wake County)
The Independent
P.O.B. 669, 27526
919-552-4112
Circulation: 3,466
Pub. Day: W (a.m.)

GRAHAM
(Alamance County)
The Alamance News
P.O.B. 431, 27253
919-228-7851
Circulation: 6,335
Pub. Day: Th (a.m.)

GREENSBORO
(Guilford County)
People and Places
P.O.B. 21807, 27420
919-373-7300
Circulation: 94,000
Pub. Days: S, T, W, Th

Triad Style
9 D Dundas Circle, 27407
919-852-8727
Circulation: 32,000
Pub. Day: W

GREENVILLE
(Pitt County)
The East Carolinian
Old South Building
East Carolina University, 27834
919-757-6366
Circulation: 12,000
Pub. Days: T & Th (a.m.)

HAMLET
(Richmond County)
The News-Messenger
P.O.B. 1207, 28345
919-997-3111
Circulation: 809
Pub. Day: Th (a.m.)

HAMPSTEAD
(Pender County)
Sounds of Pender East
P.O.B. 70, 28443
919-270-2461
Circulation: 6,174
Pub. Day: Th (a.m.)

HAVELOCK
(Craven County)
The Havelock Progress
P.O.B. 689, 28532
919-447-3173
Circulation: 3,200
Pub. Day: W (a.m.)

HAYESVILLE
(Clay County)
Clay County Progress
P.O.B. 483, 28904
704-389-8431
Circulation: 1,900
Pub. Day: Th (a.m.)

HERTFORD
(Perquimans County)
The Perquimans Weekly

P.O.B. 277, 27944
919-426-5728
Circulation: 1,959
Pub. Day: Th (a.m.)

HICKORY
(Catawba County)
The Hickory News
P.O.B. 2650, 28603
704-328-6164
Circulation: 5,950
Pub. Day: Th (p.m.)

HIGHLANDS
(Macon County)
The Highlander
P.O.B. 248, 28741
704-526-4114
Circulation: 2,834
Pub. Days: T & F (p.m.)
May-Nov
Th (p.m.) Dec-Apr

HILLSBOROUGH
(Orange County)
The News of Orange County
P.O.B. 580, 27278
919-732-2171
Circulation: 4,590
Pub. Day: W (p.m.)

JAMESTOWN
(Guilford County)
Jamestown News
P.O.B. 307, 27282
919-454-2669
Circulation: 1,320
Pub. Day: T (a.m.)

KENLY
(Johnston County)
Kenly News
P.O.B. 39, 27542
919-284-2295
Circulation: 2,543
Pub. Day: W (a.m.)

KERNERSVILLE
(Forsyth County)
Kernersville News
P.O.B. 337, 27285-0337
919-993-2161
Circulation: 5,773
Pub. Day: T & Th (a.m.)

KILL DEVIL HILLS
(Dare County)
The Outer Banks Current
P.O.B. 1836, 27948
919-441-3411
Circulation: 6,750
Pub. Day: W (a.m.)

KING
(Stokes County)
King Times-News
P.O.B. 545, 27021
919-983-3109
Circulation: 6,108
Pub. Day: W (p.m.)

LaGRANGE
(Lenoir County)
The Weekly Gazette
108 S. Caswell St., 28551
919-566-3028
Circulation: 1,290
Pub. Day: Th (a.m.)

LAURINBURG
(Scotland County)
The Laurinburg Exchange
P.O.B. 459, 28352
919-276-2311
Circulation: 8,182
Pub. Days: M-W-F (p.m.)

LIBERTY
(Randolph County)
The Liberty News
P.O.B. 69, 27298
919-622-4781
Circulation: 2,120
Pub. Day: W (a.m.)

LILLINGTON
(Harnett County)
Harnett County News
P.O.B. 939, 27546
919-893-5121
Circulation: 2,364
Pub. Day: W (a.m.)

LINCOLNTON
(Lincoln County)
Lincoln Times-News
P.O.B. 40, 28092
704-735-3031
Circulation: 9,026
Pub. Days: M-W-F (p.m.)

LOUISBURG
(Franklin County)
The Franklin Times
P.O.B. 119, 27549-0119
919-496-6503
Circulation: 7,024
Pub. Days: M & Th (a.m.)

MADISON
(Rockingham County)
The Messenger
P.O.B. 508, 27025
919-548-6047
Circulation: 8,491
Pub. Day: W (a.m.)

MANTEO
(Dare County)
The Coastland Times
P.O.B. 400, 27954
919-473-2105
Circulation: 9,606
Pub. Days: S-T-Th (a.m.)

MARSHALL
(Madison County)
The News Record
P.O.B. 369, 28753
704-649-2741
Circulation: 4,160
Pub. Day: Th (a.m.)

MARSHVILLE
(Union County)
Union News & Home
P.O.B. 100, 28103
704-624-5068
Circulation: 2,850
Pub. Day: Th (p.m.)

MATTHEWS
(Mecklenburg County)
The Southeast News
P.O.B. 1175, 28106
704-847-6397
Circulation: 2,947
Pub. Day: W (p.m.)

MEBANE
(Alamance County)
The Alamance-Orange Enterprise
P.O.B. 529, 27302
919-563-3555
Circulation: 1,682
Pub. Day: W (p.m.)

MOCKSVILLE
(Davie County)
Davie County Enterprise-Record
P.O.B. 525, 27028
704-634-2120
Circulation: 6,721
Pub. Day: Th (a.m.)

MOORESVILLE
(Iredell County)
Mooresville Tribune, Inc.
P.O.B. 300, 28115
704-664-5554
Circulation: 6,880
Pub. Day: W (p.m.)

MOREHEAD CITY
(Carteret County)
Carteret County News-Times
P.O.B. 1679, 28557
919-726-7081
Circulation: 10,528
Pub. Days: M-W-F (a.m.)

MOUNT OLIVE
(Wayne County)
Mount Olive Tribune
P.O.B. 709, 28365
919-658-9456
Circulation: 4,300
Pub. Days: Tu & F (p.m.)

MURPHY
(Cherokee County)
The Cherokee Scout
P.O.B. 190, 28906
704-837-5122
Circulation: 6,822
Pub. Days: Tu & F (p.m.)

NASHVILLE
(Nash County)
The Graphic
P.O.B. 1008, 27856
919-459-7101
Circulation: 3,789
Pub. Days: W & F (p.m.)

NEWLAND
(Avery County)
Avery Journal, Inc.
P.O.B. 128, 28657
704-733-2448
Circulation: 6,338
Pub. Day: Th (a.m.)

NORTH WILKESBORO
(Wilkes County)
The Journal-Patriot
P.O.B. 70, 28659
919-838-4117
Circulation: 14,805
Pub. Days: M & Th (p.m.)

ORIENTAL
(Pamlico County)
The Pamlico News
P.O.B. 510, 28571
919-249-1555
Circulation: N/A
Pub. Day: W (a.m.)

OXFORD
(Granville County)
Oxford Public Ledger
P.O.B. 643, 27565
919-693-2646
Circulation: 6,004
Pub. Days: M & Th (a.m.)

PILOT MOUNTAIN
(Surry County)
The Pilot
P.O.B. 223, 27041
919-368-2222
Circulation: 3,093
Pub. Day: W (p.m.)

PITTSBORO
(Chatham County)
Chatham Herald-Tribune
P.O.B. 548, 27312
919-542-4861
Circulation: 5,636
Pub. Day: Tu (p.m.)

The Chatham Record
P.O.B. 458, 27312
919-542-3013
Circulation: 1,607
Pub. Day: Th (a.m.)

PLYMOUTH
(Washington County)
The Roanoke Beacon
P.O.B. 726, 27962
919-793-2123
Circulation: 4,401
Pub. Day: W (p.m.)

RAEFORD
(Hoke County)
The News Journal
P.O.B. 550, 28376
919-875-2121
Circulation: 3,653
Pub. Day: W (a.m.)

The Public Post
P.O.B. 1093, 28376
919-875-8938
Circulation: 1,000
Pub. Day: W

RALEIGH
(Wake County)
The North Carolina Catholic
300 Cardinal Gibbons Dr., 27606-2198
919-821-9720
Circulation: 25,216
Pub. Day: Sun (a.m.)

RANDLEMAN
(Randolph County)
The Randleman Reporter
P.O. Drawer 645, 27317
919-498-4151
Circulation: 1,489
Pub. Day: Tu (a.m.)

RESEARCH TRIANGLE PARK (Durham County)
The Leader Newsmagazine
P.O.B. 12054, 27709
919-549-8209
Circulation: 6,842
Pub. Day: Th (p.m.)

ROBBINSVILLE
(Graham County)
The Graham Star
P.O.B. 68, 28771
704-479-3383
Circulation: 2,887
Pub. Day: Th (p.m.)

ROBERSONVILLE
(Martin County)
The Weekly Herald
P.O.B. 179, 27871
919-792-1181
Circulation: 905
Pub. Day: W (p.m.)

ROCKY MOUNT
(Nash County)
The Rocky Mount Record
122 NW Main St., 27804
919-997-9533
Circulation: 4,900
Pub. Day: W (p.m.)

ROXBORO
(Person County)
The Courier-Times, Inc.
P.O.B. 311, 27573
919-599-0162
Circulation: 7,717
Pub. Days: M & Th (p.m.)

RURAL HALL
(Forsyth County)
The Independent
P.O.B. 806, 27045
919-969-6076
Circulation: 1,200
Pub. Day: Th

RUTHERFORDTON
(Rutherford County)
Rutherford County News, Inc.
P.O.B. 800, 28139
704-287-3327
Circulation: 3,300
Pub. Day: W (a.m.)

SELMA
(Johnston County)
The Johnstonian-Sun
P.O.B. 278, 27576
919-965-2033
Circulation: 4,100
Pub. Day: Th (a.m.)

SHALLOTE
(Brunswick County)
The Brunswick Beacon
P.O.B. 2558, 28459
919-754-6890
Circulation: 7,020
Pub. Day: Th (a.m.)

SILER CITY
(Chatham County)
The Chatham News
P.O.B. 290, 27344
919-663-3232
Circulation: 5,049
Pub. Day: Th (a.m.)

SMITHFIELD
(Johnston County)
The Smithfield Herald
P.O.B. 1417, 27577
919-934-2176
Circulation: 13,869
Pub. Days: Tu & F (p.m.)

SNOW HILL
(Greene County)
The Standard Laconic
P.O.B. 128, 28580
919-747-3883
Circulation: 3,349
Pub. Day: W (a.m.)

SOUTHERN PINES
(Moore County)
The Pilot
P.O.B. 58, 28387
919-692-7271
Circulation: 11,110
Pub. Days: M & Th (a.m.)

SOUTHPORT
(Brunswick County)
The State Port Pilot
P.O.B. 10548, 28461
919-457-4568
Circulation: 6,098
Pub. Day: W (p.m.)

SPARTA
(Alleghany County)
The Blue Ridge Sun
P.O.B. 757, 28675
919-372-5490
Circulation: 3,194
Pub. Day: W (a.m.)

The Alleghany News
P.O.B. 8, 28675
919-372-8999
Circulation: 1,896
Pub. Day: Th (a.m.)

SPRING HOPE
(Nash County)
Spring Hope Enterprise
P.O.B. 399, 27882
Circulation: 2,700
Pub. Day: Th (p.m.)

SPRUCE PINE
(Mitchell County)
Tri-County News-Journal
P.O.B. 339, 28777
704-765-2071
Circulation: 5,895
Pub. Day: Th (a.m.)

SWANSBORO
(Onslow County)
Tideland News
P.O.B. 1098, 28584
919-326-5066
Circulation: 1,766
Pub. Day: W (p.m.)

SYLVA
(Jackson County)
The Sylva Herald & Ruralite
P.O.B. 307, 28779
704-586-2611
Circulation: 5,919
Pub. Day: Th (a.m.)

TABOR CITY
(Columbus County)
The Tabor City Tribune
P.O.B. 67, 28463
919-653-3153
Circulation: 2,823
Pub. Day: W (p.m.)

TAYLORSVILLE
(Alexander County)
The Taylorsville Times

P.O.B. 278, 28681
704-632-2532
Circulation: 6,270
Pub. Days: W (p.m.) & Sat (a.m.)

TRENTON
(Jones County)
The Jones Post
P.O.B. 117, 28585
919-448-9491
Circulation: 1,104
Pub. Day: Th (p.m.)

TROY
(Montgomery County)
Montgomery Herald
P.O.B. 426, 27371
919-576-6051
Circulation: 5,880
Pub. Day: Th (p.m.)

VANCEBORO
(Craven County)
West Craven Highlights
P.O.B. 404, 28586
919-244-0780
Circulation: 2,296
Pub. Day: Th (p.m.)

WADESBORO
(Anson County)
Anson Record & Messenger & Intelligencer
P.O.B. 959, 28170
704-694-2161
Circulation: 6,310
Pub. Days: Tu & Th (p.m.)

WAKE FOREST
(Wake County)
The Wake Weekly
P.O.B. 192, 27587
919-556-3182
Circulation: 6,970
Pub. Day: Th (a.m.)

WALLACE
(Duplin County)
The Wallace Enterprise
P.O.B. 699, 28466
919-285-2178
Circulation: 5,892
Pub. Days: M & Th (p.m.)

WARRENTON
(Warren County)
The Warren Record
P.O.B. 70, 27589
919-257-3341
Circulation: 4,718
Pub. Day: W (p.m.)

WAYNESVILLE
(Haywood County)
The Mountaineer
P.O.B. 129, 28786
704-452-0661
Circulation: 12,716
Pub. Days: M-W-Th-F (p.m.)

WENDELL
(Wake County)
Gold Leaf Farmer
P.O.B. 400, 27591
919-365-6262
Circulation: 2,676
Pub. Day: Th (a.m.)

WEST JEFFERSON
(Ashe County)
Jefferson Times
P.O.B. 808, 28694
919-246-7164
Circulation: 4,364
Pub. Days: M & Th (p.m.)

The Skyland Post
P.O.B. 67, 28694
919-246-4121
Circulation: 4,848
Pub. Day: W (a.m.)

WHITEVILLE
(Columbus County)
The News Reporter
P.O.B. 707, 28472
919-642-4104
Circulation: 10,152
Pub. Days: M & Th (p.m.)

WILLIAMSTON
(Martin County)
The Enterprise
P.O.B. 387, 27892
919-792-1181
Circulation: 5,397
Pub. Days: Tu & Th (p.m.)

WINDSOR
(Bertie County)
Bertie Ledger-Advance
P.O.B. 69, 27983
919-794-3185
Circulation: 3,748
Pub. Day: Th (p.m.)

WINSTON-SALEM
(Forsyth County)
Winston-Salem Chronicle
P.O.B. 3154, 27102
919-722-8624
Circulation: 4,894
Pub. Day: Th (a.m.)

YADKINVILLE
(Yadkin County)
The Yadkin Ripple
P.O.B. 7, 27055
919-679-2341
Circulation: 5,930
Pub. Day: Th (a.m.)

YANCEYVILLE
(Caswell County)
The Caswell Messenger
P.O.B. 100, 27379
919-694-4145
Circulation: 4,006
Pub. Day: Th (p.m.)

ZEBULON
(Wake County)
The Zebulon Record
P.O.B. 857, 27597
919-269-6101
Circulation: 2,992
Pub. Day: Th (a.m.)

OCCUPATIONS

There are far more persons employed in manufacturing related jobs than any other division of the work force, 30.4 percent of the total for the state of North Carolina. In second place, with 17.7 percent of the state total are the retail trade workers followed by total government workers (federal, state, and local) at 15.5 percent in third place.

The remaining work force is ranked in the following order: services (15.3%), construction (5.6%), wholesale trade (5.4%), transportation, communication, and utilities (4.8%), finance, insurance, and real estate (4.4%), and all other (1.0%).

Following are two charts. The first chart shows the occupational breakdown by major industry divisions, with the average employment and average weekly wage per employee for the fourth quarter of 1986.

The second chart is broken down by county to show the average employment in each major industry division for the fourth quarter of 1986.

The information in this chapter was compiled from the *Employment and Wages in North Carolina, Fourth Quarter, 1986* booklet from the Labor Market Information Division, Employment Security Commission of North Carolina, reporting insured employment figures only.

Occupational Breakdown: 4th Quarter 1986

Major Industry Divisions	*Occupation*	*Average Employment for 4th Quarter 1986*	*Average Weekly Wage per Employee*
Agriculture, Forestry & Fishing	Agricultural production—crops	5,215	210.88
	Agricultural production—livestock	6,629	295.03
	Agricultural services	11,459	235.65
	Forestry	658	201.33
	Fishing, hunting & trapping	51	229.83
Mining	Metal mining	19	313.26
	Bituminous coal & lignite mining	1	161.54
	Oil & gas extraction	8	315.88
	Nonmetallic minerals, except fuels	4,408	508.15
Construction	General building contractors	47,697	367.06
	Heavy construction contractors	23,341	377.71
	Special trade contractors	84,452	327.88
Manufacturing	Food & kindred products	48,515	339.82
	Tobacco manufactures	26,475	616.70
	Textile mill products	217,164	331.99
	Apparel & other finished products	85,819	228.13

Major Industry Divisions	Occupation	Average Employment for 4th Quarter 1986	Average Weekly Wage per Employee
	Lumber & wood products	38,360	303.58
	Furniture & fixtures	86,973	327.63
	Paper & allied products	21,878	569.71
	Printing & publishing	28,724	362.28
	Chemicals & allied products	38,357	546.89
	Petroleum Refining & related industries	774	426.48
	Rubber & misc. plastics products	32,061	421.94
	Leather & leather products	3,427	277.09
	Stone, clay, glass, & concrete products	20,306	417.17
	Primary metal industries	10,961	449.94
	Fabricated metal products	26,261	439.92
	Machinery, except electrical	56,638	547.97
	Electrical & electronic equipment	57,975	452.42
	Transportation equipment	23,571	435.01
	Instruments & related products	10,411	454.07
	Misc. manufacturing industries	6,868	316.53
Transportation, Communication, & Utilities	Local & interurban passenger transportation	3,678	255.66
	Trucking & warehousing	56,424	412.68
	Water transportation	1,514	365.46
	Transportation by air	12,413	576.39
	Pipe lines, except natural gas	115	670.38
	Transportation services	3,057	377.42
	Communication	27,696	501.57
	Electric, gas, & sanitary services	28,307	591.79
Wholesale	Wholesale trade—durable goods	90,704	488.30
	Wholesale trade—nondurable goods	59,524	425.08
Retail	Building materials & garden supplies	25,235	326.33
	General merchandise stores	67,862	179.97
	Food stores	79,520	201.89
	Automotive dealers & service stations	51,350	370.78
	Apparel & accessory stores	27,327	179.74
	Furniture & home furnishings stores	24,565	287.59
	Eating & drinking places	152,239	128.63
	Misc. retail	61,478	239.48
Finance, Insurance & Real Estate	Banking	33,512	370.83
	Credit agencies other than banks	19,299	394.07
	Security & commodity brokers, & services	3,613	840.12
	Insurance carriers	25,585	445.86
	Insurance agents, brokers & service	11,043	435.86
	Real estate	25,071	332.63
	Combined real estate, insurance, etc.	225	477.77
	Holding & other investment offices	2,379	602.41

Major Industry Divisions	Occupation	Average Employment for 4th Quarter 1986	Average Weekly Wage per Employee
Services	Hotels & other lodging places	27,442	169.24
	Personal services	27,252	217.67
	Business services	102,425	277.96
	Auto repair, services & garages	15,730	296.13
	Misc. repair services	7,949	327.86
	Motion pictures	4,490	145.46
	Amusement & recreation services	13,071	220.37
	Health services	111,430	351.21
	Legal services	11,178	444.54
	Educational services	31,949	378.30
	Social services	27,183	184.36
	Museums, botanical & zoological gardens	586	178.12
	Membership organizations	8,977	235.79
	Private households	7,967	125.53
	Misc. services	24,614	479.44
Government	Federal government	52,900	496.25
	State government	112,552	396.96
	Local government	262,533	326.98

Occupations—Average Employment in Each Major Industry Division: 4th Quarter 1986

County	*Agriculture Forestry & Fishing*	*Mining*	*Construction*	*Manufacturing*	*Transportation, Communication, & Utilities*	*Wholesale Trade*	*Retail Trade*	*Finance, Insurance & Real Estate*	*Services*	*Government*
Alamance	*	*	1,925	20,979	1,066	2,278	10,048	1,283	7,522	4,590
Alexander	*	0	*	5,413	187	127	741	114	633	959
Alleghany	32	0	157	1,094	65	*	*	37	301	538
Anson	295	*	363	4,235	341	90	902	*	387	1,478
Ashe	*	0	309	2,666	204	503	1,239	107	495	846
Avery	103	*	425	788	219	*	*	214	1,754	801
Beaufort	*	*	524	5,169	461	811	2,775	321	1,665	2,502
Bertie	352	*	131	4,511	79	*	443	106	310	992
Bladen	*	0	309	3,305	155	316	953	*	*	1,896
Brunswick	*	0	748	2,595	1,952	222	2,107	542	1,485	2,804
Buncombe	*	*	3,897	20,111	*	2,928	15,345	2,685	*	11,531
Burke	*	0	777	18,352	779	352	3,544	412	2,887	6,735
Cabarrus	*	21	2,372	16,572	1,160	585	6,897	943	*	4,893
Caldwell	*	0	911	15,094	1,099	426	3,396	430	*	3,000
Camden	21	0	*	64	10	*	94	*	40	289
Carteret	177	0	923	2,133	517	569	4,234	1,068	*	2,725
Caswell	13	0	*	767	*	3	271	27	167	1,008
Catawba	124	*	2,487	40,004	2,569	4,676	11,970	*	6,991	5,865
Chatham	207	0	471	6,374	342	499	1,432	169	813	1,291
Cherokee	78	56	316	2,951	60	201	*	124.	507	1,363
Chowan	237	0	*	1,403	140	414	798	*	779	593
Clay	32	0	103	470	*	21	182	24	101	316
Cleveland	*	255	1,143	14,456	703	1,954	4,988	726	*	3,940
Columbus	91	0	1,022	5,893	*	477	2,822	594	1,983	2,747
Craven	*	*	1,253	3,850	*	819	5,733	*	*	10,689
Cumberland	509	*	4,226	11,207	3,090	2,056	19,828	3,036	10,923	21,256
Currituck	48	0	*	104	27	32	516	58	168	601
Dare	42	0	891	354	279	218	3,119	549	1,692	1,291
Davidson	133	*	1,793	22,877	1,419	1,439	6,096	842	*	4,803
Davie	*	0	328	3,347	626	192	1,102	182	518	1,164

Duplin	1,062	*	560	5,385	163	686	1,683	*	735	2,206
Durham	264	0	4,822	27,219	4,322	2,783	14,951	4,701	32,769	13,530
Edgecombe	237	0	1,715	6,655	2,072	578	2,529	274	1,965	3,850
Forsyth	367	*	6,849	41,284	11,231	6,642	25,343	7,939	29,819	15,298
Franklin	*	*	273	2,589	74	147	1,073	172	843	1,207
Gaston	191	*	2,271	37,837	3,881	2,186	11,263	*	7,701	6,877
Gates	44	0	0	*	*	*	263	118	76	445
Graham	6	8	*	751	61	5	211	23	49	418
Granville	10	0	253	5,252	*	207	1,462	198	1,216	5,051
Greene	114	0	*	884	12	126	*	42	302	871
Guilford	*	*	13,530	60,903	10,742	18,259	37,046	*	*	22,551
Halifax	*	0	650	6,001	*	928	4,062	*	1,642	3,688
Harnett	171	*	996	4,425	259	784	3,211	441	2,288	2,655
Haywood	*	0	666	4,786	289	264	3,219	*	1,930	2,899
Henderson	*	0	1,588	6,697	1,118	807	5,004	611	3,388	3,235
Hertford	123	0	*	2,369	155	314	1,705	170	1,299	1,600
Hoke	232	0	*	3,461	30	39	483	*	222	1,399
Hyde	33	0	*	243	9	68	167	*	98	396
Iredell	*	*	2,217	16,361	*	1,535	7,185	773	4,228	4,324
Jackson	101	*	511	1,017	313	24	1,424	468	1,475	2,719
Johnston	545	*	1,860	8,837	349	768	4,256	487	*	3,595
Jones	9	5	73	*	*	81	129	*	133	403
Lee	61	36	1,316	7,067	515	709	4,558	*	1,819	2,288
Lenoir	291	0	1,820	8,057	683	1,204	4,747	783	3,360	5,843
Lincoln	*	0	527	8,030	432	468	2,256	317	837	1,916
Macon	*	62	652	1,274	271	48	1,451	260	1,015	1,124
Madison	*	0	42	613	126	*	596	*	509	815
Martin	*	0	322	3,422	198	892	1,498	*	672	1,651
McDowell	19	14	456	9,322	153	*	1,791	*	1,017	1,416
Mecklenburg	1,809	*	19,577	49,329	34,186	33,499	55,271	*	*	32,518
Mitchell	17	197	210	2,197	87	163	771	104	561	940
Montgomery	73	0	468	6,821	156	89	966	*	*	1,344
Moore	337	38	1,121	6,529	526	403	3,761	680	5,413	2,763
Nash	607	*	1,381	14,354	1,358	1,665	7,736	2,654	*	3,579
New Hanover	*	67	3,067	8,424	3,569	3,240	13,064	2,159	10,541	10,499
Northampton	*	*	299	1,307	118	255	411	50	512	1,301
Onslow	120	*	1,576	2,955	1,171	354	7,858	958	3,270	8,829

County	Agriculture Forestry & Fishing	Mining	Construction	Manufacturing	Transportation, Communication, & Utilities	Wholesale Trade	Retail Trade	Finance, Insurance & Real Estate	Services	Government
Orange	194	51	1,349	2,759	847	864	6,408	2,490	*	16,577
Pamlico	*	0	122	548	55	*	*	43	97	503
Pasquotank	*	*	432	1,300	274	659	3,111	*	*	3,306
Pender	*	0	294	531	99	197	*	186	403	1,189
Perquimans	34	0	*	511	35	*	266	41	112	473
Person	*	0	610	4,755	584	152	1,602	144	756	1,522
Pitt	*	31	2,106	8,016	*	1,906	9,392	1,467	5,375	11,500
Polk	*	0	118	1,053	41	52	412	95	720	520
Randolph	*	*	1,348	21,812	*	985	4,520	*	3,150	3,904
Richmond	139	175	421	6,245	622	369	2,827	431	*	2,456
Robeson	*	0	1,451	14,095	728	907	5,288	*	*	6,120
Rockingham	75	*	1,396	15,091	1,123	532	4,863	585	3,036	3,662
Rowan	194	69	1,663	14,737	963	1,266	7,548	*	*	5,626
Rutherford	*	0	659	10,398	1,150	521	2,876	706	*	2,652
Sampson	838	0	524	5,427	254	396	2,285	*	1,223	2,824
Scotland	188	0	*	8,772	299	260	2,225	292	1,616	1,743
Stanly	169	*	885	10,101	256	501	2,902	*	1,794	2,517
Stokes	25	*	534	1,481	222	44	769	91	*	1,444
Surry	93	*	1,874	15,841	1,200	721	4,391	560	*	3,116
Swain	9	*	*	1,033	18	118	*	35	1,486	812
Transylvania	66	*	527	3,530	*	59	1,397	272	1,295	1,165
Tyrrell	24	0	*	137	*	21	144	*	18	235
Union	1,553	*	3,424	11,429	688	1,160	4,690	*	*	3,162
Vance	66	135	431	6,681	485	492	*	256	*	2,287
Wake	*	306	15,491	24,885	11,934	14,724	39,176	*	*	43,338
Warren	5	0	141	1,283	87	71	473	*	522	811
Washington	243	0	107	608	167	*	618	74	*	1,025
Watauga	*	*	*	1,368	287	412	3,796	760	2,159	3,071
Wayne	753	0	*	7,744	*	2,043	6,708	*	4,340	8,222
Wilkes	*	*	716	9,675	832	705	*	1,129	1,937	3,092
Wilson	*	*	2,378	8,800	1,093	1,634	5,311	1,601	4,415	5,292
Yadkin	55	0	403	2,411	*	165	1,086	116	683	1,251
Yancey	9	103	158	2,524	*	14	467	*	226	715

*In tables indicates disclosure suppression.

POPULATION

In 1980, by actual census, North Carolina's population count was 5,881,385. As of July 1, 1986, the population was estimated to be 6,331,288, an increase of almost 450,000. It is projected that by the year 2000 the population will reach 6,963,552.

North Carolina's economic growth is attracting new residents from other states. In-migration accounted for 43 percent of North Carolina's population growth during the 1970s, and is expected to account for 72 percent of the state's population growth through the year 2000.

While North Carolina's booming population is the tenth largest in the nation, the state ranks twenty-eighth in geographic size—resulting in a population density considerably greater than the nation's as a whole. Yet, while three of every four Americans is a city dweller, only half of all North Carolinans live in communities of 2500 or more. About 50 percent of North Carolina's population lives in the rolling hills of the Piedmont, where the major cities and manufacturing plants are concentrated.

North Carolina's urban growth centers around medium-sized cities; eight cities have populations of more than 50,000. Much of the state's "rural" population lives on the fringes of these areas. As a result, the state offers vibrant urban centers and a wide choice of life-styles—new industries can locate in low-cost rural areas and still have access to urban services and a plentiful labor supply.

Population by County

The following chart shows actual population by county for 1980, as well as estimates for 1987, and the births and deaths for 1985 and 1987.

	Census	*Estimate*	*Births*		*Deaths*	
County	*April 1, 1980*	*July 1, 1987*	*1985*	*1986*	*1985*	*1986*
Alamance	99,319	103,855	1,290	1,311	944	993
Alexander	24,999	27,104	324	334	176	202
Alleghany	9,587	9,744	102	86	114	105
Anson	25,649	26,432	353	323	256	279
Ashe	22,325	23,399	223	210	219	234
Avery	14,409	15,126	196	190	125	125
Beaufort	40,355	43,883	595	493	471	472
Bertie	21,024	21,286	310	292	245	244
Bladen	30,491	30,881	339	379	282	307
Brunswick	35,777	44,718	661	659	372	382
Buncombe	160,934	171,457	2,054	2,107	1,714	1,744
Burke	72,504	76,548	862	875	631	640
Cabarrus	85,895	93,956	1,242	1,266	804	854
Caldwell	67,746	70,530	887	875	526	573
Camden	5,829	5,866	70	90	64	61
Carteret	41,092	51,906	737	707	445	454
Caswell	20,705	22,776	258	248	189	182

County	Census April 1, 1980	Estimate July 1, 1987	Births 1985	Births 1986	Deaths 1985	Deaths 1986
Catawba	105,208	115,573	1,490	1,405	929	930
Chatham	33,415	36,432	531	511	327	323
Cherokee	18,933	20,591	211	199	190	218
Chowan	12,558	13,519	184	181	157	183
Clay	6,619	7,305	74	73	81	74
Cleveland	83,435	86,662	1,119	1,127	768	806
Columbus	51,037	52,493	754	766	530	561
Craven	71,043	81,677	1,605	1,615	538	567
Cumberland	247,160	256,189	5,483	5,217	1,434	1,445
Currituck	11,089	13,731	177	219	130	114
Dare	13,377	19,558	250	286	146	140
Davidson	113,162	120,044	1,598	1,548	961	961
Davie	24,599	29,026	284	306	227	235
Duplin	40,952	41,801	574	546	453	416
Durham	152,785	168,015	2,449	2,526	1,426	1,385
Edgecombe	55,988	59,563	895	844	536	591
Forsyth	243,683	263,596	3,463	3,469	2,140	2,331
Franklin	30,055	34,832	427	454	299	333
Gaston	162,568	173,259	2,421	2,429	1,483	1,624
Gates	8,875	9,665	141	136	109	106
Graham	7,217	7,166	92	76	66	66
Granville	34,043	38,280	507	510	336	403
Greene	16,117	16,661	240	191	151	120
Guilford	317,154	331,897	4,315	4,520	2,802	2,814
Halifax	55,286	56,184	836	784	607	594
Harnett	59,570	64,719	1,103	1,094	506	644
Haywood	46,495	48,783	519	505	497	487
Henderson	58,580	68,605	806	755	741	695
Hertford	23,368	24,155	340	371	254	288
Hoke	20,383	23,575	332	379	147	135
Hyde	5,873	5,915	68	70	61	80
Iredell	82,538	89,371	1,099	1,176	773	821
Jackson	25,811	26,700	286	270	217	220
Johnston	70,599	79,407	1,003	1,061	694	729
Jones	9,705	9,830	154	111	92	87
Lee	36,718	42,158	640	582	414	355
Lenoir	59,819	60,285	783	791	620	593
Lincoln	42,372	46,903	565	629	391	341
Macon	20,178	23,549	168	178	178	157
Madison	16,827	17,446	365	366	283	278
Martin	25,948	26,843	452	428	317	365
McDowell	35,135	36,392	242	237	249	240
Mecklenburg	404,270	460,920	6,840	7,272	3,204	3,315
Mitchell	14,428	14,560	193	187	151	158
Montgomery	22,469	24,073	315	286	224	225
Moore	50,505	56,889	687	688	568	591

County	Census	Estimate	Births		Deaths	
	April 1, 1980	July 1, 1987	1985	1986	1985	1986
Nash	67,153	71,894	1,054	1,076	701	674
New Hanover	103,471	116,446	1,462	1,520	992	945
Northampton	22,584	22,545	291	309	259	259
Onslow	112,784	127,109	3,421	3,368	519	539
Orange	77,055	85,957	997	1,016	508	507
Pamlico	10,398	11,158	140	147	104	116
Pasquotank	28,462	30,084	446	462	262	316
Pender	22,215	25,670	325	345	224	249
Perquimans	9,486	10,701	131	156	102	109
Person	29,164	30,885	351	393	250	294
Pitt	90,146	98,567	1,395	1,433	789	763
Polk	12,984	14,726	130	111	173	181
Randolph	91,728	100,312	1,306	1,375	736	761
Richmond	45,481	46,347	584	569	449	497
Robeson	101,610	106,811	1,721	1,774	933	967
Rockingham	83,426	85,851	1,156	1,089	778	938
Rowan	99,186	105,376	1,344	1,433	1,022	1,089
Rutherford	53,787	57,375	742	734	491	615
Sampson	49,687	50,423	601	644	521	511
Scotland	32,273	33,968	514	477	309	302
Stanly	48,517	50,558	671	644	435	478
Stokes	33,086	36,013	413	437	280	287
Surry	59,449	61,882	711	710	559	599
Swain	10,283	11,042	158	163	143	128
Transylvania	23,417	26,567	277	258	208	224
Tyrrell	3,975	4,106	59	65	45	49
Union	70,380	81,335	1,126	1,143	550	571
Vance	36,748	39,059	577	589	423	425
Wake	301,327	376,337	5,135	5,390	2,276	2,137
Warren	16,232	16,488	242	231	192	206
Washington	14,801	14,500	215	216	141	152
Watauga	31,666	34,928	365	408	203	219
Wayne	97,054	97,468	1,603	1,598	889	834
Wilkes	58,657	61,058	744	722	479	560
Wilson	63,132	64,792	892	920	649	619
Yadkin	28,439	29,836	336	317	292	321
Yancey	14,934	15,988	173	167	148	148
State Total	5,881,766[(a)]	6,403,426	89,391	90,228	53,018	54,584

(a)Revised totals are 5,881,385 for the state, 22,262 for Pender County, and 91,300 for Randolph County.

Population Comparison

The major cities of the Southeast are compared below by population, rank in the United States, and the Southeast.

	July 1, 1982			April 1, 1980		
City	*Population*	*Rank in United States*	*Rank in Southeast*	*Population*	*Rank in United States*	*Rank in Southeast*
Memphis, TN	645,760	16	1	646,170	15	1
New Orleans, LA	564,561	20	2	557,927	22	2
Jacksonville, FL	556,370	23	3	540,920	23	3
Nashville-Davidson, TN	455,252	26	4	455,651	26	4
Atlanta, GA	428,153	30	5	425,022	30	5
Miami, FL	382,726	34	6	346,865	41	6
Baton Rouge, LA	361,572	41	7	346,029	42	7
CHARLOTTE, NC	323,972	48	8	315,474	49	8
Louisville, KY	293,531	50	9	298,694	50	9
Birmingham, AL	283,239	53	10	286,799	51	10
Virginia Beach, VA	282,588	54	11	262,199	57	13
Tampa, FL	276,413	55	12	271,599	54	11
Norfolk, VA	266,874	57	13	266,979	56	12
St. Petersburg, FL	241,214	61	14	238,647	59	14
Richmond, VA	218,237	66	15	219,214	65	15
Shreveport, LA	210,881	68	16	205,820	67	16
Lexington-Fayette, KY	207,668	69	17	204,165	68	17
Mobile, AL	204,586	70	18	200,452	71	19
Jackson, MS	204,195	71	19	202,895	70	18
Montgomery, AL	182,406	79	20	177,857	76	20
Knoxville, TN	175,298	84	21	175,045	77	21
Columbus, GA	174,348	85	22	169,441	88	23
Chattanooga, TN	168,016	90	23	169,728	87	22
Little Rock, AR	167,974	91	24	167,602	89	24
GREENSBORO, NC	157,337	99	25	155,642	100	25
Hialeah, FL	154,713	103	26	145,254	108	28
RALEIGH, NC	154,211	104	27	150,255	105	27
Fort Lauderdale, FL	153,755	106	28	153,279	101	26
Newport News, VA	151,240	108	29	144,903	109	29
Savannah, GA	145,699	111	30	141,655	112	31
Huntsville, AL	145,421	112	31	142,513	111	30
WINSTON-SALEM, NC	140,846	115	32	138,584	116	32
Orlando, FL	134,255	121	33	128,291	124	33
Hampton, VA	124,966	127	34	122,617	128	34
Hollywood, FL	122,051	131	35	121,323	129	35
Chesapeake, VA	119,749	135	36	114,486	137	37
Macon, GA	118,730	136	37	116,896	135	36
Portsmouth, VA	105,807	153	38	104,577	154	38
Alexandria, VA	104,276	159	39	103,217	160	39
Tallahassee, FL	102,579	166	40	101,482	166	40
Columbia, SC	101,457	169	41	101,202	168	41
DURHAM, NC	101,242	171	42	100,538	170	42
Roanoke, VA	100,187	175	43	100,220	171	43

Population of Incorporated Places

The chart below shows the actual population of incorporated places in North Carolina in 1970 and 1980, and the estimated population for 1986.

City	County Location	1970 Census	1980 Census	1986 Estimated
Aberdeen	Moore	1,592	1,945	2,347
Ahoskie	Hertford	5,105	4,887	4,911
Alamance	Alamance	NA	320	315
Albemarle	Stanly	11,126	15,110	15,218
Alexander Mills	Rutherford	988	643	615
Alliance	Pamlico	577	616	645
Andrews	Cherokee	1,384	1,621	1,739
Angier	Harnett	1,431	1,709	1,887
Ansonville	Anson	694	794	815
Apex	Wake	2,234	2,847	3,966
Arapahoe	Pamlico	212	467	501
Archdale	Guilford, Randolph	4,874	5,745	6,114
Arlington	Yadkin	711	872	920
Asheboro	Randolph	10,797	15,252	15,886
Asheville	Buncombe	57,929	53,583	60,218
Askewville	Bertie	247	227	227
Atkinson	Pender	325	298	323
Atlantic	Carteret	NA	NA	811
Atlantic Beach	Carteret	300	941	1,578
Aulander	Bertie	947	1,214	1,307
Aurora	Beaufort	620	698	737
Autryville	Sampson	213	228	241
Ayden	Pitt	3,450	4,361	4,787
Bailey	Nash	724	685	709
Bakersville	Mitchell	409	373	386
Banner Elk	Avery	754	1,087	1,082
Bath	Beaufort	231	207	242
Battleboro	Edgecombe, Nash	562	632	661
Bayboro	Pamlico	665	759	801
Beargrass	Martin	99	82	79
Beaufort	Carteret	3,368	3,826	4,584
Belhaven	Beaufort	2,259	2,430	2,512
Belmont	Gaston	5,054	4,607	5,394
Belville	Brunswick	59	102	194
Belwood	Cleveland	736	613	601
Benson	Johnston	2,267	2,792	3,047
Bessemer City	Gaston	4,991	4,787	4,933
Bethel	Pitt	1,514	1,825	1,929
Beulaville	Duplin	1,156	1,060	1,062
Biltmore Forest	Buncombe	1,298	1,499	1,623
Biscoe	Montgomery	1,244	1,334	1,434
Black Creek	Wilson	449	523	610
Black Mountain	Buncombe	3,204	4,083	4,463
Bladenboro	Bladen	783	1,428	1,535
Blowing Rock	Caldwell, Watauga	801	1,337	1,506
Boiling Springs Lake	Brunswick	245	998	1,448
Boiling Springs	Cleveland	2,284	2,381	2,405
Bolivia	Brunswick	185	252	332
Bolton	Columbus	534	563	605
Boone	Watauga	8,754	10,191	11,360

City	County Location	1970 Census	1980 Census	1986 Estimated
Boonville	Yadkin	687	1,028	1,167
Bostic	Rutherford	289	476	512
Brevard	Transylvania	5,243	5,323	5,802
Bridgeton	Craven	520	461	505
Broadway	Lee	694	908	1,127
Brookford	Catawba	590	467	483
Brunswick	Columbus	206	223	232
Bryson City	Swain	1,290	1,556	1,626
Bunn	Franklin	284	505	665
Burgaw	Pender	1,744	1,586	1,887
Burlington	Alamance	35,930	37,266	38,354
Burnsville	Yancey	1,348	1,452	1,660
Calabash	Brunswick	154	128	160
Calypso	Duplin	462	689	711
Cameron	Moore	204	225	256
Candor	Montgomery	561	868	910
Canton	Haywood	5,158	4,631	4,796
Cape Carteret	Carteret	616	944	1,236
Carolina Beach	New Hanover	1,663	2,000	2,528
Carrboro	Orange	5,058	7,336	10,080
Carthage	Moore	1,034	925	967
Cary	Wake	7,686	21,763	37,305
Casar	Cleveland	339	346	344
Cashiers	Jackson	230	553	625
Castalia	Nash	265	358	391
Caswell Beach	Brunswick	28	110	159
Catawba	Catawba	565	509	526
Centerville	Franklin	123	135	154
Cerro Gordo	Columbus	322	295	295
Chadbourn	Columbus	2,213	1,975	1,983
Chadwick Acres	Onslow	12	15	18
Chapel Hill	Durham, Orange	26.199	32,421	35,251
Charlotte	Mecklenburg	241,420	314,447	368,212
Cherryville	Gaston	5,258	4,844	4,932
China Grove	Rowan	1,788	2,081	2,159
Chocowinity	Beaufort	566	644	786
Claremont	Catawba	788	880	974
Clarkton	Bladen	662	664	816
Clayton	Johnston	3,103	4,091	5,370
Cleveland	Rowan	614	595	649
Clinton	Sampson	7,157	7,552	6,876
Clyde	Haywood	814	1,008	1,055
Coakley	Edgecombe	NA	NA	85
Coats	Harnett	1,051	1,385	1,570
Cofield	Hertford	318	465	535
Colerain	Bertie	373	284	266
Columbia	Tyrrell	902	758	828
Columbus	Polk	731	727	1,027
Como	Hertford	211	89	88
Concord	Cabarrus	18,464	16,942	28,171
Conetoe	Edgecombe	160	215	243
Conover	Catawba	3,355	4,245	4,909
Conway	Northampton	694	678	677
Corneilus	Mecklenburg	1,296	1,460	2,237
Cove City	Craven	485	500	561

City	County Location	1970 Census	1980 Census	1986 Estimated
Cramerton	Gaston	2,142	1,869	1,852
Creedmoore	Granville	1,405	1,641	1,851
Creswell	Washington	633	426	386
Crossnore	Avery	264	297	301
Dallas	Gaston	4,059	3,340	3,726
Danbury	Stokes	152	140	149
Davidson	Iredell, Mecklenburg	2,931	3,241	3,710
Dellview	Gaston	11	7	6
Denton	Davidson	1,017	949	1,086
Dillsboro	Jackson	215	179	182
Dobson	Surry	933	1,222	1,334
Dortches	Nash	686	885	978
Dover	Craven	585	600	631
Drexel	Burke	1,431	1,392	1,575
Dublin	Bladen	283	477	486
Dudley	Wayne	199	NA	278
Dundarrach	Hoke	53	NA	58
Dunn	Harnett	8,302	8,962	9,235
Durham	Durham	95,438	100,831	115,750
Earl	Cleveland	195	206	230
East Arcadia	Bladen	556	461	437
East Bend	Yadkin	485	602	629
East Laurinburg	Scotland	487	536	536
East Spencer	Rowan	2,217	2,150	2,249
Eden	Rockingham	15,871	15,672	15,658
Edenton	Chowan	4,956	5,357	5,729
Elizabeth City	Camden, Pasquotank	14,381	14,004	14,342
Elizabethtown	Bladen	1,418	3,551	3,444
Elkin	Surry, Wilkes	2,899	2,858	3,431
Elk Park	Avery	503	535	550
Ellenboro	Rutherford	465	560	587
Ellerbe	Richmond	913	1,415	1,573
Elm City	Wilson	1,201	1,561	1,674
Elon College	Alamance	2,150	2,873	4,140
Emerald Isle	Carteret	122	865	1,652
Enfield	Halifax	3,272	2,995	2,941
Erwin	Harnett	2,852	2,828	2,977
Eureka	Wayne	263	303	303
Everetts	Martin	198	213	245
Fair Bluff	Columbus	1,039	1,095	1,095
Fairmont	Robeson	2,827	2,658	2,623
Faison	Duplin	598	636	683
Faith	Rowan	506	552	659
Falcon	Cumberland, Sampson	357	339	327
Falkland	Pitt	130	118	125
Fallston	Cleveland	301	614	691
Farmville	Pitt	4,424	4,707	4,834
Fayetteville	Cumberland	53,510	59,507	71,108
Forest City	Rutherford	7,179	7,688	8,088
Fountain	Pitt	434	424	473
Four Oaks	Johnston	1,057	1,049	1,400
Foxfire	Moore	9	153	260
Franklin	Macon	2,336	2,640	3,084
Franklinton	Franklin	1,459	1,394	1,665
Franklinville	Randolph	794	607	661

City	County Location	1970 Census	1980 Census	1986 Estimated
Fremont	Wayne	1,596	1,736	1,848
Fuquay-Varina	Wake	3,576	3,110	3,860
Garland	Sampson	656	885	979
Garner	Wake	4,923	10,073	12,980
Garysburg	Northampton	231	1,434	1,379
Gaston	Northampton	1,105	883	1,025
Gastonia	Gaston	47,322	47,333	52,989
Gatesville	Gates	338	363	384
Germanton	Stokes	NA	NA	111
Gibson	Scotland	502	533	539
Gibsonville	Alamance, Guilford	2,019	2,865	3,497
Glen Alpine	Burke	797	645	667
Godwin	Cumberland	129	233	272
Gold Point	Martin	108	NA	105
Goldsboro	Wayne	26,960	31,871	34,710
Goldston	Chatham	364	353	349
Graham	Alamance	8,172	8,674	9,107
Graingers	Lenoir	NA	NA	79
Granite Falls	Caldwell	2,388	2,580	2,955
Granite Quarry	Rowan	1,344	1,294	1,579
Greenevers	Duplin	424	477	502
Greensboro	Guilford	144,076	155,642	181,039
Greenville	Pitt	29,063	35,740	41,912
Grifton	Lenoir, Pitt	1,860	2,179	2,333
Grimesland	Pitt	394	453	515
Grover	Cleveland	555	597	638
Halifax	Halifax	335	253	240
Hamilton	Martin	579	638	668
Hamlet	Richmond	4,627	4,720	6,582
Harmony	Iredell	377	470	569
Harrells	Duplin, Sampson	249	255	280
Harrellsville	Hertford	165	151	149
Harrisburg	Cabarrus	1,098	1,433	1,887
Hassell	Martin	160	109	103
Havelock	Craven	3,012	17,718	23,067
Haw River	Alamance	1,944	1,858	1,946
Hayesville	Clay	428	376	402
Haywood	Chatham	NA	190	201
Hazelwood	Haywood	2,057	1,811	1,829
Henderson	Vance	13,896	13,522	16,226
Hendersonville	Henderson	6,443	6,862	8,436
Hertford	Perquimans	2,023	1,941	2,320
Hickory	Burke, Catawba	20,569	20,757	25,558
Highlands	Macon	583	653	1,022
High Point	(a)	63,229	63,380	66,791
High Shoals	Gaston, Lincoln	563	586	663
Hildebran	Burke	521	628	639
Hillsborough	Orange	1,444	3,019	3,336
Hobgood	Halifax	530	483	496
Hoffman	Richmond	434	389	367
Holden Beach	Brunswick	136	232	349
Holly Ridge	Onslow	415	465	500
Holly Springs	Wake	697	688	772
Hollyville	Pamlico	NA	100	105

City	County Location	1970 Census	1980 Census	1986 Estimated
Hookerton	Greene	441	460	443
Hope Mills	Cumberland	1,866	5,412	8,422
Hot Springs	Madison	653	678	739
Hudson	Caldwell	2,820	2,888	3,077
Huntersville	Mecklenburg	1,538	1,294	1,378
Indian Beach	Carteret	245	54	68
Indian Trail	Union	405	811	1,030
Jackson	Northampton	762	720	709
Jackson Springs	Moore	NA	NA	248
Jacksonville	Onslow	16,289	17,056	29,012
Jamestown	Guilford	1,297	2,148	2,461
Jamesville	Martin	533	604	663
Jason	Greene	NA	NA	76
Jefferson	Ashe	943	1,086	1,146
Jonesville	Yadkin	1,659	1,752	1,711
Jupiter	Buncombe	208	NA	310
Kelford	Bertie	295	254	251
Kenansville	Duplin	762	931	977
Kenly	Johnston, Wilson	1,370	1,433	1,563
Kernersville	Forsyth	4,815	6,802	8,462
Kill Devil Hills	Dare	357	1,796	2,873
Kings Mountain	Cleveland, Gaston	8,465	9,080	9,314
Kinston	Lenoir	23,020	25,234	25,718
Kittrell	Vance	427	255	207
Knightdale	Wake	815	985	1,252
Kure Beach	New Hanover	394	611	917
LaGrange	Lenoir	2,679	3,147	3,259
Lake Lure	Rutherford	456	488	577
Lake Waccamaw	Columbus	924	1,133	1,283
Landis	Rowan	2,297	2,092	2,339
Lansing	Ashe	283	194	189
Lasker	Northampton	114	96	97
Lattimore	Cleveland	257	237	240
Laurel Park	Henderson	581	764	1,052
Laurinburg	Scotland	8,859	11,480	12,053
Lawndale	Cleveland	544	469	667
Lawrence	Edgecombe	NA	NA	106
Leggett	Edgecombe	120	99	99
Lenoir	Caldwell	14,705	13,748	14,542
Lewiston	Bertie	327	459	703
Lexington	Davidson	17,205	15,711	16,317
Liberty	Randolph	2,167	1,997	1,998
Lilesville	Anson	641	588	598
Lillington	Harnett	1,155	1,948	1,995
Lincolnton	Lincoln	5,293	4,879	5,735
Linden	Cumberland	205	365	424
Linville	Avery	NA	244	257
Littleton	Halifax	903	820	838
Locust	Stanly	1,484	1,590	1,723
Long Beach	Brunswick	493	1,844	2,961
Longview	Burke, Catawba	3,360	3,587	3,983
Louisburg	Franklin	2,941	3,238	3,636
Love Valley	Iredell	40	55	61

City	County Location	1970 Census	1980 Census	1986 Estimated
Lowell	Gaston	3,307	2,917	2,894
Lucama	Wilson	610	1,070	1,155
Lumber Bridge	Robeson	117	171	200
Lumberton	Robeson	16,961	18,241	19,830
McAdenville	Gaston	950	947	911
McDonalds	Robeson	80	117	127
McFarlan	Anson	140	133	138
Macclesfield	Edgecombe	536	504	535
Macon	Warren	179	153	157
Madison	Rockingham	2,018	2,806	2,871
Maggie Valley	Haywood	159	202	243
Magnolia	Duplin	614	592	609
Maiden	Catawba, Lincoln	2,416	2,574	2,858
Manteo	Dare	547	902	1,037
Marietta	Robeson	70	NA	189
Marion	McDowell	3,335	3,684	3,652
Marshall	Madison	982	809	807
Mars Hill	Madison	1,623	2,126	1,983
Marshville	Union	1,405	2,011	2,256
Matthews	Mecklenburg	783	1,648	5,963
Maury	Greene	421	NA	449
Maxton	Robeson, Scotland	1,885	2,711	2,821
Mayodan	Rockingham	2,875	2,627	2,544
Maysville	Jones	912	877	1,001
Mebane	Alamance, Orange	2,573	2,782	3,702
Mesic	Pamlico	369	390	412
Micro	Johnston	300	438	453
Middleburg	Vance	149	185	214
Middlesex	Nash	729	837	855
Mildred	Edgecombe	NA	NA	86
Milton	Caswell	235	235	246
Minnesott Beach	Pamlico	41	171	215
Mint Hill	Mecklenburg	2,262	7,915	12,600
Mocksville	Davie	2,529	2,637	3,487
Monroe	Union	11,282	12,639	16,203
Montreat	Buncombe	581	741	728
Mooresboro	Cleveland	453	405	405
Mooresville	Iredell	8,808	8,575	9,098
Morehead City	Carteret	5,233	4,359	6,760
Morganton	Burke	13,625	13,763	14,653
Morrisville	Wake	209	251	575
Morven	Anson	562	765	803
Mount Airy	Surry	7,325	6,962	7,197
Mount Gilead	Montgomery	1,286	1,423	1,463
Mount Holly	Gaston	5,107	4,530	4,688
Mount Olive	Duplin, Wayne	4,914	4,876	5,246
Mount Pleasant	Cabarrus	1,174	1,210	1,290
Murfreesboro	Hertford	4,418	3,007	3,235
Murphy	Cherokee	2,082	2,070	2,311
Nags Head	Dare	414	1,020	1,615
Nashville	Nash	1,670	2,678	3,530
Navassa	Brunswick	487	439	479
New Bern	Craven	14,660	14,557	18,729
New London	Stanly	285	454	505
Newland	Avery	524	722	767

City	County Location	1970 Census	1980 Census	1986 Estimated
Newport	Carteret	1,735	1,883	2,582
Newton	Catawba	7,857	7,624	8,868
Newton Grove	Sampson	546	564	574
Norlina	Warren	969	901	905
Norman	Richmond	157	252	272
North Wilkesboro	Wilkes	3,357	3,260	3,482
Norwood	Stanly	1,896	1,818	1,829
Oak City	Martin	559	475	454
Oakboro	Stanly	568	587	609
Ocean Isle Beach	Brunswick	78	143	322
Old Fort	McDowell	676	752	786
Old Sparta	Edgecombe	NA	NA	75
Oriental	Pamlico	445	536	650
Orrum	Robeson	162	167	164
Oxford	Granville	7,178	7,603	8,492
Pantego	Beaufort	218	185	181
Parkton	Robeson	550	564	577
Parmele	Martin	373	484	516
Patterson Springs	Cleveland	478	731	769
Peachland	Anson	556	506	542
Pembroke	Robeson	1,982	2,698	3,138
Pikeville	Wayne	580	662	716
Pilot Mountain	Surry	1,309	1,090	1,299
Pinebluff	Moore	570	935	1,043
Pinehurst	Moore	1,056	NA	2,620
Pine Knoll Shores	Carteret	62	646	905
Pine Level	Johnston	983	953	1,220
Pinetops	Edgecombe	1,379	1,465	1,574
Pineville	Mecklenburg	1,948	1,525	2,141
Pink Hill	Lenoir	522	644	635
Pittsboro	Chatham	1,447	1,332	1,796
Plymouth	Washington	4,774	4,571	4,896
Polkton	Anson	845	762	739
Polkville	Cleveland	494	528	631
Pollocksville	Jones	456	318	296
Powellsville	Bertie	247	320	363
Princeton	Johnston	1,044	1,034	1,210
Princeville	Edgecombe	654	1,508	1,565
Proctorville	Robeson	157	205	223
Raeford	Hoke	3,180	3,630	4,237
Raleigh	Wake	122,830	150,255	201,447
Ramseur	Randolph	1,328	1,162	1,225
Randleman	Randolph	2,312	2,156	2,424
Ranlo	Gaston	2,092	1,774	1,769
Raynham	Robeson	75	83	87
Red Oak	Nash	359	314	342
Red Springs	Robeson	3,383	3,607	3,709
Reidsville	Rockingham	13,636	12,492	12,309
Rennert	Robeson	175	178	190
Rhodhiss	Burke, Caldwell	784	727	744
Rich Square	Northampton	1,254	1,057	1,082
Richfield	Stanly	306	373	377
Richlands	Onslow	935	825	945
Roanoke Rapids	Halifax	13,508	14,702	15,467
Robbins	Moore	1,059	1,256	1,336

City	County Location	1970 Census	1980 Census	1986 Estimated
Robbinsville	Graham	777	1,370	837
Robersonville	Martin	1,910	1,981	2,007
Rockingham	Richmond	5,852	8,300	8,567
Rockwell	Rowan	999	1,339	1,480
Rocky Mount	Edgecombe, Nash	34,284	41,283	47,214
Rolesville	Wake	533	381	565
Ronda	Wilkes	465	457	436
Roper	Washington	649	795	791
Rose Hill	Duplin	1,448	1,508	1,497
Roseboro	Sampson	1,235	1,227	1,422
Rosman	Transylvania	407	512	515
Rowland	Robeson	1,358	1,841	2,003
Roxboro	Person	5,370	7,532	8,058
Roxobel	Bertie	347	278	276
Rural Hall	Forsyth	1,289	1,336	1,943
Ruth	Rutherford	360	381	411
Rutherford College	Burke	821	1,108	1,319
Rutherfordton	Rutherford	3,245	3,434	3,582
Salemburg	Sampson	669	742	719
Salisbury	Rowan	22,515	22,677	24,086
Saluda	Polk	546	607	671
Sanford	Lee	11,716	14,773	16,876
Saratoga	Wilson	391	381	379
Scotland Neck	Halifax	2,869	2,834	2,747
Seaboard	Northampton	611	687	721
Seagrove	Randolph	354	294	301
Selma	Johnston	4,356	4,762	5,129
Seven Devils	Avery, Watauga	0	54	81
Seven Springs	Wayne	188	166	168
Severn	Northampton	356	309	304
Shady Forest	Brunswick	17	43	
Shallotte	Brunswick	597	680	1,035
Sharpsburg	(b)	789	997	1,441
Shelby	Cleveland	16,328	15,310	15,508
Siler City	Chatham	4,689	4,446	4,788
Simpson	Pitt	383	407	418
Sims	Wilson	205	192	205
Smithfield	Johnston	6,677	7,288	7,656
Snow Hill	Greene	1,359	1,374	1,401
Southern Pines	Moore	5,937	8,620	9,864
Southern Shores	Dare	75	395	959
Southport	Brunswick	2,220	2,824	3,499
Sparta	Alleghany	1,304	1,687	2,078
Speed	Edgecombe	142	95	95
Spencer	Rowan	3,075	2,938	2,911
Spencer Mountain	Gaston	300	169	157
Spindale	Rutherford	3,848	4,246	4,274
Spring Hope	Nash	1,334	1,254	1,270
Spring Lake	Cumberland	3,968	6,273	7,175
Spruce Pine	Mitchell	2,333	2,282	2,424
St. Pauls	Robeson	2,011	1,639	1,891
Staley	Randolph	239	204	219
Stallings	Union	726	1,826	2,596
Stanfield	Stanly	458	463	510
Stanley	Gaston	2,336	2,341	2,612

City	County Location	1970 Census	1980 Census	1986 Estimated
Stantonsburg	Wilson	869	920	904
Star	Montgomery	892	816	799
Statesville	Iredell	20,007	18,622	19,581
Stedman	Cumberland	505	723	887
Stem	Granville	242	222	248
Stoneville	Rockingham	1,030	1,054	1,047
Stonewall	Pamlico	335	360	376
Stovall	Granville	405	417	452
Sunset Beach	Brunswick	108	304	440
Surf City	Pender	166	391	551
Swansboro	Onslow	1,207	976	1,270
Sylva	Jackson	1,561	1,699	2,055
Tabor City	Columbus	2,400	2,710	2,694
Tarboro	Edgecombe	9,425	8,634	11,109
Tar Heel	Bladen	87	118	125
Taylorsville	Alexander	1,231	1,103	1,181
Teachey	Duplin	219	373	416
Thomasville	Davidson	15,230	14,144	15,785
Topsail Beach	Pender	108	264	307
Trent Woods	Craven	719	1,177	1,768
Trenton	Jones	539	407	385
Troutman	Iredell	797	1,360	1,475
Troy	Montgomery	2,429	2,702	2,719
Tryon	Polk	1,951	1,796	1,944
Turkey	Sampson	329	417	404
Unionville	Union	NA	NA	177
Valdese	Burke	3,182	3,364	4,098
Vanceboro	Craven	758	833	950
Vandemere	Pamlico	379	335	344
Vass	Moore	885	828	888
Waco	Cleveland	245	322	353
Wade	Cumberland	315	474	527
Wadesboro	Anson	3,977	4,206	4,418
Wagram	Scotland	718	617	581
Wake Forest	Wake	3,148	3,780	4,605
Wallace	Duplin, Pender	2,905	2,903	2,980
Walnut Cove	Stokes	1,213	1,147	1,152
Walnut Creek	Wayne	81	343	413
Walstonburg	Greene	176	181	198
Warrenton	Warren	1,035	908	1,004
Warsaw	Duplin	2,701	2,910	2,993
Washington	Beaufort	8,961	8,418	9,467
Washington Park	Beaufort	517	514	553
Watha	Pender	181	196	211
Waxhaw	Union	1,248	1,208	1,342
Waynesville	Haywood	6,488	6,765	7,454
Weaverville	Buncombe	1,280	1,495	2,223
Webster	Jackson	181	200	226
Weldon	Halifax	2,304	1,844	1,724
Wendell	Wake	1,929	2,222	3,009
West Jefferson	Ashe	889	822	1,008
Whispering Pines	Moore	362	1,160	1,485
Whitakers	Edgecombe, Nash	926	924	940
White Lake	Bladen	232	968	1,122
Whiteville	Columbus	4,195	5,565	5,661

City	County Location	1970 Census	1980 Census	1986 Estimated
Wilkesboro	Wilkes	2,038	2,335	2,556
Williamsboro	Vance	NA	59	61
Williamston	Martin	6,570	6,159	6,258
Wilmington	New Hanover	46,169	44,000	54,967
Wilson	Wilson	29,347	34,424	36,767
Windsor	Bertie	2,199	2,126	2,148
Winfall	Perquimans	581	634	773
Wingate	Union	2,569	2,615	2,711
Winston-Salem	Forsyth	133,683	131,885	148,631
Winterville	Pitt	1,437	2,052	2,160
Winton	Hertford	917	825	840
Woodfin	Buncombe	2,831	3,260	3,431
Woodland	Northampton	744	861	891
Woodville	Bertie	253	212	
Wrightsville Beach	New Hanover	1,701	2,910	3,281
Yadkinville	Yadkin	2,232	2,216	2,278
Yaupon Beach	Brunswick	334	569	832
Youngsville	Franklin	555	486	562
Zebulon	Wake	1,839	2,055	2,889

(a)Davidson, Guilford, and Randolph counties.
(b)Edgecombe, Nash, and Wilson counties.
NA—Not Available
*Editor's note: Kannapolis omitted. Cabarrus and Rowan counties. 1970—NA; 1980—30,303; 1986—32,158.

50 Largest Municipalities

The 50 largest municipalities in North Carolina ranked by size, based on 1986 population estimates.

Municipality	County(ies)	July 1986 Estimate
Charlotte	Mecklenburg	368,212
Raleigh	Wake	201,447
Greensboro	Guilford	181,039
Winston-Salem	Forsyth	148,631
Durham	Durham	115,750
	Orange	
Fayetteville	Cumberland	71,108
High Point	Guilford	66,791
	Davidson	
	Randolph	
Asheville	Buncombe	60,218
Wilmington	New Hanover	54,967
Gastonia	Gaston	52,989
Rocky Mount	Nash	47,214
	Edgecombe	
Greenville	Pitt	41,912
Burlington	Alamance	38,354
Cary	Wake	37,305
Wilson	Wilson	36,767
Chapel Hill	Orange	35,251
	Durham	
Goldsboro	Wayne	34,710
Kannapolis	Cabarrus	32,158
	Rowan	
Jacksonville	Onslow	29,012
Concord	Cabarrus	28,171
Kinston	Lenoir	25,718
Hickory	Catawba	25,558
	Burke	
Salisbury	Rowan	24,086
Havelock	Craven	23,067
Lumberton	Robeson	19,830
Statesville	Iredell	19,581
New Bern	Craven	18,729
Sanford	Lee	16,876
Lexington	Davidson	16,317
Henderson	Vance	16,226
Monroe	Union	16,203
Asheboro	Randolph	15,886
Thomasville	Davidson	15,785
Eden	Rockingham	15,658
Shelby	Cleveland	15,508

Municipality	County(ies)	July 1986 Estimate
Roanoke Rapids	Halifax	15,467
Albemarle	Stanly	15,218
Morganton	Burke	14,653
Lenoir	Caldwell	14,542
Elizabeth City	Pasquotank Camden	14,342
Garner	Wake	12,980
Mint Hill	Mecklenburg	12,600
Reidsville	Rockingham	12,309
Laurinburg	Scotland	12,053
Boone	Watauga	11,360
Tarboro	Edgecombe	11,109
Carrboro	Orange	10,080
Southern Pines	Moore	9,864
Washington	Beaufort	9,467
Kings Mountain	Cleveland Gaston	9,314

Population, Past

The following figures give the population of North Carolina at each decade since 1790, when the region which became today's state of Tennessee was split off as the "Territory of the United States South of the River Ohio." Also given are figures showing the percentage increase in population for each decade and the population of North Carolina as a percentage of the entire nation's population.

Year	Population	% Increase	% of U.S.
1790	393,751		10.0
1800	478,103	21.4	9.0
1810	555,500	16.2	7.7
1820	638,829	15.0	6.6
1830	737,987	15.5	5.7
1840	753,419	2.1	4.4
1850	869,039	15.3	3.7
1860	992,622	14.2	3.2
1870	1,071,361	7.9	2.8
1880	1,399,750	30.7	2.8
1890	1,617,949	15.6	2.6
1900	1,893,810	17.1	2.5
1910	2,206,287	16.5	2.4
1920	2,559,123	16.0	2.4
1930	3,170,276	23.9	2.6
1940	3,571,623	12.7	2.7
1950	4,061,929	13.7	2.7
1960	4,556,155	12.2	2.5
1970	5,082,059	11.5	2.5
1980	5,881,385	15.7	2.6

Projected Population for 1990 by Race and Sex

County	Median Age	White Male	White Female	Non-white Male	Non-white Female	Total
Alamance	37.1	38,997	44,615	9,964	11,999	105,575
Alexander	33.1	12,897	13,326	853	826	27,902
Alleghany	37.4	4,622	5,009	80	94	9,805
Anson	33.4	6,711	7,712	5,510	6,797	26,730
Ashe	37.0	11,333	12,253	97	122	23,805
Avery	33.3	7,415	7,773	132	76	15,396
Beaufort	34.5	15,067	16,590	6,097	7,468	45,222
Bertie	33.9	3,991	4,351	5,890	7,152	21,384
Bladen	34.0	9,170	9,606	5,551	6,703	31,030
Brunswick	33.6	21,734	22,739	4,833	5,698	55,004
Buncombe	36.3	74,833	84,620	7,264	8,733	175,450
Burke	34.6	34,835	37,483	2,775	2,990	78,083
Cabarrus	35.3	40,392	44,307	5,586	6,728	97,013
Caldwell	34.2	32,962	34,876	1,683	2,065	71,586
Camden	35.0	2,101	2,149	750	878	5,878
Carteret	34.7	25,139	25,808	2,436	2,625	56,008
Caswell	34.5	7,178	7,313	4,264	4,808	23,563
Catawba	34.0	51,480	56,020	5,638	6,366	119,504
Chatham	35.9	13,929	14,849	4,195	4,604	37,577
Cherokee	37.6	9,691	10,709	364	455	21,219
Chowan	36.3	3,798	4,315	2,481	3,288	13,882
Clay	38.4	3,706	3,814	19	26	7,565
Cleveland	34.1	33,139	36,500	8,336	9,912	87,887
Columbus	34.4	16,979	18,904	7,924	9,239	53,046
Craven	28.9	31,214	29,025	11,961	13,511	85,711
Cumberland	27.3	79,476	73,176	53,093	53,868	259,613
Currituck	33.2	6,675	6,473	789	798	14,735
Dare	35.7	10,160	10,345	636	762	21,903
Davidson	34.2	52,861	57,104	5,895	6,796	122,656
Davie	34.3	13,602	14,194	1,389	1,521	30,706
Duplin	34.4	13,413	14,542	6,382	7,785	42,122
Durham	31.6	48,555	54,887	31,294	39,264	174,000
Edgecombe	32.6	13,343	15,110	14,249	18,215	60,917
Forsyth	34.5	93,679	105,323	32,368	39,770	271,140
Franklin	34.9	10,723	11,397	6,563	7,959	36,642
Gaston	33.9	73,210	81,326	10,196	12,582	177,314
Gates	36.2	2,410	2,460	2,489	2,602	9,961
Graham	34.9	3,315	3,427	209	196	7,147
Granville	35.7	11,109	11,447	8,484	8,847	39,887
Greene	33.2	4,704	4,885	3,432	3,845	16,866
Guilford	34.1	113,592	127,570	44,084	52,244	337,490
Halifax	34.5	13,442	14,929	13,235	14,998	56,604
Harnett	31.1	24,789	26,582	7,171	8,131	66,673
Haywood	38.2	23,192	25,471	481	505	49,649
Henderson	38.8	33,020	36,863	1,214	1,312	72,409
Hertford	34.3	5,062	5,500	6,419	7,474	24,455
Hoke	29.5	5,177	5,458	6,673	7,478	24,786
Hyde	33.8	2,085	2,116	782	946	5,929
Iredell	34.9	36,368	39,496	7,539	8,560	91,963
Jackson	30.9	11,404	12,486	1,514	1,635	27,039

County	Median Age	White Male	White Female	Non-white Male	Non-white Female	Total
Johnston	34.8	32,366	35,204	6,948	8,230	82,748
Jones	34.2	2,676	3,092	1,780	2,328	9,876
Lee	33.5	16,480	18,411	4,274	5,056	44,221
Lenoir	34.6	17,596	19,331	10,400	13,134	60,461
Lincoln	33.5	21,630	22,945	1,923	2,125	48,623
Macon	40.6	11,499	12,898	288	142	24,827
Madison	34.0	8,557	8,917	106	106	17,686
Martin	34.5	7,181	8,116	5,400	6,486	27,183
McDowell	34.6	16,981	18,291	713	880	36,865
Mecklenburg	33.0	160,749	174,795	67,298	79,563	482,405
Mitchell	37.9	7,020	7,513	33	45	14,611
Montgomery	34.1	9,290	9,417	2,689	3,285	24,681
Moore	37.2	22,978	25,036	5,279	6,017	59,310
Nash	34.3	24,294	26,933	10,139	12,326	73,692
New Hanover	33.2	45,561	50,097	11,567	14,142	121,367
Northampton	35.2	4,523	4,646	6,470	7,037	22,676
Onslow	23.9	56,119	40,995	20,667	14,762	132,543
Orange	28.4	34,637	38,231	7,557	8,909	89,334
Pamlico	36.4	3,876	4,207	1,548	1,817	11,448
Pasquotank	32.6	9,539	10,319	4,958	5,885	30,701
Pender	35.0	8,748	8,949	4,216	5,053	26,966
Perquimans	36.6	3,440	3,922	1,761	2,040	11,163
Person	34.5	10,447	11,497	4,443	5,150	31,537
Pitt	29.0	31,542	34,936	15,679	19,604	101,761
Polk	42.6	6,702	7,562	516	604	15,384
Randolph	34.5	46,807	50,618	2,919	3,384	103,728
Richmond	34.5	16,579	18,124	5,481	6,493	46,677
Robeson	30.8	19,372	21,541	31,296	36,574	108,783
Rockingham	34.5	33,026	36,073	8,091	9,581	86,771
Rowan	36.1	43,408	47,278	7,941	9,096	107,723
Rutherford	35.4	24,124	26,734	3,493	4,386	58,737
Sampson	34.7	15,907	17,425	8,103	9,269	50,704
Scotland	31.4	9,314	9,910	6,989	8,398	34,611
Stanly	35.6	21,456	23,584	2,894	3,400	51,334
Stokes	32.8	16,796	18,044	1,141	1,143	37,124
Surry	35.5	28,310	31,259	1,587	1,649	62,805
Swain	35.0	3,935	4,471	1,357	1,565	11,328
Transylvania	36.4	12,513	13,653	871	727	27,764
Tyrrell	34.6	1,314	1,417	614	813	4,158
Union	31.6	35,016	37,134	6,173	7,146	85,469
Vance	33.8	10,657	11,878	8,101	9,301	39,937
Wake	31.4	153,396	160,536	42,907	47,912	404,751
Warren	36.2	2,863	3,149	4,882	5,693	16,587
Washington	32.6	3,772	4,232	3,040	3,341	14,385
Watauga	28.9	17,212	18,244	361	347	36,164
Wayne	31.8	31,949	33,474	14,434	17,771	97,628
Wilkes	34.2	28,598	30,464	1,382	1,525	61,969
Wilson	33.3	19,665	22,474	10,526	12,757	65,422
Yadkin	36.4	14,032	14,859	749	727	30,367
Yancey	36.0	7,707	8,423	161	98	16,389
Total	33.2	2,410,838	2,588,491	743,408	859,078	6,601,815

PORTS AND WATERWAYS

North Carolina has two excellent deep-water ports at Morehead City and Wilmington, which have been described as the "fastest growing ports in the nation." In 1986, combined income from all port operations totaled $24.85 million, an increase of 9 percent over 1985. Combined port tonnage for calendar year 1986 totaled 7.02 million tons, an increase of 1.08 million tons over the previous year.

Two new international marketing offices were opened by the Port Authority in 1986, one in London and one in Hong Kong.

The Port of Wilmington has 6,040 feet of continuous wharf; 410,000 square feet of transit storage; 1.1 million square feet of warehouse space; and 120 acres of paved open storage. It is located along the east bank of the Cape Fear River, about 26 miles from the mouth of the river and two and one-half hours from the open sea.

The Morehead City Port has 5,300 feet of continuous wharf, 875,000 square feet of covered storage, and 14 acres of open storage. It is situated four miles from the open sea along the Newport River and Bogue Sound.

There is, in effect, a seaport 200 miles from the ocean. In 1984, the Charlotte Intermodal Terminal was opened by the Ports Authority to provide inland access. Since Charlotte is closer than competing ports to the industrial centers of western Virginia, Kentucky, Tennessee, Piedmont South Carolina, and Georgia, manufacturers can realize substantial savings by shipping containers on railroad flatcars to the Port of Wilmington.

Also of significance are two inland waterways. North Carolina is linked with the Eastern seaboard by the Intracoastal Waterway and more than 3 million tons of freight is moved through the state each year on its 12-foot channel.

Cape Fear is North Carolina's most navigable river. It connects the Port of Wilmington to Fayetteville, which is 115 miles inland.

Wanchese Seafood Industrial Park, the only government-financed project entirely devoted to seafood processing and commercial fishing in the nation, is on Roanoke Island. The park is administered and maintained by the state.

PUBLIC ASSISTANCE

The AFDC figures on the following chart represent the average monthly number of Aid to Families with Dependent Children recipients, and do not include foster-care recipients. The SSI figures represent the Supplemental Security Income to the aged, disabled, or blind persons receiving income assistance for the fiscal year. The state total was independently estimated.

County	AFDC 1984–85	AFDC 1985–86	1987 AFDC Avg. Monthly Recipients	1987 AFDC Average per Recipient	SSI and Other 1984–85
Alamance	1,341	1,350	1,290	$89.08	2,052
Alexander	155	173	172	88.68	393
Alleghany	144	147	123	88.65	381
Anson	911	986	1,003	83.10	910
Ashe	351	390	401	86.67	944
Avery	159	153	142	87.95	517
Beaufort	1,039	1,044	1,213	84.23	1,503
Bertie	1,047	1,177	1,222	82.07	1,216
Bladen	1,600	1,783	1,755	88.11	1,304
Brunswick	1,167	1,457	1,602	84.54	1,060
Buncombe	2,263	2,513	2,596	86.40	3,560
Burke	1,007	1,135	1,158	88.72	1,553
Cabarrus	1,183	1,400	1,460	84.47	1,431
Caldwell	972	1,108	1,076	88.98	1,058
Camden	124	142	148	87.73	118
Carteret	512	567	609	86.53	720
Caswell	681	628	637	88.80	771
Catawba	1,347	1,473	1,357	88.86	1,276
Chatham	462	494	500	89.00	674
Cherokee	272	345	335	87.87	828
Chowan	421	476	518	81.40	440
Clay	72	88	89	85.65	299
Cleveland	2,690	3,014	2,745	88.58	2,067
Columbus	2,684	2,859	2,867	85.83	2,630
Craven	2,091	2,280	2,324	83.92	1,877
Cumberland	10,278	10,828	10,972	85.02	4,104
Currituck	150	149	156	84.77	212
Dare	121	135	151	88.81	136
Davidson	1,586	1,710	1,772	88.37	1,428
Davie	229	263	250	90.49	494
Duplin	1,467	1,588	1,420	84.27	1,741
Durham	4,042	3,974	4,150	84.03	3,229
Edgecombe	3,757	3,844	3,936	85.33	2,116
Forsyth	7,597	7,529	7,363	83.85	4,109
Franklin	952	981	981	82.96	1,275
Gaston	4,640	5,290	5,100	87.70	2,713
Gates	313	342	332	86.69	331
Graham	151	168	177	82.25	284
Granville	861	818	820	89.29	1,383
Greene	825	888	800	84.72	408
Guilford	6,962	7,046	6,934	85.04	4,644
Halifax	4,852	5,025	5,014	85.07	2,928
Harnett	2,138	2,292	2,423	85.60	1,762
Haywood	850	998	1,013	88.57	1,207
Henderson	850	975	1,054	86.46	1,110

County	AFDC 1984–85	AFDC 1985–86	1987 AFDC Avg. Monthly Recipients	1987 AFDC Average per Recipient	SSI and Other 1984–85
Hertford	1,109	1,308	1,495	85.61	1,037
Hoke	1,284	1,379	1,395	78.88	615
Hyde	222	212	190	87.77	279
Iredell	1,589	1,828	1,782	84.39	1,346
Jackson	362	383	445	83.18	713
Johnston	1,752	1,770	1,852	84.12	2,882
Jones	445	471	406	87.73	383
Lee	968	1,033	1,139	82.06	971
Lenoir	2,483	2,806	2,826	82.73	2,496
Lincoln	721	792	744	87.60	574
Macon	102	152	438	87.33	647
Madison	381	420	1,262	83.23	872
Martin	1,125	1,126	610	83.29	1,063
McDowell	562	644	192	85.39	879
Mecklenburg	12,567	12,799	12,965	86.21	5,599
Mitchell	178	222	219	85.75	661
Montgomery	488	565	557	81.18	673
Moore	711	744	769	88.21	1,134
Nash	2,325	2,325	2,388	85.25	2,132
New Hanover	3,721	4,119	4,352	87.26	2,209
Northampton	1,888	1,943	1,910	87.02	1,218
Onslow	1,507	1,705	1,971	83.48	1,226
Orange	810	779	786	90.63	816
Pamlico	367	415	440	90.68	321
Pasquotank	1,354	1,480	1,453	86.87	710
Pender	950	1,013	1,098	86.62	851
Perquimans	513	541	564	86.07	344
Person	904	894	914	86.22	919
Pitt	4,404	4,884	5,091	83.63	3,247
Polk	115	119	131	86.90	249
Randolph	547	703	753	86.98	1,241
Richmond	1,267	1,351	1,285	83.32	1,450
Robeson	6,667	6,959	6,611	85.67	4,709
Rockingham	2,007	2,080	1,977	87.24	2,091
Rowan	1,482	1,635	1,674	83.09	1,388
Rutherford	1,295	1,424	1,466	82.84	1,546
Sampson	1,757	1,930	1,986	85.14	1,905
Scotland	2,490	2,717	2,624	83.33	1,305
Stanly	572	623	591	93.07	680
Stokes	434	488	489	89.78	575
Surry	747	845	823	88.03	1,702
Swain	391	391	411	87.17	481
Transylvania	337	391	442	85.65	437
Tyrrell	261	259	259	84.11	201
Union	1,653	1,629	1,602	81.03	935

County	AFDC 1984–85	AFDC 1985–86	1987 AFDC Avg. Monthly Recipients	1987 AFDC Average per Recipient	SSI and Other 1984–85
Vance	1,965	1,960	1,881	84.73	1,543
Wake	5,239	5,379	5,710	86.68	5,304
Warren	1,036	1,052	990	87.01	904
Washington	945	1,023	1,052	84.14	480
Watauga	340	375	368	89.72	601
Wayne	4,454	4,665	4,682	83.37	3,598
Wilkes	658	664	686	88.23	1,749
Wilson	3,231	3,542	3,855	84.90	2,291
Yadkin	276	255	290	87.70	715
Yancey	230	249	241	86.25	679
State Total	163,500	173,485	175,290	$85.46	140,768

RADIO STATIONS

Ahoskie

WQDK-FM
Rt. 1, Box 13 B
27910, 919-332-3101

WRCS-AM
Rt. 1, Box 13 B
27910, 919-332-3101

Albemarle

WABZ-FM
108 E. North St.
28001, 704-982-1010

WWWX-AM
P.O. Box 608
28001, 704-982-1020

WZKY-AM
Norman Communications, Inc.
P.O. Box 550
28002, 704-983-1580

Asheboro

WCSE-FM
Asheboro Broadcasting Co.
303 E. Salisbury St.
27203, 919-625-2187

WGWR-AM
Asheboro Broadcasting Co.
303 E. Salisbury St.
27203, 919-625-2187

Asheville

WBMU-FM
Greater Asheville Educational Radio Association
295 W. Haywood St.
28801, 704-253-1818

WCQS-FM
Western N.C. Public Radio Inc.
73 Broadway
28804, 704-253-6875

WISE-AM
WISE Radio Inc.
90 Lookout Rd.
28804, 704-257-2700

WLOS-Stereo FM
Wometco Skyway Broadcasting
288 Macon Ave.
28801, 704-255-0013

WKSF-FM
WISE Radio Inc.
90 Lookout Rd.
28804, 704-257-2700

WRAQ-AM
Greater Asheville Broadcasting Co.
70 Adams Hill Rd.
28806, 704-252-6703

WSKY-AM
Radio Asheville Inc.
P.O. Box 2956
28802, 704-253-4451

WWNC-AM
Multimedia Broadcasting Co.
P.O. Box 6447
28816, 704-253-3835

Beaufort

WBTB-AM
Crystal Coast Comm. Inc.
1400 Ocean St.
28516, 919-728-3131

Belhaven
WKJA-FM
Winfas Inc.
Rt. 2, Box 121-R
27810, 919-964-9292

Belmont
WCGC-AM
Central Broadcasting Co.
P.O. Box 888
28012, 704-825-8224

Benson
WPYB-AM
Benson Broadcasting Co.
P.O. Box 215
27504, 919-894-3009

Black Mountain
WFGW-AM
Blue Ridge Broadcasting Corp.
P.O. Box 158
28711, 704-669-8477

WMIT-FM
Blue Ridge Broadcasting Corp.
P.O. Box 158
28711, 704-669-8477

WONO-AM
Taylor Communications Inc.
P.O. Box 668
28711, 704-669-6451

Blowing Rock
WOIX-AM
Mountaineer Broadcasting Service Inc.
P.O. Box 345
28605, 704-262-1515

Boiling Springs
WGWG-FM
Gardner-Webb College
P.O. Box 876
28017, 704-434-2349

Boone
WASU-FM
Appalachian State University
Wey Hall
28608, 704-262-3170

WATA-AM
Wilkes Broadcasting Co.
P.O. Box 72
28607, 704-264-2411

Brevard
WGCR-AM
EDCO Communications
105 Mull Arcade
28712, 704-884-9427

WPNF-AM
Pisgah Broadcasting Co.
721 N. Broad St.
28712, 704-883-3511

Bridgeton
WSFL-FM
Great Southeast Broadcasters Inc.
P.O. Box 3436, New Bern
28560, 919-633-1219

Bryson City
WBHN-AM
Starcast South Inc.
P.O. Box 820
28713, 704-488-2682

Buie's Creek
WCCE-FM
Campbell University
P.O. Box 1030
27506, 919-893-5561

Burgaw
WVBS-AM
Resort Broadcasters of N.C. Inc.
P.O. Box 696
28425, 919-259-5836

WVBS-FM
201 N. Front Street, Wilmington
28402, 919-763-6611

Burlington-Graham
WBAG-AM
Falcon Communications Inc.
P.O. Box 2450
27216, 919-226-1189

WBAG-FM
Vilcom, Inc.
925 S. Main St.
27215, 919-227-4261

WBBB-AM
Research Triangle Broadcasting Ltd. Partnership
P.O. Box 1119
27215, 919-584-0126

WPCM-FM
Research Triangle Broadcasting Ltd. Partnership
P.O. Box 1119
27215, 919-584-0126

Burlington
WQRB-AM
Box 2450
27216

Burnsville
WKYK-AM
Mark Media Inc.
715 E. Main St.
28714, 704-682-3798

Camp LeJeune
WJIK-AM
Francon Inc.
239 Western Blvd., Jacksonville
28540, 919-353-9545

Canton
WPTL-AM
Skycountry Broadcasting Inc.
131 Pisgah Dr.
28716, 704-648-3576

WWIT-AM
Mountain Broadcasting Inc.
P.O. Box 1369
28716, 704-648-3588

Chadbourn
WVOE-AM
Ebony Enterprises Inc.
Rt. 3
28431, 919-654-4385

Chapel Hill
WCHL-AM
Village Broadcasting Inc.
P.O. Box 2127
27514, 919-942-8765

WRBY-AM
Carolina Triangle Broadcasting Inc.
4411 Chapel Hill Blvd., Durham
27707, 919-493-3507

WUNC-FM
U. of North Carolina at Chapel Hill
Swain Hall 044A
27514, 919-966-5454

WXYC-FM
Student Educational Broadcasting Inc.
Carolina Union, P.O. Box 51
27514, 919-962-7768

Charlotte
WAES-AM
CRB Broadcasting of N.C.
400 Radio Rd.
28216, 704-392-6191

WAME-AM
Jimmy Swaggart Evangelistic Assn.
P.O. Box 32068
28232, 704-377-5916

WBT-AM
Jefferson-Pilot Broadcasting Co.
One Julian Price Place
28208, 704-374-3751

WBCY-FM
Jefferson-Pilot Broadcasting Co.
One Julian Price Place
28208, 704-374-3751

WEZC-FM
E.Z. Communications Inc.
137 S. Kings Dr.
28204, 704-372-1104

WFAE-FM
University of North Carolina at Charlotte
UNCC
28223, 704-597-2555

WGIV-AM
Broadcast Ent. Natl.
P.O. Box 36856
28236, 704-333-0131

WGSP-AM
WGSP Inc.
219 E. Blvd.
28203, 704-375-1310

WHVN-AM
WHVN Inc.
P.O. Box 18614
28218, 704-570-1240

WIST-AM
Metrolina Broadcasting Corp.
1418 Elizabeth Avenue
28299, 704-376-3511

WLVK-FM
Capitol Broadcasting Corp.
4701 Hedgemore Dr. #801
28209, 704-529-0097

WQCC-AM
Glinter Too Inc.
4500 N. Tryon St.
28134, 704-597-1540

WROQ-FM
Sis Radio Inc.
400 Radio Rd.
28216, 704-392-6191

WSOC-AM
Cox Communications, Inc.
P.O. Box 34665
28234, 704-335-4700

WSOC-FM
Carolina Broadcasting Co.
P.O. Box 34665
28234, 704-335-4700

Cherryville
WCSL-AM
KTC Broadcasting, Inc.
106 N. Cherry St.
28021, 704-435-3297

China Grove
WRNA-AM
South Rowan Broadcasting Co.
P.O. Box 64
28023, 704-857-1101

Claremont
WCXN-AM
WCXN Inc.
P.O. Box 909
28610, 704-459-9803

WPAR-FM
Piedmont Area Radio Inc.

P.O. Box 889,
Blacksburg, VA
24060, 704-459-9803

Clayton
WHPY-AM
Clayton Broadcasting Co.
837 Hwy. 70, E.
27520, 919-553-6136

Clinton
WCLN-AM/FM
Sampson Broadcasting Co.
P.O. Box 89
28328, 919-592-6403

WRRZ-AM/FM
WRRZ Radio Co. Inc.
P.O. Box 378
28328, 919-592-2165

Concord
WEGO-AM
Concord-Kannapolis Broadcasting Co.
520 Hwy. 29 N.
28025, 704-786-9111

WPEG-FM
Concord-Kannapolis Broadcasting Co.
520 Hwy. 29 N.
28025, 704-786-9111

Cullowhee
WWCU-FM
Western Carolina University
P.O. Box 2728
28723, 704-227-7139

Dallas
WAAK-AM
Cana-Broadcasting
P.O. Box 477
28034, 704-922-3411

WSGE-FM
Gaston College Board of Trustees
P.O. Box 95, Gaston College
28034, 704-922-7688

Davidson
WDAV-FM
Trustees of Davidson College
Davidson College
28036, 704-892-2000

Derita
WHVN-AM
WHVN, Inc.
5732 N. Tryon St.
28213, 704-570-1240

WQCC-AM
Voice of Charlotte Broadcasting
400 N. Tryon St.
28213, 704-393-8741

Dobson
WYZD-AM
Dobson Broadcasting Co.
P.O. Box 797
27017, 919-386-8134

Dunn
WCKB-AM
North Carolina Central Broadcasters Inc.
Hwy. 421 E.
28334, 919-892-3133

WPYB-AM
Hwy 301 N
28334, 919-892-7003

WDKC-FM
Landsman Webster Communications of N.C. Inc.
Drawer 2247, Fayetteville
28302, 919-892-0103

Durham
WAFR-FM
Central University Community Radio Workshop Inc.
2501 Fayetteville St.
27707, 919-688-2371

WDNC-AM/FM
WDCG-AM/FM
Durham Radio Corp.
138 E. Chapel Hill St.
27702, 919-682-0318

WDUR-AM
Airways, Inc.
P.O. Box 2169
27702, 919-683-1490

WFXC-FM
Classic Ventures Ltd.
P.O. Box 2855
27705, 919-286-9327

WRTP-AM
Leathers Enterprises/Carolina Christian Comm.
4411 Chapel Hill Blvd.
27707, 919-493-3507

WSRC-AM
Carolina Radio of Durham Inc.
700 E. Club Blvd.
27702, 919-477-7331

WTIK-AM
W & W Broadcasting Co.
707 Leon St.
27702, 919-477-7351

WXDU-FM
Duke University
P.O. Box 4706, Duke Station
27706, 919-684-2957

Eden
WCBX-AM
Stone Corp.

113 N. Pierce St.
27288, 919-623-3121

WLOE-AM
Colonial Broadcasting Co.
123 Boulevard
27288, 919-623-3118

WSRQ-FM
123 Boulevard
27288, 919-623-3118

WWWI-FM
Colonial Broadcasting Co.
P.O. Box 548
27288, 919-623-3118

Edenton

WBXB-FM
Chowan Broadcasters
P.O. Box 0
27932, 919-482-3200

WZBO-AM/FM
Edenton Broadcasters
Drawer G
27932, 919-482-2103

Elizabeth City

WCNC-AM
Northeastern Carolina Communications Inc.
Parsonage St.
27909, 919-335-4379

WGAI-AM
Campbell Broadcasting Inc.
Newland Rd.
27909, 919-335-4371

WKJX-FM
North Carolina Radio Service Inc.
P.O. Box 96X
27909, 919-338-0196

WMYK-FM
Love Broadcasting
P.O. Box 429, Moyock
27958, 919-435-6138

WRVS-FM
Elizabeth State University
1001 Parkview Dr.
27909, 919-335-3517

WWOK-FM
Success Communications Inc.
P.O. Box 1418, Nags Head
27959, 919-441-9905

Elizabethtown

WBLA-AM
Bladen Broadcasting Corp.
512 Peanut Rd.
28337, 919-862-3184

Elkin

WIFM-FM
Tri-County Broadcasting Co.
Drawer 1038
28621, 919-835-2511

WJOS-AM
Tri-County Broadcasting Co.
Drawer 1038
28621, 919-835-2511

Elon College

WSOE-FM
Elon College
Box 755
27244, 919-584-9880

Fair Bluff

WNFO
Hwy. 76, W.
28439, 919-649-7325

Fairmont

WFMO-AM
P.O. Box 665
28340, 919-628-6781

WZYZ-FM
P.O. Box 665
28340, 919-628-6781

Farmville

WGHB-AM
Hwy. 121, N.
P.O. Box 229
27828, 919-753-4121

Fayetteville

WFAI-AM
Beasley Broadcasting Co.
1108-R Ramsey St.
28302, 919-483-0393

WFLB-AM
WFLB, Inc.
1338 Bragg Blvd.
P.O. Box 530
28302, 919-323-0925

WFNC-AM
Cape Fear Broadcasting Co.
1009 William Clark Rd.
28303, 919-864-5222

WIDU-AM
WIDU Broadcasting, Inc.
N. Water St.
28302, 919-483-6111

WQSM-Stereo FM
Cape Fear Broadcasting Co.
1009 William Clark Rd.
28303, 919-864-5222

Forest City

WAGY-AM
1110 Oak St.
28043, 704-245-9887

WBBO-AM/FM
1263 W. Main St.
28043, 704-245-4205

WHCH-AM
W. Main St.
28043, 704-245-4205

Franklin
WFSC-AM
Lake Emory Rd.
28734, 704-524-4418

WLTM-AM
251 Highlands Rd.
28734, 704-369-9569

WRFR-FM
Lake Emory Rd.
28734, 704-524-5395

Fuquay Varina
WAKS-AM/FM
Mohr, Engledow Broadcasting of NC, Inc.
Hwy. 55, N.
27526, 919-552-2263

Garner
WKBQ-AM
Christopher C. Maggio
1423 Creech Rd.
27529, 919-833-3324

Gastonia
WGAS-AM
MGM Broadcasting Corp.
627 Davis Park Rd.
28052, 704-865-5796

WGNC-AM
Beasley Broadcasting
1700 N. Broadcast St.
28052, 704-865-8501

WGNC-AM
Catherine McSwain
1700 Best St.
28052, 704-865-8501

WLTC-AM
Gastonia Broadcasting Service
304 N. New Hope Rd.
28054, 704-865-1280

Goldsboro
WEQR-FM
914 W. Grantham St.
27530, 919-736-1150

WFMC-AM
Hwy. 117, S.
27530, 919-734-4211

WGBR-AM
914 W. Grantham St.
27530, 919-736-1150

WGMB-FM
104 S. Marion Dr.
27530

WOKN-FM
Hwy. 117, By-Pass Goldsboro
27530, 919-734-4213

WSSG-AM
116 W. Mulberry
27530, 919-734-1300

Graham
WSML-AM
Evans Communications, Inc.
1040 Ivey Rd.
27253, 919-227-4254

WSML-AM
Acme Communications, Inc.
P.O. Box 900
27253, 919-227-4254

Granite Falls
WYCV-AM
S. Main Ext.
28630, 704-396-3361

Greensboro
WBIG-AM
Jefferson-Pilot Communications Co.
3001 Battleground Rd.
27408, 919-288-4131

WBIG-FM
Beasley Broadcast Group
4002 E. Spring Garden St.
27419, 919-855-6500

WEAL-AM
North State Broadcasting Co.
1060 Gatewood Ave.
27405, 919-272-5121

WGLD-AM
Mann Media, Inc.
4002C Spring Garden St.
27419, 919-299-1320

WKEW-AM
WKEW Partners
708 Summit Ave.
27405, 919-273-3631

WKSI-FM
Robins Communications Inc.
221 W. Meadowview Rd.
27416, 919-275-9895

WNAA-FM
North Carolina Agricultural & Technical State University
AT&T University
27411, 919-334-7936

WOJY-FM
Adelphi Broadcasting Co.
P.O. Box 8009
27419, 919-299-0346

WPET-AM
Robins Communications Inc.
221 W. Meadowview Rd.
27416, 919-275-9738

WQFS-FM
Guilford College Board of Trustees
P.O. Box 17714, Guilford College
27410, 919-294-3820

WQMG-Stereo FM
Murray Hill Broadcasting, POAG Communications Co.
1060 Gatewood Ave.
27405, 919-275-1657

WUAG-FM
University of North Carolina at Greensboro Board of Trustees
Taylor Bldg., University of North Carolina at Greensboro
27412-5001, 919-379-5450

Greenville

WBZQ-AM
Greenville Broadcasting Co. Inc.
918 Dickinson Ave.
27834, 919-752-8740

WNCT-AM/FM
Park Communications Inc.
P.O. Box 7167
27834, 919-757-0011

WOOW-AM
WOOW Inc.
304 Evans St.
27834, 919-758-1171

WRQR-Stereo FM
P.O. Box 1546
27835, 919-830-0944

WZMB-FM
ECU Media Board
Old Joyner Library, ECU
27834, 919-757-6656

Hamlet

WKDX-AM
Richmond County Broadcasting Co. Inc.
Fifth St.
28345, 919-582-2653

Havelock

WCPQ-AM
Musicradio of N.C. Inc.
331-B W. Main St.
28532, 919-447-0101

WMSQ-FM
Musicradio of N.C. Inc.
331-B W. Main St.
28532, 919-447-0101

Henderson

WHNC-AM
Rigel Inc.
Norlina Rd.
27536, 919-438-8111

WIZS-AM
Stanley H. Fox
Roanoke Ave.
27536, 919-492-3001

WYFL-FM
Bible Broadcasting Network
Norlina Rd.
P.O. Box 1240
27536, 919-438-8111

Hendersonville

WHKP-AM
Radio Hendersonville Inc.
U.S. 64 E.
28739, 704-693-9061

WHVL-AM
The Mountainaire Corp.
717 Greenville Hwy.
28739, 704-692-1600

WKIT-FM
Radio Hendersonville Inc.
U.S. 64 E.
28739, 704-693-4193

Hickory

WHKY-AM/FM
Catawba Valley Broadcasting Inc.
526 Main Ave. S.E.
28601, 704-322-5115

WIRC-AM
Westcom Ltds.
357 First Ave., N.W.
28601, 704-322-4130

WSPF-AM
Piedmont Broadcasting Co. Inc.
211 Hwy., 127 & 2nd Ave., S.E.
28601, 704-328-1731

WXRC-FM
Westcom Ltds.
357 First Ave., N.W.
28601, 704-322-1713

High Point

WGOS-FM
Ritchy Broadcasting Co.
660 N. Main St.
27261, 919-889-1466

WHPE-FM
Bible Broadcasting Network
1714 Tower Ave.
27260, 919-889-9473

WMAG-FM
Voyager Communications Inc.
164 S. Main St.
27261, 919-272-0995

WMFR-FM
Voyager Communications Inc.
164 S. Main St., 8th Fl.
27262, 919-885-2191

WOJY-FM
Mann Media
155 Northpoint Ave.
27260, 919-869-0101

WOKX-AM
Agape Ministries Inc.
P.O. Box 6334
27262, 919-884-1551

WTHP-FM
Hi Toms Broadcasting, Inc.
1418 Long St.
27262, 919-887-0983

WWIH-FM
High Point College
27262, 919-884-5440

Icard Township
WUIV-AM
Jim Jacumin
Box U
28666, 704-397-5549

Jacksonville
WIIZ-AM
Arnold Ad Ext.
28540, 919-347-6141

WJIK-AM
239 Western Blvd.
28540, 919-353-9545

WJNC-AM
Winfas Inc.
904 Lejeune Blvd.
28541, 919-455-2202

WLAS-AM
Seaboard Broadcasting Corp.
P.O. Box 760
28541, 919-455-9528

WOPY-AM
Caleb Communications Inc.
Drawer 1216
28541, 919-347-6141

WRCM-FM
Winfas Inc.
904 Lejeune Blvd.
28540, 919-455-5300

WXQR-FM
Marine Broadcasting Corp.
1011 Hargett St.
28540, 919-455-2507

Kannapolis
WGTL-AM
Fred H. Whitley Inc.
P.O. Box 148
28081, 704-933-8700

WJZR-FM
Downs Radio Inc.
910 Fairview
28081, 704-933-1121

WRKB-AM
Downs Radio Inc.
910 Fairview
28081, 704-933-1221

King
WKTE-AM
Booth-Newsom Broadcasting, Inc.
P.O. Box 465
27021, 919-983-3111

Kings Mountain
WKMT-AM
WKMT Radio
P.O. Box 1220
28086, 704-739-3671

Kinston
WELS-AM
Farmers Broadcasting Service Inc.
1312 W. Vernon Ave.
28501, 919-523-5151

WFTC-AM
HGR Broadcasting Co.
P.O. Box 609
28501, 919-522-4141

WISP-AM
Caravelle Broadcast Group of Kinston
Hwy. 70 Bypass
P.O. Box 606
28501, 919-527-1230

WKNS-FM
Lenoir Community College
P.O. Box 188
28501, 919-527-6223

WQDW-FM
Caravelle Broadcast Group of Kinston
P.O. Box 606
28501, 919-523-1230

WRNS-FM
HGR Broadcasting Co.
P.O. Box 609
28501, 919-522-4141

Laurinburg
WEWO-AM
Durham Life Broadcasting
P.O. Box 512
28352, 919-276-2911

WLNC-AM
Contempo Communications Inc.
1300 Lila Dr.
28352, 919-276-1300

WSTS-FM
Durham Life Broadcasting
P.O. Box 512
28352, 919-276-2911

Lenoir
WJRI-AM
WJRI Inc.
Morganton Blvd.
28645, 704-754-5361

WKGX-AM
Funitus City Broadcasters Inc.
P.O. Box 1080
28645, 704-754-2881

Lexington
WKOQ-FM
Davidson County Broadcasting Co. Inc.
P.O. Box 668
27293, 704-246-2716

WLXN-AM
Davidson County Broadcasting Co. Inc.
P.O. Box 668
27293, 704-246-5944

Lewisville
WSGH-AM
Golden Rule Organization Workshop Inc.
201 Progress St., Blacksburg, VA
24060, 703-552-4252

Lillington
WLLN-AM
Harnett Broadcast Inc.
E. McNeil St./Prison Camp Rd.
27546, 919-893-8313

Lincolnton
WLON-AM
Lincoln County Broadcasting Co. Inc.
Startown Rd.
28092, 704-735-8071

Louisburg
WYRN-AM
Franklin Broadcasting Co.
P.O. Box 463
27549, 919-496-3105

Lumberton
WAGR-AM
Southeastern Broadcasting Corp.
Chestnut St.
28358, 919-739-3394

WGSS-FM
P.O. Box 393
28358, 919-739-6056

WJSK-FM
Southeastern Broadcasting Corp.
Chestnut St. Ext.
28358, 919-739-3394

WKML-FM
Lumberton Broadcasting Co.
1510 W. Fifth St.
28358, 919-738-1340

WTSB-AM
Lumberton Broadcasting Co.
P.O. Box 1123
28359, 919-739-3354

Madison
WMYN-AM
P.O. Box 311
27025, 919-548-9207

Marion
WBRM-AM
Childress Broadcasting of West Jefferson
137 N. Garden St.
28752, 704-652-9500

Marshall
WMMH-AM
Marshall Broadcasting Co.
351 Skyway Dr.
28753, 704-649-3051

Mars Hill
WVMH-FM
Mars Hill College
P.O. Box 1161-C, Blackwell Hall
28754, 704-689-1259

Mayodan
WMYN-AM
Mayo Broadcasting Corp.
P.O. Box 311, Madison, N.C.
27025, 919-548-9207

Mebane
WMYT-AM
Benchmark Communications Ltd.
201 N. 4th St.
27302, 919-563-3000

Mint Hill
WCQR-FM
Mint Hill Media
P.O. Box 889, Blacksburg, VA
24060, 703-552-4252

Mocksville
WDSL-AM
WDSL Inc.
Jericho
27028, 704-634-2177

Monroe
WDEX-AM
Norris B. Mills
309 N. Main St.
28110, 704-289-9444

WIXE-AM
Monroe Broadcasting Co.
1700 Buena Vista Dr.
28110, 704-289-2525

WMAP-AM
Union Broadcasting Corp.
P.O. Box 159
28110, 704-283-8115

Mooresville
WHIP-AM
Mooresville Media Inc.
P.O. Box 600
28115, 704-664-9447

Morehead City
WMBL-AM
Ellek B. Seymour
4030 Arendell St.
28557, 919-247-2002

WMBJ-FM
Ellek B. Seymour
4030 Arendell St.
28557, 919-247-2002

Morganton
WMNC-AM
Cooper Broadcasting Co.
1103 N. Green St.
28655, 704-437-0521

WQXX-FM
Cooper Broadcasting Co.
1103 N. Green St.
28655, 704-437-0522

Mount Airy
WPAQ-AM
Ralph D. Epperson
Springs Rd.
27030, 919-786-6111

WSYD-AM
Mount Airy Broadcasters Inc.
City View Dr.
27030, 919-786-2147

Mount Olive
WDJS-AM
The Mount Olive Broadcasting Co.
P.O. Box 429
28365, 919-658-9751

Moyock
WMYK-Stereo FM
Love Broadcasting
P.O. Box 429
27958, 919-435-6138

Murfreesboro
WBCG-FM
Murfreesboro Broadcasting Corp.
Hwy. 158 & 258
27855, 919-398-4111

WYCM-AM
Murfreesboro Broadcasting Corp.
Hwy. 158 & 258
27855, 919-398-4111

Murphy
WAZZ-FM
WAZZ Inc.
P.O. Box 2684
28560, 919-637-6144

WCVP-AM
Max M. Blakemore
P.O. Box 280
28906, 704-837-2151

WKRK-AM
Childress Broadcasting Corp. of Murphy
631 Andrews Rd.
28906, 704-837-6200

WNOS-AM
James Eugene Hodges
P.O. Box 913
28560, 919-638-8888

New Bern
WAZZ-FM
P.O. Box 2684
28560, 919-637-6144

WRNB-AM
We Care Ministries Inc.
P.O. Box 2684
28560, 919-637-6144

WSFL-FM
P.O. Box 3436
28560

WSFL-Stereo FM
Highway 70 East
28560, 919-633-2406

WTEB-FM
Board of Trustees, Craven Community College
P.O. Box 885
28560, 919-638-3434

WWMG-AM
P & C Broadcasting Co.
P.O. Box 3436
28560, 919-633-0319

Newland
WJTP-AM
J. T. Parker Broadcasting Corp.
P.O. Box 1130
28657, 704-733-0188

Newport
WZYC-FM
Emerald Communications Inc.
P.O. Box WZYC, Beaufort
28516, 919-728-2019

Newton
WNNC-AM
Newton Conover Communications, Inc.
West A St.
28658, 704-464-4041

North Wilkesboro
WKBC-AM/FM
Wilkes Broadcasting Co.
400 "C" St., Radio Bldg.
28659, 919-667-2221

Oxford
WCBQ-AM
1 Broadcast Center
27565, 919-693-4121

Pinehurst
WOLV-AM
Southern Pines
28387, 919-692-6887

Plymouth
WKLX-FM
Ralph D. Epperson
Hwy. 64 By-Pass
27962, 919-793-4104

WPNC-AM
Ralph D. Epperson
Hwy. 64 By-Pass
27962, 919-793-4104

Raeford
WSMR-AM
1085 E. Central Ave.
28376, 919-875-8704

Raleigh
WCPE-FM
Educational Information Corp.
27587, 919-556-5178

WKIX-AM
Mann Media
P.O. Box 12526
27605, 919-851-2711

WKNC-FM
North Carolina State University
P.O. Box 8607, NCSU Mail Center
27695–8607, 919-737-2400

WLLE-AM
Special Markets Media Inc.
522 E. Martin St.
27601, 919-833-3874

WPJL-AM
Raleigh Radio Co. Inc.
515 Bart St.
27611, 919-834-6401

WPTF-AM
Durham Life Broadcasting Inc.
3012 Highwoods Blvd.
27604, 919-876-0674

WQDR-FM
Durham Life Broadcasting Inc.
410 S. Salisbury St.
27602, 919-832-8311

WRAL-FM
Capitol Broadcasting Co. Inc.
711 Hillsborough St., Box 10100
27605, 919-821-8701

WRZR-AM
North Carolina Electronics, Inc.
647 Maywood Ave.
27603, 919-832-1234

WSES-AM
Gregory B. Crampton, Chapter 7 Trustee
100 St. Alban's Dr. #200
27609, 919-832-1234

WSHA-FM
Shaw University
118 E. South St.
27611, 737-4847

WYLT-FM
Adelphi Broadcasting Co.
P.O. Box 12526
27605, 919-851-2711

WYYD-FM
Mann Media
P.O. Box 12526
27605, 919-851-2711

Red Springs
WYRU-AM
Carolina Sunbelt Radio Inc.
Red Springs Industrial Park
28377, 919-843-5946

Reidsville
WREV-AM
MHR Broadcasting Inc.
1009 Madison St.
P.O. Box 1050
27323–1050, 919-349-2986

WRNC-AM
Wright Broadcasting of N.C.
Harrison St. Ext.
27320, 919-342-5916

WWMO-FM
Beasley Broadcasting of Reidsville Inc.
P.O. Box 180
27320, 919-342-1333

Roanoke Rapids
WCBT-AM
WCBT Radio Inc.
Birdsong St. & Roanoke Ave.
27870, 919-537-4184

WPGT-FM
Roanoke Christian School
338 Roanoke Ave.
27870, 919-537-8333

WPTM-FM
Halifax County Broadcasting Co.
P.O. Box 910
27870, 919-536-3115

Rockingham
WAYN-AM
WAYN Inc.
1223 Rockingham Rd.
28379, 919-895-4041

WLWL-AM
Sandhills Broadcasting Co.
Old Steel Mill Rd.
28379, 919-997-2526

WRSH-FM
Richmond County Board of Education
Long Dr.
28379, 919-895-6374

Rocky Mount
WCEC-AM
Eastern Carolina Electronics Inc.
2970 Raleigh Rd.
27801, 919-977-6810

WEED-AM
Woolfson Broadcasting Corp. of Rocky Mount Inc.
P.O. Box 2267
27801, 919-443-3119

WFMA-FM
Eastern Carolina Electronics Inc.
Hwy. 97 West
27801, 919-977-6810

WRSV-FM
Woolfson Broadcasting Corp. of Rocky Mount Inc.
P.O. Box 2666
27801, 919-442-9776

WRMT-AM
CatCom Inc.
841 Weslyan Blvd.
27803, 919-442-8091

Rose Hill

WEGG-AM
Duplin County Broadcasters
RFD No. 2
28458, 919-289-2031

Roxboro

WKRX-FM
Roxboro Broadcasting Co.
P.O. Box 1176
27573, 919-599-0266

WRXO-AM
Roxboro Broadcasting Co.
P.O. Box 1176
27573, 919-599-0266

Rutherfordton

WCAB-AM
P.O. Box 511
28139, 704-287-3356

St. Pauls

WNCR-AM
U.S. Broadcasting Co.
Rt. 3, Box 169
28384, 919-865-3131

Salisbury

WNDN-FM
Catawba College
Catawba College
28144, 704-637-4456

WRDX-FM
WSTP Inc.
P.O. Box 4157
28144, 704-636-3811

WSAT-AM
Mid-Carolina Broadcasting Co.
Drawer 99,
1525 Salisbury Blvd.
28144, 704-633-0621

WSTP-AM
WSTP Inc.
1105 Statesville Blvd.
28144, 704-636-3811

Sanford

WDCC-FM
Central Carolina Technical College
1105 Kelly Dr.
27330, 919-775-5401

WFJA-FM
WWGP Broadcasting Corp.
Drawer R
27330, 919-776-9352

WSBL-AM
Radio Sanford Inc.
P.O. Box 2517
27330, 919-774-6313

WWGP-AM
WWGP Broadcasting Corp.
U.S. Hwy. 1
27330, 919-775-3525

WXKL-AM
1819 Lee St.
27330, 919-774-6955

Scotland Neck

WYAL-AM
Weldon Rd.
27874, 919-826-3114

Selma

WBZB-AM
WBZB Broadcasting Service Inc.
Hwy. 301 S.
27576, 919-965-3753

Shallote

WDZD-FM
Media Group Inc.
Suite 7, Ocean Isle Sq.
28459, 919-579-9301

WPGO-FM
Foremark Communications
P.O. Box 1550
28459, 919-754-8147

WVCB-AM
John G. Worrell
Main Hwy. 17
28459, 919-754-4512

Shelby

WADA-AM
Bello Broadcasting Co.
Drawer 1390
28150, 704-482-1390

WCCS-AM
McBrayer Springs Rd.
28150, 704-482-1390

WOHS-AM
Shelby Radio Corp.
1151 W. Dixon Blvd.
28150, 704-482-4510

WXIK-FM
Shelby Radio Corp.
1511 W. Dixon Blvd.
28150, 704-482-3966

Siler City
WNCA-AM
Chatham Broadcasting Co. of Siler City
P.O. Box 429
27344, 919-742-2135

Smithfield
WMPM-AM
Carolina Broadcasting Service
Buffalo Rd.
27577, 919-934-2434

Southport
WJYW-FM
Atlantic Broadcasting Co.
Hwy. 133, N.
28461, 919-343-0407

Southern Pines
WDLV-AM
P.O. Box 1677
28387, 919-692-6887

WEEB-AM
Younts Broadcasting Co.
P.O. Box 570
28387, 919-692-7440

WIOZ-FM
Muirfield Broadcasting Inc.
Short & Long Sts.
28387, 919-692-2107

South Gastonia
WGAS-AM
MGM Broadcasting Corp.
P.O. Box 250
28052, 704-865-5796

Southport
WJYW-FM
P.O. Box 10999
28461, 919-763-6107

Sparta
WCOK-AM
Sparta-Independence Radio Corp.
P.O. Box 637
28675, 919-372-8231

Spindale
WGMA-AM
301 West Main
28160, 704-287-5151

Spring Lake
WRZK-AM
Dr. Claye Frank
P.O. Box 707
28390, 919-497-3176

Spruce Pine
WTOE-AM
Toe River Valley Broadcasting
Hwy. 19 E
28777, 704-765-7441

Statesville
WDRV-AM
Capitol Broadcasting Corp.
212 Signal Hill Dr.
28677, 704-872-0956

WFMX-FM
Statesville Broadcasting Co. Inc.
1117 Radio Bldg.
Radio Rd.
28677, 704-872-6348

WLVK-FM
Capitol Broadcasting Corp.
4701 Hedgemore Dr., Charlotte
28209, 704-529-0097

WLVV-FM
212 Signal Hill Dr.
28677, 704-872-0956

WSIC-AM
Statesville Broadcasting Co. Inc.
1117 Radio Bldg.
Radio Rd.
28677, 704-872-6345

Swan Quarter
WHYC-FM
Hyde County Board of Education
P.O. Box 217
27885, 919-926-7201

Sylva
WRGC-AM
WNSJ Inc.
Old Waynesville Rd.
28779, 704-586-2221

Tabor City
WKSM-FM
Prorad Communications Inc.
P.O. Box 127
28463, 919-653-2131

WTAB-AM
Prorad Communications Inc.
P.O. Box 127
28463, 919-653-2131

Tarboro
WCPS-AM
Coastal Plains Broadcasting Co. Inc.
P.O. Box 100
27886, 919-823-2191

WKTC-FM
Coastal Plains Broadcasting Co. Inc.
P.O. Box 100
27886, 919-823-2985

Taylorsville
WQXZ-AM
Alexander Broadcasting Co. Inc.

Radio Rd.
28681, 704-632-4621

WTLK-AM
International Broadcasting Co. Inc.
Tower Rd.
P.O. Box 847
28681, 704-632-4214

Thomasville
WEVE-AM
Hi-Tops Broadcasting
P.O. Box 250
27360, 919-476-7701

WEYE-FM
P.O. Box 1920
27360, 919-472-0790

WTNC-AM
P.O. Box 1920
27360, 919-472-0790

WTNC-FM
Hi-Tops Broadcasting
P.O. Box 250
27360, 919-476-7701

Troy
WJRM-AM
Montgomery Broadcasting Inc.
Biscoe Rd.
27371, 919-576-8811

Tryon
WTYN-AM
Polk County Broadcasting Corp.
Lanier Dr.
28782, 803-457-4105

Valdese
WSVM-AM
Burke County Broadcasting Co.
S. Praley St.
28690, 704-874-0000

Wadesboro
WADE-AM
Carolinas Adv. Inc.
1 Radio St.
28170, 704-694-3969

Wallace
WLSE-AM
Duplin Broadcasting Co.
Hwy. 117
28466, 919-285-2187

WZKB-FM
Duplin Broadcasting Co.
Hwy. 117
28466, 919-285-2187

Wanchese
WOBR-AM/FM
WOBR Inc.
Hwy. 345, Box 400
27981, 919-473-3434

Warrenton
WARR-AM
WARR Inc.
P.O. Box 577
27589, 919-257-2121

WVSP-FM
P.O. Box 365
27589, 919-257-1909

Warsaw
WTRQ-AM
Lyn-Win Broadcasting Inc.
Rt. 2, Box 236-D
28398, 919-293-7861

Washington
WDLX-FM
Hwy. 17, S.
27889, 919-946-2162

WRRF-AM
Tar Heel Broadcasting System
P.O. Box 1707
27889, 919-946-2162

WWGN-AM
James Eugene Hodges
228 W. Main St.
27889, 919-946-1016

Waynesville
WHCC-AM
Waynesville Broadcasting Co.
139½ Main St.
28786, 704-456-8661

WQNS-FM
Waynesville Broadcasting Co.
139½ Main St.
28786, 704-456-8661

Weldon
WPTM-Stereo FM
Aurelian Springs Rd.
27890, 919-536-3115

WSMY-AM
Smiles of N.C.
Aurelian Springs Rd.
27890, 919-536-3115

Wendell-Zebulon
WETC-AM
Daystar Broadcasting Network II, Inc.
P.O. Box 1580
27591, 919-269-6113

West Jefferson
WKSK-AM
Caddell Broadcasting
P.O. Box 729
28694, 919-246-6001

Whiteville
WENC-AM
Whiteville Broadcasting Co.
Highway 701 South
28472, 919-642-2133

WQTR-FM
Whiteville Broadcasting Co.
Highway 701 South
28472, 919-642-2133

WTXY-AM
Tuffy Broadcasting Inc.
501 W. Virgil St.
28472, 919-642-8214

WYNA-FM
111 W. Washington St.
28472, 919-642-9131

Wilkesboro

WSIF-FM
Wilkes Community College
P.O. Box 120
28697, 919-667-7136

WWWC-AM
Tomlinson Broadcasting Corp. of Wilkes City
P.O. Box 580
28697, 919-667-1241

Williamston

WIAM-AM
Fargay Broadcasters Inc.
P.O. Box 590
27892, 919-792-4161

WSEC-FM
Fargay Broadcasters Inc.
Hwy. 17, N., P.O. Box 590
27892, 919-792-4161

Wilmington

WAAV-AM/FM
Cape Fear Broadcasting
211 N. Second St.
28401, 919-763-6511

WBMS-AM
Brunson Broadcasting of N.C.
118 Princess St.
28401, 919-763-4633

WGNI-FM
Cape Fear Broadcasting
211 N. Second St.
28401, 919-763-6511

WHQR-FM
Friends of Public Radio Inc.
1026 Greenfield St.
28401, 919-343-1640

WHSL-FM
Wilmington Radio Co.
P.O. Box 5307
28403, 919-763-6363

WKLM-AM
Thom's Broadcasting Co., Inc.
118 Princess St.
28401, 919-763-4633

WLOZ-FM
University of North Carolina-Wilmington
601 S. College Rd.
28403, 919-791-8224

WMFD-AM
Wilmington Radio Co.
P.O. Box 5307
28403, 919-762-4474

WWQQ-FM
Woolfson Broadcasting Corp.
P.O. Box 5157
28403, 919-763-9977

WWIL-AM
Echo Broadcasting Co., Inc.
P.O. Box 3368
28406, 919-791-9083

Wilson

WGTM-AM
Campbell Hauser Corp.
P.O. Box 3837
27893, 919-243-2188

WLLY-AM
Champion Productions Inc.
210 Beacon St.
P.O. Box 3587
27893, 919-237-5171

WRDU-FM
Voyager Communications
P.O. Box 2528
27893, 919-243-5157

WVOT-AM
Hwy. 42, E.
27893, 919-243-5157

WXYY-FM
Hwy. 42, E.
27893, 919-243-5157

Windsor

WBTE-AM
Bertie County Broadcasting Co.
Hwy. 13/17 By-Pass
P.O. Box 509
27983, 919-794-3131

WDJB-FM
Bertie County Broadcasting Co.
P.O. Box 509
27983, 919-794-3131

Winston-Salem

WAAA-AM
Media Broadcasting Corp.
P.O. Box 11197
27106, 919-767-0430

WAIR-AM
Triad Broadcasting Co., Inc.
P.O. Box 2099
27102, 919-722-1347

WBFJ-AM
Word of Life Broadcasting Inc.

3066 TrenWest Dr., Suite A
27103, 919-760-0550

WFDD-FM
Trustees of Wake Forest University
P.O. Box 7405
27109, 919-761-5257

WKZL-FM
Nationwide Communications Inc.
4405 Providence Ln.
27106, 919-725-0556

WSEZ-FM
Holiday Broadcasting Corp.
P.O. Box 2099
27102, 919-722-1347

WSJS-AM
Summit Communications, Inc.
P.O. Box 3018
27102, 919-727-8860

WSMX-AM
Power Media Communications Inc.
500 Kinard St.
27101, 919-765-1551

WSNC-FM
Board of Trustees of Winston-Salem University
P.O. Box 13062
27110, 919-761-2008

WTOB-AM
Salem Media of N.C. Inc.
8025 N. Point Blvd.
27106, 919-723-4353

WTQR-FM
Summit Radio of N.C.
P.O. Box 3018
27102, 919-727-8860

Yadkinville
WYDK-AM
Childress Radio Co.
P.O. Box 998
27055, 919-679-2063

Yanceyville
WYNC-AM
Ansum Broadcasting Corp.
Drawer J
27379, 919-694-9212

RAILROADS

North Carolina is served by twenty-one railroad companies. These companies own and/or maintain over 4,100 miles of track in the ninety-one (out of a possible 100) counties under the jurisdiction of North Carolina's Utilities Commission.

North Carolina is at the center of a rail network that links its industries with raw materials, product suppliers, and major markets throughout the eastern United States.

Railroads operating in North Carolina are listed.

Company	*Main Business Office*	*Abbreviation*
Aberdeen & Briar Patch Railway Co.	*Aberdeen, N.C.*	*ABPR*
Aberdeen & Rockfish Railway Co.	*Aberdeen N.C.*	*A&R*
Alexander Railroad Co.	*Taylorsville, N.C.*	*ARC*
Atlantic & East Carolina Railway Co.	*Washington, D.C.*	*A&EC*
Atlantic & Western Corp.	*Sanford, N.C.*	*ATW*
Beaufort & Morehead Railroad Co.	*Beaufort, N.C.*	*B&MN*
CSX Transportation (1)	*Jacksonville, Fla.*	*CSX*
Camp Lejeune Railroad Co.	*Washington, D.C.*	*CLRR*
Cape Fear Railways, Inc.	*Fort Bragg, N.C.*	*CFR*
Carolina & Northwestern Railway Co.	*Washington, D.C.*	*CNW*
Cliffside Railroad Co. (2)	*Cliffside, N.C.*	*Cliff*
Fairmont & Western Railroad Co.	*Laurinburg, N.C.*	*FWRD*
Franklin County Railroad Corp.	*Laurinburg, N.C.*	*FCYR*

Company	Main Business Office	Abbreviation
High Point, Thomasville, & Denton Railroad Co.	*Jacksonville, Fla.*	*HPT*
Laurinburg & Southern Railroad Co.	*Laurinburg, N.C.*	*LSR*
Nash County Railroad Corp.	*Laurinburg, N.C.*	*NCYR*
Norfolk & Southern Railway Co. (3)	*Norfolk, Va.*	
Red Springs & Northern Railroad Co.	*Laurinburg, N.C.*	*RSNR*
State University Railroad Co.	*Washington, D.C.*	*S.T.U.*
Warrenton Railroad Co. (4)	*Warrenton, N.C.*	*W.R.R.*
Winston-Salem Southbound Railway Co.	*Jacksonville, Fla.*	*WSS*

(1) CSX Transportation was formerly Seaboard System Railroad, Inc. The name was changed on July 1, 1986.
(2) Cliffside Railroad Company suspended its operations in March 1986.
(3) Southern Railway and Norfolk & Western Railway merged to form Norfolk & Southern Railway.
(4) Warrenton Railroad Company is authorized to operate but has been inactive since 1984.

REGIONS

North Carolina governmental activities are divided among eighteen regions. These regions, the areas they serve, their directors, addresses, and telephone numbers are listed here.

Region A
Southwestern N.C. Planning and Economic Development
(Cherokee, Clay, Graham, Haywood, Jackson, Macon, and Swain counties)
Executive Director: Bill G. Gibson
P.O. Drawer 850
Bryson City 28713
704-488-9211

Region B
Land-of-Sky Regional Council
(Buncombe, Henderson, Madison, and Transylvania counties)
Executive Director: Robert E. Shepherd
25 Heritage Drive
Asheville 28806
704-254-8131

Region C
(Cleveland, McDowell, Polk, and Rutherford counties)
Executive Director: Paul D. Hughes
P.O. Box 841
Rutherfordton 28139
919-287-2281

Region D
Region D Council of Governments
(Alleghany, Ashe, Avery, Mitchell, Watauga, Wilkes, and Yancey counties)
Executive Director: Richard Fender
P.O. Box 1820
Boone 28607
704-264-5558

Region E
Western Piedmont Council of Governments
(Alexander, Burke, Caldwell, and Catawba counties)
Executive Director: R. Douglas Taylor
30 3rd Street, NW
Old City Hall
Hickory 28601
704-322-9191

Region F
(Cabarrus, Gaston, Iredell, Lincoln, Mecklenburg, Rowan, Stanly, and Union counties)

Executive Director: Lee Armour
1 Charlottetown Center
P.O. Box 35008
Charlotte 28235
704-372-2416

Region G
Piedmont Triad Council of Governments
(Alamance, Caswell, Davidson, Guilford, Randolph, and Rockingham counties)
Executive Director: Lindsey W. Cox
Four Seasons Office Building
2120 Pinecroft Road
Greensboro 27404
919-294-4950

Region H
Pee Dee Council of Governments
(Anson, Montgomery, Moore, and Richmond counties)
Executive Director: Hal Walker
227 N. Main St.
Box 728
Troy 27371
919-576-6261

Region I
Northwest Piedmont Council of Governments
(Davie, Forsyth, Stokes, Surry, and Yadkin counties)
Executive Director: Joe Matthews
280 S. Liberty Street
Winston-Salem 27101
919-722-9346

Region J
Triangle J Council of Governments
(Chatham, Durham, Johnston, Lee, Orange, and Wake counties)
Executive Director: Bradley S. Barker
100 Park Drive
Box 12276
Research Triangle Park 27709
919-549-0551

Region K
Kerr-Tar Regional Council of Governments
(Franklin, Granville, Person, Vance, and Warren counties)
Executive Director: Neil Mallary
238 Orange
P.O. Box 709
Henderson 27536
919-492-8561

Region L
Region L Council of Governments
(Edgecombe, Halifax, Nash, Northampton, and Wilson counties)
Executive Director: Thomas W. Elkins
301 Bypass South
Box 2748
Rocky Mount 27801
919-446-0411

Region M
Region M Council of Governments
(Cumberland, Harnett, and Sampson counties)
Executive Director: Roger Sheets
P.O. Drawer 1510
Fayetteville 28302
919-323-4191

Region N
Region N Council of Governments
(Bladen, Hoke, Robeson, and Scotland counties)
Executive Director: James Perry
P.O. Box 1529
Lumberton 28358
919-738-8104

Region O
Cape Fear Council of Governments
(Brunswick, Columbus, New Hanover, and Pender counties)
Executive Director: Jerry Ramsey
P.O. Box 1491
Wilmington 28402
919-763-0191

Region P
Neuse River Council of Governments
(Carteret, Craven, Duplin, Greene, Jones, Lenoir, Onslow, Pamlico, and Wayne counties)

Executive Director: J. Roy Fogle
P.O. Box 1717
New Bern 28560
919-638-3185

Region Q
Mid-East Commission
(Beaufort, Bertie, Hertford, Martin, and Pitt counties)
Executive Director: Robert Paciocco
P.O. Drawer 1787, One Harding Square
Washington 27889
919-946-8043

Region R
Albemarle Regional Planning and Development Commission
(Camden, Chowan, Currituck, Dare, Gates, Hyde, Pasquotank, Perquimans, Tyrrell, and Washington counties)
Executive Director: Don C. Flowers, Jr.
P.O. Box 646
Hertford 27944
919-426-5753

RELIGION

The following religious denominations maintain their headquarters in North Carolina. Number of churches and membership figures are as of 1982.

Adventist: Advent Christian Church. Organized in 1860. P.O. Box 23152, Charlotte, 28212. Churches, 351; Membership, 19,715.

Baptist: United Free Will Baptist Church. Organized in 1870. Kinston College, 1000 University St., Kinston, 28501. Churches, 836; Membership, 100,000.

Moravian: Moravian Church-Southern Province. Organized in 1753. 459 South St., Winston-Salem, 27108. Churches, 56; Membership, 21,722.

Pentecostal: Pentecostal Free Will Baptist Church. Organized in 1959. Box 1568, Dunn, 28334. Churches, 133; Membership, 15,000.

RESEARCH TRIANGLE PARK

What began as a dream in the mind of North Carolina's former Governor Luther H. Hodges has grown to become the largest research center of its kind in the world.

Recognizing the value of high technology and research, and being determined that North Carolina not be behind in the international race for technological advancement, Hodges began in 1954 to formulate plans for a research center to be based in his state. A report from a committee of university professors concerning what was being done in the field of research and what they felt could be accomplished by cooperation between the three largest universities spawned the idea for a research triangle.

The word *triangle* was especially suitable for three reasons: three *counties*—Durham, Orange, and Wake—three *cities*—Durham, Chapel Hill, and Raleigh—and three *universities*—Duke University, the University of North Carolina at Chapel Hill, and North Carolina State University—are combined to form this huge industrial park. Also, if you were to draw a line on the map from Chapel Hill to Raleigh to Durham, then back again to Chapel Hill, a triangle would result.

Founded in 1959, the Park has a campus atmosphere with its woodland setting, lakes, and vast lawns, in spite of its tremendous growth. Becton Dickinson, Burroughs Wellcome, Data General, DuPont, General Electric, IBM, Northern Telecom, Sumitomo Electric, TRW, and Union Carbide are among the Park's largest tenants. Approximately 25,000 people are employed here, earning more than $600 million annually.

A second major research park is located in North Carolina, at the other end of the Piedmont Crescent. On a 2,500-acre campus beside the University of North Carolina, University Research Park is also a rapidly growing research center. Dow Jones, the Electric Power Research Institute, IBM, Southern Bell, and Union 76 are some of its corporate residents.

These two research centers are representative of North Carolina's commitment to research and development, quality education and training.

REVOLUTIONARY WAR

To provide a solution for the financial problems England suffered protecting the colonies from the French and the Indians, Parliament thought it only fair to expect the colonists to pay at least in part for their own defense and colonial administration. The New Colonial Policy, the Sugar Act, and the Currency Act caused most Americans to protest Parliamentary taxation. Six of the colonies made their objections known through their assemblies, though North Carolina was not included in this number.

The Stamp Bill was introduced into Parliament February 13, 1765, and only four members spoke against the measure. The most significant of these was Colonel Issac Barré, who stated that Americans were "Sons of Liberty" fighting the cause of all Englishmen. The Stamp Act passed March 22, 1765 and became effective November 1, 1765.

The North Carolina Assembly in October 1764 declared opposition to the Stamp Act even before William Tryon took office as the governor on April 3, 1765, mainly because it violated the principle of no taxation without representation. John Ashe, speaker of the assembly, advised Governor Tryon that the colony would "resist it to the death."

The Sons of Liberty (so named because of Barré's speech before Parliament against the Stamp Act) began to organize about this time. Included in this group were John Ashe, Cornelius Harnett, Hugh Waddell, Abner Nash, Robert Howe and other radical leaders. The North Carolina group was unique in that they were mostly from rural areas.

When the Massachusetts legislature requested delegates from all colonies to hold a congress in New York City, October 1765, North Carolina, as well as Georgia, New Hampshire and Virginia, was not represented because Governor Tryon refused to call an assembly in time to choose delegates.

The people of the area made their feelings known by forcing the stamp officer, Dr. William Houston, to resign. Still the situation became increasingly difficult as ships could not leave port, courts of law could not open, and newspapers, books and pamphlets could not be printed. When two merchant ships were seized because their clearance papers were not stamped, the struggle reached a climax.

England became aware of America's opposition and even King George III was in favor of modifying the law, and on March 18, 1766 he signed the repeal measure. England, still in need of funds for colonial defense, passed a measure called the Duty or Revenue Act on June 29, 1767 to become effective November 20 of the same year. Duties were placed on wine, lead, painters' colors, glass, and tea.

The Massachusetts Circular Letter of 1768, written by Samuel Adams, was sent to all the continental colonies, inviting them to unite in an effort to make their grievances known. North Carolina Assembly Speaker John Harvey sent a letter to the Massachusetts legislature that his assembly was ready to firmly unite with her sister colonies, an act which Governor Tryon censured. This prompted Speaker Harvey to call an assembly "independent of the governor" which unanimously agreed to nonimportation measures.

Escalating opposition caused England to repeal their tax laws, which they relented on everything but tea, and conditions improved and colonial trade with England increased.

Because of continued disagreements with the Crown, leaders of the Whigs (as opponents of British policies were now called) held many conferences throughout the colonies to work out a unified plan of action. The North Carolina Assembly created a Committee of Correspondence which took as its first stand the issuance of a statement that all of the sister colonies should be interested in Boston's cause and that a continental congress was necessary.

The Tea Act, passed by Parliament in the spring of 1773, gave the British East India Company a monopoly on the American market and proved to be the event that set off the anger of the colonists again. On the night of December 16, 1773, a large shipment of tea was dumped into the sea by Boston citizens posing as Indians.

On October 25, 1774, the so-called "earliest known instance of political activity on the part of women in the American colonies" took place in Edenton, North Carolina when 51 ladies were led by Mrs. Penelope Barker in pledging their patriotism. They signed an agreement to do everything possible to support the American cause. This event is known as the Edenton Tea Party.

The First Continental Congress met in Philadelphia, 1774, which adopted a Declaration of Rights and Grievances, a Petition to the King, and

Addresses to the People of Great Britain and also those of British America. Economic warfare was in a sense declared on the mother country with the adoption of the Continental Association.

The tension mounted between Governor Martin and the North Carolinians concerned with unity between the colonies. The Second Provincial Congress met in New Bern to elect delegates to the Second Continental Congress which would soon be convening in Philadelphia. At the same time, Governor Martin summoned the assembly to meet, at which time he denounced both groups. The groups in turn denounced the governor. Resolutions stating the people's rights to hold meetings and endorsements of safety committees were actions of the congress which were approved by the assembly. Governor Martin, enraged by their actions, dissolved the last royal assembly that ever met in North Carolina.

On April 19, 1775, General Gage attempted to seize military stores that the Whigs had gathered in Massachusetts and that action led to the battle of Lexington and Concord, the "shot heard round the world."

Safety committees in North Carolina set about preparing the state for war by requiring merchants to sell gunpowder and men were hired to mold bullets, those who did not abide by the nonimportation agreements were punished, and a thousand volunteers were requested to be ready to march at a moment's notice. Also, any person who accepted an office from the Crown was declared a public enemy.

The safety committees were responsible for the capture and destruction by fire of Fort Johnson, where Governor Martin had been trying to protect himself from the growing rebellion. He learned of their plans in time to escape to safety aboard the British *Cruizer* which was lying offshore.

The Provincial Congress resolved that the establishment of a temporary government was necessary since Governor Martin had deserted the colony and that the colony be immediately put into a state of defense.

There were three political factions in the state. The Whigs, or Patriots, were mostly small farmers and artisans who were willing to fight England to set right their grievances and even for independence. The Loyalists, also called Tories, King's Men, or Royalists, favored peaceful opposition to the Crown and opposed war at all costs. The Moravians, Quakers, and a large number of German settlers made up the neutral group.

Although the Provincial Congress continued to make military preparations, it was six months before there was any military conflict in the South. North Carolina troops first saw action in the form of aid to Virginia and South Carolina.

The one significant battle within the state at Moore's Creek Bridge was an overwhelming Whig victory. Then the tide of war turned away from North Carolina.

North Carolina's Fourth Provincial Congress took the first official state action for independence, though it was not a declaration for the state only but rather a recommendation to the Continental Congress that all the colonies declare independence.

The council of safety became the state's governing body.

Virginia's congress instructed its delegates to support independence in the Continental Congress, May 15, 1776. Richard Henry Lee urged "that these United Colonies are and of right ought to be free and independent States . . ." on June 7. This resolution was adopted by the Congress July 2, and two days later approved the final draft of the Declaration of Independence. William Hooper, Joseph Hewes, and John Penn signed the important document for North Carolina.

The Fifth Provincial Congress met at Halifax on November 12, 1776. The president chosen at that time was Richard Caswell. On December 17 the Declaration of Rights was adopted, and the North Carolina Constitution the following day. As the last official action, Richard Caswell was appointed as governor and James Glasgow as secretary.

RIVERS

A—Hiwassee. 80 miles long, flows from Northeast Georgia through Hiwassee Lake and Appalachia Lake in Northwest North Carolina into Tennessee where it flows into the Tennessee River.

B—Little Tennessee. Forms in Rabun County, Georgia, flows north and northwest across the western corner of North Carolina into Tennessee where it enters the Tennessee River.

C—French Broad. 240 miles long, forms in Transylvania County, flows through portions of Western North Carolina and Eastern Tennessee, where it joins the Holston River to form the Tennessee River.

D—New—North and South Forks. 247 miles long, formed by the junction of the North and South Forks. The South Fork rises near Blowing Rock and the North Fork rises southwest of Ashland. The two forks join to form the New River at the Ashe-Alleghany county line near the North Carolina-Virginia border. It flows through Virginia and West Virginia where it enters the Kanawha River. It is said to be the only large river in the nation that flows north.

E—Catawba. 250 miles long, rises in McDowell County, flows east and then south into South Carolina where it joins the Big Wateree Creek to form the Wateree River.

F—Yadkin. 203 miles long, rises in Watauga County near Blowing Rock, then twists and turns until it joins the Uwharrie River to form the Pee Dee River.

G—Uwharrie. Rises in northwestern Randolph County, flows south, joins the Yadkin River to form the Pee Dee River.

H—Pee Dee. 435 miles long, originates in Montgomery County, formed by the junction of the Yadkin and Uwharrie rivers, flows south through North Carolina and South Carolina where it empties into Winyah Bay.

I—Dan. Rises in Patrick County, Virginia, flows through portions of northern North Carolina and southern Virginia, into the Kerr Reservoir on the Roanoke River.

J—Deep. Forms in Guilford County and joins the Haw River in Chatham County to form the Cape Fear River.

K—Haw. 130 miles long, flows from Forsyth County northeast and then southeast until it joins the Deep River on the Chatham and Lee county line to form the Cape Fear River.

L—Cape Fear. 200 miles long, flows from the confluence of the Deep and Haw rivers on the Chatham–Lee county line southeasterly into the Atlantic Ocean.

M—Neuse. 260 miles long, flows from Durham County where it is formed by the junction of the Eno and Flat rivers southeasterly into Pamlico Sound.

N—Northeast Cape Fear. About 90 miles long, rises in Duplin County, flow south and southeast, then turns west, then south to enter Cape Fear River at Wilmington.

O—New. About 20 miles long, rises in the northwestern part of Onslow County, flows southeasterly through Camp LeJeune Marine Base into the Atlantic Ocean.

P—Tar. 179 miles long. Rises in Person County and flows southeasterly until Beaufort County where it becomes the Pamlico River.

Q—Pamlico. 33 miles long. The lower course of the Tar River, flows southeasterly into Pamlico Sound.

RIVERS

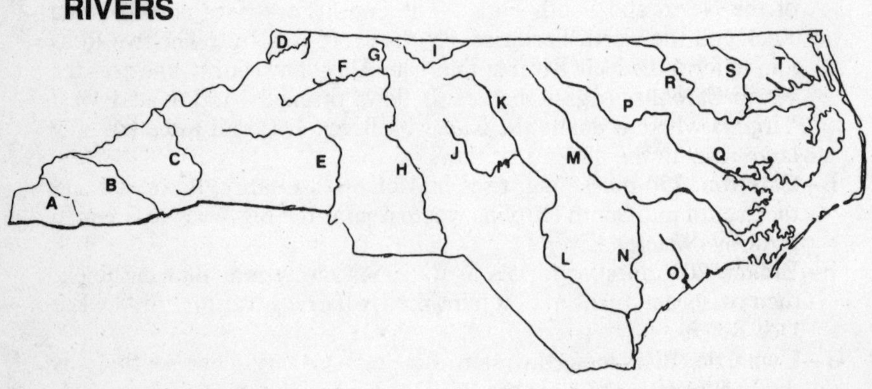

R—Roanoke. 380 miles long, forms in Montgomery County, Virginia, flows southeasterly across North Carolina and empties into Albemarle Sound.

S—Chowan. 45 miles long, formed by the Nottoway and Blackwater rivers on the Hertford-Gates county line, flows into Albemarle Sound.

T—Pasquotank. Rises in Camden County, flows southeast until it enters Albemarle Sound.

ROANOKE SETTLEMENT

The north end of Roanoke Island is the site of Sir Walter Raleigh's ill-fated attempts to establish an English community in America. It is our link with the vibrant era of Queen Elizabeth I and the golden age of the English Renaissance, a period of exploration and expansion when men of vision strove to establish colonies in distant lands to benefit the Mother Country. (Spain had already grown rich and powerful through her colonial empire.) Here on Roanoke Island, England's first serious attempt to turn her dream of empire into reality ended in failure and the strange disappearance of the colony of 1587.

EXPLORATION OF ROANOKE ISLAND

In 1584, one year after his half-brother Sir Humphrey Gilbert perished in an attempt to settle in Newfoundland, Sir Walter Raleigh obtained a patent to explore and settle in the New World. Imbued with a desire to realize his brother's dream of an English empire in America, Raleigh sent Captains Philip Amadas and Arthur Barlowe to examine the North American Coast.

They returned with glowing reports of tall trees, of land overgrown with sweet juicy grapes, and of birds so abundant that "a flocke of Cranes . . . arose under us, with such a crye redoubled by many Ecchoes, as if an armie of men had showted all together." They marveled at the rich soil and mild climate which produced three crops of corn a season in the natives' gardens. Two of these friendly robust natives, Manteo and Wanchese, returned to England with them. The land Amadas and Barlowe had explored was later named "Virginia" after Elizabeth, their Virgin Queen. The name was more than an honor; it represented Elizabeth's endorsement and support of the attempts to establish an English foothold in the New World, even in the face of all-powerful Spain.

With Raleigh's enthusiastic guidance and aid, the first colony was sent to "this paradise of the world" in 1585. It was a military venture under the command of his cousin, Sir Richard Grenville. The group chose to settle on the north end of Roanoke Island, which Amadas and Barlowe had described as "a most pleasant and fertile ground." There they built a fort under the direction of Ralph Lane and called it "the newe forte in Virginia."

When Grenville returned to England for supplies, Lane was appointed governor. Under his leadership, the group began to explore the surrounding islands and mainland, relying on Indian sources for their food supply as they expanded their quest for pearls, copper, and gold. The country was explored for a distance of about 80 miles to the south and 130 miles to the north. Thomas Hariot, an eminent geographer and scientist with the expedition, described the plant and animal life, the uses of it, and the native way of life. This data was published under the title New Found Land of Virginia, which was later expanded and supplemented by John White's watercolor drawings.

The colonists' quest for riches involved them in local Indian wars. Food became scarce, and day after day they anxiously watched the horizon for the returning supply ships. At last sails appeared, and Sir Francis Drake anchored off the inlet. Lane and his men accepted Drake's offer of ships and supplies to explore farther north for a better harbor. However, the ships were lost the next day in a storm. Weak and discouraged, the entire expedition decided to return to England with Drake.

Shortly afterward, Sir Richard Grenville, after returning to Roanoke with supplies, searched for the departed expedition. When he couldn't find it, he settled 15 men on the island with provisions for 2 years. They were to hold the country in the Queen's name until another colony could be established.

THE LOST COLONY, 1587

Immediately Raleigh began to shape plans for another colony, this time a true settlement of more than 100 men, women, and children. Raleigh appointed John White as governor, aided by 12 assistants, and directed them to settle on Chesapeake Bay. But their pilot refused to sail that far. The colonists remained on Roanoke Island, where they had stopped to look for the 15 men that Grenville had left behind the year before. They could not locate them; the only clue to their disappearance was a skeleton found near the place where the men had been left.

White and his colonists soon began to have trouble with the Indians. In a succession of skirmishes fought only a few days after the colony arrived, several colonists and Indians died.

Meanwhile, the ships were being readied for the voyage home. Governor White was persuaded to return to England for additional provisions, although he was reluctant to leave behind a newborn granddaughter, Virginia Dare. He set sail a few days after her birth.

England, when White arrived, was in imminent danger of a Spanish invasion. The danger was so great that the Queen refused to allow any large ships to leave. The two small pinnaces that were permitted to sail never reached the New World. Despite petitions to the Queen through Sir Walter Raleigh, White was unable to secure further relief for the colony.

He was finally able to sail in 1590—almost 3 years after his departure from Roanoke. When he returned, the colony had disappeared. The houses had been taken down and the settlement area enclosed within a high palisade, "very fort-like." On one prominent tree or post at the entrance to the palisade, the bark had been peeled off and the letters C R O A T O A N carved on it. The cross, a prearranged mark signifying distress or forced departure, was not there. White concluded that the colonists would be found on Croatoan Island (most of modern Ocracoke and part of Hatteras Island) or among the friendly Croatoan Indians farther inland. A series of storms and accidents forced the ships to return to England and White was unable to search for the colonists. The fate of the Lost Colony is still a mystery.

England did not successfully colonize the New World until 17 years later when a small group of hardy men and women succeeded at Jamestown. In a sense, the colony of 1587 was sacrificed to insure English victory over the Spanish Armada. But the blame should not lie entirely with England, because the colonists failed to become a part of the web of life on Roanoke Island; they did not make the best use of the offerings of the forest and sound, but relied on England for their food.

ROCKHOUNDING

North Carolina offers great variety to the rockhound and gem collector. More than 300 varieties of minerals and gems have been found here. Many old mines, once the source of commercial production, are now open to rockhounds for a daily fee.

It would be wise to check with these mines before making a trip, to determine if they are still open to the public.

Emerald
Emerald Valley Mines, Hiddenite
Hiddenite and Emerald Mine, Hiddenite
Big Crabtree Mine, Spruce Pine

Gold
Cotton Patch Mines, New London

Aquamarine
Wiseman Mine, Spruce Pine

Ruby and Sapphire
Located in Franklin:
Bonanza Mine
Caler Creek Ruby Mine
Cherokee Mine
Corundum Hill
Cowee Ruby Mine
Dale and Demko's Mine
Gibson Ruby Mine
Gregory Ruby Mine
Holbrook Ruby Mine
Houston's Sapphire Mine
Jacobs Ruby Mine
McCooks Sapphire Mine
Mason Branch Mine
Mincey Mine
Peek's Ruby Mine
Rockhound Haven Mine
Sheffield Corundum Mine
Shuler Ruby Mine
Yukon Ruby Mine

Garnet
4-K's Garnet Mine, Franklin
Mason Mountain Rhodolite Mine, Franklin

Amethyst
Shamiami Mine, Franklin

SEAT BELTS

North Carolina has a mandatory seat belt law which requires all front passengers to wear seat belts. The state also has a mandatory child restraint law which requires children 3 years old and under to be secured in a child safety seat. A child age 3 up to age 6 must ride in a safety seat or car seat belt.

SENATORS, UNITED STATES

North Carolina's two United States Senators are Jesse Helms (R) and Terry Sanford (D). Their Washington and local addresses and telephone numbers follow.

Senator Jesse Helms
403 Dirksen Senate Office Bldg.
Washington, D.C. 20510
202-224-6342

314 Century Post Office Bldg.
P.O. Drawer 2888
Raleigh, NC 27602
919-856-4630

Federal Bldg., Room 41
P.O. Box 2944
Hickory, NC 28603
704-322-5170

Senator Terry Sanford
716 Hart Senate Office Bldg.
Washington, D.C. 20510
202-224-3154

310 New Bern Ave. Room 318
P.O. Box 25009
Raleigh, 27611
919-856-4401

401 W. Trade St., Room 214
P.O. Box 3555
Charlotte, 28235
704-371-6800

212 Post Office Bldg. Otis St.
P.O. Box 2779
Asheville, 28802

SOCIAL SECURITY

Retirement, Survivors and Disability Insurance

The chart below shows the amount of monthly benefits (in thousands of dollars) in current payment status by county, type of benefit, and sex of those aged 65 and older, as of December 1986.

		Retirement Program			Survivor Program		Disability Program			Age 65 and Older	
County	Total	Retired Workers(a)	Wives or Husbands(a)	Children	Widows, Widowers, or Parents	Children	Disabled Workers	Wives or Husbands	Children	Men	Women
Alamance	$ 8,433	$ 6,093	$ 218	$ 25	$ 943	$ 308	$ 788	$ 15	$ 44	$ 2,920	$ 3,386
Alexander	1,554	1,088	51	10	171	77	140	3	14	528	654
Alleghany	743	504	37	0	111	26	57	2	6	274	308
Anson	1,703	1,126	56	9	211	163	116	5	18	629	572
Ashe	1,460	909	86	13	219	64	144	9	16	571	493
Avery	982	621	48	9	99	56	135	1	12	325	347
Beaufort	2,887	1,761	122	16	526	168	267	2	25	991	1,123
Bertie	1,304	721	59	6	277	69	144	9	20	428	493
Bladen	1,531	906	76	15	241	80	188	7	18	449	591
Brunswick	3,388	2,110	146	16	377	108	576	24	32	1,208	994
Buncombe	13,328	9,170	563	59	1,781	466	1,142	31	115	4,637	5,606
Burke	4,762	3,142	110	79	526	220	603	14	68	1,442	1,856
Cabarrus	8,165	6,095	181	41	696	302	778	14	59	2,571	3,585
Caldwell	4,136	2,631	172	16	544	218	498	9	48	1,413	1,580
Camden	337	226	30	3	29	7	33	2	6	122	132
Carteret	2,998	1,988	146	9	433	107	299	6	12	1,136	1,077
Caswell	1,009	642	32	5	139	47	129	4	10	282	406
Catawba	7,706	5,408	221	29	854	394	709	16	74	2,507	3,309
Chatham	2,143	1,447	97	13	290	69	203	8	15	679	949
Cherokee	1,615	1,064	93	12	120	60	247	10	9	621	516
Chowan	1,077	740	53	8	127	33	99	2	15	446	339
Clay	586	406	31	6	85	15	39	1	3	237	239
Cleveland	6,008	4,203	175	23	661	276	598	14	60	2,147	2,382
Columbus	3,243	1,805	131	11	665	177	369	18	67	1,062	1,209
Craven	4,117	2,613	183	14	609	218	408	18	54	1,423	1,535
Cumberland	8,419	4,707	264	54	1,318	699	1,176	47	153	2,381	2,869
Currituck	752	485	33	5	124	45	58	0	0	260	265
Dare	1,131	755	74	6	137	41	105	3	10	496	359

County	Total	Retirement Program			Survivor Program		Disability Program			Age 65 and Older	
		Retired Workers[a]	Wives or Husbands[a]	Children	Widows, Widowers, or Parents	Children	Disabled Workers	Wives or Husbands	Children	Men	Women
Davidson	7,019	4,730	220	32	863	354	746	11	64	2,484	2,644
Davie	1,787	1,197	79	2	273	68	156	5	7	623	749
Duplin	2,380	1,456	90	17	385	118	287	6	21	791	890
Durham	10,291	7,194	257	62	1,145	429	1,074	17	112	3,236	4,481
Edgecombe	3,402	2,115	112	18	536	223	362	8	27	992	1,405
Forsyth	17,597	12,438	655	83	2,131	711	1,443	16	121	5,747	7,535
Franklin	1,917	1,381	71	2	239	69	142	0	10	626	898
Gaston	12,157	8,459	308	39	1,362	596	1,242	28	124	3,968	4,882
Gates	631	397	45	3	114	30	39	1	3	240	256
Graham	501	293	29	0	77	31	58	3	10	166	183
Granville	2,144	1,369	94	39	242	176	195	2	27	740	801
Greene	631	323	32	9	182	40	38	0	5	168	275
Guilford	22,887	16,219	753	118	2,656	950	1,974	42	174	7,859	9,662
Halifax	4,192	2,596	163	42	608	217	521	13	32	1,258	1,692
Harnett	3,401	1,996	133	16	501	218	474	15	48	981	1,294
Haywood	4,061	2,679	247	17	647	130	303	10	26	1,465	1,554
Henderson	7,346	5,499	482	20	750	154	390	7	43	3,048	2,945
Hertford	1,457	909	55	11	237	57	170	5	12	498	550
Hoke	857	506	35	11	94	63	127	5	14	225	331
Hyde	353	231	15	3	63	12	25	0	3	138	155
Iredell	6,280	4,558	231	26	704	211	480	10	59	2,257	2,520
Jackson	1,715	1,082	97	11	271	57	173	6	17	641	632
Johnston	4,398	2,578	174	27	653	309	581	18	57	1,351	1,642
Jones	596	368	25	10	85	34	61	2	11	198	219
Lee	2,898	1,821	130	12	465	148	299	3	19	880	1,202
Lenoir	3,848	2,248	135	74	658	231	464	5	35	1,127	1,580
Lincoln	2,800	1,875	81	22	299	141	349	6	27	947	1,029
Macon	2,232	1,532	121	7	328	52	179	4	10	830	902
Madison	1,022	659	76	4	144	40	95	0	4	370	381
Martin	1,675	1,066	72	8	252	69	180	6	22	628	592
McDowell	2,786	1,828	98	15	348	143	309	6	40	955	983
Mecklenburg	25,981	18,025	897	117	3,370	1,167	2,196	28	180	8,755	10,758
Mitchell	1,060	708	62	4	153	24	91	5	12	427	388
Montgomery	1,644	1,055	36	9	174	44	281	8	37	536	561
Moore	5,523	3,976	375	31	579	159	353	8	43	2,264	2,081

Nash	3,923	2,447	143	14	679	220	363	17	39	1,183	1,675
New Hanover	7,364	4,887	312	33	1,051	318	679	22	62	2,489	3,006
Northampton	1,477	898	61	11	247	72	163	8	17	422	631
Onslow	3,020	1,749	130	20	479	257	328	18	39	843	1,109
Orange	3,830	2,613	187	12	544	178	268	2	26	1,350	1,653
Pamlico	727	474	50	8	111	15	59	5	5	284	230
Pasquotank	2,111	1,376	101	21	289	109	181	8	26	728	838
Pender	1,780	1,133	80	8	250	76	212	7	15	584	603
Perquimans	763	537	44	7	107	21	34	2	11	288	305
Person	2,010	1,372	82	30	216	87	194	4	23	672	763
Pitt	5,087	3,050	269	47	816	289	549	13	53	1,645	1,949
Polk	1,506	1,089	94	4	188	31	92	1	7	584	630
Randolph	6,423	4,468	183	43	675	362	616	17	59	2,093	2,521
Richmond	2,688	1,594	72	19	362	177	400	23	38	710	1,074
Robeson	5,569	3,087	189	48	808	528	784	14	110	1,550	1,914
Rockingham	6,266	4,112	175	20	824	315	726	24	68	1,756	2,681
Rowan	7,430	5,192	223	17	842	297	792	8	60	2,387	3,215
Rutherford	4,450	3,066	181	32	561	163	401	11	35	1,522	1,869
Sampson	2,968	1,811	142	13	498	156	311	8	30	965	1,138
Scotland	1,828	1,073	51	8	310	123	227	1	35	557	663
Stanly	3,792	2,818	129	20	360	105	333	8	19	1,385	1,600
Stokes	1,473	942	60	5	237	31	164	5	29	527	553
Surry	4,735	3,006	196	9	699	278	489	19	40	1,434	1,991
Swain	879	583	46	9	99	47	86	2	7	340	309
Transylvania	2,175	1,605	160	5	197	43	153	5	7	913	812
Tyrrell	311	197	20	3	68	12	12	0	0	105	151
Union	3,786	2,348	164	24	518	299	399	4	31	1,231	1,416
Vance	2,478	1,582	81	11	409	118	248	11	18	753	1,052
Wake	17,754	11,872	752	78	2,364	803	1,661	40	183	5,972	7,210
Warren	1,054	696	67	7	146	54	71	7	7	413	390
Washington	1,079	565	68	6	275	50	102	2	11	352	441
Watauga	1,605	1,093	84	9	218	68	117	5	10	637	615
Wayne	5,482	3,252	201	36	798	393	700	13	89	1,561	2,028
Wilkes	3,371	2,071	168	29	529	165	365	8	36	1,181	1,265
Wilson	4,263	2,701	178	33	695	210	402	7	38	1,407	1,751
Yadkin	1,932	1,143	91	15	311	84	267	5	16	634	704
Yancey	1,140	703	71	9	202	48	94	4	9	459	450
TOTAL	$393,509	$261,938	$15,284	$2,156	$51,882	$18,588	$38,951	$962	$3,749	$131,519	$157,032

(a) Includes special age 72 beneficiaries.

SPORTS

Baseball

The highest class of professional baseball played in North Carolina is represented by the *Charlotte Orioles* in the AA Southern Association. Charlotte is affiliated with the *Baltimore Orioles* in the American League. Charlotte's 1987 record was 85 games won and 60 games lost, for a percentage of .586.

The *Orioles* completed the 1987 season in second place in the Southern Association, having defeated Jacksonville, three games to two, in the semifinals, but losing to Birmingham in the final playoffs.

Four North Carolina universities—Duke, North Carolina, North Carolina State, and Wake Forest—are members of the Atlantic Coast Conference (ACC) of sports. The ACC baseball champions, by year, since the conference's inception, are as follows:

1954—Clemson
1955—**Wake Forest**
1956—**Duke**
1957—**Duke**
1958—Clemson
1959—Clemson
1960—**North Carolina**
1961—**Duke**
1962—**Wake Forest**
1963—**Wake Forest**
1964—**North Carolina**
1965—Maryland
1966—**North Carolina**
1967—Clemson
1968—**N.C. State**
1969—**North Carolina**
1970—Maryland
1971—Maryland
1972—Virginia
1973—**N.C. State**
1974—**N.C. State**
1975—**N.C. State**
1976—Clemson
1977—**Wake Forest**
1978—Clemson
1979—Clemson
1980—Clemson
1981—Clemson
1982—**North Carolina**
1983—**North Carolina**
1984—**North Carolina**
1985—Georgia Tech
1986—Georgia Tech
1987—Georgia Tech

Basketball

North Carolina's four Atlantic Coast Conference (ACC) basketball teams—Duke, North Carolina, North Carolina State, and Wake Forest—traditionally produce outstanding basketball teams. Tournament champions of the ACC since its inception are as follows:

1954—**N.C. State**
1955—**N.C. State**
1956—**N.C. State**
1957—**North Carolina**
1958—Maryland
1959—**N.C. State**
1960—**Duke**
1961—**Wake Forest**
1962—**Wake Forest**
1963—**Duke**
1964—**Duke**
1965—**N.C. State**
1966—**Duke**
1967—**North Carolina**
1968—**North Carolina**
1969—**North Carolina**
1970—**N.C. State**
1971—South Carolina
1972—**North Carolina**
1973—**N.C. State**
1974—**N.C. State**
1975—**North Carolina**
1976—Virginia
1977—**North Carolina**
1978—**Duke**
1979—**North Carolina**
1980—**Duke**
1981—**North Carolina**
1982—**North Carolina**
1983—**N.C. State**
1984—Maryland
1985—Georgia Tech
1986—**Duke**
1987—**N.C. State**
1988—**Duke**

Teams from North Carolina which have been champions and finalists of the National Collegiate Athletic Association's (NCAA) basketball playoffs are as follows:

1946—North Carolina placed second in finals, losing to Oklahoma A & M 40–43.
1957—North Carolina won finals, defeating Kansas 54–53.
1964—Duke placed second in finals, losing to UCLA 83–98.
1968—North Carolina placed second in finals, losing to UCLA 55–78.
1974—North Carolina won finals, defeating Marquette 76–64.
1977—North Carolina placed second in finals, losing to Marquette 59–67.
1978—Duke placed second in finals, losing to Kentucky 88–94.
1981—North Carolina placed second in finals, losing to Indiana 50–63.
1982—North Carolina won finals, defeating Georgetown 63–62.
1983—North Carolina State won finals, defeating Houston 54–52.
1986—Duke placed second in finals, losing to Louisville 69–72.

Teams from North Carolina which have been champions and finalists in the National Invitational Tournament (NIT) are as follows:

1971—North Carolina won finals, defeating Georgia 84–66.
1978—North Carolina State placed second in finals, losing to Texas 93–101.

North Carolina colleges and universities are also represented in several other basketball conferences. Members of these conferences and their 1988 final standings are:

Colonial Athletic Association

	Conference			All Games		
	W	L	Pct.	W	L	Pct.
xy-Richmond	11	3	.786	24	6	.800
George Mason	9	5	.643	20	10	.667
American U.	9	5	.643	14	14	.500
N.C.-Wilmngtn	8	6	.571	15	14	.517
Navy	6	8	.429	12	16	.429
James Madisn	5	9	.357	10	18	.357
Willim & Mry	5	9	.357	10	19	.345
East Carolina	3	11	.214	8	20	.286

Mid-Eastern Athletic Conference

	Conference			All Games		
	W	L	Pct.	W	L	Pct.
xy-**N. Cr A&T**	16	0	1.000	26	2	.929
Florida A&M	11	5	.688	22	8	.733
S. Carolina St.	10	6	.625	15	13	.536
Howard U.	9	7	.563	16	13	.552
Coppin St.	8	7	.533	13	14	.481
Morgan St.	7	8	.467	13	17	.433
Md-E. Shore	5	11	.313	7	20	.259
Bethune-Ckmn	4	12	.250	6	21	.222
Delaware St.	1	15	.063	3	25	.107

x-won regular-season title
y-won conference tournament

Southern Conference

	Conference			All Games		
	W	L	Pct.	W	L	Pct.
x-Marshall	14	2	.875	24	7	.774
Furman	11	5	.688	18	10	.643
Davidson	9	7	.563	15	13	.536
E. Tenn. St.	9	7	.563	14	15	.483
y-Tn.-Chattang	8	8	.500	20	12	.625
Appalachin St.	8	8	.500	16	13	.552
VMI	6	10	.375	13	17	.433
Citadel	5	11	.313	8	20	.286
W. Carolina	2	14	.125	8	19	.296

Sun Belt Conference

	Conference			All Games		
	W	L	Pct.	W	L	Pct.
xy-**N.C. Chrltt**	11	3	.786	22	8	.733
Va. Cmmnwlth	10	4	.714	21	11	.656
Old Dominion	9	5	.643	18	11	.621
South Alabam	8	6	.571	15	14	.517
Ala.-Birm.	7	7	.500	16	15	.516
W. Kentucky	6	8	.429	15	13	.536
South Florida	3	11	.214	6	22	.214
Jacksonville	2	12	.143	8	21	.276

Football

The highest level collegiate football played in North Carolina is represented by teams in the Atlantic Coast Conference (ACC). Champions in the ACC since its inception (North Carolina teams in bold) are:

1953—**Duke** and Maryland, tied
1954—**Duke**
1955—Maryland and **Duke,** tied
1956—Clemson
1957—**N.C. State**
1958—Clemson
1959—Clemson
1960—**Duke**
1961—**Duke**
1962—**Duke**
1963—**North Carolina** and **N.C. State,** tied
1964—**N.C. State**
1965—Clemson and **N.C. State,** tied
1966—Clemson
1967—Clemson
1968—**N.C. State**
1969—South Carolina
1970—**Wake Forest**
1971—**North Carolina**
1972—**North Carolina**
1973—**N.C. State**
1974—Maryland
1975—Maryland
1976—Maryland
1977—**North Carolina**
1978—Clemson
1979—**N.C. State**
1980—**North Carolina**
1981—Clemson
1982—Clemson
1983—Maryland
1984—Maryland
1985—Maryland
1986—**Clemson**
1987—**Clemson**

North Carolina Bowl Games

Aloha Bowl—Honolulu, Hawaii
1986—Arizona 30, North Carolina 21

Astro-Bluebonnet Bowl—Houston, Texas
1974—Houston 31, N.C. State 31
1980—North Carolina 16, Texas 7

Cotton Bowl—Dallas, Texas
1950—Rice 27, North Carolina 13
1961—Duke 7, Arkansas 6

Dixie Bowl—Birmingham, Alabama
1949—Baylor 20, Wake Forest 7

Gator Bowl—Jacksonville, Florida
1946—Wake Forest 26, South Carolina 14
1947—Oklahoma 34, N.C. State 13
1963—North Carolina 35, Air Force 0
1971—Georgia 7, North Carolina 3
1979—North Carolina 17, Michigan 15
1981—North Carolina 31, Arkansas 27

Liberty Bowl—Memphis, Tennessee
1963—Mississippi State 16, N.C. State 12
1967—N.C. State 14, Georgia 7
'973—N.C. State 31, Kansas 18
—Nebraska 21, North Carolina 17

Bowl—Miami, Florida
34, Nebraska 7
ma 48, Duke 21

Peach Bowl—Atlanta, Georgia
1970—Arizona State 48, North Carolina 26
1972—N.C. State 49, West Virginia 13
1975—West Virginia 13, N.C. State 10
1976—Kentucky 21, North Carolina 0
1977—N.C. State 24, Iowa State 14
1983—Florida State 28, North Carolina 3
1986—Va. Tech 25, N.C. State 24

Rose Bowl—Pasadena, California
1939—Southern California 7, Duke 3
1942—Oregon State 20, Duke 16 (Played at Duke)

Sugar Bowl—New Orleans, Louisiana
1945—Duke 29, Alabama 26
1947—Georgia 20, North Carolina 10
1949—Oklahoma 14, North Carolina 6

Sun Bowl—El Paso, Texas
1973—North Carolina 32, Texas Tech 28
1974—Mississippi State 26, North Carolina 24
1982—North Carolina 26, Texas 10

Tangerine Bowl—Orlando, Florida
1978—North Carolina 30, Pittsburgh 17
1979—Louisana State 34, Wake Forest 10

Golf

The game of golf was begun centuries ago in Scotland.

According to legend, golf was introduced in North Carolina in 1728 when a Fayetteville resident was observed near town swatting a feather ball.

In 1895, James W. Tufts purchased 5,000 acres of cut-over sandhills timberland and established Pinehurst, a name synonymous with fine golf.

Donald Ross, who had already designed approximately 600 courses in the nation, was hired around the turn of the century to lay out the course at Pinehurst.

North Carolina has earned the title of "Golf State, U.S.A." because of the great significance of the game and the style with which it is played in the state.

One of the most popular sports in America is showcased on the famous Number Two Course at Pinehurst, in the World Golf Hall of Fame.

The 1986 NCAA Golf Championship was won by Wake Forest University.

The champions of the Atlantic Coast Conference (ACC) since its inauguration are as follows (N.C. teams shown in bold type):

1954—**Duke**
1955—**Wake Forest**
1956—**North Carolina**
1957—**Wake Forest**
1958—**Wake Forest**
1959—**Duke**
1960—**North Carolina**
1961—**Duke**
1962—**Duke**
1963—**Wake Forest**
1964—Maryland and South Carolina, tied
1965—**North Carolina**
1966—**Duke**
1967—**Wake Forest**
1968—**Wake Forest**
1969—**Wake Forest**
1970—**Wake Forest**
1971—**Wake Forest**
1972—**Wake Forest**
1973—**Wake Forest**
1974—**Wake Forest**
1975—**Wake Forest**
1976—**Wake Forest**
1977—**North Carolina**
1978—**Wake Forest**
1979—**Wake Forest**
1980—**Wake Forest**
1981—**North Carolina**
1982—Clemson
1983—**North Carolina**
1984—**North Carolina**
1985—Georgia Tech
1986—**North Carolina**
1987—Clemson
1988—Clemson

Public Golf Courses

Asheboro
Asheboro Municipal Golf Course; 421 Country Club Rd.; 919-625-4158; 9/35/3,175.
Uwharrie Golf Course; Rt. 5; 919-857-2651; 18/72/6,480.

Asheville
Asheville Municipal Golf Course; 226 Fairway Dr., 704-298-1867; 18/72/6,412.

Banner Elk
Sugar Mountain Golf Course; Box 69; 704-898-4521; 18/64/4,000.

Belmont
Lakewood Golf Course; Lakewood Rd.; 704-825-2852; 18/71/6,098.

Bethania
Bethania Golf Course; 5801 Tobaccoville Rd.; 919-924-5226; 18/72/6,365.

Black Mountain
Black Mountain Golf Course; 225 W. State St., 704-669-2710; 18/71/6,087.

Bladenboro
Oak Grove Golf Course; Rt. 2, Box 193; 919-648-4239; 9/36/3,060.

Boone
Boone Golf Course; Hwy. 231; 704-264-8760; 18/71/6,388.
Seven Devils Golf Course; Hwy. 105; 704-963-6565; 18/71/6,240.
Willow Creek Golf Course; Box 1579; 704-963-4025; 9/27/3,600.

Boonville
Boonville Golf Course; Box 339; 919-367-7561; 9/36/3,381.

Brevard
Sherwood Forest Golf Course; P.O. Box 156, 704-885-2091; 18/3/2,260.

Brown Summit
Bryan Park Golf Course; 6275 Bryan Park Rd.; 919-621-6328; 18/72/7,183.
Monticello Golf Course; Box 457; 919-656-3211; 9/35/2,845.

Burlington
Indian Valley Municipal Golf Course; Indian Valley Drive; 919-584-7871; 18/70/6,610.
Shillelagh Golf Course; Rt. 1, Box 202; 919-449-4882; 18/70/6,231.

Caroleen
Dogwood Valley Golf Course; Box 176; 704-657-6214; 9/36/2,943.

Caswell Beach
Oak Island Country Club; 928 Caswell Beach; 919-278-5275; 18/72/6,608.

Cedar Mountain
Sherwood Forest Golf Course; Hwy. 276 South; 704-885-2091; 18/3/2,260.

Chapel Hill
Twin Lake Golf Course; 1706 Curtis Road; 919-933-1024; 9/36/3,050.

Charlotte
Cedarwood Golf Course; Hwy. 51; 704-542-0206; 18/71/6,900.
Crystal Springs Golf Course; Miller Road; 704-588-2640; 18/71/6,356.
Eastwood Golf Course; 4400 The Plaza; 704-537-7904; 18/71/6,083.
Greenbriar Hills Golf Course; 5002 Old Dowd Road; 704-392-0538; 9/34/2,600.
[illegible]est Country Club; 3018 N. Sharon [illegible] Rd., 704-536-6472; 9/35/2,775.
[illegible] Golf Course, Inc., Camp [illegible]; 704-545-4693;
Oak Hills Golf Course; Oakdale Road; 704-394-2834; 18/72/6,274.
Paradise Valley Golf Course; 10025 N. Tryon St., 704-596-2874; 9/35/2,774.
Pawtuckett Golf Course; Pawtuckett Road; 704-394-5909; 18/70/6,538.
Sunset Hills Golf Course; 800 Radio Road, 704-399-0980; 18/72/6,200.
Westport Golf Course; 251 Golf Course Dr.; 704-483-5604; 18/71/6,833.

Clayton
Plantation Golf Course; 1323 Hwy. 70 West; 919-553-5247; 9/36/3,015.
Pine Hollow Golf Course; Hwy. 70-A; 919-553-4554; 18/72/6,266.

Clemmons
Tanglewood Park; Hwy. 158 West; 919-766-6434; 18/72/6,710; 18/70/7,050.

Colfax
Sandy Ridge Golf Course; 2025 Sandy Ridge Rd.; 919-668-0408; 18/72/6,000.

Concord
Green Oaks Golf Course; Hamby Branch Rd.; 704-786-4412; 18/72/6,250.

Connelly Springs
Pine Mountain Golf Course; Rt. 1, Box 205; 704-433-4950; 18/68/5,100.

Cramerton
Lakewood Golf Course; Lakewood Rd.; 704-825-2852; 18/71/6,098.

Cullowhee
Forest Hills Country Club; Box 1599; 704-293-5442; 9/35/3,035.

Denton
Denton Golf Course; Rt. 3, Box 235; 704-869-3456; 9/36/3,100.

Denver
Westport Golf Course; 251 Golf Course Dr.; 704-483-5604; 18/71/6,833.

Dobson
Beaver Creek Golf Course; Rt. 2; 919-374-5670; 9/36/3,032.

Durham
Duke University Golf Course; Route 751; 919-684-2817; 18/72/6,900.
Hillandale Golf Course; Hillandale Rd.; 919-286-4211; 18/71/6,350.
Lakeshore Golf Course; Lumley Rd.; 919-596-2401; 18/71/6,000.

Lake-Winds Golf Course; Hwy. 501 North; 919-471-4653; 18/72/6,365.
Mike Rubish Golf City; Durham-Chapel Hill Blvd.; 919-489-9655; 9/27/984.
Westwood Golf Course; Andrews Rd.; 919-383-3896; 9/27/890.

Eden
Lyn-Rock Golf Course; 636 Valley Dr.; 919-623-6110; 18/70/5,860.

Elkin
Countryside Golf Course; Rt. 2, Box 543; 919-957-2629; 9/35/2,451.

Etowah
Etowah Valley Country Club; Box 244-A; 704-891-7022; 18/72/6,880.

Fairmont
Flag Tree Golf Course; 1000 Dogwood Dr.; 919-628-9933; 18/72/6,476.

Flat Rock
Lost Diamond Valley Golf Course; 111 High Land Lake Rd.; 704-692-0143; 9/32/2,522.

Forest City
Forest City Municipal Golf Course; Clay St.; 704-245-2474; 9/36/3,200.

Franklin
Holly Springs Golf Course; Cat Creek Rd.; 704-524-7792; 18/72/6,700.
Mill Creek Club; Rt. 1; 704-524-6458; 18/72/6,300.

Fuquay-Varina
Sippihaw Golf Course, Inc.; Rt. 4, Box 1; 919-552-9693; 18/72/6,080

Garner
Eagle Crest Golf Course; Rt. 2, Box 145; 919-772-0580; 18/71/6,253.

Gastonia
Gastonia Municipal Golf Course; Niblick Drive; 704-865-1996; 18/71/6,474.
Gastonia National Golf Course; 2801 Linwood Rd.; 704-867-9452; 18/72/6,400.
Green Valley Golf Course; Linwood Rd.; 704-739-7681; 18/72/6,545.

Goldsboro
Goldsboro Golf Course; S. Slocumb St. Ext.; 919-735-0411; 18/72/6,728.

Graham
Confederate Acres Golf Course; Woods Rd.; 919-227-4815; 18/70/6,070.

Granite Falls
Tri-County Golf Course; Rt. 2, Box 281; 704-728-3560; 18/72/6,575.

Greensboro
Bel-Aire Golf Course; Pleasant Ridge Rd.; 919-668-2413; 18/72/6,500.
Deep River Golf Course, Inc.; 555 Pegg Rd.; 919-668-2181; 18/71/6,537.
Gillespie Park Golf Course; 306 E. Florida St.; 919-373-2439; 9/37/3,465.
Longview Golf Course; 6321 Ballinger Rd.; 919-294-4018; 18/70/6,306.

Grifton
Indian Trails Golf & Country Club, Inc.; Country Club Hills; 919-524-5485; 18/72/6,335.

Hampstead
Belvedere Plantation Golf and Country Club; Box 4055; 919-270-2703; 18/72/6,500.
Chanticleer Golf Course; Hwy. 17; 919-270-2883; 18/71/6,630.

Hayesville
Chatuge Shores Golf Course; Rt. 2; 704-389-8940; 18/72/6,324.

Henderson
Kerr Lake Country Club; Neathery's Bridge Rd.; 919-492-1895; 18/72/6,432.

Hendersonville
Crooked Creek Golf Course; Crooked Creek Rd.; 704-692-2011; 18/71/6,585.

Hickory
Catawba Valley Golf; New Highway 70 East; 704-324-6304; 9/31/2,100.
Hampton Heights Golf Course; 1700 Fifth St., N.E.; 704-328-5010; 18/71/6,448.
Mountain View Golf; Hwy. 127 South; 704-294-0380; 18/72/6,500.

High Point
Blair Park Golf Course; 1901 S. Main St., 919-885-2621; 18/71/6,219.
Fairfield Golf Course; Hwy. 62 East; 919-431-2913; 9/27/2,845.
Lakewood Golf Course; 147 Old Thomasville Rd.; 919-882-2690; 9/27/683.

Oak Hollow Golf Course; 1400 Oakview Rd.; 919-869-4014; 18/72/6,429.
Sumner Hills Golf Course; Rt. 3; 919-431-1953; 18/72/6,015.

High Shoals
Gallagher Trails Golf and Swim Club; Box 10; 704-922-4208; 18/72/6,424.

Hope Mills
Cypress Lakes Golf Course; Rt.1; 919-483-0359; 18/72/6,615.

Indian Trail
Pebble Creek Executive Golf Course; Rt. 8, Hwy. 74 E; 704-821-7276; 18/54/2,251.

Jamestown
Jamestown Park Golf Course; 200 East Fork Rd.; 919-454-4912; 18/72/6,637.
Twin Oaks Golf Course; Rt. 2, Hilltop Rd.; 919-855-5278; 18/54/2,300.

Jonesville
Jonesville Golf Course; Swan Creek Rd.; 919-835-5041; 9/36/2,992.

Kernersville
Pine Knolls Golf Course; 1100 Quail Hollow Rd.; 919-993-5478; 18/72/6,346.
Pine Tree Golf Course; 1680 Pine Tree Lane; 919-993-5598; 18/71/6,800.

Kitty Hawk
Sea Scape Golf Course; Rt. 158, Box 110; 919-261-2158; 18/71/6,122.

Lake Lure
Lake Lure Municipal Golf Course; Rt. 1, Box 100; 704-625-4472; 9/35/3,011.

Lenoir
High Hills Golf Course; Rt. 6; 704-758-1403; 18/71/6,000.

Lexington
Lexington Golf Course; Country Club Dr.; 704-256-2770; 18/70/5,803.

Lillington
Pine Burr Golf Course; Hwy. 401 South; 919-893-5788; 18/72/6,537.

Lincolnton
Lincolnton Country Club; Box 541; 704-735-1382; 9/72/6,211.

Lumber Bridge
Scothurst Country Club; P.O. Box 88; 919-843-5357; 18/72/6,900.

Marion
Marion Lake Club; Hwy. 126; 18/70/6,390.

McLeansville
Cedarcrest Golf Course; Rt. 2, Box 149; 919-697-8251; 18/70/5,682.

Mebane
Arrowhead Golf Course; Mebane-Oaks Rd.; 919-563-5255; 18/72/6,555.

Mocksville
Twin Cedars Golf Course; Twin Cedars Rd.; 704-634-5824; 18/71/6,623.

Monroe
Monroe Golf Course; Hwy. 601 S.; 704-289-3041; 9/36/3,200.

Mooresville
Mooresville Municipal Golf Course; West Wilson Ave.; 704-663-2539; 18/71/6,348.

Morganton
Quaker Meadow Golf Course, Inc.; Rt. 10, Box 3; 704-437-2677; 18/71/6,702.

Mt. Airy
White Pines Country Club; Rt. 5; 919-786-6616; 9/36/3,500.

Mt. Holly
Green Meadows Golf Course; Kelly Rd.; 704-827-9264; 18/70/5,591.

Mt. Olive
Southern Wayne Country Club; Box 127; 919-658-4269; 18/71/6,100.

Murphy
Cherokee Hills Golf Course; Harshaw Rd.; 704-837-5853; 18/72/6,092.

New Bern
Carolina Pines Country Club; Carolina Pines Blvd.; 919-447-7121; 18/71/6,955.
Fairfield Harbour Country Club; 750 Broad Creek Rd.; 919-638-8011; 18/72/6,563.
River Bend Plantation Country Club; Shoreline Drive; 919-638-2819; 18/71/6,750.

Newland
Mountain Glen Golf Course; P.O. Box 326; 704-733-5804; 18/72/6,790.

N. Wilkesboro
Rock Creek Country Club; Rt. 2, Box 440; 919-696-2146; 9/36/2,931.

Old Fort
Old Fort Golf Course; Golf Course Rd.; 704-668-4256; 9/36/3,202.

Olivia
Ponderosa Golf Course; P.O. Box 208; 919-499-4013; 18/73/6,642.

Pembroke
Riverside Country Club; Jacobs Road; 919-521-2100; 18/72/6,200.

Pfafftown
Grandview Golf Course; Box 237; 919-924-8229; 18/71/6,329.

Pinebluff
Pines Golf and Resort Club; US 1 S; 919-281-4530; 18/72/6,605.

Pine Hall
Riverview Golf Course; Box 8; 919-548-6908; 9/35/3,309.

Pineville
Crystal Springs Golf Course; Hwy. 51; 704-588-2640; 18/71/6,356.

Raeford
Arabia Golf Course; Box 151; 919-875-3524; 18/71/6,013.

Raleigh
Cheviot Hills Golf Course; 7301 North Blvd.; 919-876-9920; 18/71/6,500.
Raleigh Golf Association; 1527 Tryon Rd.; 919-772-9987; 9/35/2,670.
Wil-Mar Golf Course, Inc.; Rt. 5, Box 257-F; 919-266-9146; 18/71/6,000.

Randleman
Green Acres Golf Course; 311 Exit at US 220; 919-498-2247; 9/34/2,630; 18/68/5,290.

Reidsville
Wolf Creek Golf Course; 1222 Fillman Dr.; 919-349-7660; 9/35/3,100.

Roaring Gap
Roaring Gap Golf Course; 919-363-2861; 18/72/6,400.

Robbins
Riverside Country Club; Box 428; 919-464-3686; 18/72/6,804.

Rockingham
Loch Haven Golf Course; Sandhill Rd.; 919-895-9797; 18/71/5,800.
Richmond Pines Country Club; US 1 N; 919-895-3279; 18/72/6,267.

Rocky Mount
Green Hills Golf Course; Rt. 5, Box 282; 919-443-7103; 9/36/3,070.
Ru-Bob Par Three & Driving Range; Old Wilson Rd.; 919-446-9444; 9/27/1,000.

Rutherfordton
Cleghorn Golf Course; Cox Rd.; 704-286-9117; 18/72/7,200.
Meadowbrook Golf Course; Rt. 4, Box 184-D; 704-863-2690; 18/72/6,800.
Rutherford Municipal Golf Course; Hospital Drive; 704-287-3406; 9/36/3,000.

Salisbury
Corbin Hills Golf Course; Box 964; 704-636-0672; 18/72/6,639.
Foxwood Golf Course; Rt. 1, Box 382-A; 704-637-2528; 18/72/6,175.
McCanless Golf Course; Rt. 10, Box 27; 704-637-1235; 18/70/5,519.
Rolling Hills Golf Course; Sunset Drive; 704-633-8125; 18/72/6,056.

Sanford
Carolina Lakes; Hwy. 87; 919-499-5421; 18/70/6,337.
Sanford Golf Course; Rt. 5, Box 678; 919-776-0415; 18/71/6,069.

Selma
Cardinal Country Club; Rt. 3, Box 350-1; 919-284-3647; 18/72/6,218.

Shelby
Challenger 3 Golf Course & Drive; 1650 Post Rd.; 704-482-5061; 18/54/2,989.
Royster Memorial Golf Course; 901 West Sumter St.; 704-482-4996; 9/35/2,815.

Siloam
River Mont Golf Course; Rt. 1, Box 136; 919-374-2384; 18/72/6,013.

Southern Pines
Hyland Hills Golf & Country Club; 1420 US 1 N.; 919-692-7581; 18/72/6,726.
Knollwood Fairways; Midland Rd.; 919-692-3572; 9/35/2,752.
Southern Pines Country Club; Country Club Dr.; 919-692-6551; 18/71/5,478; 9/34/2,568.

Southport
Fox Squirrel Country Club; Boiling Springs Lakes; 919-845-2625; 18/72/6,762.

Spring Hope
Peachtree Hills Country Club; P.O. Box 267; 919-478-5745; 9/35/2,718.

Statesville
Lakewood Golf Course, Inc.; Rt. 14, Box 58; 704-873-6441; 18/72/5,486.
Twin Oaks Golf Course; 3250 Twin Oaks Dr.; 704-872-3979; 18/72/6,368.

Stokesdale
Dawn Acres Golf Course; Hwy. 68; 919-643-5397; 18/71/6,365.

Stoneville
Dan Valley Golf Course; Rt. 2; 919-548-6808; 9/35/3,001.
Ponderosa Golf Course; Rt. 3, P.O. Box 573; 919-573-9025; 9/35/2,680.

Taylorsville
Brushy Mountain Golf Course; Lenoir Rd.; 704-632-7502; 18/72/6,637.

Vass
Woodlake Country Club; Lobelia Rd.; 919-245-4686; 18/72/7,017.

Wake Forest
Paschal Golf Course, Inc.; Box 571; 919-556-5861; 9/35/2,575.

Walnut Cove
Hemlock Golf Course; Power Dam Rd.; 919-591-7934; 18/70/5,400.

Warrenton
Warrenton Golf & Country Club; Box 14B, Rt. 3; 919-257-9303; 9/36/3,165.

Waynesville
Lake Junaluska Golf Course; 19 Golf Course Rd.; 704-456-8201; 9/35/2,872.

West Jefferson
Mountain Aire Golf Course; Golf Course Rd., 919-877-4716; 9/35/2,800.

Whitakers
Hickory Meadows Golf Course; Rt. 1, Box 88; 919-437-0591; 18/71/6,500.

Whiteville
Land 'O Lakes Golf Course; County Road 1546; 919-642-5757; 18/70/6,093.

Willow Springs
Hidden Valley Golf Course; Rt. 2; 919-639-4071; 18/72/6,562.

Wilmington
Duck Haven Golf Course; 1202 Eastwood Rd.; 919-791-7983; 18/72/6,431.
Wilmington Municipal Golf Course; 311 Wallace Ave.; 919-791-0558; 18/71/6,890.

Wilson
Wedgewood Golf Course; Old Stantonsburg Rd.; 919-237-4761; 18/72/6,358.

Winston-Salem
Heather Hills Executive Golf Course; 3801 Heathrow Dr.; 919-788-5785; 18/62/3,800.
Hillcrest Golf Course; 2450 Stratford Rd.; 919-765-9961; 27/72/6,840.
Reynolds Park Golf Course; Reynolds Park Rd.; 919-788-9876; 18/71/6,504.
Wilshire Golf Course; 1570 Bridgeton Rd.; 919-788-7016; 18/72/6,406.
Winston Lake Park Golf Course; New Walkertown Rd.; 919-727-9659; 18/71/6,374.

Winton
Old Mill Golf & Country Club; Rt. 1, Box 18-A; 919-358-4671; 9/36/3,255.

Zebulon
Windy Hill; Rt. 2; 919-496-4397; 9/27/1,315.
Zebulon Country Club; Rt. 3, Box 118; 919-269-8311; 18/72/5,646.

North Carolina Sports Hall of Fame

The North Carolina Sports Hall of Fame was begun in 1962 when the Sports Award Committee of the Charlotte Chamber of Commerce appointed officers and directors, and members of the Atlantic Coast Sports Writers Association were polled for nominations for inductees.

Currently the Hall of Fame momentos are stored in the North Carolina Museum of History in Raleigh. It is hoped that the museum will be expanded in the not too distant future and there will be space for a permanent exhibit of the memorabilia.

1963
Jim Beatty, distance runner
Wes Ferrell, baseball
Charlie Justice, football
Estelle Lawson Page, golf
Clarence Parker, football

1964
Everett Case, baseball
Fred Crawford, football
Rick Ferrell, baseball
Enos Slaughter, baseball
Wallace Wade, football

1965
Robert A. ("Bob") Fetzer, coach and athletic director
Jack McDowall, football, basketball, coach, and athletic director
Harvie Ward, Jr., golf

1966
William D. Murray, football coach
Billy Joe Patton, golf
Lee Petty, NASCAR driver
Tom Zachary, baseball

1967
Alvin ("General") Crowder, baseball
Murray Greason, captained football & baseball, basketball coach
George McAfee, football
Ray Reeve, sportscaster
Dave Sime, sprinter, Olympian

1968
Jack Cobb, basketball
Richard S. Tufts, golf
Douglas ("Peahead") Walker, football coach
Hoyt Wilhelm, baseball

1969
Dugan Aycock, golf
Eddie Cameron, basketball & football coach, football player
Billy Goodman, baseball
Sam Jones, basketball

1970
Leon Brogden, high school coach
Horace ("Bones") McKinney, basketball & coach
Clarence Stasavich, football coach

1971
Roman Gabriel, football
Bob Jamieson, high school coach
Sonny Jurgensen, football
Jim Weaver, ACC commissioner, athletic director

1972
Maxine Allen, bowling
John Baker, Jr., football
Dickie Hemric, basketball
Dan Hill, football, athletic director

1973
Walter ("Buck") Leonard, baseball
Gaylord Perry, baseball
Jim Perry, baseball
Richard Petty, NASCAR driver
Floyd ("Chunk") Simmons, decathlon Olympian
Art Weiner, football

1974
Earle Edwards, football coach
Clayton Heafner, golf
Jim ("Catfish") Hunter, baseball

1975
Vic Bubas, basketball coach
Meadowlark Lemon, basketball
John ("Buddy") Lewis, baseball
Leroy Walker, Olympic track team head coach

1976
George Barclay, football coach
Peggy Kirk Bell, golf

Tommy Byrne, baseball
Dr. Angus ("Monk") McDonald, three-sports star, football quarterback
Mickey Walsh, steeplechase trainer

1977
Johnny Allen, baseball
Dick Herbert, sports writer
Lee Stone, high school coach
Tony Waldrop, track

1978
Forrest ("Smokey") Burgess, baseball
Clarence ("Bighouse") Gaines, basketball coach
Bob Gantt, college football, high school basketball
Allen Morris, tennis
Johnny Palmer, golf

1979
Billy Ray Barnes, football, baseball
Jack King, trap & skeet shooter
Ronnie Shavlik, basketball
Ernie Shore, baseball

1980
Smith Barrier, sports journalist
Johnny Mackorell, football, coach & athletic director
Dale Morey, golf, basketball
Pat Preston, football
Jethro Pugh, football

1981
Raymond Floyd, golf
Sam Ranzimo, basketball
Dean Smith, basketball coach
Burgess Whitehead, baseball

1982
Junior Johnson, NASCAR driver
Glen ("Ted") Mann, baseball, sport information director
John ("Red") O'Quinn, football, football manager
David Thompson, basketball

1983
Dr. Lenox Baker, sports medicine
Clyde King, baseball, basketball, baseball manager
Luther Lassiter, billiards
Whitey Lockman, baseball, baseball manager
Jeff Mullins, basketball, Olympian

1984
Walt Bellamy, basketball, Olympian
Marge Burns, golf
Ellis Hagler, football & golf coach
Wallace Shelton, high school coach

1985
Willis Casey, athletic director, swimming coach
Whitt Cobb, basketball, tennis, track
Roger Craig, baseball player, coach & manager
Red Wilson, coach, high school & small college levels

1986
No Awards were presented this year.

1987
Skip Alexander, golf
Bobby Bell, football
C. D. Chesley, T.V. producer
Jack Coombs, baseball
Francis Rogallo, inventor of the flexible-wing hang glider

North Carolina High School State Champions: 1985–86

The state champions for high school athletics and their coaches are as follows, as reported by the North Carolina High School Athletic Association, P.O. Box 3216, Chapel Hill, 27515, 919-962-2345.

Fall 1987

Football	1A	Murphy	David Gentry
	2A	Whiteville	Bill Hewitt
	3A	Shelby	Jim Taylor
	4A	Garner	Hal Stewart
Cross-Country, Men's	1A/2A	Monroe	Tommy Harris
	3A	Sun Valley	Jim Sanders
	4A	Pine Forest	Mickey Stoker
Cross-Country, Women's	1A/2A	East Davidson	Larry Espinosa
	3A	Washington	Bill White
	4A	Chapel Hill	Jack Morgan
Women's Tennis	1A/2A	Mount Airy	Betty Smith
	3A	Madison-Mayodan	Frank Sparks
	4A	Goldsboro	Anne Webb
Women's Golf		Pinecrest	Jim Parkins
Volleyball	1A	Edneyville	Lisa Rhodes
	2A	Mount Airy	Ginger Crissman-Ashley
	3A	Trinity	Cathy Claris
	4A	Tuscola	Susan Hartsell
Men's Soccer	1A/2A/3A	Charlotte Catholic	Bill Finneyfrock
	4A	Athens Drive	Greg Welsh

Winter 1988

Indoor Track, Men's		Hillside	Russell Blunt
Indoor Track, Women's		Grimsley	Russell Woodward
Men's Basketball	1A	St. Pauls	John Gibbs
	2A	Lexington	James Daye
	3A	Bartlett Yancey	Lindsey Page
	4A	A. C. Reynolds	Jim Sziksai
Women's Basketball	1A	Hayesville	Darryl McClure
	2A	Bandys	Mike Matheson
	3A	Trinity	Renee Hayes
	4A	Vance	Dottie Cobb
Wrestling	1A/2A	Mitchell	Steve Atwood
	3A	T. Wingate Andrews	Wally Burke
	4A	Cary	Jerry Winterton
Men's Swimming		C. E. Jordan	Jim Maxwell
Women's Swimming		Grimsley	Durante Griffin

Spring 1987			
Men's Golf	1A/2A	Southwest Guilford	Dave Hardison
	3A	Ragsdale	Herb Pike
	4A	Jacksonville	Ray Durham
Men's Tennis	1A/2A	Lexington	Gary Whitman
	3A	T.C. Roberson	Mike Everhart
	4A	Asheville	Brigitte Worden
Women's Track	1A/2A	Albemarle	Agnes Maske
	3A	Cummings	Ralph Holloway
	4A	Grimsley	Russ Woodward
Men's Track	1A/2A	Hendersonville	David Pierce
	3A	Sun Valley	Jim Sanders
	4A	Hillside	Russell Blunt
Women's Soccer		Page	Zack Osborne
Baseball	1A	Hallsboro	Charles Sanderson
	2A	Greene Central	James Fulghum
	3A	North Gaston	Terry Radford
	4A	Broughton	Brinkley Wagstaff
Softball	1A	Bath	Walt Davis
	2A	South Granville	Jimmy Fleming
	3A	Southern Durham	Andy Andrews
	4A	Northern Nash	Mickey Bridgers

STATE PARKS

The North Carolina Park System is operated by the Department of Natural Resources and Community Development through its Division of Parks and Recreation.

Listed below are the names, mailing addresses, phone numbers, locations and acreage, and a brief summary of the features of each.

Boone's Cave, C/o North Carolina State Parks, West District Office, Route 2, Box 224M, Troutman, 28166, 704-528-6514; 14 miles W of Lexington by US 64 and NC 150; 110 acres. Legendary hide-out of Daniel Boone on the Yadkin River, contains an 80-foot tunnel for visitor exploration, over 30 species of wildflowers, hiking and picnicking available.

Carolina Beach, P.O. Box 475, Carolina Beach, 28428, 919-458-8206; 10 miles S of Wilmington off Hwy. 421; 1,773 acres. Self-guiding nature trail, Venus's-flytrap, 5 other insect-eating plants, over 30 kinds of trees, shrubs, and flowering plants; excellent fishing and boating in the Cape Fear River and adjoining waterways.

Cliffs-of-the-Neuse, Rt. 2, P.O. Box 50, Seven Springs, 28578, 919-778-6234; 14 miles SE of Goldsboro off NC 111; 608 acres. River bluff layered with rocks and sediment containing fossil shells and bones; creative dioramas and audiovisuals in visitor center and museum.

Crowder's Mountain, Rt. 1, P.O. Box 159, Kings Mountain, 28086, 704-867-1181; 6 miles W of Gastonia off 29–74 on SR 1125; 1,966 acres. King's Mountain area, site of Revolutionary War battle; 90 species of birds, including 20 species of warbler, seasonally.

Duke Power, Rt. 2, P.O. Box 224M, Troutman, 28166, 704-528-6350; 10 miles S of Statesville on SR 1330; 1,458 acres. Located on the northern shore of Lake Norman, largest man-made lake in the state; lakeshore campground, swimming, boating and fishing for black crappie, striped and white bass, channel catfish, and yellow perch.

Eno River, Rt. 2, P.O. Box 436-C, Durham, 27705, 919-383-1686; 3 miles NW of Durham off SR 1569; 1,965 acres. Nature hiking, camping, winter canoeing and rafting along a 14-mile section of the Eno River; suspension bridge allows access to both sides of the park.

Falls Lake, 12700 Six Forks Rd., Raleigh, 27609, 919-847-7183; 7 miles N of Raleigh off US I-64 E on Six Forks Rd. to SR 2003; 11,000 acre lake with 230 miles of shoreline. Interim facilities for boating, swimming, fishing and picnicking; commercial marina; fishing for largemouth bass, bluegill, crappie, and catfish.

Fort Fisher State Recreation Area, c/o Carolina Beach State Park, P.O. Box 475, Carolina Beach, 28428, 919-458-8206; 5 miles S of Carolina Beach off SR 421; 237 acres. Seashell collecting, nature study, swimming, and fishing.

Fort Macon, P.O. Box 127, Atlantic Beach, 28512, 919-726-3775; 2 miles E of Atlantic Beach on SR 1190; 389 acres. Ocean recreation and Civil War history with 150-year-old fort.

Goose Creek, Rt. 2, P.O. Box 372, Washington, 27889, 919-923-2191; 10 miles E of Washington off SR 1334; 1,327 acres. Outstanding natural features are natural sand beaches along Pamlico River and stately live oaks draped with Spanish Moss; freshwater fishing for bass, bluegill, perch; saltwater in the Pamlico River for croaker, bluefish, and flounder.

Hammocks Beach, Rt. 2, P.O. Box 295, Swansboro, 28584, 919-326-4881; 4.5 miles W of Swansboro off NC 242; 892 acres. On Bear Island, accessible only by private boat or free passenger ferry; surf swimming; bathhouse; snack bar; channel and surf fishing for bluefish, croaker, flounder, speckled trout, drum, red channel bass.

Lake James, on eastern side of Lake James, near Morganton, under construction. Will offer a public beach, primitive campsites, and nature trails. For more information contact NC Dept. of Natural Resources and Community Development, Division of Parks and Recreation, P.O. Box 27687, Raleigh, 27611-7687, 919-733-4181.

Hanging Rock, P.O. Box 186, Danbury, 27016, 919-593-8480; 5 miles W of Danbury off SR 1101; 5,862 acres. Panoramic view, sparkling mountain streams, waterfalls, and cascades; over 300 species of mountain flora; rock climbing allowed on Moore's and Cook's Walls.

Jockey's Ridge, P.O. Box 592, Nags Head, 27959, 919-441-7132; Nags Head—US 158 Bypass; 385 acres. The highest sand dune on the East Coast; favorite spot for hang gliders and anyone wanting an exhilarating view of North Carolina coast.

Jones Lake, Rt. 2, P.O. Box 945, Elizabethtown, 28337, 919-588-4550; 4 miles N of Elizabethtown on NC 242, 2,208 acres. Shaded by huge old trees and cooled by a clear lake; variety of recreational facilities.

Jordan Lake, Rt. 2, P.O. Box 159, Apex, 27502, 919-362-0586; off US 64 W of Apex; 13,900 acre lake with 150 miles of shoreline. Interim recreation facilities for boating, swimming, sailing, and picnicking; commercial marina; fishing for largemouth and striped bass, bluegill, and crappie.

Kerr Lake, Rt. 3, P.O. Box 800, Henderson, 27536, 919-438-7791; N of Henderson; 2,609 acres divided into seven parks. Over 1,000 campsites; swimming, fishing, boating, sailing, water skiing; special events, spring art show, summer folk art and craft festival, camping crafts fair, amateur striped bass fishing tournament, and Governor's Cup Invitational Regatta in June; three commercial marinas.

Lake Waccamaw, Rt. 1, P.O. Box 63, Kelly, 28448, 919-669-2928; 6 miles S of Lake Waccamaw off US 74-76; 9,219 acres. Limited interim day use.

Medoc Mountain, Rt. 3, P.O. Box 219G, Enfield, 27823, 919-445-2280; 15 miles SW of Roanoke Rapids off NC 561; 2,286 acres. On the fall of the Piedmont and Coastal Plain; unusual mixture of plant and animal species; bluegill, largemouth bass, pickerel, red breast sunfish, Roanoke bass are abundant in Little Fishing Creek.

Merchant's Millpond, Rt. 1, P.O. Box 141A, Gatesville, 27938, 919-357-1191; 6 miles NE of Gatesville on SR 1403; 2,508 acres. Southern swamp forest with massive gum trees and cypresses; canoeing all year from millpond down Bennetts Creek; overnight canoe trips for organized groups by advance arrangement with park superintendent; pond fishing for largemouth bass, crappie, catfish, chain pickerel, shad; winter stopover for migrating waterfowl.

Morrow Mountain, Rt. 5, P.O. Box 430, Albemarle, 28001, 704-982-4402; 7 miles E of Albemarle off NC 24-27-73 on SR 1719; 4,641 acres. Within the ancient Uwharrie Range, which sprawls across four counties; on Pee Dee River and Lake Tillery; variety of recreational facilities; panoramic views, and miles of hiking, nature, and bridle trails.

Mt. Jefferson, P.O. Box 48, Jefferson, 28640, 919-246-9653; 1.5 miles S of Jefferson on US 221; 541 acres. A magnificent oak-hickory forest; is a National Natural Landmark; purple rhododendron, mountain laurel, and azalea; open May through October.

Mt. Mitchell, Rt. 5, P.O. Box 700, Burnsville, 28714, 704-675-4611; 30 miles NE of Asheville off Blue Ridge Parkway on NC 128; 1,459 acres. Highest peak east of Mississippi River, 6,684 feet; 18 miles of hiking trails, including 22-station Balsam Trail near the top of the mountain.

New River, P.O. Box 48, Jefferson, 28640, 919-982-2587; 8 miles SE of Jefferson off NC 88 on SR 1588; 532 acres. On 26 mile stretch of the New River; interim facilities at four access sites for primitive and canoe camping, hiking, fishing, and nature study.

Pettigrew, Rt. 1, P.O. Box 336, Creswell, 27928, 919-797-4475; 9 miles S of Creswell off US 64 on SR 1166; 17,368 acres. Lake Phelps, located here, is teeming with largemouth bass, white perch, channel catfish, and various panfish; ideal sailing conditions; wintering and nesting area for the Canada goose and several species of ducks.

Pilot Mountain, Rt. 1, P.O. Box 21, Pinnacle, 27043, 919-325-2355; 24 miles N of Winston-Salem off US 52; 3,768 acres. Name comes from large quartzite monadnock that rises 1,500 feet above surrounding area. Park is in two sections connected by a 5-mile, 300-foot wide woodland corridor for hiking and horseback riding. Climbing allowed on Little Pinnacle Wall.

Raven Rock, Rt. 3, P.O. Box 1005, Lillington, 27546, 919-893-4888; 6 miles W of Lillington off US 421 on SR 1314; 2,752 acres. A massive rock outcrop 152 feet high, jutting out at a 45° angle over the Cape Fear River; highland trees and shrubs mix with typical Piedmont vegetation; canoe wilderness camping; excellent river and creek fishing for catfish, largemouth bass, variety of sunfish.

Singletary Lake, Rt. 1, P.O. Box 63, Kelly, 28448, 919-669-2928; 12 miles SE of Elizabethtown on NC 53; 1,221 acres. Used primarily for organized group camping; mess hall and kitchen, campers' cabins, washhouses; boating, fishing, swimming open to camping groups. Headquarters for State Lakes: White, Waccamaw, Salter's, Singletary, and Bay Tree Lakes.

South Mountains, Rt. 1, P.O. Box 206, Connelly Springs, 28612, 704-433-4772; 18 miles S of Morganton on SR 1904; 5,783 acres. High Shoals Waterfall tumbles 80 feet into mountain stream; interim facilities for primitive camping, nature study, hiking, and trout fishing.

Stone Mountain, Star Rt. 1, P.O. Box 17, Roaring Gap, 28668, 919-957-8185; 7 miles SW of Roaring Gap off US 21 on SR 1002 to SR 1749; 11,285 acres. A dome-shaped granite mass rising 600 feet above its base; 17 miles of trout streams; rugged terrain with hiking trails and rock climbing.

Theodore Roosevelt, P.O. Box 127, Atlantic Beach, 28512, 919-726-3775; 7 miles S of Atlantic Beach on SR 1201; 265 acres. Coastal plain brackish marsh and maritime forest lands given by the family of our 26th president; abundant bird life; unique plant life. Coastal environment interpreted by live exhibits and multimedia programs at Marine Resources Center–Bogue Banks.

Waynesboro, Route 2, Box 50, Seven Springs, 28578, 919-778-6234; off US 117 Bypass in Goldsboro; 146 acres. Picnicking, fishing, and hiking along Neuse River, day use only.

Weymouth Woods, 400 N Ft. Bragg Rd., Southern Pines, 28387; 2 miles S of Southern Pines off US 1 on SR 2074; 628 acres. Sandhills Nature Preserve established to preserve and protect a small segment of the specially adapted plant and animal communities of the Sandhills Region. Interpretive displays in museum: subterranean life, beaver pond, "Sounds of the Night." Numerous migratory songbirds; 600 species of plants; scheduled trail walks Mon.–Sat.

Wm. B. Umstead (Crabtree), Rt. 8, P.O. Box 130, Raleigh, 27612, 919-787-3033; 10 miles W of Raleigh on US 70; 3,979 acres. Located within Research Triangle area; family camping, organized group camp, lake fishing, hiking trails, bridle trails, summer naturalist; interpretive programs.

Wm. B. Umstead (Reedy Creek), 1800 Harrison Ave., Cary, 27511, 919-467-7259; 11 miles W of Raleigh on I-40; 1,355 acres. Also within Research Triangle area; organized group camp, lake fishing, hiking trails, bridle trails.

STATE SYMBOLS

The following list and illustrations present the state symbols, nickname, and flag.

Flower
Dogwood

Bird
Cardinal

Fish
Channel Bass

Nickname
"The Tar-Heel State"

Tree
Pine

Mammal
Gray Squirrel

Song
"The Old North State"

Motto
"To Be Rather Than To Seem."

Seal

TAXES

Persons residing in North Carolina are subject to the following state taxes: personal income tax; occupational license taxes; intangible taxes; sales and use tax; cigarette tax; soft drink tax; alcoholic beverage taxes; motor vehicle taxes; inheritance taxes.

On the local level the taxes are as follows: occupational license taxes; property taxes; real estate transfer taxes; sales and use taxes; occupancy tax.

The state sales and use tax rate of 3 percent is levied on purchases of tangible commodities, room and cottage rentals, laundry and dry cleaning services and certain utility services.

Sales of motor vehicles, boats, and aircraft are taxable at a 2 percent rate with a maximum tax of $300 per single article.

Sales of farm, mill, and laundry machinery, equipment, and accessories thereto are taxed at a rate of 1 percent with a maximum tax of $80 per single article. Fuel sold to farmers, manufacturers and laundries is taxable at a 1 percent rate.

All counties levy a 2 percent local sales and use tax on transactions (other than sales of taxable utility services) subject to the 3 percent state rate.

State Sales and Use Tax: Comparative statement of Gross Collections and Gross Retail Sales, by Counties

	Gross Collections[a]			*Gross Retail Sales*[b]	
County	*February 1987 through January 1988*	*February 1986 through January 1987*	*Percent increase (decrease)*	*Calendar year 1987*	*Calendar year 1986*
Alamance	$ 21,405,495	$ 20,554,731	4.14	$ 982,978,315	$ 949,673,135
Alexander	2,133,691	1,987,627	7.35	99,739,345	94,638,123
Alleghany	960,575	903,428	6.33	41,859,489	41,525,498
Anson	2,096,424	1,956,322	7.16	98,576,292	93,339,568
Ashe	2,765,202	2,575,118	7.38	119,156,532	108,278,242
Avery	2,370,533	2,183,312	8.58	102,453,800	92,001,984
Beaufort	6,408,694	6,143,973	4.31	319,186,111	314,512,294
Bertie	1,244,456	1,154,877	7.76	65,948,066	62,198,721
Bladen	2,430,225	2,145,138	13.29	141,599,174	125,155,263
Brunswick	7,875,628	7,347,530	7.19	292,777,796	268,129,198
Buncombe	39,314,450	35,545,109	10.60	1,621,017,456	1,510,597,805
Burke	8,980,014	8,303,952	8.14	406,825,217	388,200,185
Cabarrus	15,470,206	13,839,094	11.79	628,902,322	580,375,988
Caldwell	9,132,408	8,202,578	11.34	428,199,895	403,577,258
Camden	265,650	256,825	3.44	13,541,939	12,897,934
Carteret	9,574,829	9,120,622	4.98	400,762,834	387,294,246
Caswell	718,905	627,533	14.56	33,601,211	31,364,371
Catawba	29,876,882	27,139,639	10.09	1,351,709,317	1,275,815,844
Chatham	3,872,579	3,631,313	6.64	179,403,182	172,423,838
Cherokee	3,538,705	3,557,947	(.54)	147,636,909	149,663,486

County	Gross Collections(a) February 1987 through January 1988	February 1986 through January 1987	Percent increase (decrease)	Gross Retail Sales(b) Calendar year 1987	Calendar year 1986
Chowan	$ 1,824,733	$ 1,722,449	5.94	$ 73,323,261	$ 74,128,271
Clay	576,994	556,019	3.77	30,939,448	32,222,734
Cleveland	13,590,525	11,850,364	14.68	627,976,701	559,229,652
Columbus	7,373,626	8,182,228	(9.88)	318,307,675	350,641,233
Craven	12,594,337	11,920,237	5.66	526,493,518	512,726,054
Cumberland	42,395,977	40,441,761	4.83	1,810,442,204	1,737,783,342
Currituck	1,356,685	1,223,088	10.92	69,826,188	70,451,422
Dare	9,430,386	8,102,164	16.39	351,167,386	305,971,099
Davidson	15,673,542	14,605,190	7.31	810,908,658	767,487,670
Davie	2,771,631	2,633,625	5.24	139,427,877	134,927,626
Duplin	4,167,246	3,836,736	8.61	198,397,341	182,687,772
Durham	41,941,078	39,617,875	5.86	1,479,500,938	1,429,695,437
Edgecombe	6,658,976	6,181,161	7.73	329,359,224	310,502,418
Forsyth	77,119,024	71,368,168	8.06	3,111,407,695	2,911,811,263
Franklin	2,630,590	2,519,319	4.42	145,874,882	140,623,525
Gaston	27,541,718	24,912,807	10.55	1,324,723,943	1,199,511,343
Gates	462,651	437,989	5.63	30,863,798	30,248,871
Graham	677,889	675,736	.32	27,832,968	27,957,602
Granville	3,702,580	3,381,856	9.48	163,700,169	153,601,519
Greene	942,541	850,745	10.79	53,646,604	49,300,330
Guilford	100,552,992	92,415,262	8.81	4,802,988,688	4,544,640,751
Halifax	8,335,276	7,950,757	4.84	359,389,747	355,910,860
Harnett	7,259,315	6,818,770	6.46	347,390,185	337,260,442
Haywood	8,972,095	8,195,582	9.47	388,883,349	361,262,522
Henderson	12,945,193	12,196,893	6.14	586,929,738	563,640,554
Hertford	3,532,467	3,427,930	3.05	171,748,131	169,258,786
Hoke	1,208,528	1,162,176	3.99	56,363,489	53,385,023
Hyde	525,368	522,481	.55	23,489,181	23,462,917
Iredell	15,818,182	14,624,135	8.16	797,362,002	761,661,643
Jackson	3,375,351	3,153,366	7.04	142,373,381	134,814,717
Johnston	11,025,225	10,208,389	8.00	563,756,661	529,513,696
Jones	568,288	496,219	14.52	29,144,577	26,996,946
Lee	9,932,218	9,176,420	8.24	442,523,418	417,014,918
Lenoir	11,701,187	11,910,793	(1.76)	513,507,557	508,815,695
Lincoln	5,464,753	5,173,245	5.63	244,450,137	231,639,486
Macon	4,235,813	4,080,283	3.81	165,485,531	162,241,535
Madison	956,794	960,958	(.43)	45,126,087	44,011,321
Martin	4,005,524	3,762,692	6.45	143,053,561	137,241,476
McDowell	3,927,962	3,758,112	4.52	187,459,257	177,757,992
Mecklenburg	162,714,546	151,364,196	7.50	8,016,747,464	7,526,725,898
Mitchell	2,207,769	2,098,750	5.19	107,813,848	101,139,567
Montgomery	2,470,205	2,444,382	1.06	120,692,822	120,511,975
Moore	10,277,898	8,687,790	18.30	436,336,187	378,581,486
Nash	16,637,996	15,649,298	6.32	778,712,528	743,954,559
New Hanover	31,714,700	28,835,049	9.99	1,412,696,389	1,336,956,303
Northampton	995,169	999,060	(.39)	55,061,057	56,723,602
Onslow	15,245,367	15,007,311	1.59	630,844,528	634,552,597
Orange	14,209,875	13,615,303	4.37	573,771,745	548,508,745
Pamlico	848,273	782,591	8.39	39,838,752	37,196,327
Pasquotank	6,594,973	6,334,517	4.11	282,100,712	277,563,209

County	Gross Collections(a)			Gross Retail Sales(b)	
	February 1987 through January 1988	*February 1986 through January 1987*	*Percent increase (decrease)*	*Calendar year 1987*	*Calendar year 1986*
Pender	$ 1,886,971	$ 1,725,020	9.39	$ 88,593,987	$ 85,994,316
Perquimans	641,772	529,334	21.24	32,496,107	27,985,904
Person	3,652,738	3,383,664	7.95	161,963,919	154,782,188
Pitt	19,690,515	18,185,655	8.27	874,839,964	831,082,548
Polk	1,087,711	939,638	15.76	48,147,516	43,992,779
Randolph	12,060,513	10,846,753	11.19	544,363,877	505,784,150
Richmond	6,050,535	5,509,853	9.81	264,295,751	247,051,420
Robeson	12,723,982	11,545,291	10.21	597,548,908	548,766,915
Rockingham	11,680,456	10,955,655	6.62	487,890,266	460,200,307
Rowan	16,568,984	15,285,846	8.39	699,495,197	666,946,246
Rutherford	8,407,983	7,572,012	11.04	464,203,165	422,672,808
Sampson	5,774,348	5,466,515	5.63	275,539,617	260,333,260
Scotland	4,948,073	4,793,907	3.22	205,891,406	204,879,709
Stanly	7,755,331	7,460,125	3.96	381,796,917	363,188,040
Stokes	2,465,428	2,094,367	17.72	109,800,499	93,879,594
Surry	10,958,279	10,151,364	7.95	546,503,721	508,587,724
Swain	1,063,805	1,018,803	4.42	53,065,348	52,283,742
Transylvania	3,383,325	3,317,071	2.00	122,892,213	119,840,196
Tyrrell	296,798	275,345	7.79	15,913,925	15,325,431
Union	12,676,346	11,545,427	9.80	614,197,724	568,721,915
Vance	6,436,693	6,239,881	3.15	277,676,137	276,134,183
Wake	114,374,421	109,966,420	4.01	4,703,825,264	4,529,986,736
Warren	1,055,411	1,050,242	.49	52,547,656	52,061,638
Washington	1,471,019	1,291,239	13.92	76,504,010	70,538,085
Watauga	7,461,897	7,028,698	6.16	305,825,121	293,371,857
Wayne	15,920,635	15,226,004	4.56	745,152,831	710,818,009
Wilkes	8,330,198	7,444,346	11.90	369,034,652	345,442,212
Wilson	13,827,813	12,782,848	8.17	668,285,213	605,325,615
Yadkin	2,847,074	2,707,139	5.17	139,002,652	135,902,327
Yancey	1,488,966	1,406,281	5.88	61,588,599	59,252,722
Foreign	126,715,331	110,213,403	14.97	3,902,037,733	3,616,665,483
Sales tax on utility services***	299,916,375	189,536,805	6.00	—	—
Use tax on motor vehicles, airplanes, boats	24,725,098	24,356,006	1.52		
Totals	$1,591,472,408	$1,479,859,850	7.54	$59,456,956,284	$56,223,915,771

Note: Detail may not add to totals due to rounding.

(a) State sales and use taxes remitted in the months shown. Merchants filing monthly remit taxes to the State in the month following the month in which sales occur. Merchants filing semimonthly remit taxes to the State 10 days following the end of the half-month period in which sales occur.

(b) Total taxable and nontaxable sales reported on sales and use tax report forms. Data reflect sales by merchants during the calendar year for merchants filing monthly reports, and sales during the period January 16 through the following January 15 for merchants filing semimonthly reports.

(c) Tax on utility services is remitted quarterly. Utility sales not presently tabulated.

Property Tax

This figure represents the total amount of property taxes levied by all local jurisdictions in the county for the fiscal year. The tax is levied on all real and tangible personal property. Personal property includes machinery and equipment, inventories, household property, motor vehicles, etc. There are certain exemptions and exclusions. Preferential treatment is given for certain stored agricultural products. Property taxes are collected by the county and by the component jurisdictions—cities, school districts, and other special districts. County sums differ from the state total due to rounding.

County	Property Tax Levies (000's) 1984–85	Property Tax Levies (000's) 1985–86	County	Property Tax Levies (000's) 1984–85	Property Tax Levies (000's) 1985–86
Alamance	$ 24,097	$ 26,441	Guilford	$ 109,459	$ 129,699
Alexander	3,562	3,748	Halifax	10,523	11,625
Alleghany	1,235	1,347	Harnett	9,699	10,045
Anson	4,675	5,273	Haywood	8,734	9,188
Ashe	3,208	3,791	Henderson	11,480	12,584
Avery	2,478	3,226	Hertford	4,245	4,504
Beaufort	6,914	7,249	Hoke	3,438	3,647
Bertie	2,790	3,734	Hyde	1,555	1,591
Bladen	5,508	6,174	Iredell	16,212	16,735
Brunswick	15,035	16,157	Jackson	3,989	4,168
Buncombe	41,357	46,346	Johnston	13,062	14,057
Burke	13,683	13,933	Jones	1,245	1,295
Cabarrus	18,056	19,840	Lee	9,859	10,772
Caldwell	12,456	13,738	Lenoir	10,946	11,956
Camden	845	858	Lincoln	8,426	8,657
Carteret	10,197	11,040	Macon	4,342	4,342
Caswell	2,307	2,379	Madison	2,185	2,511
Catawba	23,230	24,783	Martin	7,052	7,966
Chatham	6,644	7,280	McDowell	5,232	5,777
Cherokee	2,141	2,228	Mecklenburg	199,040	215,975
Chowan	2,404	2,697	Mitchell	2,184	2,496
Clay	914	888	Montgomery	4,123	4,794
Cleveland	14,717	15,250	Moore	11,861	12,727
Columbus	8,305	8,788	Nash	14,013	15,592
Craven	11,526	12,191	New Hanover	35,995	39,904
Cumberland	43,218	43,931	Northampton	3,972	4,214
Currituck	3,178	3,892	Onslow	13,474	14,567
Dare	11,188	12,183	Orange	21,086	23,917
Davidson	18,837	19,045	Pamlico	1,774	1,864
Davie	4,874	5,233	Pasquotank	4,436	4,932
Duplin	6,425	6,639	Pender	4,661	5,545
Durham	58,538	66,653	Perquimans	1,687	1,812
Edgecombe	10,564	11,666	Person	6,434	6,649
Forsyth	87,382	89,868	Pitt	21,697	23,480
Franklin	5,455	5,998	Polk	2,498	2,540
Gaston	35,603	37,882	Randolph	15,613	17,671
Gates	1,407	1,568	Richmond	7,286	7,769
Graham	717	1,056	Robeson	15,604	17,110
Granville	6,230	7,144	Rockingham	19,383	20,415
Greene	2,698	2,831	Rowan	16,691	19,268

County	Property Tax Levies (000's) 1984–85	Property Tax Levies (000's) 1985–86	County	Property Tax Levies (000's) 1984–85	Property Tax Levies (000's) 1985–86
Rutherford	$ 10,640	$ 11,547	Vance	$ 5,605	$ 6,251
Sampson	9,176	9,527	Wake	128,271	143,177
Scotland	6,815	7,398	Warren	2,558	3,131
Stanly	9,529	9,918	Washington	2,578	2,854
Stokes	7,362	7,970	Watauga	6,412	7,632
Surry	11,686	12,235	Wayne	14,483	15,955
Swain	888	917	Wilkes	8,180	8,376
Transylvania	6,162	6,594	Wilson	15,952	16,812
Tyrrell	1,065	1,231	Yadkin	4,041	4,256
Union	15,856	16,576	Yancey	1,424	2,076
			Total	1,468,476	1,603,761

1986 Individual Income Tax

Counties	Number of Taxpayers: Taxable	Number of Taxpayers: Non-taxable	Adjusted Gross Income[a]: Total	Adjusted Gross Income[a]: Average[b]	Computed Tax Due: Total	Computed Tax Due: Average[c]
Alamance	60,397	6,809	$ 1,052,764,485	$15,665	$ 43,152,331	$ 714
Alexander	14,000	1,608	210,810,080	13,507	8,127,075	581
Alleghany	4,492	714	59,048,536	11,342	2,165,713	482
Anson	11,472	1,572	163,139,164	12,507	5,795,295	505
Ashe	10,141	1,773	134,700,100	11,306	4,916,943	485
Avery	6,765	1,058	96,750,946	12,367	3,654,732	540
Beaufort	19,573	3,480	310,797,557	13,482	12,175,334	622
Bertie	8,555	1,499	117,841,025	11,721	4,178,203	488
Bladen	11,433	2,126	167,994,392	12,390	6,101,690	534
Brunswick	19,737	3,724	321,605,479	13,708	12,458,587	631
Buncombe	86,749	13,571	1,528,191,148	15,233	62,281,463	718
Burke	39,045	4,500	666,332,475	15,302	27,788,479	712
Cabarrus	49,872	6,119	868,555,704	15,512	35,259,381	707
Caldwell	37,801	4,363	582,461,547	13,814	22,689,624	600
Camden	2,521	407	38,772,903	13,242	1,531,721	608
Carteret	22,923	3,914	372,630,200	13,885	14,604,414	637
Caswell	8,527	1,052	125,695,713	13,122	4,849,907	569
Catawba	67,389	7,571	1,222,510,320	16,309	51,329,489	762
Chatham	18,222	2,497	301,986,236	14,575	12,343,804	677
Cherokee	8,521	1,523	111,463,791	11,098	3,973,662	466
Chowan	6,265	1,045	97,695,205	13,365	3,700,539	591
Clay	3,046	539	40,073,589	11,178	1,413,366	464
Cleveland	43,735	5,609	716,658,039	14,524	28,544,466	653
Columbus	20,541	3,779	325,923,432	13,401	12,612,032	614
Craven	30,753	6,190	514,958,825	13,939	19,977,620	650
Cumberland	86,284	16,060	1,431,486,291	13,987	55,106,400	639
Currituck	5,178	795	83,082,328	13,910	3,258,347	629
Dare	9,991	1,558	180,903,101	15,664	7,572,598	758
Davidson	64,186	7,603	1,049,886,623	14,625	42,146,997	657
Davie	14,208	1,874	268,315,455	16,684	11,423,227	804
Duplin	17,537	3,311	263,684,904	12,648	10,180,616	581
Durham	87,174	10,601	1,805,136,976	18,462	78,054,474	895

Counties	Number of Taxpayers: Taxable	Number of Taxpayers: Non-taxable	Adjusted Gross Income[a]: Total	Adjusted Gross Income[a]: Average[b]	Computed Tax Due: Total	Computed Tax Due: Average[c]
Edgecombe	26,845	3,845	$ 417,601,781	$ 13,607	$ 15,815,718	$ 589
Forsyth	145,934	17,544	3,245,813,098	19,855	143,386,690	983
Franklin	14,948	2,064	229,048,860	13,464	8,786,048	588
Gaston	91,879	11,082	1,600,502,993	15,545	65,569,138	714
Gates	3,330	518	53,444,063	13,889	2,156,057	647
Graham	2,798	532	34,111,235	10,244	1,178,149	421
Granville	17,485	2,320	268,835,350	13,574	10,274,891	588
Greene	6,188	1,073	86,546,612	11,919	3,126,275	505
Guilford	186,948	22,467	4,060,425,890	19,389	178,232,465	953
Halifax	22,844	3,601	351,091,572	13,276	13,382,453	586
Harnett	26,044	4,012	392,871,575	13,071	14,824,695	569
Haywood	22,690	3,952	375,080,816	14,079	15,286,659	674
Henderson	34,836	6,096	610,535,644	14,916	25,140,807	722
Hertford	9,158	1,526	139,483,888	13,055	5,221,248	570
Hoke	8,154	1,306	111,201,116	11,755	3,800,292	466
Hyde	2,111	571	28,424,816	10,598	1,015,090	481
Iredell	48,659	6,324	819,963,800	14,913	32,987,978	678
Jackson	10,370	1,773	158,916,387	13,087	6,361,978	613
Johnston	36,681	5,641	574,706,895	13,579	22,262,606	607
Jones	3,886	845	52,666,892	11,132	1,830,430	471
Lee	21,488	2,784	389,543,576	16,049	15,935,219	742
Lenoir	27,798	4,519	462,149,054	14,300	18,146,807	653
Lincoln	24,928	2,950	430,841,205	15,455	17,795,767	714
Macon	10,234	2,005	141,308,000	11,546	5,109,894	499
Madison	6,626	1,394	85,673,683	10,683	3,046,107	460
Martin	11,244	2,052	166,678,356	12,536	6,206,539	552
McDowell	17,780	2,285	270,635,439	13,488	10,568,337	594
Mecklenburg	255,572	30,811	5,921,985,021	20,679	262,319,121	1,026
Mitchell	7,002	1,068	102,648,545	12,720	3,935,862	562
Montgomery	11,348	1,466	168,203,735	13,127	6,399,938	564
Moore	29,143	4,194	546,356,133	16,389	22,781,496	782
Nash	36,109	5,109	638,642,917	15,494	25,935,221	718
New Hanover	56,417	8,292	1,157,315,382	17,885	49,846,188	884
Northampton	8,245	1,446	116,072,125	11,977	4,225,167	512
Onslow	33,196	8,285	472,479,392	11,390	16,930,312	510
Orange	40,333	5,378	853,108,695	18,663	37,388,701	927
Pamlico	4,697	960	70,019,643	12,378	2,646,726	563
Pasquotank	12,545	2,046	203,028,390	13,915	7,926,495	632
Pender	10,726	1,798	170,233,068	13,593	6,488,951	605
Perquimans	4,077	823	55,259,961	11,278	1,962,994	481
Person	14,842	1,841	229,946,086	13,783	9,070,377	611
Pitt	44,813	6,583	791,744,688	15,405	31,710,952	708
Polk	6,928	1,133	137,038,329	17,000	5,963,052	861
Randolph	54,032	6,221	864,015,535	14,340	34,683,805	642
Richmond	19,519	2,927	298,074,934	13,280	11,269,467	577
Robeson	42,750	7,009	607,534,342	12,210	21,803,871	510
Rockingham	44,093	5,515	729,876,141	14,713	29,606,870	671
Rowan	53,273	6,884	890,562,934	14,804	35,709,924	670
Rutherford	27,214	3,888	401,877,481	12,921	15,221,413	559
Sampson	20,345	3,757	299,142,692	12,412	10,974,518	539
Scotland	14,044	1,778	230,577,099	14,573	8,851,023	630

Counties	Number of Taxpayers: Taxable	Non-taxable	Adjusted Gross Income(a): Total	Average(b)	Computed Tax Due: Total	Average(c)
Stanly	26,970	3,393	$ 429,960,567	$ 14,161	$ 16,946,880	$ 628
Stokes	17,449	2,328	294,962,665	14,914	12,112,178	694
Surry	32,521	5,035	501,067,386	13,342	19,346,112	595
Swain	3,924	867	47,062,058	9,823	1,599,423	408
Transylvania	12,293	1,929	217,032,310	15,260	8,980,049	731
Tyrrell	1,464	377	18,399,844	9,994	615,277	420
Union	38,836	4,774	679,562,352	15,583	27,537,118	709
Vance	18,521	2,362	282,784,036	13,541	10,774,422	582
Wake	208,309	24,453	4,873,736,933	20,939	217,657,290	1,045
Warren	6,286	990	83,365,367	11,458	2,899,681	461
Washington	6,224	1,182	104,313,264	14,085	4,169,695	670
Watauga	14,092	2,346	218,076,017	13,267	8,404,523	596
Wayne	41,526	6,935	649,290,262	13,398	24,842,311	598
Wilkes	30,035	4,127	464,462,768	13,596	17,854,674	594
Wilson	32,184	4,834	559,211,806	15,106	22,360,976	695
Yadkin	15,597	2,225	242,814,167	13,624	9,486,128	608
Yancey	7,071	1,225	100,947,081	12,168	3,890,547	550
Other ****	151,929	22,340	2,092,070,873	12,005	85,488,165	563
Total	3,255,413	454,859	$58,604,822,189		$2,419,434,756	

Note: Returns are tabulated in county of residence designated by taxpayer without further clerical scrutiny.
(a) Adjusted gross income is not reduced by adjusted gross loss.
(b) Adjusted gross income divided by total number of taxpayers.
(c) Total tax due divided by number of taxpayers filing taxable returns.

TELEVISION STATIONS

Archdale
WGHP-TV (Channel 8)
Taft Broadcasting
2005 Francis St.
27263, 919-841-8888

Asheville
WHNS-TV (Channel 21)
Pappas Telecasting of the Carolinas
521 College St.
28801, 704-258-2100

WLOS-TV (Channel 13) ABC
Wometco Skyway Broadcasting Co.
P.O. Box 2150
28802, 704-255-0013

Burlington
WRDG (Channel 16)
Bass Mountain Rd.
Snow Camp
27349, 919-376-6016

Chapel Hill
WUND-TV (Channel 2)
U.N.C.
910 Raleigh Rd.
27514, 919-962-8191

WUNE-TV (Channel 17)
U.N.C.
910 Raleigh Rd.
27514, 919-962-8191

WUNF-TV (Channel 33)
U.N.C.
910 Raleigh Rd.
27514, 919-962-8191

WUNG-TV (Channel 58)
U.N.C.
910 Raleigh Rd.
27514, 919-962-8191

WUNJ-TV (Channel 39)
U.N.C.
910 Raleigh Rd.
27514, 919-962-8191

Charlotte
WBTV (Channel 3) ABC
Jefferson-Pilot Broadcasting Co.
One Julian Price Place
28208, 704-374-3500

WCCB-TV (Channel 18)
WCCB-TV, Inc.
1 Television Place
28205, 704-372-1800

WPCQ-TV (Channel 36)
Channel 36 Partners, Channel 36, Inc.
P.O. Box 18665
28218, 704-536-3636

WSOC-TV (Channel 9) ABC
Cox Communications Broadcasting Co.
P.O. Box 34665
28234, 704-335-4700

Durham
WTVD (Channel 11) CBS
Capital Cities
Communications, Inc.
P.O. Box 2009,
411 Liberty St.
27702, 919-683-1111

Fayetteville
WKFT (Channel 40)
Central Carolina Television, Inc.
230 Donaldson St.
28301, 919-323-4040

Greensboro
WFMY-TV (Channel 2) CBS
Harte-Hanks Communications
P.O. Box TV2
27420, 919-379-9639

WGGT (Channel 48)
Guilford Telecasters, Inc.
330 S. Greene St.
27401, 919-274-4848

WLXI-TV (Channel 61)
P.O. Box TV61
27420, 919-855-5610

Greenville
WNCT-TV (Channel 9) CBS
3221 Evans St.
27834, 919-756-3180

Hickory
WHKY-TV (Channel 14)
526 Main Ave. SE
28601, 704-322-5115

High Point
WGHPiedmont-TV (Channel 8)
P.O. Box TV 8
27420, 919-841-8888

New Bern
WCTI-TV (Channel 12) ABC
400 Glenburnie Dr.
P.O. Box 2325
28560, 919-637-2111

Raleigh
WRAL-TV (Channel 5) ABC
Capitol Broadcasting Co.
P.O. Box 12000
27605, 919-821-8500

WPTF-TV (Channel 28) NBC
Durham Life Broadcasting Service, Inc.
410 S. Salisbury St.
27602, 919-832-8311

Washington
WITN-TV (Channel 7) NBC
WITN-TV, Inc.
Highway 17
27889, 919-946-3131

Wilmington
WECT-TV (Channel 6) NBC
Atlantic Telecasting Corp.
322 Shipyard Blvd.
28401, 919-791-8070

WWAY (Channel 3) ABC
Clay Broadcasting Corp.
P.O. Box 2068
28402, 919-762-8581

Winston-Salem
WNRW-TV (Channel 45)
Act III Broadcasting
3500 Myer-Lee Dr.
27101, 919-722-4545

WXII-TV (Channel 12) NBC
700 Coliseum Dr.
27106, 919-721-9944

PUBLIC/EDUCATIONAL TV STATIONS

Asheville
WUNF-TV (Channel 33)
University of North Carolina Board of Governors
P.O. Box 3508, Chapel Hill
27514, 919-962-8191

Chapel Hill
WUNC-TV (Channel 4)
University of North Carolina Board of Governors
P.O. Box 3508
27514, 919-962-8191

Charlotte
WTVI-TV (Channel 42)
Charlotte-Mecklenburg Public Broadcasting Authority
42 Coliseum Dr.
28205, 704-372-2442

Columbia
WUND-TV
27925, 919-962-8191

Concord
WUNG-TV
28025, 919-962-8191

Greenville
WUNK-TV
27834, 919-962-8191

Jacksonville
WUNM-TV
28540, 919-962-8191

Linville
WUNE-TV
28646, 919-962-8191

Wilmington
WUNJ-TV (Channel 39)
University of North Carolina Board of Governors
P.O. Box 3508, Chapel Hill 27514, 919-962-8191

Winston-Salem
WUNL-TV (Channel 26)
University of North Carolina Board of Governors
P.O. Box 2688, Chapel Hill 27514, 919-962-8191

TIME ZONE

The state of North Carolina lies entirely within the Eastern Time Zone.

TOURIST ATTRACTIONS

In addition to the following tourist attractions, also see Festivals and Events, Forts, Historic Sites, Museums, National Forests, National Historic Landmarks, National Parks, National Wildlife Refuges, Rockhounding and State Parks.

ASHEBORO

North Carolina Zoological Park. 1,371 acres of land that is the first natural habitat zoo in the U.S. Open daily. 919-879-5606.

ASHEVILLE

Folk Art Center. Located on the Blue Ridge Parkway east of Asheville. The center displays native crafts and tools with demonstrations, exhibits and museum. 704-298-7928.

Thomas Wolfe Memorial. Frame residence famous as Dixieland in Thomas Wolfe's *Look Homeward Angel* and was boyhood home of the author. 704-253-8304.

University Botanical Gardens. Native flora may be viewed on the 10-acre tract on the UNC-Asheville campus. 704-258-5200.

BAKERSVILLE

Roan Mountain. World's largest natural garden of crimson-purple rhododendron. Peak bloom mid-June. 704-682-6146.

BEAUFORT

Historic Beaufort. Restored historic dwellings and public buildings with beautiful waterfront. Adjoining the restoration grounds is the **N.C. Maritime Museum** featuring maritime displays and artifacts. 919-728-5225.

BLOWING ROCK

Moses H. Cone Memorial Park. Blue Ridge Parkway recreational area with crafts center in manor house; fishing, hiking and bridle trails. 704-295-3782.

Mystery Hill. Between Blowing Rock and Boone. Mystery Hill defies the law of gravity; also craft and mountain life exhibits on display. 704-264-2792.

Tweetsie Railroad. Narrow gauge steam locomotives pull sightseeing train. Amusement park, frontier village. Open June-October. 704-264-9061.

BURNSVILLE

Mt. Mitchell. The highest peak (6,684 ft.) in Eastern America. Observation tower. 704-675-4611.

CARTHAGE

House in the Horseshoe. Plantation home of Philip Alston, Whig leader, and was scene of Whig-Tory skirmishes in 1780–81. 919-947-2051.

CHAPEL HILL

Patterson's Mill Country Store. Quaint store of 1880–1930 vintage with pharmacy, doctor's office and N.C. crafts. 919-493-8149.

CHARLOTTE

Carowinds. Family entertainment complex astride the N.C.-S.C. line which features rides, shows and historic attractions. Open May-October. 704-588-2600.

Latta Place. River plantation of James Latta, c. 1800; built in the Federal style. 704-875-2312.

CHEROKEE

Magic Waters. Water theme park with rides and entertainment. Open May-Labor Day. 704-497-4311.

Santa's Land. Zoo, toy and gift shops, and rides. 704-497-9191.

CLEMMONS

Tanglewood Park. A 1,100-acre park with golf, swimming, camping and riding. Former estate of William and Kate B. Reynolds who bequeathed it for recreational use. 919-766-0591.

CRESWELL

Somerset Place. Plantation built in the 1830s by Josiah Collins II; located on shore of Lake Phelps, and was a gathering place for fashionable society. Picnic facilities in adjoining Pettigrew State Park. 919-797-4560.

DURHAM

Duke Homestead. Home (1852) and tobacco factory (1869) of the Duke family whose name is synonymous with tobacco, electric power and philanthropy. Museum, exhibits and visitor center with film. 919-477-5498.

Duke University. Located on Duke University campus is the gothic **Duke Chapel** with a carillon of 50 bells in the 210-ft. tower. On west campus are the **Sarah P. Duke Memorial Gardens** featuring formal and informal plantings of flowers and shrubs. Peak bloom is April. The **Duke University Museum of Art** is located on the east campus. 919-684-2323.

Stagville Preservation Center. Exhibits, research and educational instruction on the art of preservation. 919-477-9835.

EDENTON

Historic Edenton. A waterfront setting, restored homes and gardens may be toured. The **Penelope Barker House,** c. 1782, is headquarters for Historic Edenton. 919-482-3663.

Iredell House. Built in 1759, home of James Iredell who was Attorney General of N.C. and later named by George Washington to the U.S. Supreme Court. 919-482-2637.

ELIZABETH CITY

Elizabeth City Historic District. A 30-block district with antebellum commercial buildings. 919-335-4365.

FAYETTEVILLE

Market House. A national historic landmark built in 1838 as a produce market. 919-483-8133.

FONTANA

Fontana Dam. Highest dam (480 ft.) in TVA system impound 30-mile-long Fontana Lake and has observation points and visitor center. 704-498-2211.

FRANKLIN

Franklin Gem and Mineral Museum. Housed in a 150-year-old jail, museum has fossils, minerals, and gems from N.C. Open May-October. 704-369-7831.

Gold City. Reconstructed mining village with restaurant, craft shop and chairlift. 704-369-9183.

GILEAD

Town Creek Indian Mound. Reconstructed 16th century Indian ceremonial center with temples and mortuary. Visitor center-museum. 919-439-6802.

GREENSBORO

Water Country. 45-acre water theme park. Open May-early September. 919-852-9721.

HALIFAX

Historic Halifax. Site of first official action by a colony for independence and site of the adoption of N.C.'s first state constitution. Tours through restored 18th and 19th century buildings. Visitor center-museum and archaeological exhibits. 919-583-7191.

HERTFORD

Newbold-White House. The oldest house in the state, located on a 7-acre site, the home was built c. 1680, and is part of the Historic Albemarle Tour. 919-426-7567.

HIGHLANDS

Whiteside Mountain. Highest sheer cliffs in Eastern America; accessible via US 64. Open April-December. 704-526-3765.

HIGH POINT

Southern Furniture Exposition Bldg. This facility has been the hub of the furniture manufacturing industry since 1921. 919-889-6144.

HILLSBOROUGH

Antique Music and Wheels. Collection of musical instruments and old automobiles. 919-732-7136.

KANNAPOLIS

Cannon Visitor Center. Exhibits demonstrate textile products and art. Free plant tours weekdays. 704-938-3200.

KENANSVILLE

Historic Kenansville. Over 25 homes in the town have passed their 100th birthday. A fine example of Greek Revival architecture is the plantation home of the late Thomas Kenan II, known as **Liberty Hall.** 919-296-0254.

KERNERSVILLE

Korner's Folly. The 22-room house is built on seven levels; top floor was converted into a theatre in 1897, making it the first "Little Theatre" in the U.S. 919-993-4521.

KINSTON

The Richard Caswell Memorial and *CSS Neuse*. Grave of N.C.'s first constitutionally elected governor, and site of remains of the ram *Neuse*, one of two iron-clad gunboats completed in N.C. 919-522-2091.

KURE BEACH

Fort Fisher. Site of the largest land-sea battle fought up until the time it fell in 1865. Visitor center-museum, earthworks and items from Confederate blockade runners. 919-458-5538.

LINVILLE

Grandfather Mountain. Highest peak (5,964 ft.) in Blue Ridge range has mile-high swinging bridge connecting two peaks. Hiking trails, recreational and camping areas and wildlife habitats. Hang gliding daily, weather permitting. 704-733-2013.

Linville Caverns. Stalactites and stalagmites along an underground river. 704-756-4171.

MAGGIE VALLEY

Ghost Town. Theme park on mountain overlooking Maggie Valley with frontier village and stagecoach rides. Open May-October. 704-926-0256.

MANTEO

Elizabethan Gardens. Formal and informal plantings with fine collection of antique garden ornaments. 919-473-3234.

Elizabeth II. Designed in the 16th century-style and named for the ship which brought the first English colonists to America. Costumed interpreters and visitor center with exhibits on the Roanoke Voyages. 919-473-1144.

MURFREESBORO

Historic Murfreesboro. The 12-block historic district includes 18th and early 19th century structures on this early river port on the Meherrin River. 919-398-4886.

MURPHY

Fields of the Wood. The Church of God of Prophecy Memorial has the Ten Commandments carved in stone covering the mountainside. 704-837-2242.

NEW BERN

Historic New Bern. Founded in 1710, the city has many historic sites including the **Attmore-Oliver House** (c. 1790). 919-637-3111.

Tryon Palace. Residence of the colonial governor and meeting place of the colonial assembly and later the first state capitol. The complex includes restorations of Georgian buildings and gardens on the palace grounds designed in the manner of 18th-century English gardens. 919-638-5109.

NEWTON GROVE

Bentonville Battleground. Markers, trenches, Harper House Field Hospital restoration and visitor center-museum on site of largest Civil War battle fought in N.C. 919-594-0789.

PINEHURST

World Golf Hall of Fame. Contemporary structure houses golf artifacts, photographs and memorabilia of golfing greats. 919-295-6651.

PINEVILLE

James K. Polk Memorial. Restored log house where the 11th President of the U.S. was born November 2, 1795. Visitor center-museum. 704-889-7145.

RALEIGH

Historic Oakwood. The historic district is one of the finest examples of intact Victorian neighborhoods in the country. Walking tour includes 50 historic points of interest. 919-833-3005.

Mordecai Historical Park. This unique park contains the **Andrew Johnson Birthplace,** home of the 17th President of the U.S. The Greek Revival **Mordecai House** is a museum for historical activities and study. 919-834-4844.

REIDSVILLE

Chinqua-Penn Plantation and Gardens. Country estate and gardens built by the Penn family of tobacco industry fame. Owned by UNC-Greensboro. 919-349-4576.

ROSE HILL

Duplin Wine Cellars. N.C.'s oldest and largest winery offers a look at wine-making; free wine-tasting and tour. 919-289-3888.

SALISBURY

Historic Salisbury. The 23-block national register historic district includes homes, offices and an historic downtown. 704-636-0103.

SEAGROVE

Seagrove Pottery. Pottery-making from native clays is produced as it was in the 18th century. Museum displays works from as early as 1750. 919-625-6121.

SEDALIA

Charlotte Hawkins Brown Memorial. Contributions of N.C. Afro-American citizens are remembered at the site of Palmer Memorial Institute. Visitor center. 919-733-7862.

SOUTHPORT

Brunswick Town. Ruins of colonial seaport and St. Philip's Church and earthworks of Fort Anderson. Visitor center-museum. 919-371-6613.

SPENCER

Spencer Shops. Once Southern Railways central repair shops; now the N.C. Transportation Museum which displays the development of transportation in the state. 704-636-2889.

STANFIELD

Reed Gold Mine. Gold was discovered in 1799 by 12-year-old Conrad Reed at the site. Reconstructed ore-crushing mill, underground mine tunnels, panning area and visitor center. 704-786-8337.

STATESVILLE

Fort Dobbs. Built in 1756, the fort was named for Royal Governor Arthur Dobbs. Visitor center, recreational facilities and exhibits. 704-873-5866.

TARBORO

Tarboro Historic District National Recreation Trail. 45-block historic district with headquarters at the Blount-Bridgers House. 919-823-8121, ext. 249.

VALLE CRUCIS

Mast General Store. The store, founded in 1883, is a good example of an old general store. 704-963-6511.

WILLIAMSBORO

St. John's Episcopal Church. Parish established in 1746 and is the oldest frame church in the state. 919-693-5547.

WILMINGTON

Airlie Gardens. Azaleas, camellias and huge live oaks on scenic drives around lakes. Peak bloom in April. 919-763-9991.

Chandler's Wharf. Historic ships, museum, shops and restaurants show Wilmington's waterfront as it was in the 19th century. 919-343-1406.

Greenfield Gardens. A municipal park features native shrubs, trees and azaleas. 919-762-2611.

Historic Wilmington. A tour of historic sites includes the **Governor Dudley Mansion** (c. 1825) home of the first N.C. governor elected by popular vote. The **St. John's Museum of Art** features an outstanding permanent art collection housed in the St. John's Lodge (c. 1804), which is the oldest Masonic Lodge in the state. 919-762-2511.

Orton Plantation. Stately mansion and gardens established in 18th century as rice plantation. 919-371-6851.

Poplar Grove Plantation. One of the oldest (c. 1850) peanut producing plantations in the state and a good example of a coastal plantation home. 919-686-9503.

USS North Carolina Battleship Memorial. 35,000-ton battleship is a war memorial to the men and women of the U.S. military services in World War II. An "Immortal Showboat" sound and light spectacular is presented during the summer. 919-762-1829.

WINDSOR

Hope Plantation. Restored mansion built by Governor David Stone, c. 1803. 919-794-3140.

WINSTON-SALEM

Bethabara. The site of the first Moravian settlement in the state. Restored buildings are on the site and represent outstanding examples of Moravian architecture in America. 919-924-8191.

Stroh Brewery Company. Facility is the largest plant under one roof in N.C., and produces 4 million barrels of beer annually. Reservations required for large groups. 919-788-6710, ext. 252.

Whitaker Park. America's leading cigarettes are made in this plant. Tours 8:00 a.m.-10:00 p.m. weekdays; reservations required for large groups. 919-773-5718.

LIGHTHOUSES

N.C. has a variety of lighthouses, each with a unique history. Following is a list of the state's most prominent lighthouses. **Bald Head.** Bald Head Island. Built in 1817 and stands 109 ft. tall. **Bodie Island.** Bodie Island, Cape Hatteras National Seashore. 150 ft. in height, visitor center, nature trails. **Cape Hatteras.** Buxton, Cape Hatteras National Seashore. Tallest lighthouse in America at 208 ft. **Cape Lookout.** Core Banks, Cape Lookout National Seashore. 160 ft. and still operational. **Ocracoke.** Ocracoke Island, Cape Hatteras National Seashore. 76 ft. high and the oldest lighthouse in the national seashores, built in 1823.

NORTH CAROLINA STATE GOVERNMENT COMPLEX

Raleigh has served as the state's capital since 1792. The state government complex is located in downtown Raleigh and includes many points of interest. The **Governor's Mansion** is considered one of the nation's outstanding examples of Victorian architecture. The **State Capitol** is a classic Greek Revival building located on the 6-acre Capitol Square and houses the Governor's office. The **State Legislative Building** is the only building in the country devoted exclusively to the legislative branch of state government. The **Capital Area Visitor Center** has information on Raleigh attractions, events and self-guided tours. 919-733-3456.

REGIONAL BEACH ACCESS FACILITIES

Available at ten sites located along North Carolina's barrier islands. Parking, handicapped facilities and dune crossovers to the beach are provided. For more information and site locations, contact the Division of Coastal Management. 919-733-2293.

SNOW SKIING AREAS

Appalachian Ski Mountain. Near Blowing Rock and Boone. Vertical drop 365 ft., 8 slopes, 3 chairlifts, 3 surface lifts. Snowmaking, rentals, ski school, weekday and group rates, food, night skiing; 704-295-7828. **Beech Mountain.** Near Banner Elk, Blowing Rock and Boone. Vertical drop 830 ft., 12 slopes, 6 chairlifts, 2 surface lifts. Snowmaking, rentals, ski school, weekday and group rates, food, lounge, nursery, entertainment, night skiing, ice skating, off-season activities; 704-387-2011. **Cataloochee.** Near Maggie Valley and Waynesville. Vertical drop 740 ft., 8 slopes, 1 chairlift, 2 surface lifts. Snowmaking, rentals, ski school, weekly and group rates, food, lounge, entertainment, night skiing, off-season activities; 704-926-0285. **Fairfield-Sapphire Valley.** Near Cashiers. Vertical drop 425 ft., 4 slopes, 1 chairlift, 2 surface lifts. Snowmaking, rentals, ski school, weekday and group rates, food, lodging, lounge, nursery, entertainment, night skiing, ice skating, off-season activities; 704-743-3441. **Hawksnest.** Near Banner Elk, Blowing Rock and Boone. Vertical drop 619 ft., 5 slopes, 2 chairlifts, 2 surface lifts. Snowmaking, rentals, lounge, ski school, weekday and group rates, food, night skiing; 704-963-6561. **Hound Ears.** Near Banner Elk, Blowing Rock and Boone. Vertical drop 107 ft., 2 slopes, 1 chairlift, 1 surface lift. Snowmaking, rentals, ski school, group rates, lodging, food, off-season activities. Fri-Mon, only; 704-963-4321. **Mill Ridge.** Near Banner Elk, Blowing Rock and Boone. Vertical drop 225 ft., 5 slopes, 1 chairlift, 1 surface lift. Snowmaking, rentals, ski school, group rates, food, entertainment, night skiing; 704-963-4500. **Scaly Mountain.** Scaly Mountain Vertical drop 225 ft., 4 slopes, 1 chairlift, 1 surface lift. Snowmaking, rentals, ski school, weekday and group rates, food, entertainment, night skiing; 704-526-3737. **Sugar Mountain.** Near Banner Elk, Blowing Rock and Boone. Vertical drop 1200 ft., 16 slopes, 4 chairlifts, 3 surface lifts. Snowmaking, rentals, ski school, weekday and group rates, food, lodging, nursery, lounge, entertainment, night skiing, off-season activities;

704-898-4521. **Wolf Laurel.** Near Mars Hill. Vertical drop 700 ft., 9 slopes, 1 chairlift, 3 surface lifts. Snowmaking, rentals, ski school, weekday and group rates, food, lodging, lounge, night skiing, off-season activities; 704-689-4111.

VEHICLE REGISTRATIONS

The North Carolina Department of Motor Vehicles reports a total of 5,190,922 vehicles licensed in the state as of March, 1988. This total includes house trailers, special mobile equipment, wreckers, jeeps, and other identified vehicles, though they are not included on the following chart in the interest of space.

In addition to the county totals, towns with a population of over 2,500 have been included.

County and Town	*Autos*	*Trucks*	*Buses*	*Trailers*	*Motor-cycles*	*Tractor Trucks*	*Total*
Alamance	63,790	18,215	567	9,164	1,080	669	94,196
Burlington	37,099	9,392	160	5,195	599	697	53,533
Graham	11,082	3,503	353	1,284	198	54	16,614
Alexander	13,585	6,007	138	2,616	273	120	22,890
Alleghany	4,760	2,218	78	711	68	26	7,915
Anson	10,999	4,300	198	1,422	202	191	17,377
Wadesboro	5,936	1,952	167	726	89	118	9,027
Ashe	10,694	5,433	149	1,182	172	72	17,828
Avery	7,147	3,564	117	883	106	93	12,044
Beaufort	20,931	8,313	258	4,897	331	245	35,199
Washington	11,579	3,890	220	2,340	194	104	18,445
Bertie	9,611	3,688	215	1,664	160	196	15,595
Bladen	13,968	5,631	228	2,123	155	197	22,411
Brunswick	23,934	10,230	249	4,247	413	246	39,658
Buncombe	93,611	29,950	689	10,195	1,775	760	137,997
Asheville	54,397	14,495	627	4,834	916	519	76,300
Burke	38,402	14,658	308	6,161	702	417	61,012
Morganton	21,449	7,802	272	2,830	350	157	33,054
Valdese	4,834	1,755	11	800	90	89	7,616
Cabarrus	52,385	16,721	367	8,125	992	659	79,839
Concord	28,096	8,772	299	4,868	516	548	43,420
Kannapolis	21,344	5,737	66	2,391	419	51	30,228
Caldwell	36,203	14,599	326	6,347	748	673	59,201
Granite Falls	7,044	3,045	26	1,136	160	49	11,518
Lenoir	22,283	8,727	266	3,988	417	549	36,420
Camden	3,013	1,375	61	624	39	35	5,189
Carteret	25,224	9,046	207	5,287	441	96	40,646
Beaufort	5,033	1,824	145	1,015	52	15	8,138
Morehead City	7,544	2,102	38	1,273	91	26	11,177
Caswell	10,184	4,059	178	897	157	34	15,576
Catawba	66,533	23,565	493	12,456	1,312	1,735	106,689
Hickory	37,057	12,179	118	7,852	698	1,432	59,652
Newton	10,993	3,749	321	1,666	228	121	17,185
Chatham	20,025	7,900	239	3,173	399	169	32,109
Siler City	6,752	2,570	33	1,128	122	105	10,768
Cherokee	9,376	4,697	121	1,229	172	42	15,792
Chowan	6,481	2,261	85	1,254	79	86	10,309
Edenton	5,591	1,853	82	983	63	55	8,687

VEHICLE REGISTRATIONS

County and Town	Autos	Trucks	Buses	Trailers	Motor-cycles	Tractor Trucks	Total
Clay	3,275	1,646	42	512	49	2	5,574
Cleveland	43,343	15,658	454	5,646	664	420	66,562
Kings Mountain	10,437	3,812	45	1,461	206	336	16,405
Shelby	24,379	8,106	370	3,084	311	225	36,665
Columbus	25,200	9,887	359	3,704	291	259	39,846
Whiteville	8,439	2,906	322	1,136	95	52	12,997
Craven	36,842	11,987	360	6,170	753	229	56,764
New Bern	23,571	7,215	330	4,265	334	152	36,159
Cumberland	114,484	31,398	901	9,902	2,940	513	161,350
Fayetteville	93,842	25,042	852	8,018	2,055	662	131,467
Spring Lake	7,477	2,119	18	538	261	17	10,511
Currituck	6,206	3,061	84	1,411	97	51	11,058
Dare	11,456	4,726	70	2,165	226	47	18,872
Davidson	67,892	24,541	501	11,861	1,475	754	107,741
Lexington	32,055	11,327	400	6,679	659	595	52,023
Thomasville	19,586	6,424	74	2,532	416	168	29,427
Davie	15,718	6,179	135	2,583	285	130	25,187
Duplin	19,445	8,555	264	2,789	275	295	31,784
Wallace	3,764	1,616	13	604	57	70	6,163
Durham	97,471	21,168	650	8,683	1,315	457	130,432
Durham	95,613	20,103	632	8,194	1,274	474	126,984
Edgecombe	27,133	9,486	244	3,481	389	176	41,107
Rocky Mount	10,704	2,757	39	1,215	150	52	14,992
Tarboro	10,933	4,577	186	1,632	124	111	17,641
Forsyth	158,213	37,497	1,355	16,475	2,823	1,768	219,285
Kernersville	19,149	6,021	47	2,631	390	174	28,600
Winston-Salem	117,978	25,276	1,210	12,292	1,956	1,850	161,346
Franklin	16,630	6,711	209	2,012	235	128	26,090
Louisburg	7,471	2,928	182	903	107	99	11,753
Gaston	90,891	28,308	576	10,176	1,654	1,565	134,018
Belmont	9,079	2,494	23	963	150	24	12,819
Bessemer City	5,682	2,117	18	681	127	22	8,710
Cherryville	6,126	2,208	20	1,624	78	1,187	11,298
Cramerton	1,112	295	9	71	17		1,511
Dallas	6,769	2,641	32	950	149	40	10,655
Gastonia	46,059	12,824	431	4,131	811	229	64,884
Lowell	1,693	571	6	156	33	5	2,473
Mount Holly	7,070	2,344	15	846	155	18	10,531
Gates	4,452	1,886	116	813	64	96	7,469
Graham	3,140	1,866	48	652	44	42	5,912
Granville	17,859	6,829	227	1,985	269	103	27,404
Oxford	10,379	3,700	209	972	136	110	15,575
Greene	6,885	2,821	149	991	79	25	11,006
Guilford	203,601	45,583	1,390	23,553	3,093	2,872	281,862
Greensboro	137,270	27,002	1,079	15,553	1,906	2,027	185,950
High Point	47,574	11,477	273	8,805	756	1,927	71,233
Halifax	25,821	8,092	319	3,090	461	177	38,181
Enfield	3,909	1,081	10	278	55	27	5,375
Roanoke Rapids	12,413	3,990	33	1,701	260	114	18,625
Scotland Neck	2,518	778	9	297	25	15	3,665
Harnett	30,322	11,562	327	4,045	530	205	47,271
Dunn	10,745	3,874	27	1,467	166	150	16,513
Erwin	3,206	1,014	15	384	73	8	4,732
Haywood	23,449	11,155	183	4,082	442	114	39,837
Canton	7,482	3,541	16	1,423	147	50	12,802
Waynesville	9,786	4,822	149	1,643	176	96	16,833
Henderson	38,066	12,803	270	4,972	758	391	57,941
Hendersonville	23,809	6,849	219	2,576	436	121	34,435

County and Town	Autos	Trucks	Buses	Trailers	Motor-cycles	Tractor Trucks	Total
Hertford	10,699	3,644	216	1,800	141	197	16,826
Ahoskie	5,503	1,816	53	893	72	148	8,557
Murfreesboro	2,742	838	22	481	35	53	4,199
Hoke	8,838	3,316	139	910	197	45	13,530
Raeford	7,022	2,454	136	700	158	44	10,573
Hyde	2,332	1,253	52	494	36	23	4,209
Iredell	50,264	17,758	387	8,680	1,148	589	79,295
Mooresville	14,273	4,919	47	2,591	287	110	22,388
Statesville	29,280	9,720	320	4,850	658	536	45,620
Jackson	11,328	5,399	139	1,474	271	48	18,858
Cullowhee	2,288	956	9	275	70	7	3,642
Johnston	40,812	16,715	418	6,618	573	323	65,889
Clayton	7,240	2,826	20	1,097	141	22	11,433
Selma	5,384	2,047	15	886	62	65	8,515
Smithfield	8,553	3,015	338	1,241	117	77	13,429
Jones	4,086	1,863	80	824	55	68	7,020
Lee	22,379	7,567	177	2,695	383	223	33,649
Sanford	22,162	7,508	178	2,723	367	232	33,398
Lenoir	29,550	9,236	300	4,628	359	213	44,586
Kinston	23,140	6,853	272	3,577	256	207	34,560
Lincoln	25,239	10,273	241	4,300	520	254	41,083
Lincolnton	14,530	5,342	206	2,221	278	140	22,845
Macon	11,460	5,869	118	1,702	211	60	19,742
Madison	7,367	3,879	171	875	134	33	12,547
Martin	11,979	4,587	165	2,287	185	145	19,456
Williamston	6,739	2,606	146	1,369	105	67	11,095
McDowell	16,962	7,260	189	1,976	276	93	26,971
Marion	12,135	4,924	174	1,296	200	62	18,935
Mecklenburg	291,535	58,890	1,912	29,050	3,479	5,458	392,807
Charlotte	256,079	56,006	1,862	27,634	2,870	6,664	353,266
Davidson	3,698	966	11	753	64	51	5,580
Mitchell	7,196	3,348	117	697	135	39	11,625
Spruce Pine	4,138	1,756	17	462	86	28	6,544
Montgomery	10,764	4,814	136	1,634	184	99	17,727
Moore	32,597	10,764	306	3,193	632	143	47,967
Southern Pines	7,550	1,488	17	438	98	8	9,659
Nash	39,991	12,874	442	5,723	553	709	60,609
Rocky Mount	23,796	6,347	184	3,587	286	820	35,211
New Hanover	63,331	16,579	386	8,364	957	462	90,605
Wilmington	56,628	14,456	383	7,318	818	545	80,604
Northampton	9,853	3,789	216	1,446	142	130	15,690
Onslow	45,633	15,445	383	5,880	1,434	227	69,452
Jacksonville	29,606	9,238	357	3,492	784	120	43,884
Midway Park	1,889	424	1	121	79	1	2,527
Tarawa Terrace	1,592	245		29	55		1,925
Orange	46,250	10,764	412	3,812	932	137	62,643
Chapel Hill	28,699	4,510	132	2,038	564	254	36,383
Pamlico	5,256	2,520	75	1,290	105	48	9,367
Pasquotank	14,220	4,727	176	2,116	245	99	21,746
Elizabeth City	14,570	4,828	173	2,163	261	113	22,278
Pender	12,644	5,396	164	2,496	157	100	21,096
Perquimans	4,848	1,983	88	953	73	50	8,082
Person	15,737	6,374	152	1,619	245	63	24,308
Roxboro	12,092	4,437	148	1,127	190	65	18,137
Pitt	49,487	13,872	461	6,827	832	240	72,135
Ayden	4,168	1,455	10	630	70	19	6,387
Farmville	3,962	1,254	11	616	55	53	5,993
Greenville	31,630	7,569	421	3,977	512	223	44,595

VEHICLE REGISTRATIONS

County and Town	Autos	Trucks	Buses	Trailers	Motor-cycles	Tractor Trucks	Total
Polk	8,279	2,904	73	809	170	43	12,427
Randolph	54,163	21,517	503	10,505	1,151	983	89,329
Asheboro	22,035	7,983	408	3,694	410	231	34,949
Richmond	20,894	7,724	248	2,612	342	295	32,279
Hamlet	5,928	1,908	100	621	94	17	8,705
Rockingham	11,944	4,210	133	1,400	202	94	18,090
Robeson	46,308	16,795	585	3,990	910	375	69,262
Lumberton	19,737	6,638	471	1,944	387	159	29,475
Red Springs	4,041	1,318	17	301	58	30	5,792
Rockingham	46,658	15,446	366	5,495	664	478	69,520
Reidsville	19,115	6,257	51	2,096	270	76	28,003
Eden	13,808	3,889	46	1,417	187	298	19,801
Rowan	57,348	18,068	427	9,873	1,153	739	88,138
Salisbury	30,189	8,628	307	5,423	553	705	46,062
Spencer	1,773	393	2	173	34	2	2,390
Rutherford	28,719	10,413	276	3,360	410	310	43,796
Forest City	9,622	3,078	20	1,358	135	184	14,501
Rutherfordton	7,256	2,874	108	849	105	81	11,349
Spindale	2,434	693	107	246	30	26	3,554
Sampson	24,375	9,475	299	3,828	319	317	38,802
Clinton	11,157	3,823	260	1,788	121	187	17,421
Scotland	15,239	4,628	189	1,430	272	87	21,921
Laurinburg	11,070	3,200	176	1,068	174	100	15,846
Stanly	27,056	10,581	250	4,527	706	275	43,614
Albemarle	12,572	4,401	221	2,000	301	162	19,755
Stokes	18,753	8,060	184	2,427	437	83	30,095
Surry	33,640	13,345	326	4,606	597	581	53,355
Elkin	5,282	1,826	17	624	91	33	7,907
Mount Airy	18,112	7,135	41	2,807	310	524	29,089
Swain	4,611	2,400	108	689	131	11	8,017
Transylvania	12,943	5,147	121	1,902	258	32	20,635
Brevard	7,543	2,634	108	946	132	14	11,507
Tyrrell	1,504	707	40	387	11	33	2,696
Union	41,624	16,716	434	6,496	912	478	67,156
Monroe	21,080	8,439	378	3,228	442	256	34,074
Vance	18,949	6,118	197	2,233	246	183	28,065
Henderson	17,198	5,388	194	2,150	217	216	25,497
Wake	242,996	64,230	2,183	26,637	3,729	1,321	343,815
Cary	26,676	4,026	26	2,330	434	51	33,752
Fuquay Varina	6,498	2,438	29	989	113	36	10,165
Garner	11,924	3,894	16	1,681	257	37	17,959
Raleigh	167,143	42,711	2,033	18,082	2,259	1,464	235,587
Wake Forest	7,868	2,794	20	1,032	128	46	11,982
Warren	7,764	3,010	146	908	93	67	12,061
Washington	6,590	2,658	126	1,687	129	113	11,362
Plymouth	4,088	1,609	111	1,199	78	69	7,193
Watauga	15,901	6,147	206	1,628	300	161	24,519
Boone	9,402	3,183	197	920	166	93	14,058
Wayne	47,436	15,479	472	6,956	789	449	72,169
Goldsboro	32,930	9,434	444	4,508	629	368	48,759
Mount Olive	5,963	2,255	12	869	68	50	9,272
Wilkes	31,965	12,605	336	4,586	581	632	50,939
North Wilkesboro	10,735	4,079	36	1,569	161	218	16,886
Wilson	34,037	10,690	362	4,759	435	443	51,015
Wilson	25,091	6,986	339	3,424	304	709	37,059
Yadkin	16,337	6,757	179	2,331	328	82	26,179
Yancey	7,128	3,683	124	888	101	81	12,111
TOTALS	3,463,465	1,099,825	31,639	456,979	60,187	44,834	5,190,922

VOTERS, REGISTERED

County	Total 1986	Demo-crats 1986	Repub-licans 1986
Alamance	51,476	36,201	12,638
Alexander	16,056	7,744	7,327
Alleghany	6,431	4,826	1,439
Anson	11,000	10,198	727
Ashe	15,023	7,943	6,524
Avery	8,486	1,895	6,408
Beaufort	20,511	16,552	3,539
Bertie	11,139	10,525	499
Bladen	16,722	15,418	1,133
Brunswick	24,572	16,584	7,247
Buncombe	89,722	58,442	26,769
Burke	35,462	21,497	12,119
Cabarrus	43,146	27,715	13,819
Caldwell	32,803	17,056	13,460
Camden	3,133	2,952	156
Carteret	24,312	15,351	7,409
Caswell	11,383	10,448	836
Catawba	54,110	27,030	22,972
Chatham	20,615	15,508	4,299
Cherokee	12,965	7,500	4,859
Chowan	6,495	5,569	787
Clay	5,532	2,673	2,392
Cleveland	38,054	29,747	7,082
Columbus	29,406	26,628	2,525
Craven	28,688	21,168	6,463
Cumberland	78,314	59,136	15,660
Currituck	6,038	5,226	602
Dare	10,124	7,313	2,056
Davidson	57,075	31,439	23,207
Davie	13,801	5,758	7,557
Duplin	19,070	16,896	2,071
Durham	89,244	69,093	15,064
Edgecombe	28,952	25,465	3,077
Forsyth	134,802	84,971	41,728
Franklin	15,973	13,841	1,936
Gaston	73,019	47,189	22,583
Gates	5,442	5,254	151
Graham	5,579	2,967	2,444
Granville	16,262	14,821	1,220
Greene	7,839	7,310	469
Guilford	175,078	113,917	51,963
Halifax	26,646	24,608	1,658
Harnett	25,650	20,552	4,766
Haywood	25,153	19,206	5,305
Henderson	36,219	16,014	18,157
Hertford	13,417	12,395	904
Hoke	8,525	7,983	487
Hyde	3,123	2,841	232
Iredell	44,513	28,838	13,897
Jackson	14,786	9,803	4,276
Johnston	34,236	26,947	6,609
Jones	5,415	5,092	288
Lee	18,322	14,696	3,196
Lenoir	28,258	23,459	4,521
Lincoln	24,838	15,700	8,142
Macon	13,780	7,911	5,087
Madison	11,010	7,490	3,166
Martin	12,368	11,148	1,060
McDowell	17,637	12,056	4,781
Mecklenburg	248,276	150,642	83,614
Mitchell	9,640	2,137	7,318
Montgomery	12,255	8,955	2,965
Moore	29,647	15,843	12,226
Nash	34,589	26,706	7,276
New Hanover	54,321	36,385	16,052
Northampton	12,388	12,105	262
Onslow	30,720	23,106	6,223
Orange	48,197	35,724	9,108
Pamlico	6,229	5,357	745
Pasquotank	12,767	10,556	1,746
Pender	12,844	10,617	1,953
Perquimans	4,782	4,281	416
Person	13,768	12,283	1,276
Pitt	43,507	33,776	8,357
Polk	9,346	5,133	3,584
Randolph	47,281	21,002	24,018
Richmond	20,319	17,979	2,121
Robeson	47,614	43,909	3,039
Rockingham	39,444	29,898	7,904
Rowan	47,609	27,865	17,492
Rutherford	26,720	19,493	6,441
Sampson	28,684	18,938	9,334
Scotland	12,921	10,807	1,501
Stanly	25,652	15,016	9,385
Stokes	20,850	11,862	8,339
Surry	28,987	18,334	9,744
Swain	7,115	4,885	1,906
Transylvania	14,171	7,620	5,322
Tyrrell	2,152	1,981	152
Union	32,827	22,793	8,733
Vance	19,163	17,668	1,316
Wake	186,848	125,365	50,153
Warren	10,225	9,836	339
Washington	7,499	6,921	468
Watauga	23,169	11,397	9,757
Wayne	38,455	30,343	7,396
Wilkes	35,057	14,221	19,471
Wilson	30,497	25,443	4,695
Yadkin	15,908	6,226	9,167
Yancey	10,797	6,623	3,664
Totals	3,080,990	2,114,536	836,726

Source: NC State Board of Elections

WAR BETWEEN THE STATES

As it became more apparent that the South would secede from the Union, the majority of North Carolinians were still in favor of resolving regional differences through peaceful means, rather than disunion. Compared to other Southern states, particularly those of the Deep South, North Carolina did not contain many large plantations, since the soil was not well suited to growing cotton, the backbone of the plantation economy. Residents in the eastern section of North Carolina did own a few slaves, but not in the large numbers that landowners in other states did. The mountainous terrain of the western section of the state did not lend itself to slaveholding, since most farms there were small, family run operations.

It was President Abraham Lincoln's request to North Carolina authorities on April 15, 1861, to furnish 75,000 troops to quell the southern "insurrection" that convinced most North Carolinians that secession was indeed the only solution to the problem. Governor John W. Ellis replied to Mr. Lincoln's request, "I can be no party to this wicked violation of the laws of the country and to this war upon the liberties of a free people. You can get no troops from North Carolina." On May 20, North Carolina seceded from the Union.

Before the War was finished, more than 125,000 North Carolina men and boys had served with the Confederacy. In addition, the state furnished two members of President Jefferson Davis's cabinet: Thomas Bragg, the Attorney General, and George Davie, also the Attorney General two years later. Two Lieutenant-Generals, six Major-Generals, and twenty-five Brigadier-Generals also called North Carolina home before they volunteered for the Confederate cause. Eight more men were Brigadier Governors in the state militia, four of whom served the Confederacy as Adjutant-Generals.

Depending upon how one defines a battle or an engagement, there were at least 85 skirmishes of large and small importance on North Carolina soil. The heaviest years of fighting were 1862 and 1865. In early 1862, Union forces seized Roanoke Island, New Bern, and Fort Macon, thereby, in effect, occupying much of the eastern portion of the state.

By the end of May 1863, most Confederate troops operating in North Carolina had been sent to Virginia in anticipation of Robert E. Lee's invasion of Pennsylvania. Of the 15,301 Confederate soldiers killed or wounded at Gettysburg in early July, over 4,000 were from North Carolina. While 1863 saw the continuation of Federal occupation of the eastern part of the state, the western, mountainous sections, although relatively untouched by the enemy, witnessed a serious wave of desertions. Opposition to conscription was rampant. The irony of the situation is that Federal authorities failed to capitalize on the problem and, for the most part, left the west alone. As one authority has said, by the end of 1863 North Carolina was truly at the mercy of the enemy.

In April 1864, Confederate forces recaptured Plymouth, which had been occupied by Union forces since late 1862. Just as rapidly, they lost the town—on October 27, 1864—when the ironclad ship, the *Albermarle*, defending the town was torpedoed and sunk.

The last major battle for North Carolina was at Bentonville, from March 19 to 21, 1865. The Confederates lost 2,825 men there, to 1,646 Union casualties. Over the next few weeks, several skirmishes were fought across the South, before General Lee finally surrendered at Appomattox on April 9. On April 26, Governor Johnston surrendered his 30,000-man army to General Sherman at the Bennett farmhouse west of Durham. Johnston's surrender effectively ended the major resistance to the Union in North Carolina, although as late as May a few reports continued of minor altercations.

WATERFALLS

Because of its high altitudes in the western part of the state, North Carolina contains some of the highest and most picturesque waterfalls in the nation. Brief descriptions of the most noteworthy of these falls follow.

Bridal Veil Falls. This picturesque falls cascades over US 64 near Highlands. Cars drive under the falls. Height, 120 feet.

Connestee Falls. On US 276 about 6 miles south of Brevard. Twin falls, each about 110 feet. Picnic grounds with fireplaces, shelters and spring water. Walkway to base of falls. On private property. FEE.

Cullasaja Falls. On US 64 between Highlands and Franklin. Cascades about 250 feet.

Douglas Falls. On Forest Road #74, 13 miles east of Barnardsville. Located in Craggy Mountain Scenic Area. The road ends in a parking area, where a trail leads to the falls. Height, 70 feet.

Dry Falls. On US 64, 3 miles west of Highlands. A paved trail leads to the falls from the parking area where visitors can walk behind the falls.

Glen Falls Scenic Area. On US 106, 2 miles south of Highlands. A short trail from the parking area leads to the falls. Height, 50 feet.

Hickory Nut Falls. 3/4 mile west of Chimney Rock parking area. Trail leads from parking area, and one from Sky Lounge (elevator landing on top of rock). More than 400 feet high. Privately maintained. Admission.

High Falls. Near US 64 on Horse Pasture River. Turn left on Bohaney Road near Lake Sapphire between Toxaway and Cashiers. Height, 125 feet.

Leatherwood and Bald Springs Falls. On Forest Road #1244, 10 miles north of Hayesville. Located on Fires Creek. Picnicking is available. Height, 100 feet.

Linville Falls. Just off Blue Ridge Parkway and US 221-N.C. 105, 1.6 miles. Spectacular double level falls and gorge. Surrounded by Pisgah National Forest. Donated to National Park Service by John D. Rockefeller, Jr. Comfort Station.

Looking Glass Falls. On US 276 in Pisgah National Forest between Wagon Road Gap and Brevard. Parking space on highway and short walk to bottom of falls. Height, 85 feet.

Maiden Hair Falls. 4 miles south of Brevard, 1 mile off US 276. Old water wheel. Private property. Height, 100 feet.

Moore Cove Falls. On US 276, 10.4 miles north of Brevard. Falls located about 300 feet up trail from the parking area. A foot bridge crosses the creek beside the highway providing access to the falls.

Rainbow Falls. Near US 64 on Horse Pasture River. Turn at Whitewater Falls sign near Oakland. Over 200 feet.

Toxaway Falls. Between Rosman and Cashiers on US 64. Highway goes over top of falls, which cascade 123 feet.

Walker Falls. 10 miles east of Barnardsville on Forest Road #74. Adjacent to Walker Cove Research Natural Area. Height, 75 feet.

Whitewater Falls. 2 levels. Upper falls cascades 411 feet and believed to be highest in Eastern America. Whitewater falls are located off US 64 on an unpaved road near Oakland between Cashiers and Lake Toxaway. 10-mile road from US 64 to Whitewater Falls passes 4 other falls.

WRIGHT BROTHERS

Just after the turn of the century, the lonesome dunes of Kitty Hawk became a hub of activity, when two brothers, Wilbur and Orville Wright, made them the proving ground for their experiments with flight.

The Wright brothers were born and raised in the Midwest, and from childhood had a keen interest in science. Their inspiration to pursue the problems of flight came from Otto Lilienthal, the "father of gliding." Through gliding experiments in his native Germany, Lilienthal had been the first to explain why curved wing surfaces were superior to flat wing surfaces in flying machines. Wilbur and Orville began to experiment, gathering information about lift, balance, and the warping and twisting of wings.

To test their theories they needed a place with fairly constant winds. By checking records from the Weather Bureau at Washington, D.C., they decided on Kitty Hawk. The brothers carried on experiments with their gliders here in 1900, 1901, and 1902, improving each model over the preceding one. They made more than a thousand glider flights from the top of Kill Devil Hill, setting many records for distances and time in the air.

By 1903 Wilbur and Orville felt that they had conquered the problems of flight and were ready to test their theories on a motor-driven, heavier-than-air machine. On December 17, 1903, their flying machine lifted off the level sand a few hundred feet north of Kill Devil Hill and moved forward under its own power. The plane was in the air about 12 seconds and traveled some 120 feet. Although the distance and the length of time in the air seem short, this was the first successful, powered, man-carrying airplane flight in history. The age of aviation had dawned. A young industrialized society welcomed this new mode of transportation unaware of the benefits and problems it would bring.

ZIP CODES

NORTH CAROLINA

Place	Zip
Aberdeen, Moore	28315
Advance, Davie	27006
Ahoskie, Hertford	27910
Union	27910
Airport, Charlotte	28219
Alamance, Alamance	27201
Albemarle, Stanly	28001
Albertson, Duplin	28508
Alexander, Buncombe	28701
Alexis, Gaston	28006
Alliance, Pamlico	28509
Almond, Swain	28702
Altamahaw, Alamance	27202
Anderson, Kitty Hawk	27949
Andrews, Cherokee	28901
Angier, Harnett	27501
Ansonville, Anson	28007
Apex, Wake	27502
Aquone, Macon	28703
Arapahoe, Pamlico	28510
Ararat, Surry	27007
Archdale, High Point	27263
Arden, Buncombe	28704
Ardmore, Winston-Salem	27113
Arrowood, Charlotte	28217

Ash, Brunswick 28420
Asheboro, Randolph 27203
Farmer 27203
ASHEVILLE, Buncombe 28802
Biltmore 28813
Court House 28807
Downtown 28802
Glenrock 28812
Grace 28814
Haywood Road 28806
Oteen 28815
West Asheville 28816
Atando, Charlotte 28206
Atkinson, Pender 28421
Atlantic, Carteret 28511
Atlantic Beach, Carteret 28512
Atlantic Christian College, Wilson 27893
Aulander, Bertie 27805
Aurora, Beaufort 27806
Autryville, Sampson 28318
Avon, Dare 27915
Ayden, Pitt 28513
Aydlett, Currituck 27916
Azalea, Wilmington 28406
Badin, Stanly 28009
Bahama, Durham 27503
Bailey, Nash 27807
Bakersville, Mitchell 28705
Balfour, Henderson 28706
Balsam, Jackson 28707
Balsam Grove, Transylvania 28708
Banner Elk, Avery 28604
Valle Crucis (Watauga Co.) 28619
Barber, Rowan 27008
Barco, Currituck 27917
Barium Springs, Iredell 28010
Barnardsville, Buncombe 28709
Barnesville, Robeson 28319
Bat Cave, Henderson 28710
Bath, Beaufort 27808
Battleboro, Nash 27809
Bayboro, Pamlico 28515
Bear Creek, Chatham 27207
Beaufort, Carteret 28516
Belews Creek, Forsyth 27009
Belhaven, Beaufort 27810
Bellarthur, Pitt 27811
Belmont, Gaston 28012
Catawba Heights 28012
North Belmont 28012
Belvidere, Perquimans 27919
Bennett, Chatham 27208
Benson, Johnston 27504
Berkeley, Goldsboro 27530
Berkeley Sta Boxes, Goldsboro 27532
Bessemer City, Gaston 28016
Bethabara, Winston-Salem 27116
Bethania, Forsyth 27010
Bethel, Pitt 27812
Bethlehem, Hickory 28601
Beulaville, Duplin 28518
Biggs Park, Lumberton 28358
Biltmore, Asheville 28813
Biscoe, Montgomery 27209
Black Creek, Wilson 27813
Black Mountain, Buncombe 28711
Black Mountain Sanatorium 28711
Black Mountain Sanatorium, Black Mountain 28711
Bladenboro, Bladen 28320
Blanch, Caswell 27212
Blounts Creek, Beaufort 27814
Blowing Rock, Watauga 28605
Boger City, Lincolnton 28092
Boiling Spring Lakes, Southport 28461
Boiling Springs, Cleveland 28017
Gardner Webb College 28017
Bolivia, Brunswick 28422
Bolton, Columbus 28423
Bonlee, Chatham 27213
Bonnie Doone, Fayetteville 28303
Boomer, Wilkes 28606
Boone, Watauga 28607
Downtown 28607
Boonville, Yadkin 27011
Bostic, Rutherford 28018
Bowdens, Duplin 28322
Brasstown, Clay 28902
Brevard, Transylvania 28712
Bridgeton, Craven 28519
Broadway, Lee 27505
Browns Summit, Guilford 27214
Brunswick, Columbus 28424
Bryson City, Swain 28713
Buies Creek, Harnett 27506
Bullock, Granville 27507
Bunn, Franklin 27508
Bunnlevel, Harnett 28323
Burgaw, Pender 28425
Burlington, Alamance 27215
Main Office Boxes 27216
Glen Raven 27215
North Burlington 27215
Burnsville, Yancey 28714
Butner, Granville 27509
Butters, Bladen 28324
Buxton, Dare 27920
Bynum, Pittsboro 27228
Calabash, Shallotte 28459
Calypso, Duplin 28325
Camden, Camden 27921
Cameron, Moore 28326
Overhills (Harnett Co.) 28326
Johnsonville (Harnett Co.) 28326
Cameron Village, Raleigh 27605
Camp Lejeune, Jacksonville 28542
Candler, Buncombe 28715
Candor, Montgomery 27229
Canton, Haywood 28716
Cape Fear, Wilmington 28401
Carmel Commons, Charlotte 28211
Caroleen, Rutherford 28019
Carolina Beach, New Hanover 28428
Carolina Hills, Fletcher 28732
Carrboro, Orange 27510
Carthage, Moore 28327
Cary, Wake 27511
Casar, Cleveland 28020
Cashiers, Jackson 28717
Castalia, Nash 27816
Castle Hayne, New Hanover 28429
Casville, CPO Ruffin 27326
Catawba, Catawba 28609
Catawba Heights, Belmont 28012
Cedar Falls, Randolph 27230
Cedar Grove, Orange 27231
Cedar Island, Carteret 28520
Cedar Mountain, Transylvania 28718
Central Falls, Randolph 27232
Century, Raleigh 27602
Cerro Gordo, Columbus 28430
Chadbourn, Columbus 28431
Chapel Hill, Orange 27514
Eastgate 27514
Franklin Street 27514
Glen Lennox 27514
CHARLOTTE, Mecklenburg 28230
Airport 28219

Arrowood 28217
Atando 28206
Carmel Commons 28211
Derita 28221
Downtown 28230
Eastway 28218
Elizabeth 28204
First Union 28202
Freedom 28266
Idlewild 28229
Mint Hill 28212
Myers Park 28207
North Charlotte 28225
Park Road 28220
Plaza 28299
Providence Square 28211
Randolph 28222
Sedgefield 28209
Sharon 28210
Starmount 28224
UNCC 28223
University Park 28297
Cherokee, Swain 28719
Cherry Point, Havelock 28533
Cherryville, Gaston 28021
Chimney Rock, Rutherford 28720
China Grove, Rowan 28023
Chinquapin, Duplin 28521
Chocowinity, Beaufort 27817
Claremont, Catawba 28610
Clarendon, Columbus 28432
Clarkton, Bladen 28433
Emerson 28433
Clayton, Johnston 27520
Clemmons, Forsyth 27012
Cleveland, Rowan 27013
Cliffside, Rutherford 28024
Climax, Guilford 27233
Clinton, Sampson 28328
Clyde, Haywood 28721
Coats, Harnett 27521
Cofield, Hertford 27922
Coinjock, Currituck 27923
Colerain, Bertie 27924
Coleridge, Randolph 27234
Colfax, Guilford 27235
College, Durham 27708
Collettsville, Caldwell 28611
Colon, Lee 27236
Columbia, Tyrrell 27925
Columbus, Polk 28722
Comfort, Jones 28522
Como, Hertford 27818
Concord, Cabarrus 28025
Wil-Mar Park 28025
Conetoe, Edgecombe 27819
Connellys Springs, Burke 28612
Conover, Catawba 28613
Conway, Northampton 27820
Cooleemee, Davie 27014
Corapeake, Gates 27926
Cordova, Richmond 28330
Cornelius, Mecklenburg 28031
Corolla, Currituck 27927
Cottonade, Fayetteville 28303
Council, Bladen 28434
Court House, Asheville 28807
Cove City, Craven 28523
Crabtree Valley, Raleigh 27622
Cramerton, Gaston 28032
Cranberry, Avery 28614
Creedmoor, Granville 27522
Creston, Ashe 28615
Creswell, Washington 27928
Crisp, Macclesfield 27852
Crossnore, Avery 28616
Crouse, Lincoln 28033
Crumpler, Ashe 28617
Culberson, Cherokee 28903
Cullowhee, Jackson 28723
Cumberland, Cumberland 28331
Cumnock, Sanford 27237
Currie, Pender 28435
Currituck, Currituck 27929
Dallas, Gaston 28034
Dana, Henderson 28724
Danbury, Stokes 27016
Davidson, Mecklenburg 28036
Davis, Carteret 28524
Deep Gap, Watauga 28618
Deep Run, Lenoir 28525
Delco, Columbus 28436
Denton, Davidson 27239
Denver, Lincoln 28037
Derita, Charlotte 28221
Dillsboro, Jackson 28725
Dobson, Surry 27017
Dover, Craven 28526
Downtown, Asheville 28813
Downtown, Boone 28607
Downtown, Charlotte 28230
Downtown, Salisbury 28144
Draper, Eden 27288
Drexel, Burke 28619
Dublin, Bladen 28332
Dudley, Wayne 28333
Duke, Durham 27706
Dunn, Harnett 28334
Durants Neck, Hertford 27930
DURHAM, Durham 27702
College 27708
Duke 27706
East Durham 27703
Forest Hills 27707
Lakewood 27707
North Durham 27704
Northgate 27701
Parkwood 27707
Research Triangle Park 27709
Shepard 27707
Wellons Village 27703
West Durham 27705
Eagle Rock, Wake 27523
Eagle Springs, Moore 27242
Earl, Cleveland 28038
East Bend, Yadkin 27018
East Carolina University, Greenville 27834
East Durham, Durham 27703
East Fayetteville, Fayetteville 28301
East Flat Rock, Henderson 28726
Eastgate, Chapel Hill 27514
East Goldsboro, Goldsboro 27530
East Lake, Dare 27931
East Laurinburg, Laurinburg 28352
East Rocky Mount, Rocky Mount 27801
East Spencer, Rowan 28039
Eastway, Charlotte 28218
Eden, Rockingham 27288
Draper 27288
Spray 27288
Edenton, Chowan 27932
Edgemont, Lenoir 28645
Edneyville, Henderson 28727
Edward, Beaufort 27821
Efland, Orange 27243
Elizabeth, Charlotte 28204
Elizabeth City, Pasquotank 27909
Federal Building 27909
Elizabethtown, Bladen 28337
Elkin, Surry 28621
Elk Park, Avery 28622
Ellenboro, Rutherford 28040
Ellerbe, Richmond 28338
Elm City, Wilson 27822
Elon College, Alamance 27244
Emerson, Clarkton 28433
Emerywood, High Point 27262
Enfield, Halifax 27823
Engelhard, Hyde 27824
Englewood, Rocky Mount 27801

Enka, Buncombe 28728
Ennice, Alleghany 28623
Ernul, Craven 28527
Erwin, Harnett 28339
Ether, Montgomery 27247
Etowah, Henderson 28729
Eure, Gates 27935
Eureka, Fremont 27830
Eutaw, Fayetteville 28303
Everetts, Martin 27825
Evergreen, Columbus 28438
Fair Bluff, Columbus 28439
Fairfield, Hyde 27826
Fairmont, Robeson 28340
McDonald 28340
Fairview, Buncombe 28730
Faison, Duplin 28341
Faith, Rowan 28041
Falcon, Cumberland 28342
Falkland, Pitt 27827
Falls, Raleigh 27609
Fallston, Cleveland 28042
Farmer, Asheboro 27203
Farmville, Pitt 27828
FAYETTEVILLE,
Cumberland 28302
Bonnie Doone 28301
Cottonade 28304
East Fayetteville 28301
Eutaw 28303
Fort Bragg 28307
Haymount 28305
Lafayette 28309
Lakedale 28306
Methodist College 28301
Newbold 28301
Pope AFB 28308
Womack Army
Hospital 28307
Federal Building,
Elizabeth City 27909
Ferguson, Wilkes 28624
First Union, Charlotte 28202
Five Point, Raleigh 27628
Flat Rock, Henderson 28731
Fleetwood, Ashe 28626
Fletcher, Henderson 28732
Carolina Hills 28732
Fontana Dam,
Graham 28733
Forest City,
Rutherford 28043
Forest Hills, Durham 27707
Fort Bragg,
Fayetteville 28307
Fountain, Pitt 27829
Four Oaks, Johnston 27524
Four Seasons,
Hendersonville 28739
Frank, Newland 28657
Franklin, Macon 28734
Franklin Street,
Chapel Hill 27514
Franklinton, Franklin 27525
Franklinville,
Randolph 27248
Freedom, Charlotte 28266
Fremont, Wayne 27830
Eureka 27830
Friendly, Greensboro 27404
Frisco, Dare 27936
Fuquay-Varina, Wake 27526
Furnitureland,
High Point 27264
Gardner Webb College,
Boiling Springs 28017
Garland, Sampson 28441
Garner, Wake 27529
Main Street 27529
Garysburg,
Northampton 27831
Gaston, Northampton 27832
Gastonia, Gaston 28052
Main Office Boxes 28053
West Gastonia 28052
Gates, Gates 27937
Gatesville, Gates 27938
George, Northampton 27833
Germanton, Stokes 27019
Gerton, Henderson 28735
Gibson, Scotland 28343
Gibsonville, Guilford 27249
Glade Valley,
Alleghany 28627
Glen Alpine, Burke 28628
Glendale Springs,
Ashe 28629
Glendon, Moore 27251
Glen Lennox,
Chapel Hill 27514
Glen Raven,
Alamance 27215
Glenrock, Asheville 28802
Glenville, Jackson 28736
Glenwood, McDowell 28737
Gloucester, Carteret 28528
Godwin, Cumberland 28344
Golden Gate,
Greensboro 27405
Gold Hill, Rowan 28071
Goldsboro, Wayne 27530
Berkeley 27530
Berkeley Sta Boxes 27532
East Goldsboro 27530
Grantham 27530
Seymour Johnson
AFB 27531
Goldston, Chatham 27252
Grace, Asheville 28814
Graham, Alamance 27253
Grandy, Currituck 27939
Granite Falls,
Caldwell 28630
Granite Quarry,
Rowan 28072
Grantham, Goldsboro 27530
Grantsboro, Pamlico 28529
Grassy Creek, Ashe 28631
Grayson, Ashe 28632
Greenmountain,
Yancey 28740
GREENSBORO,
Guilford 27420
Friendly 27404
Golden Gate 27405
Guilford College 27410
Hilltop 27417
Plaza 27429
Spring Valley 27416
Summit 27415
Tate Street 27435
West Market Street 27402
Greenville, Pitt 27834
East Carolina
University 27834
Gregory, Shawboro 27973
Grifton, Pitt 28530
Grimesland, Pitt 27837
Grover, Cleveland 28073
Guilford College,
Greensboro 27410
Gulf, Chatham 27256
Gumberry,
Northampton 27838
Halifax, Halifax 27839
Hallsboro, Columbus 28442
Hamilton, Martin 27840
Hamlet, Richmond 28345
Hampstead, Pender 28443
Hamptonville, Yadkin 27020
Harbinger, Currituck 27941
Harkers Island,
Carteret 28531
Harmony, Iredell 28634
Harrells, Sampson 28444
Harrellsville, Hertford 27942
Harris, Rutherford 28074
Harrisburg, Cabarrus 28075
Hassell, Martin 27841
Hatteras, Dare 27943
Havelock, Craven 28532
Cherry Point 28533
Haw River, Alamance 27258
Hayesville, Clay 28904
Haymount,
Fayetteville 28305
Hays, Wilkes 28635
Haywood Road,
Asheville 28806
Hazelwood, Haywood 28738
Henderson, Vance 27536
Hendersonville,
Henderson 28739

Main Office Boxes 28793
Four Seasons 28739
Southside 28739
Henrico, Northampton 27842
Henrietta, Rutherford 28076
Hertford, Perquimans 27944
Durants Neck 27930
Hickory, Catawba 28601
Main Office Boxes 28603
Bethlehem 28601
Lenoir Rhyne 28601
Longview 28601
Viewmont 28601
Hiddenite, Alexander 28636
Highfalls, Moore 27259
Highlands, Macon 28741
HIGH POINT, Guilford 27261
Archdale (Randolph Co.) 27263
Emerywood 27262
Furnitureland 27264
High Shoals, Gaston 28077
Hildebran, Burke 28637
Hillsborough, Orange 27278
Hilltop, Greensboro 27417
Hobbsville, Gates 27946
Hobgood, Halifax 27843
Hobucken, Pamlico 28537
Hoffman, Richmond 28347
Holden Beach, Supply 28462
Hollister, Halifax 27844
Holly Ridge, Onslow 28445
Surf City (Pender Co.) 28445
Topsail Beach (Pender Co.) 28445
Holly Springs, Wake 27540
Hookerton, Greene 28538
Hope Mills, Cumberland 28348
Horse Shoe, Henderson 28742
Hot Springs, Madison 28743
Hubert, Onslow 28539
Hudson, Caldwell 28638
Huntersville, Mecklenburg 28078
Hurdle Mills, Person 27541
Husk, Ashe 28639
Icard, Burke 28666
Idlewild, Charlotte 28229
Indian Trail, Union 28079
Ingold, Sampson 28446
Iron Station, Lincoln 28080
Ivanhoe, Sampson 28447
Jackson, Northampton 27845
Jackson Park, Kannapolis 28081
Jackson Springs, Moore 27281
Jacksonville, Onslow 28540
Camp Lejeune 28542
McCutcheon Field 28545
Midway Park 28544
Naval Hospital 28542
New River Plaza 28540
Northwoods 28540
Tarawa Terrace 28543
James City, New Bern 28560
Jamestown, Guilford 27282
Jamesville, Martin 27846
Jarvisburg, Currituck 27947
Jefferson, Ashe 28640
Johnsonville, Cameron 28326
Jonas Ridge, Burke 28641
Jonesboro Heights, Sanford 27330
Jonesville, Yadkin 28642
Julian, Guilford 27283
Kannapolis, Cabarrus 28081
Jackson Park 28081
Midway 28081
Kelford, Bertie 27847
Kelly, Bladen 28448
Kenansville, Duplin 28349
Kenly, Johnston 27542
Kernersville, Forsyth 27284
Kill Devil Hills, Dare 27948
King, Stokes 27021
King Charles, Raleigh 27620
Kings Mountain, Cleveland 28086
Kinston, Lenoir 28501
Main Office Boxes 28502
Park View 28501
Kipling, Harnett 27543
Kittrell, Vance 27544
Kitty Hawk, Dare 27949
Anderson 27949
Knightdale, Wake 27545
Knotts Island, Currituck 27950
Kure Beach, New Hanover 28449
Lafayette, Fayetteville 28304
LaGrange, Lenoir 28551
Lakedale, Fayetteville 28306
Lake Junaluska, Haywood 28745
Lake Lure, Rutherford 28746
Lake Toxaway, Transylvania 28747
Lakeview, Moore 28350
Lake Waccamaw, Columbus 28450
Lakewood, Durham 27707
Landis, Rowan 28088
Lansing, Ashe 28643
Lasker, Northampton 27848
Lattimore, Cleveland 28089
Laurel Hill, Scotland 28351
Laurel Springs, Alleghany 28644
Laurinburg, Scotland 28352
East Laurinburg 28352
Lawndale, Cleveland 28090
Lawsonville, Stokes 27022
Leasburg, Caswell 27291
Leicester, Buncombe 28748
Leland, Brunswick 28451
Lemon Springs, Lee 28355
Lenoir, Caldwell 28645
Edgemont 28645
Whitnel 28645
Lenoir Rhyne, Hickory 28601
Lewiston Woodville, Bertie 27849
Woodville 27849
Lewisville, Forsyth 27023
Lexington, Davidson 27292
Liberty, Randolph 27298
Lilesville, Anson 28091
Lillington, Harnett 27546
Lincolnton, Lincoln 28092
Boger City 28092
Linden, Cumberland 28356
Linville, Avery 28646
Linville Falls, Burke 28647
Linwood, Davidson 27299
Little Switzerland, McDowell 28749
Littleton, Halifax 27850
Locust, Stanly 28097
Long Beach, Southport 28461
Longisland, Catawba 28648
Longview, Hickory 28601
Longwood, Brunswick 28452
Louisburg, Franklin 27549
Lowell, Gaston 28098
Lowgap, Surry 27024
Lowland, Pamlico 28552
Lucama, Wilson 27851
Lumber Bridge, Robeson 28357
Lumberton, Robeson 28358
Biggs Park 28358
Lynn, Polk 28750
Macclesfield, Edgecombe 27852
Crisp 27852
Macon, Warren 27551
Madison, Rockingham 27025
Maggie Valley, Haywood 28751
Magnolia, Duplin 28453
Maiden, Catawba 28650
Main Office Boxes, Burlington 27216
Main Office Boxes, Gastonia 28053

Main Office Boxes, Hendersonville 28793
Main Office Boxes, Hickory 28603
Main Office Boxes, Kinston 28502
Main Street, Garner 27529
Mamers, Harnett 27552
Manns Harbor, Dare 27953
Manson, Warren 27553
Manteo, Dare 27954
Maple, Currituck 27956
Maple Hill, Pender 28454
Marble, Cherokee 28905
Margarettsville, Northampton 27853
Marietta, Robeson 28362
Marion, McDowell 28752
Marshall, Madison 28753
Walnut 28753
Marshallberg, Carteret 28553
Mars Hill, Madison 28754
Marshville, Union 28103
Marston, Richmond 28363
Matthews, Mecklenburg 28105
Maury, Greene 28554
Maxton, Robeson 28364
Mayodan, Rockingham 27027
Maysville, Jones 28555
McAdenville, Gaston 28101
McCain, Hoke 28361
McCutcheon Field, Jacksonville 28545
McDonald, Fairmont 28340
McFarlan, Anson 28102
McGrady, Wilkes 28649
McLeansville, Guilford 27301
Mebane, Alamance 27302
Meredith College, Raleigh 27602
Merritt, Pamlico 28556
Merry Hill, Bertie 27957
Method, Raleigh 27606
Methodist College, Fayetteville 28301
Micaville, Yancey 28755
Micro, Johnston 27555
Middleburg, Vance 27556
Middlesex, Nash 27557
Midland, Cabarrus 28107
Midway, Kannapolis 28081
Midway Park, Jacksonville 28544
Millbrook, Raleigh 27658
Millers Creek, Wilkes 28651
Mill Spring, Polk 28756
Milton, Caswell 27305
Milwaukee, Northampton 27854
Mineral Springs, Union 28108
Minneapolis, Avery 28652
Mint Hill, Charlotte 28212
Misenheimer, Stanly 28109
Mocksville, Davie 27028
Moncure, Chatham 27559
Monroe, Union 28110
Sutton Park 28110
Montezuma, Avery 28653
Montreat, Buncombe 28757
Mooresboro, Cleveland 28114
Mooresville, Iredell 28115
Moravian Falls, Wilkes 28654
Mordecai, Raleigh 27604
Morehead City, Carteret 28557
Morganton, Burke 28655
Morrisville, Wake 27560
Morven, Anson 28119
Mountain Home, Henderson 28758
Mount Airy, Surry 27030
White Plains 27030
Mount Gilead, Montgomery 27306
Mount Holly, Gaston 28120
Mount Mourne, Iredell 28123
Mount Olive, Wayne 28365
Mount Pleasant, Cabarrus 28124
Mount Tabor, Winston-Salem 27106
Mount Ulla, Rowan 28125
Moyock, Currituck 27958
Murfreesboro, Hertford 27855
Murphy, Cherokee 28906
Myers Park, Charlotte 28207
Nags Head, Dare 27959
Nakina, Columbus 28455
Naples, Henderson 28760
Nashville, Nash 27856
Naval Hospital, Jacksonville 28542
Navassa, Wilmington 28404
Nebo, McDowell 28761
Neuse, Raleigh 27661
Neuse Forest, New Bern 28560
New Bern, Craven 28560
James City 28560
Neuse Forest 28560
West New Bern 28560
Newbold, Fayetteville 28301
Newell, Mecklenburg 28126
New Hill, Wake 27562
Newland, Avery 28657
Frank 28657
New London, Stanly 28127
Newport, Carteret 28570
New River Plaza, Jacksonville 28540
Newton, Catawba 28658
Newton Grove, Sampson 28366
Norlina, Warren 27563
Norman, Richmond 28367
North, Winston-Salem 27115
North Belmont, Belmont 28012
North Burlington, Burlington 27215
North Charlotte, Charlotte 28225
North Durham, Durham 27704
Northgate, Durham 27701
North Hills, Raleigh 27619
North Roxboro, Roxboro 27573
Northside, Granville 27564
North Wilkesboro, Wilkes 28659
Northwoods, Jacksonville 28540
Norwood, Stanly 28128
Oakboro, Stanly 28129
Oak City, Martin 27857
Oak Park, Raleigh 27612
Oak Ridge, Guilford 27310
Ocean Isle Beach, Shallotte 28459
Ocracoke, Hyde 27960
Old Fort, McDowell 28762
Olin, Iredell 28660
Olivia, Harnett 28368
Oriental, Pamlico 28571
Orrum, Robeson 28369
Oteen, Asheville 28815
Otto, Macon 28763
Overhills, Cameron 28326
Oxford, Granville 27565
Palmyra, Halifax 27859
Pantego, Beaufort 27860
Park Road, Charlotte 28220
Parkton, Robeson 28371
Park View, Kinston 28501
Parkwood, Durham 27707
Parkwood, Wilson 27893
Parmele, Martin 27861
Patterson, Caldwell 28661
Paw Creek, Mecklenburg 28130
Peachland, Anson 28133
Pelham, Caswell 27311
Pembroke, Robeson 28372
Pendleton,

Northampton 27862
Penland, Mitchell 28765
Penrose, Transylvania 28766
Pfafftown, Forsyth 27040
Pikeville, Wayne 27863
Pilot Mountain, Surry 27041
Pinebluff, Moore 28373
Pine Hall, Stokes 27042
Pinehurst, Moore 28374
Pine Level, Johnston 27568
Pineola, Avery 28662
Pinetops, Edgecombe 27864
Pinetown, Beaufort 27865
Pineville, Mecklenburg 28134
Piney Creek, Alleghany 28663
Pink Hill, Lenoir 28572
Pinnacle, Stokes 27043
Pisgah Forest, Transylvania 28768
Pittsboro, Chatham 27312
Bynum 27228
Plaza, Charlotte 28299
Plaza, Greensboro 27429
Pleasant Garden, Guilford 27313
Pleasant Hill, Northampton 27866
Plumtree, Avery 28664
Plymouth, Washington 27962
Point Harbor, Currituck 27964
Polkton, Anson 28135
Polkville, Cleveland 28136
Pollocksville, Jones 28573
Pope AFB, Fayetteville 28308
Poplar Branch, Currituck 27965
Potecasi, Northampton 27867
Powells Point, Currituck 27966
Powellsville, Bertie 27967
Princeton, Johnston 27569
Proctorville, Robeson 28375
Prospect Hill, Caswell 27314
Providence, Caswell 27315
Providence Square, Charlotte 28211
Purlear, Wilkes 28665
Raeford, Hoke 28376
RALEIGH, Wake 27611
Cameron Village 27605
Century 27602
Crabtree Valley 27622
Falls 27609
Five Point 27628
King Charles 27620
Meredith College 27602
Method 27606
Millbrook 27658
Mordecai 27604
Neuse 27661
North Hills 27619
Oak Park 27612
State University 27695
Ramseur, Randolph 27316
Randleman, Randolph 27317
Randolph, Charlotte 28222
Red Oak, Nash 27868
Red Springs, Robeson 28377
Reidsville, Rockingham 27320
Research Triangle Park, Durham 27709
Rex, Robeson 28378
Reynolda, Winston-Salem 27109
Rhodhiss, Caldwell 28667
Richfield, Stanly 28137
Richlands, Onslow 28574
Rich Square, Northampton 27869
Ridgecrest, Buncombe 28770
Ridgeway, Warren 27570
Riegelwood, Columbus 28456
Roanoke Rapids, Halifax 27870
Roaring Gap, Alleghany 28668
Roaring River, Wilkes 28669
Robbins, Moore 27325
Robbinsville, Graham 28771
Robersonville, Martin 27871
Rockingham, Richmond 28379
Rockwell, Rowan 28138
Rocky Mount, Edgecombe 27801
East Rocky Mount 27801
Englewood (Nash Co.) 27801
Wesleyan College (Nash Co.) 27801
Westridge (Nash Co.) 27801
West Rocky Mount (Nash Co.) 27801
Rocky Point, Pender 28457
Rodanthe, Dare 27968
Roduco, Gates 27969
Rolesville, Wake 27571
Ronda, Wilkes 28670
Roper, Washington 27970
Roseboro, Sampson 28382
Rose Hill, Duplin 28458
Rosman, Transylvania 28772
Rougemont, Durham 27572
Rowland, Robeson 28383
Roxboro, Person 27573
North Roxboro 27573
Roxobel, Bertie 27872
Ruffin, Rockingham 27326
Casville (Caswell Co.) 27326
Rural Hall, Forsyth 27045
Rutherford College, Burke 28671
Rutherfordton, Rutherford 28139
Saint Pauls, Robeson 28384
Salem, Winston-Salem 27108
Salemburg, Sampson 28385
Salisbury, Rowan 28144
Downtown 28144
Salter Path, Carteret 28575
Saluda, Polk 28773
Salvo, Dare 27972
Sandy Ridge, Stokes 27046
Sanford, Lee 27330
Cumnock 27237
Jonesboro Heights 27330
Sapphire, Transylvania 28774
Saratoga, Wilson 27873
Saxapahaw, Alamance 27340
Scaly Mountain, Macon 28775
Scotland Neck, Halifax 27874
Scotts, Iredell 28699
Scottville, Ashe 28672
Scranton, Hyde 27875
Seaboard, Northampton 27876
Seagrove, Randolph 27341
Sealevel, Carteret 28577
Sedalia, Guilford 27342
Sedgefield, Charlotte 28209
Selma, Johnston 27576
Semora, Caswell 27343
Seven Springs, Wayne 28578
Severn, Northampton 27877
Seymour Johnson AFB, Goldsboro 27531
Seymour Johnson AFB, Goldsboro 27530
Shallotte, Brunswick 28459
Calabash CPO 28459
Ocean Isle Beach 28459
Sunset Beach 28459
Shannon, Robeson 28386
Sharon, Charlotte 28210
Sharpsburg, Nash 27878
Shawboro, Currituck 27973
Gregory 27973
Shelby, Cleveland 28150
Shepard, Durham 27707
Sherrills Ford, Catawba 28673
Shiloh, Camden 27974
Siler City, Chatham 27344

Siloam, Surry 27047
Simpson, Pitt 27879
Sims, Wilson 27880
Skyland, Buncombe 28776
Smithfield, Johnston 27577
Smyrna, Carteret 28579
Sneads Ferry, Onslow 28460
Snow Camp, Alamance 27349
Snow Hill, Greene 28580
Sophia, Randolph 27350
Southern Pines, Moore 28387
South Mills, Camden 27976
Southmont, Davidson 27351
Southport, Brunswick 28461
Boiling Spring Lakes 28461
Long Beach 28461
Southside, Hendersonville 28739
Sparta, Alleghany 28675
Speed, Edgecombe 27881
Spencer, Rowan 28159
Spindale, Rutherford 28160
Spray, Eden 27288
Spring Hope, Nash 27882
Spring Lake, Cumberland 28390
Spring Valley, Greensboro 27416
Spruce Pine, Mitchell 28777
Stacy, Carteret 28581
Staley, Randolph 27355
Stanfield, Stanly 28163
Stanley, Gaston 28164
Stantonsburg, Wilson 27883
Star, Montgomery 27356
Starmount, Charlotte 28224
State Road, Surry 28676
Statesville, Iredell 28677
West Statesville 28677
State University, Raleigh 27695
Stedman, Cumberland 28391
Stella, Carteret 28582
Stem, Granville 27581
Stokes, Pitt 27884
Stokesdale, Guilford 27357
Stoneville, Rockingham 27048
Stonewall, Pamlico 28583
Stony Point, Alexander 28678
Stovall, Granville 27582
Stumpy Point, Dare 27978
Sugar Grove, Watauga 28679
Summerfield, Guilford 27358
Summit, Greensboro 27415
Sunbury, Gates 27979
Sunset Beach, Shallotte 28459
Supply, Brunswick 28462
Holden Beach 28462
Surf City, Holly Ridge 28445
Sutton Park, Monroe 28110
Swannanoa, Buncombe 28778
Warren Wilson College 28778
Swan Quarter, Hyde 27885
Swansboro, Onslow 28584
Swepsonville, Alamance 27359
Sylva, Jackson 28779
Tabor City, Columbus 28463
Tapoco, Graham 28780
Tarawa Terrace, Jacksonville 28543
Tarboro, Edgecombe 27886
Tar Heel, Bladen 28392
Tate Street, Greensboro 27435
Taylorsville, Alexander 28681
Teachey, Duplin 28464
Terrell, Catawba 28682
Thomasville, Davidson 27360
Thurmond, Wilkes 28683
Tillery, Halifax 27887
Timberlake, Person 27583
Toast, Surry 27049
Tobaccoville, Forsyth 27050
Todd, Ashe 28684
Topsail Beach, Holly Ridge 28445
Topton, Cherokee 28781
Townsville, Vance 27584
Traphill, Wilkes 28685
Trenton, Jones 28585
Trinity, Randolph 27370
Triplett, Watauga 28686
Troutman, Iredell 28166
Troy, Montgomery 27371
Tryon, Polk 28782
Tuckasegee, Jackson 28783
Turkey, Sampson 28393
Turnersburg, Iredell 28688
Tuxedo, Henderson 28784
Tyner, Chowan 27980
Unaka, Cherokee 28908
UNCC, Charlotte 28223
Union, Ahoskie 27910
Union Grove, Iredell 28689
Union Mills, Rutherford 28167
University of NC, Wilmington 28403
University Park, Charlotte 28297
Valdese, Burke 28690
Vale, Lincoln 28168
Valle Crucis, Banner Elk 28691
Vanceboro, Craven 28586
Vandemere, Pamlico 28587
Vass, Moore 28394
Vaughan, Warren 27586
Viewmont, Hickory 28601
Vilas, Watauga 28692
Waco, Cleveland 28169
Wade, Cumberland 28395
Wadesboro, Anson 28170
Wagram, Scotland 28396
Wake Forest, Wake 27587
Wakulla, Robeson 28397
Walkertown, Forsyth 27051
Wallace, Duplin 28466
Wallburg, Davidson 27373
Walnut, Marshall 28753
Walnut Cove, Stokes 27052
Walstonburg, Greene 27888
Wanchese, Dare 27981
Warne, Clay 28909
Warrensville, Ashe 28693
Warrenton, Warren 27589
Warren Wilson College, Swannanoa 28778
Warsaw, Duplin 28398
Washington, Beaufort 27889
Watha, Pender 28471
Waughtown, Winston-Salem 27117
Waves, Dare 27982
Waxhaw, Union 28173
Waynesville, Haywood 28786
Weaverville, Buncombe 28787
Webster, Jackson 28788
Welcome, Davidson 27374
Weldon, Halifax 27890
Wellons Village, Durham 27703
Wendell, Wake 27591
Wentworth, Rockingham 27375
Wesleyan College, Rocky Mount 27801
West Asheville, Asheville 28816
West Durham, Durham 27705
West End, Moore 27376
Westfield, Surry 27053
West Gastonia, Gastonia 28052
West Jefferson, Ashe 28694
West Market Street, Greensboro 27402
West New Bern, New Bern 28560
Westridge, Rocky Mount 27801
West Rocky Mount,